Also available for instructors:

INSTRUCTOR'S MANUAL/TEST BANK
Multiple Choice, True/False, and Short Answer

Larry J. Siegel

CRIMINOLOGY

CRIMINOLOGY

SECOND EDITION

Larry J. Siegel
UNIVERSITY OF NEBRASKA, OMAHA

West Publishing Company
ST. PAUL   NEW YORK   LOS ANGELES   SAN FRANCISCO

Cover: "Estate" by Robert Rauschenberg, ©1963.
         Philadelphia Museum of Art: Given by the
         Friends of the Philadelphia Museum of Art

Production credits: copyediting by Chris Thillen
                      text and cover design by Paula Schlosser
                      artwork by Alice Thiede
                      indexing by Lois Oster
                      composition by Graphic World

Library of Congress Cataloging-in-Publication Data

Siegel, Larry J.
   Criminology.

   Includes bibliographical references and index.
   1. Crime and criminals.   2. Crime and criminals—
United States.   I. Title.
HV6025.S48   1986   364   85-20351
ISBN 0-314-93511-8
1st Reprint—1986

To Rachel, Andrew and Eric Siegel
and Therese J. Libby

Contents

CHAPTER **2**

The Criminal Law and Its Processes 24

CHAPTER 3 # Measuring Criminal Behavior 50

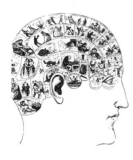

CHAPTER **7**

Sociological Approaches: Social Structure Theories   184

CHAPTER **8**

Sociological Approaches: Social Process Theories   218

CHAPTER **9**

Sociological Approaches: Social Conflict Theory 256

SECTION III CRIME TYPOLOGIES

CHAPTER 11 Economic Crimes: Street Crime 334

CHAPTER **12 Economic Crimes: Organizational Criminality** 360

CHAPTER 13 Public Order Crime 400

section IV THE CRIMINAL JUSTICE SYSTEM 436

CHAPTER 14 Overview of the Criminal Justice System 438

CHAPTER 15 The Police 474

CHAPTER 16 The Adjudicatory Process 518

CHAPTER 17 Corrections 562

Preface

Criminology is being offered today as an area of study on hundreds of college campuses around the nation. It is a dynamic field, constantly changing to reflect legal decisions, scientific research, national surveys, policy changes, and academic thought and writing. Because the field is so dynamic, *Criminology* has been updated to incorporate the changes that have occurred since the first edition was published in 1983.

This new edition focuses on changes in the crime rate, law, theory, and knowledge about the major forms of crime. Its emphasis is on contemporary criminology, but it contains significant historical information as well. It attempts to provide a balanced, objective view of a complex, highly diversified field of study.

The major features of the text are described below.

Goals and Objectives

A criminology course is normally a student's first opportunity to study the nature of criminal behavior. The text for use in such a course must be comprehensive, logically organized, easily understood, and reflective of the major research efforts in the field. Consequently, the objectives of the second edition of *Criminology* are: first, to be as objective as possible, presenting the many diverse views that characterize criminology and reflect its interdisciplinary nature; second, to achieve a balance in presenting material, not allowing any single viewpoint to dominate its content; third, to be thorough, presenting the most important works in criminological literature; and fourth, to make the text interesting and readable, thus encouraging students to pursue further study in the field.

The book analyzes criminology in depth by examining historical data, statistical information, journal articles, scholarly works, and government documents. Throughout the text, **Close-Ups** are used to focus on critical issues, illustrate important research, discuss leading legal cases, and present programs and policies in the criminal justice system. The Close-Ups will help students and instructors develop meaningful classroom discussions on criminological issues.

Major Changes in This Edition

Since the first edition was published, numerous changes have occurred in the study of criminology: the crime rate has begun to drop; conservative views have become more influential; legal decisions have expanded police power; and important discoveries have been made in such diverse areas as identifying career criminals, serial murder, and the link between drug use and crime. There is a growing swing in public policy, from emphasis on the rights of individuals and the offender's need for care and treatment to emphasis on social control, protection of society, and concern for the victims of crime.

This second edition takes into account the evolution of criminology by updating the discussion of law, public policy, theory, and crime measurement. The outline from the first edition remains the same, with two notable exceptions. A new chapter (4) has been added to review current data on criminals and victims. In addition, chapter 11, Economic Crimes: Organizational Criminality, was included to provide in depth coverage of criminal behavior involving organizational activity such as price fixing, environmental crimes, and computer crime.

Section I provides a framework for studying criminology. The first chapter introduces the field and discusses its most basic concepts: the definition of crime, the components of criminology, and ethical issues in criminology. The second chapter reviews the criminal law and includes new material on the concept of criminal defenses. The last two chapters include detailed discussion on how criminologists measure crime rates and what crime data tells us about the nature and extent of criminal behavior. Chapter 4 contains a detailed discussion of the habitual criminal, female offenders, and race and criminal behavior, as well as a discussion of victimization risk.

Section II discusses criminological theory. It contains chapters covering the most important areas of criminological thought, including classical, psychological, biological, and sociological theories. All material has been updated and new sections on socialization and crime, unemployment and crime, corporal punishment, and television and behavior have been added.

Section III is devoted to the major forms of criminal behavior. It includes chapters on violence, theft, and public order crimes. Current information on serial murder, cause of rape, drugs and crime, family violence, burglary, and arson is presented. This section contains a new chapter called "Economic Crimes: Organizational Criminality," which discusses white-collar and organized crime.

Section IV focuses on the criminal justice system. Its opening chapter provides an overview of the entire system, and is followed by individual chapters on the police, court, and correctional processes. New material has been added on models of justice, police patrol, police use of deadly force, sentencing practices, use of plea bargains, time served in prison, effectiveness of probation and parole, private industry in prison, and so on. Every effort has been made to update legal cases as well as information on policy and practices within the system.

This text has been carefully structured to cover the material in a comprehensive, balanced, and objective fashion.

Distinctive Features

In addition to updating and improving the overall quality and quantity of the substantive material, this edition has some distinct pedagogical features that should help the students to better understand the study of criminology.

1. **Photos, charts, and illustrations.** More illustrations, charts, and photographs are used throughout this edition. They are designed to help students visualize components of criminology and to organize the text material.

2. **Chapter Outline.** Each chapter begins with an outline of all subject headings in the chapter. The material is thus concisely organized for the student and instructor.

3. **Key Terms.** Following each chapter outline is a list of key terms used by professional criminologists. A good vocabulary of concepts will help the student become better acquainted with the field of criminology.

4. **Close-Ups.** Every chapter contains Close-Ups to illustrate important research, surveys, policy, academic ideas, or case studies. They are designed to be current, controversial, informative, and thought provoking. Each Close-Up is accompanied by discussion questions designed to stimulate classroom discussions.

5. **Chapter Summary.** Each chapter concludes with a summary of the most significant topics, issues and concepts in the chapter. The student thus has the opportunity to concentrate on the chapter's material in a summarized form.

6. **Instructor's Manual.** An instructor's manual is provided to help the busy instructor prepare and plan the course.

Acknowledgments

Many people helped make this book possible. Those who reviewed the first edition and made suggestions that I followed to the best of my ability include: Bonnie Berry, University of Miami; James A. Black, University of Tennessee; Stephen J. Brodt, Ball State University; Edward Green, Eastern Michigan University; Dennis E. Hoffman, University of Nebraska-Omaha; Gerrold Hotaling, University of New Hampshire; Joseph Jacoby, Bowling Green State University; James J. McKenna, Villanova University; Paul E. Tracy, Northeastern University; and Charles B. Vedder, Stetson University.

I would also like to thank others who provided me with ideas and material. They include: Spencer Rathus; John Laub; James Kane; Pete Kuchel; Marvin Zalman; David Friedrichs; Chris Eskridge; Sam Walker; Janet Porter; James Fyfe; Frank Cullen; Jim Garofolo and Ed McGarrell and the staff at the Hindelang Research Center in Albany, New York; Marty Schwartz; Joseph Weis; Linda Saltzman; Chuck Fenwick; and Bob Regoli. Special thanks are due to my wonderful executive editor, Mary Schiller, who has worked with me on numerous projects and to Catherine Maggio, the production editor, who did a professional job on putting this book together. My sincere thanks to Willa Martin, Senior Research Associate at TJL Legal Research, Inc., Omaha, Nebraska for her inexhaustible patience and technical assistance.

I Concepts of Crime and Criminology

S ECTION I OF THIS book introduces students to the field of criminology and its most basic subject matter. It covers the concept of crime, the nature of law, and the extent of criminal behavior.

The first chapter provides an overview of criminology. Who are criminologists? What do they do? How do they perceive their field of study? Chapter 1 also discusses the various components of the field. Like many other academic disciplines, criminology contains various subdisciplines that practitioners can specialize in: victimology, penology, sociology of law, crime measurement, and so on. Students will learn that there is no unified view of criminology, but rather conflicting concepts of the field and its subject matter.

The section's second chapter focuses on the criminal law. It introduces the major components of the law: the definition of crimes, the concept of intent, and the defenses to criminal accusations. Students will find that simply engaging in an act that is outlawed by society may not mean a person has committed a crime. All the elements of criminal law must be considered before an action is labelled criminal.

The final two chapters review the various sources of crime data and discuss what they tell us about criminals and their victims. Chapter 3 reviews the methods used to measure crime and gives an overview of the extent of crime in the United States. Chapter 4 focuses on the individual characteristics of criminals and victims and evaluates the influence of important social traits— age, race, sex, economic status—on the likelihood of becoming a criminal or victim. Measuring criminal behavior patterns is the basis for criminological theory. The way crime is organized, its trends and patterns, has profoundly influenced the way criminologists view the causes of crime. The validity of criminological theory is bound up in the validity of crime measurement.

1 Crime and Criminology

CHAPTER OUTLINE

KEY TERMS

capital punishment
recidivism
crime
criminal behavior
law
justice
criminologists
criminology
Cesare Lombroso
criminological enterprise

theories
white-collar crime
crime typology
criminal justice system
deviant behavior
decriminalized
consensus view of crime
sanctioned
violation of natural law
mala in se crime

statutory crime
mala prohibitum crime
moral entrepreneurs
classical theorists
positivists
conflict approach
radical criminology
interactionist view of crime
symbolic interactionist

Introduction

- A serial murderer terrorizes a city, striking at random. His behavior patterns have the police baffled. Why do some people turn to random violence as a way of life?
- The United States Supreme Court upholds the legality of the death penalty. Opponents of **capital punishment** view the decision as a step backward in society's moral development. Supporters see the decision as a major victory in the fight against crime. Who is right?
- Prisons don't seem to work. Many former inmates repeat their criminal activities soon after they leave confinement **(recidivism).** Yet judges are incarcerating convicted offenders at an ever increasing rate. What is wrong with our correctional system?
- Black citizens charge that they are discriminated against by white-dominated police departments, courts, and correctional agencies. Is this true? If so, what can be done about it?
- The attorney for a man accused of trying to assassinate the president claims his client is not guilty because he is mentally ill. Should we excuse a criminal act if it is a product of mental illness?

Crime, criminal behavior, law and **justice** are topics that have long fascinated people. Books, films, television, and newspapers are constantly flooded with fact and fiction about crime and criminals. As with the weather, everyone has an opinion about crime, but no one seems to be able to do much about it.

Criminologists are people who earn their living thinking about crime. Unlike the general public, whose opinions about crime are colored by personal experiences, biases, and values, criminologists bring the scientific method to bear on the study of crime and justice. These well-informed and highly trained observers of social phenomena use established research methodologies to objectively examine issues relating to crime and its consequences.

Criminology is the scientific approach to the study of criminal behavior and society's subsequent reaction to it.

This text will review criminology and analyze its major areas of inquiry. It focuses on the nature and extent of crime, the cause of crime, crime patterns, and crime control. This chapter introduces criminology. How is it defined? What are its goals? What major issues face its practitioners? What ethical issues face those wishing to conduct criminological research?

What is Criminology?

Criminology is the scientific approach to the study of criminal behavior. In their classic definition, Edwin Sutherland and Donald Cressey, two prominent criminologists, state:

> Criminology is the body of knowledge regarding crime as a social phenomenon. It includes within its scope the processes of making laws, of breaking laws, and of reacting toward the breaking of laws. . . . The objective of criminology is the development of a body of general and verified principles and of other types of knowledge regarding this process of law, crime, and treatment.[1]

Sutherland and Cressey's definition includes the most important areas of interest to criminologists: the development of criminal law and its use to define crime, the cause of law violations, and the methods used to control criminal behavior. Also important is their use of the term *verified principles* to signify the use of the scientific method in criminology. Many people study crime without using established methods of scientific inquiry. These people are not criminologists but journalists, commentators, critics, social thinkers, and so on. Criminologists use scientifically verified methods to pose research questions (*hypotheses*), gather data, create theories, and test their validity. They use every method of established social science inquiry: analysis of existing records, experimental designs, surveys, historical analysis, and so on. It is the rigid adherence to the scientific method that sets the professional criminologist apart from the layman interested in the study of crime.

Criminology: an Interdisciplinary Science

Criminology is interdisciplinary. Few academic centers grant graduate degrees in criminology (Florida State University, for example). Therefore most criminologists have been trained in diverse fields, most commonly sociology, but also political science, psychology, economics, and the natural sciences. In fact, **Cesare Lombroso,** often called the "father of criminology," was a medical doctor.[2]

For most of the twentieth century, criminology's primary orientation was sociological. However, in the 1980s it has been deeply influenced by the contributions of persons in several diverse fields. For example, biologists and physicians have studied the physical characteristics of criminal offenders to isolate particular traits that seem to produce law-violating behavior. In a similar vein, psychologists and other members of the mental health profession have focused on the mental processes that are thought to produce violent behavior. Other contributions are being made by historians and political economists who study the history of law and the evolving definition of crime.

The diverse, heterogeneous nature of criminology has created some confusion over whether it should be considered an independent academic discipline or a subfield of a larger, more well established discipline, such as sociology or even psychology. Vincent Webb and Dennis Hoffman suggest that a field becomes a discipline ". . . if it has subject matter of its own. In other words, a field of study is recognized as a discipline when it establishes that it has a body of knowledge that is distinct and autonomous."[3] Some critics charge that criminology has not yet achieved the stature of an independent academic discipline, that it remains an amalgam of information and ideas from various subject areas. However, two distinguished criminologists, Marvin Wolfgang and Franco Ferracutti, counter that criminology is in fact a separate discipline that integrates knowledge from many fields because "it has accumulated its own set of organized data and theoretical conceptualizations that use the scientific method, approach to understanding, and attitude in research."[4]

Thus, criminology can be viewed as an integrated approach to studying criminal behavior. Though it combines elements of many other fields, its practitioners devote their primary interest to understanding the true nature of law, crime, and justice.

The Criminological Enterprise

Regardless of their background or training, criminologists are primarily interested in studying crime and criminal behavior. As Wolfgang and Ferracutti put it:

> *A criminologist is one whose professional training, occupational role, and pecuniary reward are primarily concentrated on a scientific approach to, and study and analysis of, the phenomenon of crime and criminal behavior.*[5]

Within the broader arena of criminology are several subareas, which taken together make up the **criminological enterprise.** Criminologists may specialize in a subarea, in the same way that a psychologist might specialize in development, perception, personality, psychopathology, and so on.

CRIMINAL STATISTICS

The subarea of criminal statistics involves measuring the amount and trends of criminal activity. How much crime occurs annually? Who commits it? When and where does it occur? Which crimes are the most serious (see Close-Up)? Criminologists interested in criminal statistics try to create valid and reliable measurements of criminal behavior. For example, they might review the records of police and court agencies. They survey large samples of citizens to determine the percentage of law violators who escape detection by the justice system. They also study the victims of crime to draw conclusions about the true number of criminal acts. The various measures of criminal behavior and their interpretation will be reviewed in chapters 3 and 4.

SOCIOLOGY OF LAW

The sociology of law is a subarea of criminology concerned with the role of social forces in shaping criminal law and, concomitantly, the role of criminal law in shaping society. Criminologists study the history of legal thought in an effort to understand how particular laws developed into their current form. For example, criminal laws controlling theft, rape, drug abuse, and so on evolved into their present state after years of change. How such modern crimes as racketeering, computer fraud, and price fixing developed are also subjects of particular interest to criminologists. Similarly, the impact of law and its application on human behavior is an important area of criminological study. What effect does passing a tough new drunk-driving or gun-control law have on people's illegal use of alcohol and guns? What effect does capital punishment have on the murder rate? These too are questions studied by criminologists. The criminal law will be discussed further in chapter 2.

THE ETIOLOGY OF CRIME

The etiology of crime focuses on the actual causes of criminal behavior. A question that has tormented criminologists from the first is, Why do people engage in criminal acts? Why, when they know their actions can bring harsh punishment and social disapproval, do they steal, rape, and murder? In short, why do people behave the way they do? Does crime have a social or an individual basis? Is it a psychological, biological, social, political, or economic phenomenon? Criminologists usually bring their personal beliefs and backgrounds to bear when they study the issue. Consequently, there are diverse **theories** of crime causation, each reflecting the orientation of its creator. Psychologically trained criminologists view crime as a function of personality, development, social learning, or cognition. Biologically oriented criminologists study the biochemical, genetic, and neurological linkages to crime. Sociologically trained criminologists look at the social forces producing criminal behavior.

Despite important strides, understanding the cause of crime remains a difficult problem. Criminologists are still unsure why, given similar conditions, one person elects criminal solutions to his or her problems while another conforms to accepted social rules of behavior. Further, when attempts have been made to understand crime rates and trends, faulty data and unsound research methods have prevented criminologists from developing any firm conclusions. Understanding the nature and causes of crime is a goal that has so far eluded its seekers.

Closely related to understanding the cause of criminality is predicting it. If criminologists could isolate crime producing phenomena, then they should be able to predict whether a particular individual would become crime-prone. For example, if a significant number of individuals with chemical X in their bloodstream were found to be violence-prone, we might predict that all people with X would become violent, even if they had not yet done so. Prediction is extremely controversial, and criminologists engaged in research that could lead to crime prediction have been challenged by many of their colleagues, who fear that such efforts could result in labeling and stigmatizing innocent people because of suspicions about their future actions.

Despite these disagreements, most criminologists agree that the cause of the crime must be understood if society is to deal with it effectively. The various theories of crime causation will be discussed in chapters 5 through 9.

CRIMINAL BEHAVIOR SYSTEMS

The criminal behavior systems subarea of criminology involves describing and researching specific criminal types. For example, Marvin Wolfgang's famous study, *Patterns in Criminal Homicide,* is considered a landmark analysis of the nature of homicide and the relationship between victim and offender (see chapter 10).[6] Edwin Sutherland's analysis of business-related offenses helped coin a new phrase— **white-collar crime**—to describe economic crime activities.

The study of criminal behavior also involves research on the links between different types of crime and criminals. This is known as **crime typology.** Unfortunately, existing typologies often disagree, so no standard exists within the field. Some typologies focus on the criminal, suggesting the existence of offender groups such as professional criminals, psychotic criminals, occasional criminals, and so on. Others focus on the crimes, clustering them into categories such as property crimes, sex crimes, and so on. Chapters 10 through 13 discuss particular crime categories, including violent, economic, and public order crimes.

PENOLOGY

The penology subarea of criminology focuses on efforts to correct and control known criminal offenders. Criminologists have long been interested in crime control. Stephen Schafer defined criminology as follows:

> *Criminology, in general terms, is the study of crimes, criminals, and victims. . . . Yet, as criminology is usually understood, its scope does not cover all phases of lawbreaking and all aspects of the crime problem. . . . Criminal etiology is one of the two major dynamic parts of criminology. It is the study of factors and producing elements of crime. . . . Penology and correction is the other dynamic part of criminology. It is the study of the consequences of crime; it analyzes how to change the lawbreaker to be a law-abiding member of society and how to repair the damage or harm caused to the victim of crime.*[7]

Crime Seriousness

How does the public view the seriousness of crime? The National Survey of Crime Severity measured public perceptions of the severity of 204 illegal events ranging from "playing hooky" to killing twenty people with a bomb. The survey results follow.

HOW DO PEOPLE RANK THE SEVERITY OF CRIME?

Severity of score and offense

72.1. Planting a bomb in a public building. The bomb explodes and twenty people are killed.

52.8. A man forcibly rapes a woman. As a result of physical injuries, she dies.

43.2. Robbing a victim at gunpoint. The victim struggles and is shot to death.

39.2. A man stabs his wife. As a result, she dies.

35.7. Stabbing a victim to death.

35.6. Intentionally injuring a victim. As a result, the victim dies.

33.8. Running a narcotics ring.

27.9. A woman stabs her husband. As a result, he dies.

26.3. An armed person skyjacks an airplane and demands to be flown to another country.

25.9. A man forcibly rapes a woman. No other physical injury occurs.

24.9. Intentionally setting fire to a building causing $100,000 worth of damage.

22.9. A parent beats his young child with his fists. The child requires hospitalization.

21.2. Kidnapping a victim.

20.7. Selling heroin to others for resale.

19.5. Smuggling heroin into the country.

19.5. Killing a victim by recklessly driving an automobile.

17.9. Robbing a victim of $10 at gunpoint. The victim is wounded and requires hospitalization.

16.9. A man drags a woman into an alley, tears her clothes, but flees before she is physically harmed or sexually attacked.

16.4. Attempting to kill a victim with a gun. The gun misfires and the victim escapes unharmed.

15.9. A teenage boy beats his mother with his fists. The mother requires hospitalization.

15.5. Breaking into a bank at night and stealing $100,000.

14.1. A doctor cheats on claims he makes to a federal health insurance plan for patient services.

13.9. A legislator takes a bribe from a company to vote for a law favoring the company.

13.0. A factory knowingly gets rid of its waste in a way that pollutes the water supply of a city.

12.2. Paying a witness to give false testimony in a criminal trial.

12.0. A police officer takes a bribe not to interfere with an illegal gambling operation.

12.0. Intentionally injuring a victim. The victim is treated by a doctor and hospitalized.

11.8. A man beats a stranger with his fists. He requires hospitalization.

11.4. Knowingly lying under oath during a trial.

11.2. A company pays a bribe to a legislator to vote for a law favoring the company.

10.9. Stealing property worth $10,000 from outside a building.

10.5. Smuggling marijuana into the country for resale.

10.4. Intentionally hitting a victim with a lead pipe. The victim requires hospitalization.

10.3. Illegally selling barbiturates, such as prescription sleeping pills, to others for resale.

10.3. Operating a store that knowingly sells stolen property.

Thus, an important goal of criminology is to suggest strategies for crime control and then help implement these policies in the real world. While the development of the field of criminal justice has caused some overlap to occur in this area, modern criminologists have continued their efforts to develop new crime control programs and policies. However, this activity is not without controversy.

Some criminologists view crime control as involving rehabilitation and treatment. Their efforts are directed at providing behavior alternatives for would-be criminals and treatment for individuals convicted of law violations to help them "go straight." In general, rehabilitation-and-treatment-oriented criminologists make up the liberal branch of the field. They view the criminal as someone society

10.0. A government official intentionally hinders the investigation of a criminal offense.

9.7. Breaking into a school and stealing equipment worth $1,000.

9.7. Walking into a public museum and stealing a painting worth $1,000.

9.6. Breaking into a home and stealing $1,000.

9.6. A police officer knowingly makes a false arrest.

9.5. A public official takes $1,000 of public money for his own use.

9.4. Robbing a victim of $10 at gunpoint. No physical harm occurs.

9.3. Threatening to seriously injure a victim.

9.2. Several large companies illegally fix the retail prices of their products.

8.6. Performing an illegal abortion.

8.5. Selling marijuana to others for resale.

8.5. Intentionally injuring a victim. The victim is treated by a doctor but is not hospitalized.

8.2. Knowing that a shipment of cooking oil is bad, a store owner decides to sell it anyway. Only one bottle is sold and the purchaser is treated by a doctor but not hospitalized.

7.9. A teenage boy beats his father with his fists. The father requires hospitalization.

7.7. Knowing that a shipment of cooking oil is bad, a store owner decides to sell it anyway.

7.5. A person, armed with a lead pipe, robs a victim of $10. No physical harm occurs.

7.4. Illegally getting monthly welfare checks.

7.3. Threatening a victim with a weapon unless the victim gives money. The victim gives $10 and is not harmed.

7.3. Breaking into a department store and stealing merchandise worth $1,000.

7.2. Signing someone else's name to a check and cashing it.

6.9. Stealing property worth $1,000 from outside a building.

6.5. Using heroin.

6.5. An employer refuses to hire a qualified person because of that person's race.

6.4. Getting customers for a prostitute.

6.3. A person, free on bail for committing a serious crime, purposefully fails to appear in court on the day of his trial.

6.2. An employee embezzles $1,000 from his employer.

5.4. Possessing some heroin for personal use.

5.4. A real estate agent refuses to sell a house to a person because of that person's race.

5.4. Threatening to harm a victim unless the victim gives money. The victim gives $10 and is not harmed.

5.3. Loaning money at an illegally high interest rate.

5.1. A man runs his hands over the body of a female victim, then runs away.

5.1. A person, using force, robs a victim of $10. No physical harm occurs.

4.9. Snatching a handbag containing $10 from a victim on the street.

4.8. A man exposes himself in public.

4.6. Carrying a gun illegally.

4.5. Cheating on federal income tax return.

4.4. Picking a victim's pocket of $100.

4.2. Attempting to break into a home but running away when a police car approaches.

3.8. Turning in a false fire alarm.

3.7. A labor union official illegally threatens to organize a strike if an employer hires nonunion workers.

3.6. Knowingly passing a bad check.

3.6. Stealing property worth $100 from outside a building.

3.5. Running a place that permits gambling to occur illegally.

3.2. An employer illegally threatens to fire employees if they join a labor union.

2.4. Knowingly carrying an illegal knife.

cont'd

has failed; someone under social, psychological, or economic stress; someone who can be helped if society is willing to pay the price. Rehabilitation-oriented criminologists advocate such measures as improved educational opportunities, job training, counseling, community corrections, and the like to reduce the crime rate. Their work will be reviewed in chapters 6, 7, and 8.

In opposition to this view, conservative criminologists argue that crime can only be prevented through a strict policy of social control. As chapter 5 will explain, they advocate such measures as the threat of capital punishment, mandatory prison sentences, and increased police presence.

Finally, radical criminologists view crime control as a political function. If

Crime Seriousness—cont'd

2.2. Stealing $10 worth of merchandise from the counter of a department store.

2.1. A person is found firing a rifle for which he knows he has no permit.

2.1. A woman engages in prostitution.

1.9. Making an obscene phone call.

1.9. A store owner knowingly puts "large" eggs into containers marked "extra-large."

1.8. A youngster under sixteen years old is drunk in public.

1.8. Knowingly being a customer in a place where gambling occurs illegally.

1.7. Stealing property worth $10 from outside a building.

1.6. Being a customer in a house of prostitution.

1.6. A male, over sixteen years of age, has sexual relations with a willing female under sixteen.

1.5. Taking barbiturates, such as sleeping pills, without a legal prescription.

1.5. Intentionally shoving or pushing a victim. No medical treatment is required.

1.4. Smoking marijuana.

1.3. Two persons willingly engage in a homosexual act.

1.1. Disturbing the neighborhood with loud, noisy behavior.

1.1. Taking bets on the numbers.

1.1. A group continues to hang around a corner after being told to break up by a police officer.

0.9. A youngster under sixteen years old runs away from home.

0.8. Being drunk in public.

0.7. A youngster under sixteen years old breaks a curfew law by being out on the street after the hour permitted by law.

0.6. Trespassing in the backyard of a private home.

0.3. A person is a vagrant. That is, he has no home and no visible means of support.

0.2. A youngster under sixteen years old plays hooky from school.

In deciding severity, people seem to take into account such factors as—

- The victims' ability to protect themselves
- The extent of injury and loss
- For property crimes, the type of business or organization the property is stolen from
- The offender's relationship to the victim

Interestingly, white-collar crimes, such as consumer fraud, cheating on income taxes, pollution by factories, price fixing, and accepting bribes, are viewed at least as seriously as many conventional property and violent crimes.

Within particular categories of crime, severity assessments are affected by factors such as whether injury occurred and the extent of property loss. For example, all burglaries are not scored at the same severity level because of the differing characteristics of each event (even though all the events fit into the same crime category).

DISCUSSION QUESTIONS:

1. How would you rate the seriousness of crimes?
2. Should punishments be based on citizens' perceptions of crime seriousness?

SOURCE. "The Seriousness of Crime: Results of a National Survey," Center for Studies in Criminology and Criminal Law, University of Pennsylvania. In National Institute of Justice *Report to the Nation on Crime and Justice* (Washington, D.C.: 1983), forthcoming.

society were structured in an equitable fashion, they argue, then the need for committing crime would disappear. Radical criminologists work for social change and political awareness. Their work will be reviewed in chapter 9. Since penology is an important part of the criminological enterprise, the agencies and processes of justice will be discussed in chapters 14 through 17.

VICTIMOLOGY

Victimology focuses on the victims of crime. The popularity of victimology can be traced to the early work of Hans von Hentig and later work by Stephen Schafer.[8]

The study of victimology is concerned with the natural extent of victimization, the victim's role in the criminal process, and the protection of victims.

These authors were among the first to suggest that victims play an important role in the criminal process, that their actions may actually precipitate crime, and that the study of crime is not complete unless the victim's role is considered.

In recent years criminologists have devoted ever increasing attention to the victim's role in the criminal process. The areas of particular interest include: using victim surveys to measure the nature and extent of criminal behavior (chapter 3), calculating the actual costs of crime to victims (chapter 4), creating probabilities of victimization risk (chapter 4), studying victim culpability or precipitation of crime (chapter 10), and designing services for the victims of crime (chapter 15).

Victimology remains a relatively new branch of criminology. It is undergoing rapid change and the materials throughout the book reflect its influence on the criminological enterprise.

Criminology and Criminal Justice

In the late 1960s, interest in the so-called crime problem gave rise to the development of academic programs devoted to studying the **criminal justice system.** Although the terms *criminology* and *criminal justice* may seem similar, there are major differences between them.

According to Marvin Zalman, criminology explains the *etiology* (origin), extent, and nature of crime in society, whereas criminal justice refers to the agencies of social control that deal with crime and delinquency. Zalman further suggests that while criminologists are mainly concerned with crime and its consequences, criminal justice scholars are engaged in describing, analyzing, and explaining the behavior of the agencies of justice—police departments, courts, and correctional facilities.[9]

Since both fields are crime-related, some overlap exists between them. Criminologists, especially those interested in penology, must be aware of how the agencies of justice operate and how they influence crime and criminals. Similarly, criminal justice experts cannot begin to design programs of crime prevention or rehabilitation without understanding something of the nature of crime. Hence, it is common for criminal justice programs to feature courses on criminology and for criminology courses to evaluate the agencies of justice.

The tremendous interest in criminal justice has led to the creation of more than a thousand justice-related academic programs; not surprisingly, these programs are often staffed by criminologists. Thus, it seems possible for the two fields not only to coexist but to help each other grow and develop.

Criminology and Deviance

Criminology is also sometimes confused with the study of deviant behavior. However, significant distinctions can be made between these areas of scholarship.

Deviant behavior is behavior that departs from social norms.[10] Included within the broad spectrum of deviant acts are behaviors ranging from committing murder or rape to being a nudist or eating with one's fingers in public.

Crime and deviance are often confused; however, not all crimes are deviant and not all deviant acts are crimes. For example, using "soft drugs" such as marijuana may be illegal, but is it deviant? As we shall see in chapter 13, a significant percentage of U.S. youth have used or are using drugs. Therefore, to argue that all crimes are behaviors that depart from the norms of society is probably erroneous.

Similarly, many deviant acts are not criminal. For example, suppose someone observes a person drowning and makes no effort to save that person. This behavior could not legally be considered criminal (see chapter 2). Though society would probably condemn the person's behavior as immoral and deviant, it could not take legal action (unless the observer was a lifeguard!).

In sum, many criminal acts, but not all, fall within the concept of deviance. Similarly, some deviant acts, but not all, are considered crimes.

Two issues that involve deviance are of particular interest to criminologists: How do deviant behaviors become crimes? When should crimes be considered only deviant behaviors and therefore not subject to state sanction?

The first issue involves the historical development of law. Many acts that are legally forbidden today were once considered merely unusual or deviant behavior. For example, the sale and possession of marijuana was legal in this country until 1937, when it became illegal under federal law (see chapter 13). To understand the nature and purpose of law, criminologists study the process by which crimes are created from deviance. Marijuana use was banned because of an extensive lobbying effort by Harry Anslinger, head of the Federal Bureau of Narcotics, who used magazine articles, public appearances, and public testimony to sway public opinion against marijuana use.[11] In one famous article, which appeared in 1937, Anslinger told how "an entire family was murdered by a youthful [marijuana] addict in Florida. . . . with an ax he had killed his father, mother, two brothers, and a sister."[12] As a result of these efforts a deviant behavior, marijuana use, became a criminal behavior; and previously law abiding citizens were now defined as criminal offenders.

Criminologists also consider whether outlawed behaviors have evolved into social norms and, if so, whether they should be either legalized or have their penalties reduced (**decriminalized**). For example, there has been frequent debate over legalizing such acts as possession of firearms, marijuana use, abortion, gambling, and prostitution. If an illegal act becomes a norm, should society reevaluate its criminal status and let it become merely an unusual or deviant act? Conversely, if scientists show that a normative act such as smoking or drinking poses a serious health hazard, should it be made illegal? Many recent efforts, both pro and con, have been made to control morally questionable behavior and restrict the rights of citizens to freedom of their actions.

In sum, criminologists are concerned with the concept of deviance and its relationship to criminality. The shifting definition of deviant behavior is closely associated with our concepts of crime.

Crime and Criminology

Professional criminologists usually align themselves with one of several schools of thought or perspectives on their field. Each perspective maintains its own view of what constitutes criminal behavior and what causes people to engage in criminality. This diversity of thought is not unique to criminology; biologists, psychologists, sociologists, historians, economists, and most natural and social science professionals disagree among themselves about critical issues in their fields. Considering the multidisciplinary nature of criminology, it is not surprising that conflicting views exist within it.

It is also common for criminologists to disagree on the nature and definition of crime itself. A criminologist's choice of orientation or perspective depends in part on his or her definition of crime. Thus, the beliefs and research orientations of most criminologists are related to their conceptualizations of crime. This section discusses the three most common concepts of crime and analyzes their relation to criminological schools of thought.

THE CONSENSUS VIEW OF CRIME

The origin of the **consensus view of crime** can be traced to the functionalist school of sociology.[13] Functionalism emphasizes the contributions each part of society makes to the whole. According to the functionalist model, the varied parts of a society are organized into an integrated structure, and change in one area or institution exerts a powerful influence on others. In a perfectly integrated culture, social stability exists and societal members agree on norms, goals, rules, and values. In a maladapted society, upheaval and unrest are common, and social goals confused and unclear. The functionalist model also suggests that society's members have a standard set of rules and values to guide their daily lives and activities. The existing legal code reflects and codifies these generally agreed-upon conduct norms.

From the functionalist viewpoint, the criminal law reflects the mainstream of society's values, beliefs and opinions. Crimes are defined as violations of the criminal law and are believed to be behaviors repugnant to all elements of society. This is referred to as the *consensus view of crime* since it implies that there is general agreement among a majority of citizens on what behaviors should be outlawed by the criminal law, and henceforth be viewed as crimes.

Several attempts have been made to create a concise, yet thorough and encompassing, consensus definition of crime. The eminent criminologists Edwin Sutherland and Donald Cressey have taken the popular stance of linking crime with the criminal law:

> *Criminal behavior is behavior in violation of the criminal law. . . . [I]t is not a crime unless it is prohibited by the criminal law [which] is defined conventionally as a body of specific rules regarding human conduct which have been promulgated*

by political authority, which apply uniformly to all members of the classes to which the rules refer, and which are enforced by punishment administered by the state.[14]

This approach to crime implies that its definition is a function of the beliefs, morality, and direction of the existing legal power structure. Note also Sutherland and Cressey's statement that the criminal law is applied "uniformly to all members of the classes to which the rules refer." This statement reveals the authors' faith in the concept of an ideal legal system that can deal adequately with all classes and types of people. This leading consensus view makes crime essentially a legal concept.

Crime and Criminal Law. The consensus view, then, generally links the concept of crime to the substantive criminal law. That is, crimes are viewed as acts that violate the accepted legal code of the jurisdiction in which they occur.

Wayne LaFave and Austin Scott define the criminal law as "that law (1) [which] for the purpose of preventing harm to society (2) declares what conduct is criminal and (3) prescribes the punishment to be imposed for such conduct."[15]

Three parts of this definition are worth noting: (1) prevention of harm, (2) criminal conduct, and (3) punishment. The first part, prevention of harm, implies that the purpose of criminal law is to protect society from acts that might otherwise hurt its members and institutions; damage and loss of property and physical injury are examples of harm associated with crime. From this perspective, the criminal law can be viewed as a collection of rules of conduct that, if obeyed, will produce an orderly and just society. Laws mediate the differences within society and allow social life to continue unimpeded. Crimes can be viewed as unconventional behavior in opposition to the will of the majority, behavior legally forbidden to all citizens. Thus, in the consensus model, criminal law serves a *social control* function.

The second part, criminal conduct, refers to the specific acts outlawed or forbidden by the criminal code. Each act in the criminal code contains separate elements. For an individual's behavior to be considered criminal, it must loosely match the specific criteria contained in the criminal law. For example, if someone steals money by forcibly breaking into your house, his act may contain the elements of the crime of burglary; if instead he threatens you personally with a gun and takes your wallet, his act most likely possesses the elements of the crime of robbery. Deciding whether an act is criminal is more complex than it may seem, so the elements of crimes will be described more explicitly in chapter 2's discussion of criminal law.

The final part, punishment, points out that the incentive people have to obey the rules of conduct contained in the criminal code is the knowledge that they will be punished, or **sanctioned,** if convicted of a law violation. There cannot be a crime without a corresponding punishment, nor can someone be punished without having been convicted of committing a crime. Moreover, society gives the right to punish law violators to the duly authorized government with legal control over the particular area.

The consensus model of crime is probably accepted by a majority of practicing criminologists and is the one most often used in criminology texts. Nonetheless, various issues confuse it, especially the relationship of crime to morality. Let us now examine that issue in more depth.

Crime and Morality. Crime, as it is defined by the consensus model, seems closely intertwined with morality. Since both crime and immorality are considered violations of accepted societal principles of right and wrong, it seems logical to view crime as a type of immoral behavior. Consequently, law violators can be regarded as bad, evil, or wicked people. Similarly, if we view criminals as caring little for the rights of others, it is only fitting that society punish them harshly. Yet the link between crime and morality is often tenuous and confusing. To understand the consensus model better, we will examine this issue further.

Many acts declared to be crimes by legal codes are behaviors that under some circumstances could be considered legal and moral. For example, most state criminal codes would find a friendly neighborhood poker game illegal, because it involves the crime of unlicensed gambling. Yet it is difficult for poker players to view gambling as immoral, especially since the same state's legal code may allow gambling at horse tracks or licensed casinos. Pornography is another area in which definitions of law and morality often seem confused. A state code may outlaw obscene material that displays nude people engaging in sexual conduct, yet may allow the showing of nationally distributed films or the sale of magazines that seem to display just such conduct (for example, consider the content of *Playboy* magazine).

Confounding the issue further is the fact that a great deal of unethical, socially undesirable, or immoral behavior is not criminal. For example, students may consider racism, sexism, profiteering, lying, and personal selfishness more immoral than betting on football games or smoking marijuana; nonetheless, only the last two behaviors are usually considered illegal. Another example of this situation is state laws that hold that a passerby is not legally required to help an accident victim. Many might find such casual disregard for another's life and safety highly immoral.

Thus, it seems safe to conclude that not all law violations are immoral and not all immoral behaviors are law violations.

Why does such confusion arise? Probably because of the dualistic nature of consensus criminal law. Some illegal acts, referred to as **violations of natural law** or **mala in se crimes,** are rooted in the core values inherent in Western civilization. Natural laws are designed to control such behaviors as inflicting physical harm on others (assault, rape, murder), taking possessions that rightfully belong to another (larceny, burglary, robbery), or harming another person's property (malicious damage, trespass).

Another type of crime, sometimes called **statutory crime** or **mala prohibitum crime,** involve breaking laws passed by legislative bodies that reflect current mores, norms, and opinions of society. In essence, statutory crimes are believed to violate today's morality as expressed by the "right-thinking" members of society. These **moral entrepreneurs** (as the sociologist Howard Becker calls them) believe it their duty to lobby and convince lawmakers that some particular behavior offends the conscience of the majority.[16] Hence, crimes are periodically *created* to control behaviors practiced by millions of otherwise law abiding people. During our lifetime, controversy has swirled around laws legalizing (or outlawing) abortions, guns, drug use, gambling, and prostitution. Often, acts are outlawed (or legitimized) because relatively few powerful and vocal people convince lawmakers that they represent a far larger constituency than they actually do.

While it may often be easy to link natural laws to a basic concept of morality, it is much more difficult to do so in the case of statutory law. Crime, therefore, is a concept that constantly changes relative to a particular culture and often independently from any absolute moral code. Consequently, as will be discussed later in this chapter, many criminologists charge that the consensus concept of crime does not really represent an accurate picture of public opinion.

Criminology and the Consensus View of Crime. Currently, two schools of criminology use the consensus definition of crime: **classical theorists** and **positivists.** Though they share a similar view of crime, these two schools of thought differ in many respects. The major assumptions of the more conservative classical criminologists are: (a) people have free will to choose criminal or conventional means to get the goods and services they desire; (b) the threat of punishment will *deter* people from choosing criminal solutions; and (c) society can control criminal behavior by making the pain of punishment outweigh the pleasure of criminal gain. Classical criminologists believe that society can prevent crime by increasing the effectiveness of the criminal justice system, establishing stricter penalties for law violation, and incapacitating known criminals for extended periods of time. The classical perspective will be discussed in greater detail in chapter 4.

In contrast, liberal positivist criminologists believe that behavior is determined by external forces over which people have little control. Positivists use the empirical scientific method, borrowed from the natural sciences, to investigate crime promoting conditions or factors. Some positivist criminologists focus on the individual biological and psychological traits of offenders; their work will be discussed in chapter 6.[17] In contrast to this view, sociological criminologists believe aspects of the social environment exert a powerful crimogenic (crime producing) influence on human behavior. Some sociological criminologists concern themselves with poverty and class structure and their effect on criminal behavior. Other sociological criminologists focus on the association between crime and social processes such as peer relations, education, and family relationships. The former approach is referred to as the *social structure perspective*; the latter, as the *social process perspective*.

In sum, the difference between liberal positivist and conservative classical criminologists concerns the issue of free will versus determinism. Both groups agree crime is an act that violates the basic values and beliefs of conventional society. Classical theorists argue that criminals choose to violate the law for reasons of greed and personal gain. Positivists believe that law violations are a function of uncontrollable mental, physical, or social conditions.

THE CONFLICT VIEW OF CRIME

In the 1970s, another perspective on the nature of crime and justice developed popularity in the United States and Europe. In opposition to the consensus view, the **conflict approach** depicted society as a collection of diverse groups—owners, workers, professionals, students, minority groups, and so on—who were in conflict with one another about a number of issues. Groups able to assert their political and economic power use the law and the criminal justice system to advance their own causes. Criminal laws, therefore, are viewed as acts created to protect the "haves" from the "have-nots." Conflict criminologists often compare and contrast the harsh penalties exacted on people for taking property (burglary, larceny) with the minor penalties for illegal business practices (polluting the environment, securities violations). Moreover, they charge that while the poor go to prison for minor law violations, the wealthy are given lenient sentences for even the most serious breaches of law. Thus, the conflict perspective of crime is more socioeconomic and political than legal, since it views the definition of crime as being affected by wealth, power, and position and not by moral consensus or for the control of social disruption. In their overview of the conflict approach, Eugene Doleschal and Nora Klapmuts have this to say about the nature of crime:

> *Official crime and the detected criminal are produced and maintained by social forces that have little or nothing to do with the harmfulness of actual behavior. The most successful criminals . . . are rarely caught, rarely prosecuted, and rarely punished . . . . These are persons with power or access to power, the rich and the intelligent. The less successful criminals are more likely to be . & . punished. . . . They are the powerless, the poor, the unintelligent.* [18]

In a similar vein, Richard Quinney has stated:

> *Crime as a legal definition of human conduct is created by agents of the dominant class in a politically organized society. . . . Definitions of crime are composed of behaviors that conflict with the interests of the dominant class.* [19]

Crime, according to this definition, is a political concept designed to protect the power and position of the upper classes at the expense of the poor. Even crimes prohibiting violent acts such as rape and murder may have political undertones: Banning violent acts insures domestic tranquility and guarantees that the anger of the poor and disenfranchised classes will not be directed at the wealthy capitalists who exploit them.

According to conflict criminologists, the key to achieving success is power. Groups that attain power, usually through wealth and position, can control the behavior of others and gain a disproportionate share of what society has to offer.

A number of conflict theorists look to the philosophical-political-economic writings of the German philosopher Karl Marx for their inspiration. Marx viewed social life as being controlled by *economic determinism*; that is, the nature of society—its art, music, religion, lifestyles, and concepts of law and crime—is deeply influenced by its economic system. [20] Conflict theorists influenced by Marx believe the U.S. justice system was created to serve the capitalist class and fix power in the hands of the wealthy. This sub-area of the conflict perspective is often called **radical criminology.** The conflict school of criminology will be discussed in greater detail in chapter 9.

THE INTERACTIONIST VIEW OF CRIME

The **interactionist view of crime** traces its antecedents to the **symbolic interactionist** school of sociology, first popularized by George Herman Mead, Charles Horton Cooley, and W.I. Thomas. [21] This position holds that: (1) people act according to their own interpretations of reality, according to the meaning things have for them; (2) they learn the meaning of a thing from the way others react to it, either positively or negatively; and (3) they reevaluate and interpret their own behavior according to the meaning and symbols they have learned from others.

With respect to crime, the interactionist view falls somewhere between the consensus and conflict perspectives. Unlike the consensus model, the interactionist view portrays crime and law as independent from the concept of an absolute moral code. According to this perspective, the definition of crime reflects the preferences of people who hold social power in a particular legal jurisdiction and who use their influence to impose their definition or right and wrong on the rest of the population. Criminals are individuals whom society chooses to label as outcasts or deviants because they have violated social rules. The classic statement on this matter has been supplied by sociologist Howard Becker, who claims that "the deviant is one to whom that label has successfully been applied; deviant behavior is behavior people so label." Thus, the prevailing interactionist view is that crimes are outlawed behaviors simply because society defines them that way and not because they are inherently evil acts.

Even then, most serious mala in se crimes such as murder or theft may be viewed as violations of current social concerns and not as breaches of absolute human morality. For example, while U.S. culture abhors and prohibits the willful taking of another person's life and labels this act murder, it condones such actions under certain circumstances—during wartime, in self-defense, when a law-enforcement agent believes a criminal fleeing from arrest is dangerous to himself or others, or when a person is executed after conviction for a capital crime. Furthermore, in other cultures and at other times, acts we consider criminal have been viewed as conventional behavior, and people our society views as conventional have been considered criminal. For example, whereas making a big corporate profit may be applauded in the United States as sound business practice, it would be considered a criminal act in Russia, China, or some other socialist countries.

The interactionist view of crime can also be compared with the conflict perspective. They are similar in that both suggest that behavior is outlawed when it offends the sensibilities of citizens who maintain the social, economic, and political power necessary to have the law conform to their interests or needs. However, unlike the conflict view, the interactionist perspective does not attribute capitalist economic and political motives to the process of defining crime. Instead, interactionists see the criminal law as conforming to the beliefs of moral entrepreneurs who use their influence to shape the legal process in the way they see fit.[22] Laws against pronography, prostitution, and drugs are believed to be motivated more by moral crusades than by capitalist sensibilities. Consequently, interactionists are concerned with shifting moral and legal standards and *social relativism.*

Although the interactionist perspective provides a way of looking at crime, it is actually more concerned with the social consequences of law violation. As Becker comments:

> *We are not so much interested in the person who commits a deviant act once as in the person who sustains a pattern of deviance over a long period of time, who makes of deviance a way of life, who organizes his identity around a pattern of deviant behavior.*[23]

To the interactionist, crime has no meaning unless people react to it, labeling perpetrators as deviant and setting them on a course of sustained criminal activity. The one-time criminal, if not caught or labeled, can simply return to a "normal" way of life with little permanent damage—the college boy who tries marijuana does not view himself, nor do others view him, as a criminal or a drug addict. Only when prohibited acts are recognized and sanctioned do they become important, life transforming incidents. Consequently interactions believe that society should intervene as little as possible in the lives of law violators lest they be labeled and stigmatized. The labeling process will be reviewed in chapter 7.

PERSPECTIVES IN CRIMINOLOGY

The consensus view of crime dominated criminological thought until the late 1960s. Criminologists devoted themselves to learning why lawbreakers violated the rules of society. The criminal was viewed as an outlaw who, for one reason or another, flauted the rules defining acceptable conduct and behavior.

In the 1960s the interactionist perspective gained prominence. The rapid change U.S. society was experiencing made traditional laws and values questionable. Many criminologists were swept along in the social revolution of the 1960s, and likewise embraced an ideology that suggested that crimes reflected rules imposed by a conservative majority on nonconforming members of society. At the same time, more radical scholars gravitated toward conflict explanations. Today, in the more conservative 1980s, it seems that the consensus view of crime is again predominant. However, each position still has many followers. It is our position that criminologists' personal definitions of crime dominate the rest of their thinking, research efforts, and attitudes toward their profession. Thus, U.S. criminologists have taken different directions in their quest for understanding crime and its control.

Considering these differences, it is possible to take elements from each school of thought to formulate an integrated definition of crime:

> *Crime is a violation of societal rules of behavior as interpreted and expressed by a criminal code created by people holding social and political power. Individuals who violate these rules are subject to sanctions by state authority, social stigma, and loss of status.*

This definition combines the consensus view's position that the criminal law defines crimes with the conflict perspective's emphasis on political power and control and the interactionist view's concepts of stigma. Thus, crime as defined here is a political, social, and economic function of modern life.

Ethical Issues in Criminology

A critical issue facing students of criminology involves recognizing the field's political and social consequences. All too often, criminologists forget the social responsibility they bear as experts in the area of crime and justice. When acted upon by government agencies, their pronouncements and opinions become the basis for sweeping social policy; thus, the lives of millions of people are influenced by criminological research data. During our lifetime, we have witnessed debates over gun control, capital punishment, and mandatory sentences. While some criminologists have successfully argued for massive social service programs to reduce the crime rate, others consider it a waste of time. By holding themselves up to be experts on law violating behavior, criminologists place themselves in a position of power; the potential consequences of their actions are enormous. Therefore, they must be aware of the ethics of their profession and be prepared to defend their work in the light of public scrutiny. Major ethical issues include the following: What is to be studied? Who is to be studied? How should studies be conducted?

Under ideal circumstances, when criminologists choose a subject for study they are guided by their own scholarly interests, by pressing social needs, by the availability of accurate data, and by other, similar concerns. Nonetheless, in recent years a great influx of government and institutional funding has influenced the direction of criminological inquiry. Major sources of monetary support include the

Justice Department's National Institute of Justice (NIJ) and the Office of Juvenile Justice and Delinquency Prevention (OJJDP). Both the National Science Foundation (NSF) and the National Institute of Mental Health (NIMH) have been prominent sources of government funding. Private foundations such as the Ford Foundation have also played an important role in supporting criminological research.

Though the availability of research money has spurred criminological inquiry, it has also, as indicated, affected the directions research has taken. Since state and federal governments provide a significant percentage of available research monies, they may also dictate the areas that can be studied. A potential conflict of interest arises when the institution funding research is itself one of the principal subjects of the research process. There also may exist a not-so-subtle influence on the criminologist seeking research funding: if criminologists are too critical of the government's role in the crime process, perhaps they will be barred from receiving further financial help. This situation appears even more acute when we consider that criminologists typically work for universities or public agencies and are under pressure to bring in a steady flow of research funds or to maintain the continued viability of their agency. Even when criminologists maintain discretion of choice, the direction of their efforts may not be truly objective. For example, John Galliher and James McCartney show that funding agencies have supported a positivistic concept of delinquency by their tendency to support research oriented toward discovering external factors that cause youths to become law violators.[24]

Austerity programs and budget cutbacks have severely limited the government's current role in funding social science research. It will be interesting to observe changes in the direction and objectivity of future criminological research efforts.

A second major ethical issue in criminology concerns who is to be the subject of inquiries and study. Too often, criminologists have focused their attention on the poor and minorities while ignoring the middle-class criminal, white-collar crime, organized crime, and government crime. Critics have charged that by "unmasking" the poor and desperate, criminologists have justified any harsh measures taken against them.[25] For example, social scientists have suggested that criminals have a lower IQ than the average citizen and that minority status is the single greatest predictor of criminality.[26] Though such research is often methodologically unsound and admittedly tentative, it can focus attention on the criminality of one element of the community while ignoring others. Also, subjects are often misled about the purpose of the research. When white and black youngsters are asked to participate in a survey of their behavior they are rarely told in advance that the data they provide may later be used to prove the existence of significant racial differences in their self-reported crime rates. Should subjects be told what the true purpose of a survey is? Would such disclosures make meaningful research impossible?

Criminological research may also endanger the lives and privacy of its subjects. Laud Humphreys's well-known study *Tea Room Trade* involved his observation of gay sexual encounters in public restrooms.[27] Humphreys, who posed as a homosexual, recorded the license plate numbers of his subjects and later contacted them for interviews. When criminologists conduct such observation, should they identify themselves and state the purpose of their research? The homosexuals Humphreys observed were personally endangered, since their identities were recorded when they participated in an illegal act. Though Humphreys refused to cooperate with police authorities, the potential for harm was still there. By deceiving the men he observed, did Humphreys violate an unwritten ethical rule of social science? How far should criminologists go when collecting data? Is it ever permissible to deceive subjects in order to collect data?

Criminology Today

What critical issues face the field of criminology and what does the future hold in store?

In the 1980s we have so far witnessed a marked change in the ideological orientation of the field, from liberal to conservative thinking. For example, a major theme currently being explored by criminologists is how best to use legal punishment in controlling or deterring crime (see chapter 5). Similarly, criminologists have identified a violence-prone career criminal type and suggest that such people be separated from the rest of society (chapter 4). Whereas liberals in the 1960s and 1970s sought to define the social factors that produced crime, conservatives in the 1980s are less concerned about what causes crime and more concerned about what can be done to prevent it. Consequently, efforts are now being made to identify chronic offenders and develop a means of controlling them, rather than to plan methods of treating offenders and provide alternatives to their criminality.

Though the ideological emphasis of criminology seems to be changing, significant numbers of liberal thinkers still maintain that the forces producing crime lie outside of personal control. They contend that if crime rates are to be reduced, the answer lies not in punishing individual offenders, but in improving neighborhoods, upgrading schools, strengthening families, and so on. Thus, in the 1980s we have witnessed much ideological polarization within criminology.

We have also seen an increased emphasis on the victim's role in the crime problem during the 1980s. Victimization statistics have become a prominent method of identifying crime rates and trends. The relationship between the victim and criminal has become the focus of some study. Increased attention has been given to the personal characteristics of victims and criminals, to assess the way crimes occur and society's reaction to them. For example, one prominent study has shown that when a murder case has a black criminal and a white victim, the criminal is more likely to receive the death penalty than if the offender and victim are both of the same race (see chapter 5).

In step with the conservative leanings of the field has been an increased focus on nonsocial causes of criminal behavior. A liberal view would hold that we are all born equal, but that social forces such as poverty, racism, and lack of opportunity propel some into a life of crime. Though among the earliest explanations of criminality, biological and psychological causes are once again being studied by some criminologists, who seek to explain the prevalence of violent and antisocial behavior patterns in our society (chapter 6). Concern for public safety has precipitated research studies designed to find the key to discovering the personal factors that precipitate uncontrollable, violent behavior patterns. Since these crimes often seem random and unexplainable, it seems logical that some personal aberration can account for them.

Finally, criminology seems to be maturing as an area of scientific study. Both the literature and the research of the field grow more scientifically advanced each year; criminology is as sophisticated as any other social science. Criminologists are feeling greater pressure to master the techniques of electronic data analysis; thus, the body of knowledge about criminality and crime patterns continues to grow. And though some constants have been discovered, great controversy still exists over how data should be interpreted and what the findings actually mean.

These major issues should continue to be focal concerns for criminology through the 1980s. We might expect to see diminished concern about the causes of crime and an increased focus on social control mechanisms. It seems ironic that only a few short years ago the most important new trend in criminology was the influence of radical thinking and the questioning of traditional values and relationships. A shift in the opposite direction is occurring, and the recent research and policies reviewed in this text reflect that change.

Summary

Criminology is the scientific approach to the study of criminal behavior and society's reaction to it. It is essentially an interdisciplinary field; many of its practitioners were originally trained as sociologists, psychologists, economists, political scientists, historians, and natural scientists. In the late 1960s, criminal justice programs were created to examine and improve the U.S. system of justice. Today, many criminologists work in criminal justice educational programs, and the two fields are mutually dedicated to understanding the nature and control of criminal behavior.

Included among the various subareas that make up the criminological enterprise are criminal statistics, the sociology of law, the etiology of crime, criminal behavior systems, and penology.

In viewing crime, criminologists use one of three perspectives: the consensus view, the conflict view, and the interactionist view. The consensus view is that crime is illegal behavior defined by the existing criminal law, which reflects the values and morals of a majority of citizens. Crimes are behaviors prohibited so that society can operate in an orderly fashion. The conflict view is that crime is behavior created so that economically powerful individuals can retain their control over society. The interactionist view portrays criminal behavior as a relativistic, constantly changing concept that reflects society's current thinking about deviant behavior. According to the interactionist view, criminal behavior is behavior so labeled; criminals are people society chooses to label as outsiders, or deviants.

Criminologists must critically examine the way they conduct research. To obtain data, criminologists often mislead people as to the true purpose of their efforts. Criminologists must be concerned with the ethics of their profession.

Criminology is undergoing great change in the 1980s. A swing in the direction, from liberal and radical approaches to a more conservative outlook, appears to be in motion.

Notes

1. Edwin Sutherland and Donald Cressey, *Principles of Criminology*, 6th ed. (Philadelphia: J.B. Lippincott, 1960), p. 3.
2. See Marvin Wolfgang, "Cesare Lombroso," in *Pioneers in Criminology*, ed. Herman Mannheim (Montclair, N.J.: Patterson Smith, 1970), pp. 232–71.
3. Vincent Webb and Dennis Hoffman, "Criminal Justice as an Academic Discipline," *Journal of Criminal Justice* 6 (1978):349.
4. Marvin Wolfgang and Francis Ferracuti, *The Subculture of Violence* (London: Social Science Paperbacks, 1967), p. 20.
5. Ibid., p. 27.
6. Marvin Wolfgang, *Patterns in Criminal Homicide* (Philadelphia: University of Pennsylvania Press, 1958).
7. Stephen Schafer, *Introduction to Criminology* (New York: McGraw-Hill, 1976), p. 3.
8. Hans Von Hentig, *The Criminal and His Victim* (New Haven: Yale University Press, 1948); Stephen Schafer, *The Victim and His Criminal* (New York: Random House, 1968).

9. Marvin Zalman, *A Heuristic Model of Criminology and Criminal Justice* (Chicago: Joint Commission on Criminology Education and Standards, University of Illinois, Chicago Circle, 1981), pp. 9–11.

10. Charles McCaghy, *Deviant Behavior* (New York: MacMillan, 1976), pp. 2–3.

11. Edward Brecher, *Licit and Illicit Drugs* (Boston: Little Brown, 1972), pp. 413–16.

12. Ibid., p. 414.

13. Jon Shepherd, *Sociology* (St. Paul: West Publishing Co., 1981), p. 11.

14. Edwin Sutherland and Donald Cressey, *Criminology*, 8th ed. (Philadelphia: Lippincott, 1970), p. 8.

15. Wayne LaFave and Austin Scott, *Criminal Law* (St. Paul: West Publishing Co., 1972), p. 5.

16. Howard Becker, *Outsiders: Studies in the Sociology of Deviance* (New York: Free Press, 1963).

17. See Leonard Hippchen, *The Ecologic-Biochemical Approaches to Treatment of Delinquents and Criminals* (New York: Van Nostrand Reinhold, 1978).

18. Eugene Doleschal and Nora Klapmuts, "Toward a New Criminology," *Crime and Delinquency* 5 (1973):607.

19. Richard Quinney, *Criminology* (Boston: Little Brown, 1975), pp. 37–41.

20. David Greenberg, *Crime and Capitalism* (Palo Alto, Calif.: Mayfield, 1981), pp. 13–15.

21. See Herbert Blumer, *Symbolic Interactionism* (Englewood Cliffs, N.J.: Prentice-Hall, 1969).

22. Becker, *Outsiders*, p. 9.

23. Ibid.

24. John Galliher and James McCartney, "The Influence of Funding Agencies on Delinquency Research," *Social Problems* 21 (1974):77–90.

25. See Greenberg, *Crime and Capitalism*, pp. 1–15.

26. Michael Hindelang and Travis Hirschi, "Intelligence and Delinquency: A Revisionist Review," *American Sociological Review* 42 (1977):471–486.

27. Laud Humpherys, *Tea Room Trade* (Chicago: Aldine, 1975).

2 The Criminal Law and Its Processes

CHAPTER OUTLINE

Introduction

Criminal Law and Civil Law

Functions of the Criminal Law
Exerts Social Control
Banishes Personal Retribution
Expresses Public Opinion and Morality
Deters Criminal Behavior
Punishes Transgressors
Maintains Social Order

Historical Development of Law and Crime
Origins of English Law
Common Law in America

Felony and Misdemeanor

The Legal Definition of a Crime
Actus Reus
Mens Rea

Defenses: Excuse and Justification
Ignorance or Mistake
Insanity
Intoxication
Duress
Necessity
Self-Defense
Entrapment

Reforming the Criminal Law

Summary

KEY TERMS

criminal law
civil law
burden of proof
beyond a reasonable doubt
preponderance of the evidence
substantive criminal law
folkways
mores
retribution
mala in se
mala prohibitum
deter

shire
hundreds
tithing
ecclesiastic
circuit judge
common law
stare decisis
criminal attempt
arson
decriminalize
felony

misdemeanor
actus reus
mens rea
general intent
specific intent
transferred intent
constructive intent
strict-liability crime
excuse
justification
guilty but insane

Introduction

In chapter 1, the concept of crime was viewed from various criminological perspectives. We saw that much disagreement exists among criminologists about the true nature of criminal behavior. Similarly, the role of law in defining crime is open to debate. Some view law as a mechanism of social control; others see it as expressing the beliefs, values, and morals of society; still others believe it is a device to maintain the status quo and insure that the wealthy and powerful keep their advantageous positions in society.

Despite these differences, it is the existing criminal law that defines crime in U.S. society. Each state government, as well as the federal government, has its own criminal code, developed over many generations and incorporating moral beliefs, social values, and political and economic developments and needs. The criminal law is a living document, constantly evolving to keep pace with society. However, if the existing criminal law had to be classified, it would be viewed as a set of rules designed to maintain the social fabric and, albeit slowly, to reflect public opinion. There is little question that U.S. criminal law reflects the consensus/functionalist viewpoint.

In modern society, the rule of law governs the form and direction of almost all human interaction. Business practices, family life, education, property transfer, inheritance, and other common forms of social relations must conform to the rules set out by the legal code. Most importantly for our purposes, the law defines behaviors society labels as criminal. As noted in chapter 1, most criminologists have adopted the legal definition of crime in their research and writing. Consequently, it is important for students of criminology to have a basic understanding of the law and its relationship to crime and deviance.

This chapter will review the nature and purpose of the law, chart its history, and discuss its elements.

Criminal Law and Civil Law

Law can be divided into two broad categories—**criminal law** and **civil law.** Civil law is all law other than criminal law, such as tort law (the law of personal wrongs and damage), property law (the law governing transfer and ownership of property), and contract law (the law of personal agreements).

There are several differences between criminal law and civil law. First, the main purpose of criminal law is to give the state the power to protect the public from harm by punishing individuals whose actions threaten the social order. In civil law, the harm or injury is considered a private wrong, and the main concern is to compensate individuals for harm done to them by others. In a criminal action, the state initiates the legal proceedings by bringing charges and prosecuting the violator. If it is determined that the criminal law has been broken, the state can impose punishment, such as imprisonment, probation (community supervision by the court), or a fine payable to the state. In a civil action, however, the injured person must initiate proceedings. In a successful action, the injured individual usually receives money to compensate for the harm done.

Another major difference is the **burden of proof** required to establish the defendant's liability. In criminal matters, the defendant's guilt must be proved **beyond a reasonable doubt.** In a civil case, the defendant is required to pay damages if a **preponderance of the evidence** finds that he or she committed the wrong. Establishing guilt by a preponderance of the evidence is easier than establishing it beyond a reasonable doubt.[1]

Although major differences exist between criminal law and civil law, there are also many similarities, particularly in the area of tort law. A tort is a civil action in which an individual asks to be compensated for personal harm. The harm may be either physical or mental and includes such acts as trespass, assault and battery, libel, and slander. Because some torts are similar to some criminal acts, a person can possibly be held both criminally and civilly liable for one action. For example, if one man punches another, it is possible for the assailant to be charged by the state with assault and battery—and imprisoned if found guilty—and also sued by the victim in a tort action in which he could be required to pay monetary damages. Perhaps the most important similarity is that criminal law and civil law have a common purpose. Both attempt to control people's behavior by setting limits on what acts are permissible; both accomplish this through state-imposed sanctions. Table 2.1 summarizes the similarities and differences between tort law and criminal law.

TABLE 2.1
A comparison of criminal and tort law

Similarities
Both criminal and tort law seek to control behavior.
Sanctions are imposed in both laws.
Similar areas of legal action exist; for example, personal assault and control of white-collar offenses such as environmental pollution.

Differences

Criminal Law	Tort Law
Crime is a public offense.	Tort is a civil or private wrong.
The sanction associated with criminal law is incarceration or death.	The sanction associated with a tort is monetary damages.
The right of enforcement is with the state.	The individual brings action.
The government ordinarily does not appeal.	Both parties can appeal.
Fines go to the state.	The individual receives damages as compensation for harm done.

Functions of the Criminal Law

The **substantive criminal law** is a written code defining crimes and their punishments. In U.S. society, the state and federal governments have developed their own unique criminal codes. Though all the codes are different, the terms they use and the behaviors they are designed to control are often quite similar.

Regardless of which culture or jurisdiction created them, or when, criminal codes have several distinct functions. The most important of these are described below.

EXERTS SOCIAL CONTROL

The primary purpose of the criminal law is to control the behavior of people within its jurisdiction. The criminal law is a written statement of rules to which people must conform their behavior. Every society also maintains unwritten rules of conduct—ordinary customs and conventions referred to as **folkways,** and universally followed behavior norms and morals, or **mores.** However, it is the criminal law that formally prohibits behaviors believed by those in political power to threaten societal well-being, or to challenge their own authority. For example, in our society the criminal law incorporates centuries-old prohibitions against the following behaviors harmful to others: taking the possessions of another person, physically harming another person, damaging another person's property, and cheating another person out of his or her possessions. Similarly, the law prevents actions that challenge the legitimacy of the government, such as planning its overthrow, collaborating with its enemies, and so on. Whereas violations of mores and folkways may be informally punished by any person, control of the criminal law is given to those in political power.

BANISHES PERSONAL RETRIBUTION

By delegating enforcement to others, the criminal law controls an individual's need to seek **retribution** or vengeance, against those who violate his or her rights. By punishing people who infringe on the rights, property, and freedom of others, the law shifts the burden of revenge from the individual to the state. As Oliver Wendell Holmes states, this prevents "the greater evil of private retribution."[2] Though state retaliation may offend the sensibilities of many citizens, it is greatly preferable to a system in which people would have to seek justice for themselves.

EXPRESSES PUBLIC OPINION AND MORALITY

The criminal law also reflects constantly changing public opinions and moral values. As noted in chapter 1, **mala in se** crimes such as murder and forcible rape are almost universally prohibited, but the prohibition of legislatively created **mala prohibitum** crimes such as traffic law and gambling violations changes according to shifting social conditions and attitudes. The criminal law is used to codify these changes. For example, if a state government decides to legalize certain previously outlawed behaviors, such as gambling or marijuana possession, it will amend the state's criminal code. Thus, the criminal law defines the boundaries between current concepts of moral and immoral behavior and allows people to guide their activities accordingly.

The law's ability to reflect prevailing public opinion and morality is subject to much debate. The consensus view of crime is that the content of the criminal law reflects prevailing public opinion. However, an interactionist interpretation of law holds that its moral content is controlled by small but powerful interest groups. Similarly, a conflict theorist sees the law's moral content as reflecting the control of the "haves" over the "have-nots" in society. There is little question that an important goal of the criminal law is to express a moral viewpoint that defines the boundaries of socially acceptable behavior. It is the source of that viewpoint that is often the focus of controversy.

DETERS CRIMINAL BEHAVIOR

The criminal law's social control function is realized through its ability to **deter** potential law violators. The threat of punishment associated with violating the law is designed to prevent crimes before they occur. During the Middle Ages public executions were held to drive this point home. Today, the criminal law's impact is felt through news accounts of long prison sentences and an occasional execution. Does the law's deterrent power work as intended? This controversial question will be explored in chapter 5.

Before the 19th century, legal punishment often consisted of physical pain intended to prevent further law violations.

PUNISHES TRANSGRESSORS

The criminal law grants the government the ability to sanction offenders. Violations of folkways and mores are the province of all citizens, but criminal violations fall solely under the jurisdiction of political agencies. Those violating mores and folkways can be subject to social disapproval, whereas criminal law violators alone are subject to physical coercion and punishment.

Legal punishment, as previously noted, is thought to deter would-be criminals. We punish criminals in the belief that they will become convinced that further law violation will have painful consequences. Before the nineteenth century, most punishments used physical pain to achieve this effect. Today we either incarcerate criminals or execute the most serious offenders. Does punishment have its desired effect? This important question will be reviewed in chapter 5.

MAINTAINS SOCIAL ORDER

All legal systems are designed to support and maintain the boundaries of the social order they serve. In medieval England the law protected the feudal system by defining an orderly system of property transfer and ownership. At the other end of the legal spectrum, laws in socialist or communist nations protect the primacy of the state by strictly curtailing profiteering and individual enterprise. Our own capitalist system is also supported and sustained by the criminal law.

In a sense, the content of the criminal law reflects the economic/political system more than it represents some idealized moral code. In U.S. society, by meting out punishment to those who damage or steal property, the law promotes the activities needed to sustain an economy based on the accumulation of wealth. It would be impossible to conduct business through the use of contracts, promissory notes, credit, banking, and so on unless the law protected private capital. In fact, the criminal law has not always protected commercial enterprise; if one merchant cheated another, it was considered a private matter. Then in 1473, in the *Carrier's Case,* an English court ruled that a merchant who held and transported merchandise for another was guilty of theft if he kept the goods for his own purposes.[3] Prior to the *Carriers' Case,* the law did not consider it a crime for people to keep something that was already in their possession. Breaking with legal precedent, the British court recognized that the new English mercantile trade system could not be sustained if property rights had to be individually enforced. To this day, the substantive criminal law prohibits such business-related acts as larceny, fraud, embezzlement, and commercial theft. Without the law to protect it, the free enterprise system could not exist.

Historical Development of Law and Crime

The concept of law has been present throughout history. In primitive societies, custom and folkways were the equivalents of law. Each group had its own set of customs, which were usually created to deal with situations that arose in daily living. These customs would often be followed long after the reason for their origin was forgotten. Many customs had the force of law and eventually developed into formal or written law.[4]

Hammurabi's Code in Babylonia (2000 B.C.) and the Mosaic Code of the Israelites (1200 B.C.) are among the most famous of the early formal laws. The Mosaic Code not only is the law of the Jews but also is a basis for the U.S. legal system. As Rene A. Wormser points out, "the law of the Jews became one of the chief root sources of both the law of the Continent of Europe and the English law upon which ours is directly based."[5] The Ten Commandments, which are part of the Mosaic Code, exemplify this point. The commandments proscribing killing, stealing, perjury, and adultery precede by several thousand years the same laws found in the U.S. legal system.

Mosaic law, early Greek law, Roman law, and the canon law of the early Catholic church have together greatly contributed to the foundation of U.S. law. However, the major building block for the United States is the English common law. The following discussion focuses on its historical development.

ORIGINS OF ENGLISH LAW

Before the Norman Conquest in 1066, the legal system among the early English (Anglo-Saxons) was very decentralized. Each county **(shire)** was divided into units called **hundreds,** which were groups of one hundred families. The hundred was divided into groups of ten called **tithings.** The tithings were responsible for maintaining order among themselves; petty cases were tried by the hundred group, and only the most serious and important cases were heard by the county courts. The county courts were presided over by local clergymen and church officials known as **ecclesiastics.** Therefore, the law varied in substance from county to county, hundred to hundred, and tithing to tithing. Except for the law of crimes, there was very little written law. Custom and law were one and the same to the Anglo-Saxons.

Crimes during this period were viewed as personal wrongs, and compensation therefore was often paid to the victims. If payment was not made, the victims' families would attempt to forcibly collect damages or seek revenge. The result could be a blood feud between two opposing families.

The recognized crimes were theft, violence, and disloyalty to one's feudal lord. They included treason, homicide, rape, property theft, assault (putting another in fear) and battery (wounding another). For treasonous acts, the punishment was death. However, for many other acts, including both theft and violence, compensation could be paid to the victim. For example, even a homicide could be settled by paying compensation to the deceased's family, unless the crime was carried out by poison or ambush—in that case it was punished by death. For killing in an open fight, a sum *(bot)* was paid; part of it (the *wer*) went to the king, and the remainder (the *wite*) went to the deceased's kin. A scale of compensation existed for lesser injuries such as the loss of an arm or an eye. Important persons, churchmen, and nuns received a greater degree of restitution than the general population. Theft during the Anglo-Saxon era could result in slavery for the thieves and their families. If caught in the act of fleeing with the stolen goods, the thief could be killed. Thus, to a great degree, criminal law was designed to provide an equitable solution to what was considered a private dispute.

The Norman Conquest. After the Norman Conquest in 1066, William the Conqueror, the Norman leader, did not immediately change the substance of Anglo-Saxon law.[6] At the outset of William's reign, justice was administered as it had been in previous centuries. The church courts handled acts that might be considered sin, and the local baron or the county courts dealt with most secular violations. However, to secure control of the countryside and to insure military supremacy over his newly won lands, William replaced the local judiciary with royal administrators who dealt with the most serious breaches of the peace. Since the royal administrator could not continually be present in each community, a system was developed in which each judge rode in a circuit throughout England, holding court in each county several times a year. When court was in session, the royal officials would summon a number of citizens who would, on their oath, tell of the crimes and serious breaches of the peace that had occurred since the judge's last visit. The royal judge then decided what to do in each case, using local custom and rules of conduct as his guide. If, for example, a local farmer had stolen his neighbor's cow, he might be executed if those before him had suffered that fate for a similar offense. However, if in previous cases the thief had been forced to make restitution to the victim, then that judgment would be rendered in the present case.

At first, the judicial process was haphazard, lacking formalized rules or procedures. Judges did not have a professional identity and viewed themselves as agents of royal authority rather than as arbitrators or dispensers of law. Juries, which began to develop about this time, were groups of local citizens on whom the judges called not only to decide the facts of the case but also to investigate the crimes, accuse suspected offenders, and even give testimony at the trial. Gradually, royal prosecutors came into being. These representatives of the Crown submitted evidence and brought witnesses to testify before the jury. But not until much later was the accused in a criminal action allowed to bring forth witnesses to rebut charges; and not until the eighteenth century was oath taking by witnesses required. Few formal procedures existed, and both the judge and the prosecutor felt free to intimidate witnesses and jurors when they considered it necessary.

The Common Law. The present English system of law came into existence during the reign of Henry II (1154–1189). Henry also used traveling judges, better known as **circuit judges.** These judges traveled a specific route known as a circuit and heard the cases that previously had been under the jurisdiction of local courts. This practice was the main factor contributing to the growth of the common law.

As it is used today, the term **common law** refers to a law common to all subjects of the land, without regard for geographic or social differences.[7] As best they could, Henry's judges applied a national law instead of the law that held sway in local jurisdictions. This attempt was somewhat confused at first, from having to take into account both local custom and the Norman conquerors' feudal law. However, as new situations arose, judges took advantage of legal uncertainty by either inventing new solutions or borrowing from the laws of European countries. During formal and informal gatherings, the circuit judges shared these incidents, talked about unique cases, and discussed their decisions, thus developing an oral tradition of law. Together these incidents, filtered through the national court system, eventually produced the common law.

Thus, common law is judge-made law, or case law. It is the law found in previously decided cases. Crimes such as murder, burglary, arson, and rape are common-law crimes—they were initially defined and created by judges.

Coexistent with the common-law system is the law of precedent, otherwise known as **stare decisis.** *Stare decisis* means "to stand by decided cases" and is used by the courts to determine the outcome of future cases. In other words, courts are bound to follow the law established in previously decided cases unless the law is overruled by a higher court.

Common Law and Statutory Law. The common law was and still is the law of the land in England. In most instances, the common law retained traditional Anglo-Saxon concepts. For example, the common law originally defined *murder* as the unlawful killing of another human being with malice aforethought.[8] By this definition, for offenders to be found guilty of murder, they must (1) have planned the crime and (2) have intentionally killed the victim out of spite or hatred. However, this general definition proved inadequate to deal with the many situations in which one person took another's life. Over time, to bring the law closer to the realities of human behavior, English judges added other forms of murder: killing someone in the heat of passion; killing someone out of negligence; and killing someone in the course of committing another crime, such as during a robbery. Each form of murder was given a different title (i.e., manslaughter, felony murder) and provided with a different degree of punishment. Thus, the common law was a constantly evolving legal code.

In some instances, the creation of a new common-law crime can be traced back to a particular case. For example, an unsuccessful attempt to commit an illegal act was not considered a crime under early common law. The modern doctrine that **criminal attempt** can be punished under law can be traced directly back to 1784 and the case of *Rex* v. *Scofield.* In that case, Scofield was charged with having put a lit candle and combustible material in a house he was renting with the intention of burning it down; however, the house did not burn. He defended himself by arguing that an attempt to commit a misdemeanor was not actually a misdemeanor. In rejecting this argument, the court stated: "The intent may make an act, innocent in itself, criminal; nor is the completion of an act, criminal in itself, necessary to constitute criminality."[9] After *Scofield*, attempt became a common-law crime, and today most U.S. jurisdictions have enacted some form of criminal attempt law.

When the situation required it, the English parliament enacted legislation to supplement the judge-made common law. Violations of these laws are referred to as *statutory crimes.* For example, in 1723 the Waltham Black Act punished with death offenses against rural property, from the poaching of small game to arson, if the criminal was armed or disguised.[10] Moreover, the act eroded the rights of the accused; it allowed the death sentence to be carried out without a trial if the accused failed to surrender when ordered to do so. The underlying purpose of the act was the British Parliament's desire to control the behavior of peasants whose poverty forced them to poach on royal lands. In the Black Act, then, the British ruling class created a mechanism for protecting its property and position of social power.

Statutory laws usually reflect existing social conditions. They deal with issues of morality such as gambling, sexual activity, and drug-related offenses. Sometimes they reflect changes in technology or social custom. For example, a whole series of statutory laws, such as those concerning embezzlement and fraud, were created to protect the well-being of British, and later American, business enterprise.[11] Chapter 10 will discuss these crimes in greater detail.

COMMON LAW IN AMERICA

Before the American Revolution, the colonies, then under British rule, were subject to the law handed down by English judges. After the colonies acquired their independence, they adapted and changed the English law when necessary to fit their needs. In many states, legislatures standardized such common-law crimes as murder, burglary, arson, and rape by putting them into statutory form. In other states, comprehensive penal codes were passed, thus abolishing the common-law crimes. An example of this process of modifying the common law can be found in the Massachusetts statute defining **arson.** The common-law definition of *arson* is "the malicious burning of the dwelling of another." Massachusetts has expanded this definition by passing legislation defining *arson* as "the willful and malicious setting fire to, or burning of, *any building or contents* thereof *even if they were burned by the owner.*"[12] (Emphasis added.)

As in England, whenever the common law proved inadequate to deal with changing social and moral issues, the colonists supplemented it with legislative statutes, creating new elements in the various state and federal legal codes. As noted, early in the nation's history it was both legal and relatively easy to obtain narcotics such as heroin, opium, and cocaine.[13] Their use became habits of the middle class. However, public and governmental concern arose over the use of narcotics by immigrants, such as the Chinese, who had come to the United States to build railroads and work in mines. Eventually, changes in public sentiment resulted in the 1914 passage of the Harrison Act, which outlawed trade in opium and its derivatives. Later, in 1937, pressure from federal law enforcement officials led to passage of the Marijuana Tax Act, which outlawed the sale or possession of that substance.

We can see in the case of marijuana how the statutory law is subject to change. When use of "pot" became widespread among the middle class in the 1960s, several states revised their laws and effectively **decriminalized** possession of marijuana. Thus, the statutory law began to reflect the views of individual states' legislatures on the use of soft drugs by their citizens. In some states, marijuana possession is still punished by many years in prison; in others, by a small fine.

In summary, much of English common law has become part of the criminal codes of the various state governments and the federal government. In addition, it has from time to time been supplemented by statutes that reflect current moral issues and public opinion.

Felony and Misdemeanor

As they exist today, criminal laws can be classed as either felonies or misdemeanors. The distinction between the two types of crime is based on the seriousness of the crime. A **felony** is a serious offense, whereas a **misdemeanor** is a minor one. Crimes such as murder, rape, and burglary are felonies; crimes such as assault and battery, petty larceny, and disturbing the peace are misdemeanors.

State statutes define what constitutes a felony or misdemeanor—thus, the definition varies from jurisdiction to jurisdiction. Most states define a felony as a crime punishable by death or imprisonment in a state prison, and a misdemeanor as a crime punishable by fine or imprisonment in a local jail.

Some states, however, distinguish between a felony and a misdemeanor on the basis of prison term as opposed to place of imprisonment. Under this model of classification, a felony is usually defined as a crime punishable by death, or imprisonment for more than one year; and a misdemeanor as all other crimes punished by less than a year of confinement. Some common felonies and misdemeanors are discussed in the next Close-Up.

The Legal Definition of a Crime

Newspapers often tell us about people who admit at trial that they committed the act they are accused of, yet are not found guilty of the crime. In most instances, this occurs because state or federal prosecutors have not proven that their behavior falls within the legal definition of a crime. To fulfill the legal definition, all elements of the crime must be proven. For example, in Massachusetts the crime of burglary is defined as:

> Whoever breaks and enters a dwelling house in the nighttime, with intent to commit a felony, or whoever, after having entered with such intent, breaks into such dwelling house in the nighttime, any person being lawfully therein, and the offender being armed with a dangerous weapon at the time of such breaking or entry, or so arming himself in such house or making an actual assault on a person lawfully therein, commits the crime of burglary.[14]

Note that burglary has the following elements:

- It happens at night.
- It involves breaking or entering or both.
- It happens at a dwelling house.
- The accused is armed or arms himself or herself after entering the house or commits an actual assault on a person lawfully in the house.
- The accused intends to commit a felony.

In order for the state to prove a crime occurred, and the defendant committed it, the prosecutor must show that the accused engaged in the *actus reus* and had the *mens rea* or intent to commit the act. The **actus reus** (guilty act) can be either an aggressive act such as a person's taking money, burning a building, or shooting someone; or a failure to act when there is a legal duty to do so, such as a parent's neglecting to seek medical attention for a sick child. The **mens rea** (guilty mind), refers to an individual's state of mind at the time of the act or, more specifically, the person's *intent* to commit the crime.

For most crime, both the actus reus and the mens rea must be present for the act to be considered a crime. For example, if Albert decides to kill Bob and then takes a gun and shoots Bob, Albert can be convicted of the crime of murder, because both elements are present. Albert's shooting of Bob is the actus reus; his decision to kill Bob is the mens rea. However, if Albert only thinks about shooting Bob but does nothing about it, the element of actus reus is absent; and no crime has been committed. Thoughts of committing an act do not alone constitute a crime.

Let us now turn our attention to a closer examination of these issues.

ACTUS REUS

As mentioned, the *actus reus* is the criminal act itself. For an act to be considered illegal, the action must be voluntary. For example, if one person shoots another, that certainly could be considered a voluntary act. However, if the shooting occurs while the person holding the gun is having an epileptic seizure or a heart attack or while the person is sleepwalking, he or she will not be held criminally liable, because the act was not voluntary. But if the individual knew of such a condition and did not take precautions to prevent the act from occurring, then the person could be held responsible for the criminal act. For instance, if Tom has an epileptic seizure while he is hunting and his gun goes off and kills Victor, Tom will not be held responsible for Victor's death. But if Tom knew of his condition and further knew that a seizure could occur at any time, he could be convicted of the crime because it was possible for him to foresee the danger of handling a gun, yet he did nothing about it. Thus, the central issue concerning voluntariness is whether the individual has control over his or her actions.

A second type of actus reus is the failure to act when there is a legal duty to do so. A legal duty arises in three common situations:

1. Relationship of parties based on status. These relationships include parent/child and husband/wife. If a husband finds his wife unconscious because she took an overdose of sleeping pills, he has a duty to try to save her life by seeking medical aid. If he fails to do so and she dies, he can be held responsible for her death.

2. Imposition by statute. For example, some states have passed laws that require a person involved in an automobile accident to stop and help the other parties involved.

3. Contractual relationship. These relationships include lifeguard/swimmer, doctor/patient, and babysitter/child. Because lifeguards have been hired to insure the safety of swimmers, they have a legal duty to come to the aid of drowning persons. If a lifeguard knows a swimmer is in danger and does nothing about it and the swimmer drowns, the lifeguard is legally responsible for the swimmer's death.

The duty to act is a legal and not a moral duty. The obligation arises from the relationship between the parties or from explicit legal requirements. For example, a private citizen who sees a person drowning is under no legal obligation

Common-Law Crimes

The substantive law defines crimes and prescribes the punishments that can be imposed on people engaging in criminal activity. Though each state uses its own definitions, enough similarity exists among them to suggest a general formula for defining most common criminal activities. Below, some familiar illegal acts are set out and an example of each is given.

CRIMES AGAINST THE PERSON

First-degree murder—unlawful killing of another human being with malice aforethought and with premeditation and deliberation.

Second-degree murder—unlawful killing of another human being with malice aforethought but without premeditation and deliberation.

Voluntary manslaughter—intentional killing committed under extenuating circumstances that mitigate the killing, such as killing in the heat of passion after being provoked.

Involuntary manslaughter—unintentional killing, without malice, that is neither excused nor justified, such as homicide resulting from criminal negligence.

Battery—unlawful touching of another with intent to cause injury.

Assault—intentional placing of another in fear of receiving an immediate battery.

Rape—unlawful sexual intercourse with a female without her consent.

Statutory rape—sexual intercourse with a female who is under the age of consent.

Robbery—wrongful taking and carrying away of personal property from a person by violence or intimidation.

EXAMPLES

A person buys some poison and pours it into a cup of coffee another is drinking, intending to kill that person. The motive—to get the insurance benefits of the victim.

A person intending to greatly harm another after a disagreement in a bar hits that person in the head with a baseball bat and the victim dies as a result of the injury. Hitting someone hard with a bat is known to cause serious injury. Because the act was committed in spite of this fact, it is second-degree murder.

A husband coming home early from work finds his wife in bed with another man. The husband goes into a rage and shoots and kills both lovers with a gun he keeps by his bedside.

After becoming drunk, a person drives a car at high speed down a crowded street and kills a pedestrian.

A person seeing someone sitting in his favorite seat in the cafeteria goes up to that person and pushes him out of the seat.

A person aims an unloaded gun at another who believes the gun is loaded and says she is going to shoot.

After a party a man offers to drive a young female acquaintance home. He takes her to a wooded area and despite her protests forces her to have sexual relations with him.

A boy, aged eighteen, and his girlfriend, aged fifteen, have sexual relations. Though the victim voluntarily participates, her age makes her incapable of legally consenting to have sexual relations.

A man armed with a loaded gun approaches another man on a deserted street and demands his wallet.

to save that person. Although we may find it morally reprehensible, the private citizen could walk away and let the swimmer drown without facing legal sanctions.

In any discussion of the actus reus of a crime, it should be mentioned that in some circumstances words are considered acts. In the crime of sedition, the words of disloyalty constitute the actus reus. Further, if a person falsely yells "fire" in a crowded theater and people are injured in the rush to exit, that person is held responsible for the injuries, because his or her word constitutes an illegal act.

INCHOATE (INCOMPLETE) OFFENSES

Attempt—an intentional act for the purpose of committing a crime that is more than mere preparation or planning of the crime. However, the crime is not completed.

Conspiracy—voluntary agreement between two or more persons to achieve an unlawful object or to achieve a lawful object using means forbidden by law.

Solicitation—efforts by one person to encourage another person to commit or attempt to commit a crime by means of advising, enticing, inciting, ordering, or otherwise.

EXAMPLES

A person intending to kill another places a bomb in the second person's car so that it will detonate when the ignition key is used. The bomb is discovered before the car is started. Attempted murder has been committed.

A drug company sells larger-than-normal quantities of drugs to a doctor, knowing that the doctor is distributing the drugs illegally. The drug company is guilty of conspiracy.

A person offers another a hundred dollars to set fire to a third person's house. The person requesting that the fire be set is guilty of solicitation, whether the fire is set or not.

CRIMES AGAINST PROPERTY

Burglary—breaking and entering of a dwelling house of another in the nighttime with the intent to commit a felony.

Arson—intentional burning of a dwelling house of another.

Larceny—taking and carrying away the personal property of another with the intent to steal the property.

Embezzlement—fraudulent appropriation of another's property by one already in lawful possession.

Receiving stolen goods—receiving of stolen property with the knowledge that the property is stolen and with the intent to deprive the owner of the property.

EXAMPLES

Intending to steal some jewelry and silver, a person breaks a window and enters another's house at ten o'clock at night.

A person, angry that her boss did not give her a raise, goes to her boss's house and sets fire to it.

While a woman is shopping, she sees a diamond ring displayed at the jewelry counter. When no one is looking, the woman takes the ring and walks out of the store.

A bank teller receives a cash deposit from a customer and places it in the cash drawer with other deposits. A few minutes later, he takes the deposit out of the cash drawer and keeps it by placing it in his pocket.

A "fence" accepts some television sets from a thief with the intention of selling them, knowing that the sets have been stolen.

DISCUSSION QUESTIONS

1. Do you know the definitions used for crimes such as burglary, murder, or rape in your jurisdiction?
2. Why is robbery considered a violent crime and not a property crime?
3. Should statutory rape be considered as serious as forcible rape?
4. What is the difference between *malice aforethought* and *premeditation*?

SOURCE. Therese J. Libby, J.D., president, TJL Legal Research Inc.

MENS REA

In most situations, for an act to constitute a crime it must be done with criminal intent—otherwise known as *mens rea*. Intent in the legal sense can mean carrying out an act intentionally, knowingly, and willingly. However, the definition also encompasses situations in which recklessness or negligence establishes the required criminal intent.

Some crimes require specific intent and other require general intent. The type of intent needed to establish criminal liability varies depending on how the crime is defined. Most crimes require a **general intent,** or an intent to commit the crime. Thus, when Ann picks Bill's pocket and takes his wallet, her intent is to steal. **Specific intent,** on the other hand, is an intent to accomplish a specific purpose as an element of the crime. It involves an intent in addition to the intent to commit the crime. For example, burglary is the breaking and entering of a dwelling house in the nighttime with the intent to commit a felony. The breaking and entering aspect requires a general intent; the intent to commit a felony is a specific intent. Thus, if Dan breaks and enters Emily's house because he intends to steal Emily's diamonds, Dan is guilty of burglary. However, if Dan merely breaks and enters Emily's house but has no intent to commit a crime once inside, Dan cannot be convicted of burglary, because he lacked specific intent.

In some instances, criminal intent exists although it appears there is no intent to commit the act. This situation occurs when the result is not desired but is substantially certain to occur. For example, if Kim for the purpose of killing John poisons the punch bowl at John's party and John and his guests die as a result of drinking the punch, Kim is said to have intentionally killed both John and his guests. This is so because Kim was substantially certain that the others at the party would drink the punch and be poisoned along with John.

The concept of mens rea also encompasses the situation in which a person intends to commit a crime against one person but injures another party instead. For instance, if Sam, intending to kill Larry, shoots at Larry but misses and kills John, Sam is guilty of murdering John even though he did not intend to. This is known as **transferred intent.** Under this doctrine, the original criminal intent is transferred to the unintended victim.

Mens rea is also found in situations in which harm has resulted because a person has acted negligently or recklessly. Criminal negligence is often found in situations involving drunken driving. If a drunken driver speeding and zigzagging from left to right hits and kills another person, criminal negligence exists. Negligence involves a person's acting unreasonably under the circumstances. In the case of drunken driving, the law maintains that a reasonable person would not drive a car when drunk and thus unable to control the vehicle. The intent that underlies the finding of criminal liability for an unintentional act is known as **constructive intent.**

Exceptions to the Mens Rea Requirement. As mentioned, in most cases both the actus reus and the mens rea must be present before a person can be convicted of a crime. However, several crimes defined by statute do not require mens rea. The actor is guilty simply by doing what the statute prohibits; mental intent does not enter the picture. These offenses are known as **strict-liability crimes,** or *public welfare offenses.* Health and safety regulations, traffic laws, and narcotic control laws are strict-liability statutes.

The underlying purpose of these laws is to protect the public. For example, in the case of *United States* v. *Dotterweich,* the Supreme Court upheld the conviction of a drug company president for misbranding drugs, an act in violation of the federal Food, Drug, and Cosmetic Act. Dotterweich, as president, was in general charge of the business but had not personally mislabeled the drugs; his employees had done the labeling. The Court, finding Dotterweich liable for the illegal actions of his employees, maintained that strict-liability legislation "dispenses with the conventional requirement for criminal conduct awareness of some wrongdoing. In the interest of the larger good it puts the burden of acting at hazard upon a person otherwise innocent but standing in responsible relation to a public danger."[15] Dotterweich was fined $500 and given sixty days probation.

Defenses: Excuse and Justification

As mentioned, the legal definition of crime includes the concept of criminal responsibility, or mental intent. Therefore, if a person whose mental state is affected commits a criminal act, it is possible for the person to defend his or her law-violating actions. When this happens, the person is said to have an **excuse**— meaning the person lacks the intent required to be held criminally responsible for his or her actions. Insanity, intoxication, necessity, and duress are among the types of excuse defenses.

Another type of defense is that of **justification.** Here, the individual usually admits committing the criminal act but maintains that the act was justified and that he or she therefore should not be held criminally liable. Among the justification defenses are self-defense and entrapment.

Persons standing trial for criminal offenses may defend themselves by claiming either that their actions were justified under the circumstances or that their behavior can be defended by their lack of mens rea. If their claims are accepted by judge or jury, then they cannot be held responsible for violating the law and they will be found "not guilty as charged." We will now examine some of these defenses and justifications in greater detail.

IGNORANCE OR MISTAKE

As a general rule, ignorance of the law is no excuse. However, courts have recognized that ignorance can be an excuse if the government fails to make enactment of a new law public, or if the offender relied on an official statement of the law that was later deemed incorrect.

Ignorance or mistake can be an excuse if it negates an element of a crime. For example, if Andrew purchases stolen merchandise from Eric but is unaware that the material was illegally obtained, he cannot be convicted of receiving stolen merchandise because he had no intent to do so. But if Rachel attempts to purchase marijuana from a drug dealer and mistakenly purchases hashish, she can be convicted of a drug charge because she intended to purchase illegal goods.[16]

Ignorance or mistake does not excuse crime when there is some evil intent. However, this creates a conflict when the evil was purely of moral and not legal consequence. For example, some cases of statutory rape (sexual relations with minor females) have been defended on the grounds that the perpetrator was ignorant of their victim's true age. This defense has been allowed in states where sex between consenting adults is legal under the rationale that if a reasonable mistake had not been made, no crime would have occurred. Nonetheless, if the mistake seems unreasonable (for example, if the victim was a preteen) the original charge will stand.[17]

INSANITY

Insanity is a defense to criminal prosecution in which the defendants' state of mind negates their criminal responsibility. A successful insanity defense results in a verdict of "not guilty by reason of insanity." Insanity here is a legal category. As used in U.S. courts, it does not necessarily mean that persons using the defense are mentally ill or unbalanced, only that their state of mind at the time the crime was committed made it impossible for them to have the necessary intent to satisfy the legal definition of a crime. Thus, a person can be diagnosed a psychopath or psychotic but still be judged legally sane. However, it is usually left to psychiatric testimony in court to prove a defendant legally insane.

A person found to be legally insane at the time of trial is placed in the custody of state mental health authorities until diagnosed as sane. Sometimes, a person who was sane when he or she committed a crime becomes insane soon afterward. In that instance, the person receives psychiatric care until capable of standing trial and is then tried on the criminal charge, since the person actually had mens rea at the time the crime was committed. On rare occasions, persons who were legally insane at the time they committed a crime become rational soon afterward. In that instance, the state can neither try them for the criminal offense nor have them committed to a mental health facility. The test used to determine whether a person is legally insane varies between jurisdictions. U.S. courts have used one of four tests: (1) the M'Naghten Rule, (2) the Irresistible Impulse Test, (3) the Durham Rule, and (4) the Substantial Capacity Test.

The M'Naghten Rule. In 1843, the English court established the M'Naghten Rule, also known as the *right-wrong test.* Daniel M'Naghten, believing Edward Drummond to be Sir Robert Peel, the prime minister of Great Britain, shot and killed Drummond (Peel's secretary). At his trial for murder, M'Naghten claimed that he could not be held responsible for the murder because his delusions had caused him to act. The jury agreed with M'Naghten and found him not guilty by reason of insanity. Because of the importance of the people involved in the case, the verdict was not well received. The British Parliament's House of Lords reviewed the decision and requested the court to clarify the law with respect to insane delusions. The court's response became known as the M'Naghten Rule:

> *To establish a defense on the ground of insanity, it must be proved that at the time of the committing of the act the party accused was labouring under such a defect of reason from disease of the mind, as not to know the nature and quality of the act he was doing; or, if he did know it, that he did not know he was doing what was wrong.*[18]

Essentially, the M'Naghten Rule maintains that an individual is insane if he or she is unable to tell the difference between right and wrong because of some mental disability.

The M'Naghten Rule is a widely used test for legal insanity in the United States. In about half of the states, this rule is the legal test when an issue of insanity is presented. However, over the years, much criticism has arisen concerning M'Naghten. First, great confusion has surfaced over such terms as *disease of the mind, know,* and the *nature and quality of the act.* These terms have never been properly clarified. Second, critiques, mainly from the mental health profession, have pointed out that the rule is unrealistic and narrow in that it does not cover situations in which people know right from wrong but cannot control their actions.

The Irresistible Impulse Test. Because of questions about M'Naghten, approximately fifteen state jurisdictions have supplemented the M'Naghten Rule with another test, known as the Irresistible Impulse Test.[19] This test allows the defense of insanity to be used for situations in which defendants were unable to control their behavior because of a mental disease. Thus, the defendants do not have to prove that they did not know the difference between right and wrong, only that they could not control themselves at the time of the crime.

The Durham Rule. The Durham Rule, also known as the *products test*, originated in New Hampshire in 1871. In 1954, the United States Court of Appeals for the District of Columbia applied the New Hampshire test in the case of *Durham* v. *United States.* The court held "that an accused is not criminally responsible if his unlawful act was the product of mental disease or defect."[20] The benefit of applying this test is that it allows psychiatrists, as expert witnesses, to have greater input about the defendant's mental condition. Critics of the Durham Rule argue that because the term *product* is not defined, the jury has no standard for judging the evidence and must therefore rely on the psychiatrist's decision. Although the Durham Rule was once used in several states, it has since been abandoned in all states except New Hampshire.

The Substantial Capacity Test. The newest test for insanity is the Substantial Capacity Test, which was originally a section of the American Law Institute's *Model Penal Code.* It has, over the years, become increasingly popular with U.S. courts. The rule states:

> *A person is not responsible for criminal conduct if at the time of such conduct as a result of mental disease or defect he lacks substantial capacity either to appreciate the criminality [wrongfulness] of his conduct or to conform his conduct to the requirement of law.*[21]

The Substantial Capacity Test is essentially a combination of the M'Naghten Rule and the Irresistible Impulse Test. It is, however, broader in its interpretation of insanity for it requires only a lack of substantial capacity instead of complete impairment, as in M'Naghten and the Irresistible Impulse Test. This test also differs in that it uses the term *appreciate* instead of *know,* the term used in M'Naghten. The federal government and about half the states now use the Substantial Capacity Test.

The Insanity Controversy. Much discussion over the years has concerned the purpose and appropriateness of the insanity defense. Many critics of the defense maintain that inquiry into a defendant's psychological makeup is inappropriate at the trial stage; they would prefer that the issue be raised at the sentencing stage, after guilt or innocence has been determined.

Opponents also charge that criminal responsibility is separate from mental illness and that the two should not be equated. It is a serious mistake, they argue, to consider criminal responsibility as a trait or quality that can be detected by a psychiatric evaluation.

Moreover, some criminals avoid punishment because they are erroneously judged by psychiatrists to have mental illnesses. Conversely, some people who are found not guilty by reason of insanity because they suffer from a mild personality disturbance are incarcerated as mental patients far longer than they would have been imprisoned if they had been convicted of a criminal offense.

John Hinckly's successful insanity defense provoked a public outcry and prompted some jurisdictions to revamp their legal definitions of insanity.

Advocates of the insanity defense say that it serves a unique purpose. Most successful insanity verdicts result in the defendant's being committed to a mental institution until he or she has recovered. The general assumption, according to two legal authorities, Wayne LaFave and Austin Scott, is that the insanity defense makes it possible to single out for special treatment certain persons who would otherwise be subjected to further penal sanctions following conviction. LaFave and Scott further point out that an alternative view maintains that the "real function of the insanity defense is to authorize the state to hold those who must be found not to possess the guilty mind, even though the criminal law demands that no person be held criminally responsible if doubt is cast on any material element of the offense charged."[22]

The insanity plea was thrust into the spotlight when John Hinckley's unsuccessful attempt to kill President Ronald Reagan was captured by news cameras. Hinckley was found not guilty by reason of insanity. Public outcry against this seeming miscarriage of justice prompted some states to revise their insanity statutes. New Mexico, Georgia, Alaska, Delaware, Michigan, Illinois, and Indiana, among other states, have created the defense plea of **guilty but insane,** in which the defendant is required to serve the first part of his or her sentence in a hospital, and once "cured," to be sent to prison. In 1984, the federal government revised its criminal code to restrict insanity as a defense solely to individuals who are unable to understand the nature and wrongfulness of their acts; a defendant's irresistible impulse will no longer be considered. The burden of proof has made an important shift from the prosecutor's need to prove sanity to the defendant's need to prove insanity.[23]

Although such backlash against the insanity plea is intended to close supposed legal loopholes allowing dangerous criminals to go free, the public's fear may be misplaced. It is estimated that fewer than 1 percent of all cases use the insanity plea. Moreover, evidence shows that relatively few insanity defense pleas are successful. Even if the defense is successful, the offender must be placed in a secure psychiatric hospital or the psychiatric ward of a state prison. Since many defendants who successfully plead insanity are nonviolent offenders, it is certainly possible that their hospital stay will be longer than the prison term they would have received if convicted of the crimes they were originally accused of.[24]

Despite efforts to ban its use, the insanity plea is probably here to stay. Most crimes require mens rea, and unless we are willing to forego that standard of law, we will be forced to find not guilty those people whose mental state makes it impossible for them to rationally control their behavior.

INTOXICATION

Intoxication, which includes the taking of alcohol or drugs, is generally not considered a defense. However, there are two exceptions to this rule. First, an individual who becomes intoxicated either by mistake, through force, or under duress can use involuntary intoxication as a defense.

Second, voluntary intoxication is a defense when specific intent is needed and the person could not have formed the intent because of his or her intoxicated condition. For example, if a person breaks and enters another's house but is so drunk that he cannot form the intent to commit a felony, the intoxication is a defense against burglary.

DURESS

Duress is a defense to a crime when the defendant commits an illegal act because the defendant or a third person has been threatened by another with death or serious bodily harm if the act is not performed. For example, if Pete, holding a gun on Jerry, threatens to kill Jerry unless he breaks into and enters Bill's house, Jerry has a defense of duress for the crime of breaking and entering.

This defense, however, does not cover the situation in which defendants commit a serious crime such as murder to save themselves or others. The reason for this exception is that the defense is based on the social policy that, when faced with two evils (harm to oneself or violating the criminal law), it is better to commit the lesser evil in order to avoid the threatened harm. In the situation of murder versus threatened harm, however, the taking of another's life is considered the greater of the two evils.

NECESSITY

The defense of necessity is applied in situations in which a person must break the law in order to avoid a greater evil caused by natural physical forces (storms, earthquakes, illness). This defense is only available when committing the crime is the lesser of two evils. For example, a person lacking a driver's license is justified in driving a car to escape a fire.

However, as the famous English case *Regina* v. *Dudley and Stephens* indicates, necessity does not justify the intentional killing of another.[25] In that case, three sailors and a cabin boy had been shipwrecked and floating in the open seas in a lifeboat. After nine days without food and seven without water, Dudley and Stephens killed the cabin boy and the three sailors ate his body and drank his blood. Four days later the sailors were rescued. The court acknowledged that the cabin

CLOSE-UP

Justifiable Homicide?

The following classic legal case concerns the issue of whether homicide is justified to save a life. The courts have ruled that there is no right, generally, to take the life of another to save someone else, even in a common disaster.

The American ship *William Brown* left Liverpool for Philadelphia on March 13, 1841. It carried a crew of seventeen and sixty-five passengers, Scotch and Irish emigrants. On April 19, near Newfoundland, the ship struck an iceberg and began rapidly to fill with water. The longboat and the jollyboat were lowered. The captain, eight men of the crew, and one passenger got into the jollyboat. The remaining nine members of the crew, including Holmes, a seaman, and thirty-two passengers, got into the longboat. Thirty-one passengers went down with the ship (one having died previously). The longboat leaked and was overcrowded, but it remained afloat for about twenty-four hours. The wind rose and the sea became rough. Following the first mate's direction that man and wife should not be parted and women should be spared, the crew threw overboard fourteen of the male passengers—all the male passengers on board except two married men and a small boy. Two women were either thrown over or jumped after their brother. The passengers were not informed or consulted about what was to be done. None of the crew was thrown over. The next morning the longboat was sighted by a ship, and everyone yet on board was saved. Holmes was charged and convicted of manslaughter.

DISCUSSION QUESTIONS:

1. Can the taking of a human life ever be morally justified?

2. What would you have done in Holmes's place?

SOURCE. *United States* v. *Holmes*, 26 F. Cas. 360 (1824).

---

boy most likely would have died naturally because he was in the weakest condition, but nevertheless judged the killing unjustified. (See the following Close-Up on justifiable homicide.)

SELF-DEFENSE

Defense of the Person. At times, an individual is justified in using force against another to protect himself or herself. When that happens, the person claims to have acted in self-defense and is therefore not guilty of the harm done. If the defendant was justified in using force, self-defense excuses such crimes as murder, manslaughter, and assault and battery.

The law, however, has set limits as to what is reasonable and necessary self-defense. First, defendants must have a reasonable belief that they are in danger of death or great harm and that it is necessary for them to use force to prevent harm to themselves. For example, if Mary threatens to kill Jan but it is obvious that Mary is unarmed, Jan is not justified in pulling her gun and shooting Mary. However, if Mary, after threatening Jan, reaches into her pocket as if to get a gun and Jan then pulls her gun and shoots Mary, Jan could claim self-defense, even if it is discovered that Mary was unarmed. In this situation, Jan had a reasonable belief that harm was imminent and that it was necessary to shoot first to avoid injury to herself.

Second, the amount of force used must be no greater than that necessary to prevent personal harm. For instance, if Steve punches Ben, Ben could not justifiably hit Steve with an iron rod. Ben could, however, punch Steve back if he believed Steve was going to continue punching.

Another issue arises concerning self-defense in situations in which deadly force may be necessary: Does a person have a duty to avoid using deadly force against an attacker by retreating if possible? U.S. courts are split on this issue. The majority of states maintain that the person attacked does not have to retreat, even if he or she can do so safely. This position is based on the policy that a person should not be forced to act in a humiliating or cowardly manner. However, many states do require that a person try to retreat, if it is possible to do so safely, before using deadly force. Even in most of these jurisdictions, however, people are not required to retreat if attacked in their homes or offices.

The rules concerning self-defense also apply to situations involving defense of a third person. Thus, if a person reasonably believes that another is in danger of unlawful bodily harm from an assailant, the person may use the force necessary to prevent the danger.

The self-defense concept received national publicity when, on 22 December 1984, Bernard Goetz shot four would-be robbers on a subway car in New York. Despite some concern over the interracial nature of the incident (Goetz is white and his assailants black), public support seemed overwhelmingly on the side of self-defense. At first the New York grand jury failed to indict Goetz on a shooting charge, although two of the injured robbers were shot in the back. Later, public support swung the other way and Goetz was indicted in the case.

Defense of Property. Using force to defend one's property from trespass or theft is allowable if the force is reasonable. This means that the case of force should be a last resort after requests to stop interfering with the property have failed or after legal action has failed. Also, the use of deadly force is not considered reasonable when only protection of property is concerned. This is based on the social policy that human life is more important than property.

ENTRAPMENT

Entrapment is another defense that excuses a defendant from criminal liability. The entrapment defense is raised when the defendant maintains that law enforcement officers induced him or her to commit a crime. The defendant would not have committed the crime had it not been for trickery, persuasion, or fraud on the officers' part. In other words, if law enforcement officers plan a crime, implant the criminal idea in a person's mind, and pressure that person into doing the act, the person may plead entrapment.

This situation is different from that in which an officer simply provides an opportunity for the crime to be committed but the defendant is willing and ready to do the act. For example, if a plainclothes police officer poses as a potential customer and is approached by a prostitute, no entrapment has occurred. However, if the same officer approaches a young woman and persuades her to commit an act of prostitution, the defense of entrapment is appropriate.

In the famous ABSCAM case, federal agents posing as Arab businessmen recorded efforts by high-ranking government officials to solicit bribes as payment for using their influence in Congress. Though the federal agents were disguised and seemed to encourage the bribe attempts, courts ruled that their actions did not involve entrapment, since the agents were merely providing an opportunity for the bribe attempts to be made and not planting the criminal idea in the minds of the government officials.

However, in the equally famous DeLorean case, the jury believed John DeLorean was entrapped by the FBI since an informer acting on their behalf originally suggested the idea of importing cocaine. Though DeLorean was a willing participant in the $24 million deal, the idea started with an agent of the government and he was therefore found not guilty.

Reforming the Criminal Law

In recent years, many states and the federal government have been examining their substantive criminal law. Since the law, in part, reflects public opinion regarding various forms of behavior, what was a crime forty years ago may not be considered so today. In some states, crimes such as possession of marijuana have been decriminalized—given reduced penalties. Such crimes may be punishable by a fine instead of a prison sentence. Other former criminal offenses, such as vagrancy, have been legalized—all criminal penalties have been removed. And, in some jurisdictions, penalties have been toughened, especially for violent crimes such as rape and assault. Still other states have changed their laws to reflect public awareness of social realities. For example, Nebraska has changed its law against rape to one banning sexual assault. Whereas the common-law crime of rape concerns a sexual assault of a female by a male, Nebraska's new law recognizes that sexual assaults can also take place between people of the same sex.

The most important criminal law reform has been the Federal Comprehensive Crime Control Act of 1984 (effective 1 November 1986). The act standardizes sentences, changes the concept of probation, revamps the insanity plea, and creates new substantive laws. For example, the act prohibits convicted criminals from profiting from their misdeeds by selling their stories to the media. The revised code calls for profits from such sales to be given to a special fund to benefit the victims of crime. The code also imposes monetary penalties for federal crimes. Without question, this act's most important provisions are in the sentencing area. Here, it eliminates indeterminate sentences, phases out parole, and makes sentences fairer and more certain. A sentencing commission will be established to determine sentencing guidelines; it is hoped this will alleviate the problem of sentencing disparity by limiting judicial discretion. Although controversial because of such provisions as governmental appeal, pretrial detention restrictions, and use of the death penalty, the new act should be a great improvement over present federal criminal code regulations.

The future direction of the criminal law in the United States remains unclear. More attention probably will be paid to the substantive nature of criminal law, particularly because of its importance in the preservation of society. We can also anticipate both expansions and contractions in the criminal law itself. Certain actions will be adopted as criminal and given more attention, such as white-collar crime, juvenile delinquency, crimes by corporations, and political corruption. Other offenses, such as habitual drunkenness, traffic violations, illegal drug use, and petty criminal offenses, may be reduced in importance or removed entirely from the criminal law system. In addition, efforts will probably be made to develop a system of judicially fixed sentences, to abolish parole, and to make criminal sentencing fairer and more certain for the justice system, the public, and the offender.

Summary

The substantive criminal law is a set of rules that specifies the behavior society has outlawed. The criminal law can be distinguished from the civil law on the basis that the former involves powers given to the state to enforce social rules while the latter controls interactions between private citizens. The criminal law serves important purposes: it represents public opinion and moral values, it enforces social controls, it deters criminal behavior and wrongdoing, and it banishes private retribution.

The criminal law used in U.S. jurisdictions traces its origin to the English common law. Common law was formulated during the Middle Ages when King Henry II's judges began to use precedents set in one case to guide actions in another; this system is called *stare decisis*. In the U.S. legal system, common-law crimes have been codified by lawmakers into state and federal penal codes. Today, most crimes fall into the category of felony or misdemeanor. Felonies are serious crimes usually punished by a prison term, whereas misdemeanors are minor crimes that carry a fine or a light jail sentence. Common felonies include murder, rape, assault with a deadly weapon, and robbery; misdemeanors include larceny, simple assault, and possession of small amounts of drugs.

Every crime has specific elements. In most instances, these elements include the actus reus (guilty act), which is the actual physical part of the crime—for example, taking money or burning a building. In addition, most crimes also contain a second element, the mens rea (guilty mind), which refers to the state of mind of the individual who commits a crime—more specifically, the person's intent to do the act.

At trial, a person can claim to have lacked mens rea and, therefore, not to be responsible for the criminal actions. One type of defense is excuse for mental reasons, such as insanity, intoxication, necessity, or duress. Another defense is justification by reason of self-defense, or entrapment.

Of all defenses, insanity is perhaps the most controversial. In most states, persons using an insanity defense claim that they did not know what they were doing when they committed a crime or that their mental state did not allow them to tell the difference between right and wrong (the M'Naghten Rule). Insanity defenses in the remaining jurisdictions include the claims that criminal actions were a product of mental illness, that the offender was motivated by an irresistible impulse, or that the offender lacked the substantial capacity to conform his or her conduct to the criminal law. Regardless of the insanity defense used, critics charge that mental illness is separate from legal responsibility and that the two should not be equated. Supporters counter with the argument that the insanity defense allows mentally ill people to avoid penal sanctions.

The criminal law is undergoing constant reform. Some acts are being decriminalized—having their penalties reduced—while other laws are being revised to make penalties for some acts more severe. One major revision effort is the modernization of the federal criminal code.

Notes

1 For example, see Brinegar v. United States, 338 U.S. 160 (1949); Speiser v. Randall, 357 U.S. 513 (1958); In re Winship, 397 U.S. 358 (1970).

2 Oliver Wendell Holmes, *The Common Law*, ed. Mark De Wolf (Boston: Little Brown, 1881), p. 36.

3 *Carrier's Case*, Y.B. 13 Edw. 4, f. 9, pl. 5 (Star Chamber and Exchequer Chamber, 1473), discussed at length in Jerome Hall, *Theft, Law and Society* (Indianapolis: Bobbs-Merrill, 1952), chap. 1.

4 The criminal law concepts and terminology in this chapter are a synthesis of those contained in Fred Inbau, James Thompson, and James Zagel, *Criminal Law and Its Administration* (Mineola, N.Y.: Foundation Press, 1974); Wayne LaFave and Austin

Scott, *Handbook on Criminal Law* (St. Paul: West Publishing Co., 1982); and Sanford Kadish and Monrad Paulsen, *Criminal Law and Its Processes* (Boston: Little Brown, 1975).

5 Rene Wormser, *The Story of Law*, rev. ed. (New York: Simon and Schuster, 1962).

6 See generally Arthur Rossett and Donald Cressey, *Justice by Consent* (New York: J.B. Lippincott, 1976), pp. 48–50.

7 Wormser, *The Story of Law*.

8 LaFave and Scott, *Handbook on Criminal Law*, pp. 528–29.

9 Caldwell 397 (1784), cited in LaFave and Scott, *Handbook on Criminal Law*, p. 422.

10 9 George I C. 22, 1723, cited in Douglas Hay, "Crime and Justice in Eighteenth and Nineteenth Century England," in *Crime and Justice*, vol. 2, ed. Norval Norris and Michael Tonrey (Chicago: University of Chicago Press, 1980), p. 51.

11 Jerome Hall, *Theft, Law and Society* (Indianapolis: Bobbs-Merrill, 1952), chap. 1, is generally considered the best source for the history of common-law theft crimes.

12 Mass. Gen. Laws Ann. (West 1982) ch. 266, pp. 1–2.

13 See generally Alfred Lindesmith, *The Addict and the Law* (New York: Vintage Books, 1965), chap. 1.

14 Mass. Gen. Laws Ann. (West 1983). ch. 266, p. 14.

15 320 U.S. 277 (1943).

16 LaFave and Scott, *Handbook on Criminal Law*, p. 356.

17 Ibid., p. 361.

18 8 Eng. Rep. 718 (1843).

19 Kadish and Paulsen, *Criminal Law and Its Processes*, pp. 215–16.

20 94 U.S. App. D.C. 228, 214 F. 2d 862 (1952).

21 *Model Penal Code* § 401 (1952).

22 LaFave and Scott, *Handbook on Criminal Law*, p. 516.

23 Comprehensive Crime Control Act of 1984—Pub. L. No. 98–473, § 403.

24 Samuel Walker, *Sense and Nonsense About Crime* (Monterey, Calif.: Brooks Cole, 1985), p. 120.

25 Regina v. Dudley and Stephens, 14 Q.B. 273 (1884).

3 Measuring Criminal Behavior

CHAPTER OUTLINE

KEY TERMS

surveys
samples
populations
random selection
questionnaire studies
interviews
self-report surveys

victimization surveys
cohort study
recidivism
official crime statistics
Uniform Crime Report (UCR)
index crimes

Part I offenses
Part II offenses
deterred
incapacitated
known group method
National Crime Survey (NCS)

Introduction

An important goal of criminology is to measure the nature and extent of criminal behavior. There are several reasons for this goal. For one thing, accurate measurement of criminal behavior trends is necessary if criminologists are to effectively evaluate policy initiatives in the criminal justice system. For example, if a state legislature enacts a law banning the private possession of unlicensed handguns, an important research question is: What effect does this legal measure have on the state's violent crime rate? Criminologists might be called on to study the issue. One possible approach might be to compare the state's violent crime rate before and after the gun control law took effect. If the number of violent crimes decreases soon after the law's passage, this may indicate that the handgun bill is a viable crime reduction technique. If, however, the handgun bill does not produce an appreciable change in the violent crime rate, rethinking the problem is in order. Perhaps the measure did not go far enough. Or perhaps legislation alone cannot influence the use of illegal handguns. Without accurate information, crime control policy cannot be effectively evaluated.

Measuring criminal behavior patterns is also important for everyday decision making in the justice system. For example, police chiefs need information on trends in illegal behavior if they are to make reasoned decisions on resource allocation, staffing, and patrol distribution. It would be foolish to put the largest contingent of police on the street at noon if most crimes occur at three o'clock in the morning. Similarly, surveys of inmates released from prison can help correctional authorities predict the likelihood that a particular type of offender will succeed in the outside world. This information can be used to select for early release programs those inmates who stand the best chance for success.

Measuring criminal behavior is also essential if the root causes of crime are to be discovered. As chapters 5 through 9 will show, criminologists have devoted great effort to explaining the causes of crime. This task could not be undertaken unless accurate indicators of the crime rates could be produced and the personal characteristics—age, sex, race—of offenders collected. Who commits crime, where it is committed, and how often it is committed have a great deal of bearing on efforts to determine *why* it occurs.

Thus, in measuring criminal behavior, criminologists have three primary objectives: understanding the nature of the criminal offender, evaluating the effectiveness of criminal justice programs, and aiding decision making in the legal system.

This chapter focuses on the measurement of crime. It contains a brief discussion of some methods used by criminologists to collect crime-related data, and an analysis of crime trends. In the following chapter, the major forms of crime data—self-reports, record studies, and victimization surveys—will be analyzed to learn something about the nature of criminals and their victims.

Acquiring Crime Data

Criminologists have used a wide variety of research techniques to measure the nature and extent of criminal behavior. To understand and evaluate criminal behavior statistics, it is important to develop some knowledge of how these data are collected. It is also important to understand the methods used in criminology because this understanding provides insight into how professional criminologists approach various problems and questions in their field.

SURVEY RESEARCH

A great deal of crime measurement is based on **surveys.** Survey researchers study **samples**—limited numbers of people representative of entire groups of people who share similar characteristics, called **populations.** For example, a criminologist might measure a sample of 300 prison inmates drawn from the population of 500,000 inmates in the United States; in this case, the sample represents the entire population of U.S. inmates. Or a sample of burglary incidents could be taken from the city of Miami; here, the sample would represent the population of Miami burglaries.

It is assumed that the characteristics of people in a carefully selected sample will be quite similar to those of the population at large. Therefore, any information gathered about the sample can be generalized to the population. This is the key to survey research: If a sample is accurately selected, it is a microcosm of the population from which it is taken. Consequently, sampling eliminates the need to measure large numbers of people to get accurate information about them. To obtain representative samples, criminologists randomly select them from populations. **Random selection** involves choosing subjects by chance so that all members of a population have an equal probability of being selected for study. For example, the name of every prison inmate could be placed on a list and every hundredth one selected. A table of random numbers can also be used to select subjects.

Survey research can be designed to measure the attitudes, beliefs, values, personality traits, and behavior of participants. Self-report surveys are geared toward measuring participants' criminal activity; victimization surveys seek information from people who have been victims of crime; attitude surveys may look at the views of varied groups such as prostitutes, students, drug addicts, police offenders, judges, or juvenile delinquents.

Most survey data are gathered through questionnaires or interviews. **Questionnaire studies** ask participants to answer in writing questions created by the researchers. These items are contained in a survey instrument. **Interviews** require that the researcher or an assistant discuss the questions with participants and then jot down or otherwise record answers.

Some surveys are close-ended—the participant has a limited choice of answers to a particular item. Consider the following example:

"A Fetus is a Living Creature, and Therefore Abortions Should be Made Illegal."

Strongly agree   Agree   Unsure   Disagree   Strongly disagree

In this example, survey participants would be asked to select the answer that best represented their view on abortion. In an interview, the researcher would read the question and then mark the response on an interview schedule. The benefit of the close-ended survey is that it is uniform, is easy to code and analyze, and provides consistency in comparisons of people's answers.

The open-ended survey asks respondents to say or write in their own words their feelings, attitudes, opinions, or beliefs about a subject. An example of an open-ended question is:

What is Your Opinion About the Death Penalty for Convicted Murderers?

Open-ended questions give participants more latitude in their answers and can elicit much more information from them than close-ended items. However, answers are difficult to analyze, and meaningful comparison of different answers presents problems.

Survey research is an excellent method for describing the characteristics of large numbers of people. Moreover, statistical analysis of carefully drawn samples enables researchers to generalize their data from small groups to large populations. Since questions and methods are standardized for all subjects, experimenter bias is less likely to interfere with the validity of the data.

The most serious drawback to surveys is their assumption that an individual's response will be valid and accurate. Though efforts are usually made to insure the validity of questionnaire items, it is difficult to guard against people who either deliberately lie and misrepresent information or are unsure of answers and give mistaken responses. Moreover, surveys are limited when the area to be studied involves the way people interact with one another, or other topics an individual may not be able to judge personally. Despite these drawbacks, surveys continue to be an extremely popular method of gathering criminological data.

This chapter will focus on two types of crime measurement surveys: **self-report surveys,** in which criminal offenders are asked about their lawviolating behaviors, and **victimization surveys,** in which the victims of crime provide information on their experiences.

RECORDS AND EXISTING DATA SOURCES

Criminological researchers frequently use records of social organizations such as hospitals, schools, welfare departments, courts, police departments, and prisons.

Agency records provide a rich source of criminological information. School records usually contain data on a student's academic performance, attendance record, IQ, disciplinary problems, and teacher ratings. Hospitals record incidents of drug use, suspicious wounds, and child abuse. Police files contain reports of criminal activity, arrest data, personal information on suspects, victim reports, actions taken by police officers, and so on. Court records allow researchers to compare the personal characteristics of offenders with the outcomes of their court appearances—conviction rates and types of sentence. Prison records contain information on inmates' personal characteristics, adjustment problems, disciplinary records, rehabilitation efforts, length of sentence served, and so on.

Information from several diverse sources is often cross-referenced by criminologists to determine if a relationship exists among seemingly independent variables. For example, youths' school achievement and disciplinary files can be cross-indexed with their police records to find out whether youths who manifest problems in their school careers also engage in delinquent or criminal acts.

Criminologists who conduct record studies use either primary or secondary data sources. Primary data are generated by delving into the actual files of police agencies, courts, prisons, schools, and so on. Information from these sources can then be analyzed by use of computers and complex statistical designs. For example, a criminologist exploring the relationship between socioeconomic status and criminal behavior might obtain police department files; look at the occupation, education, and income of all people arrested in a single year; and then compare characteristics of this sample with those of a group of nonoffenders.

Secondary data are originally gathered by government agencies and research foundations and then reanalyzed by criminologists. Census Bureau data, Labor Department employment data, reports of state correctional departments, and so on have all been used by criminologists in their research. The most important of these sources is the Uniform Crime Report (UCR), compiled by the Federal Bureau of Investigation.[1] The UCR is an annual report that reflects the number of crimes reported by citizens to local police departments and the number of arrests made by police agencies in a given year. The UCR is probably the most important source of official crime statistics, and we will focus on its findings later in this chapter.

One important type of research that makes use of records is called a **cohort study.**[2] Here, criminologists select a sample of people born at a particular time— say, all boys born in Boston in 1960—and chart their lives through hospital, school, police, and other records for a certain period of time. For the sample just described, the criminologist might be able to determine the personal characteristics of boys who are likely to fail in school; whether boys who fail in school are more likely to be arrested by police; which arrested boys are likely to be petitioned to court; which court-processed boys become institutionalized; and whether institutionalized boys are more likely than noninstitutionalized ones to repeat their criminal offenses **(recidivism).**

Some important cohort studies have been undertaken in the past few years; because of their importance, chapter 4 will be devoted to the results of the most significant studies.

Official Crime Statistics

The term **official crime statistics** refers to the records of offenders and offenses processed by police, court, and correctional agencies. Criminologists use these records to study both crime rates and offenders' characteristics.

As mentioned earlier, sometimes primary data sources are used. Often, criminologists delve into local agency records to measure the activities and characteristics of local criminal offenders. Using these regional studies usually restricts the scope of the findings to the particular jurisdiction that supplied the data. However, it is not unusual for criminologists to draw general conclusions about the nature of crime from these restricted samples.

When criminologists seek information on national crime trends, they usually turn to the Uniform Crime Report. Because the UCR is considered the most significant source of official crime statistics, we will focus on it here.

THE UNIFORM CRIME REPORT (UCR)

As indicated earlier, the FBI's **Uniform Crime Report (UCR)** is the best known and most widely cited source of criminal statistics.[3] The FBI receives and compiles reports from over 15,000 police departments serving a majority of the United States population. Its major unit of analysis involves the **index crimes:** murder and nonnegligent manslaughter, forcible rape, robbery, aggravated assault, burglary, larceny, arson, and auto theft. The FBI tallies and annually publishes the number of reported offenses by city, county, standard metropolitan statistical area (SMSA), and geographical divisions of the United States. In addition to these statistics, the UCR provides information on the number and characteristics of individuals who have been arrested and the number and location of assaults on police officers.

The methods used to compile the UCR are quite complex. Each month, law enforcement agencies report the number of index crimes known to them. A count of these crimes, which are also known as **Part I offenses,** is taken from records of all complaints of crime received by law enforcement agencies from victims, officers who discovered the infractions, or other sources (see the Close-Up on UCR crimes).

UCR Crimes and Definitions

Crime	Definition	Facts
HOMICIDE	Causing the death of another person without legal justification or excuse.	Homicide is the least frequent violent crime. 93% of the victims were slain in single-victim situations. At least 55% of the murderers were relatives or acquaintances of the victim. 24% of all murders occurred or were suspected to have occurred as the result of some felonious activity.
RAPE	Unlawful sexual intercourse with a female, by force or without legal or factual consent.	Most rapes involved a lone offender and a lone victim. About 36% of the rapes were committed in the victim's home. 58% of the rapes occurred at night, between 6 p.m. and 6 a.m.
ROBBERY	Unlawful taking or attempted taking of property that is in the immediate possession of another, by force or threat of force.	Robbery is the violent crime that typically involves more than one offender (in about half of all cases). Slightly less than half of all robberies involved the use of a weapon. Less than 2% of the robberies reported to the police were bank robberies.
ASSAULT	Unlawful intentional inflicting, or attempted inflicting, of injury upon the person of another. *Aggravated assault* is the unlawful intentional inflicting of serious bodily injury or unlawful threat or attempt to inflict bodily injury or death by means of a deadly or dangerous weapon with or without actual infliction of injury. *Simple assault* is the unlawful intentional inflicting of less than serious bodily injury without a deadly or dangerous weapon or an attempt or threat to inflict bodily injury without a deadly or dangerous weapon.	Simple assault occurs more frequently than aggravated assault. Assault is the most common type of violent crime.
BURGLARY	Unlawful entry of any fixed structure, vehicle, or vessel used for regular residence, industry,	42% of all households burglaries occurred without *forced* entry.

Whenever complaints of crime are determined through investigation to be unfounded or false, they are eliminated from the actual count. The number of "actual offenses known" is reported to the FBI whether or not anyone is arrested for the crime, the stolen property is recovered, or prosecution is undertaken. In addition, each month law enforcement agencies report the total crimes that were cleared. Crimes are cleared in two ways: (1) when at least one person is arrested, charged, and turned over to the court for prosecution, or (2) by exceptional means, when some element beyond police control precludes the physical arrest of an offender (e.g., they flee the country). Data on the number of clearances involving

Crime	Definition	Facts
	or business, with or without force, with the intent to commit a felony or larceny.	In the burglary of more than 3 million American households, the offenders entered through an unlocked window or door or used a key (for example, a key "hidden" under a doormat). About 34% of the no-force household burglaries were known to have occurred between 6 a.m. and 6 p.m. Residential property was targeted in 67% of reported burglaries; nonresidential property accounted for the remaining 33%. Three-quarters of the nonresidential burglaries for which the time of occurrence was known took place at night.
LARCENY (THEFT)	Unlawful taking or attempted taking of property other than a motor vehicle from the possession of another, by stealth, without force and without deceit, with intent to permanently deprive the owner of the property.	Pocket picking and purse snatching most frequently occur inside nonresidential buildings or on street locations. Unlike most other crimes, pocket picking and purse snatching affect the elderly as much as other age groups. Most personal larcenies with contact occur during the daytime, but most household larcenies occur at night.
MOTOR VEHICLE THEFT	Unlawful taking or attempted taking of a self-propelled road vehicle owned by another, with the intent of depriving the owner of it permanently or temporarily.	Motor vehicle theft is relatively well reported to the police because reporting is required for insurance claims and vehicles are more likely than other stolen property to be recovered. About three-fifths of all motor vehicle thefts occurred at night.
ARSON	Intentional damaging or destruction or attempted damaging or destruction by means of fire or explosion of the property without the consent of the owner, or of one's own property or that of another by fire or explosives with or without the intent to defraud.	Single-family residences were the most frequent targets of arson. More than 17% of all structures where arson occurred were not in use.

SOURCE. Bureau of Justice Statistics, *Report to the Nation on Crime and Justice* (Washington, D.C.: Bureau of Justice Statistics, 1983), pp. 2–3.

only the arrest of offenders under the age of eighteen, data on the value of property stolen and recovered in connection with Part I offenses, and detailed information pertaining to criminal homicide are also reported.

Arrest data, which include the age, sex, and race of persons arrested, are reported monthly by crime category for both Part I and Part II offenses. **Part II offenses,** while excluding traffic violations, include all other crimes except those classified as Part I.

The UCR employs three methods to express crime data. First, the number of crimes reported to the police and arrests made are expressed as raw figures (for

The Uniform Crime Reports are compiled from crimes reported to police agencies around the nation.

$86 \mid 125 \text{ million}$

example, 1,004,372 motor vehicle thefts occurred in 1983). Second, percent changes in the amount of crime between years is computed (for example, robbery decreased 8.4 percent between 1982 and 1983). Finally, crime rates per 100,000 people are computed. That is, when the UCR indicates that the murder rate was 8.3 in 1983, it means that about 8 people in every 100,000 fell victim to murder between 1 January and 31 December of 1983. The equation used is:

$$\frac{\text{Number of reported crimes}}{\text{Total U.S. population}} \times 100,000 = \text{rate per 100,000}$$

$8.6 \quad 86 \text{ murders}$

Crime Trends in the United States

Studies have indicated that a gradual increase in the crime rate, especially in the area of violent crime, occurred from 1830 to 1860. Following the Civil War, this rate increased significantly for about fifteen years. Then, from 1880 to the time of the first World War, with the possible exception of the years immediately preceding and following the war, the number of reported crimes decreased. After a period of readjustment, the crime rate steadily declined until the depression (about 1930), whereupon another general increase, or crime wave, was recorded.[4] Crime rates increased gradually following the 1930s until the 1960s, when the growth rate became much greater. The homicide rate, which had declined from the 1930s to the 1960s, also began a period of sharp increase.

The upswing in the crime rate continued through the 1970s until 1980, when more than 13 million index crimes were reported—a rate of 5,899 per 100,000 people.[5] However, in 1981, almost no increase was reported in the recorded number of index crimes. The violence rate rose only 1 percent over the previous year's, and the property crime rate remained about the same. Between 1981 and 1984 the rate steadily declined with overall drops of 7 percent in 1983 and 7 percent in 1984 when slightly more than 11.1 million crimes were reported to police. (Despite these declines, the FBI reported that the crime rate did increase in the last 3 months of 1984 and went up an additional 3 percent in the first 6 months of 1985.)[6]

As table 3.1 indicates, the overall crime rate peaked in 1980 when 5,931 crimes were reported per 100,000 population and over 13,360,000 criminal incidents were reported to police. Since then there has been a steady decrease in most crime categories. One notable exception is the rape rate, which increased 6 percent in 1984. However, this increase may be a result of the women's movement, which has encouraged victims to report sexual assaults to police. Consequently, the increased rape rate may reflect reporting changes rather than an actual crime increase.

How can the stabilization and decline of the crime rate be explained? There are several reasons for this dramatic change in what many people had believed to be an ever-expanding circle. For one thing, the population has been aging. The postwar "baby boom" generation reached their teenage years in the 1960s, just as the violent crime rate began a sharp increase. Since (as we will see in chapter 4) both the victims and perpetrators of violent crime tend to fall in the 18–25 age category, the rise in crime reflected the age structure of society. With the "graying" of society in the 1980s, and a decline in the birth rate, it is not surprising that the crime rate has also declined. However, the children of baby-boomers will be reaching "prime" crime age toward the end of the decade and some forecasters predict a corresponding rise in the crime rate.

A second explanation for the decline in the crime rate can be attributed to the "get-tough" crime control policies instituted in the past few years. More people than ever are being locked in the nation's prisons and jails, almost 500,000 by the end of 1985. Tough sentencing policies, including mandatory prison terms for some crimes, coupled with the abolition of parole, have helped account for a rapid increase in the prison population. Some experts believe that this new conservative attitude toward criminal justice has helped reduce the crime rate. Potential criminals are **deterred** through fear of punishment; convicted ones are **incapacitated** in prison. Although it is often difficult to establish a direct link between crime rates and punishment levels (see chapter 6), those favoring tough crime control policies view the current drop in the crime rate as more than a coincidence.

Of course, a third possibility is that the information local police send to the FBI is inaccurate. Though, as we shall discuss later in this chapter, police have been accused of "fudging" crime statistics, it is unlikely that the drop in the crime rate can be attributed solely to police mismanagement of crime data. First, declines in the murder rate (see the following Close-Up) have corresponded with declines in the overall crime rate, and murder statistics are usually considered highly accurate. Second, other sources of criminal statistics, most notably victim surveys (see later in this chapter), also indicate an overall downtrend in crime.

In sum, during the first part of the 1980s the overall crime rate has declined. However, with a rise in the teenage population during the end of the decade, the crime rate may eventually begin another upward move.

The Nature of Crime

Perhaps the most important fact in criminology is that certain stable trends in the crime rate appear year after year. Because these are social trends, they are considered evidence that crime is a sociological phenomenon and thus must be analyzed through social research and analysis.

SEASON AND CLIMATE

Most reported crimes occur during the warm summer months of July and August. One possible explanation for this warm weather trend is that people spend more

TABLE 3.1 Index of crime, United States, 1974–1984

Population[a]	Crime index total[b]	Violent crime[c]	Property crime[d]	Murder and nonnegligent manslaughter	Forcible rape	Robbery	Aggravated assault	Burglary	Larceny theft	Motor vehicle theft
Number of offenses:[d]										
1974—211,392,000	10,253,400	974,720	9,278,700	20,710	55,400	442,400	456,210	3,039,200	5,262,500	977,100
1975—213,124,000	11,256,600	1,026,280	10,230,300	20,510	56,090	464,970	484,710	3,252,100	5,977,700	1,000,500
1976—214,659,000	11,315,600	988,410	10,327,200	18,780	57,180	422,450	489,990	3,099,800	6,264,800	962,600
1977—216,332,000	10,950,700	1,013,270	9,937,400	19,120	63,610	407,440	523,100	3,062,700	5,900,500	974,200
1978—218,059,000	11,174,000	1,068,280	10,105,800	19,560	67,720	421,580	559,430	3,119,300	5,985,900	1,000,600
1979—220,099,000	12,211,200	1,188,870	11,022,300	21,460	76,510	474,680	616,220	3,318,200	6,595,300	1,108,800
1980—225,349,264	13,366,100	1,323,400	12,042,700	23,040	83,130	558,750	658,480	3,784,300	7,130,800	1,127,700
1981—229,146,000	13,384,500	1,340,540	12,043,900	22,520	82,630	585,480	649,910	3,768,800	7,188,300	1,086,800
1982—231,534,000	12,933,700	1,301,500	11,632,200	21,010	78,900	546,200	655,380	3,437,200	7,136,400	1,058,600
1983—233,981,000	12,070,200	1,237,980	10,832,200	19,310	78,920	500,220	639,530	3,120,800	6,707,000	1,004,400
1984—236,158,000	11,881,800	1,273,280	10,608,500	18,690	84,230	485,010	685,350	2,984,400	6,591,900	1,032,200
Rate per 100,000 inhabitants:[d]										
1974	4,850.4	461.1	4,389.3	9.8	26.2	209.3	215.8	1,437.7	2,489.5	462.2
1975	5,281.7	481.5	4,800.2	9.6	26.3	218.2	227.4	1,525.9	2,804.8	469.4
1976	5,271.4	460.5	4,811.0	8.8	26.6	196.8	228.3	1,444.0	2,918.5	448.4
1977	5,062.0	468.4	4,593.6	8.8	29.4	188.3	241.8	1,415.7	2,727.5	450.3
1978	5,124.3	489.9	4,634.4	9.0	31.1	193.3	256.5	1,430.5	2,745.1	458.9
1979	5,548.1	540.2	5,007.9	9.7	34.8	215.7	280.0	1,507.6	2,996.5	503.8
1980	5,931.3	587.3	5,344.0	10.2	36.9	247.9	292.2	1,679.3	3,164.3	500.4
1981	5,841.0	585.0	5,256.0	9.8	36.1	255.5	283.6	1,644.7	3,137.0	474.3
1982	5,586.1	562.1	5,024.0	9.1	34.1	235.9	283.1	1,484.5	3,082.2	457.2
1983	5,158.6	529.1	4,629.5	8.3	33.7	213.8	273.3	1,333.8	2,866.5	429.3
1984	5,031.3	539.2	4,492.1	7.9	35.7	205.4	290.2	1,263.7	2,791.3	437.1
1984					34.5	215	346	1344	3000	507

a. Populations are Bureau of the Census provisional estimates as of July 1, except April 1, 1980, preliminary census counts, and are subject to change.

b. Due to rounding, the offenses may not add to totals.

c. Violent crimes are offenses of murder, forcible rape, robbery, and aggravated assault. Property crimes are offenses of burglary, larceny theft, and motor vehicle theft. Data are not included for the property crime of arson.

d. Annual totals for years prior to 1983 have been adjusted and may not be consistent with those in prior editions of this publication.

All rates were calculated on the offenses before rounding.

SOURCE: Federal Bureau of Investigation, *Uniform Crime Report* 1984.

Murder Rates

Murder rates have been charted since the beginning of the century by the FBI and National Center for Health Statistics. Since they are considered the most accurate criminal statistics, they provide a good picture of overall crime trends.

Three major trends can be seen in the murder rate. From 1903 to 1933, the rate rose from 1.1 to 9.7 homicides per 100,000 U.S. citizens. Between 1934 and 1958, it fell to 4.5. From 1961 to 1980, it rose again to 11.0. Since 1980, the murder rate has declined to slightly less than 8.0 per 100,000. This trend helps validate the decline in the overall crime rate that has occurred since 1980.

Many factors are believed to have influenced the murder rate. During World War II the rate declined, only to increase sharply after the war ended (1945–47). The depression years were the time of a marked increase in murders. The postwar baby-boomers' coming of age in the sixties coincided with another murder rate increase. The return to capital punishment in the eighties has coincided with a murder rate decline.

DISCUSSION QUESTIONS

1. What factors in today's society influence the murder rate?

2. Why do murder rates increase in the aftermath of wars?

SOURCE. Bureau of Justice Statistics, *Report to the Nation on Crime and Justice* (Washington, D.C.: U.S. Government Printing Office, 1983), p. 10. Updated with *Uniform Crime Report 1983* and *Uniform Crime Report 1984* statistics.

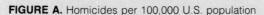

FIGURE A. Homicides per 100,000 U.S. population

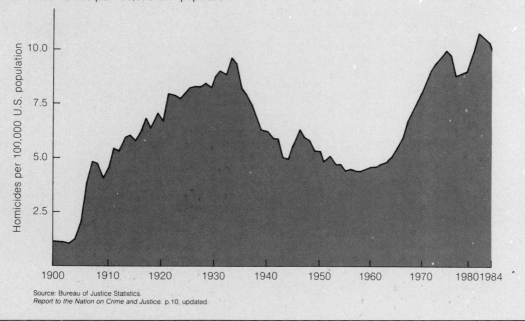

Source: Bureau of Justice Statistics.
Report to the Nation on Crime and Justice. p.10, updated.

time outdoors during these months, making themselves easier targets. Similarly, homes are left vacant more often during the summer, making them more vulnerable to property crimes. Two exceptions to this trend are murders and robberies, which occur frequently in December and January (though rates are also high during the summer).

POPULATION DENSITY

Table 3.2 shows the relationship between crime rate and population density. Areas with low per capita crime rates tend to be rural. Large urban areas have by far the

TABLE 3.2.

Crime rate, area, 1983
(Rate per 100,000
inhabitants)

Offense	Total United States	Metropolitan area	Rural counties	Other cities
Crime index total	5,158.6	5,852.3	1,881.0	4,629.4
Modified crime index total				
Violent crime	529.1	627.2	161.2	315.3
Property crime	4,629.5	5,225.1	1,719.8	4,314.1
Murder	8.3	9.1	5.8	5.0
Forcible rape	33.7	38.9	15.1	21.1
Robbery	213.8	272.9	16.6	49.4
Aggravated assault	273.3	306.2	123.7	239.8
Burglary	1,333.8	1,501.5	655.9	1,039.5
Larceny-theft	2,866.5	3,200.3	963.8	3,085.5
Motor vehicle theft	429.3	523.4	100.1	189.1

SOURCE. Federal Bureau of Investigation, *Uniform Crime Report 1983*, p. 42.

highest crime rates. Exceptions to this trend are low-population resort areas with high transient or seasonal populations—such as Atlantic City, New Jersey and Nantucket, Massachusetts.

It is interesting that the increase in crime in the 1970s was greater in rural and suburban areas than in larger cities—this trend might be a result of the youthful population in these areas.

REGION

Definite differences are apparent in regional crime rates. Western states have a significantly higher crime rate in almost all crime categories than that found in other regions of the country. The one notable exception is the southern states, who traditionally have the highest murder rate (in chapter 9, murder in southern areas is discussed further).

CLEARANCES

Crimes are cleared when perpetrators are arrested and turned over for prosecution. Traditionally, about 20 percent of all reported index crimes are cleared by arrest. Marked differences in clearance rates can be seen between property and violent crimes. As table 3.3 indicates, violent crimes are much more likely to be solved than property crimes. This reflects the greater resources police have available to solve the more serious violent crimes and the availability of witnesses to identify offenders. When Part II offenses are included, about 10.2 million people are arrested annually.

Criticisms of the Uniform Crime Report

Despite its importance and wide use by criminologists, the accuracy of the UCR has been heavily criticized. The three greatest areas of concern—reporting practices, law enforcement practices, and methodological problems—are discussed below.

REPORTING PRACTICES

One major concern of criminologists is that many serious crimes are not reported by victims to police and therefore do not become part of the UCR. The reasons

Crowded metropolitan areas experience the highest reported crime rates.

for not reporting vary. Some people do not have property insurance and therefore believe it is useless to report theft-related crimes. In other cases, the victim may fear reprisals from the offender's friends or family.

Several national surveys have attempted to discover why citizens decide not to report delinquent or criminal acts. In 1966, the President's Commission on Law Enforcement and the Administration of Justice sponsored one such effort. Using a nationally drawn sample of 10,000 citizens, the commission found that the most common concerns were that the "police couldn't do anything about the matter," that "it was a private—not criminal—affair," that the person "was not sure if the real offenders would be caught," and that the "police wouldn't want to be bothered."[7]

In a study conducted by the National Crime Survey (NCS), a large, nationally drawn sample of citizens was used to determine what factors relate to the reporting of, or the failure to report, criminal activity (the NCS will be discussed later in this chapter).[8] The NCS data reveal that the reasons given for not reporting crime varied according to the type of criminal behavior examined. Victims of robbery said they did not report the crime because it "was a private matter" (20 percent) or because "nothing could be done" (23 percent). Assaults remained unreported because people felt "they were a private matter" (34 percent).[9] Most people who did not report crimes such as robbery, burglary, and larceny did so because they believed "nothing could be done" and the "victimization was not important enough."

In an analysis of NCS data, Michael Hindelang and Michael Gottfredson found that for each category of personal, household, and business victimization, completed criminal acts were more often reported than attempted victimizations.[10] Similarly, the seriousness of delinquent or criminal activity influenced reporting; for example, the use of a weapon in the crime increased the likelihood that police

TABLE 3.3.
Index crimes cleared by
arrest, 1983

Crime type	Number arrested	Percent cleared
Violent crimes		
Murder	20,310	76
Assault	298,830	61
Rape	34,080	52
Robbery	146,170	26
Total	499,390	46
Property crimes		
Burglary	475,800	15
Larceny	i,315,000	19
Motor vehicle theft	119,400	15
Arson	19,800	17
Total	1,930,000	18
Total arrests	2,429,400	21

SOURCE. Federal Bureau of Investigation, *Uniform Crime Report 1983,* pp.
160-170.

would be notified. As the value of monetary loss increased, so did the probability
that the act would be reported.[11]

Hindelang and Gottfredson found that the personal characteristics of the victim
also influenced reporting habits. As a general rule, the victim's age was strongly
related to failure to report crimes—victims under thirty-five were much less likely
to report crimes than those over thirty-five. Racial differences were found to be
minor except among the youngest victims (those twelve to nineteen years old);
whites were less likely to report crimes than blacks. Family income was found to
be directly related to crime reporting—as income rose, so too did the probability
that victims would contact police. Whether or not the criminal was an acquaintance
of the victim did not seem to affect the likelihood of the crime's being reported.

LAW ENFORCEMENT PRACTICES

The way police departments record and report criminal and delinquent activity
also affects the validity of UCR statistics. For example, in New York City for the
period 1948–52, burglaries rose from 2,726 to 42,491, and larcenies increased from
7,713 to 70,949.[12] These increases were found to be related to the change from a
precinct to a centralized reporting system for crime statistics. A new central reporting system instituted in Philadelphia in 1952 resulted in a sharp rise in index
crimes—from 16,773 in 1951 to 28,560 in 1953.[13] How police interpret the definitions of index crimes may also affect reporting practices.[14] For example, police
in Boston were found to report only completed rapes to the FBI, while those in
Los Angeles reported completed rapes, attempted rapes, and sexual assaults. Reporting practices helped account for the fact that the rape rate in Los Angeles is
far higher than that in Boston.

A recent study by Lawrence Sherman and Barry Glick for the Police Foundation
found that local police departments make systematic errors in UCR reporting.[15]
All 196 departments surveyed counted an arrest only after a formal booking procedure, although the UCR requires arrests to be counted if the suspect is released
without a formal charge. Similarly, 29 percent did not include citations and 57

percent did not include summonses, though the UCR requires it. An audit of arrests found an error rate of about 10 percent in every Part I offense category.

Of a more serious nature are allegations that police officials may deliberately alter reported crimes to put their departments in a more favorable light with the public. David Seidman and Michael Couzens suggest that police administrators, interested in lowering the crime rate and thus improving their departments' images, may falsify crime reporting by deliberately undervaluing the cost of stolen goods so that an index larceny will be relegated to a nonreportable offense category.[16] Thus, it is possible that political issues can help to raise or lower crime rates.

Finally, increased police efficiency and professionalism may actually help increase crime rates. As more sophisticated computer-aided technology is developed for police work, and as the education and training of police employees increases, so too might their ability to record and report crimes, thereby producing higher crime rates.

METHODOLOGICAL PROBLEMS

Methodological issues also add to the problem of the UCR's validity. Leonard Savitz has collected a list of twenty such issues, including:

1. No federal crimes are reported.
2. Reports are voluntary and vary in accuracy and completeness.
3. Not all police departments submit reports.
4. The FBI uses estimates in its total crime projections.
5. If multiple crimes are committed by an offender, only the most serious is recorded. Thus, if a narcotics addict rapes, robs, and murders a victim, only the murder is recorded as a crime.
6. For some crimes, each act is listed as a single offense. Thus, if a man robs six people in a bar, it's listed as one robbery; but if he assaulted them it would be listed as six assaults.
7. Uncompleted acts are lumped together with completed ones.
8. There are important differences between the FBI's definition of a crime and those used in a number of states.[17]

Future of the Uniform Crime Report. What does the future of the UCR look like? A recent report prepared by a private consulting firm for the Justice Department recommended some important changes that may eventually be adopted by the FBI:

- Instead of submitting statements of the kinds of crime that individual citizens reported to the police and summary statements of resulting arrests, local police agencies would provide a brief account of each incident to a central national office. The central office would then use these accounts to calculate an area's crime rate.
- In addition to normal reporting procedures, 300 agencies serving more than 100,000 people, and a sample of at least 300 smaller departments, would provide detailed reports on Part I crimes. Reports also would be made on numerous additional crimes, such as kidnapping, blackmail, extortion, and bribery. This would allow a national data base on the nature of crime, victims, and criminals to be developed.

• The third change would impose more stringent auditing techniques to insure the accuracy and completeness of the material being submitted by the police.[18]

If adopted, these changes may bring about greater uniformity in cross-jurisdictional reporting and improve the accuracy of official crime data.

Self-Report Studies

The questionable validity of official data has been a serious problem for criminologists. If they base their work on inaccurate data, then all subsequent theory and policy decisions will be biased and misleading. Two sociologists, Roger Hood and Richard Sparks, have commented on the problem of uncertainty:

> In relying on this [official] data the theorist is faced with two problems. First, he must estimate to what extent those convicted differ from those who have committed identical acts but have not been caught or prosecuted. Secondly, he must try to disentangle those factors which explain criminal behavior from those which explain why a person has become officially processed as a delinquent or a criminal.[19]

The problems associated with official statistics have led many criminologists to seek alternative sources of information in assessing the true extent of crime patterns. In addition, official statistics do not say much about the personality, attitudes, and behavior of individual criminals. Official statistics may illustrate broad concepts, such as trends in the relative frequency of crime; but they are an inadequate source of information about narrower theoretical issues, such as the relationship between the individual personality and criminal behavior. Thus, alternative sources of information about criminal behavior are needed to help determine its true extent, develop valid theories and test them, and make effective policy.

One frequently employed alternative to official statistics is the self-report study. Self-report studies are designed to allow participants to reveal information about their violations of the law. The studies have many different formats. For example, the criminologist can approach people who have been arrested by police, or even prison inmates, and interview them about their illegal activities. Subjects can also be first telephoned at home and then mailed a survey form. Most often, self-report surveys are administered to large groups through a mass distribution of questionnaires. The names of subjects can be requested, but more commonly they remain anonymous. The basic assumption of self-report studies is that the anonymity of the respondents and the promise of confidentiality backed by academic credentials will encourage people to accurately describe their illegal activities. Thus, self-reports are viewed as a mechanism to get at the *dark figures of crime,* the figures missed by official statistics.

Most self-report studies have focused on juvenile delinquency and youth crime, for two reasons.[20] First, it is more convenient to survey youths than adults. The school provides a setting in which literally thousands of subjects can be reached simultaneously, all of them with the means to respond to a research questionnaire at their disposal (pens, desks, time). Second, since attendance is mandatory, a school-based self-report survey is usually considered a reliable estimate of the activities of all youths in a given community. Self-reports have also been used to examine the offense histories of prison inmates and identify factors that can predict criminal behavior patterns.

Self-reports make it possible to assess the number of people in the population who have committed illegal acts, and the frequency of their law violations. Since most self-report instruments also contain items measuring subjects' attitudes, values, personal characteristics, and behaviors, the data obtained from them can be used for various purposes, such as testing theories, measuring attitudes toward crime, and so on.

Self-report studies, then, allow criminologists to identify people who commit criminal acts but are able to evade detection and never figure in the official crime statistics. Self-reports provide a broader picture of the distribution of criminality, since they do not depend on the offender's being apprehended. Furthermore, since many criminologists believe that class bias exists in the criminal justice system, self-reports allow criminologists to evaluate the distribution of criminal behavior across class lines. One important goal of self-report studies is to determine whether differences exist in the law-violating behaviors of upper-, middle-, and lower-class individuals. This issue has major importance for the study of the causes of criminal behavior (see chapters 7, 8, and 9).

SELF-REPORT DATA

As mentioned, most self-report instruments have gathered data from groups of high school students. In general, they indicate that the number of youths who break the law is far greater than had previously been believed. In fact, when truancy, alcohol consumption, petty theft, and soft drug use are included in self-report scales, almost everyone tested is found to have violated some law.[21]

Self-report studies indicate that the most common offenses are truancy, alcohol abuse, use of a false ID, shoplifting or larceny under $5, fighting, marijuana use, and damage to the property of others. It has been estimated that almost 90 percent of all youths commit delinquent and criminal acts. In fact, several studies have suggested that there is actually little difference between the behavior of incarcerated youths and that of typical high school students. It is not unusual for self-reports to find alcohol and drug abuse, theft, violence, and damage rates of more than 50 percent among suburban, rural, and urban high school youths. What is surprising is the consistency of these findings in samples taken from southern, eastern, mid-western, and western states.

When the results of recent self-report surveys are compared with various studies conducted over a twenty-year period, a uniform pattern emerges. The use of drugs and alcohol increased markedly in the 1970's and then leveled off in the 1980's; theft, violence, and damage-related crimes seem more stable. Although a self-reported crime wave has not occurred, neither has there been any visible reduction in teenage delinquency. For example, when Rosemary Sarri compared self-report data collected in the late 1960s with similar data from the late 1970s, she found that involvement in serious crimes by both males and females had remained stable, while involvement in such acts as alcohol abuse, marijuana use, and driving while intoxicated had increased.[22]

Self-report studies can tell us many things about delinquent offenders who are not apprehended by the police. For example, a national study by Franklyn Dunford and Delbert Elliott found that only about 24 percent of all serious, chronic juvenile offenders were apprehended by police, and overall only 8 percent of all youths admitting delinquent acts were ever arrested.[23] So self-reports can provide a significant amount of information about youthful offenders that cannot be found in the official statistics.

A Self-Report Instrument

Most self-report surveys are similar to the one illustrated below. Some ask subjects to check the appropriate spaces, while others allow them to write in the precise number of times they engaged in each criminal act. Note that this sample survey limits the reporting period to the past twelve months. Some surveys ask subjects to report their lifetime involvement in crime, while others use both techniques.

Surveys are also likely to contain items not directly related to criminal activity—for example, items requesting information on such diverse topics as subjects' self-image; intelligence; personality; attitudes toward family, friends, and school; and leisure activities. Self-report surveys also gather personal information on subjects' family background, social status, race, and sex.

SAMPLE SURVEY Please indicate how often in the past twelve months you did each act. (Check the best answer).

	Never did act	One time	2–5 times	6–9 times	10–13 times	14–17 times	18+ times
1. Stole something worth less than $50							
2. Stole something worth more than $50							
3. Snorted or sniffed heroin							
4. Injected heroin							
5. Used amphetamine pills (such as uppers, crystal meth, dex)							
6. Shot up amphetamines							
7. Got drunk on beer							
8. Got drunk on hard liquor							
9. Got drunk on wine							
10. Used marijuana (pot)							
11. Used downers (valium, or librium, darvon, thorazine, etc.)							
12. Used psychedelics (LSD, mescaline)							
13. Used cocaine							
14. Been in a fistfight							
15. Carried a weapon such as a gun or knife							
16. Fought someone using a weapon							
17. Stole a car							
18. Used force to steal							
19. (For boys) Forced a girl to have sexual relations against her will							
20. Driven a car while drunk or high							
21. Damaged property worth more than $10							

DISCUSSION QUESTIONS

1. Do you think subjects would honestly answer these questions if they were promised anonymity and confidentiality?

2. Have you participated in any of the acts listed in the sample survey?

SOURCE. Sample survey form from Larry Siegel and Spencer Rathus.

CRITIQUE OF SELF-REPORT STUDIES

Though self-report studies had a profound effect on criminological theory in the 1960s and 1970s (see chapter 7), their methodology has been criticized for various reasons. Critics of self-report studies frequently suggest that it is unreasonable to expect young people to candidly admit illegal acts. They have nothing to gain, and the ones taking the greatest risk are the ones with official records. On the other hand, some young people may exaggerate their delinquent acts, forget some of them, or be confused about what is being asked.

We cannot be certain how valid self-report studies are, because we have nothing reliable to measure them against. Correlation with official reports is expected to be low, because the inadequacies of such reports were largely responsible for researchers' asking youths themselves about their criminality in the first place.

Most self-reports have been used with youthful offenders who are not involved in adult criminality. Many, as you have seen, contain an overabundance of trivial offenses—skipping school, running away, using a false ID—often lumped together with serious crimes to form a "total crime index."[24] Consequently, comparisons between groups can be highly misleading. Moreover, even if a large percentage of a school population voluntarily participates in a self-report, researchers can never be sure that the remaining few who refuse to participate or are absent that day do not engage in most of the serious crimes in the community.

Various techniques have been used to verify self-report data. The most common is to compare the answers youths give with their official police records.[25] A typical approach is to ask youths if they have ever been arrested for or convicted of a delinquent act and then check their official records against their self-reported responses. A number of studies using this method have found a remarkable uniformity between self-reported answers and official records.

Other methods are also used to test the validity of self-reports.[26] The **known group method** compares incarcerated youths with "normal" groups to see whether the former report more delinquency. Peer informants—friends who can verify the honesty of a subject's answers—are used. Subjects are tested twice to see if their answers remain the same (called *testing across time*). The questions are designed to reveal respondents who are lying on the exam—for example, an item might say: "I have never done anything wrong in my life." In general, these efforts have validated self-report studies.

In what is probably the most thorough analysis of self-report methodologies, Michael Hindelang, Travis Hirschi, and Joseph Weis closely reviewed the literature concerning the reliability and validity of self-reports and conducted their own independent analysis using data gathered in Seattle, Washington and other sites.[27] They concluded that the problems of accuracy in self-reports are "surmountable"; that self-reports are more accurate than most criminologists believe; and that self-reports and official statistics are quite compatible:

> *The method of self reports does not appear from these studies to be fundamentally flawed. Reliability measures are impressive and the majority of studies produce validity coefficients in the moderate to strong range.*[28]

Thus self-reports continue to be used as a standard method of delinquency research. Many of the studies discussed in chapter 5–9 rely on self-reports for their data.

Victimization Studies: The National Crime Survey

The third component in the crime measurement triad is the victimization survey. Rather than depending on the agencies of justice or the criminals themselves for data, victim surveys measure the extent of criminal behavior by focusing on its target—the victims. Several significant efforts have had victims of crime tell of their experiences.[29] However, a recent national effort, the National Crime Survey, is by far the most complex and far-reaching. Consequently, this discussion will focus primarily on that survey.

The **National Crime Survey (NCS)** is collected by the United States Bureau of the Census in cooperation with the Bureau of Justice Statistics of the U.S. Department of Justice. In the national survey, samples of housing units are selected on the basis of a complex, multistage sampling technique.[30]

The total annual sample size for the national surveys is about 60,000 households, containing about 136,000 individuals. The total sample is composed of six independently selected subsamples, each with about 10,000 households with 22,000 individuals. Each subsample is interviewed twice a year about victimizations suffered in the preceding six months. For example, in January, 22,000 individuals (in 10,000 households) and representatives from more than 8,000 businesses are interviewed. In the following month—and in each of the four succeeding months—an independent probability sample of the same size is interviewed. In July, the housing units originally interviewed in January are revisited, and interviews are repeated; likewise, the original February sample units are revisited in August, the March units in September, and so on. Each time they are interviewed, respondents are asked about victimizations suffered during the six months preceding the month of interview.

The data reported represent estimates of crimes occurring in the United States, based on weighted sample data. It is possible to make these estimates because a probability sample of respondents was surveyed. The interview completion rate in the national sample is about 95 percent or more of those selected to be interviewed in any given period; hence, population estimates are relatively unbiased.

The NCS data have been used to determine the nature and extent of crime in the United States. Survey data are subjected to elaborate statistical analysis to estimate the amount of crime occurring in the nation as a whole. This procedure presents a picture of the crime problem without the methodological problems that plague the Uniform Crime Report. In fact, NCS data indicate that only 45 percent of violent crimes, 24 percent of personal crimes of theft, and 38 percent of household crimes are brought to the attention of police. Many citizens reported that, among other reasons, they failed to contact police because they "felt nothing could be done" or because they believed the criminal act "just wasn't important enough" to bother authorities.

Thus, NCS data account for many more criminal acts than those reported in the UCR. This is not to say that NCS data alone can be considered the "official" crime statistics. Victimization data are, of course, limited to crimes in which a victim exists and cannot be used to measure such victimless crimes as drug use and gambling. Nor can NCS data accurately account for crimes such as fraud, embezzlement, or tax violations, in which the respondents themselves may have participated. And, of course, national statistics are merely estimates that may be subject to error and must be interpreted accordingly.

SELECTED FINDINGS

The most recent data from the National Crime Survey indicate that about 35.5 million crimes, including both completed acts and attempts, occurred in 1984—

approximately four times as many as reported by the UCR. Rape, personal robbery, and assault, as figure 3.1 indicates, made up 15 percent of these crimes (about 6 million incidents), while larceny, probably the least serious crime, accounted for 50 percent of the total. It is important that NCS data indicate crime rates have changed very little in the past five years.

Table 3.4 illustrates the number of crimes and the percentage of victims reporting crime to the police for the personal and household crimes investigated by the NCS. It can be plainly seen that the number of criminal acts recorded by the NCS far exceeds those found in FBI data. For example, whereas the FBI tallies one million Part I violent acts, the NCS records about 3.5 million comparable offenses (and, unlike FBI data, NCS data exclude murder). In a similar vein, the FBI estimates that about 10 million property crimes occur annually, but the NCS figure is about 35 million.

In addition to the volume of crime, the most dramatic evidence contained in table 3.5 is the significant number of crimes *not* reported to police: about half the rapes, robberies, and burglaries; and more than half the assaults and larcenies. Only "successful" auto thefts are generally reported (90 percent), and these because state law requires it and the parties are generally insured. When victims are asked why they did not report crime, they usually respond that it was a private matter, they did not want to get involved, and so on.

Table 3.5 indicates the estimated crime rate for NCS offenses controlling for population density. The rates per offense type are significantly higher than UCR estimates, but the two data sources are similar with respect to geographic representation.

Large cities have far higher violent and property crime rates than less densely populated areas. The differences are most dramatic with respect to violent crimes—metropolitan rape and robbery rates are three and four times as high as in rural

FIGURE 3.1

Percent distribution of victimizations, by sector and type of crime.

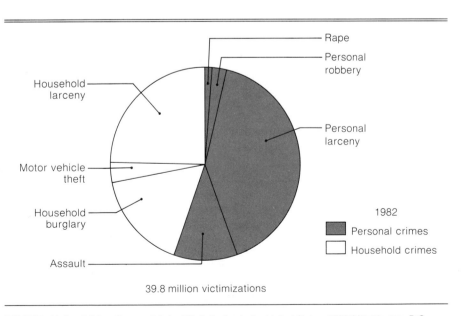

39.8 million victimizations

SOURCE. National Crime Survey, *Criminal Victimization in the United States, 1979* (Washington, D.C.: Government Printing Office, 1981), p. 3, updated.

TABLE 3.4   Estimated number of personal and household victimizations and percent not reported to police

Type of victimization	1975 Esti-mated number	1975 Percent not re-ported	1976 Esti-mated number	1976 Percent not re-ported	1976 Esti-mated number	1976 Percent not re-ported	1978 Esti-mated number	1978 Percent not re-ported
Personal victimizations								
Rape and attempted rape	151,055	44	145,193	47	154,237	42	171,145	49
Robbery	1,121,374	46	1,110,639	46	1,082,936	44	1,038,074	49
Robbery and attempted robbery with injury	353,493	34	360,700	36	386,405	33	330,843	33
Serious assault	207,114	33	175,660	32	214,670	24	179,905	29
Minor assault	146,380	37	185,041	39	171,735	45	150,939	37
Robbery without injury	467,595	41	453,867	40	412,505	35	408,833	44
Attempted robbery without injury	300,285	69	296,071	67	284,026	70	298,398	72
Assault	4,176,056	54	4,343,261	52	4,663,827	55	4,730,097	56
Aggravated assault	47590,080	44	1,694,941	41	1,737,774	47	1,707,883	46
With injury	543,175	34	588,672	37	541,411	37	576,731	36
Attempted assault with weapon	1,046,905	49	1,106,269	43	1,196,363	51	1,131,152	51
Simple assault	2,585,976	60	2,648,320	59	2,926,053	60	3,022,214	62
With injury	687,352	51	691,534	53	755,780	51	755,125	51
Attempted assault without weapon	1,898,624	63	1,956,786	60	2,170,273	63	2,267,089	66
Personal larceny with contact	513,952	65	497,056	63	461,014	62	549,967	64
Purse snatching	119,096	36	91,595	32	87,937	36	111,475	44
Attempted purse snatching	60,912	B	55,535	B	46,687	B	65,568	B
Pocket picking	333,943	72	349,926	70	326,390	66	372,924	66
Personal larceny without contact	15,455,660	73	16,021,110	73	16,469,154	74	16,492,446	74
Household victimizations								
Burglary	6,688,964	51	6,663,422	51	6,766,010	50	6,698,581	52
Forcible entry	2,251,869	27	2,277,063	29	2,300,292	27	2,199,925	29
Unlawful entry without force	2,959,734	62	2,826,599	60	2,962,705	60	2,911,696	61
Attempted forcible entry	1,477,361	67	1,559,760	66	1,503,013	67	1,586,959	67
Larceny	9,156,711	72	9,300,854	72	9,415,533	74	9,344,239	75
Under $50	5,615,914	84	5,601,954	84	5,443,697	85	5,177,916	87
$50 or more	2,707,605	46	2,745,097	47	2,851,831	52	3,125,604	54
Amount not ascertained	277,922	81	299,350	78	410,196	82	395,943	77
Attempted	555,270	76	654,454	73	709,808	73	644,776	77
Vehicle theft	1,418,725	28	1,234,644	30	1,296,759	31	1,364,549	33
Completed	910,253	8	759,816	11	797,671	11	860,016	11
Attempted	508,472	63	474,828	61	499,089	63	504,533	71
Business victimizations								
Robbery	261,725	9	297,516	12	X	X	X	X
Burglary	1,518,339	18	1,576,242	25	X	X	X	X

a.   Subcategories may not sum to total because of rounding.   X = figures not available.
b.   Figures are rounded.

areas (though the assault ratio is only about 1.5 to 1). Both NCS and UCR data indicate that crime occurs more frequently in warmer summer months than during the winter. In the following Close-Up, NCS data are analyzed to describe the typical American household that experiences crime.

1979		1980		1981		1982		1983[b]		1984[b]	
Esti-mated number	Percent not re-ported	Esti-mated number	Percent not re-ported	Esti-mated number	Percent not re-ported	Esti-mated number	Percent not re-ported	Esti-mated number	Percent not re-ported	Esti-mated number	Percent not re-ported
191,739	48	173,770	57	177,541	42	152,570	45	154,000	53	180,000	44
1,115,870	42	1,209,039	41	1,380,962	43	1,333,620	42	1,149,700	47	1,117,000	45
381,245	35	415,615	28	440,075	31	414,353	29	377,000	X	419,000	X
203,300	32	210,410	22	215,204	23	212,725	24	187,000	X	214,000	X
177,946	38	205,205	34	224,871	39	201,629	35	190,000	X	205,000	X
470,846	34	478,035	38	595,194	39	584,781	38	457,000	X	436,000	X
263,778	67	315,388	64	345,693	66	334,486	62	315,000	X	262,000	X
4,845,822	54	4,747,256	52	5,023,806	53	4,972,832	51	4,600,000	54	4,657,000	56
1,768,683	44	1,706,745	43	1,795,702	44	1,754,184	39	1,517,000	43	1,673,000	47
599,136	36	587,530	36	590,542	33	586,718	29	537,000	59	596,000	61
1,169,547	49	1,119,215	46	1,205,160	50	1,167,466	44	980,000	X	1,077,000	X
3,077,139	59	3,040,511	57	3,228,104	58	3,218,648	58	3,083,000	X	2,984,000	X
795,483	46	849,984	49	842,949	46	858,958	47	824,000	X	788,000	X
2,281,656	64	2,190,527	60	2,385,154	62	2,359,690	62	2,259,000	X	2,197,000	
510,790	64	557,760	63	604,875	58	577,125	66	563,000	64	530,000	68
119,548	40	143,626	40	146,330	38	131,429	40	127,000	X	91,000	X
46,707	B	55,168	B	48,975	B	46,467	B	50,000	X	34,000	X
344,535	70	358,966	69	409,571	62	399,229	71	386,000	X	404,000	X
15,861,378	74	14,758,069	71	15,273,714	72	14,975,908	71	14,095,000	74	13,259,000	74
6,684,018	51	6,973,932	48	7,392,603	47	6,662,843	49	6,063,000	51	5,643,000	51
2,154,639	27	2,462,080	26	2,587,098	23	2,104,087	24	1,903,000	X	1,844,000	X
3,109,280	60	3,033,163	57	3,078,168	59	2,932,122	59	2,607,000	X	2,478,000	X
1,420,099	67	1,478,690	64	1,727,337	64	1,626,634	65	1,553,000	X	1,321,000	X
10,631,289	74	10,466,874	72	10,174,660	73	9,704,598	72	9,144,000	75	8,750,000	73
5,726,441	86	5,060,050	86	4,903,484	86	4,613,488	87	4,429,000	X	3,982,000	X
3,666,796	55	4,150,033	55	4,032,487	56	3,963,988	55	3,699,000	X	3,791,000	X
562,414	77	500,321	70	507,655	75	443,905	75	410,000	X	394,000	X
675,639	75	756,469	72	731,033	73	683,217	75	576,000	X	583,000	X
1,392,837	30	1,380,796	29	1,438,980	33	1,376,866	26	1,264,000	31	1,340,000	31
920,158	13	936,593	12	890,898	12	946,887	10	810,000	X	836,000	X
472,679	36	444,203	64	548,082	65	429,979	63	454,000	X	505,000	X
X	X	X	X	X	X	X	X	X	X	X	X
X	X	X	X	X	X	X	X	X	X	X	X

SOURCE. McGarrell and Flanagan, *Sourcebook of Criminal Justice Statistics, 1984* (Washington, D.C.: U.S. Government Printing Office, 1985), preliminary draft, updated with *Criminal Victimization 1984* (Washington, D.C.: U.S. Government Printing Office, 1985).

A CRITIQUE OF THE NATIONAL CRIME SURVEY

Though the NCS eliminates the UCR's major methodological drawback—victims' failure to report crime—it too has problems that mitigate its value.[31] First, the NCS cannot measure crimes in which the victim may have participated, such as

TABLE 3.5 Estimated rate of personal and household victimization[a]

Type of victimization	Core cities within standard metropolitan statistical areas	Areas within standard metropolitan statistical areas, but outside of core cities	Areas outside of standard metropolitan statistical areas	Total
Personal victimizations (Rate per 100,000 persons 12 years of age or older)				
Rape and attempted rape	153	53	53	81
Robbery	1,334	577	327	708
Robbery with injury	359	190	136	220
Serious assault	188	95	70	113
Minor assault	171	95	66	107
Robbery without injury	630	241	118	310
Attempted robbery without injury	345	146	72	177
Assault	3,210	2,614	2,175	2,638
Aggravated assault	1,256	835	767	931
With injury	372	290	286	311
Attempted assault with weapon	885	545	482	619
Simple assault	1,954	1,778	1,407	1,708
With injury	540	441	401	456
Attempted assault without weapon	1,413	1,338	1,006	1,252
Personal larceny with contact	629	243	105	306
Purse snatching	154	62	7	70
Attempted purse snatching	58	20	2	25
Pocket picking	418	162	95	212
Personal larceny without contact	9,473	8,529	5,902	7,945
Household victimizations (Rate per 100,000 households)				
Base	25,165,280	32,696,835	27,342,931	85,205,046
Burglary	10,270	7,146	6,370	7,820
Forcible entry	3,731	2,241	1,581	2,469
Unlawful entry without force	3,802	3,142	3,467	3,441
Attempted forcible entry	2,737	1,763	1,321	1,909
Larceny	13,874	11,098	9,452	11,390
Under $50	5,975	5,404	4,912	5,415
$50 or more	6,094	4,426	3,595	4,652
Amount not ascertained	663	469	453	521
Attempted	1,142	799	493	802
Vehicle theft	2,744	1,484	736	1,616
Completed	1,863	1,040	504	1,111
Attempted	881	444	231	505

a. Subcategories may not sum to total because of rounding.

SOURCE. McGarrell and Flanagan, *Sourcebook of Criminal Justice Statistics, 1984* (Washington, D.C.: U.S. Government Printing Office, 1985).

drug use, gambling, fraud, and so on. Second, it is only an estimate of crime patterns that probably occurred and should not be interpreted to mean that the crimes actually took place.

The NCS also may suffer from victims' underreporting or overreporting of crime. They may underreport because they have forgotten an incident or perhaps were not even aware of it—for example, a victim may have thought he misplaced his wallet when it was actually stolen. Victims may know the offender and mistakenly believe they will get the offender in trouble if they discuss the incident with interviewers. Some victims may be embarrassed by the crime and may not wish to discuss it with anyone.

Overreporting can result from victims' misinterpretation of noncriminal incidents. For example, an open front door may be viewed as evidence of attempted burglary when it was actually the result of carelessness on the part of a family member. Victims may wish to show their cooperation by interpreting minor incidents—being jostled or pushed in the schoolyard, for example—as assaults or attacks.

It is also possible that bias, miscoding or misinterpretation of fact, or interviewer error affect the validity of NCS data. Some interviewers may believe they have to record crimes to justify their continued employment.

Though the NCS is not flawless, it represents a major criminological achievement. As you will see in the following section, its findings, together with self-reports and UCR data, can help criminologists better understand the nature of crime in the United States.

Summary

Measuring crime is a major goal of criminology. Crime data are usually acquired from surveys of victims and criminals or from records of criminal justice agencies.

Official crime statistics are composed of data from the records of police, court, and correctional agencies. The best-known official data source is the Uniform Crime Report (UCR), compiled by the Federal Bureau of Investigation. The UCR compiles crimes reported to local police agencies, crimes cleared, and arrests made. The UCR indicates that large cities, warm weather months, and southern and western states have disproportionately high crime rates. About 12 million crimes are reported annually in the UCR.

Self-report studies ask subjects to tell about their law-violating behavior. Self-reports indicate that the crime rate is much higher than previously believed.

Victimization surveys ask the victims of crimes about their personal experiences. One study, the National Crime Survey, indicates that about 40 million crimes occur annually.

All three sources of crime statistics have methodological flaws that undermine their validity. The UCR has been criticized because of underreporting by victims, police mismanagement of criminal statistics, and methodological problems. Self-reports rely on the honesty of the respondents, who may or may not wish to reveal their behavior. They have also been criticized for containing trivial acts that are not "real crimes." Victimization data may contain flaws derived from victims' misinterpretation of events, forgetfulness, and so on.

Nonetheless, all three sources—official crime statistics, self-report studies, and victimization surveys—agree that the crime rate has been declining since 1980. This dramatic reversal may be attributed to a lowering of the age structure, get-tough criminal justice policies, or even methodological problems in the way crime statistics are gathered.

Notes

1 Federal Bureau of Investigation, *Crime in the United States, 1983* (Washington, D.C.: U.S. Government Printing Office, 1984). Hereafter cited as FBI, *Uniform Crime Report* in footnotes and referred to in text as Uniform Crime Report (UCR). Uniform Crime

Households Touched by Crime

In addition to individual analysis, since 1981 the NCS has computed the number of households touched by crime. A household is considered "touched by crime" if during the year it experienced a burglary, auto theft, or household larceny, or if any member was raped, robbed, assaulted, or the victim of a personal larceny.

At the time of this writing, the 1983 household statistics were available, and they reflect the continuing decline in overall crime rate. As table A indicates, about 23.6 million households experienced victimization in 1983, a decline of about 7 percent from the previous year. Despite this decline, more than a quarter of all American families experienced some type of victimization in 1983.

TABLE A. Households touched by crime

	1983		1982		Relative percent change 1982–83
	Number of households	Percent	Number of households	Percent	
Households touched by all crimes	23,621,000	27.4	24,989,000	29.3	−7
Violent crime	4,400,000	5.1	4,776,000	5.6	−9
Rape	128,000	0.1	136,000	0.2	−6
Robbery	981,000	1.1	1,196,000	1.4	−19
Assault	3,620,000	4.2	3,835,000	4.5	−7
Aggravated	1,301,000	1.5	1,415,000	1.7	−9
Simple	2,568,000	3.0	2,712,000	3.2	−6
Larceny	16,983,000	19.7	17,835,000	20.9	−6
Personal	11,230,000	13.0	11,821,000	13.9	−6
With contact	533,000	0.6	574,000	0.7	−7
Without contact	10,836,000	12.6	11,381,000	13.4	−6
Household	7,706,000	8.9	8,181,000	9.6	−7
Burglary	5,268,000	6.1	5,865,000	6.9	−11
Motor vehicle theft	1,193,000	1.4	1,358,000	1.6	−13
Crimes of high concern[a]	7,681,000	8.9	8,521,000	10.0	−11
Total	86,146,000	100.0%	85,178,000	100.0%	—

NOTE: Detail does not add to total because of overlap in households touched by various crimes. Percent change is based on unrounded figures.
a. Rape, robbery, assault, burglary.

Report data are supplemented with preliminary data from the 1984 crime survey released by the FBI.

2 For a general review of the subject, see David Farrington, "Longitudinal Research on Crime and Delinquency," in *Crime and Justice*, vol. 1, ed. Norval Morris and Michael Tonry (Chicago: University of Chicago Press, 1979), pp. 288–348.

3 This section adapted from FBI *Uniform Crime Reports 1983*, pp. 1–5.

4 Clarence Schrag, *Crime and Justice: American Style* (Washington, D.C.: U.S. Government Printing Office, 1971).

5 FBI, *Uniform Crime Report 1983*, p. 41.

6 FBI, *Uniform Crime Report 1984*, preliminary report. Updated with information provided by the FBI, 1985.

7 Philip Ennes, *Criminal Victimization in the United States*, field survey 2 (Report on a

Table B illustrates the characteristics of households touched by crime. The following trends can be viewed in the data:

RACE OF HOUSEHOLD HEAD

- 4.6% of all black households had members who were victims of serious violent crime (rape, robbery, or aggravated assault), almost twice the percentage for white households (2.4%).
- Black households were more vulnerable than white households to burglary (8.5% vs. 5.8%).
- About the same percentage of white households as black households suffered thefts of objects from places away from the home (at work, in restaurants, etc.); however, a higher percentage of black than of white households suffered thefts of objects from around the home (excluding burglaries).

FAMILY INCOME

- The fraction of all families touched by a crime of violence or theft varied by size of income; about a fourth (26%) of all low-income families were victimized compared with about a third (35%) of all high-income families.[1]
- Households with annual incomes of $25,000 or more a year had the greatest risk of being touched by crimes of theft. A fourth (25%) of these households suffered thefts during 1983, compared with 16% of households with incomes under $7,500.

PLACE OF RESIDENCE

- For most personal crimes, the aggregate victimization experience of suburban households was closer to that of urban households than that of rural households. (For burglary and household larceny, however, the opposite was true). For example, suburban households are victimized by personal larceny without contact about as often as urban households but much more frequently than rural households.

- A third (33%) of all urban households were touched by a crime of violence or theft in 1983.
- There was little difference in the percentages of urban and suburban households victimized by the theft of objects away from the home, but urban households were more likely than their suburban counterparts to be victims of theft from around the home.
- The percentage of urban households touched by violent crime by strangers was more than double that for rural households (4.8% vs. 1.9%).
- The biggest relative difference between urban and suburban households was for robbery; the urban estimate is more than twice the suburban estimate, despite the small absolute difference between them (2.1% vs. 9.9%).
- The biggest relative difference between suburban and rural households was for motor vehicle theft; the percentage of rural households victimized by this crime was only half that of suburban households (0.7% vs. 1.4%).

SIZE OF HOUSEHOLD

The size of a household is an important factor in assessing its vulnerability to crime. Overall, the more people in a household, the greater its vulnerability, although this tendency is more pronounced for personal crimes than for household crimes. (Larger households have more members at risk for personal crimes; but each household, regardless of size, is the unit at risk for household crimes.)

- 1 in 5 single-person households was touched by crime in 1983 (table B).
- 2 in 5 households with six or more members were touched by crime.
- The percentage touched by crime varied most by size of household for personal larceny, and varied least by size of household for burglary.

[1] In this report households with annual incomes of less than $7,500 are considered low-income households; those with incomes of $7,500–$14,999, medium; $15,000–$24,999, medium high; and $25,000 or more, high.

cont'd

National Survey by President's Commission on Law Enforcement and Criminal Justice, Washington, D.C., 1967).

8 Edmund McGarrell and Timothy Flanagan, *Sourcebook of Criminal Justice Statistics 1984* (Washington, D.C.: U.S. Government Printing Office, 1985), table 3.6.

9 Ibid.

10 Michael Hindelang and Michael Gottfredson, "The Victim's Decision Not to Involve the Criminal Justice Process," in *Criminal Justice and the Victim*, ed. William F. McDonald, (Beverly Hills, Calif.: Sage Publications, 1976), pp. 57–74.

11 Ibid., pp. 71–73.

12 Paul Tappan, *Crime, Justice and Corrections* (New York: McGraw-Hill, 1960).

13 Daniel Bell, *The End of Ideology* (New York: Free Press, 1967), p. 152.

14 Duncan Chappell, Gilbert Geis, Stephen Schafer, and Larry Siegel, "Forcible Rape: A

Households Touched by Crime—cont'd

TABLE B. Percent of households touched by crime by selected characteristics, 1983

	Race of head		Annual family income				Place of residence		
	White	Black	Under $7,500	$7,500-$14,999	$15,000-$24,999	$25,000 or more	Urban	Suburban	Rural
Any NCS crime	26.9%	31.8%	24.7%	25.9%	27.9%	32.4%	32.5%	28.4%	21.6%
Violent crime	4.9	6.5	5.9	4.9	4.9	5.3	6.5	5.2	3.7
Rape	0.1	0.2	0.3	0.1	0.1	0.1	0.2	0.1	0.2
Robbery	1.0	2.3	1.6	1.2	1.1	0.9	2.1	0.9	0.5
Assault	4.1	4.7	4.5	4.0	4.0	4.6	4.8	4.5	3.3
Aggravated	1.4	2.5	1.8	1.6	1.4	1.4	2.0	1.5	1.1
Simple	3.0	2.5	3.1	2.7	2.9	3.5	3.2	3.3	2.4
Property crime									
Personal larceny	13.0	13.1	9.1	10.9	13.7	18.3	14.8	14.3	9.9
Burglary	5.8	8.5	8.2	6.0	5.4	5.6	8.0	5.8	4.7
Household larceny	8.8	10.1	8.7	9.4	9.2	9.3	10.9	8.8	7.4
Motor vehicle theft	1.3	2.1	1.1	1.3	1.6	1.6	2.1	1.4	0.7
Serious violent crime[1]	2.4	4.6	3.4	2.7	2.5	2.3	4.0	2.4	1.7
Crimes of high concern[2]	8.6	11.7	10.7	8.6	8.2	8.9	11.9	8.8	6.3
Total larceny[3]	19.6	20.4	15.7	18.3	20.6	24.9	22.3	20.9	16.0

NOTE: Detail does not add to total because of overlap in households touched by various crimes.
[1]Rape, robbery, aggravated assault.
[2]Rape, robbery, assault by stranger, or burglary.
[3]Personal larceny, household larceny.

In 1983, 70 million people lived in households touched by crime. Even though this number represents a decline from the previous year, it indicates that crime remains a pervasive social problem in the American culture.

DISCUSSION QUESTIONS

1. Has your household been "touched by crime"? Did you tell the police about it?

2. Does the fact that 27 percent of American households fall victim to crime shock you? Is that number more or less than you expected?

3. Is the fact that wealthier households are the more likely victims of crime surprising? Or does this relate to the fact that wealthy victims are more likely to live in the city or suburbs?

SOURCE. Adopted from Bureau of Justice Statistics, *Households Touched by Crime, 1983* (Washington, D.C.: National Institute of Justice, 1984).

Comparative Study of Offenses Known to the Police in Boston and Los Angeles," in *Studies in the Sociology of Sex*, ed. James Henslin (New York: Appleton Century Crofts, 1971), pp. 169–93.

15 Lawrence Sherman and Barry Glick, "The Quality of Arrest Statistics," *Police Foundation Reports* 2 (1984):1–8.

16 David Seidman and Michael Couzens, "Getting the Crime Rate Down: Political Pressure and Crime Reporting," *Law and Society Review* 8 (1974):457.

17 Leonard Savitz, "Official Statistics," in *Contemporary Criminology*, ed. Leonard Savitz and Norman Johnston, (New York: John Wiley, 1982), pp. 3–15.

18 New York Times, "Study Faults FBI Crime Statistics, Proposes Changes," *Omaha World Herald*, 20 June 1985.

19 Roger Hood and Richard Sparks, *Key Issues in Criminology* (New York: McGraw-Hill, 1970), p. 72.

20 A pioneering effort in self-report research is A.L. Porterfield, *Youth in Trouble* (Fort Worth, Tex.: Leo Potishman Foundation, 1946). For a review, see Robert Hardt and George Bodine, *Development of Self-Report Instruments in Delinquency Research: A Conference Report* (Syracuse, N.Y.: Syracuse University Youth Development Center, 1965). See also Fred Murphy, Mary Shirley, and Helen Witner, "The Incidence of Hidden Delinquency," *American Journal of Orthopsychology* 16 (1946):686–96.

21 For example, the following studies have noted the great discrepancy between official statistics and self-report studies. Maynard Erickson and LaMar Empey, "Court Records, Undetected Delinquency and Decision-Making," *Journal of Criminal Law, Criminology and Police Science* 54 (1963):456–69; Martin Gold, "Undetected Delinquent Behavior," *Journal of Research in Crime and Delinquency* 3 (1966):27–46; James Short and F. Ivan Nye, "Extent of Unrecorded Delinquency, Tentative Conclusions," *Journal of Criminal Law, Criminology and Police Science* 49 (1958):296–302; David Farrington, "Self-Reports of Deviant Behavior: Predictive and Stable?" *Journal of Criminal Law and Criminology* 64 (1973):99–110; Michael Hindelang, "Causes of Delinquency: A Partial Replication and Extension," *Social Problems* 20 (1973):471–87.

22 Rosemary Sarri, "Gender Issues in Juvenile Justice," *Crime and Delinquency* 29 (1983):381–97.

23 Franklyn Dunford and Delbert Elliott, "Identifying Career Criminals Using Self-Reported Data," *Journal of Research in Crime and Delinquency* 21 (1984):57–86.

24 See generally James Hackler and Melanie Lautt, "Systematic Bias in Measuring Self-Reported Delinquency," *Canadian Review of Sociology and Anthropology* 6 (1969): 92–106.

25 See, for example, Harwin Voss, "Ethnic Differentials in Delinquency in Honolulu," *Journal of Criminal Law, Criminology and Police Science* 54 (1963):322–327; Erickson and Empey, "Court Records"; H.B. Gibson, Sylvia Morrison, and D.J. West, "The Confession of Known Offenses in Response to a Self-Reported Delinquency Schedule," *British Journal of Criminology* 10 (1970):277–80; John Blackmore, "The Relationship between Self-Reported Delinquency and Official Convictions amongst Adolescent Boys," *British Journal of Criminology* 14 (1974):172–76.

26 See, for example, Spencer Rathus and Larry Siegel, "Crime and Personality Revisited: Effects of MMPI Sets in Self-Report Studies," *Criminology* 18 (1980):245–51; John Clark and Larry Tifft, "Polygraph and Interview Validation of Self-Reported Deviant Behavior," *American Sociological Review* 31 (1966):516–23.

27 Michael Hindelang, Travis Hirschi, and Joseph Weis, *Measuring Delinquency* (Beverly Hills, Calif.: Sage Publications, 1981).

28 Ibid., p. 196.

29 The data contained in the following sections were originally presented in National Crime Survey, *Criminal Victimization in the United States 1982* (Washington, D.C., U.S. Government Printing Office, 1984). These data are supplemented by analyses in McGarrell and Flanagan, *Sourcebook of Criminal Justice Statistics 1984.*

30 See generally James Levine, "The Potential for Crime Over-Reporting in Criminal Victimization Surveys," *Criminology* 14 (1976):307–330; Richard Sparks, "Surveys of Victimization—An Optimistic Assessment," in *Crime and Justice, An Annual Review of Research*, vol. 3, ed. Michael Tonry and Norval Morris (Chicago: University of Chicago Press, 1981), pp. 1–60.

31 Ibid.

4 Victims and Criminals

CHAPTER OUTLINE

Introduction

Social Class and Crime

Age and Crime

Sex and Crime: The Female Criminal

Explaining Female Criminality

Race and Crime

Causes of Racial Disparity in Crime

The Chronic Offender: Career Criminals

Wolfgang's "Delinquency in a Birth Cohort"

Birth Cohort Follow-up

Birth Cohort II

Incapacitating Chronic Offenders

Chronic Offenders Today

Crime Victimization

Victim Characteristics

Crime Characteristics

Criminals and Victims: A Review

Summary

KEY TERMS

chronic offender

career criminal

victimization risk

social class

instrumental crimes

expressive crimes

social structure

aging out process

masculinity hypothesis

chivalry hypothesis

subculture of violence

cohort

chronic recidivists

selective incapacitation

Introduction

What do the various sources of criminological statistics tell us about crime in America? What is known about the nature of crime, criminals, and their victims? What sociological trends or patterns exist in the crime rate that can help us understand the causes of crime?

These questions are among the most important issues in the criminological literature. They focus attention on the root causes of crime and provide the raw material criminological theory is based on. Though each of the major sources of crime statistics (described in chapter 3) has its limitations, they share enough common ground to allow concrete inferences to be drawn about the nature of crime.

Therefore, this chapter will pull together the three crime measures to analyze the social forces influencing crime trends—age, class, sex, and race. Then criminal statistics will be used to analyze a major concept in criminological literature—the **chronic offender** or **career criminal.** It is alleged that not only can the population be subdivided into criminals and noncriminals, but that the offending population itself can be further subdivided into one-time (or occasional) criminals and chronic offenders, a small group of people who are responsible for a disproportionate share of the offending population.

Finally, the victim of crime will be the focus of analysis. Who are the victims? What factors increase **victimization risk?** What are the economic costs of crime to victims?

Social Class and Crime

A most important issue in the criminological literature is the relationship between **social class** and crime. Traditionally, crime has been thought to be a lower-class phenomenon. After all, people at the bottom of the social structure have the greatest incentive to commit crimes. Those unable to obtain desired goods and services through conventional means may consequently resort to theft and other illegal activities—such as the sale of narcotics—to obtain them; these activities are referred to as **instrumental crimes.** Those living in poverty areas are also believed to engage in disproportionate amounts of violent crime as a means of expressing their rage, frustration, and anger against society. Rates of **expressive crimes,** such as rape and assault, may also be higher in poverty areas because those engaging in violence can develop an alternative source of positive self-image by viewing themselves as tough, strong, or "bad." If this is so, the cause of crime would be related to a person's place in the **social structure.**

Official statistics indicate that crime rates in inner-city, high-poverty areas are generally higher than those in suburban or wealthier areas. As you may recall, crime rates in urban areas are significantly higher than those in suburban and rural counties. Studies using aggregate police statistics (arrest records) have consistently shown that crime rates in lower-class areas are higher than in wealthier neighborhoods.[1]

One problem with accepting these findings at face value is that the relationship between official crime and social class may be more a function of law enforcement practices and not actual criminal behavior patterns. Police may devote more resources to poverty areas and consequently apprehension rates may be higher there. Similarly, police may be more likely to formally arrest and prosecute lower-class citizens than those in the middle and upper classes, which may account for the lower classes' overrepresentation in the official statistics.

Because of these factors, self-report data have been used extensively to test the class-crime relationship. If people in all social classes self-report similar crime patterns, but only those in the lower class are formally arrested, that would explain the higher crime rates in lower-class neighborhoods. However, if lower-class people report greater criminal activity than their middle- and upper-class peers, it would indicate that the official statistics are an accurate representation of the crime problem.

As mentioned previously, most self-report studies have been conducted with youths. Surprisingly, the first self-report studies, specifically those conducted by James Short and F. Ivan Nye, did not find a direct relationship between social class and youth crime.[2] They found that socioeconomic class was related to official processing by police, court, and correctional agencies, but not to the actual commission of crimes. For example, Short and Nye found that criminal behavior had no relationship to class when they used self-reports as the criterion of delinquency, but that it had a clear relationship when they used institutionalization. In addition, factors generally associated with lower-class membership, such as broken homes, were found to be related to institutionalization but not to admissions of delinquency. Ivan Nye, James Short, and Virgil Olsen studied two areas of the nation and several schools. Using the father's occupation as an indicator of class, they were unable to support the contention that a relationship exists between self-reported delinquency and socioeconomic class.[3]

In another study, Robert Dentler and Lawrence Monroe found no relationship between amount of admitted delinquency and class.[4] Most researchers did conclude, however, that lower-class youths were more likely to receive official notice from the justice system. Therefore, they appear to be overrepresented as official delinquents. Middle-class delinquency, on the other hand, remained hidden.

For more than twenty years after the use of self-reports became widespread, a majority of self-report studies agreed that a class-crime relationship did not exist.[5] In the definitive work in this area, Charles Tittle, Wayne Villemez, and Douglas Smith reviewed 35 studies containing 363 separate estimates concerning the relationship between class and crime.[6] They concluded that little if any support exists for the contention that crime is primarily a lower-class phenomenon. Consequently, Tittle and his associates argued that official statistics probably reflect class bias in the processing of the lower class.[7] The Tittle review is usually cited by criminologists as the strongest statement refuting the claim that the lower class is disproportionately criminal.

Recent Research on Class and Crime. These findings have significantly affected criminological theory. If crime is not purely a function of social class, and if there are no significant distinctions in the crime rate across economic class lines, then it is evident that the causes of crime must be found in social experiences common to all people—poor family environment, peer pressure, school failure, stigma and labeling, and so on. Consequently, sociological theories were developed (discussed in chapter 7) that focus on social processes—and not social structure—as the primary cause of crime.

However, not all criminologists agree with Tittle's findings. That faction usually points to the inclusion of trivial offenses, for example using a false ID, in most self-report instruments. They contend that although middle- and upper-class youths may appear to be as delinquent as those in the lower class, it is only because they frequently engage in trivial offenses. However, if only serious Part I offenses are considered, these criminologists believe that lower-class youths will be found more delinquent, and a true class-crime relationship should emerge.

The most widely cited evidence that a class-crime relationship exists can be found in the work of Delbert Elliott and his colleagues Suzanne Ageton and David Huizinga. Using a carefully drawn national sample of 1,726 youths ages eleven to seventeen and a sophisticated self-report instrument, Elliott and Ageton found lower-class youths to be much more likely than middle-class youths to engage in serious delinquent acts such as burglary, assault, robbery, sexual assault, and vandalism.[8] Moreover, lower-class youths were much more likely than middle-class youths to have committed "numerous" serious personal and property crimes (more than two hundred). These findings forced Elliott and Ageton to conclude that self-report data give findings about class and crime that are actually similar to those of official data. Furthermore, the authors charge that studies showing middle- and lower-class youths to be equally delinquent rely on measures weighted toward minor crimes (for example, using a false ID or skipping school). When serious crimes like burglary and assault are used in the comparison, lower-class youths are significantly more delinquent.

In a follow-up study, Elliott and Huizinga again found that middle-class youths (males) are much less likely to commit serious crime than lower-class youths. There were substantial class differences in both the prevalence and incidence of serious crime.[9]

So the weight of recent evidence seems to point to the concurrence of self-report and official criminal statistics—crime is more prevalent among the lower class. However, this is not the final word on the issue. In a landmark study, *Measuring Delinquency*, Michael Hindelang, Travis Hirschi, and Joseph Weis found that a relationship between social class and crime was nonexistent in *both* self-report and official data. They concluded:

> *There is no apparent systematic bias in either self-report or official measures of delinquency at the individual level associated with social class of sufficient magnitude to produce misleading results if one measure of delinquency rather than the other were used.*[10]

Thus, while some criminologists argue that crime is primarily a lower-class phenomenon, others believe that it is spread throughout the social structure. In an important recent work, three prominent criminologists show that the relationship between social class and crime is weak and that both self-report data and official statistics are relatively unbiased. Consequently, studies that rely on official statistics may be more accurate than some critics would like to believe.

If these results seem confusing, don't worry—they should be. The relationship between social class and crime has perplexed professional criminologists for over thirty years. The debate is still far from settled.

Age and Crime

Crime is a young person's game. Criminologists Travis Hirschi and Michael Gottfredson state, "Age is everywhere correlated with crime. Its effects on crime do not depend on other demographic correlates of crime."[11] In other words, regardless of economic status, marital status, race, sex, and so on, younger people commit crime more often than their older peers.

FIGURE 4.1

Age and criminal
behavior

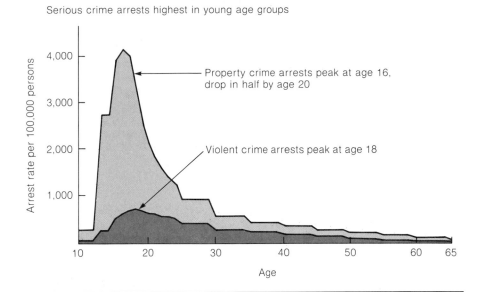

Serious crime arrests highest in young age groups

Property crime arrests peak at age 16,
drop in half by age 20

Violent crime arrests peak at age 18

Arrest rate per 100,000 persons

Age

SOURCE. *FBI Uniform Crime Reports,* 3-year average, 1978-80. *Report to the Nation on Crime and
Justice,* Bureau of Justice Statistics, p. 32.

Official arrest data indicate that people under twenty are the most likely to
commit property and violent crimes. Property crime arrests peak at sixteen, while
violent crime arrests predominate at age eighteen (see figure 4.1).

Findings of the National Crime Survey (NCS) duplicate the official crime
data. When victims are asked to estimate the age of their assailants in crimes
involving personal contact (rape, personal larceny, robbery, assault), they report
that offenders between eighteen and twenty years old are about three times as
likely to commit crimes than those twenty-one years old or over. Those described
as twelve to seventeen years old were twice as likely to violate the law as those
twenty-one years old or over. This pattern has been shown by John Laub to be
consistent since 1973 (see figure 4.2).[12]

The question that emerges from these data is "What happens to the youthful
offenders as they mature?" It is evident that most law violators between sixteen
and twenty-one years old forego their criminal behavior when they become adults
(or adult crime rates would equal those of juvenile offenders); this is referred to as
the **aging out process.** For some, aging out may be a consequence of socialization
and changing social roles. As adolescents mature, the demands of job and family
may reduce opportunities they have for criminal behavior; job and family replace
peers and gangs as reference groups. When they enter the workplace, former
delinquents can substitute conventional for illegitimate opportunity structures—
they "go straight." Others, apprehended by police, are serving long terms in the
nation's prison systems and lack the opportunity to commit crime. Those who are
less fortunate appear as statistics in police homicide or drug-related death files. In
any event, regardless of their sex, race, economic class, or other factors, younger
people are more likely to violate the law, but will reduce their criminal activity
as they mature.

FIGURE 4.2

Estimated annual rates of offending in total personal crimes

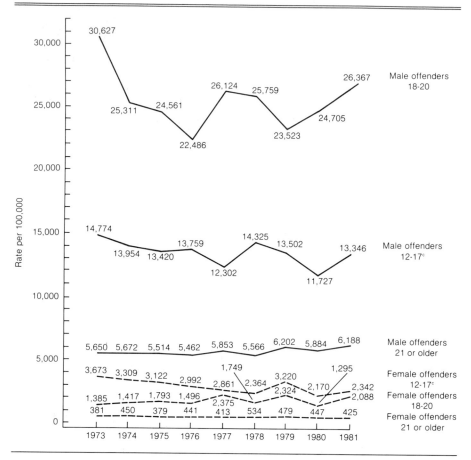

[a]Includes perceived age of lone offender and perceived age of oldest multiple offender.

[b]Excluded are incidents (about 10 percent of the total) in which the victim did not know whether there was one or more than one offender and incidents involving offenders of "mixed" sexes.

[c]The numerator of the rates of offending for 12–17-year-olds excludes incidents (about 1 percent of the total) in which the offender was perceived by the victim to be under 12 years of age. The denominator of the rate is the number of 12–17-year-olds in the general population.

SOURCE. John Laub, *Juvenile Criminal Behavior in the United States: An Analysis of Offender and Victim Characteristics,* Working Paper 25, Michael J. Hindelang Criminal Justice Research Center (Albany, N.Y., 1983), p.25.

Sex and Crime: The Female Criminal

The three major forms of criminal statistics generally agree that male crime rates are considerably higher than those of females. The NCS indicates that the personal crime rate of male offenders eighteen to twenty years old was an astounding 26,367 per 100,000; the rate for females eighteen to twenty years old was 2,088 per 100,000—about a tenth as much (see figure 4.2). In other words, in approximately 87 percent of all cases of violent personal crime, victims identified the offender as being male.[13]

The Uniform Crime Report (UCR) arrest statistics also indicate the predominance of male criminality. The overall male-female arrest ratio is usually about four male offenders to one female offender; for violent crimes the ratio is closer to nine males to one female.

Despite this disparity, increases in female criminality during the past decade have been greater than those in male criminality. While the male arrest rate declined 3.8 percent in 1975–1984, the female rate increased almost 17 percent. And though the overall crime rate has decreased in recent years, declines in male crime have been greater than those in female crime.[14]

Recent self-report studies also show significant male-female differences. Rosemary Sarri found that while male-female ratios for minor offenses (truancy) were quite similar, they showed major discrepancies for serious crimes such as assault and burglary.[15] Delbert Elliott's National Youth Survey and the national survey by Jay Williams and Martin Gold also found that males commit more serious crimes. Hindelang, Hirschi, and Weis concluded that if the methodological problems that beset self-reports could be solved, their results would mirror official crime data—males commit much more serious crime than females.[16]

EXPLAINING FEMALE CRIMINALITY

Traditional criminological literature recognized differences between male and female crime. Early views portrayed the female criminal as an emotional, physical, or psychological aberration. The most notable theoretical work was Cesare Lombroso's 1895 book, *The Female Offender*.[17] Lombroso argued that whereas women generally were more passive and less criminal than men, there was a small group of female criminals who lacked "typical" female traits of "piety, maternity, underdeveloped intelligence, and weakness."[18]

Lombroso also stated that women were lower on the evolutionary scale than men, more childlike, less sensitive, and less intelligent.[19] Women who committed crimes (most often prostitution and other sex-related offenses) could be distinguished from "normal" women by physical characteristics—excessive body hair, wrinkles, crow's feet, and abnormal cranium, for example.[20] In physical appearance as well as in emotionality, delinquent females appeared closer to both criminal and noncriminal men than to other women. Lombroso's theory became known as the **masculinity hypothesis.**

Later theorists portrayed the female criminal as either a sexually controlling or sexually naive person, manipulating men for profit or being manipulated by them. Otto Pollack, writing fifty years after Lombroso, viewed the female criminal as a devious creature whose criminality was masked because criminal justice authorities were reluctant to take action against her. Pollack's theory is referred to as the **chivalry hypothesis.** Pollack charged that rather than being manipulated and exploited by men, female criminals were the exploiters and instigators who encouraged their male companions to pursue criminal careers.[21]

In the fifties and sixties, criminological literature portrayed adolescent female offenders as troubled individuals, alienated at home, who pursued crime as a means of compensating for their disrupted personal lives.[22] The streets became a "second home" to girls whose physical and emotional adjustment was hampered by a strained home life, marked by such conditions as absent fathers, overly competitive mothers, and so on.

In the seventies, several influential works, most notably Freda Adler's *Sisters in Crime*[23] and Rita James Simon's *The Contemporary Woman and Crime*, revolutionized thinking on the causes of female crime.[24] Their research focused attention on the changing role of women in society and its relationship to female crime rates. Both Adler and Simon believed that the traditionally lower crime rate for women could be explained by their "second-class" economic and social position. They further contended that, as women's social roles changed and their lifestyles became more like those of their male counterparts, their criminal activity would also become more like that of males. Criminologists, responding to this research, began to refer to the "new female criminal."

The rapid increase in the female crime rate during the 1970s gave support to the social and economic development model of the new female criminal. However, the relationship between female liberation and crime has been a hotly debated topic in the criminological community. Some scholars, most notably Darrell Steffensmeier and Renee Hoffman Steffensmeier, Joseph Weis, Carol Smart, Steven Box, and Chris Hale, conclude that the emancipation of women may have had relatively little influence on female crime rates.[25] In other words, they believe that rising female crime rates may not reflect economic or social changes. Other scholars contend that female crime rates are rising because police today may be more willing to formally arrest and process female offenders, that female liberation has brought an end to the chivalry hypothesis. Moreover, say these researchers, the offense patterns of women are still quite different from those of men. Men are still committing a disproportionate share of serious crimes such as robbery, burglary, and assault.

For these reasons, theories of criminal behavior have usually focused on male offenders. Though some prominent theoretical models give equal weight to both male and female crime, female criminality is normally treated as a separate issue. If female crime rates continue to grow, it is likely that theoreticians will pay closer attention to the nature of female criminality.

Race and Crime

All three sources of criminal statistics provide evidence that minority group members commit more crimes, especially violent crimes, than the general population. The UCR tells us that although black citizens make up 12 percent of the general population, they account for about 46 percent of the violent crime arrests and 30 percent of the property crime arrests, as well as a disproportionate number of Part II arrests.[26]

We could argue that since the UCR statistics represent arrest data, the minority crime rate might be a reflection of racism and discrimination by police. Therefore, criminologists have sought validation for the racial differences in the official crime statistics by analysis of NCS and self-report data.

The NCS supplies racial data on crimes in which victims were able to observe their attackers—rape, assault, and robbery. In table 4.1, NCS data are compared to UCR arrest data collected in 1982. Blacks are identified as committing a dis-

TABLE 4.1
Race and violent crime: NCS and UCR data—1982

Crime Category	UCR		NCS	
	% White	% Black	% White	% Black
Rape	50	48	68	28
Robbery	41	58	44	47
Assault	60	38	69	27

SOURCE. *Crime in the United States, 1982*, p. 186; *Criminal Victimization in the United States, 1982*.

proportionate share of personal violent crimes. Nonetheless, the proportions are somewhat less than reported in the UCR arrest statistics, especially for the crime of rape. This could mean that police are more likely to arrest black suspects for that crime, or that women attacked by black offenders are more likely to report the crime to police. Also, rape tends to be an intraracial crime and black women are more likely to report rapes to police (67 percent) than white women (50 percent).

CAUSES OF RACIAL DISPARITY IN CRIME

Racial differences in the crime rate is an extremely sensitive issue. Before NCS data were available, liberal-radical criminologists denounced UCR data as reflecting discriminatory arrest practices. However, today most criminologists recognize that recorded differences in the black-white crime rate cannot be explained away solely by differential treatment within the criminal justice system.[27]

How can these disparities be explained? One approach has been to trace the black experience in America. Some criminologists view black crime as a function of socialization in a society where the black family was torn apart and black culture destroyed in such a way that recovery has proven impossible. James P. Comer, in *American Violence and Public Policy*, a 1985 update of the National Commission on the Causes and Prevention of Violence, argues that the early slave experiences left a wound that has been deepened by racism and lack of opportunity.[28] Children of the slave society were thrust into a system of forced dependency and negative self-feelings. Comer writes that it was a system that promoted powerful forces for identification with an aggressor (slave master and other whites) and ambivalence and antagonism toward one's self and group. After emancipation, blacks were shut out of the social and political mainstream. Frustrated, angry, they were isolated in segregated communities, turning within for support. Their entire American experience provided for negative self-images, anger, and rage. Comer states:

> *In reaction to failure, the most vibrant and reactive often become disrupted and violent in and out of schools both individually and in groups or gangs. Neighborhoods and communities of adequately functioning families are then overwhelmed by the reactive and most troubled individuals and families. Models of violence and other troublesome behavior for children abound in relatives, friends, and neighbors unsuccessful in previous generations.*[29]

According to Comer, the intraracial nature of black violence is in reaction to an "inability to cope with the larger society or to identify with black and white leaders and institutional achievements. Frustration and anger is taken out on people most like self."[30]

In his influential book, *Criminal Violence, Criminal Justice*, Charles Silberman also views the problem as a function of the black experience in this country—"an experience that differs from that of other ethnic groups." Silberman's provocative argument is that black citizens have learned to be violent because of their treatment in U.S. society. First, they were violently uprooted from their African homeland. Then their slavery was maintained by violence. After emancipation, their lower-class position was enforced by violent means, such as intimidation by the Ku Klux Klan. To strike back meant harsh retaliation by the white-controlled law. Moving to northern cities, blacks suffered two burdens unknown to other migrants: their color and their heritage of slavery. After all, the color black in U.S. culture connotes sinister, dirty, evil, or bad things, while white stands for goodness and purity (the good guys always wear white hats; social outcasts are blacklisted; brides wear white and witches wear black). Consequently, to survive and reach cultural and personal fulfillment, blacks have developed their own set of norms, values, and traditions. In the 1960s, many blacks began to adopt the image, first developed in Southern folklore and myth, of being "bad" in their personal lives. After 350 years of fearing whites, Silberman writes, "black Americans have discovered that the fear runs the other way, that whites are intimidated by their very presence; it would be hard to overestimate what an extraordinarily liberating force this discovery is . . . 350 years of festering hatred has come spilling out."[31]

According to Silberman, black violence does not have a cathartic effect—instead of dissipating rage, violence appears to create even more aggression. And, as blacks continue to get a greater share of prosperity, it is ironic that their violence rate may increase because of increased anger and alienation on the part of those who did not share in the gains of American society.

Criminologists Marvin Wolfgang and Franco Ferracuti speculate that the black experience has promoted the development of a **subculture of violence** in inner-city ghetto areas. Membership in the subculture demands the use of physical force as solutions for everyday encounters.[32] The subculture of violence and counterarguments to it will be discussed further in chapter 10.

Most theories put forward to explain black-white crime differentials are open to criticism. According to Barry Sample and Michael Philip, the true relationship between race and crime may contain elements of economic differences, social disorganization, aspects of personality, effects of physical and biological characteristics, subcultural adaptations, and the legacy of racism and discrimination.[33] Consequently, further research is needed to develop a comprehensive theoretical explanation of black-white crime rate differences.

The Chronic Offender: Career Criminals

An important and controversial issue in criminology during the seventies and eighties has been the discovery of the chronic offender, or career criminal. Researchers, using self-report and official data, have found that the offender population can be divided into a larger group of one-time or occasional criminals, and a small group of hard-core career offenders. This latter group commits a far greater share of the crime rate than their numbers warrant. Moreover, they are involved in the most serious and violent crimes, including armed robberies, burglaries, and assaults.

The importance and controversy surrounding the chronic offender concept involves its policy implications. If only a small group of people—the chronic offenders—commits enormous amounts of crime, it follows that if these people were incapacitated for long periods of time, their absence from society would have an appreciable effect on the crime rate. This thinking has been embraced by conservative criminologists, who believe that punishment is the best means to deter crime (see chapter 5). A justice policy based on the chronic offender concept demands that career criminals be set apart from society based on their demonstrated threat to public safety and the high probability that they will engage in serious crime in the future. Such thinking has dominated justice policy in the 1980s.

The chronic offender concept is the result of research using both official and self-report data. Some important works on this topic will be discussed in detail below.

WOLFGANG'S "DELINQUENCY IN A BIRTH COHORT"

The concept of the chronic career offender is most closely associated with the research efforts of Marvin Wolfgang and his associates at the University of Pennsylvania.[34] In 1972, Wolfgang, Robert Figlio, and Thorsten Sellin published a landmark study, *Delinquency in a Birth Cohort,* which has profoundly influenced the very concept of the criminal offender.

Wolfgang, Figlio, and Sellin used official records to follow the criminal careers of a **cohort** of 9,945 boys born in Philadelphia, Pennsylvania, in 1945, from the time of their birth until they reached eighteen years of age in 1963. Official police records were used to identify delinquents. About one-third of the boys (3,475) had some police contact. The remaining two-thirds (6,470) had none. Each delinquent's actions were given a seriousness weight based on the Wolfgang-Sellin Delinquency Index, which provides a weighted score for every delinquent act.[35] The weighting of delinquent acts allowed the researchers to differentiate, for example, between a simple assault requiring no medical attention for the victim and a serious assault in which the victim needed hospitalization.

Wolfgang and his colleagues obtained data from school records, including subject IQ scores and measures of academic performance and conduct. Socioeconomic status was determined by locating the residence of each member of the cohort and assigning him the median family income for that area.

The most well-known discovery of Wolfgang and associates was that of the so-called chronic offender. The cohort data indicated that 54 percent (1,862) of the sample's delinquent youths were repeat offenders, while the remaining 46 percent (1,613) were one-time offenders. However, the repeaters could be further categorized as nonchronic recidivists and **chronic recidivists.** The former consisted of 1,235 youths who had been arrested more than once but less than five times, and who made up 35.6 percent of all delinquents. The latter were a group of 627 boys arrested *five times or more* who accounted for 18 percent of the delinquents and 6 percent of the total sample of 9,945.[36]

It was the chronic offenders (known today as "the chronic 6 percent") who were involved in the most dramatic amounts of delinquent behavior; they were responsible for *5,305 offenses, or 51.9 percent of all offenses.* Even more striking was the involvement of chronic offenders in serious criminal acts. Of the entire sample, they committed 71 percent of the homicides, 73 percent of the rapes, 82 percent of the robberies, and 69 percent of the aggravated assaults.

Wolfgang and his associates found that arrest and court experience did little to deter the chronic offender. In fact, disposition was inversely related to chronic offending—the stricter the disposition chronic offenders received, the more likely they would be to engage in repeated criminal behavior. Strict dispositions also increased the probability that further court action would be taken. Two factors stood out as encouraging recidivism—the seriousness of the original offense and the severity of disposition.

BIRTH COHORT FOLLOW-UP

In a more recent analysis, Wolfgang and his associates followed a 10 percent sample of the original cohort (974 subjects) through their adulthood to age thirty. They divided the sample into three groups: those who had been juvenile offenders only, those who were adult offenders only, and persistent offenders (those who had offenses in both time periods). Those classified as chronic juvenile offenders in the original birth cohort made up 70 percent of the "persistent" group. They had an 80 percent chance of becoming adult offenders and a 50 percent chance of being arrested four or more times as adults. In comparison, subjects with no juvenile arrests had only an 18 percent chance of being arrested as an adult. The chronic offenders also continued to engage in the most serious crimes. Though they accounted for only 15 percent of the follow-up sample, the former chronic delinquents were involved in 74 percent of all arrests and 82 percent of all serious crimes, such as homicide, rape, and robbery. Clearly, chronic juvenile offenders continue their law-violating careers as adults.

BIRTH COHORT II

The subjects who made up Wolfgang's original birth cohort were born in 1945. How have behavior patterns changed in subsequent years? To answer this question, Wolfgang and associates selected a new, larger birth cohort, born in Philadelphia in 1958, and followed them until their maturity. The 1958 cohort is larger than the original. It has 28,338 subjects—13,811 males and 14,527 females.

Only preliminary data are available on the 1958 cohort, but it has already generated some important findings. Although the proportion of delinquent youths is about the same as that in the 1945 cohort, those in the larger sample were involved in 20,089 delinquent arrests. Chronic offenders (five or more arrests for juveniles) made up 7.5 percent of the 1958 sample (compared with 6.3 percent in 1945) and 23 percent of all delinquent offenders (compared with 18 percent in 1945). Chronic female delinquency was relatively rare—only 1 percent of the females in the survey were chronic offenders.

Chronic male delinquents continued to commit more than their share of criminal behavior. They accounted for 61 percent of the total offenses and a disproportionate amount of the most serious crimes: 61 percent of the homicides, 76 percent of the rapes, 73 percent of the robberies, and 65 percent of the aggravated assaults. The chronic female offender was less likely to be involved in serious crimes.

It is interesting that the 1958 cohort, as a group, was involved in significantly more serious crime than the 1945 group. For example, their violent offense rate (149 per 1,000 in the sample) was three times higher than the rate for the 1945 cohort (which was 47 per 1,000 subjects).

The 1945 cohort study found that chronic offenders dominate the total crime rate and continue in their law-violating careers as adults. The newer cohort study is showing that the chronic offender syndrome is being maintained in a group of subjects who were born thirteen years later than the original cohort and, if anything, are more violent than their older brothers. Finally, the efforts of the justice system seem to have little preventive effect on the behavior of chronic offenders: the more often a person was arrested, the more likely he or she was to be arrested again. For males, 26 percent of the entire group had one violent arrest, of that 26 percent, 34 percent went on to a second violent offense, 43 percent of the three-time losers went on to a fourth arrest, and so on.

Wolfgang's research has had a major effect on criminological thought. Subsequent efforts have in part duplicated Wolfgang's Pennsylvania study.[37] The chronic career criminal has become an accepted element of criminological thought and criminal justice policy. The question remains, "If we can identify chronic offenders, what should we do about them and how can they be controlled?"

INCAPACITATING CHRONIC OFFENDERS

A self-report study involving 2,000 convicted offenders in Texas, Michigan, and California led senior Rand Corporation researcher Peter Greenwood to advocate a policy of **selective incapacitation** as a means of controlling career criminals.[38] According to Greenwood, career criminals usually share the following characteristics:

- Incarceration for more than half the two-year period preceding the most recent arrest
- A prior conviction for the crime that is being predicted
- Juvenile conviction prior to age sixteen
- Commitment to a state or federal juvenile facility
- Heroin or barbiturate use in the two-year period preceding the current arrest
- Heroin or barbiturate use as a juvenile
- Employment for less than half the two-year period preceding the current arrest

Greenwood believes that if judges used these characteristics in calculating prison sentences, both the prison population and the crime rate would be significantly reduced. For example, using California inmates, Greenwood estimates that selective incapacitation of offenders on the basis of these seven variables would result in a 15-percent decrease in the robbery rate and a concomitant 5-percent drop in the number of inmates convicted of robbery.

Greenwood's policy of selective incapacitation has become quite controversial. Two leading criminologists, Andrew von Hirsch and Don Gottfredson, suggest that if used it can lead to imprisonment of those falsely identified as high-risk offenders and result in release of dangerous criminals mistakenly identified as low-risk offenders.[39] In addition, von Hirsch and Gottfredson suggest that (1) the self-report data Greenwood uses are unreliable, (2) Greenwood's study examines only incarcerated robbers and burglars, and (3) Greenwood does not acknowledge that many robberies and burglaries are committed in groups and that incarcerating one participant will only cause the gang to find a new one.

In addition to these problems, Greenwood's formula relies on legally irrelevant personal information, such as prior employment record, which would be excluded at a sentencing hearing. Also, self-reports of drug use could not be obtained from offenders who were going to be sentenced to prison.

A different approach to incapacitation, based on criminal career patterns rather than personal characteristics, may avoid some of the problems associated with selective incapacitation. This approach relies on recent empirical research on criminal careers by Alfred Blumstein, Jacqueline Cohen, Marcia and Jan Chaiken, and others.[40] These researchers found that the main variables in creating an effective crime control strategy involved empirical estimates of average individual arrest and crime rates, and the average lengths of criminal careers. They also attempted to identify variations in criminal careers associated with the nature of the current crime and with prior criminal record.[41]

FIGURE 4.3

Expected crime reduction from prison terms of varying length (in years) imposed after any conviction for different target offenses

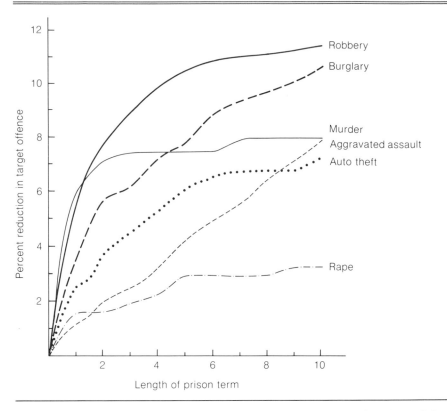

SOURCE. Jacqueline Cohen, *Incapacitating Criminals: Recent Research Findings* (Washington, D.C.: National Institute of Justice, 1983).

The research goal of Blumstein and his colleagues was to identify classes of offenders who, on the average, would remain criminally active at high rates. In Blumstein and Cohen's analysis of criminal career patterns for arrestees in Washington, D.C., convicted robbery and burglary defendants emerged as prime candidates for incapacitation. They commit these offenses, on average, at relatively high rates, and have relatively short careers. Short prison terms for these offenders can potentially consume a large percentage of their expected careers, thereby reducing robbery and burglary rates.

Figure 4.3 illustrates the different crime reductions achievable, based on Jacqueline Cohen's District of Columbia data, for prison terms of different lengths. When relatively short terms after any conviction are considered, focusing on robbery convictions offers relatively larger crime reduction benefits than aiming at other offenses.

According to Cohen, minimum two-year terms imposed on all adult defendants convicted of robbery would result in an 8-percent reduction in robberies by adults, while increasing the prison population by 7 percent.

Like Peter Greenwood's selective incapacitation research, this alternative approach is at an early stage. If it can be perfected, it may avoid some of the ethical pitfalls of selective incapacitation. Based solely on present and past criminal records, it is less susceptible to attack for reliance on controversial personal variables; and since sentencing policies would apply uniformly to groups of similar offenders—a form of targeted collective incapacitation—objections of unjust, unequal punishment have less force.

CHRONIC OFFENDERS TODAY

The work of Wolfgang and his associates, of Peter Greenwood and Alfred Blumstein, and so on has made the chronic offender a central focus of criminology in the 1980s. This work has had an important influence on the justice system and the way it views strategies for crime control. Around the country, legal jurisdictions are developing sentencing policies designed to incapacitate serious offenders for long periods of time without hope of probation or parole. The nation's prison system is filled to capacity. Yet, supporters view the recent decline in the crime rate as justification for these policies. Discovery of the chronic offender has reshaped the American justice system (see the Close-Up on habitual offenders).

Crime Victimization

National Crime Survey data allow us to examine the criminal incident from the victim's perspective. Who has the greatest chance of becoming a crime victim? Under what circumstances is victimization most likely to take place? What are the costs of crime? The NCS data have proven indispensable in understanding the nature of the criminal act.

VICTIM CHARACTERISTICS

For over a decade, the victimization patterns measured by the NCS have been remarkably uniform.[42] Some of the most important differences in the social and economic characteristics of victims of violent personal crimes are presented in

Contrary to popular perception, the elderly actually have the lowest risk of becoming victims of personal crimes.

Habitual Offenders

What are the personal characteristics of career criminals? To answer this question, Joan Petersilia, Peter Greenwood, and Marvin Lavin studied the criminal careers of forty-nine prison inmates in California who could be classified as habitual offenders.

They found that the sample of forty-nine habitual offenders reported committing over 10,500 crimes of the nine types considered: auto theft (1,492), purse snatching (25), grand theft (993), burglary (2,331), robbery (855), aggravated assault (188), forgery (995), drug sales (3,620), and rape (6). Since the average criminal career was about twenty years long, and half the time was spent in prison, the average respondent committed about twenty crimes per year of street time.

The researchers found that the sample could be further broken down into (a) *intensive offenders* (16) who identified themselves as career criminals and consciously directed their activities toward criminality, and (b) *intermittent offenders* (33) who were opportunistic and did not view themselves as criminals. The following characteristics of the two groups describe the distinctions between intensive and intermittent offenders:

JUVENILE CRIMINALITY

- A larger percentage of intensives than intermittents reported committing a serious crime before the age of thirteen.
- A larger percentage of intermittent offenders were incarcerated before the age of eighteen.

CRIMINAL SOPHISTICATION

- Intensive offenders did more precrime planning than did intermittent offenders.
- As juveniles, a majority of the intensives committed crimes without partners; almost all intermittents used partners.
- Burglary was considerably more profitable to the intensives than to the intermittents.

PROSECUTORIAL TREATMENT

- Prosecutors threatened a greater proportion of intensives than intermittents with the filing of prior felony convictions as special allegations, but there was no difference between the two types in the actual charging of priors.

DRUGS AND ALCOHOL INVOLVEMENT

- Those involved with alcohol alone were preponderantly the intermittent type.
- A greater proportion of intensives than intermittents were involved with drugs, alone or combined with alcohol.

figure 4.4. During 1982, victimization was more common among youths, males, divorcees, blacks, poor and unemployed people, and government employees.

The relationship between race, sex, and age of crime victims is further explored in table 4.2. There we can see the striking differences in victimization risk associated with these sociological variables. First, though many people believe that the elderly face the greatest risk of being crime victims, table 4.2 shows that the nation's teenagers and young adults are most likely to become the victims of violent and theft-related crimes. For example, the violent crime victimization rate of a black male teenager (90.5) is more than *twenty times greater* than that of an elderly white female (4.0), and those teenagers' risk of theft victimization (114.7) is more than five times as great. These data show that crime victims and offenders share the same sociological characteristics.

Another important relationship uncovered by NCS data is the relationship between personal wealth and victimization. Figure 4.5 shows that as personal wealth increases, a person's chance of becoming a victim of violence and household crime decreases, but their chance of becoming a victim of personal thefts and larcenies increases. This may be interpreted to mean that criminals seek out personal and household victims within their own economic environment, but choose to victimize people within that environment who have the greatest economic means.

SOCIOECONOMIC FACTORS

- The intermittent type was more likely to be better employed.

USE OF VIOLENCE

- A moderately larger proportion of intensives than intermittents injured their victims.
- Intensives manifested much more violence in their personal lives than intermittents.

MOTIVATION

- Contrary to expectations, there were few differences between the two types in their motivation for crime. The primary motivations seemed to be (a) drug and alcohol abuse, (b) peer influence, and (c) poor employment records.

ARREST, CONVICTION, AND INCARCERATION RATES

- The average intensive offender experienced a few more arrests during his total career than did the average intermittent. However, during their adult career periods, intensive offenders were arrested for only 4 percent of their self-reported nondrug felonies, while intermittents were arrested for 21 percent. Intermittents were thus five times more likely to be arrested.
- Intermittent offenders had moderately higher conviction and incarceration rates per nondrug arrest than intensive offenders.

The researchers found that rehabilitation of these offenders was problematic and that deterrence strategies (chapter 5) would not work. They advocated a policy of long-term incapacitation.

The continuing criminal activity of the forty-nine habitual offenders in the face of frequent arrests, convictions, and incarcerations is an indication of the inability of previous rehabilitation, deterrence, and prevention efforts to curtail their criminal behavior. The primary alternative for counteracting such offenders is a greater reliance on incapacitation. Incapacitation policies are intended to insure the conviction and prolonged incarceration of serious habitual offenders, once arrested. The rationale is obvious: Offenders cannot commit crimes against the community while in prison, and they are not likely to be able to make up for lost time after release if the probability of reincarceration is high. But an incapacitation policy is both unfair and highly expensive if an undue number of inappropriate offenders are given long prison terms. Thus, the effectiveness of this approach rests largely on the ability of the criminal justice system to distinguish among offenders and identify those most deserving of lengthy imprisonment.

DISCUSSION QUESTIONS

1. Should career criminals be given mandatory life sentences after a third felony conviction?
2. Should the death penalty be given to habitual criminals who commit crimes like rape and robbery but not murder?

SOURCE. Joan Petersilia, Peter Greenwood, and Marvin Lavin, *Criminal Careers of Habitual Felons* (Washington, D.C.: U.S. Government Printing Office, 1978), pp. I–XV.

Beyond these findings, the NCS tells us that married and widowed people are less likely to be victimized than divorced and single people. Surprisingly, people over twenty-five with some college education were more likely than those with less schooling to be the victims of violent crime or personal larceny. Unemployed people were more likely to be victims of crime than those who held jobs. Finally, people who lived in large households (six or more members) and rented rather than owned their dwellings had much higher victimization rates than those residing with fewer people and buying their own homes.

The picture that emerges of the crime victim, then, is a young, poor, minority male, who is unemployed and living with a large family that is renting an apartment. From chapter 3 data, we also know that the victim lives in a large city, probably in the south or west, and most likely will not bother to let police know about his or her victimization.

CRIME CHARACTERISTICS

The NCS data can be used to tell us something about the nature of the criminal offense itself. One important finding is that a significant amount of crime involves relatives and acquaintances. The UCR has also traditionally shown that a significant

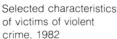

FIGURE 4.4

Selected characteristics
of victims of violent
crime, 1982

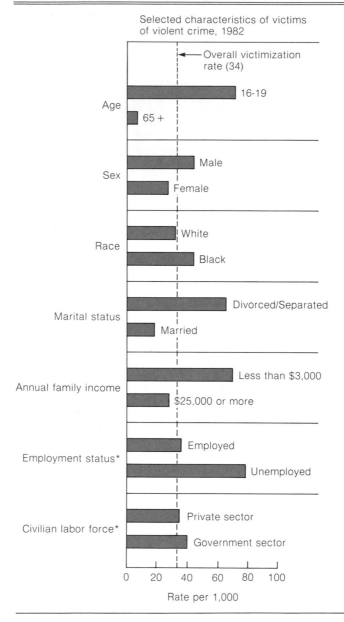

Selected characteristics of victims
of violent crime, 1982

NOTE: The differences between the rates within categories are statistically significant. Rate differences between categories may or may not be significant.

*Limited to labor force participants age 16 and over

SOURCE. *Criminal Victimization in the United States*, p. 2.

number of murder cases involve family and friends. For example, in 1983 only 15 percent of murders could be classified as involving strangers. Unfortunately, the UCR does not collect data on the victim-offender relationship for other crime categories. However, the NCS shows that only 64 percent of all other personal offenses involved strangers. This means that more than one-third of rapes, robberies, and assaults were committed by someone the victim was acquainted with.

TABLE 4.2
Victimization rates

Race, sex, and age of victims	Rate per 1,000 population in each age group	
	Crimes of violence	Crimes of theft
White		
Male		
12-15 (6,149,000)	61.1	140.1
16-19 (6,576,000)	89.3	136.0
20-24 (8,856,000)	85.9	149.4
25-34 (16,735,000)	56.0	106.8
35-49 (16,874,000)	24.3	74.0
50-64 (14,053,000)	12.1	46.3
65 and over (9,468,000)	6.9	25.3
Female		
12-15 (5,875,000)	41.5	122.8
16-19 (6,493,000)	51.8	126.9
20-24 (9,018,000)	50.9	124.7
25-34 (16,752,000)	35.5	86.1
35-49 (17,348,000)	17.4	76.8
50-64 (15,581,000)	7.9	47.6
65 and over (13,710,000)	4.0	21.9
Black		
Male		
12-15 (1,068,000)	80.8	125.3
16-19 (1,100,000)	90.5	114.7
20-24 (1,276,000)	85.4	141.1
25-34 (2,062,000)	66.4	122.3
35-49 (1,832,000)	36.6	71.3
50-64 (1,336,000)	21.8	54.8
65 and over (849,000)	[a]14.2	19.1
Female		
12-15 (1,065,000)	37.9	105.5
16-19 (1,153,000)	62.9	99.0
20-24 (1,485,000)	61.4	68.7
25-34 (2,487,000)	39.4	105.0
35-49 (2,266,000)	18.8	58.4
50-64 (1,699,000)	11.0	56.4
65 and over (1,285,000)	[a]9.1	26.9

NOTE: Numbers in parentheses refer to population in the group.

[a]Estimate, based on about 10 or fewer sample cases, is statistically unreliable.

SOURCE. *Criminal Victimization in the United States, 1982*, p. 27.

This relationship is even more striking for divorced women, who report that they were acquainted with their attacker in 36 percent of rapes, 43 percent of robberies, and 72 percent of assaults. These data, however, must be interpreted with caution. The NCS respondents may be reluctant to report attacks by family or friends for fear of implicating them. Thus, it is possible that the number of crimes involving friends and family is even higher than that reported by the victim data.

The NCS also finds that most violent crimes occur at night, between 6:00 P.M. and 6:00 A.M. Though it is harder to establish the time of property crimes, most were distributed equally throughout the day and night—except for motor vehicle theft, which usually (65 percent) occurred at night.

Most violent crimes (42 percent) took place in an outdoor public area such

FIGURE 4.5

Victimization rates: Personal crimes of violence and theft, by race and annual family income, 1982

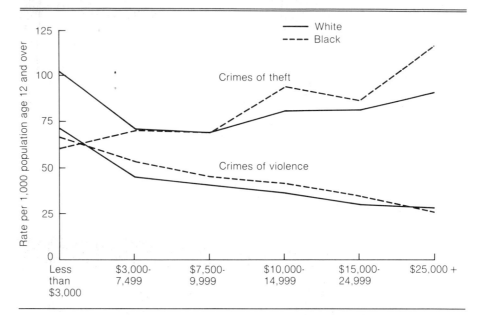

SOURCE. *Criminal Victimization in the United States, 1982,* p. 7.

as a street or park. About 15 percent took place in public buildings and 5 percent in schools. Only 24 percent occurred in or near the victim's home. However, a substantial number of violent acts involving nonstrangers occurred in the home as compared to stranger-to-stranger offenses (26 percent versus 5 percent).

Most violent acts (89 percent) involved a single victim and offender (71 percent). Again, when victims were attacked by an acquaintance it was more likely to be a single-offender incident (85 percent) than when the incident involved a stranger (62 percent).

In about one-third of all violent crimes a weapon was used, and in about three-fourths the victims attempted to defend themselves. The NCS data indicate that those who used physical force to protect themselves were more likely to suffer serious injury (16 percent) than those who did absolutely nothing (12 percent). However, victims who took nonviolent evasive action (6 percent) or tried to talk themselves out of their predicament (6 percent) were the least likely to suffer serious injury (see the Close-Up on the economic costs of crime).

In sum, victimization risk is related to exposure to crimogenic conditions. People who place themselves in jeopardy by frequenting public places in the evening are more likely to become crime victims than those who stay home. Thus, the inner-city youth who goes to the park in the evening has a far greater victimization potential than the female senior citizen who goes home and locks her door in the evening.

Criminals and Victims: A Review

The various sources of criminal statistics paint a consistent picture of crime in America. Below, some of the more salient points are summarized:

- The crime rate has declined. After years of rapid expansion, most crime categories have peaked. Some criminologists believe crime rates will begin

FIGURE 4.6

Victimization rates:
Household crimes, by
annual family income,
1982

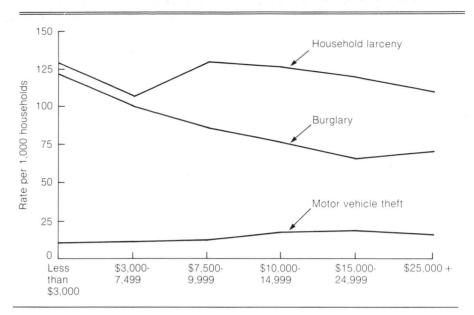

SOURCE. *Criminal Victimization in the United States, 1982*, p. 7.

to rise when the children of the baby-boomers reach eighteen, sometime around 1990.

- Many people—about half—do not report crime to police, believing that "nothing can be done" or that they "shouldn't get involved."
- Crime occurs more often in large cities than in suburban or rural areas. Population density is related to crime rates. People living in low-income areas are more likely to commit crime, and to become its victims. However, households touched by crime tend to be relatively wealthier.
- Crime occurs more often in summer, in the evening, and in western and southern regions. The geographic and temporal patterns show that crime is not a random event.
- People who commit crime are disproportionately young, male, minority group members, and poor. The victims of crime also share these characteristics. Although middle- and upper-class citizens commit their share of crime, the poor seem to commit more serious and violent crimes.
- The elderly are actually quite safe in our society; young people have a much higher victimization rate than those over sixty-five.
- Crime tends to be intraracial. Blacks victimize blacks, whites victimize whites, and so on.
- Victims put themselves at risk by frequenting public places in the evening.
- The costs of crime are immense. Direct economic loss is about $10 billion annually. Indirect costs and the cost of the "underground economy" may approach $300 billion.
- The police cannot do much about crime. About 20 percent of all crimes are solved by the police. The more serious the crime, the more likely police are to solve it.

The Economic Costs of Crime

What are the major economic costs of crime? The reading below discusses some of the major victim losses identified by the NCS and other data sources:

In 1981, the most recent year for which data are available, the total direct economic loss to victims of personal and household crimes measured by the NCS was $10.9 billion (table A). This estimate includes the value of cash and property taken, property damage, and medical expenses sustained by victims of violent crimes. Nearly 75 percent of the total loss, or $8.1 billion, resulted from household crimes, and household burglary alone caused more than a third of the total loss, $4.1 billion (table B).

TABLE A Economic loss to victims of personal and household crimes

Year	Total loss in current dollars*	Total loss in 1981 constant dollars*
All crimes		
1981 (31,802,300)	10,911	10,911
1980 (30,409,700)	10,086	11,133
1975 (30,707,400)	5,568	9,409
Personal crimes		
1981 (16,371,000)	2,782	2,782
1980 (15,270,000)	2,362	2,608
1975 (16,378,500)	1,531	2,587
Crimes of violence		
1981 (1,742,500)	651	651
1980 (1,493,400)	507	560
1975 (1,409,300)	329	556
Crimes of theft		
1981 (14,628,400)	2,130	2,130
1980 (13,776,600)	1,855	2,047
1975 (14,969,200)	1,202	2,031
Household crimes		
1981 (15,431,300)	8,129	8,129
1980 (15,139,700)	7,724	8,525
1975 (14,328,900)	4,037	6,822

* Dollars in millions

In comparison to 1981, the loss was $10.1 billion for 1980 and $5.6 billion for 1975 (table A). The 1981 cost of crime estimate was 8.2 percent higher than that for 1980 and 96.0 percent above the 1975 aggregate cost. However, a 10.4 percent increase in consumer prices between 1980 and 1981 eliminated any meaningful difference between these two annual estimates. Whereas a 69.0 percent increase in consumer prices from 1975 to 1981 sharply reduced the real increase in crime costs for these years, the aggregate cost in 1981 still was significantly higher than in 1975. This increase chiefly was the result of a rise in losses from household crimes. Accompanying this increase was a 1.1 million upswing in the number of burglaries and household larcenies in which economic loss was sustained.

Other major findings for 1981 include:

- More than 93 percent of the 1981 aggregate loss from crime ($10.2 billion out of $10.9 billion) occurred as a result of crimes in which there was no victim-offender contact, i.e., burglary, household larceny, motor vehicle theft, and personal larceny without contact (table B).
- The aggregate loss from attempted and completed motor vehicle theft, including vehicle damage, was $2.8 billion, substantially exceeding that for household larceny ($1.2 billion) or any of the individual personal crimes. Also, the highest median loss for any crime, $1,500, was associated with motor vehicle theft. The median value in 1981 of completed (successful) motor vehicle thefts, excluding property damage losses, was $2,100.
- Among the three violent crimes, the largest total economic loss, $421 million, was a result of robbery. Although rape appeared to have the largest median economic loss in 1981 among the three violent crimes, in fact the median losses for these crimes did not differ significantly from one another.
- Economic losses from personal larceny without contact, measured at $2.1 billion, substantially exceeded those for each of the other personal crimes, primarily because of its prevalence. About 70 percent of all personal crimes involve theft without contact.

- A small group of chronic offenders may account for a significant amount of the crime rate. Incapacitating these people may help reduce crime. However, research shows that chronic offending is amplified rather than diminished by arrest.

Summary

Official, victim, and self-report data provide information on the nature of crime and its victims.

TABLE B Economic losses of personal and household crimes

Type of crime	Total loss (in millions)		Median loss (in hundreds)
	In current dollars	In 1981 constant dollars	
Personal sector			
1981 (16,371,000)	2,782	2,782	45
1980 (15,270,000)	2,362	2,608	40
1975 (16,378,500)	1,531	2,587	22
Crimes of violence			
1981 (1,742,500)	651	651	80
1980 (1,493,400)	507	560	77
1975 (1,409,300)	329	556	43
Rape			
1981 (56,100)	20	20	145
1980 (50,600)	23	25	50
1975 (53,700)	15	25	30
Robbery			
1981 (954,600)	421	421	85
1980 (757,600)	283	312	85
1975 (758,400)	184	311	43
Assault			
1981 (731,900)	210	210	64
1980 (685,200)	200	221	65
1975 (597,100)	130	220	43
Crimes of theft			
1981 (14,628,400)	2,130	2,130	40
1980 (13,776,600)	1,855	2,047	40
1975 (14,969,200)	1,202	2,031	20
Personal larceny with contact			
1981 (538,700)	64	64	50
1980 (479,400)	43	47	39
1975 (460,900)	34	57	30
Personal larceny without contact			
1981 (14,089,700)	2,066	2,066	40
1980 (13,297,200)	1,812	2,000	40
1975 (14,508,300)	1,168	1,974	20
Household sector			
1981 (15,431,300)	8,129	8,129	65
1980 (15,139,700)	7,724	8,525	60
1975 (14,328,900)	4,037	6,822	40
Burglary			
1981 (5,309,000)	4,127	4,127	160
1980 (4,958,300)	3,561	3,930	150
1975 (4,831,000)	1,624	2,745	85

Continued

Among the issues of importance to criminologists, none is as important or confusing as the relationship between social class and crime. Although it seems logical that poor people commit crime, the data provide a rather confusing picture. Some studies indicate that lower-class citizens do in fact commit more crime than the upper classes, but others show that wealth and status are unrelated to criminality. If so, then other social forces aside from wealth must be influencing criminal behavior.

The data also show that young people, males, and minorities are more likely to commit crime than older people, females, and whites. Explanations for these

The Economic Costs of Crime—cont'd

TABLE B Economic losses of personal and household crimes—continued

	Total loss (in millions)		
Type of crime	In current dollars	In 1981 constant dollars	Median loss (in hundreds)
Household larceny			
1981 (9,039,900)	1,249	1,249	40
1980 (9,150,700)	1,310	1,446	40
1975 (8,397,300)	608	1,028	20
Motor vehicle theft			
1981 (1,082,500)	2,754	2,754	1,500
1980 (1,030,700)	2,854	3,150	1,300
1975 (1,100,500)	1,806	3,052	830

- The median loss to victims of personal larcenies, some $40, was lower than the median loss to victims of the three violent crimes, about $80.

The UCR also helps us understand the cost of crime. The 1983 statistics (table C) provide this information on the economic impact:

The average cost per crime reported in the UCR was much higher than that recorded for NCS offenses. This probably reflects that victims tend to report crimes in which their economic loss is greatest.

Beyond these losses, the full cost of crime must take into account the "underground economy" not included in either the UCR or NCS. This involves prostitution, gambling, drug sales, computer fraud, tax cheating, pilferage, the illegal sale of alcohol, etc., and is estimated by Carl Simon and Anne Witte to amount to between $170 and $300 billion in 1980. Counting an inflation rate of 5 percent, the 1986 figures would be between $230 and $400 billion.

Crime has other hidden costs, some of them almost incalculable—higher insurance rates, medical costs, lost work time, increased cost of retail goods due to pilferage losses, lost tax revenues on sales of illegal goods, and treatment center costs (e.g., narcotics and alcohol rehabilitation). The entire cost of the criminal justice system, estimated at over $30 billion, is another economic cost of crime.

TABLE C Estimated value of loss due to Part I crimes, 1983

Crime	Loss
Robbery	$ 323,000,000
Burglary	2,700,000,000
Larceny	2,300,000,000
Motor vehicle theft	4,000,000,000
Arson	795,000,000
Total	$10,118,000,000

So, in addition to the human suffering caused by crime, its economic costs have a major effect on U.S. society.

SOURCE. Carl Simon and Ann Witte, *Beating the System: The Underground Economy* (Boston: Auburn House, 1982); Bureau of Justice Statistics, *The Economic Costs of Crime* (Washington, D.C.: U.S. Government Printing Office, 1984); FBI, *Crime in the United States, 1983*.

differences usually focus on the socialization process. For example, women may be less violence-prone than men because their social role has stressed obedience and gentility as opposed to the male machismo. Some criminologists believe that the women's movement has so altered women's role in society that their crime rates will begin to parallel those of male criminals.

Another phenomenon discovered in the crime data is that of chronic offenders. Several studies have shown that a small group of men commit a significant portion of all crimes. The most well known research was conducted by Marvin Wolfgang with a cohort of boys drawn from Philadelphia in 1945. Peter Greenwood of the Rand Corporation has suggested that these chronic offenders be incapacitated for long periods of time.

Victim research helps us understand the nature of victimization in our society. Victims tend to have the same characteristics as criminals, that is, they are young, minority, male, and poor. Studies show that victimization is related to the risks— such as going out at night to public places—victims take.

Notes

1 See, for example, the cohort study conducted by Marvin Wolfgang (discussed later in this chapter).

2 James Short and F. Ivan Nye, "Reported Behavior as a Criterion of Deviant Behavior," *Social Problems* 5 (1958):207–13.

3 Ivan Nye, James Short, and Virgil Olsen, "Socio-economic Status and Delinquent Behavior," *American Journal of Scoiology* 63 (1958):381–89.

4 Robert Dentler and Lawrence Monroe, "Social Correlates of Early Adolescent Theft," *American Sociological Review* 63 (1961):733–43.

5 See generally John Clark and Eugene Wenninger, "Socio-economic Class and Area as Correlates of Illegal Behavior Among Juveniles," *American Sociological Review* 27 (1962):826–34; William Arnold, "Continuities in Research: Scaling Delinquent Behavior," *Social Problems* 13 (1965):59–66; LaMar Empey and Maynard Erickson, "Hidden Delinquency and Social Status," *Social Forces* 44 (1966):546–54; Jay Williams and Martin Gold, "From Delinquent Behavior to Official Delinquency," *Social Problems* 20 (1972):209–229; Richard Johnson, "Social Class and Delinquency," *Criminology* 18 (1980):86–93. See also Terence Thornberry and Margaret Farnsworth, "Social Correlates of Criminal Involvement: Further Evidence of the Relationship between Social Status and Criminal Behavior," *American Sociological Review* 47 (1982):505–518.

6 Charles Tittle, Wayne Villemez, and Douglas Smith, "The Myth of Social Class and Criminality: An Empirical Assessment of the Empirical Evidence," *American Sociological Review* 43 (1978):643–56.

7 Ibid.

8 Delbert Elliott and Suzanne Ageton, "Reconciling Race and Class Differences in Self-Reported and Official Estimates of Delinquency," *American Sociological Review* 45 (1980):95–110.

9 Delbert Elliott and David Huizinga, "Social Class and Delinquent Behavior in a National Youth Panel: 1976–1980," *Criminology* 21 (1983):149–77.

10 For a similar view, see John Braithwaite, "The Myth of Social Class and Criminality Reconsidered," *American Sociological Review* 46 (1981):35–58; Michael Hindelang, Travis Hirschi and Joseph Weis, *Measuring Delinquency* (Beverly Hills, Calif.: Sage Publishing Co., 1981), p. 196.

11 Travis Hirschi and Michael Gottfredson, "Age and the Explanation of Crime," *American Journal of Sociology* 89 (1983):552–84, at 581.

12 John Laub, "Juvenile Criminal Behavior in the United States: An Analysis of Offender and Victim Characteristics," Working Paper 25, Michael J. Hindelang Criminal Justice Research Center, Albany, N.Y., 1983, p. 25.

13 Bureau of Justice Statistics, *Criminal Victimization in the United States, 1982* (Washington, D.C.: National Institute of Justice, 1984), p. 47.

14 Federal Bureau of Investigation, *Crime in the United States, 1983* (Washington, D.C.: U.S. Government Printing Office, 1984), p. 176. Herein cited as *Uniform Crime Reports, 1983.*

15 Rosemary Sarri, "Gender Issues in Juvenile Justice," *Crime and Delinquency* 29 (1983):381–97.

16 Elliott and Ageton, "Reconciling Race and Class Differences in Self-Reported and

Official Estimates of Delinquency"; Williams and Gold, "From Delinquent Behavior to Official Delinquency"; Hindelang, Hirschi, and Weis, *Measuring Delinquency.*

17 Cesare Lombroso, *The Female Offender,* (New York: Appleton Publishers, 1920).

18 Ibid., p. 122.

19 Ibid.

20 Ibid., pp. 51–52.

21 Otto Pollak, *The Criminality of Women* (Philadelphia: University of Pennsylvania, 1950).

22 Gisela Konopka, *The Adolescent Girl in Conflict* (Englewood Cliffs, N.J.: Prentice-Hall, 1966); Clyde Vedder and Dora Somerville, *The Delinquent Girl* (Springfield, Ill.: Charles C. Thomas, 1970).

23 Freda Adler, *Sisters in Crime* (New York: McGraw-Hill, 1975).

24 Rita James Simon, *The Contemporary Woman and Crime* (Washington, D.C.: U.S. Government Printing Office, 1975).

25 Darrell Steffensmeier and Renee Hoffman Steffensmeier, "Trends in Female Delinquency," *Criminology* 18 (1980):62–85; see also idem, "Crime and the Contemporary Woman: An Analysis of Changing Levels of Female Property Crime, 1960–1975," *Social Forces* 57 (1978):566–84; Joseph Weis, "Liberation and Crime: The Invention of the New Female Criminal," *Crime and Social Justice* 1 (1976):17–27; Carol Smart, "The New Female Offender: Reality or Myth," *British Journal of Criminology* 19 (1979):50–59; Steven Box and Chris Hale, "Liberation/Emancipation, Economic Marginalization or Less Chivalry," *Criminology* 22 (1984):473–78.

26 FBI, *Uniform Crime Reports 1983,* p. 187.

27 Daniel Georges-Abeyie, "Definitional Issues: Race, Ethnicity and Official Crime/Victimization Rates," in D. Georges-Abeyie, ed. *The Criminal Justice System and Blacks* (New York: Clark Boardman, 1984), p. 12; Robert Sampson, "Race and Criminal Violence: A Demographically Disaggregated Analysis of Urban Homicide," *Crime and Delinquency* 31 (1985):47–82.

28 James Comer, "Black Violence and Public Policy," in *American Violence and Public Policy,* Lynn Curtis, ed. (New Haven, Conn.: Yale University Press, 1985), pp. 63–86.

29 Ibid., p. 80.

30 Ibid., p. 81.

31 Charles Silberman, *Criminal Violence, Criminal Justice* (New York: Random House, 1979), pp. 153–65.

32 Marvin Wolfgang and Franco Ferracuti, *The Subculture of Violence* (London: Tavistock, 1967).

33 Barry Sample and Michael Philip, "Perspectives on Race and Crime in Research and Planning," in Georges-Abeyie, ed., *The Criminal Justice System and Blacks,* (New York: Clark Boardman, 1984), pp. 21–36.

34 Marvin Wolfgang, Robert Figlio, and Thorsten Sellin, *Delinquency in a Birth Cohort* (Chicago: University of Chicago Press, 1972).

35 See Thorsten Sellin and Marvin Wolfgang, *The Measurement of Delinquency* (New York: Wiley, 1964), p. 120.

36 Paul Tracy and Robert Figlio, "Chronic Recidivism in the 1958 Birth Cohort" (Paper presented at the American Society of Criminology meeting, Toronto, October 1982); Marvin Wolfgang, "Delinquency in Two Birth Cohorts," in *Perspective Studies of Crime and Delinquency,* Katherine Teilmann Van Dusen and Sarnoff Mednick, eds. (Boston: Kluwer-Nijhoff, 1983), pp. 7–17. The following sections rely heavily on these sources.

37 Described in Tracy and Figlio, "Chronic Recidivism in the 1958 Birth Cohort"; Lyle Shannon, *Assessing the Relationship of Adult Criminal Careers to Juvenile Careers: A Summary* (Washington, D.C.: U.S. Department of Justice, 1982); D.J. West and David P. Farrington, *The Delinquent Way of Life* (London: Hienemann, 1977); Donna Hamparian, Richard Schuster, Simon Dinitz, and John Conrad, *The Violent Few* (Lexington, Mass.: Lexington Books, 1978); Franklyn Dunford and Delbert Elliott, "Identifying Career Offenders Using Self-Reported Data," *Journal of Research in Crime and Delinquency* 21

(1984):57–86; Stephen VanDine, John Conrad, and Simon Dinitz, *Restraining The Wicked* (Lexington, Mass.: Lexington Books, 1979).

38 Peter Greenwood, *Selective Incapacitation* (Santa Monica, Calif.: Rand Corporation, 1982).

39 "Selective Incapacitation: New Solution or Old Myth," *Criminal Justice Newsletter,* April 25, 1983:3–4.

40 Alfred Blumstein and Elizabeth Graddy, "Prevalence and Recidivism in Index Arrests: A Feedback Model," *Law and Society Review* 16 (1982): 265–90; Jan Chaiken and Marsha Chaiken, *Varieties of Criminal Behavior* (Santa Monica, Calif.: Rand Corporation, 1982); Alfred Blumstein and Jacqueline Cohen, "Estimation of Individual Crime Rates from Arrest Records," *Journal of Criminal Law and Criminology* 70 (1979):561–85.

41 This section was taken from Jacqueline Cohen, *Incapacitating Criminals: Recent Research Findings* (Washington, D.C.: National Institute of Justice, 1983).

42 Data in this section come from Bureau of Justice Statistics, *Criminal Victimization in the United States, 1982.*

II Theories of Crime Causation

AN IMPORTANT GOAL OF the criminological enterprise is to create valid and accurate theories of crime causation. Social scientists have defined theory as:

- A general statement or set of statements that explain many different facts by reference to underlying principles and relationships. *
- A statement that organizes a set of concepts in a meaningful way by explaining the relationship among the concepts. †

Criminologists have sought to collect vital facts about crime and interpret them in a scientifically meaningful fashion. By developing empirically verifiable statements, or hypotheses, and organizing them into theories of crime causation, they hope to identify the root causes of crime. Since the late nineteenth century, criminological theory has pointed to various underlying causes of crime. The earliest theories generally attributed crime to a single underlying cause: atypical body build, genetic abnormality, insanity, physical anomalies, poverty, and so on. Later theories attributed crime causation to multiple factors: poverty, peer influence, school problems, family dysfunction, etc.

In this section, theories of crime causation are grouped into five chapters. Chapters 5 and 6 focus on individual traits. They hold that crime is either a freewill choice made by an individual, or it is a function of personal psychological or biological maladaption, or both. Chapters 7 through 9 investigate theories based in sociology. These theories portray crime as a function of the structure, process, and conflicts of social living.

The goal of this section is to present the rich historical traditions and the current state of criminological theory. This section also describes the efforts being made by criminologists of various academic disciplines to uncover the true causes of crime and to suggest methods of eliminating it.

---

*Reece McGee, *Sociology*, 2nd ed. (New York: Holt, Rinehart & Winston, 1980), p. 540.

†Ian Robertson, *Sociology*, 2nd ed. (New York: Worth, 1981), p. 16.

5 Classical and Neoclassical Theories: Conservative Criminology

CHAPTER OUTLINE

Introduction

Foundations of Classical Theory

Cesare Beccaria

Jeremy Bentham

The First Prominence of Classical Criminology

The Fall and Resurrection of Classical Criminology

Deterrence

General Deterrence

Deterrence and Perceived Threat

Research on Deterrence

An Analysis of the General Deterrence Concept

Incapacitation and Special Deterrence

Research on Incapacitation and Special Deterrence

Selective Incapacitation

A Critique of Incapacitation

The Death Penalty

Arguments For the Death Penalty

Arguments Against the Death Penalty

Research on Capital Punishment

A Critique of the Death Penalty

Retribution

Just and Painful

Just Desert

Policy Implications of Classical Theory

Law

Police

Sentencing

Capital Punishment

Corrections

Summary

KEY TERMS

rehabilitation

Cesare Beccaria

Jeremy Bentham

utility

Benthamism

Declaration of the Rights of Man

indeterminate prison sentence

modern classical

neoclassical

conservative

deterrence

general deterrence

special deterrence

partial deterrence

absolute deterrence

particular deterrence

generalized deterrence

selective deterrence

incapacitation

death penalty

retribution

just desert

blameworthy

presumptive sentencing

sentencing guidelines

Furman v. *Georgia*

Gregg v. *Georgia*

justice model

Introduction

The classical approach to crime causation has several basic elements: (1) people in society have free will to choose criminal or conventional solutions to meet their needs or settle their problems; (2) criminal solutions may be more attractive than conventional ones, because they usually require less work for a greater payoff; (3) a person's choice of criminal solutions may be controlled by fear of society's reaction to such acts; (4) the more *severe, certain,* and *swift* the reaction, the better it can control criminal behavior; (5) the most efficient crime prevention device is punishment sufficient to make crime an unattractive choice. Thus, the basic premise of classical theory is that all men and women have the potential to be criminals if not kept in check by fear of punishment.

The classical view was one of the first formal criminological doctrines. It was originally developed in the mid-eighteenth century and provided the impetus for the penal reform movements of the nineteenth century.[1] Its roots can be traced to the philosophies of John Locke and Jean Jacques Rousseau, who recognized the rights of all people to be equal under law and called for the state to protect people's natural rights to "life, liberty, and property."[2] Though these philosophers believed state-administered punishment was necessary to protect rights, they believed it should not be cruel, excessive, or capricious.

By the end of the nineteenth century, the popularity of the classical approach began to decline; and by mid-twentieth century, the perspective was held in disrepute with most criminologists. During this period, positivist criminology in all its various forms (see the next three chapters) reached ascendancy in criminological circles. Uncontrollable external factors—poverty, IQ, education, home life—were believed to be the true causes of criminality; the concept of punishing people because of life situations they couldn't control seemed foolish and cruel. Progress in psychological treatment and counseling led to a mood in U.S. and European correctional circles that stressed the **rehabilitation** of known criminals and the prevention of crime by treatment rather than punishment. Criminologists who continued to advocate punishment as a means of crime control were considered conservative, reactionary, and vindictive.

Then, in the 1970s and into the 1980s, the classical approach began to enjoy a resurgence of popularity with a growing conservative segment of the criminological community. Concurrently, modern classical thinking began to influence a growing number of crime prevention policies in such areas as criminal sentences and punishments. Today, the classical approach is a potent theoretical and policy-making perspective.

This chapter will review the philosophical underpinnings of the classical approach and briefly trace its history. Then it will review in depth the five most important themes of modern classical theory: deterrence, incapacitation, the death penalty, retribution, and just desert. Finally, the chapter will breifly review how classical theory has influenced policy making in the area of criminal justice.

Foundations of Classical Theory

When classical theory was being formulated, the existing systems of punishment, law, and justice were chaotic. Although there was general agreement as to what acts constituted crimes, the penalties on law violators were often arbitrary, discretionary, and cruel. In France, the *Criminal Ordinance of 1670* was the first attempt to codify legal sanctions. It limited the arbitrary power of judges; but in several instances it did not specify a penalty, giving the magistrate discretion to increase or diminish punishments according to the circumstances of the case.[3]

Beccaria was an Italian economist and jurist who condemned confiscation, capital punishment, and torture.

Punishments included public flogging, branding, beheading, burning, and worse. Even simple wanderers and vagabonds had by the sixteenth century come to be viewed as dangerous and were subject to these extreme penalties. Well-known clergymen such as Martin Luther called for rulers to "pursue, beat, strangle, hang and torture" offenders, since rulers were the representatives of divine retribution.[4] In England, by 1829, the number of crimes punished by the death penalty was in the hundreds.[5]

The mid-eighteenth century was also a time when many great social philosophers began to call for rethinking the prevailing concepts of law and justice. While a majority still advocated that the harshest possible penalties be meted out to law violators, others argued for a more rational approach to punishment. They stressed that the relationship between crimes and their punishment should be balanced and fair. Rather than cruel public executions designed to frighten people into obedience, reformers called for a more moderate and just approach to penal sanctions.[6] Two of these reformers, **Cesare Beccaria** and **Jeremy Bentham,** can be considered the founders of the classical approach.

CESARE BECCARIA

Cesare Bonesana, Marquis of Beccaria, was born into an aristocratic family in Milan, Italy, in 1738.[7] Beccaria was a firm advocate of the principle of **utility,** which maintains that people are basically rational creatures who choose their own courses of action. Humans, according to this view, want to achieve pleasure and avoid pain. Crimes must therefore provide some pleasure to the criminal. It follows that to deter crime one must administer pain in an appropriate amount to counterbalance the pleasure obtained from crime. In keeping with his utilitarian views, Beccaria stated: "The fundamental principle that should govern the creation and maintenance of laws is 'the greatest happiness to be shared by the greatest number of people.'"[8]

Beccaria viewed law and justice as conditions similar to those the French philosopher Jean Jacques Rousseau described in his concept of the social contract: a set of rules that guarantee life, liberty, and happiness to all people. Beccaria stated: "weary of living in a continual state of war, and of enjoying a liberty rendered useless by the uncertainty of preserving it, [people] sacrificed a part so that they might enjoy the rest of it in peace and safety."[9] Yet, he did not suggest that people obey laws freely, sacrificing a portion of their personal liberty merely to promote the common good. Since people are egotistical and self-centered, they must be goaded by the fear of punishment, which provides a tangible motive for them to obey the law and suppress the despotic spirit in every person.

On Punishment. Beccaria believed that for a criminal penalty to achieve its purpose, the pain it inflicted had only to exceed the advantage that could be obtained from the crime it sought to control. In calculating the relationship between crime and punishment, the law should take into account the "certainty of punishment and loss of good the crime might have produced."[10] Certainty of punishment, rather than severity, is of the greatest import for deterrence.

Beccaria is credited with almost single-handedly causing the abolition of that most odious punishment—torture—which was used to obtain confessions from the accused or punish the convicted. He pointed out to world leaders how torture enabled the "robust scoundrel" who would resist it to go free, while condemning the innocent person who happened to be weak. Torture, Beccaria claimed, put the innocent in a position in which they could lose (if they confessed to a false accusation) and the guilty in a position in which they could gain (if they resisted torture and were absolved of a wrong).

Beccaria firmly believed that severe, brutal punishment was unnecessary. He suggested that people could adapt to even the most hideous punishment. "The severity of punishment," he wrote, "of itself emboldens men to commit the very wrong it is supposed to prevent."[11] Moreover, when punishment is very severe, criminals will commit additional crimes, since they have nothing more to lose. It is not surprising that Beccaria was a staunch opponent of the indiscriminate use of capital punishment and believed the death penalty should be used only on rare occasions.

Crime and Punishment. Rather than stress the cruelty of punishment to control criminality, Beccaria believed it would be more effective to closely link crime with its consequences in the minds of would-be criminals. Of greatest importance to Beccaria was establishing the proper proportions between crimes and punishments. There are several reasons for this approach. Most importantly, if two crimes that do not equally injure society are punished equally, then people will not be deterred from committing the greater of the two crimes. For example, if both bank robbery and murder were punished by death, a bank robber would have little reason to refrain from killing any witnesses to the robbery. To be effective, the punishment for a crime must be justified by the harm done.

In conclusion, Beccaria states the following theorem:

In order for punishment not to be in every instance, an act of violence of one or many against a private citizen, it must be essentially public, prompt, necessary, the least possible in the given circumstances, proportionate to the crimes, dictated by the laws.[12]

Beccaria's principles of justice have continued to influence criminological thinking for two hundred years.

JEREMY BENTHAM

The second major philosophical influence on the classical school was the British philosopher Jeremy Bentham.[13] Born in 1748 to a well-to-do family, Bentham spent his life trying to develop a system of scientific jurisprudence and legislation. His writings made his thoughts so famous at home and abroad that when he died in 1833, **Benthamism** continued intact as a philosophical system for more than fifty years.[14] In addition, his philosophy had an important effect on British policy and governmental strucutre.

Bentham's Notion of Utility

Nature has placed mankind under the governance of two sovereign masters, pain and pleasure. . . . they govern us in all we do, in all we say, in all we think: every effort we can make to throw off our subjection will serve but to demonstrate and confirm it.[15]

This statement briefly summarizes Bentham's thought on the nature of human behavior. Actions are evaluated by their tendency to produce advantage, pleasure, and happiness and to avoid or prevent mischief, pain, evil, or unhappiness.

Bentham created a *moral calculus* for estimating the likelihood that any individual would engage in a particular act. It involves a balancing test—weighing the possibility that an act will cause current or future pleasure against the possibility that it will create current or future pain. Since human judgment is so complex, Bentham provides hundreds of independent factors to be considered and evaluated; they include "the pleasures of wealth . . . , the pleasures of skill . . . , the pleasures of benevolence . . . , the pleasures of piety . . . , the pains of desire . . . , disappointment . . . , of the senses [hunger, thirst]."[16]

Law and Punishment. Bentham believed that the purpose of all law is to produce and support the total happiness of the community it serves. Since punishment is in itself harmful, its existence is only justified if it promises to prevent greater evil than it creates. Punishment, therefore, has four main objectives: (1) to prevent all criminal offenses; (2) when it cannot prevent a crime, to convince the offender to commit a less serious one; (3) to insure that a criminal uses no more force than necessary; (4) to prevent crime as cheaply as possible. He derived six rules to guide punishment:

1. *The value of the punishment must not be less in any case than what is sufficient to outweigh that of the profit of the offence.*
2. *The greater the mischief of the offence, the greater is the expense which it may be worth while to be at, in the way of punishment.*
3. *Where two offences come in competition, the punishment for the greater offence must be sufficient to induce a man to prefer the less.*
4. *The punishment should be adjusted in such a manner to each particular offence,*

> *that for every part of the mischief there may be a motive to restrain the offender from giving birth to it.*
>
> 5. *The punishment ought in no case to be more than what is necessary to bring it into conformity with the rules here given.*
> 6. *That the quantity actually inflicted on each individual offender may correspond to the quantity intended for similar offenders in general, the several circumstances influencing sensibility ought always to be taken into account.* [17]

These rules are the theoretical concepts underlying what is known today as classical criminology.

THE FIRST PROMINENCE OF CLASSICAL CRIMINOLOGY

Classical criminology as formulated by Beccaria and Bentham was a significant force in jurisprudence and legal policy for over a hundred years. The belief that punishment should fit the crime and that people should be punished for what they did and not to satisfy the whim of a capricious judge or ruler was widely accepted throughout Europe and the United States. The most stunning example of how the classical philosophy was embraced in Europe occurred in 1789, when France's postrevolutionary Constituent Assembly adopted these ideas in the **Declaration of the Rights of Man:**

> *the law has the right to prohibit only actions harmful to society. . . . The law shall inflict only such punishments as are strictly and clearly necessary. . . . no person shall be punished except by virtue of a law enacted and promulgated previous to the crime and applicable according to its terms.* [18]

Similarly, a prohibition against "cruel and unusual punishments" was incorporated in the Eighth Amendment to the U.S. Constitution. Thus, the use of tortures and harsh punishments was largely abandoned in the nineteenth century. The practice of incarcerating criminals and structuring prison sentences to fit the severity of crime was a reflection of classical criminology.

THE FALL AND RESURRECTION OF CLASSICAL CRIMINOLOGY

The classical perspective controlled U.S. and European judicial philosophy during much of the late eighteenth and the nineteenth centuries. Men and women were sentenced to prisons in outlying areas to serve their punishment. Capital punishment was still widely used but slowly began to be employed for only the most serious crimes. The byword was "let the punishment fit the crime." However, in the late nineteenth century and into the twentieth century, positivist criminologists (see the next three chapters) began to dispute the classical school's belief in free will. Positivist criminologists and correctional reformers argued that the cause of people's criminal behavior was beyond their control and that treatment and rehabilitation, not punishment, were the keys to preventing crime. Criminals began to be viewed as maladjusted and ill rather than greedy or pleasure seeking.

As early as 1866 in Massachusetts and 1877 in New York, the **indeterminate prison sentence** was legislated into being.[19] Under this model, prisoners were confined for at least a short stay but after the minimum sentence was up, they were kept in prison only until the authorities believed them rehabilitated sufficiently to be released. This sentencing philosophy became the most widespread in the United States and indicated the triumph of the positivist/rehabilitation theory over the classical/punishment approach.

At mid-twentieth century, liberal, rehabilitation-oriented criminology began to replace classical views as the dominant approach in American jurisprudence. Though classical principles still controlled much of the legal process, and though some political candidates such as Richard Nixon ran on "law and order" planks, professional criminologists generally rejected classical criminology.[20]

Then, in the late 1970s and into the 1980s, three factors rekindled interest in classical criminology. First, there was disenchantment with the failure of positivist criminology to isolate specific crime producing traits or factors. Second, the rehabilitation of known criminals, considered a cornerstone of positivist policy, came under attack; a number of national surveys (the most well known being Robert Martinson's *What Works?*) failed to uncover examples of rehabilitation programs that seemed to prevent future criminal activity.[21] Finally a tremendous increase in the reported crime rate, as discussed in chapter 3, as well as serious disturbances in the nation's prisons, produced a great deal of fear in all corners of society.

To many criminologists, reviving the classical concepts of social control and punishment made more sense than futilely trying to rehabilitate criminals.[22] (See Close-Up titled "Could Successful Rehabilitation Reduce the Crime Rate?") As a group, these social thinkers are referred to as **modern classical, neoclassical,** or conservative criminologists.

Despite its current prominence, modern classical theory is divided into different segments. Though criminologists may personally embrace the classical model, they may actually favor only one of its particular views while rejecting the others. In the following sections, the most prominent concepts of the classical view are discussed. Each is an independent concept that stands (or falls) on its own. However, the sum of these concepts is considered the heart of classical theory.

Deterrence

One of the most significant and oft-debated issues of modern classical criminology involves **deterrence.** This concept is usually divided into two parts—**general deterrence** and **special deterrence.** The former has been defined as "the inhibiting effect of sanctions on the criminal activity of people other than the sanctioned offender."[23] Put another way, it is alleged that potential criminals' perception that they will be punished for law violations causes them to be afraid to commit crimes. The term *special deterrence* refers to the inhibiting effect of punishment on the convicted criminal. The theory of special deterrence holds that if pain of punishment, such as a prison sentence, exceeds the benefits of crime, a one-time criminal will not repeat the law-violating behavior. Since the issue of special deterrence is linked to incarceration, it will be discussed later; the present analysis will deal only with general deterrence.

GENERAL DETERRENCE

Modern classical thinkers argue that an inverse relationship should exist between crime rates and the severity, certainty, and celerity (speed) of legal sanctions. In other words, if the punishment for a crime is increased and if the effectiveness and

Could Successful Rehabilitation Reduce the Crime Rate?

Ernest Van Den Haag is a well-known advocate of modern classical criminology. He has long championed the need for punishment to reduce crime rates and give criminals their just deserts. Conversely, he is skeptical about the worth of treatment-oriented programs in rehabilitating criminals.

In a widely read paper, Van Den Haag poses the question, "Could successful rehabilitation programs reduce the crime rate?" That is, if every known criminal could be successfully rehabilitated, would it appreciably influence the annual number of crimes taking place in the United States?

Van Den Haag thinks not. First, rehabilitation programs can only be used to control people who have already been caught. They are useless against both first offenders who have never been apprehended and habitual criminals who evade the net of justice.

But, even if recidivists (repeat offenders) committed almost all crimes and rehabilitation programs were uniformly successful in treating them, Van Den Haag still believes that rehabilitation cannot work. The number of persons engaged in any activity, legal or illegal, depends on the comparative net advantage they expect. For example, people become dentists because they expect profit, a respected social standing, and other benefits. Consequently, every dentist who retires, dies, or changes occupations is replaced by another because the need for dentistry remains constant. If many dentists were removed from the profession, a temporary disruption of services might result, but eventually the increased advantages of the field (since the patient-to-dentist ratio would now have increased) would draw recruits to the field.

By analogy, new car thieves, drug dealers, and burglars would be drawn to their respective "fields" if all current practitioners were "retired" through rehabilitation efforts. As long as there exists an advantage—in wealth, power, pleasure, and social gain—in committing crime, there will also exist a ready pool of recruits willing to take advantage of it.

Van Den Haag believes that crime can be controlled only through decreasing its advantages. When punishments are severe enough and the chance of apprehension great, only then will crime be reduced. Rehabilitation is doomed to failure. He concludes:

Our only hope for reducing the burgeoning crime rate lies in decreasing the expected net advantage of committing crimes (compared to lawful activities) by increasing the cost through increasing the expected severity of punishments and the probability of suffering them. The cost is low enough now to make crime pay for a rising number of persons, because of legal practices which were justified by the hope of rehabilitation and the mistaken idea that rehabilitation could reduce the crime rate. These legal practices, which have made the threats of the law less than daunting, must be abandoned if we are to reduce the crime rate. Probation must become exceptional. Parole and indeterminate sentences must be abolished, and so must judicial sentencing discretion and the numerous other programs meant to reduce the crime rate by rehabilitation. Punishment must become predictable. A higher apprehension and conviction rate is also needed, and could readily be produced by changes in counter-productive legal and judicial practices which make "the incarceration of even the most obviously guilty criminal . . . a task comparable to landing a barracuda with a trout-rod and a dry-fly." I believe we will move in that direction. Meanwhile, it may help if we stop relying on such dead-end streets as rehabilitation and the practices connected with it.

SOURCE. Ernest Van Den Haag, "Could Successful Rehabilitation Reduce the Crime Rate," *Journal of Criminal Law and Criminology* 73:1022–1035 (1985).

efficiency of the justice system in enforcing the law prohibiting that act is improved, then the number of people engaging in that act should decline.

The factors of severity, certainty, and celerity influence one another. For example, if a crime—say, robbery—is punished very severely but few robbers are ever caught or punished, it is likely that the severity of punishment for robbery will not deter people from robbing. On the other hand, if the certainty of apprehension and conviction is increased by modern technology, more efficient police work, or some other factor, then even minor punishments might deter the potential robber.

Legal punishments were once public spectacles intended to impress observers with the law's power.

HUDIBRAS.

Another issue influencing the probability of deterrence is the level of crime prevention desired by lawmakers. In some cases, society desires **partial deterrence** of an act; in this case, the act is not eliminated but restricted or controlled in some way. For example, the fifty-five-miles-per-hour speed law might cause offenders to violate the law by going sixty, when before they would have gone seventy-five. A law banning the sale of alcohol on Sunday might restrict public intoxication to Monday through Saturday.

In contrast, **absolute deterrence** is intended to totally eliminate a particular criminal act. For example, passage of a law requiring a mandatory life sentence for the sale of heroin would be construed as a measure seeking absolute deterrence of that act.

William Bowers, a sociologist, has distinguished further among types of possible deterrent effects.[24] **Particular deterrence** refers to the situation in which increasing punishment for a certain type of offense decreases the rate of that particular crime. **Generalized deterrence** refers to the condition in which increasing punishment for a particular offense reduces the rate for that offense plus those for several related criminal activities. This phenomenon may be explained by the fact that if people have a general impression that all punishments have increased, they may forego participating even in criminal acts whose penalties have been unchanged. In addition, Bowers identifies **selective deterrence,** in which increasing punishment for a particular offense reduces the rate of another offense that it was not designed to reduce.

DETERRENCE AND PERCEIVED THREAT

The underlying assumption of the general deterrence model is that people are fully aware of the punishments associated with criminal acts and choose to forego law-violating behaviors because of those punishments. If people were unaware of the pains associated with criminal sanctions, then the force of punishment would have no effect on them.

Very little research has been done to determine if people really are aware of criminal penalties. One study found that among a general population sample, respondents could correctly answer only 25 to 30 percent of questions measuring knowledge of criminal penalties. However, when prisoners were asked the same questions, they answered 57 percent correctly.[25] These data seem to suggest that correct information on criminal penalties is not a deterrent per se.

Michael Geerken and Walter Gove have tried to place the perception issue of deterrence into a theoretical framework.[26] Their major contribution is the observation that the way people know and find out about the certainty and severity of punishment is a major contributing factor to the effectiveness of general deterrence. They argue that "the more members of the social system rely on the mass media for their information about criminal behavior, the greater the effects of the deterrence system."[27] Geerken and Gove believe that if people hear about crime and punishment from newspapers, television, radio, and the like, they develop an exaggerated view of the effectiveness of law enforcement and the severity of punishment, because media sources tend to report on crimes that have been solved and offenders who have been punished. Furthermore, since mass media report on individual cases, the deterrent effect is often graphic. In this case, deterrent measures should be effective.

Conversely, Geerken and Gove maintain that "the more members of a social system have detailed knowledge about crime, the more specific the deterrence message and the less efficient the deterrence system."[28] People in high crime areas learn about the possibility of being punished for their criminal acts directly from active law violators. Therefore, they are more likely to be aware that the system of justice and punishment is less effective than the media make it out to be. Also, in high crime jurisdictions, strain on criminal justice resources produces a condition in which the probability of deterring a particular crime is lower than it would be in areas where the police and courts could devote more attention and resources to individual cases.

Geerken and Gove's research is supported by a recent study of drug dealing by Sheldon Ekland-Olson, John Lieb, and Louis Zurcher.[29] These researchers found that the relationship between perceived threat and deterrence was highly complex, involving interpersonal relationships and situational factors. For example, they found in their interviews of drug dealers, that if a set of personal relationships was unlikely to be affected by an arrest, the perceived severity of the arrest was low—"just a hassle." If, however, it was believed that an arrest would threaten a friendship circle or criminal operating network, the threat of arrest was taken quite seriously and arrests were to be avoided at all costs. Sanction severity was thus situationally determined.

Ekland-Olson and his associates also found that the fear of sanctions tends to increase solidarity among criminal groups.[30] Certainty of punishment becomes a function of how much trust exists among associates in crime. Personal relationships can be manipulated, that is a criminal can deal only with people of proven character to reduce perceptions of punishment certainty. In sum, those interested in deterrence must take into account the dynamics of criminal interaction when they attempt to understand the crime prevention effect of punishment.

RESEARCH ON DETERRENCE

Much research has been carried out to determine whether deterrent measures such as arrest and legal punishments affect people's behavior. Some studies make use of aggregate data sources such as the Uniform Crime Reports (UCR) or prison statistics (see chapter 3), while others create perceptual data through survey methods. These two methods will be discussed separately. (Additional research has focused on the deterrent effect of the death penalty; because of the importance of the topic, it will be discussed separately later in this chapter.)

Aggregate Data Research. Criminologists who use aggregate data compare arrest, conviction, and sentencing data with crime rates. For example, in one study conducted in California, Solomon Kobrin and his associates found that the frequency of arrest (arrest probability) had a significant effect on crime rates.[31] Similar findings were reported by Charles Tittle and Alan Rowe in a study of arrest probability in Florida.[32] Their data suggested that the deterrent effect of criminal justice action was greatest where the probability of arrest was at least 0.30. They interpreted their findings to mean that a threshold level of arrest probability is needed before a deterrent effect can occur, and that level is about 30 percent.

The relationship between apprehension rates and crime rates is far from simple. For example, Edwin Zedlewski found that such a relationship existed between the amount of police resources available and some crime rates (burglary) but not others (larceny). Moreover, Zedlewski found—using victimization (NCS) data—a significant relationship between apprehension risk and crime rates that did not exist when he used official (UCR) data. Using NCS data, he found that every 1 percent increase in arrest probability would produce a corresponding 1.8 percent decrease in property offenses.[33]

However, not all research efforts show a positive deterrent effect. For example, in an oft-cited study, Theodore Chiricos and Gordon Waldo used the UCR and national prisoner statistics to analyze deterrent effects.[34] They computed a measure of certainty of imprisonment for six index crimes by finding the ratio of prison admissions for one year to the average number of crimes known to the police. Their data reveal an inconsistent relationship between certainty and severity of punishment and crime rate. Even in the case of homicide, Chiricos and Waldo found little relationship between the certainty and severity of punishment and the crime rate.

In general, however, most research studies have found a negative association between crime rates and deterrent factors such as arrest and probability of sanction. That is, the greater the deterrent measures employed, the lower the crime rate. Nonetheless, this conclusion must be accepted with some degree of caution, since a variety of factors may bias findings. In a highly regarded analysis of deterrence research, Daniel Nagin argues that several factors interfere with proper interpretation of research data.

The way data is recorded by various jurisdictions may influence perceived relationships. "Jurisdictions that record fewer reported crimes and/or unfound [disregard] more recorded crimes will tend to have lower crime rates and higher measure of such sanction rates."[35] A police department may inflate crime clearance rates to improve its image. Similarly, if the crime rate increases, prosecutors are more likely to allow serious criminals to plead guilty to lesser charges, thus giving the false impression that as crime rates go up the probability of imprisonment also increases.

In addition, Nagin argues that researchers assume that crime and sanctions affect one another (higher crime rates lead to → higher sanctions which lead to → reduced crime, resulting in → lower sanctions, which will lead to → higher crime rates in a → never-ending cycle). This assumption may be erroneous.

Finally, Nagin argues that the deterrent effect of sanctions may reflect the effect of incapacitation and not real fear of punishment. That is, by heavily sanctioning offenders through incarceration, society will place the most serious offenders in prison and thereby reduce the crime rate. What appears to be a deterrent effect is actually an effect of incapacitation.

Perceptual Research. Because of the problems inherent in using aggregate data, modern classical criminologists have turned to another type of research—perceptual research—to study deterrent effects. This approach uses self-report surveys to ask people directly whether they feel that they will be caught if they engage in some crime, and whether they actually engage in that crime. Deterrence is supported if people who feel they will be arrested or punished for an act will also refrain from engaging in that act. Deterrence is contradicted if prior perceptions of punishment have little or no effect on subsequent behavior.

In recent years several perceptual studies have been conducted to test deterrence. Unfortunately, their results have neither uniformly supported nor contradicted deterrence theory. In one such study, Harold Grasnick and George Bryjak surveyed 400 people to determine whether perceived certainty and severity of punishment were related to criminality.[36] They found that the deterrence effect is most noticeable among people who believe they are (1) certain to be arrested for a crime and (2) certain to be punished severely if arrested. Put another way, people fear getting arrested more if they also believe they are likely to be treated severely rather than with leniency. In a similar research effort Grasnick, and his associates found that perceived certainty and severity of punishment were significantly related to the deterrence of past criminal behaviors and also to estimations of whether the person would engage in future criminal behavior.[37]

In a national survey of almost two thousand subjects, Charles Tittle found that perception of informal sanctions was a more effective determinant of deterrence than perception of formal sanctions.[38] Tittle concluded that social control seems to be rooted almost entirely in how people perceive negative reactions from interpersonal acquaintances (family, friends), while formal sanctions (arrest, prison) are irrelevant in an immediate sense. Only experienced offenders seemed to fear societal punishment, causing Tittle to conclude that legal sanctions do no more than supplement informal control processes by influencing a small segment of "criminally inclined" persons.

Other studies support this finding. For example, Matthew Silberman found that specific offenses were unaffected by deterrent measures but that commitment to conventional morality provided a general deterrent effect.[39] In a similar vein, Linda Anderson, Theodore Chiricos, and Gordon Waldo found a strong inverse relationship between marijuana use and certainty of punishment (that is, people certain of punishment did not use pot). Informal sanctions and peer disapproval were more important deterrents than fear of formal punishment.[40]

Panel Studies. A major problem of perceptual research is the causal ordering of the data. It is actually not surprising that people who have already committed criminal acts report that they do not feel threatened by legal sanctions. To show that the threat of legal punishment inhibits behavior, a researcher must prove that law-breakers felt no threat before they engaged in criminal acts.

A few studies have attempted to accomplish this goal by measuring an intact group, or *panel,* of subjects over time. The deterrence concept would be supported if (1) people's perceptions of sanctions can be shown to remain stable between measurements, and (2) those who at first feared the deterrent effect of the law later refrained from engaging in criminal behaviors. Several studies have explored this issue. In one study, Donna Bishop surveyed 2,147 high school students at a nine-month interval.[41] Although her data indicate that perceptions of deterrence are not stable, a significant deterrent effect was indicated by her data. Bishop concludes that current behavior choices influence subsequent criminal involvement. It seems that once criminal activity is initiated, it tends to be followed by a reassessment of the likelihood of getting caught—perceptions of risk are lowered, in turn promoting further criminality.

In contrast to Bishop's assessment, similar research by Raymond Paternoster and his associates,[42] and by W. William Minor and Joseph Harry,[43] found little evidence that perceptions of punishment actually deter crime. All three studies agree, however, that perceptions of deterrence change over time and that studies measuring deterrent effects must be longitudinal. In other words, to accurately measure deterrence, subjects must be measured over time. Studies using a single measure of criminal behavior and perceptions of deterrence, such as those mentioned earlier, may be methodologically unsound. In sum, evidence so far has not given unqualified support to the crime prevention properties of general deterrence.

AN ANALYSIS OF THE GENERAL DETERRENCE CONCEPT

General deterrence is the heart of classical criminology. Modern classical theorists like Ernest Van Den Haag believe that the purpose of the law and justice system is to create a "threat system":

> *Criminal laws prohibit some acts and try to deter from them by conditional threats which specify the punishments of persons who were not deterred. Sufficiently frequent imposition of these punishments by courts of law makes the threats credible. If the community feels that they are deserved, punishments also gratify its sense of justice, and help to legitimize the threat system of the criminal law by stigmatizing crime as morally odious.*[44]

The legal threat of punishment should, on the face of it, deter lawbreakers through fear of punishment. Who among us can claim that they never had an urge to commit crime that was deterred by fear of discovery and its consequences? Nonetheless, few studies show that perceptions of deterrence or deterrent measures actually reduce the propensity to commit crime or lower the crime rate. There is some indication that an increase in the arrest or conviction rate (or in the belief that an arrest or conviction will occur) is correlated with a decrease in crime, but the relationship is far less perfect than classical theorists would like us to believe.

How can this discrepancy be explained? First, deterrence theory demands a rational weighing and shifting of costs and benefits by the potential offender. There is reason to believe that in many instances criminals are desperate people acting under the influence of drugs and alcohol, or suffering from personality disorders. Surveys of inmates show a significant proportion were under the influence of drugs at the time they committed the crime they were punished for. It is likely that general deterrence would have little influence on these offenders.

Secondly, many offenders are members of what Ken Auletta calls the "under class"—people cut off from society, lacking the education, skills, and other personality traits they need to be in demand in the modern economy.[45] Can such desperate people be deterred by fear of punishment? What alternatives are open to them? Can we reasonably expect that people who have little chance of improving themselves through legitimate means will be deterred by an abstract fear of distant laws?

Third, as Beccaria's famous equation tells us, the threat of punishment involves not only its severity but its certainty and speed. Our legal system is not very effective. Chapter 3 noted that only 10 percent of serious offenses are cleared by police. As apprehended offenders are processed through all the stages of the criminal justice system (see chapter 13), the odds of their receiving serious punishment for committing an index crime approach 40 to 1. As Geerken and Gove point out, these lessons are not lost on people involved in serious criminal behavior.

So, although general deterrence remains an intriguing concept—and is certainly responsible for reducing the crime rate—it seems an unlikely device for eliminating crime per se. Besides, who would want to live in a society whose laws were certain, swift, and severe enough to eliminate all law violations?

Incapacitation and Special Deterrence

Incapacitation is a policy advocated by modern classical criminologists who believe that a small number of dangerous criminals commit a large percentage of the nation's crimes. To inhibit crime and protect its victims, say these criminologists, crime-prone individuals should be incapacitated for long periods of time. Advocates of *special deterrence* believe this experience should be so awful that these criminals will never repeat their criminal acts.

The best-known advocate of incapacitation/special deterrence is the political scientist James Q. Wilson. In his widely read book, *Thinking about Crime,* Wilson is both critical of positivist/rehabilitation views and supportive of strict punishment and confinement.[46]

Wilson believes liberal positivist/rehabilitation measures have failed. He argues that though many theories seek to find social, economic, and psychological causes of crime, "none will supply a plausible basis for the advocacy of public policy."[47] Positivist theories are faulty, he alleges, because they direct our attention toward social conditions and variables that cannot be easily changed. If, for example, poverty is found to be a cause of crime, it is not clear how society can do anything about criminality, since poverty is an ever-present social condition. If young males are viewed as more likely to commit crimes, it means little for policy makers, since "men cannot be changed into women or made to skip over their adolescent years."[48]

Wilson asks the question, "What measures can be used to prevent crime without regard to the reasons why people engage in it in the first place?" In his opinion, punishment and incapacitation are the answers. He charges that a small number of people commit a great proportion of crimes, and that these individuals do not fear punishment even though they are frequently arrested. Wilson says the problem lies with the courts and correctional agencies who, because of their desire to rehabilitate criminals, have neglected their job of protecting the public. Rehabilitation is not the answer because (1) treatment plans don't seem to work and (2) different people who commit the same crime often receive different sentences, thus violating the offenders' and public's sense of justice.

Wilson therefore argues for the abandoning of rehabilitation and the embracing of classical theory:

> *Criminals may be willing to run greater risks (or they may have a weaker sense of morality) than the average citizen, but if the expected cost of crime goes up without a corresponding increase in the expected benefits then the would-be criminal—unless he or she is among that small fraction of criminals who are utterly irrational—engages in less crime.*[49]

He suggests that the following policies be adopted to reduce crime:

- Devote the resources of the criminal courts to the issue of sentencing.
- Create uniform sentencing practices.
- Make every conviction for nontrivial offenses entail a penalty that involves incarceration (which he calls "deprivation of liberty").
- Let deprivation of liberty make use of community-based programs that enable the inmate to work or receive treatment. However, the prospects for rehabilitation should not be allowed to govern the length of sentence.
- Make conviction for a subsequent offense invariably lead to an increased term of deprivation of liberty. Penalties would be designed to fit the crime, with some discretion given to a judge to evaluate the circumstances of the case.

In conclusion, Wilson says:

> *Some persons will shun crime even if we do nothing to deter them, while others will seek it out even if we do everything to reform them. Wicked people exist. Nothing avails except to set them apart from innocent people. And many people, neither wicked nor innocent, but watchful, dissembling and calculating of their opportunities, ponder our reaction to wickedness as a cue to what they might profitably do.*[50]

RESEARCH ON INCAPACITATION AND SPECIAL DETERRENCE

Research on the benefits of incapacitation and special deterrence has again met with mixed results. Using data from Wolfgang's cohort study of 9,945 boys in Philadelphia, Steven Clarke found that only 1 to 4 percent of all known index crimes were avoided by the incapacitation of juveniles.[51] David Greenberg employed prison and FBI index crime data to estimate the effect of imprisonment on crime rates.[52] He determined that if the prison population were cut in half, the crime rate would go up only 4 percent at most; if prisons were entirely eliminated, crime might increase 8 percent. Looking at this relationship from another perspective, if the average current prison sentence (two years) were increased 50 percent, the crime rate might be reduced only 4 percent. Greenberg says:

> *Prisons may be terribly unpleasant, psychologically destructive, and at times dangerous to life and limb, but there is no compelling evidence that imprisonment substantially increases (or decreases) the likelihood of subsequent criminal involvement.*[53]

Issac Erlich obtained similar results in a study of prison rates and incapacitation; he estimated that a 50-percent reduction in average time served would result in only a 4.6-percent increase in property crime and a 2.5-percent increase in violent crime.[54] In fact, in a recent study, Lee Bowker found that an *increase* in incarceration rates may actually lead to an increase in crime rate.[55]

One of the few studies to show a crime prevention effect of incapacitation was conducted in New York by Shlomo Shinnar and Reuel Shinnar. In contrast to previous research, the study concluded that a policy of mandatory prison sentences of five years for violent crime and three for property offenses could reduce the reported crime rate by a factor of four or five.[56]

Similarly, a study by Stephan Van Dine, Simon Dinitz and John Conrad estimated that a mandatory prison sentence of five years for any felony offense could reduce the murder, rape, robbery and serious assault rates by 0.17 percent. A similar sentence limited to repeat felons would reduce the rate of these crimes by 0.6 percent.[57]

SELECTIVE INCAPACITATION

As you may recall, the concept of incapacitation was further defined by Peter Greenwood of the Rand Corporation.[58] Greenwood suggests that incapacitation could be an effective crime reduction strategy if it was employed against a specific offender population. In his study of over 2,000 inmates serving time for theft offenses in California, Michigan, and Texas, he found that the selective incapacitation of chronic offenders could reduce the rate of robbery offenses 15 percent while actually lowering the number of offenders incarcerated for that crime by 5 percent.

Earlier (chapter 4) it was noted that although the concept of selective incapacitation has piqued the interest of many criminologists, it is not without its detractors. For example, Samuel Walker also suggests that selective incapacitation produces potential errors in identifying chronic offenders. He also questions the enormous economic costs a policy of selective incapacitation might produce—$60 to $75 billion for new prison construction and between $12 and $24 billion in annual maintenance fees. In addition, Walker cites possible due process considerations: is it fair to incapacitate someone in part because they were unemployed before their crime?[59]

In sum, Greenwood's selective incapacitation concept has been embraced by some criminologists, but it has inherent flaws that have been identified by others.

A CRITIQUE OF INCAPACITATION

The incapacitation philosophy has had a powerful influence on criminological theory and policy. As noted in chapter 3, the recent decline in the crime rate has been attributed partly to the great numbers of people who are now incapacitated. Yet, incapacitation is not without its drawbacks.

First, incapacitating criminals is terribly expensive—costs today are between $5 and $10 billion. Even if incarceration could reduce the crime rate, the costs would be enormous. At a time of deficits and austerity, would American taxpayers be willing to spend billions on new prison construction and annual maintenance fees?

Second, there is little evidence that incapacitating criminals will deter them from future criminality, and even more reason to believe that the opposite will occur. A recent federal survey found that the more prior incarceration experiences inmates had, the more likely they were to recidivate (and return to prison) within 12 months of their release.[60] In some jurisdictions, but not all, the longer the prison sentence the inmate served, the more likely they were to return to prison. Whatever reason the person had to commit crime before their incarceration, there is little to suggest that a prison sentence will improve their lot. The criminal label precludes their entry into many legitimate occupations and solidifies their attachment to criminal careers.

Finally, as Charles Silberman suggests, the economics of crime suggest that if money can be made from criminal activity, there will always be someone to take the place of the incarcerated offender.[61] New criminals will be recruited and trained, offsetting any benefit accrued by incarceration.

The Death Penalty

One of the most controversial aspects of modern classical theory is the employment of the **death penalty** as a punishment for murder and other capital crimes. The death penalty contains aspects of general deterrence, special deterrence, and incapacitation. Though the execution of convicted criminals has been common throughout human history, it is a topic that has long perplexed social thinkers. This section will review the arguments for and against capital punishment and briefly describe research on its effectiveness.

ARGUMENTS FOR THE DEATH PENALTY

Various arguments have been offered in support of the death penalty by modern classical thinkers. One is that executions have always been used, that it is inherent in human nature to punish the wicked. The Bible describes methods of executing criminals. Many moral philosophers and religious leaders, such as Thomas More, John Locke, and Immanuel Kant, did not oppose the death penalty; neither did the framers of the U.S. Constitution.[62]

The death penalty also seems to be in keeping with the current mode of dispensing punishment. The criminal law exacts proportionately harsher penalties for crimes based on their seriousness; logic says that this practice is testimony to a retributionist philosophy. Therefore, the harshest penalty for the most severe crime represents a logical step in the process.

Modern classical thinkers also argue that the death penalty is sometimes the only real threat available to deter crime. For example, prison inmates serving life sentences can be controlled only if they are aware that further transgressions can lead to death. Or a person committing a crime that carries with it a long prison sentence might be more likely to kill witnesses if not deterred by the threat of death.

Death is the ultimate incapacitation. Some offenders are so dangerous that they can never be safely let out in society. The death penalty is a sure way of preventing these people from ever harming others.

In summary, supporters view capital punishment as the ultimate deterrent to crime. They believe that so serious a sanction prevents many potential criminals from taking the lives of innocent victims. The justification for the death penalty, therefore, relies on the premise that sacrificing the life of a few evil people will save the lives of many innocent ones.

ARGUMENTS AGAINST THE DEATH PENALTY

Opponents of the death penalty argue that "social vengeance by death is a primitive way of revenge which stands in the way of moral progress."[63] Its inherent brutality places it in violation of the Eighth Amendment of the U.S. Constitution, which prohibits "cruel and unusual punishment."

Opponents also object to the finality of the death penalty. It is quite possible for an innocent person to be convicted of crime; once the person is executed, the mistake can never be rectified. "It is better that a thousand guilty go free than one innocent man be executed" is a statement abolitionists often make. (See Close-Up titled "Brutalization or Deterrence.")

The discretionary nature of the death penalty also draws criticism from opponents of the death penalty. Legal scholar Charles Black argues that "arbitrary discretion pervades every road to the chair."[64] The prosecutor has the unreviewable power to decide what to charge the defendant with and later makes the decision whether to allow the accused to plead guilty to a lighter sentence. The jury, before it finds a person guilty, must deal with such thorny legal issues as premeditation and insanity, issues legal scholars have not precisely understood or defined. In murder cases, the jury is almost always told it can find the defendant guilty of a "lesser included offense" (for example, second-degree rather than first-degree murder), and their decision is not reviewable by higher authority. Clemency by executive pardon, the final stage in the process, is entirely discretionary. "The net result," concludes Black, "is that no one knows why 500 or so people on death row have really been picked for this agony, in a country where a homicide occurs every twenty-six minutes."[65]

Opponents of the death penalty charge that it has been employed in a discriminatory fashion. Between 1930 and 1967, 3,859 alleged criminals were executed in the United States. Of those executed, 53.5 percent were black and 45.4 white. This trend has not changed; in 1985, out of about 1,500 prisoners on death row, about half were black, Hispanic, or native American.[66] (See Close-Up entitled "Race and The Death Penalty.")

Abolitionists claim that capital punishment has never proven to be a deterrent any more than has life in prison. In fact, capital punishment may encourage murder, since it sets an example of violence and brutality.

In addition to the points above, the following have been offered as arguments against using the death penalty as a deterrent:[67]

- Murder is an act of anger and frustration.
- Murder is often the result of alcohol abuse.
- Murderous assaults typically involve *face saving,* or the maintenance of a favorable identity in the presence of threats, insults, or demands.
- Victims are often intoxicated.
- In order to deter, the death penalty must cause people to put themselves in the shoes of the offender. Since executed murderers are usually portrayed as brutal sadists, it is unlikely that the calculating, rational potential murderer will identify with them.

Brutalization or Deterrence?

"The lesson of the execution, then, may be to devalue life by the example of human sacrifice. Executions demonstrate that it is correct and appropriate to kill those who have greatly offended us. . . . In effect, the message of the execution may be lethal vengeance, not deterrence."*

If it is acceptable for the state to execute people who offend it, is it not possible that potential killers will view this as a message that it is morally reasonable to kill people who have offended them? This is a question posed by William Bowers and Glenn Pierce, experts on the death penalty.

The core of the Bowers-Pierce argument is the *alternative identification process*. They argue that deterrence theorists are accurate when they suggest that potential murderers identify with the actors in an execution. However, they differ with the prevailing view as to which actor the murderers identify with. According to Bowers and Pierce, killers view the victim of their crime as being similar to the executed person—someone who has offended a very powerful force and is made to suffer for it.

Furthermore, evidence suggests that people may imitate violent acts and that both self-destruction (suicide) and the harming of others is prompted by well-publicized accounts of suicides and executions. Thus, executions might have a *brutalization effect*, which prompts more rather than fewer murders.

Bowers and Pierce substantiate their claims by pointing to research data indicating that states that have abandoned the death penalty experience lower murder rates than neighboring areas that maintain it. Moreover, they cite evidence that soon after a well-publicized execution takes place, the murder rate increases, indicating that executions have a direct, immediate effect on the homicide rate.

To directly test their position, Bowers and Pierce examined the effect of the death penalty on homicides in New York state, employing as data the monthly homicide

figures from January 1907 through August 1964 (a year after the last execution took place) and monthly execution data from January 1906 through August 1963. They find a brutalizing effect of at least two extra homicides in the month following an execution, with some carry-over effect in the following month. Moreover, their research leads them to believe that the brutalization effect is most likely to occur among violence-prone potential killers rather than the population at large. Although further research is needed, Bowers and Pierce fear that if executions of the hundreds of people on death row now were to begin in earnest, the cost to innocent bystanders would be outstanding.

DISCUSSION QUESTIONS

1. Do you believe that physically assaulting an opponent is ever justified?

2. Is life in prison more brutal or less brutal than executions?

3. Do you think murderers identify with the executioner or the executed?

SOURCE. William Bowers and Glenn Pierce, "Deterrence or Brutalization: What Is the Effect of Executions," *Crime and Delinquency* 26 (1980):453–84. *(William Bowers and Glenn Pierce, 1980).

RESEARCH ON CAPITAL PUNISHMENT

Various studies have tested the assumption that capital punishment deters violent crime. One type of study looks at the immediate effect of an execution on the murder rate. If capital punishment does have a deterrent effect, the reasoning goes, then it should occur immediately after a well-publicized execution has taken place. One of the first noteworthy studies of this type was conducted in Philadelphia in 1935 by Robert Dann. He chose five highly publicized executions of convicted murderers in different years and determined the number of homicides in the sixty-day periods before and after each execution. Each 120-day period had approximately the same number of homicides, as well as the same number of days on which homicides occurred. Dann's rationale was that if capital punishment does deter crime, this deterrent effect should cause a drop in the number of homicides in the days immediately following an execution. However, his study revealed that an average of 4.4 more homicides occurred during the sixty days following an execution than during those preceding it, suggesting that the overall impact of executions might actually increase the incidence of homicide. Dann concluded that no deterrent effect was demonstrated. In a more recent study on the immediate effect of executions in Britain from 1858 to 1914, David Phillips found a temporary deterrent effect based on the publicity following the execution.[68]

Another type of research compares the murder rates of states that have abolished the death penalty with the rates of those that maintain it. In 1952, using this approach, Karl Schuessler analyzed eleven states' murder rates for the years 1930 to 1949.[69] Schuessler examined annual data for homicide rates and execution risks (the numbers of executions for murder per thousand homicides per year) and concluded that homicide rates and execution risks move independently of each other. Extending this analysis to include the examination of European countries before and after the abolition of the death penalty, Schuessler found nothing in the data to suggest that homicide trends were influenced by the abolition of capital punishment.

One of the most noted capital punishment studies was conducted by Thorsten Sellin in 1959.[70] Contiguous states were grouped in sets of three so that at least one in the group differed from the others in maximum penalties for homicide; in each set, at least one state did not provide the death penalty and at least one state did. Within these clusters of similar jurisdictions, the homicide rate in states with capital punishment was compared with the homicide rate in states without a mandatory death penalty. Since the homicide trends in all states studied were found to be similar regardless of whether the death penalty was provided, Sellin concluded that capital punishment did not appear to influence the reported rate of homicide.

Another contiguous-state analysis was carried out in 1969 by Walter Reckless, who compared seven states in which the death penalty had been abolished with nine states in which it still applied.[71] Using data from the 1967 Uniform Crime Reports, Reckless compared rates of murder, aggravated assault, and combined violent crimes. He found that five out of seven abolition states had lower crime rates than contiguous states that used the death penalty, while the remaining two sets of states tied. Reckless concluded that the death penalty was not an effective deterrent to capital crimes.

Recently, advanced econometric statistical analysis has been used to determine the relationship of execution and murder rates for the nation as a whole. The most widely cited study is Isaac Ehrlich's 1975 work, which made use of national crime and execution data.[72] According to Ehrlich, the perception of execution risk is an important determinant of whether one individual will murder another. As a result of his analysis, Ehrlich concluded that each additional execution per year in the United States would save seven or eight people from being victims of murder.

Ehrlich's research has been widely cited by advocates of the death penalty as empirical proof of the deterrent effect of capital punishment. However, subsequent research by William Bowers and Glenn Pierce, who replicated Ehrlich's analysis but used a somewhat different statistical technique, showed that his approach merely confirms previous findings that capital punishment is no more effective as a deterrent than life imprisonment.[73]

In sum, studies that have attempted to show the actual effect of capital punishment on the murder rate indicate that the execution of convicted criminals has

Race and the Death Penalty

An important criticism of the death penalty is that it has traditionally been given to a disproportionate number of minority citizens. This issue is still with us today.

Some recent research indicates that the death penalty is not used in a discriminatory fashion, but an important study conducted by Raymond Paternoster in South Carolina found that race does play a role in death penalty sentences. However, Paternoster's research focuses attention on the race of the victim as well as the criminal. Table A was constructed with data from Paternoster's study. It indicates that blacks who kill whites have over a 4.5 times greater risk of having the prosecutor seek the death penalty than do blacks who kill blacks. Paternoster found that the overall probability of a death sentence being requested for killers of blacks is 0.163, while for killers of whites it is 0.438, or 2.5 times greater. When the race of the victim is ignored, the chance of blacks and whites receiving the death penalty is almost equal. Thus, it is race of the victim and not of the offender that is most likely to bring about the death penalty. Similarly, Paternoster found that prosecutors in rural counties were more likely to ask for the death penalty than those in urban areas. In sum, extralegal factors seem to play a major role in the decision to seek the death penalty.

TABLE A. Probability of prosecutor seeking death penalty by race of offender and victim

Offender/victim combination	Probability of death requests	
	All homicides	Capital murders*
Black kills white	.365	.486
White kills white	.079	.389
Black kills black	.009	.105
White kills black	.130	.438

*Capital cases are aggravated murders; they are the only cases in which death can be sought.

DISCUSSION QUESTIONS:

1. How can the effect of a victim's race be minimized in capital punishment decision making?
2. Does discrimination in the sentencing of the death penalty make the death penalty inherently cruel and unusual punishment?

SOURCE. Raymond Paternoster, "Race of The Victim and Location of Crime: The Decision to Seek the Death Penalty in South Carolina," *Journal of Criminal Law and Criminology* 74 (1983):754–85. (Table A adapted from p. 767.)

relatively little effect as a deterrent measure. Nevertheless, many people still hold to the efficacy of the death penalty as a crime deterrent, and recent Supreme Court decisions have heralded a resumption of its use.

A CRITIQUE OF THE DEATH PENALTY

The death penalty is a cornerstone of classical theory; the ultimate punishment should deter the most serious crime. Yet, there is little sound evidence that the death penalty has much influence over murder rates. How can we explain this discrepancy? Many factors may come into play here, but the nature of the victim-criminal relationship in murder transactions is still the most likely culprit. Although stranger-versus-stranger murders are increasing, in chapter 3 we noted that most murderers knew their victims. Family conflicts, lovers' quarrels, and so on precipitate many homicides. The passions and involvements may obstruct the deterrent power of the law. Similarly, many murders occur during felonies such as holdups and burglaries. An offender surprised in the act of committing a crime, perhaps under the influence of alcohol or drugs, may be far removed from the law's deterrent power.

Finally, the discretion involved in the decision to seek the death penalty makes its use morally questionable. We as a society might thirst for revenge against the brutal killer, but we must also recognize that many of the country's most notorious murderers—Richard Speck, Charles Manson, Sirhan Sirhan, James Earl Ray, Wayne Williams, Juan Corona, and David Berkowitz (Son of Sam)—did not get the death penalty. As Raymond Paternoster points out, racial and geographic (differences) may play a greater role in receiving the death penalty than does the seriousness of the crime. Approximately 14,000 people who commit murder are apprehended by the police each year; of these, only a few hundred are condemned to death. Who these people are and why they are condemned to death are serious moral issues.

Retribution

Classical theory also holds that people should be punished solely because their law violations deserve punishment or retribution. This view is based on the work of philosopher Immanuel Kant—who argued that rational people deserve punishment because the law promises to punish crime, and that offenders bring its wrath on themselves when they violate social rules.[74] Criminals deserve the dignity of being treated as rational, intelligent people; they enjoy a right to punishment. Moreover, punishment restores social equilibrium by taking away any unfair advantages criminals gained by violating the law.

Retribution remains a theme championed by many modern classical legal scholars and philosophers. Those who hold this view maintain that people should be punished for what they've actually done, not for what they might do or what others may do. Retributionists propose a system of punishment that tries to square the gain a criminal makes from illegal activity with the loss suffered by the victim or by society as a whole. Since crime benefits one person at the expense of others, it is only fair to return the situation to its original state by penalizing the transgressor, and by doing no more and no less. They charge that wrongdoers deserve punishment for their misdeeds. If people were sanctioned for any other reason (for example, for deterrence or rehabilitation), then they would be little different from animals who are trained to meet the needs of their owners. Such a condition opens the way for a totalitarian state to undertake forcible "improvements" of its citizens without regard to whether their behavior has made them criminally or morally liable to social control.[75]

Retributionists maintain that the concept of deterrence is illogical and dangerous, because it is not absolutely necessary that the person punished even have committed the crime for deterrence to work. As C. S. Lewis has stated, rehabilitation-oriented treatment is equally dysfunctional:

> To be taken without consent from my home and friends; to lose my liberty; to undergo all those assaults on my personality which modern psychotherapy knows how to deliver; to be remade after some pattern of "normality" hatched in a Viennese laboratory to which I never professed allegiance; to know that the process will never end until either my captors have succeeded or I grown wise enough to cheat them with apparent success—who cares whether this is called Punishment or not? That it includes most of the elements for which any punishment is feared—shame, exile, bondage and years eaten by the locust—is obvious.[76]

In an oft-cited statement of classical thought, J. D. Mabbott holds that retribution is the most logical basis for punishing criminals.[77] In his refutation of the concepts of deterrence and rehabilitation, Mabbott poses these questions: If it could be shown that a particular criminal had not been improved by punishment and that no would-be criminals had been deterred by knowledge of the punishment, would that prove the punishment was unjust? Or suppose an innocent person went to prison and came out a much better, more successful person than before and that many potential criminals were influenced by this fate; would the results justify punishing an innocent person? Mabbott concludes that punishing people for reasons other than that they deserve retribution is inherently unfair; it is essential that inflicting a punishment not be determined by some notion that it will do the criminal or society some "good."

K. G. Armstrong argues that retributive punishment is not revenge; revenge is private and personal and requires no authority to control its direction.[78] Retribution instead involves the lawful action of the state to protect society, reform the criminal, and recover for society—by force where necessary—what a "reluctant debtor" owes it.

Retributionists argue that punishments are fair and necessary in a just society. First, punishment assures law-abiding people that they are not assuming an unfair burden by their compliance with the conventional rules of society. Second, punishment assures compliance with rules that insure an orderly society and fair distribution of goods and services. Third, punishment is society's way of creating equilibrium among its members and institutions. If a person acquires an unfair advantage by disobeying rules law-abiding citizens respect, then matters cannot be set straight until that advantage is erased.

JUST AND PAINFUL

The retributive ideal has received a recent boost from Graeme Newman's book, *Just and Painful.*[79] Newman, a strict retributionist, argues that society should return to using corporal punishment for sanctioning offenders. He approves of using electroshocks to punish offenders because (1) they are over with quickly, (2) they have no lasting effect, and (3) they can easily be adjusted to fit the severity of a crime. Some of Newman's other ideas include:

- Acute corporal punishment should be introduced to fill the gap between the severe punishment of prison and the nonpunishment of probation.
- For the majority of property crimes, the preferred corporal punishment is that of electric shock because it can be scientifically controlled and calibrated and is less violent in its application when compared with other corporal punishments, such as whipping.
- For violent crimes in which the victim was terrified and humiliated, and for which a local community does not wish to incarcerate, a violent corporal punishment should be considered, such as whipping. In these cases, humiliation of the offender is seen as justifiably deserved.
- Every effort should be made to develop a split system of criminal justice: one system for the punishment of *crimes*, and one for the punishment of *criminals.*
- After an offender has committed a number of repeated offenses, or when the combined injury and damage of crimes reach a certain amount, he will be treated as a criminal deserving incarceration.

Just Desert

A more current version of retribution exists in the concept of **just desert.** Whereas the two positions seem almost identical, *desert* appears to be a more pleasant and less threatening term than *retribution*, which has often been closely linked with revenge. The just desert position has been most clearly spelled out by criminologist Andrew Von Hirsch in *Doing Justice*, the report of the Committee for the Study of Incarceration, a study group funded by several private foundations in the mid-1970s. In his report, Von Hirsch is generally critical of the rehabilitation/positivist criminology philosophy. He charges:

- The character or size of a penal institution has little to do with its effectiveness.
- Probation (community supervision) does not seem more effective than prison.
- More intensive supervision on the street does not seem to curb recidivism.
- Vocational training has proven ineffective.
- Small community-based programs are no more effective than traditional programs.
- Social science has not proven that the best possible correctional treatment program is superior to no treatment at all.[80]

Von Hirsch therefore offers the concept of desert as a theoretical model to guide justice policy:

To say someone "deserves" to be rewarded or punished is to refer to his past conduct and assert that its merit or demerit is reason for according him pleasant or unpleasant treatment.[81]

The logic of this concept is contained in these three statements:

1. Those who violate others' rights deserve to be punished.
2. We should not deliberately add to human suffering; punishment makes those punished suffer.
3. However, punishment may prevent more misery than it inflicts; this conclusion reestablishes the need for desert-based punishment.[82]

This utilitarian view is the key to the desert approach: Punishment is needed to preserve the social equity disturbed by crime; nonetheless, severity of punishment should be commensurate with the seriousness of crime.

Desert theory is also concerned with the rights of the accused. It alleges that the rights of the person being punished should not be unduly sacrificed for the good of others (as with deterrence). The offender should not be treated as more (or less) **blameworthy** than is warranted by the character of his or her offense. For example, Von Hirsch asks the following question: If two crimes, A and B, are equally serious, but if severe penalties are shown to have a deterrent effect only with respect to A, would it be fair to punish the person who has committed crime A more harshly simply to deter others from committing the crime? Conversely, imposing a slight sentence for a serious crime would be unfair, because it would treat the offender as being less blameworthy than he or she is.

In sum, the just desert model suggests that retribution justifies punishment because people deserve what they get for past deeds.[83] Punishment based on deterrence or incapacitation is wrong because it involves an offender's future actions, which cannot accurately be predicted. Punishment should be the same for all people who commit the same crime. Criminal sentences based on individual needs or characteristics are inherently unfair since all people are equally blameworthy for their misdeeds.

As we shall see in the following sections, the concept of desert-based justice has strongly influenced criminal justice policy makers.

Policy Implications of Classical Theory

In recent years, classical criminology has had a great effect on policy making in the U.S. justice system. Modern classical concepts such as deterrence, incapacitation, and just desert have played an important role in criminal justice operations. This section will briefly review how classical theory influences policy making.

LAW

Classical theory has had an important influence on people's thoughts about the relationship between law, punishment, and crime. It is evident that policy makers accept the idea that punishment has a deterrent effect when they use tough criminal sentences in an effort to control crime. One striking example of this trend has been in the area of gun control. Some states have toughened penalties in order to deter violent crimes. Michigan's Felony Firearms Statute adds a mandatory two years in prison to the sentence of any person convicted of a crime in which a gun was used.[84] Similarly, the Bartley-Fox gun law in Massachusetts provides a one-year mandatory prison term for simply carrying an unregistered firearm.[85] Research indicates that the Michigan law has not reduced violent crime in the city of Detroit, while the Massachusetts law has reduced the use of handguns but promoted the use of other weapons in violent crimes. Despite the lack of success of these efforts, it is evident that today's lawmakers still rely on the threat of penalties as a front-line crime deterrent. Increasing numbers of state jurisdictions are imposing longer mandatory sentences with the hope of deterring crime. This issue will be discussed further in chapter 16.

POLICE

The very nature of police operations seems to embody classical principles. Their mission of crime prevention is aided by the deterrent effect of their visibility and presence on potential criminals. Their easily recognizable uniforms and patrol cars serve as constant reminders that criminal violations can result in apprehension and serious punishments.

The police have undertaken several projects to determine whether they actually provide a deterrent to crime. The most famous study was conducted in Kansas City, Missouri.[86] To evaluate the effectiveness of police patrols, fifteen independent police beats or districts were divided into three groups: the first retained normal police patrol; the second (*proactive*) was supplied with two to three times the normal amount of patrol forces; the third (*reactive*) eliminated its preventive patrol entirely, and police officers responded only when summoned by citizens to the scene of a crime.

Surprisingly, data from the Kansas City study indicated that these variations in patrol techniques had little effect on the crime patterns in the fifteen locales. The presence or absence of patrol did not seem to affect residential or business burglaries, auto thefts, larcenies involving auto accessories, robberies, vandalism, or other criminal behavior. Variations in police patrol techniques appeared to have little effect on citizens' attitudes toward the police, their satisfaction with police, or their fear of future criminal behavior.

Despite the setback dealt to classical theory by the Kansas City Study, a recent study by Lawrence Sherman and Richard Berk has rekindled the belief that police actions may actually deter crime.[87] Sherman and Berk evaluated a program the Minneapolis Police Department created to control domestic (spousal) violence and abuse. In the program, police officers randomly assigned suspects to one of three response categories: (1) formal arrest, (2) "advice" such as counseling and media-tion, and (3) an order that the suspect must leave the premises for eight hours. The results of the project were tracked for six months, using official data and victim reports. Sherman and Berk report that people subjected to the harshest response, arrest, were less likely to become involved in violence than those who were merely advised. The authors conclude:

> . . . arrest and initial incarceration alone may produce a deterrent effect, regardless of how the courts treat such cases, and that arrest makes an independent contribution to the deterrence potential of the criminal justice system.[88]

In sum, though the Kansas City Study questioned the general deterrent effect of police work, recent research developed by Sherman and Berk indicates that police procedures could produce a special deterrent effect.

SENTENCING

As mentioned earlier in this chapter, some studies indicate that the conviction rate has an inverse relationship with crime rates. Thus, the fear of being found guilty in a court of law may have a deterrent effect on potential criminals. None-theless, the methodological problems in measuring a true deterrent effect make it impossible to realistically conclude that sentencing risk deters crime.

Despite this uncertainty, classical philosophy has recently had a tremendous effect on sentencing. Advocate of incapacitation and just desert have influenced some state legislators to pass strict sentencing guidelines that abolish early release from prison (parole) and also insure that most convicted offenders will serve some time in prison for their acts (mandatory sentencing). In addition, a number of states, including California, Indiana, Illinois and Maine, has passed **presumptive sentencing** laws.[89] These laws guarantee that most people sent to prison for a particular crime will get the same sentence and will serve the entire sentence without early release or parole (although there is usually a provision for time off for good behavior). Most presumptive sentencing statutes allow judges to add time to a sentence for a particularly serious crime or subtract time if the circumstances warrant it. However, the presumption is that offenders will get the sentence they deserve and that all similar offenders will serve the same number of years in prison.

Other state jurisdictions—including Michigan, Washington, and Minnesota—are drafting **sentencing guidelines** that instruct judges on the appropriate sentence for a particular crime. Sentencing guidelines follow the theory of just desert because they are designed to uphold the principle that offenders who commit like crimes should receive like penalties (see chapter 16).

CAPITAL PUNISHMENT

The most important development related to the classical approach in sentencing has been the revived use of the death penalty to deter murder and punish criminals. Throughout the history of the United States, the death penalty was freely used when judges or juries thought it was warranted. Then, in 1972, the United States Supreme Court, in its **Furman v. Georgia** decision, ruled that the discretionary imposition of the death penalty was cruel and unusual punishment under the Eighth and Fourteenth Amendments of the Constitution.[90] This case not only questioned whether capital punishment is a more effective deterrent than life imprisonment, but it also challenged the very existence of the death penalty on the grounds of its brutality and finality.

The Court did not rule out the use of capital punishment as a penalty; rather, it objected to the arbitrary and capricious manner in which it was imposed. After *Furman*, many states changed statutes that had previously allowed juries discretion in imposing the death penalty. In some states, this was accomplished by enacting statutory guidelines for jury decisions; in others, the death penalty was made mandatory for certain crimes only. Despite these changes in statutory law, no further executions were carried out while the Supreme Court pondered additional cases concerning the death penalty.

In July 1976, the Supreme Court ruled on the constitutionality of five states' death penalty statutes. In the first case, **Gregg v. Georgia,** the Court found valid the Georgia statute that held that a jury must find at least one "aggravating circumstance" out of ten before the death penalty can be imposed in murder cases.[91] In the *Gregg* case, for example, the jury imposed the death penalty after establishing beyond a reasonable doubt the presence of two aggravating circumstances:

1. The murder was committed while the offender was engaged in the commission of two other capital felonies.
2. The offender committed the murder for the purpose of receiving money and other financial gains (an automobile).

The Court also upheld the constitutionality of a Texas statute on capital punishment in *Jurek* v. *Texas*[92] and of a Florida statute in *Proffitt* v. *Florida.*[93] These statutes are similar to Georgia's in that they limit sentencing discretion not only by specifying the crimes for which capital punishment can be handed down, but also by stipulating criteria concerning the circumstances surrounding the crimes. For example, the Texas statute requires that the death sentence be imposed only if the jury, in a proceeding following the verdict, responds in the affirmative to two and sometimes three of the following questions:

1. Whether the conduct of the defendant that caused the death of the deceased was committed deliberately and with the reasonable expectation that the death of the deceased or another would result.
2. Whether a probability exists that the defendant will commit criminal acts of violence that constitute a continuing threat to society.
3. If raised by the evidence, whether the conduct of the defendant in killing the deceased was unreasonable in response to the provocation, if any, offered by the deceased.

However, the Supreme Court declared that mandatory death sentences were unconstitutional.

In the late 1970s and early 1980s a more conservative Supreme Court has eased the way for executions by lifting some of the legal roadblocks to capital punishment, such as the seating of jurors who are opposed to the death penalty.[94] At the time of this writing, about 1,500 people are on death row. Capital punishment has become a fairly commonplace event in American culture, and its supporters point to the declining murder rate as evidence of its success.

CORRECTIONS

Classical theory has also influenced the correctional process. Criminologist David Fogel's **justice model** of corrections has been adopted in several jurisdictions.[95] Fogel calls for the elimination of parole, or of any release based on an inmate's "rehabilitation" success. He instead advocates flat (determinate) sentences, and prisons as places for punishment rather than treatment. Fogel believes that an inmate's sense of justice must be raised lest they feel victimized by the system. If everyone is treated equally and fairly, then even the severest punishment will be acceptable; but if inmates perceive that benefits and privileges are being unequally distributed, then their sense of injustice will outweigh any possible benefits of correctional rehabilitation efforts.

The justice model has had an important influence on correctional policy in the 1980s. Most importantly, it has been used as a justification when state legislators wish to abolish parole or create more restrictive sentences. The justice model has become the cornerstone of corrections in the 1980s (see chapter 14).

Summary

Classical theory assumes that each person has the free will to choose whether to commit criminal acts. However, people are influenced by their fear of the criminal penalties associated with being caught and convicted for law violations. The more severe, certain, and swift the punishment, the more likely it is to control crime.

The classical approach is rooted in the utilitarian philosophy of Cesare Beccaria and Jeremy Bentham. These eighteenth-century social philosophers argued that punishment should fit the crime. Though firmness was necessary, punishments should not exceed the actual cost of crime. Beccaria was particularly influential as a spokesman against torture and the use of capital punishment.

Classical criminology influenced policy making for almost a hundred years. Punishments were tailored to fit criminal acts. Use of the death penalty was limited. The growth of positivist criminology, which stressed external causes of crime and rehabilitation of known offenders, reduced the popularity of the classical approach in the twentieth century. However, classical criminology recently has become more popular with U.S. criminologists. Several classical concepts have been advocated as useful for the understanding of crime and its control.

Deterrence theory relates to the concept that an inverse relationship should exist between punishment and crime. However, a number of factors confound the relationship. For example, if people don't believe they will be caught, even harsh punishment may not deter crime. Deterrence theory has been criticized on the grounds that it wrongfully assumes that criminals make a rational choice before committing crimes, ignores the intricacies of the criminal justice system, and does not take into account the social and psychological factors that may influence criminality. Research designed to test the validity of the deterrence concept has not indicated that deterrent measures actually reduce the crime rate.

Another classical concept involves incapacitation and special deterrence; its proponents hold that the crime rate can be reduced if dangerous people are locked up for extended periods and punished so severely that they never commit crimes again. The leading advocate of the incapacitation philosophy is the political scientist James Q. Wilson. Research efforts have not provided clear-cut proof that increasing the number of people in prison—and increasing prison sentences—will reduce crime rates.

Another aspect of classical criminology, one that combines elements of deterrence and incapacitation, is the increased use of the death penalty to prevent murder and other capital crimes. People in favor of capital punishment argue that it is the ultimate deterrent, that it causes the criminal to suffer as the victim did, and that it prevents killers from ever threatening innocent people again. People opposed to capital punishment reject its brutality, the discriminatory way in which it is applied, and its finality. Empirical research has not proven that the death penalty reduces the murder rate, and some recent efforts by William Bowers and Glenn Pierce indicate that executions might even cause an increase in the murder rate.

The fourth branch of classical criminology includes the theories of retribution and just desert. Advocates of these theories suggest that the punishment should fit the crime. The justice system should be modified so that criminals serve their entire sentences behind bars. Desert-oriented criminologists advocate the abolition of parole and the widespread use of flat or determinate sentences.

Classical theory has been influential in shaping public policy. The criminal law is designed to deter potential criminals and fairly punish those who have been caught engaging in illegal acts. Police forces have operated to deter and prevent crime. Some courts have changed sentencing policies to adapt to classical principles, and the U.S. correctional system seems geared toward incapacitation and special deterrence. Recently, the Supreme Court has once again legalized the death penalty; and its renewed use is testimony to the importance of classical theory.

Notes

1 Francis Edward Devine, "Cesare Beccaria and the Theoretical Foundations of Modern Penal Jurisprudence," *New England Journal on Prison Law* 7 (1982):8–21.

2 John Locke, *Two Treatises on Government*, 2d ed. (London: P. Lasslett, 1970, pp. 313–81.

3 Marcello Maestro, *Voltaire and Beccaria* (New York: Octagon, 1972), p. 2.

4 Ysabel Rennie, *The Search for Criminal Man* (Lexington, Mass.: Lexington Books, 1978), p. 8.

5 Ibid., p. 9.

6 Cited in James Heath, *Eighteenth Century Penal Theory* (New York: Oxford University Press, 1963), p. 98.

7 Cesare Beccaria, *On Crimes and Punishments*, 6th ed., trans. Henry Paolucci (Indianapolis: Bobbs-Merrill, 1977).

8 Ibid., p. 8.

9 Ibid., p. 11.

10 Ibid., p. 13.

11 Ibid., p. 43.

12 Ibid., p. 99.

13 Jeremy Bentham, *A Fragment on Government* and *An Introduction to the Principle of Morals and Legislation*, ed. Wilfred Harrison (Oxford: Basil Blackwell, 1967).

14 Ibid., p. xi.

15 Ibid., p. 21.

16 Ibid., p. 152.

17 Adapted from Rennie, *Search for Criminal Man*, p. 22.

18 Ibid., p. 23.

19 Vincent Webb and Roy Roberg, *Issues in Corrections* (St. Paul, Minn.: West Publishing, 1981), p. 52.

20 Ibid., p. 22.

21 Robert Martinson, "What Works?—Questions and Answers about Prison Reform," *Public Interest* 35 (1974):22–54.

22 Ronald Bayer, "Crime, Punishment and the Decline of Liberal Optimism," *Crime and Delinquency* 27 (1981):190.

23 Alfred Blumstein, Jacqueline Cohen, and Daniel Nagin, *Deterrence and Incapacitation: Estimating the Effects of Criminal Sanctions on Crime Rates* (Washington, D.C.: National Academy of Science, 1978), p. 3.

24 William Bowers, "A Causal Framework for the Analysis of Deterrence and Related Processes," in *Crime Prevention and Social Control,* ed. Ronald Akers and Edward Sagarin (New York: Praeger, 1974), pp. 22–38. See also William Chambliss, "Types of Deviance and the Effectiveness of Legal Sanctions," *Wisconsin Law Review* 1967 (1967):703–719.

25 Carol Crowther, "Crimes, Penalties and Legislatures," *Annals of the American Academy of Political and Social Sciences* 381 (1969):147–58.

26 Michael Geerken and Walter Gove, "Deterrence: Some Theoretical Considerations," *Law and Society Review* 9 (1975):497–514.

27 Ibid., p. 505.

28 Ibid., p. 507.

29 Sheldon Ekland-Olson, John Lieb, and Louis Zurcher, "The Paradoxical Impact of Criminal Sanctions: Some Microstructural Findings," *Law and Society Review* 18 (1984):159–78.

30 Ibid., p. 175.

31 Solomon Kobrin, E.W. Hansen, S.G. Lubeck, and R. Yeaman, *The Deterrent Effectiveness of Criminal Justice Sanction Strategies: Summary Report* (Washington, D.C.: Government Printing Office, 1972).

32 Charles Tittle and Alan Rowe, "Certainty of Arrest and Crime Rates: A Further Test of the Deterrence Hypothesis," *Social Forces* 52 (1974):455–62.

33 Edwin Zedlewski, "Deterrence Findings and Data Sources: A Comparison of the Uniform Crime Reports and the National Crime Surveys," *Journal of Research in Crime and Delinquency* 20 (1983):262–76.

34 Theodore Chiricos and Gordon Waldo, "Punishment and Crime: An Examination of Some Empirical Evidence," *Social Problems* 18 (1970):200–217.

35 Blumstein, Cohen, and Nagin, *Deterrence and Incapacitation,* p. 4.

36 Harold Grasnick and George Bryjak, "The Deterrent Effect of Perceived Severity of Punishment," *Social Forces* 59 (1980):471–91.

37 Harold Grasnick and D.J. Green, "Legal Punishment, Social Disapproval and Internalization as Inhibitors of Illegal Behavior," *Journal of Criminal Law and Criminology* 71 (1980):325–35.

38 Charles Tittle, *Sanctions and Social Deviance* (New York: Praeger, 1980).

39 Matthew Silberman, "Toward a Theory of Criminal Deterrence," *American Sociological Review* 41 (1976):442–61.

40 Linda Anderson, Theodore Chiricos, and Gordon Waldo, "Formal and Informal Sanctions: A Comparison of Deterrent Effects," *Social Problems* 25 (1977):103–114. See also Maynard Erickson and Jack Gibbs, "Objective and Perceptual Properties of Legal Punishment and Deterrence Doctrine," *Social Problems* 25 (1978):253–64.

41 Donna Bishop, "Deterrence: A Panel Analysis," *Justice Quarterly* 1 (1984):311–28.

42 Raymond Paternoster, Linda Saltzman, Gordon Waldo, and Theodore Chiricos, "Estimating Perceptual Stability and Deterrent Effects: The Role and Perceived Legal Punishment in the Inhibition of Criminal Involvement," *Journal of Criminal Law and Criminology* 74 (1983):270–97.

43 W. William Minor and Joseph Harry, "Deterrent and Experiential Effects in Perceptual Deterrence Research: A Replication and Extension," *Journal of Research in Crime and Delinquency* 19 (1982):190–203.

44 Ernest Van Den Haag, "The Criminal Law as a Threat System," *Journal of Criminal Law and Criminology* 73 (1982):709–785.

45 Ken Auletta, *The Under Class* (New York: Random House, 1982).

46 James Q. Wilson, *Thinking about Crime* (New York: Basic Books, 1975).

47 Ibid., p. 53.

48 Ibid., p. 55.

49 Ibid., p. 197.

50 Ibid., p. 235.

51 Steven Clarke, "Getting 'em Out of Circulation: Does Incarceration of Juvenile Offenders Reduce Crime?" *Journal of Criminal Law and Criminology* 65 (1974):528–35.

52 David Greenberg, "The Incapacitative Effects of Imprisonment: Some Estimates," *Law and Society Review* 9 (1975):541–80.

53 Ibid., p. 558.

54 Isaac Erlich, "Participation in Illegitimate Activities: An Economic Analysis," *Journal of Political Economy* 81 (1973):521–67.

55 Lee Bowker, "Crime and the Use of Prisons in the United States: A Time Series Analysis," *Crime and Delinquency* 27 (1981):206–212.

56 Reuel Shinnar and Shlomo Shinnar, "The Effects of the Criminal Justice System on the Control of Crime: A Quantitative Approach," *Law and Society Review* 9 (1975):581–611.

57 Stephan Van Dine, Simon Dinitz and John Conrad, *Restraining the Wicked: The Dangerous Offender Project* (Lexington, Mass.: Lexington Books, 1979.)

58 Peter Greenwood, *Selective Incapacitation* (Santa Monica, Calif.: Rand Corp., 1982).

59 Samuel Walker, *Sense and Nonsense about Crime* (Monterey, Calif.: Brooks Cole, 1985), pp. 56–63.

60 John Wallerstedt, *Returning to Prison*, Bureau of Justice Statistics Special Report (Washington, D.C.: U.S. Department of Justice, 1984).

61 Charles Silberman, *Criminal Violence, Criminal Justice* (New York: Random House, 1978), p. 196.

62 See, for example, Ernest Van Den Haag, *Punishing Criminals: Concerning a Very Old and Painful Question* (New York: Basic Books, 1975), pp. 209–211; Walter Berns, "Defending the Death Penalty," *Crime and Delinquency* 26 (1980):503–511.

63 Kilman Shin, *Death Penalty and Crime* (Fairfax, Virginia: George Mason University, 1978), p. 1.

64 Charles Black, "Objections to S. 1382, a Bill to Establish Rational Criteria for the Imposition of Capital Punishment," *Crime and Delinquency* 26 (1980):441–53.

65 Ibid., p. 442.

66 "Ruling May Halt All Executions in 7 States," *Omaha World Herald*, 1 February 1985, p. 1; Bureau of Justice Statistics, *Capital Punishment, 1983* (Washington, D.C.: National Institute of Justice, 1984).

67 William Bowers and Glenn Pierce, "Deterrence or Brutalization: What Is the Effect of Executions," *Crime and Delinquency* 26 (1980):453–84.

68 Robert Dann, "The Deterrent Effect of Capital Punishment," (Philadelphia: *Friends Social Service Series #29*, 1935); David Phillips, "The Deterrent Effect of Capital Punishment," *American Journal of Sociology* 86 (1980):139–48; Hans Zeisel, "A Comment on the 'Deterrent Effect of Capital Punishment' by Phillips," *American Journal of Sociology* 88 (1982):167–69.

69 Karl Schuessler, "The Deterrent Influence of the Death Penalty," *Annals of the Academy of Political and Social Sciences* 284 (1952):54–62.

70 Thorsten Sellin, *The Death Penalty* (Philadelphia: American Law Institute, 1959).

71 Walter Reckless, "Use of the Death Penalty," *Crime and Delinquency* 15 (1969):43.

72 Isaac Erlich, "The Deterrent Effect on Capital Punishment: A Question of Life and Death," *American Economic Review* 65 (1975):397–417.

73 William B. Bowers and Glenn Pierce, "The Illusion of Deterrence in Isaac Erlich's Research on Capital Punishment," *Yale Law Journal* 85 (1975):187–208.

74 For an analysis of Kant's work, see Gray Cavender, "Justice, Sanctioning and the Justice Model," *Criminology* 22 (1984):203–213.

75 J.B. Hawkins, "Punishment and Moral Responsibility," *Modern Law Review* 7 (1944):205–208.

76 C.S. Lewis, "The Humanitarian Theory of Punishment," *20th Century* 3 (1948-1949):4–16.

77 J.D. Mabbott, "Punishment," *Mind* 49 (1939):152–67.

78 K.G. Armstrong, "The Retributionist Hits Back," *Mind* 70 (1961):471–90.

79 Graeme Newman, *Just and Painful* (New York: MacMillan, 1983), pp. 139–43.

80 Andrew von Hirsch, *Doing Justice* (New York: Hill and Wang, 1976).

81 Ibid., pp. 15–16.

82 Ibid., pp. 15–16.

83 Thomas Honderich, "On Justifying Protective Punishment," *British Journal of Criminology* 22 (1982):268–75.

84 Colin Loftin and David McDowall, "One with a Gun Gets You Two: Mandatory Sentencing and Firearms Violence in Detroit," *Annals, AAPS* 455 (1981):158–68.

85 Glenn Pierce and William Bowers, "The Bartley-Fox Gun Law's Short-Term Impact on Crime in Boston," *Annals, AAPS* 455 (1981):128–37.

86 George Kelling, Tony Pate, Duane Dieckman, and Charles Brown, *The Kansas City Preventive Patrol Experiment: A Summary Report* (Washington, D.C.: Police Foundation, 1974).

87 Lawrence Sherman and Richard Berk, "The Specific Deterrent Effects of Arrest for Domestic Assault," *American Sociological Review* 49 (1984):261–72.

88 Ibid., p. 271.

89 Stephen LaGoy, Fred Hussey, and John Kramer, "A Comparative Assessment of Determinate Sentencing in Four Pioneer States," *Crime and Delinquency* 24 (1980):385–400.

90 408 U.S. 238, 92 S.Ct. 2726, 33 L.Ed. 2d 346 (1972).

91 428 U.S. 153, 96 S.Ct. 2909, 49 L.Ed. 2d 859 (1976).

92 428 U.S. 262, 96 S.Ct. 2950, 49 L.Ed. 2d 929 (1976).

93 428 U.S. 325, 96 S.Ct. 3001, 49 L.Ed. 2d 944 (1976).

94 Woodson v. North Carolina, 428 U.S. 280 (1976); Roberts v. Louisiana, 428 U.S. 325 (1976).

95 David Fogel, *We Are the Living Proof: The Justice Model for Corrections* (Cincinnati: Anderson, 1975).

6 Biological and Psychological Theories of Crime Causation

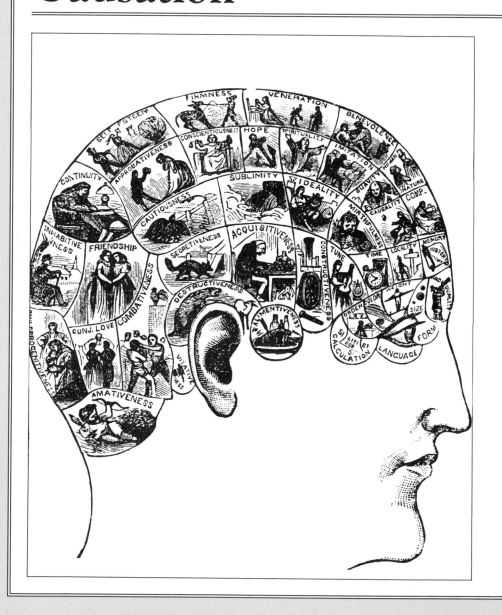

CHAPTER OUTLINE

Introduction

Foundations of Biocriminology

Cesare Lombroso and Criminal Man

Lombroso's Contemporaries

Theories of Heredity

Body-Build Theories

Modern Biocriminology and Sociobiology

Biochemical Factors

Neurophysiological Studies

Genetic Influences

Evaluation of the Biological Perspective

Psychological Theory of Crime

Early Psychological Theory

Psychoanalytic Perspective: Sigmund Freud

Post-Freudian Psychoanalytic Theory

Psychoanalysis and Criminal Behavior

Cognitive Theory

Behavior Theory and the Social Learning Approach

Psychobiological Perspective

Crime and Personality Traits

A Critique of Psychological Theories

Individual-Oriented Theory and Social Policy

Summary

KEY TERMS

biocriminology

psychocriminology

Cesare Lombroso

atavistic anomaly

moral anomaly

E.O. Wilson

sociobiology

mental degenerate

psychoanalytic perspective

cognitive theory

social learning

behavior modeling

psychobiologist

Sigmund Freud

repression

fixated

Carl Jung

inferiority complex

identity crisis

schizophrenia

August Aichorn

social learning

Albert Bandura

sociopath

psychopath

classification center

medical model

Introduction

The preceding chapter explained how criminologists of the classical school maintain that criminals choose to violate the law after carefully weighing the benefits and consequences of their illegal activities. Not all criminologists are convinced, however, that this calculated thought process actually takes place. Since the middle of the nineteenth century, social scientists have suggested that uncontrollable environmental factors may significantly influence behavior patterns. Physical make-up, mental and psychological status, family structure, and socioeconomic conditions have all been viewed as contributing to behavior tendencies. As a group, social scientists who believe a person's behavior is controlled by outside forces and not his or her personal decision-making processes are referred to as *positivists.*

The earliest positivist theories of crime causation focused on the criminal's biological makeup and psychological makeup. Theories about the former suggest that criminals have unique biophysical properties that motivate their antisocial behavior **(biocriminology),** while theories about the latter are more concerned with the relationship to criminal behavior of psychological factors such as mental stability, intelligence, learning, and moral development **(psychocriminology).** Although biological and psychological theories were among the earliest criminological perspectives, their advocates are still quite active today.

In general, the pioneers of biocriminology and psychocriminology held that the classical approach was an inadequate explanation of crime, because it failed to explain why one person chooses to commit crime while others adhere to conventional values and beliefs. Positivists maintained that whereas most people living under similar conditions are subject to the same socialization process, only a small minority become seriously delinquent or criminal. Therefore, some personal trait must separate the deviant members of society from the nondeviant. These personal differences explain why, when faced with the same life situations, one person commits crime while another attends school, church, and neighborhood functions. All people may be aware of and even fear the sanctioning power of the law, but some are unable to control their urges and passions. These people commit crimes of violence and destruction.

As a rule, no single biological or psychological concept is thought to be adequate as an explanation of all criminality. Rather, as common sense would suggest, each offender is considered unique physically and mentally; consequently, there must be different explanations for their different behaviors. For example, one person may have had a very ordinary childhood and yet have "learned" to be violent through personal experiences in adolescence. Another offender may be suffering from a neurological problem, while a third may have a blood chemistry disorder believed to be related to antisocial activity. Criminologists who focus on the individual see many explanations for crime, since, in fact, there are many differences among criminal offenders.

Biocriminologists and psychocriminologists are not overly concerned with legal definitions of crime. Their studies focus on basic human behavior and drives—aggression, violence, lack of concern for others, depression, and so on.

This chapter will first review the history and current status of biocriminology. This perspective holds that criminals have in their physical makeup properties that make them crime prone. Then the chapter will turn to a discussion of psychological theory; such theories view crime as a product of personality, learning, and mental processes. In the following two chapters, sociological positivism will be discussed.

Foundations of Biocriminology

Biological explanations of criminal behavior first became popular during the middle part of the eighteenth century. At that time, there was considerable ferment in the scientific community. A great deal of interest developed in *positivism*—the use of the scientific method and empirical analysis to study behavior. While classical penologists such as Beccaria and Bentham were trying to explain people's behavior through armchair analysis and logic, others attempted to apply the scientific method to the study of criminal behavior. One natural avenue of inquiry was the association between biophysical makeup and crime.

The earliest biocriminologists were concerned with the shape of the head and body. *Physiognomists* such as J. K. Lavater studied the facial features of criminals to determine whether the shape of ears, nose, and eyes and the distance between them were associated with antisocial behavior. *Phrenologists* such as Franz Joseph Gall and Johann K. Spurzheim studied the shape of the skull and bumps on the head to determine whether these physical attributes were linked to criminal behavior. Phrenologists believed that external cranial characteristics dictate which areas of the brain control physical activity. Their primitive techniques and quasi-scientific methods have been thoroughly discredited.

CESARE LOMBROSO AND CRIMINAL MAN

With the publication of Charles Darwin's *Origin of Species* in 1859, the scientific quest to unlock the secrets of human origin and behavior received considerable momentum. In Italy, an Italian physician, **Cesare Lombroso,** was studying the cadavers of executed criminals in an effort to scientifically determine whether law violators were physically different from people of conventional values and behavior.

Lombroso (1835–1909), known as the "father of criminology," was a doctor who served much of his career in the Italian army. His army experience gave him ample opportunity to study the physical characteristics of soldiers convicted and executed for criminal offenses. Later, he studied inmates at institutes for the criminally insane at Pavia, Pesaro, and Reggio Emilia.[1]

Lombrosian theory can be outlined in a few simple statements.[2] First, Lombroso believed that serious offenders, those who engaged in repeated assault- or theft-related activities, were born to be criminals. These *crimogenic* people have inherited physical problems that impel them into a life of crime.

Second, said Lombroso, criminals suffer from **atavistic anomalies**—physically, they are throwbacks to more primitive times when people were savages. For example, criminals were believed to have the enormous jaws and strong canine teeth common to carnivores and savages who devour raw flesh. In addition, Lombroso compared criminals' behavior to that of the mentally ill and those suffering some forms of epilepsy.

According to Lombrosian theory, crimogenic traits can be acquired through *indirect heredity*, from a "degenerate family with frequent cases of insanity, deafness, syphilis, epilepsy, and alcoholism among its members." Direct heredity—being related to a family of criminals—is the second primary cause of crime. In addition to heredity, environmental conditions can promote crime—alcoholism, lack of education, temperature swings (hot temperatures were related to violent crime), and imitation of well-publicized crimes. Thus, while Lombroso believed that inherited biological factors are the primary cause of criminality, he also recognized that environment can affect antisocial behavior.

Other Criminal Types. In his later writings, Lombroso estimated that only one-third of law violators were born criminals.[3] He identified several other antisocial types that round out the criminal universe. Of these, the most prominent is the *criminaloid,* who differs from the born criminal by a relative lack of atavistic traits. Criminaloids are drawn into crime by their greed and the desire for easy wealth and then become enmeshed in its clutches. They are the pickpockets, swindlers, con men, and smugglers that plague society. Though more intelligent and physically superior to born criminals, their contact with them in prison, coupled with a love of alcohol, causes criminaloids to develop into habitual criminals who cannot be distinguished from more serious types.

Lombroso also identified the *insane criminal,* an exaggerated born criminal who commits impulsive, obscene, and cruel acts. *Criminals by passion* are the opposite of the born criminal.[4] They are characterized by an excessive number of noble traits—integrity, sensibility, altruism, and affection. Passionate criminals may kill someone who has dishonored their family or has been unfaithful to them. In almost all cases, their crime is murder; and it is not uncommon for their suicide to follow that crime. Finally, *occasional criminals,* or *pseudo-criminals,* are those who do not seek to commit crimes but are drawn into doing so for insignificant reasons.

Lombroso's work is regarded today as historical curiosity, not scientific fact. His research methodology has been discredited. He did not use control groups from the general population to compare his results. Many of the traits he assumed to be inherited are not really genetically determined. Moreover, many of the biological features he identified could be caused by deprivation in surroundings and diet. That is, even if certain biological traits were related to crime, they might be products not of heredity but of some environmental condition such as poor nutrition or health care. Thus, it is conceivable that both criminal behavior and biological abnormality might be caused by the same unidentified environmental factor.

LOMBROSO'S CONTEMPORARIES

Lombroso's theories sparked great controversy and won him avid supporters as well as serious critics. One of his critics, Charles Goring (1870–1919), found Lombroso's methods imprecise and inadequate. In *The English Convict,* published in 1913, Goring described his use of the *biometric method* to study three thousand English convicts.[5] The biometric method applies precise statistical tests to the study of human characteristics.

Goring rejected Lombroso's claims of biological determinism. In measuring such traits as distance between the eyes, head circumference, weight, hearing, and hair and eye color, he found little difference in the physical characteristics of criminals and noncriminals. Goring discovered, however, that criminal behavior bore a significant relationship to a condition he referred to as "defective intelligence." Consequently, Goring believed that criminal behavior was inherited and could therefore best be controlled by regulating the reproduction of families exhibiting such traits as "feeblemindedness, epilepsy, insanity, and defective social instinct."[6]

A contemporary of Lombroso and Goring, Raffaele Garofalo (1852–1934) occupies a theoretical middle ground between them. On the one hand, he shared Lombroso's belief that certain physical characteristics indicate a criminal nature. For example, he stated that among criminals "a lower degree of sensibility to physical pain seems to be demonstrated by the readiness with which prisoners submit to the operation of tattooing."[7] But despite his respect for Lombroso, Garofalo argued that no proof of the existence of a criminal or delinquent type had been produced and that murderers and other serious criminals manifest many different physical traits. Garofalo explained deviant behavior with his concept of *psychic*, or *moral, anomaly*—the criminal's lack of compassionate and altruistic feelings, a lack that has an organic root. The moral anomaly, said Garofalo, is a psychic force found more frequently in so-called inferior races and transmitted through heredity. Though environment plays a role in the development of criminality, internal factors predominate. They include the "instincts" that are congenital or inherited or that are acquired in early infancy and thereafter become inseparable from the "psychic organism."

Finally, Garofalo recognized the differences among individual criminals and suggested that criminals be classified as murderers, who are totally lacking in humanity, or as lesser criminals, who in turn should be classified as violent criminals, thieves, and lascivious criminals (sexual offenders).

Enrico Ferri (1856–1929) is identified along with Lombroso and Garofalo as part of "the holy three of criminology." A student of Lombroso, Ferri believed that a number of biological, social, and organic factors caused delinquency and crime.[8]

As late as 1939, Ernest Hooton, a supporter of Lombroso, argued that the criminal was biologically and socially inferior. "In every population," Hooton concluded, "there are hereditary inferiors in mind and in body as well as physical and mental deficients. . . . Our information definitely proves that it is from the physically inferior element of the population that native born criminals from native parentage are mainly derived."[9] According to Hooton, the social and environmental factors associated with crime include low-status occupations, divorce, and lack of education. The physical factors associated with criminality are tattooing, thin hair, straight hair, red-brown hair, low sloping foreheads, mixed eye color (a sign of racial impurity), thin lips, long thin necks, and several other features. These concepts are no longer taken seriously.

THEORIES OF HEREDITY

Another early branch of biocriminology focused on human heredity and its relationship to deviant behavior. This position held that physical traits may indeed produce criminal behavior and that possession of physical abnormalities can be transmitted genetically from one generation to the next. The result is crime-producing, crimogenic families.

Advocates of this *psychobiological*, or inheritance, theory studied the family trees of criminal and delinquent offenders. They traced the activities of several generations of families believed to have an especially large number of criminal members. The most famous of these studies involved the Jukes and the Kallikaks. Richard Dugdale's book, *Crime, Pauperism, Disease and Heredity* (1910), and Arthur Estabrook's later work, *The Jukes in 1915*, traced the history of the Jukes, a family responsible for a disproportionate amount of crime. Dugdale concentrates his efforts on one branch of the family tree, the offspring of Ada Jukes, whom he labeled the "mother of criminals." Dugdale succeeded in locating over 1,000 of her descendants and found that they included 280 paupers, 60 thieves, 7 murderers, 140 criminals, 40 persons with venereal disease, 50 prostitutes, and other assorted deviants. Estabrook studied the Jukes family even more closely and accumulated data on 2,000 members. He found an additional 170 paupers, 118 criminals, 378 prostitutes, and still more assorted deviants.[10]

In an associated effort, Henry Goddard studied the offspring of Martin Kallikak, who lived during the time of the American Revolution. Kallikak first had an illegitimate son by a woman of "low-born" family and then married into a "good" family. Goddard located 480 relations of the illegitimate offspring and 496 descendants of Kallikak's marriage. The former group contained substantially more deviant and criminal members than the latter group. The immediate implication of these studies was that undesirable hereditary characteristics, even in distant relatives, were enough to condemn succeeding generations of a family to a life of criminal degeneracy. Again, criminals were seen as being "born and not made."[11]

Studies like these were taken quite seriously in their time. Of course, the writings of the heredity school are no longer considered valid. Even if more families like the Jukeses or Kallikaks could be located, this alone would not prove that psychodegeneracy is a cause of crime. Considering the thousands of family bloodlines within the United States, it can be expected that a few will produce a disproportionate number of deviants. Furthermore, many of the "best" families have produced murderers and thieves. Finally, the heredity theory provides no explanation why many members of psychodegenerate families live perfectly normal lives and become productive members of their communities.

BODY-BUILD THEORIES

Another independent branch of biocriminology was the body-build, or *somatotype*, school. Advocates of this approach argued that criminals manifest distinct physiques that make them susceptible to particular types of criminal behavior.

One of the first criminologists to link body type with delinquency was Ernst Kretschmer. He identified two distinct types, the *cyclothyme* and the *schizothyme*. Cyclothymes are spontaneous and lack sophistication. They are soft-skinned, with little muscle, and are kindhearted, tractable, sociable, talkative, and sometimes rash. Schizothymes have strong reactions and are apathetic and wayward in their nature. Their build is either tall and flat or wide, muscular, and strong. Kretschmer believed that cyclothymes were less serious delinquents and criminals and that schizothymes were more serious ones.[12]

William H. Sheldon also linked body type to delinquency.[13] In his analysis of youth, Sheldon discovered the existence of three basic body types. *Mesomorphs* have well-developed muscles and an athletic appearance. They are active, aggressive, and sometimes violent and are the most likely to become criminals. *Endomorphs* have heavy builds and are slow moving. They are known for lethargic behavior. *Ectomorphs* are tall and thin, less social, and more intellectual than the other types. Sheldon believed that most people maintained in their physical structure elements of all three body builds. He classified convicted offenders according to their body builds in a process he called *somatotyping*. Sheldon also believed there was a strong relationship between somatotype and psychiatric disorder.

Recent studies of the relationship of body build to delinquency were conducted by Sheldon Glueck and Eleanor Glueck. The Gluecks used Sheldon's three body types and added a fourth, a "balanced type" that included boys with no discernible dominant body type. In a lengthy research effort involving large samples of delinquent and nondelinquent boys, the Gluecks found that mesomorphs were disproportionately represented among delinquent boys (60.1 percent versus 30.7 percent).

Conversely, only 14.4 percent of the delinquents were ectomorphic; but 39.6 percent of the nondelinquents were ectomorphic.[14]

The Gluecks claim that a disproportionate number of delinquent youths may be mesomorphs because their strength and agility enable them to carry out the demands of the delinquent role. Endomorphs may be too slow and clumsy, and ectomorphs too fragile, to be successful delinquents. Recently, however, B. R. McCandless and his associates found no significant relationship between body build and self-reported delinquency. The link between physique and delinquency seems tenuous at best.[15]

Modern Biocriminology and Sociobiology

What seems no longer tenable at this juncture is any theory of human behavior which ignores biology and relies exclusively on socio-cultural learning. . . . Most social scientists have been wrong in their dogmatic rejection and blissful ignorance of the biological parameters of our behavior[16]

Biological explanations of crime fell out of favor in the early twentieth century. During this period, criminologists became concerned about the psychological and social factors associated with crime (discussed in this chapter and the three following chapters). The work of Lombrosians and other biocriminologists was viewed as methodologically unsound, racist, and generally invalid.

Then, in the early 1970s, spurred by the publication of *Sociobiology*, by **E. O. Wilson,** the biological basis for crime once again emerged into the limelight.[17] **Sociobiology** differs from earlier theories of behavior in that it stresses that biological and genetic conditions affect the perception and learning of social behaviors, which in turn are linked to existing environmental structures. Sociobiologists view biology, environment, and learning as mutually interdependent factors. Thus, problems in one area can be altered by efforts in another. For example, people suffering from learning disorders can be given special tutoring to improve their reading skills. In this view, then, people are biosocial organisms whose personalities and behaviors are influenced by physical as well as environmental conditions.

Influenced by sociobiology, modern biocriminologists charge that traditional criminologists ignore the biological basis for human behavior. Sociologically trained criminologists disregard all the advances made in the sciences of biology and experimental psychology. Furthermore, traditional criminologists seem content to study reports of behavior, either through surveys or self-reports, rather than to observe the actual human behaviors they are allegedly concerned with.

Modern biocriminological theory has several outstanding principles. First, it rejects assumptions that all humans are born with equal potential to learn and achieve *(equipotentiality)* and that thereafter their behavior is controlled by social forces. Whereas traditional criminologists suggest (either explicitly or implicitly) that all people are born equal and that their parents, schools, neighborhoods, and friends control their subsequent development, biocriminologists argue that no two people are alike (with rare exceptions such as identical twins) and that the combination of human genetic traits and the environment produces individual behavior patterns.

A second critical focus of modern biocriminology is its position on learning. All social behavior, including criminal behavior, is learned. Each individual organism is believed to have a unique potential for learning. The physical and social environment interact to either limit or enhance an organism's capacity for learning. People learn through a process involving the brain and central nervous system. Learning is not controlled by social interactions but by biochemistry and cellular interaction. Learning can take place only when physical changes occur in the brain.

C. Ray Jeffrey, a well-known biocriminologist, provides this model of behavior:

$$\text{Genetic code} \times \text{Environment} =$$
$$\text{Brain code} \times \text{Environment} = \text{Behavior}$$

He explains his position in this way:

> *Genetic codes and brain codes are of a biochemical nature, involving the biochemical structure of genes and of neural transmission in the brain. The type of behavior (response) exhibited by an organism depends on the nature of the environment (stimulus) and the way in which the stimulus is coded, transmitted, and decoded by the brain and nervous system. . . .*
>
> *We do not inherit behavior any more than we inherit height or intelligence. We do inherit a capacity for interaction with the environment. Sociopathy and alcoholism are not inherited, but a biochemical preparedness for such behaviors is present in the brain which, if given a certain type of environment, will produce sociopathy or alcoholism.*[18]

Jeffrey and other biocriminologists have been in the forefront of promoting biological research in criminology.

The following subsections will examine some of the more important issues in modern biocriminology.[19] First, we will look at how biochemical factors are believed to affect the learning of proper behavior patterns. Then we will turn to the relationship of brain function and crime. Finally, we will briefly consider current ideas about genetic factors and crime.

In reading this material, you should remember that biocriminology is a relatively new field. Many of the studies reported on here are case histories involving a few select subjects. Relatively few biocriminological studies involve rigorous scientific sampling, control group comparisons, and other validity checks. Therefore, rather than critiquing each study individually, it might be simpler to state that they represent conditional first attempts to study a complex phenomenon. If indeed there is a biosocial basis for crime, its undisputed proof will be for future research efforts to uncover.

BIOCHEMICAL FACTORS

One major area of biocriminological interest involves biochemical factors, such as those produced by diet, environmental contaminants, and allergies. Though drugs and alcohol have also been linked to crime, they will be discussed in a later chapter (chapter 13).

Vitamin and Mineral Deficiencies. Sociobiologists maintain that minimum levels of vitamins and minerals are needed for brain growth, especially in the early years of life. Abnormal behavior can result from lack of these necessary vitamins and minerals. If people with normal needs for vitamins do not consume food that satisfies these needs, they will suffer from *vitamin deficiency*. If people have genetic

Bio-criminologists have linked eating junk food and sweets to violent and aggressive behavior.

conditions that cause greater-than-normal needs for vitamins and minerals, they are said to suffer from *vitamin dependency.*

People with vitamin deficiency or dependency can manifest many physical, mental, and behavioral problems. They may suffer severe distortions in seeing, hearing, and other special senses. For example, alcoholics often suffer from thiamine deficiency because of their poor diets and consequently are susceptible to the serious, often fatal Wernicke-Korsakoff disease.[20]

Research studies examining the relationship between crime and vitamin deficiency/dependency have seemed to find a close link between antisocial behavior and insufficient quantities of some B vitamins—B^3 and B^6—and vitamin C. In addition, studies have purported to show that a major proportion of all schizophrenics and children with learning and behavior disorders are dependent on vitamin B^3 and B^6.[21] Leonard Hippchen, a leading biocriminologist, found that medical research has identified vitamin B^3 dependency as a major cause of hyperactivity among youth.

In another study on the effect of diet on such crime-related acts as aggression and hostility, J. Kershner and W. Hawke evaluated the effect that a high-protein, low-carbohydrate, sugarless diet, supplemented by megavitamins, had on children labeled as having behavior problems.[22] Kershner and Hawke asked the subjects' parents to evaluate their children on thirteen behavior qualities, including hyperactivity, aggression, and attention span. The researchers discovered that children had significantly improved behavior patterns and that improved diet was the most important factor in producing positive change.

Some recent efforts have continued to observe the effect of diet on behavior. For example, Stephen Schoenthaler conducted an experiment with 276 incarcerated youths to determine whether a change in the amount of sugar in their diet would have a corresponding influence on their behavior within the institutional setting.[23] In the experiment, several dietary changes were made: sweet drinks were replaced with fruit juices; table sugar was replaced with honey; breakfast cereals with high sugar content were eliminated; molasses was substituted for sugar in cooking; and so on. Schoenthaler found that these changes produced a significant reduction in disciplinary actions within the institution: the number of assaults, thefts, fights, and disobedience within the institution declined about 45 percent. It is important to note that these results were consistent when such factors as age, previous offense record, and race of the offender were considered.

These are but a few of hundreds of current studies to determine whether there is a link between biochemistry and behavior. As a whole, these efforts seem to be saying that in every segment of society there are violent, aggressive, and amoral people and that improper food, vitamin, and mineral intake may be responsible for their antisocial behavior.

Hypoglycemia. *Hypoglycemia* occurs when glucose (sugar) in the blood falls below levels necessary for normal and efficient brain functioning. The brain is sensitive to the lack of blood sugar because it is the only organ that obtains its energy solely from combustion of carbohydrates. Thus, when the brain is deprived of blood sugar, it has no alternate food supply to call upon, and its metabolism slows down, impairing its function. Symptoms of hypoglycemia include irritability, anxiety, depression, crying spells, headaches, and confusion.

Research studies have linked hypoglycemia to outbursts of antisocial behavior and violence. As early as 1943, D. Hill and W. Sargent linked murder to hypoglycemia.[24] Several studies have related assaults and fatal sexual offenses to hypoglycemic reactions.[25]

Hypoglycemia has also been connected with a syndrome characterized by aggressive and assaultive behavior, glucose disturbance, and brain dysfunction. Studies of jailed inmates and prison inmate populations have found a higher than normal level of hypoglycemia.[26]

Testosterone. *Testosterone* is a principal male steroid hormone. It controls secondary sex characteristics such as facial hair and voice timbre in males. Evidence suggests that its production levels may be strongly related to criminal aggressiveness in human males. L. E. Kreuz and R. M. Rose found in a sample of inmates that testosterone levels were higher in men who committed violent crimes than in the other prisoners, though results of comparisons with a noncriminal control group were nonsignificant.[27] Nonetheless, other studies, especially those by Richard Rada, could not distinguish between violent and nonviolent offenders on the basis of their testosterone levels.[28]

Despite the uncertainty of evidence linking testosterone to crime, drugs decreasing testosterone levels have been used to treat male sex offenders. Sarnoff Mednick and Jan Volavka warn that the long-term side effects of such treatment are still problematic.[29] In a similar vein, administration of the female hormone *estrogen* to sexually active men has led to a decrease in their sexual potency. Consequently, estrogen and another female hormone, progesterone, have also been used to manage sex offenders.[30]

Allergies. Sociologists are also concerned with the effect of cerebral allergies and neuroallergies on criminal and otherwise deviant behavior. In general, allergies are defined as unusual or excessive reactions of the body to a foreign substance.[31] For example, hay fever is an allergic reaction caused when pollen cells enter the body and are fought or neutralized by the body's natural defenses. The result of the battle is itching, red eyes, and active sinuses. *Cerebral allergies* cause an excessive reaction of the brain, whereas *neuroallergies* affect the nervous system.

Neuroallergies and cerebral allergies are believed to cause the allergic person to produce enzymes that attack wholesome foods as if they were dangerous to the body.[32] They may also cause swelling of the brain, which can produce mental, emotional, and behavioral problems including hyperemotionality, aggressiveness, and violent behavior. Neuroallergy and cerebral allergy problems have also been linked to hyperactivity in children, which may portend antisocial behavior and the labeling of children as potential delinquents. The foods most commonly involved in producing such allergies are cow's milk, wheat, corn, chocolate, citrus, and eggs; however, about three hundred other foods have been identified as allergens.

The potential seriousness of the problem has been raised by studies linking the average consumption of one suspected cerebral allergen—corn—to cross-national homicide rates.[33]

Environmental Contaminants. Recently, biocriminologists have begun to focus on the effects of environmental contaminants on behavior. Increasing amounts of lead, copper, cadmium, mercury, and inorganic gases such as chlorine and nitrogen dioxide have been found in the ecosystem. At high levels, these substances can cause severe illness or death; at more moderate levels, they have been linked to emotional and behavioral disorders.[34]

Some studies have linked food additives to crime. For example, C. Hawley and R. E. Buckley claim that food dyes and artificial colors and flavors can produce hostile, impulsive, and otherwise antisocial behavior in youths.[35]

Other research efforts have been directed at measuring the influence of lead on youths' behavior. For example, in one study of hyperactive children who manifested conduct problems and other antisocial behavior, Oliver David and his associates found that lead in the bloodstream may have had an important role in explaining the onset of the behavior.[36]

Lighting may be another important environmental influence on antisocial behavior. Research projects have suggested that radiation from artificial light sources such as fluorescent tubes and television sets may produce antisocial, aggressive behavior.[37]

NEUROPHYSIOLOGICAL STUDIES

Another area of sociobiology of particular interest to criminology is *neurophysiology*, or the study of brain activity. In most instances, the research focus has been on the *electroencephalogram* (EEG), which measures the electronic pulses of the brain. The EEG has been used to compare patterns of activity found in criminal and noncriminal populations. Yet, this is only one aspect of neurocriminology. This section will discuss various brain function patterns that have been related to criminality.

Minimal Brain Dysfunction. *Minimal brain dysfunction* (MBD) is related to an abnormality in cerebral structure. It has been defined as abruptly appearing, maladaptive behavior that interrupts the lifestyle and life flow of an individual. In its most serious form, MBD has been linked to serious antisocial acts, an imbalance in the urge-control mechanisms of the brain, and chemical abnormality. Included within the category of minimal brain dysfunction are several abnormal behavior patterns, including dyslexia, visual perception problems, hyperactivity, poor attention span, temper tantrums, and aggressiveness.

One type of minimal brain dysfunction that has been of great concern to biocriminologists manifests itself through episodic periods of explosive rage. This form of the disorder is considered an important cause of such behavior as wife beating, child abuse, suicide, aggressiveness, and motiveless homicide. One perplexing feature of this syndrome is that people who are afflicted with it often maintain warm and pleasant personalities between episodes of violence.

Some studies have attempted to measure the presence of minimal brain dysfunction in offender populations. R. D. Robin and his associates found that 60 percent of a sample of suicidal adolescents exhibited brain dysfunction on psychological tests.[38] Similarly, R. R. Monroe found that almost all prison subjects he tested manifested significant neurophysiologic dysfunction.[39] L. T. Yeudall studied sixty criminal patients and found that they were characterized by lateral brain dysfunction of the dominant hemisphere of the brain. His data helped him predict with 95-percent accuracy the recidivism of violent criminals.[40]

Of interest to both educators and criminologists is the relationship between MBD and the so-called learning-disabled child. Research has shown that although *learning-disabled* (LD) children violate the law at the same rate as non-LD children, they are overrepresented in official arrest and juvenile court statistics.[41]

EEG Abnormality. As explained earlier, the electroencephalogram (EEG) records the electrical impulses given off by the brain. Measurements of the EEG reflect the activity of neurons located in the cerebral cortex. The rhythmic nature of this brain activity is determined by mechanisms that involve subcortical structures, primarily the thalmus portion of the brain. The EEG represents a signal composed of various rhythms and transient electrical discharges, commonly called brain waves, which can be recorded by electrodes placed on the scalp. The frequency is given in cycles per second, measured in hertz (Hz), and usually ranges from 0.5 to 30 Hz.

In what is considered the most significant investigation of EEG abnormality and crime, a randomly selected group of 335 violent delinquents was divided into those who were habitually violent and those who had committed a single violent act. While 65 percent of the habitually aggressive had abnormal EEG recordings, only 24 percent of the second group had recordings that deviated from the norm. When the records of individuals who had had brain damage, were mentally retarded, or were epileptic were removed from the sample, the percentage of abnormality among boys who had committed a solitary violent crime was the same as that of the general population, about 12 percent. However, the habitually aggressive subjects still showed 57-percent abnormality.[42]

Other research efforts have linked abnormal EEG recordings to antisocial behavior in children. Although about 5 to 15 percent of normal youths have abnormal EEG readings, about 50 to 60 percent of those with behavior disorders display abnormal recordings. In studies of problem children, about half were found to have abnormal EEG activity. Behaviors highly correlated with abnormal EEG included poor impulse control, inadequate social adaptation, hostility, temper tantrums, and destructiveness.[43]

Studies of adults have associated slow and bilateral brain waves with hostile, hypercritical, irritable, nonconforming, and impulsive behavior. Psychiatric patients with EEG abnormalities have been reported to be highly combative and to suffer episodes of rage. Studies of murderers have shown that a disproportionate number manifest abnormal EEG rates.[44]

There is evidence that abnormal EEG readings are linked to violent behavior, but a great many studies have found little relationship between the two.[45] In addition, research that concludes that abnormal EEG readings are associated with violence has lacked the precision needed to give it predictive value. For example, even if half of all violence-prone people had abnormal EEG ratings, there would still be too many nonviolent people with abnormal EEGs for researchers to conclude that EEG abnormality was a cause of violence.

Other Brain Dysfunctions. It is possible that brain disease can also be related to violent crime. The presence of brain tumors has been linked to a wide variety of psychological problems, including personality changes, hallucinations, and psychotic episodes. There is evidence that people with tumors are prone to depression, irritability, temper outbursts, and even homicidal attacks.[46]

Clinical case studies of patients suffering from brain tumors indicate that they may undergo behavior changes so great that previously docile people attempt to seriously harm their families and friends; when the tumor is removed, their behavior returns to normal.[47]

One well-known case involved Charles Whitman, who, after killing his wife and his mother, barricaded himself in a tower at the University of Texas with a high-powered rifle and proceeded to kill fourteen people and wound twenty-four others before he was killed by police. An autopsy revealed that Whitman suffered from a malignant infiltrating tumor. Whitman had previously experienced uncontrollable urges to kill and had actually gone to a psychiatrist seeking help for his problems. He kept careful notes documenting his feelings and his inability to control his homicidal urges, and left instructions for his estate to be given to a mental health foundation so it could study mental problems such as his. Nevertheless, it is still uncertain whether Whitman's tumor actually caused his behavior.[48]

In addition to brain tumors, head injuries caused by accidents such as falls or auto crashes have been linked to personality reversals marked by outbursts of antisocial and violent behavior. A variety of central nervous system diseases including cerebral arteriosclerosis, epilepsy, senile dementia, Korsakoff's syndrome, and Huntington's corea have also been associated with memory deficiency, orientation loss, and affective (emotional) disturbances dominated by rage, anger, and increased irritability.[49]

GENETIC INFLUENCES

The earliest biocriminological studies stressed the genetic basis of criminality. Today, biocriminologists are still concerned with the role heredity plays in producing crime-prone people. Evidence exists that animals can be bred to have aggressive traits; pit bulldogs, fighting bulls, and fighting cocks have been selectively mated to produce superior predators. Of course, no similar data are available for people, but some studies have attempted to document genetic factors associated with criminality. The most important of these studies are examined next.

Chromosome Studies: The XYY Controversy. Chromosomes—microscopic structures contained in cell nuclei—carry the basic genetic material, genes. Human beings normally have forty-six chromosomes, of which forty-four determine the shape and structure of the body and two determine sex. The typical male chromosome contingent is recorded as 46, XY; and the female, as 46, XX.[50]

Sometimes an individual possesses greater or fewer than the normal chromosome complement because of problems encountered soon after the onset of life. Of concern are males who have an extra Y chromosome—the 47, XYY syndrome. Males can also possess an extra X chromosome (47, XXY), but this condition is of less importance to criminology.

Several early studies on the XYY phenomenon reported XYY males to be very tall individuals with a disproportionate inclination to commit crimes of violence.[51] Surveys of tall men in institutions for the mentally ill and prisons suggested that the rate of persons found to have an extra Y chromosome was greater than the rate estimated for the population at large.[52] The XYY syndrome received a great deal of publicity when Richard Speck, the convicted killer of eight nurses in Chicago, was said to be an XYY. There was much public concern that all XYYs were potential killers and should be closely controlled. Civil libertarians expressed fear that all XYYs could be labeled dangerous and violent regardless of whether they had engaged in violent activities.[53] (Later research found that Speck did not actually have an extra Y chromosome.)

The most current research has cast doubt on the XYY hypothesis. Biocriminologists have found that the proportion of XYYs in the prison population is not significantly higher than in the population at large (about 1 in 700 male births). However, some evidence shows that the number of XYY males in secure mental hospitals is higher than would be expected by chance alone.[54]

A cohort study was recently conducted in Denmark in which the cohort consisted of all the 31,436 men born in Copenhagen in the years 1944 through 1947.[55] All tall men over 184 centimeters—about 6 feet—were visited in their homes and asked to give blood samples and undergo chromosome analysis. Twelve XYY men were identified. It was found that they had little or no recorded evidence of violent behavior. The XYYs did engage in more criminal behavior than the non-XYY males of their height, age, and class; and there was some evidence that their EEG patterns were somewhat abnormal; but the fact that they had not engaged in violence seriously damaged the hypothesized association of XYY and violence. Though further research is being conducted on the link between XYY and violence, the issue has become less important.

Twin Studies. If in fact inherited traits cause criminal behaviors, it should be expected that twins would be quite similar in their antisocial activities. However, since twins are usually brought up in the same household and exposed to the same set of social conditions, it would be difficult to determine whether their behavior was a result of biological, sociological, or psychological conditions. Biocriminologists have tried to overcome this dilemma by comparing identical, monozygotic (MZ) twins with fraternal, dizygotic (DZ) twins of the same sex.[56] MZ twins are genetically identical, while DZ twins have only half their genes in common. If heredity does determine criminal behavior, we should expect that MZ twins would be much more similar in their antisocial activities than DZ twins.

The earliest studies conducted on the behavior of twins detected a significant relationship between the criminal activities of MZ twins and a much lower association between those of DZ twins. In a review of relevant studies conducted between 1929 and 1961, Sarnoff Mednick and Jan Volavka found that, overall, 60 percent of MZ twins shared criminal behavior patterns (if one twin was criminal, so was the other), while only 30 percent of DZ twins were similarly related.[57] These findings may be viewed as powerful evidence that a genetic basis for criminality exists.

More recent studies have supported these basic findings, though the level of association found between the behaviors of MZ twins is somewhat lower than previously thought. For example, Karl Christiansen studied 3,586 male twin pairs and found a 52-percent concordance for MZ pairs and a 22-percent concordance for DZ pairs. This result suggests that the identical MZ twins may share a genetic characteristic that increases the risk of their engaging in criminality.[58]

Similarly, David Rowe and D. Wayne Osgood analyzed the factors that influence the correlation between self-reported delinquency and delinquency of friends in a sample of twin pairs.[59] They evaluated three distinct factors: genetic variations, common environmental influences that affect family members equally, and specific environmental factors that influence the individual uniquely. They found that genetic influences actually explain greater variation in delinquency rates than the other variables. However, this does not mean that delinquents are genetically inferior or damaged. For example, the genetic component could be manifested through intelligence (IQ), and thus linked to delinquency through school failure and academic underachievement.

Can we conclude from this evidence that criminality is genetically predetermined? Mednick and Volavka offer several explanations for the MZ twins' higher criminality relationship. Say, for example, that a physical characteristic such as height were related to committing crimes; MZ twins would more likely both be tall than DZ twins, since height is genetically transmitted. Or, say that alcohol addiction increased the probability that someone would engage in antisocial behavior; it is possible that alcohol addiction is related to genetic factors more likely to be shared by MZ twins than by DZ twins. Put another way, a relationship between genetics and criminality might be accomplished through the influence of some undisclosed intervening variable. However, the authors conclude that:

> Despite the limitations of the twin method, the results of these studies are compatible with the hypothesis that genetic factors account for some of the variance associated with antisocial behavior.[60]

Adoption Studies. Another approach that has been used to determine whether heredity influences criminality has focused on the behavior of adopted children. The logic behind this line of inquiry is that if children's behavior is more similar to that of their biological parents than to that of their adoptive parents, then the idea of a genetic basis for criminality would be supported. If, on the other hand, adoptees are more similar to their adoptive parents than their biological parents, an environmental basis for crime would seem more valid.

Several studies indicate that some relationship may exist between biological parents' behavior and the behavior of their children, even when their contact has been infrequent. In one major study, Barry Hutchings and Sarnoff Mednick analyzed 1,145 male adoptees born in Copenhagen, Denmark between 1927 and 1941; of these, 185 had criminal records.[61] After following up on 143 of the criminal adoptees and matching them with a control group of 143 noncriminal adoptees, Hutchings and Mednick found that the criminality of the biological father was a strong predictor of the child's criminal behavior. Moreover, the researchers found that when *both* the biological and the adoptive father were criminal, the probability that the youth would engage in criminal behavior greatly expanded. Consequently, the authors concluded that both biological and environmental factors influence crime. These results were duplicated in studies by Sarnoff Mednick and his associates, using a sample of 14,427 adoptees born in Denmark between 1924 and 1947.[62]

Findings from twin and adoption studies have not refuted the hypothesis that there is some genetic basis to criminality. Although the evidence is not conclusive, it has been used to give preliminary support to the association of heredity, environment, and criminality.

EVALUATION OF THE BIOLOGICAL PERSPECTIVE

Biological explanations of crime raise some challenging questions for criminology. These theories have been challenged by critics, who suggest they are racist and dysfunctional. If biology can explain the cause of street crimes such as assault, murder, or rape, the argument goes, and if the poor and minority group members commit a disproportionate number of such acts, then by implication biological theory says that members of these groups are biologically different or inferior. Biological theory is challenged because it seemingly ignores the effect of a crime-producing social environment. Furthermore, biological theory seems to divide people into criminals and noncriminals on the basis of their physical makeup, and ignores that almost everyone has engaged in some type of illegal activity at some time.

Modern biocriminologists, however, believe that their approach should not be confused with Lombrosian, deterministic biology. Rather than suggest that there are born criminals and noncriminals, they maintain that some people carry within them the potential to be violent or antisocial and that environmental conditions can sometimes trigger antisocial responses. This would explain why some otherwise law-abiding citizens engage in a single, seemingly unexplainable antisocial act and, conversely, why some people with long criminal careers often engage in conventional behavior.

Biological explanations may also account in part for cultural discrepancies in crime rates. The environment is viewed as a triggering mechanism; and it is possible that people living in high-poverty, high-crime inner-city areas are more likely to experience crime-producing stimuli than people living in more affluent neighborhoods. Moreover, wealthier citizens are better equipped to compensate for adverse biological conditions by diet, treatment, medication, and education. For example, in a wealthy school district, parents of a child who is suffering from a minimal brain dysfunction may avail themselves of special education and treatment programs unavailable in less affluent districts.

The major drawback to the biological perspective, as indicated earlier, is lack of adequate empirical testing. In most research efforts, sample sizes are relatively small and poorly chosen. Even more serious is the fact that a great deal of biocriminological research is conducted with samples of adjudicated offenders who have been placed in clinical treatment settings. Thus, we can never be sure whether findings apply only to offenders who have been convicted of crimes and placed in treatment or to the population of criminals as a whole. Consequently, the true relationship being measured could be that between biological traits and arrest or conviction, not between biological traits and criminality. Thus, a great deal more research is needed if biological explanations of crime are to be considered truly

Crime and Human Nature

In their book, *Crime and Human Nature*, James Q. Wilson and Richard Herrnstein synthesize elements of classical theory with biological and psychological concepts. In this controversial work they propose a theory of criminal behavior which holds that people choose criminal solutions when they believe that the rewards (material gain, peer approval, etc.) for their actions will outweigh any negative consequences (punishment, pangs of conscience, disapproval of onlookers, and so on). Various factors influence the decision to commit crime: the strength of the rewards, their certainty or delay, and the way rewards are valued and reinforced. But in general, Wilson and Herrnstein assume that criminal behavior is controlled by its consequences.

Wilson and Herrnstein argue that inherited constitutional factors influence the decision to commit crime. More specifically, they find that such individual factors as a low IQ, an abnormal body-type, and an impulsive personality predispose a person to choose criminal behaviors. Similarly, they agree with the evidence that criminal behavior tendencies are inherited through genetic transference. In sum, the authors believe that the factors predicting criminal behavior are genetic, and it follows that the decision to choose crime is also influenced by heredity.

Wilson and Herrnstein do not ignore social factors, however. They find that a poor and disrupted home life is a strong predictor of criminal behavior, whereas educational and community experiences have a more peripheral effect. Nonetheless, they believe that social variables have only a secondary or contributing influence on crime. People who have inherited impulsive and aggressive personality traits and limited intelligence will choose to commit crime. Since these tendencies are inherited it is no surprise that crime sometimes runs in families.

Wilson and Herrnstein believe that punishment can help convince an offender not to commit crime; but that the best defense to crime would be to help families reaffirm a sense of morality to their children. Crime-producing physical traits can be counteracted by a family life that stresses conventional values and teaches that crime is counterproductive.

Critics will be quick to point out that most studies showing that constitutional factors predispose people to commit crime are flawed, but *Crime and Human Behavior* should have a major effect on the criminological community.

DISCUSSION QUESTIONS:

1. Do you believe that crime can be inherited?
2. Do criminals have unique physical and mental characteristics?

SOURCE. James Q. Wilson and Richard Herrnstein, *Crime and Human Behavior* (New York: Simon and Schuster, 1985).

---

valid. However, as the following Close-Up, "Crime and Human Nature", suggests, biocriminology still has some influential supporters among leading criminologists.

Psychological Theory of Crime

Psychologists, psychiatrists, and other mental health professionals have long played an active role in formulating criminological theory. In their quest to understand and treat all varieties of abnormal mental conditions, psychologists have encountered clients whose behavior falls within categories society has labeled criminal, deviant, violent, and antisocial. Since psychologists view all human behavior as a function of some mental process, it is not surprising that they would conclude that many criminal behaviors can be traced to personality disturbances. However, not even the staunchest supporter of psychological theory would suggest that all criminals are mentally ill, psychotic, psychopathic, or insane. Though some criminals are considered to possess highly disturbed personalities and therefore are not to be held legally responsible for their criminal activities, these criminals make up only a small percentage of offenders. Psychologists do, however, trace the onset of criminality to a person's mental process and, therefore, argue that criminologists will never understand the cause of criminality unless they determine the psychological processes that motivate it.

EARLY PSYCHOLOGICAL THEORY

The earliest "psychological" view was that criminals were possessed by evil spirits or demons. Later theories suggested that mental illness and insanity were inherited and that deviants were inherently mentally damaged by reason of their inferior genetic makeup.

An early pioneer of the concept of insanity was the English physician Henry Maudsley (1835–1918). Maudsley believed that insanity and criminal behavior were strongly linked: "Crime is a sort of outlet in which their unsound tendencies are discharged; they would go mad if they were not criminals, and they do not go mad because they are criminals."[63]

Maudsley was a firm believer that criminal-producing mental traits are inherited, leading to long lines of crime-prone **mental degenerates.** He stated that people who become criminals do not have the "aptitude of the higher industrial classes" and that they are "deficient in the power of attention . . . have bad memories and make slow progress in learning." Furthermore, Maudsley found criminals to be "inherently vicious," to "steal and lie with a skill hard to believe," to be "hopeless pupils," and to come from families in which insanity or some allied condition prevailed. In sum, Maudsley believed insanity to be a condition, passed from one generation to the next, that rendered the affected incapable of controlling their aggressive behavior.

Today, most psychologists do not believe that insanity is inherited. When they study crime, psychocriminologists usually address basic issues of human behavior: Why do people engage in violence and aggression? Is there such a thing as a criminal personality? Do childhood experiences influence adult criminality? However, as we shall see, there is by no means unanimity among psychologists over the answers to these questions.[64] Some psychologists view antisocial behavior from a **psychoanalytic perspective**—their focus is on early childhood experience and its effect on personality. Others use **cognitive theory** to explain crime—their view is that people's moral development is the key to understanding behavior. Behaviorists stress **social learning** and **behavior modeling** as the keys to criminality. **Psychobiologists** are concerned with the links among biological processes, human personality, and criminality. The following sections will review each of these perspectives independently.

PSYCHOANALYTIC PERSPECTIVE: SIGMUND FREUD

Psychoanalytic psychology is the creation of the Viennese doctor **Sigmund Freud** (1856–1939). Psychoanalysis has become the most well-known and often-used theory of personality development.[65] Though many mental health professionals still use Freud's approach, there have been numerous efforts by his successors to expand, contradict, and reassess his pioneering concepts.

Structure of Mind and Personality. According to Freudian theory, the human mind performs three separate functions. The *conscious* mind is the aspect of the mind that people are most aware of—hunger, pain, thirst, desire. The *preconscious* mind contains elements of experiences that are out of awareness but can be brought back to consciousness at any time—memories, experiences. The *unconscious* part of the mind contains biological desires and urges that cannot readily be experienced as thoughts. Part of the unconscious contains feelings about sex and hostility, which people keep below the surface of consciousness by a process called **repression.**

Freud also postulated a three-part structure for the human personality. The *id*, the primitive part of people's mental makeup, is present at birth. It represents unconscious biological drives for sex, food, and other life-sustaining necessities. The id follows the *pleasure principle*—it requires instant gratification without concern for the rights of others.

The *ego* develops early in life, when an infant begins to learn that its wishes cannot be instantly gratified. The ego is that part of the personality that compensates for the demands of the id by helping people guide their actions to remain within the boundaries of social convention. The ego is guided by the *reality principle*—it takes into account what is practical and conventional by societal standards.

The *superego* develops as a result of incorporating within the personality the moral standards and values of parents, community, and significant others. It is the moral aspect of people's personalities; it passes judgments on their behavior.

All three parts of the personality operate to control behavior. People's id might demand pleasures, such as premarital sex; the superego makes them feel guilty for these desires; the ego works out a compromise—they can engage in some sexual activities, but they should not go "too far" or else they may "get in trouble."

Development. Freud postulates that the most basic human drive, or instinct, present at birth is *Eros*, the instinct to preserve and create life. Eros is expressed sexually. Consequently, very early in their development, humans experience sexuality, which is expressed in the seeking of pleasure through various parts of the body. During the first year of life, a child attains pleasure by sucking and biting; Freud called this the *oral stage*. During the second and third years of life, the focus of sexual attention is on the elimination of bodily wastes—the *anal stage*. The *phallic stage* occurs during the third year of life; children now focus their attention on their genitals. Males begin to have sexual feelings for their mother (the Oedipus complex) and girls for their fathers (the Electra complex). *Latency* begins at age six; during this period, feelings of sexuality are repressed until the *genital stage* begins at puberty; this marks the beginning of adult sexuality.

If conflicts are encountered during any of the psychosexual stages of development, a person can become **fixated** at that point. The person will as an adult exhibit behavior traits characteristic of those encountered during infantile sexual development. For example, an infant who does not receive enough oral gratification during the first year of life is likely as an adult to engage in such oral behavior as smoking, drinking, or drug abuse or to be clinging and dependent in personal relationships. Thus, the root of adult behavior problems can be traced to problems developed in the earliest years of life.

POST-FREUDIAN PSYCHOANALYTIC THEORY

Freud's view of the mind and personality has influenced several competing versions of psychoanalytic theory.[66] For example, **Carl Jung** (1875–1961), one of Freud's inner circle, developed *analytical psychology*. According to Jungian theory, an important aspect of the human psychic structure is the *collective unconscious*. This comes to people by way of heredity and contains primitive images, a sort of racial memory of the past experience of the human species. Although these primitive images, or *archetypes*, remain unconscious, they influence human thought and emotion.

Alfred Adler (1870–1937) is credited with being the founder of *individual psychology*. Adler coined the term **inferiority complex.** Most people have feelings of inferiority, Adler claimed, and compensate for them with a drive for superiority. Adler recognized that self-awareness plays an important part in personality and that people have a *creative self*, exhibited by the desire to overcome obstacles and develop individual potential.

Erik Erikson's (1902–1984) theory of *psychosocial development* holds that humans go through eight stages of ego development. From birth to one year, the infants learn to trust their mothers and become acclimated to their surroundings. Later stages find individuals trying to master fundamental skills, learning careers, becoming committed to love, being creative, and, finally, exhibiting wisdom and dignity. Erikson identified the **identity crisis**—a period of serious personal questioning people undertake in an effort to determine their own values and sense of direction.

PSYCHOANALYSIS AND CRIMINAL BEHAVIOR

Freud did not spend much time theorizing about crime. He did link criminality to an unconscious sense of guilt a person retains because of his childhood Oedipus complex. He states:

> *In many criminals, especially youthful ones, it is possible to detect a very powerful sense of guilt which existed before the crime, and is therefore not its result but its motive. It is as if it was a relief to be able to fasten the unconscious sense of guilt onto something real and immediate.*[67]

However, following Freud, psychoanalysts have generally linked criminality to abnormal mental states produced by early childhood trauma.

Within classical Freudian theory, two mental conditions are thought to produce antisocial activity. A *neurosis* is a disorder characterized by extreme anxiety. It represents the feeling that repressed, unacceptable impulses may break through and take control. A more extreme form of mental disturbance is *psychosis*, abnormal behavior that impairs everyday functioning. Psychosis occurs when the primitive id functions take control of the personality.

Psychotics are people who manifest disturbances of thought, mood, and behavior. There are various specific psychotic disorders; of those, **schizophrenia** is perhaps most often linked to crime. Schizophrenics exhibit illogical and incoherent thought processes and a lack of insight into their behavior. They may experience delusions and hallucinate. For example, they may see themselves as agents of the devil, avenging angels, or the recipients of messages from animals and plants. David Berkowitz, the "Son of Sam" or "44-calibre killer," exhibited these traits. *Paranoid schizophrenics* suffer complex behavior delusions involving wrong-doing or persecution—they think everyone is out to get them.

The psychoanalyst whose work is most closely associated with using these concepts to explain criminality is **August Aichorn**.[68] After examining many delinquent youths, this Viennese doctor concluded that societal stress, though damaging, could not alone result in a life of crime unless a predisposition existed that prepared youths psychologically for antisocial acts. He labeled this state *latent delinquency*. Latent delinquency is found in youngsters whose personality requires them (1) to seek immediate gratification (to act impulsively), (2) to consider satisfaction of their personal needs more important than relating to others, and (3) to satisfy instinctive urges without consideration of right and wrong (that is, they lack guilt).

Psychoanalyst David Abrahamsen views the criminal as an id-dominated person who suffers from the inability to control impulsive, pleasure seeking drives.[69] Perhaps because they suffered unhappy experiences in childhood, or had families who could not provide proper love and care, criminals suffer from weak or damaged egos that make them unable to cope with conventional society. In its most extreme form, criminality may be viewed as a form of psychosis that prevents offenders from appreciating the feelings of their victims or controlling their own impulsive needs for gratification.

Psychiatrist Seymour Halleck views criminality as a manifestation of feelings of oppression and the inability of people to do much about it. Criminality actually allows troubled people to survive by producing positive psychic results: it helps them to feel free and independent, it gives them the possibility of excitement and the chance to use their skills and imagination, it provides them with the promise of positive gain, it allows them to blame others for their predicament (for example, the police), and it gives them a chance to rationalize their sense of failure ("If I hadn't gotten into trouble, I could have been a success").[70]

The views of psychoanalysts like Abrahamsen and Halleck are supported by research which shows that many serious, violent offenders suffer from some sort of personality disturbance. James Sorrells' well-known study of juvenile murderers, "Kids Who Kill," found that many homicidal youths could be described in such terms as "overtly hostile," "explosive or volatile," "anxious," and "depressed."[71] Likewise, in a recent study of forty-five males accused of murder, Richard Rosner and his associates found that 75 percent could be classified as having some mental illness, including schizophrenia.[72] However, as the following Close-Up entitled "Crime and Mental Disorder" suggests, there is little evidence that mentally ill people are generally violent or criminal.

It is evident from these statements that the psychoanalytic model of the criminal offender depicts an aggressive, frustrated person dominated by events that occurred early in childhood.

COGNITIVE THEORY

Cognitive psychologists are concerned with people's mental processes—how they perceive and mentally represent the world they live in. They study problem solving, idea formation, dreams, and so on. The leading developers of this school were Wilhelm Wundt (1832–1920), Edward Titchener (1867–1927), and William James (1842–1920). The cognitive perspective contains several subgroups. *Gestalt* psychology is concerned with perception of the world in whole units rather than individual pieces. The *moral and intellectual development* branch is concerned with how adults morally represent and reason about the world. *Humanistic psychology* stresses self-awareness and "getting in touch with feelings."

Moral and Intellectual Development Theory. The moral and intellectual development branch of cognitive psychology is perhaps the most important for criminological theory. Jean Piaget (1896–1980), the founder of this approach, hypothesized that people's reasoning processes develop in an orderly fashion, beginning at birth and continuing until they are twelve years old and older.[73] At first, during the *sensormotor stage*, children respond to the environment in a simple manner, seeking interesting objects and developing their reflexes. By the fourth

Crime and Mental Disorder

The psychoanalytic perspective links serious, violent criminal behavior to psychosis. Ac- cording to this view, people suffering from schizophrenia, paranoia, and so on will be more likely to commit violent, aggressive crimes. Conversely, a disproportionate number of people who commit violent crimes are probably suffering from some type of severe personality disturbance. Just how accurate is this view? That is, are the mentally ill more likely to become involved in crime than the mentally sound?

To answer this question, psychologists John Monahan and Henry Steadman reviewed the existing body of lit- erature on the relationship between mental disorder and crime. They found that the rate of mental disorder in a population must be thought of as either being the *true rate* (or the percentage of the population mentally ill) or the *treated rate* (the percentage of the population under treatment for mental illness). Some of the findings are summarized below.

There are two kinds of studies of the true and treated rates of crime and mental disorder. The first kind looks at "pure" cases, in which rates of mental disorder are computed for groups of criminals or crime rates are computed for groups of the mentally disordered. That is, the study covers people who are "purely" in one category and inquires as to those who also fall into the other category.

The second kind of study considers "mixed" cases— persons who are being treated as both criminal and

mentally disordered. These persons fall into various le- gal categories of "mentally disordered offenders."

PURE CASES OF CRIMINAL BEHAVIOR OR MENTAL DISORDER

Findings from the available research on the true and treated rates of mental disorder among criminals—and the true and treated rates of crime among the disor- dered—are summarized in table A.

The scant research into mental disorder among per- sons who have been arrested ("true criminals") sug- gests that their rates of disorder are no higher than those of the general American population of comparable social class.

Several surveys have been made of the rates of men- tal disorder among persons in jails and prisons ("treated criminals"). These studies have reported rates of serious mental disorder ranging from 1 to 7 percent, whereas

TABLE A Studies of pure cases of criminal behavior or mental disorder

Relationship at issue	Amount of evidence	Findings compared with matched groups in the general population
True disorder among true criminals	Little	No higher
True crime among truly disordered	None	—
True crime among treated disordered	Much	No higher
Treated disorder among true criminals	None	—
True disorder among treated criminals	Much	No higher
Treated crime among truly disordered	None	—
Treated disorder among treated criminals	Little	No comparison data
Treated crime among treated disordered	Little	Unclear

and final stage, the *formal operations stage*, they have developed into mature adults who can use logic and abstract thought.

Lawrence Kohlberg has applied the concept of moral development to issues in criminology.[74] He suggests that people travel through stages of moral development, during which their decisions and judgments on issues of right and wrong are made for different reasons. It is possible that serious offenders have a moral orientation that differs from that of law-abiding citizens. Kohlberg's stages of development are:

STAGE 1—Right is obedience to power and avoidance of punishment.
STAGE 2—Right is taking responsibility for oneself, meeting one's own needs, and leaving to others the responsibility for themselves.

rates of less severe mental disorders range from 15 to 20 percent. (Such questionable categories as sociopathy, alcoholism, and drug addiction are not included in these figures.) When comparing these rates with those found in surveys of the general population, it is necessary to recognize that jail and prison inmates are disproportionately persons of lower social class, and that such persons have disproportionately high rates of mental disorder. The conclusion that emerges: the rate of mental disorder among inmate populations does not exceed the rate of mental disorder among groups of comparable social class in the general community.

The following conclusions from the research appear justified:

- The arrest rate of mentally disordered offenders after their release from mental hospitals is very similar to the arrest rate of pure mental patients with a comparable prehospital arrest record.
- It is questionable how many persons legally adjudicated to be mentally disordered offenders are suffering from true mental disorder. The most frequent diagnosis given to mentally disordered sex offenders, for example, is "sexual deviation."
- The subsequent conviction rate of mentally disordered offenders (based on the little data that exist) is consistent with what one would predict from a knowledge of their criminal history and demographic characteristics.
- Likewise, the factors relating to the rehospitalization of pure mental patients (e.g., the number of times they have been hospitalized in the past) also seem to relate to the rehospitalization of mentally disordered offenders.

MIXED CASES OF CRIMINAL BEHAVIOR AND MENTAL DISORDER

Studies of cases of persons treated simultaneously for criminal behavior and mental disorder lead to the conclusion that rates of crime and mental disorder are about what one would expect from a knowledge of their demographic characteristics and their experience with the mental health and criminal justice systems.

"Mentally disordered offenders" is an umbrella term, covering four legal categories: (1) persons judged incompetent to stand trial, (2) persons found not guilty by reason of insanity, (3) mentally disordered sex offenders, and (4) persons transferred from prison to a mental hospital.

IMPLICATIONS

The correlates of crime among the mentally disordered appear to be the same as the correlates of crime among any other group: age, gender, race, social class, and prior criminality. Likewise, the correlates of mental disorder among criminal offenders appear to be the same as those in other populations: age, social class, and previous disorder. Populations characterized by the correlates of both crime and mental disorder (e.g., low social class) can be expected to show high rates of both, and they do.

It does appear from the data that, if one could excise approximately half the population of state mental hospitals (those with prior arrest records), then the remaining patients, on their release, would be no more criminal than the rest of us. However, the data do not reveal how this can be done without transferring many of these people to jails and prisons, and thereby aggravating the problems of those institutions.

In sum, Monahan and Steadman found little evidence that the mentally ill are any more criminal than the rest of society.

DISCUSSION QUESTIONS

1. Does the finding that crime rates among the mentally ill are equivalent to those of the general population invalidate psychoanalytic theory?
2. Should a person who is evaluated as mentally ill by clinical personnel but legally sane under the law be responsible for their criminal actions?

SOURCE. Adapted from John Monahan and Henry Steadman, *Crime and Mental Disorder*. National Institute of Justice Research in Brief, Washington, D.C., September 1984. Footnotes omitted.

STAGE 3—Right is being good in the sense of having good motives, having concern for others, and "putting yourself in the other person's shoes."

STAGE 4—Right is maintaining the rules of a society and serving the welfare of the group or society.

STAGE 5—Right is based on recognized individual rights within a society with agreed-upon rules—a social contract.

STAGE 6—Right is an assumed obligation to principles applying to all humankind, principles of justice, equality, and respect for human personality.

Kohlberg classifies people according to the stage on this continuum at which their moral development has ceased to grow. In studies conducted by Kohlberg and his associates, criminals have been found to be significantly lower in their moral judgment development than noncriminals of the same social background.[75] The majority of noncriminals were classified in stages three and four, whereas a majority of criminals fell in stages one and two. Moral development theory, then, suggests that people who obey the law simply to avoid punishment or who have outlooks mainly characterized by self-interest are more likely to commit crimes than those who view the law as something that benefits all of society and who sympathize with the rights of others. Moral development theory suggests that growth to a higher stage of moral judgment probably insulates a person against criminal behavior. This is a relatively new field, and research efforts to examine its principles have not been extensive.

BEHAVIOR THEORY AND THE SOCIAL LEARNING APPROACH

Behavior theory maintains that human actions are developed through learning experiences. Rather than focus on unconscious personality traits or cognitive development patterns produced early in childhood, behavior theorists are concerned with the actual behaviors people engage in during the course of their daily lives. The major premise of behavior theory is that people alter their behavior according to the reactions it receives from others. Consequently, behavior is constantly being shaped by life experiences. With respect to criminal activity, the behaviorist viewpoint is that crimes, especially violent acts, are learned responses to life situations and do not necessarily represent abnormal or morally immature responses.

Social Learning Theory. The **social learning** branch of behavior theory is the one most relevant to criminology, since it stresses the acquisition of violent and aggressive behavior patterns.[76] Social learning theorists, most notably **Albert Bandura,** argue that people are not actually born with the ability to act violently but that they learn to be aggressive through their life experiences. These experiences include observing others acting aggressively to achieve some goal or watching others being rewarded for violent acts on television, in movies, and so on. Simply put, people learn to act aggressively when as children they model their behavior after the violent acts of adults. Later in life, these violent behavior patterns persist in social relationships.

In the social learning view, psychological or biological factors may predispose a person toward violence, but the activation of a person's violent tendencies is achieved by factors in the environment. Therefore, Albert Bandura claims, the specific forms that aggressive behavior takes, the frequency with which it is expressed, the situations in which it is displayed, and the specific targets selected for attack are largely determined by social learning factors.

Social Learning and Violence. Social learning theorists view violence as something learned through a process called behavior modeling. In modern society, aggressive acts are usually modeled after three principal sources. Most prominent is the behavior model reinforced by family members. Bandura reports that studies of family life show that children who use aggressive tactics have parents who use similar behaviors when dealing with others.

A second influence on the social learning of violence is provided by environmental experiences. People who reside in areas in which violence is a daily oc-

Television and Behavior

One important social learning hypothesis is that children model their behavior after the behavior of characters they see on television. It matters little if they are real-life or cartoon figures, as long as they are rewarded for their aggressive behavior and the children can identify in some way with them. This relationship is particularly important when we consider the amount of violence on television programs. For example, when researchers at Pennsylvania University's Annenberg School of Communications monitored the number of programs containing violence and the number of violent acts per program from 1967 to 1979, they found that weekend daytime programming, usually directed at children, has the most violent content.

There are several competing explanations for the effects television is said to have on behavior:

- Observational learning occurs when the violence seen on television is copied by the child viewer. Children learn to be violent from television in the same way that they learn cognitive and social skills from their parents and friends.
- Television violence increases the arousal levels of viewers and makes them more prone to act aggressively. Studies measuring the galvanic skin response of subjects—a physical indication of arousal based on the amount of electricity conducted across the palm of the hand—show that viewing violent television shows led to increased arousal levels in young children.
- Television violence promotes attitude changes, which can then result in behavior changes. Watching television violence promotes such negative attitudes as suspiciousness and the expectation that the viewer himself or herself will become involved in violence. Attitudes of frequent television viewers toward aggression become positive when they see violence as a common and socially acceptable behavior.
- Television violence helps already aggressive youths justify their behavior. It is possible that, instead of *causing violence,* television helps violent youths rationalize their behavior as a socially acceptable and common activity.
- Television violence may disinhibit aggressive behavior, which is normally controlled by other learning processes. Disinhibition takes place when adults are viewed as being rewarded for violence, and when

violence is seen as socially acceptable. This contradicts previous learning experiences in which violent behavior was viewed as wrong.

The evidence that watching violence on television is correlated with personal expressions of violence seems overwhelming. Hundreds of studies on the issue have been conducted. With few exceptions, they found that television has both an immediate, short-term influence and a lasting, long-term effect on behavior.

This evidence should not be interpreted to mean that all violent people became that way from watching television, or that watching television will automatically make a person violent. Millions of people watch violent films and television programs without ever becoming violent themselves. Some carefully conducted studies in which the television viewing of youths was observed over time have failed to show a significant link between watching violence on television and personal aggressive behavior. But the evidence does suggest that some people *are* influenced by television and that both parents and television executives should at least be sensitive to this problem.

DISCUSSION QUESTIONS

1. Should violent programs aimed at children be banned from network television?
2. Have you ever been influenced by a particularly violent television show or film?

SOURCE. D. Pearl, L. Bouthilet, and D. Lazar, eds., *Television and Behavior,* vols. 1 and 2 (Washington, D.C.: U.S. Government Printing Office, 1982).

currence are more likely to act violently than those whose subcultural affiliations stress conventional behavior.

A third source of behavior modeling is provided by the mass media. It has been commonplace for films and television shows to graphically depict violence. Moreover, violence is often portrayed as an acceptable behavior, especially for heroes who never have to face legal consequences for their actions. For example, David Phillips found the homicide rate increases significantly immediately after a heavyweight championship prize fight.[77] (See Close-Up entitled "Television and Behavior.")

Studies indicate that observing violence on TV can precipitate personal acts of violence.

What triggers violent acts? Various sources have been investigated by social learning theorists. One position is that a direct, pain-producing physical assault will usually trigger a violent response. Yet the relationship between painful attacks and aggressive responses has been found to be inconsistent; whether people counterattack in the face of physical attack depends in part on their skill in fighting and their perception of the strength of their attackers.

Verbal taunts and insults have also been linked to aggressive responses. People who are predisposed to aggression by their learning experience are likely to view insults from others as a challenge to their social status and to react with violence.

Still another violence-triggering mechanism is a perceived reduction in one's life conditions. Prime examples of this phenomenon are riots and demonstrations in poverty-stricken ghetto areas. Studies have shown that discontent also produces aggression in the more successful members of lower-class groups who have been led to believe they can succeed but have been thwarted in their aspirations. It is still uncertain how this relationship is constructed; however, it is apparently complex. No matter how deprived some individuals are, they will not resort to violence. It seems evident that people's perceptions of their relative deprivation have differing effects on their aggressive responses.

In summary, social learning theorists have said that the following four factors help produce violence and aggression:

1. An event that heightens arousal—such as a person's frustrating or provoking another through physical assault or verbal abuse.
2. Aggressive skills—learned aggressive responses picked up from observing others, either personally or through the media.
3. Expected outcomes—the belief that aggression will somehow be rewarded.

> Rewards can come in the form of reducing tension or anger, gaining some financial reward, building self-esteem, or gaining the praise of others.

4. Consistency of behavior with values—the belief, gained from observing others, that aggression is justified and appropriate given the circumstances of the current situation.

PSYCHOBIOLOGICAL PERSPECTIVE

Psychobiologists, or *physiological psychologists*, search for relationships among changes in brain cells, nervous system activity, and mental processes. They have used research techniques like electrical stimulation of areas of the brain to demonstrate that particular parts of the brain control a wide range of emotional and behavioral activity, ranging from sexuality to aggression.

Psychologists also have studied the effects of hormone and cell activity on behavior. Since these efforts are quite similar to those of biocriminologists, discussed earlier in this chapter, they need not be repeated here. However, two issues relating to biological psychology are of particular relevance to criminology and should be given some mention: the psychopathic personality and mental ability and crime.

The Psychopath. It has become commonplace for psychocriminologists to view morally indifferent people who have frequent brushes with the law as **sociopaths** or **psychopaths** (these terms are used interchangeably).[78] Clinicians view psychopaths as aggressive, dangerous, antisocial individuals who act in an unthinking and callous manner. They lack insight into their behavior and are likely to feel little remorse for their violent, aggressive, or criminal acts. Psychopaths neither learn from their mistakes nor are influenced by punishments. Though they may appear charming and may have at least average intelligence, they lack emotional depth and are incapable of loving others. Psychopaths have been described as having an unstable, transient lifestyle without long-term commitments. Nonetheless, they do not display clinically significant intellectual or psychiatric symptoms. Perhaps their most important feature is a low level of anxiety, which contributes to their lack of remorse or guilt over their misdeeds.

Psychopaths are likely to be very dangerous. If a person has no feelings for others and often acts on impulse, it follows that there will be little to bar him or her from expressing antisocial behavior. It is not surprising, therefore, that research studies show that people evaluated as psychopaths are significantly more criminal and violence-prone when compared to nonpsychopathic control groups. Moreover, as Robert Hare and Jeffrey Jutai report, psychopaths may continue their criminal careers long after other offenders "burn out" or "age out" of crime.[79] Psychopathy has also been linked to serious violent crimes such as mass murder or serial murder; this topic will be discussed further in chapter 9. Psychopaths are continually in trouble with the law, and therefore are likely to wind up in penal institutions. It has been estimated that up to 30 percent of all inmates can be classified as psychopaths or sociopaths, but a more realistic figure is probably 10 percent.[80] Nonetheless, not all psychopaths become criminals; conversely, most criminals are not psychopaths.

Psychopathy and Physical Traits. There are several suspected causes of the psychopathic personality. Some psychologists believe that early development and nurturing contribute to the condition. Among the suspected causes are a sociopathic father, parental rejection and lack of love during childhood, loss of a parent during childhood, and inconsistent discipline. The early relationship between mother and child is also quite significant. Children who lack the opportunity to form an attachment to a mother-figure in the first three years of life, who suffer sudden separation from the mother-figure, or who see changes in the mother-figure are most likely to develop psychopathic personalities.

Although developmental factors are a suspected cause of psychopathy, physical traits have also been linked to the antisocial personality.[81] One particular psycho-biological concern is the link between psychopathy and the activity of the *autonomic nervous system (ANS)*. The ANS mediates physiological activities associated with emotions and is manifested in such measurements as heartbeat rate, blood pressure, respiration, muscle tension, pupillary size, and electrical activity of the skin (called *galvinac skin resistance*, or *GSR*).

Some evidence indicates that psychopaths have lower skin conductance levels and fewer spontaneous responses than normal subjects. Research shows that this relationship is slight and inconsistent, but some recent studies do indicate the possibility that psychopaths have lower levels of arousal to environmental stimulations such as noises and pain than do control subjects. Similarly, psychopaths have been found to be less likely to show physiological signs that they are apprehensive about threatened pain and punishment than normal subjects. Put simply, psychopaths seem to react differently to physical sensations than nonpsychopaths. Research has been undertaken to determine whether psychopaths are therefore unlikely to experience anxiety and to be deterred by punishment. It has been found that clinically defined psychopaths who have had their levels of arousal increased through injections of the hormone adrenalin do in fact begin to respond as normal subjects do. It is possible that some psychopaths are thrill seekers who engage in high-risk activities to raise their general neurological level to a more optimal state.[82]

IQ and Criminality. A second biopsychological issue relating to crime is the controversy over the suspected relationship between intelligence and criminality. Some criminologists have maintained that many delinquents and criminals have a below-average intelligence quotient (IQ) and that low IQ is a cause of their criminality.

Early criminologists believed that low intelligence was a major cause of crime and delinquency. Criminals were believed to be inherently substandard in intelligence and thus naturally inclined to commit more crimes than more intelligent persons. If authorities could determine which individuals had low IQs, they might identify potential criminals before they committed socially harmful acts. Since social scientists had a captive group of subjects in training schools and penal institutions, they began to measure the correlation between IQ and crime by testing adjudicated offenders. Thus, inmates of penal institutions were used as a test group around which numerous theories about intelligence were built, leading ultimately to the *nature versus nurture* controversy that is still going on today. These concepts are discussed in some detail in the following sections.

Nature Theory. The nature theory argues that intelligence is largely determined genetically, that ancestry determines IQ, and that low intelligence as demonstrated by low IQ is linked to behavior, including criminal behavior.

When the newly developed IQ tests were administered to inmates of prisons and juvenile training schools in the first decades of the century, the nature position gained support, because a very large proportion of the inmates scored low on the tests. Henry Goddard found during his studies in 1920 that many institutionalized persons were what he considered "febbleminded"; he concluded that at least half of all juvenile delinquents were mental defectives.[83] Goddard's results were challenged in 1931, when Edwin Sutherland evaluated IQ studies of criminals and delinquents and noted significant variation in their findings.[84] The discrepancies were believed to reflect refinements in testing methods and scoring rather than differences in the mental ability of criminals.

In 1926, William Healy and Augusta Bronner tested a group of delinquent boys in Chicago and Boston and found that 37 percent were subnormal in intelligence. They concluded that delinquents were five to ten times more likely to be mentally deficient normal boys.[85]

These and other early studies were embraced as proof that low IQ scores indicated potentially delinquent children and that a correlation existed between innate low intelligence and deviant behavior.[86] IQ tests were believed to measure the inborn genetic makeup of individuals, and many criminologists accepted the idea that individuals with substandard IQs were predisposed toward delinquency and adult criminality.

Nurture Theory. The rise of culturally sensitive explanations of human behavior in the 1930s led to the nurture school of intelligence. This theory states that intelligence must be viewed as partly biological but primarily sociological. Nurture theorists discredited the notion that persons commit crimes because they have low IQs. Instead, they postulated that environmental stimulation from parents, relatives, social contacts, schools, peer groups, and innumerable others create a child's IQ level and that low IQs result from an environment that also encourages delinquent and criminal behavior. Thus, if low IQ scores are recorded among criminals, these scores may reflect the criminals' cultural background, not their mental ability.

Studies challenging the assumption that people automatically committed criminal acts because they had below-average IQs began to appear as early as the 1920s. John Slawson studied 1,543 delinquent boys in New York institutions and compared them with a control group of New York City boys in 1926.[87] Slawson found that although 80 percent of the delinquents achieved lower scores in abstract verbal intelligence, delinquents were about normal in mechanical aptitude and nonverbal intelligence. These results indicated the possibility of cultural bias in portions of the IQ tests. He also found that there was no relationship between the number of arrests, the types of offenses, and IQ.

Kenneth Eels and his associates found that tests used in the 1950s systematically underestimated the abilities of children of the working class. They argued that traditional intelligence tests predict who will succeed in a school system that makes use of abstract ideas and experiences that only middle-class children are likely to have: "There are reasoning abilities in the lower class that schooling could capitalize on if it were redesigned to be less verbal and culture-laden."[88] Robert Rosenthal and Lenore Jacobsen further debunked the notion that academic success and IQ scores were linked.[89]

Recent Trends. There is still great controversy over the nature of IQ and its relationship to criminal behavior. Many well-known scientists have come forward to claim that IQ is a function of genetic inheritance.

The new heredity theorists, particularly Arthur Jensen and Richard Herrnstein, argue that genetic factors account for much of the variability in intelligence as measured by standard IQ scores and that environmental factors account for little.[90] Jensen argues that race is the key to IQ differences; Herrnstein believes that social class is the determining factor. Both agree that the observable gap in intelligence between blacks and whites and lower- and middle-class groups will remain fixed as long as the environmental conditions with which heredity interacts do not change. Thus, although both men believe that intelligence has a genetic basis, they do not deny the influence of environmental factors.

Recently, however, social scientists have countered arguments based on heredity. In their study of black children adopted by white families, Sandra Scarr and Richard Weinberg found that social environment plays the dominant role in determining the average IQ level of the black children. Black adoptees scored as high on IQ tests as white adoptees in other studies. They conclude: "The dramatic increase in the IQ mean and the additional finding that placement and adoptive family characteristics account for a major portion of the IQ differences . . . suggest that the IQ score of these children is malleable."[91]

Scarr and Weinberg are currently conducting a long-term study of adoptees in Minnesota.[92] Their sample includes both black and white children adopted into middle-class families. A longitudinal study of these youths confirms that racial differences do not account for a major portion of IQ performance and that black and interracial children brought up in middle-class culture and schools perform as well as other adopted children in similar environments.[93] Thus, recent evidence seems to point to the influence of environment on IQ.

The contention that IQ scores are strongly related to crime has received support from Travis Hirschi and Michael Hindelang.[94] After reexamining several important research studies—Hirschi's own 1969 effort (see chapter 7), the work of Marvin Wolfgang and colleagues (see chapter 4), and research conducted by Joseph Weis—Hirschi and Hindelang conclude that "the weight of evidence is that IQ is more important than race and social class" for predicting criminal and delinquent involvement. Furthermore, they reject the notion that IQ tests are race- and class-biased (favoring middle-class whites) and therefore invalid. They find major differences between criminals and noncriminals within *similar* racial and socioeconomic class categories. Their major contention is that low IQ increases the likelihood of criminal behavior through its effect on school performance. That is, youths with low IQs do poorly in school, and school failure and academic incompetence are highly related to delinquency, and later to adult criminality.

These findings have been supported by research conducted by Terrie Moffitt, William Gabrielli, Sarnoff Mednick, and Fini Schulsinger.[95] Using results obtained from longitudinal studies conducted in Denmark, the researchers found a significant relationship between low IQ and delinquency. They conclude that children with a low IQ may be likely to engage in delinquent behavior because their poor verbal ability is a handicap in the school environment:

> *Such initial experiences may contribute to later delinquency in many ways: by creating a negative attitude toward authority, by inducing a child to seek rewards in less socially desirable settings, or by making a child more sensitive to the effects of delinquent peer pressure when peers provide an important source of esteem.*[96]

The true relationship between intelligence and crime is far from being settled.

CRIME AND PERSONALITY TRAITS

So far, this section has viewed the concept of personality development and its relationship to criminality from four different psychological perspectives—the psychoanalytic, the cognitive, the behavioral, and the biological. All agree that human beings have the potential to develop abnormal, destructive personality characteristics, although they disagree on the process by which such development takes place.

To simplify the process by which psychologists evaluate personality, standardized tests have been constructed to measure traits associated with abnormal symptoms. Thus, instead of a time-consuming clinical evaluation, subjects can be given a test to determine the structure of their personality.

Two types of personality tests predominate in the evaluation of the criminal personality—projective techniques and personality inventories. Projective techniques require a subject to react to an ambiguous picture or shape by describing what it represents or by telling a story about it. The Rorschach Inkblot Test and the Thematic Apperception Test (TAT) are examples of two widely used projective tests. Such tests are given by clinicians trained to interpret responses and categorize them according to established behavioral patterns. However, such tests must be given individually by highly trained clinicians; and the analysis of responses is sometimes subject to individual interpretation.

The second frequently used method of psychological testing is the personality inventory. These tests require subjects to agree or disagree with groups of questions in a self-administered survey. The most widely used psychological test is the Minnesota Multiphasic Personality Inventory, commonly called the MMPI. Developed by R. Starke Hathaway and J. Charnley McKinley, the MMPI has subscales that purport to measure many different personality traits, including psychopathic deviation (Pd scale), schizophrenia (Sc), and hypomania (Ma).[97]

Elio Monachesi and R. Starke Hathaway pioneered the use of the MMPI to predict criminal behavior. They concluded that scores on some of the MMPI scales, especially the Pd scale, predicted delinquency. In one major effort, they administered the MMPI to a sample of ninth grade boys and girls in Minneapolis and found that Pd scores had a significant relationship to later delinquent involvement. Similar studies have been conducted by Hathaway, Monachesi, Lawrence Young, and William Kvaraceus and, more recently, Michael Hindelang, Joseph Weis, Spencer Rathus, and Larry Siegel.[98]

Despite the time and energy put into using MMPI and other scales to predict crime and delinquency, the results have proved inconclusive. Three surveys of the literature of personality testing—one by Karl Schuessler and Donald Cressey (covering the pre-1950 period), another by Gordon Waldo and Simon Dinitz (covering the period 1950–1965), and another, more recent survey by David Tennenbaum—found little evidence that personality traits could indeed predict criminal involvement.[99]

A CRITIQUE OF PSYCHOLOGICAL THEORIES

Psychological theories are useful as explanations of the behavior of deeply disturbed, impulsive, or destructive people. However, they are limited as general explanations of criminality. For one thing, the phenomenon of crime and delinquency is so

The Criminal Personality Revisited

Despite the apparent failure of personality tests to show a linkage between personality traits and crime, a study by Samuel Yochelson, a psychiatrist, and Stanton Samenow, a psychologist, has allegedly identified the existence of a "criminal personality."

After conducting in-depth interviews with 240 men under observation and treatment in St. Elizabeth's Hospital in Washington, D.C., Yochelson and Samenow conclude that a criminal personality exists. "It is not the environment that turns a man into a criminal" they argue, "it is a series of choices that he makes starting at a very early age."

Among the rather surprising conclusions the authors reach is that the criminal personality is imprinted at birth and is relatively unaffected by parental influences. In fact, they conclude that it is more likely that young criminals have a profound and negative effect on their families than that their families have a negative effect on them.

Further investigations led Yochelson and Samenow to draw the following conclusions about the criminal personality: People who have a criminal mind seek the excitement associated with law violation and scorn those living a "safe," socially productive life. They go out of their way to make friends with criminal groups and will do anything to win the approval of their criminal peers. In school, they try to exploit every situation for their own benefit. Later, at work, they exhibit the same abnormal, self-serving relationships.

Criminals are not specialists. By the time they are apprehended, they have committed hundreds of offenses of every type—property, assault, sex—but have not been arrested.

Most importantly, Yochelson and Samenow believe they have uncovered criminal thinking patterns strongly related to antisocial behavior:

The criminal lives in a world where there is no loyalty or trust, even in relation to others like him. Untrustworthy himself, he demands that others trust him. If he happens to earn others' trust, he exploits it. He depends on others but does not see his own dependence. To him, this exhibits weakness and places him in jeopardy. He claims he can live without interdependence but demands that others provide him with whatever he wants. The criminal does not know how to get along with responsible people from day to day; he generally occupies the extremes of total withdrawal or inappropriate intimacy. He is intolerant of others' shortcomings but reacts angrily when anyone finds fault with him. Instead of friendships, the criminal seeks avenues of triumph. People are to be used, conquered, controlled like pawns, exploited, and then discarded when they can no longer serve a purpose useful to him. Only rarely does the

widespread that to claim that all criminals are psychologically disturbed is to make that claim against a vast majority of people.

Individual-Oriented Theory and Social Policy

Individual-oriented theories have profoundly influenced social policy. Since the 1920s it has become commonplace to offer psychological treatment to offenders before, during, and after a criminal conviction. For example, beginning in the 1970s, pretrial programs have sought to divert offenders into nonpunitive rehabilitative programs designed to treat rather than punish them. Based on some type of counseling regime, diversion programs are commonly used with first offenders, nonviolent offenders, and so on.

At the trial stage, judges commonly order psychological profiles of convicted offenders for planning a treatment program. Should they be kept in the community? Do they need a more secure confinement to deal with their problems?

If correctional confinement is called for, inmates are commonly evaluated at a **classification center** in order to measure their personality traits or disorders. Correctional facilities almost universally require inmates to partake in some form of psychological therapy: group therapy, individual analysis, transactional analysis, and so on. Parole decisions may be influenced by the prison psychologist's evaluation of the offender's adjustment.

criminal genuinely "like" another person. His liking is based on someone's agreeing with him, building him up, assisting him in his plans, or at least not interfering with him. He also "likes" someone he can exploit. His very characteristics preclude his genuinely loving anyone. He regards kindness as weakness. Although he expresses fragments of sentimentality, the criminal cold-bloodedly uses the very people he professes to love.

Most of all, the criminal fears being put down by other people. A putdown occurs when someone fails to gratify his every desire or fulfill his every expectation. Any inconvenience is regarded as a personal affront. What a noncriminal habitually shrugs off reduces the power-thrusting, controlling criminal to a zero. The zero state, which is far more encompassing than the noncriminal's inferiority feelings, reflects the criminal's extremes in thinking and his misconception of himself and the outside world. He is either a colossus or a nothing. He regards himself as a zero when the world does not accord him the status that he thinks he deserves and things are not going according to plan. On such occasions, the criminal believes that everyone looks on him as a nothing and that this state is permanent. The seeming finality and futility of such a state are intolerable to him, and he usually responds with criminal acts, as well as with anger and with determination to reassert his status as "somebody" rather than continue to be (by his definition) a "nobody." Life for the criminal is a series of anger reactions to surmount his fear of being a nothing.

The antidote to the zero state is not constructive activity but a cutoff of fear, an angry reaction, and a search for excitement (crime). Anger is a basic component of the criminal's personality; it is pervasive, although not always apparent to others.

These therapists suggest that law violators, to be rehabilitated, must be taught to give up their amoral way of life and to operate on a new, moral basis. They see criminals as having three choices: continue in crime, commit suicide, or change totally to a legitimate lifestyle. Yochelson and Samenow suggest that criminals can learn to change by first developing self-insight and then learning to give up their criminal ideas and thought patterns.

Yochelson and Samenow's work is highly controversial, since it not only is critical of all other psychological and sociological theories but also suggests that criminals are inherently different from noncriminals.

DISCUSSION QUESTIONS

1. Could criminals actually have different personalities than noncriminals?
2. How would Yochelson and Samenow explain the difference between a heroin user, a rapist, and an embezzler?

SOURCE. Samuel Yochelson and Stanton Samenow, *The Criminal Personality* vol. 1 (New York: Jason Aronson, 1977), Quotes from vol. I; pp. 119, 131.

Biologically oriented therapy is just now being used in the criminal justice system. Programs have altered diet, changed lighting, compensated for learning disabilities, treated allergies, and so on. Results of these experiments have been mixed.

In sum, for most of the twentieth century the criminal justice system has used a **medical model,** or rehabilitation philosophy, in dealing with law violators. The theory has two prongs: First, primary prevention programs seek to relieve personal problems before they manifest themselves as crime. Thousands of family therapy organizations, substance abuse clinics, mental health associations, and so on are operating around the United States. Referrals to these are made by teachers, employers, courts, welfare agencies, etc. It is assumed that if a person's problems can be treated before they become overwhelming, some future crimes will be prevented.

Secondary prevention programs provide aid and counseling to youths and adults after they have violated the law. Attendance in such programs may be a mandatory requirement of a probation order, part of a diversionary sentence, or as aftercare at the tail end of a prison sentence.

Beyond these efforts, the law recognizes the psychological aspects of crime when it permits the insanity plea as an excuse for criminal liability or when it permits trial delay because of mental incompetency.

This medical model is now under attack. The alleged failure of rehabilitation programs, heralded by research efforts indicating that "nothing seems to work," caused many criminologists and policy makers to turn to the more conservative classical measures described in chapter 5. Today the rehabilitation model is at a crossroads, challenged on one side by critics who believe punishment and not treatment is the proper response to criminality and on the other by criminologists who charge that rehabilitation efforts are self-defeating, since they label and stigmatize clients as sick or crazy (see chapter 7).

Despite the widely heralded death of the treatment model, psychological and biological efforts continue to flourish. It is ironic that although the evidence is inconclusive that crime is a function of individual maladaptation, the justice system continues to rely on individual therapy as a major form of crime prevention.

Summary

The earliest positivist criminologists were biologists. Led by Cesare Lombroso, these early researchers believed some people manifested primitive traits that made them born criminals. Today, their research is debunked because of poor methodology, testing, and logic.

Other pioneering biological research portrayed criminality as an inherited trait passed from one generation of criminals to another. Still another early direction of biocriminology focused on the body build of criminals. Otto Kretschmer and later William Sheldon along with Sheldon and Eleanor Glueck believed that the human body could be classified on the basis of size and musculature. Criminals and delinquents were believed to have well-developed muscles and an athletic appearance, a type known as mesomorphic.

Biological views fell out of favor in the early twentieth century. In the 1970s, spurred by the publication of E. O. Wilson's *Sociobiology*, several criminologists again turned to study of the biological basis of criminality. For the most part, the effort has focused on the cause of violent crime. Interest has centered on several areas: (1) biochemical factors such as diet, allergies, hormonal imbalances, and environmental contaminants such as lead; (2) neurophysiological factors such as brain disorders, EEG abnormalities, tumors, and head injuries; and (3) genetic factors such as the XYY chromosome and inherited traits. Biocriminology is in its infancy, and no definitive studies have been undertaken.

Psychological attempts to explain criminal behavior have their historical roots in the concept that all criminals are insane or mentally damaged. This position is no longer accepted. Today, there are four main psychological perspectives. The psychoanalytic view, the creation of Sigmund Freud, links aggressive behavior to personality conflicts developed in childhood. In the worst case, conflict leads to a severe behavior disorder called psychosis. According to some psychoanalysts, psychotics are aggressive, unstable people who can easily become involved in crime.

Cognitive psychology is concerned with human development and how people perceive the world. Criminality is viewed as a function of improper moral development. In contrast, learning theorists see criminality as a learned behavior. Children who are exposed to violence and see it rewarded may become violent as adults. Physiological psychologists link psychological traits with biological factors. One important area of study has been the psychopath, a person who lacks emotion and concern for others. Another issue is the relationship of IQ to criminality. This controversial issue has been resurrected once again with the publication of research studies purporting to show that criminals have lower IQs than noncriminals.

Psychologists have developed standardized tests with which to measure personality traits. One avenue of research has been to determine whether criminals and noncriminals manifest any differences in their responses to test items. Three major reviews of the literature have failed to find any direct link of criminality and personality.

Notes

1 Marvin Wolfgang, "Cesare Lombroso," in *Pioneers in Criminology*, ed. Hermann Mannheim (Montclair, N.J.: Patterson Smith, 1970), pp. 232–71.

2 See generally Cesare Lombroso, *Crime, Its Causes and Remedies* (Montclair, N.J.: Patterson Smith, 1968).

3 Gina Lombroso-Ferrero, *Criminal Man According to the Classification of Cesare Lombroso* (Montclair, N.J.: Patterson Smith, 1972), p. 100.

4 Ibid., p. 118.

5 Charles Goring, *The English Convict: A Statistical Study, 1913* (Montclair, N.J.: Patterson Smith, 1972).

6 Edwin Driver, "Charles Buckman Goring," in *Pioneers in Criminology*, ed. Hermann Mannheim (Montclair, N.J.: Patterson Smith, 1970), p. 440.

7 Raffaele Garofalo, *Criminology*, trans. Robert Miller (Boston: Little, Brown, 1914), p. 92.

8 Enrico Ferri, *Criminal Sociology* (New York: D. Appleton, 1909).

9 Ernest Hooton, *The American Criminal* (Cambridge, Mass.: Harvard University Press, 1939), p. 309.

10 Richard Dugdale, *The Jukes* (New York: Putnam, 1910); Arthur Estabrook, *The Jukes in 1915* (Washington, D.C.: The Carnegie Institute of Washington, 1916). The studies in this section are described in Stephen Schafer, *Introduction to Criminology* (Reston, Va.: Reston Publishing, 1976), pp. 60–61.

11 Henry Herbert Goddard, *The Kallikak Family: A Study in the Heredity of Feeble-Mindedness* (New York: Macmillan, 1927).

12 Ernst Kretschmer, *Physique and Character*, trans. W. J. H. Spratt (London: Keegan, Paul, Trench, Trubner, 1925).

13 William Sheldon, *Varieties of Delinquent Youth* (New York: Harper & Bros., 1949).

14 Sheldon Glueck and Eleanor Glueck, *Of Delinquency and Crime* (Springfield, Ill.: Charles C. Thomas, 1974), p. 2.

15 B. R. McCandless, W. S. Persons, and A. Roberts, "Perceived Opportunity, Delinquency, Race and Body Build among Delinquent Youth," *Journal of Consulting and Clinical Psychology* 38 (1972):281.

16 Pierre van den Bergle, "Bringing Beast Back In: Toward a Biosocial Theory of Aggression," *American Sociological Review* 39 (1974):779.

17 E. O. Wilson, *Sociobiology* (Cambridge, Mass.: Harvard University Press, 1975).

18 C. Ray Jeffrey, "Criminology as an Interdisciplinary Behavioral Science," *Criminology* 16 (1978):161–62.

19 Material in these subsections relies heavily on Leonard Hippchen, "Some Possible Biochemical Aspects of Criminal Behavior," *Journal of Behavioral Ecology* 2 (1981):1–6; Sarnoff Mednick and Jan Volavka, "Biology and Crime," in *Crime and Justice*, ed. Norval Morris and Michael Tonry (Chicago: University of Chicago Press, 1980), pp. 85–159; Saleem Shah and Loren Roth, "Biological and Psychophysiological Factors in Criminality," in *Handbook of Criminology*, ed. Daniel Glazer (Chicago: Rand McNally, 1974), pp. 125–40.

20 Leonard Hippchen, ed., *Ecologic-Biochemical Approaches to Treatment of Delinquents and Criminals* (New York: Von Nostrand Reinhold, 1978), p. 14.

21 Ibid.

22 J. Kershner and W. Hawke, "Megavitamins and Learning Disorders: A Controlled Double-blind Experiment," *Journal of Nutrition* 109 (1979):819–26.

23 Stephen Schoenthaler and Walter Doraz, "Types of Offenses Which Can Be Reduced in an Institutional Setting Using Nutritional Intervention," *International Journal of Biosocial Research* 4 (1983):74–84; and idem, "Diet and Crime," *International Journal of Biosocial Research* 4 (1983):29–39; see also A.G. Schauss, "Differential Outcomes among Probationers Comparing Orthomolecular Approaches to Conventional Casework Counseling," (Paper presented at the Annual Meeting of the American Society of Criminology, Dallas, Texas, 9 November 1978); A. Schauss and C. Simonsen, "A Critical Analysis of the Diets of Chronic Juvenile Offenders, Part I," *Journal of Orthomolecular Psychiatry* 8 (1979):149–57. See also A. Schauss, J. Bland, and C. Simonsen, "A Critical Analysis of the Diets of Chronic Juvenile Offenders, Part II," *Journal of Orthomolecular Psychiatry* 8 (1979):222–26; A. Hoffer, "Children with Learning and Behavioral Disorders," *Journal of Orthomolecular Psychiatry* 5 (1976):229.

24 D. Hill and W. Sargent, "A Case of Matricide," *Lancet* 244 (1943):526–27.

25 E. Podolsky, "The Chemistry of Murder," *Pakistan Medical Journal* 15 (1964):9–14.

26 J. A. Yaryura-Tobias and F. Neziroglu, "Violent Behavior Brain Dysrhythmia and Glucose Dysfunction, a New Syndrome," *Journal of Orthopsychiatry* 4 (1975):182–88.

27 L. E. Kreuz and R. M. Rose, "Assessment of Aggressive Behavior and Plasma Testosterone in a Young Criminal Population," *Psychosomatic Medicine* 34 (1972):321–32.

28 Richard Rada, "Plasma Androgens in Violent and Non-Violent Sex Offenders," *Bulletin of the American Academy of Psychiatry and the Law* 11 (1983):149–58; R. T. Rada, D. R. Laws, and R. Kellner, "Plasma Testosterone Levels in the Rapist," *Psychosomatic Medicine* 38 (1976):257–68.

29 Sarnoff Mednick and Jan Volavka, "Biology and Crime."

30 J. Money, "Influence of Hormones on Psychosexual Differentiation," *Medical Aspects of Human Sexuality* 2 (1968):32–42.

31 H. E. Amos and J. J. P. Drake, "Problems Posed by Food Additives," *Journal of Human Nutrition* 30 (1976):165.

32 Ray Wunderlich, "Neuroallergy as a Contributing Factor to Social Misfits: Diagnosis and Treatment," in *Ecologic-Biochemical Approaches to Treatment of Delinquents and Criminals,* ed. Leonard Hippchen (New York: Von Nostrand Reinhold, 1978), pp. 229–53.

33 A. R. Mawson and K. J. Jacobs, "Corn Consumption, Tryptophan, and Cross-National Homicide Rates," *Journal of Orthomolecular Psychiatry* 7 (1978):227–30.

34 A. Schauss, *Diet, Crime and Delinquency* (Berkeley, Calif.: Parker House, 1980).

35 C. Hawley and R. E. Buckley, "Food Dyes and Hyperkinetic Children," *Academy Therapy* 10 (1974):27–32.

36 Oliver David, Stanley Hoffman, Jeffrey Sverd, Julian Clark, and Kytja Voeller, "Lead and Hyperactivity. Behavior Response to Chelation: A Pilot Study," *American Journal of Psychiatry* 133 (1976):1155–58.

37 John Ott, "The Effects of Light and Radiation on Human Health and Behavior," in *Ecologic-Biochemical Approaches to Treatment of Delinquents and Criminals,* ed. Leonard Hippchen (New York: Von Nostrand Reinhold, 1978), pp. 105–83. See also A. Kreuger and S. Sigel, "Ions in the Air," *Human Nature,* July (1978):46–47; Harry Wohlfarth, "The Effect of Color Psychodynamic Environmental Modification on Disciplinary Incidents in Elementary Schools Over One School Year: A Controlled Study," *International Journal of Biosocial Research* 6 (1984):44–53.

38 R. D. Robin, R. M. Sarles, T. J. Kenney, B. J. Reynolds, and F. P. Heald, "Adolescents Who Attempt Suicide," *Journal of Pediatrics* 90 (1977):636–38.

39 R. R. Monroe, *Brain Dysfunction in Aggressive Criminals* (Lexington, Mass.: D. C. Heath, 1978).

40 L. T. Yeudall, *Childhood Experiences as Causes of Criminal Behavior* (Senate of Canada, Issue no. 1, Thirteenth Parliament, Ottawa, Canada, 1977).

41 C. Murray, *The Link between Learning Disabilities and Juvenile Delinquency* (Washington, D. C.: Government Printing Office, 1976), p. 65. See also B. Claire McCullough, Barbara Zaremba, and William Rich, "The Role of the Juvenile Justice System in the

Link between Learning Disabilities and Delinquency," *State Court Journal* 3 (1979):45; Hill and Sargent, "A Case of Matricide."

42 D. Williams, "Neural Factors Related to Habitual Aggression—Consideration of Differences between Habitual Aggressives and Others Who Have Committed Crimes of Violence," *Brain* 92 (1969):503–20.

43 R. S. Aind and T. Yamamoto, "Behavior Disorders of Childhood," *Electroencephalography and Clinical Neurophysiology* 21 (1966):148–56.

44 Z. A. Zayed, S. A. Lewis, and R. P. Britain, "An Encephalographic and Psychiatric Study of 32 Insane Murderers," *British Journal of Psychiatry* 115 (1969):1115–24.

45 K. E. Moyer, *The Psychobiology of Aggression* (New York: Harper & Row, 1976).

46 Ibid., pp. 24–25.

47 H. D. Kletschka, "Violent Behavior Associated with Brain Tumors," *Minnesota Medicine* 49 (1966):1853–55.

48 R. Johnson, *Aggression in Man and Animals* (Philadelphia: Saunders, 1972), p. 79.

49 C. E. Lyght, ed., *The Merck Manual of Diagnosis and Therapy* (West Point, Pa.: Merck, 1966).

50 This section relies heavily on Shah and Roth, "Biological and Psychophysiological Factors in Criminality," pp. 134–40; Lee Ellis, "Genetics and Criminal Behavior," *Criminology* 20 (1982):43–67.

51 A. A. Sandberg, G. F. Koepf, T. Ishiara, T. S. Hauschka, "An XYY Human Male," *Lancet* 262 (1961):488–89.

52 Shah and Roth, "Biological and Psychophysiological Factors in Criminology," p. 135.

53 T. R. Sarbin and L. E. Miller, "Demonism Revisited: The XYY Chromosome Anomaly," *Issues in Criminology* 5 (1970):195–207.

54 Shah and Roth, "Biological and Psychophysiological Factors in Criminality," p. 137.

55 Mednick and Volavka, "Biology and Crime," p. 93.

56 Ibid., p. 94.

57 Ibid., p. 95.

58 See Sarnoff A. Mednick and Karl O. Christiansen, *Biosocial Bases in Criminal Behavior* (New York: Gardner Press, 1977).

59 David Rowe and D. Wayne Osgood, "Heredity and Sociological Theories of Delinquency: A Reconsideration," *American Sociological Review* 49 (1984):526–40.

60 Mednick and Volavka, "Biology and Crime," p. 97.

61 Barry Hutchings and Sarnoff A. Mednick, "Criminality in Adoptees and Their Adoptive and Biological Parents: A Pilot Study," in *Biosocial Bases in Criminal Behavior*, ed. S. A. Mednick and K. O. Christiansen (New York: Gardner Press, 1977).

62 Sarnoff Mednick, William Gabrielli, and Barry Hutchings, "Genetic Influences in Criminal Behavior: Evidence from an Adoption Cohort," in *Perspective Studies of Crime and Delinquency*, Katherine Teilmann Van Dusen and Sarnoff Mednick, eds. (Boston: Kluver-Nijhoff, 1983), pp. 39–57; K.S. Van Dusen, S. Mednick, S. Gabrielli, and B. Hutchings, "Social Class and Crime in An Adoption Cohort," *Journal of Criminal Law and Criminology* (1983).

63 See Peter Scott, "Henry Maudsley," in *Pioneers in Criminology*, ed. Hermann Mannheim (Montclair, N.J.: Patterson Smith, 1970), p. 212.

64 See generally Spencer Rathus, *Psychology* (New York: Holt, Rinehart and Winston, 1984).

65 See generally Donn Byrne and Kathryn Kelly, *An Introduction to Personality* (Englewood Cliffs, N.J.: Prentice-Hall, 1981).

66 This section adapted from Rathus, *Psychology*, pp. 412–20.

67 Sigmund Freud, "The Ego and the Id," in *Complete Psychological Works of Sigmund Freud*, vol. 19 (London: Hogarth, 1948), p. 52.

68 August Aichorn, *Wayward Youth* (New York: Viking Press, 1935).

69 David Abrahamsen, *Crime and the Human Mind* (New York: Columbia University Press, 1944), p. 137; see generally, Fritz Redl and Hans Toch, "The Psychoanalytic Per-

spective," in *Psychology of Crime and Criminal Justice*, ed. Hans Toch (New York: Holt, Rinehart and Winston, 1979), pp. 193–95.

70 Seymour Halleck, *Psychiatry and the Dilemmas of Crime* (Berkeley, Calif.: University of California Press, 1971).

71 James Sorrells, "Kids Who Kill," *Crime and Delinquency* 23 (1977):312–20.

72 Richard Rosner, "Adolescents Accused of Murder and Manslaughter: a Five Year Descriptive Study," *Bulletin of The American Academy of Psychiatry and The Law* 7 (1979):342–51.

73 See generally Jean Piaget, *The Moral Judgement of the Child* (London: Keagan Paul, 1932).

74 Lawrence Kohlberg, *Stages in the Development of Moral Thought and Action* (New York: Holt, Rinehart and Winston, 1969).

75 L. Kohlberg, K. Kauffman, P. Scharf, and J. Hickey, *The Just Community Approach in Corrections: A Manual* (Niantic, Conn.: Connecticut Department of Corrections, 1973).

76 This discussion is based on three works by Albert Bandura: *Aggression: A Social Learning Analysis* (Englewood Cliffs, N.J.: Prentice-Hall, 1973); *Social Learning Theory* (Englewood Cliffs, N.J.: Prentice-Hall, 1977); "The Social Learning Perspective: Mechanisms of Aggression," in *Psychology of Crime and Criminal Justice*, ed. H. Toch (New York: Holt, Rinehart and Winston, 1979), pp. 198–236.

77 David Phillips, "The Impact of Mass Media Violence on U.S. Homicides," *American Sociological Review* 48 (1983):560–68.

78 See generally Albert Rabin, "The Antisocial Personality—Psychopathy and Sociopathy," in *The Psychology of Crime and Criminal Justice*, ed. Hans Toch (New York: Holt, Rinehart and Winston, 1979), pp. 236–51.

79 Robert Hare and Jeffery Jutai, "Criminal History of the Male Psychopath: Some Preliminary Data," in Tielmann, Van Dusen, and Mednick, eds., *Perspective Studies of Crime and Delinquency*, pp. 225–36.

80 Seymour Halleck, *Psychiatry and the Dilemmas of Crime* (New York: Harper & Row, 1967), pp. 99–115.

81 See generally Mednick and Volavka, "Biology and Crime," pp. 105–23.

82 Rathus, *Psychology*, p. 545.

83 Henry Goddard, *Efficiency and Levels of Intelligence* (Princeton, N.J.: Princeton University Press, 1920).

84 Edwin Sutherland, "Mental Deficiency and Crime," in *Social Attitudes*, ed. Kimball Young (New York: Henry Holt, 1931), chap. 15.

85 William Healy and Augusta Bronner, *Delinquency and Criminals: Their Making and Unmaking* (New York: MacMillan, 1926).

86 See C. Burt, "The Inheritance of Mental Ability," *American Psychologist* 13 (1958): 1–15.

87 John Slawson, *The Delinquent Boys* (Boston: Budget Press, 1926).

88 Kenneth Eels, et al., *Intelligence and Cultural Differences* (Chicago: University of Chicago Press, 1951), p. 181.

89 Robert Rosenthal and Lenore Jacobsen, *Pygmalion in the Classroom* (New York: Holt, 1968).

90 See generally Arthur Jensen, *Bias in Mental Testing* (New York: Free Press, 1979); see also Arthur Jensen, "How Much Can We Boost IQ and Scholastic Achievement?" *Harvard Educational Review* 39 (1969):1–123.

91 Sandra Scarr and Richard Weinberg, "I.Q. Test Performance of Black Children Adopted by White Families," *American Psychologist* 31 (1976):726–39.

92 Sandra Scarr and Richard Weinberg, "The Minnesota Adoption Studies: Genetic Differences and Malleability," *Child Development* 54 (1983):260–67.

93 For an opposing view, see Joseph Horn, "The Texas Adoption Project: Adopted Children and Their Intellectual Resemblance to Biological and Adoptive Parents," *Child Development* 54 (1983):268–75.

94 Travis Hirschi and Michael Hindelang, "Intelligence and Delinquency: A Revisionist Review," *American Sociological Review* 42 (1977):471–586.

95 Terrie Moffitt, William Gabrielli, Sarnoff Mednick, and Fini Schulsinger, "Socioeconomic Status, IQ, and Delinquency," *Journal of Abnormal Psychology* 90 (1981): 152–56.

96 Ibid., p. 155. For a similar finding, see L. Hubble and M. Groff, "Magnitude and Direction of WISC-R Verbal Performance IQ Discrepancies Among Adjudicated Male Delinquents," *Journal of Youth and Adolescence* 10 (1981):179–83.

97 See generally R. Starke Hathaway and Elio Monachesi, *Analyzing and Predicting Juvenile Delinquency with the MMPI* (Minneapolis: University of Minnesota Press, 1953).

98 R. Starke Hathaway, Elio Monachesi, and Lawrence Young, "Delinquency Rates and Personality," *Journal of Criminal Law, Criminology and Police Science* 51 (1960):443–60; Michael Hindelang and Joseph Weis, "Personality and Self-Reported Delinquency: An Application of Cluster Analysis," *Criminology* 10 (1972):268; Spencer Rathus and Larry Siegel, "Crime and Personality Revisited," *Criminology* 18 (1980):245–51.

99 Karl Schuessler and Donald Cressey, "Personality Characteristics of Criminals," *American Journal of Sociology* 55 (1950):476–84; Gordon Waldo and Simon Dinitz, "Personality Attributes of the Criminal: An Analysis of Research Studies 1950–1965," *Journal of Research in Crime and Delinquency* 4 (1967):185–201; David Tennenbaum, "Research Studies of Personality and Criminality," *Journal of Criminal Justice* 5 (1977):1–19.

Sociological Approaches: Social Structure Theories

CHAPTER OUTLINE

KEY TERMS

cartographic school of criminology

culture of poverty

under class

social structure theory

cultural deviance theory

cultural transmission theory

culture conflict theory

strain theory

strain

transitional neighborhood

social disorganization

conduct norm

theory of anomie

goals

means

subcultural strain theory

status frustration

middle-class measuring rods

short-run hedonism

group autonomy

reaction formation

differential opportunity

Introduction

The preceding chapter reviewed positivist theories of crime causation in which the main focus of attention was on the individual. This chapter and the next two turn to sociological explanations of criminality. As a group, they emphasize the role social institutions, structures, and processes play in shaping human behavior. This chapter reviews sociological theories that emphasize the relationship between people's social status and their criminal behavior. In the following chapter, the focus will be shifted to theories that analyze social processes and institutions and their influence on crime and deviance.

There are many reasons why sociology has been the predominant approach of U.S. criminologists during the twentieth century. First, it has long been evident that varying patterns of criminal behavior exist within the social structure. Some geographic areas are more prone to violence and serious theft-related crimes than others (see chapter 3). Criminologists have attempted to discover why such patterns exist and how they can be eliminated. Explanations of crime as an individual-oriented phenomenon fail to explain these apparent discrepancies in the crime rate. For example, if violence, as some criminologists suggest, is related to chemical or chromosome abnormality, then how do they explain why some areas of the city experience more violence than others? If violence has a biological origin, shouldn't it be distributed more evenly throughout the social structure?

Further, sociology is concerned with social change and the dynamic aspects of human behavior. It seeks to account for changes in technology, norms, values, institutions, and structures and their subsequent effect on individual and group behavior. As early as 1887, Ferdinand Tonnies distinguished between *Gemeinschaft* (community) and *Gesellschaft* (society).[1] The former is the preindustrial folk society based on tradition, folkways, and intimate human contact. The latter, the modern industrial society, is characterized by impersonal relationships, competition, and the erosion of kinship. A similar model of society was constructed by Emil Durkheim in his conception of *mechanical solidarity* and *organic solidarity*.[2] Mechanical solidarity characterizes the society that keeps its structure intact by consensus among its members concerning appropriate values, norms, rules, and so on (similar to Gesellschaft). In contrast, organic solidarity marks social systems in which members are dependent on one another because of close personal ties and highly specialized roles.

These concepts are still useful today because the changing structure of modern postindustrial society continues to have a tremendous effect on intergroup and interpersonal relationships.[3] For example, one change has been the reduced influence of the family and the increased stress on individuality, independence, and isolation. It is not surprising that family disruption and personal alienation have been linked to some forms of criminality.

Still another important social change has been the rapid increase in technology and its influence on the social system. One outcome has been the need for more service, technological, and white-collar workers and fewer blue-collar and agricultural workers. People who lack the requisite social and educational training, who are the victims of racial prejudice and class bias, have found that the road to success through upward occupational mobility has become almost impassable. Lack of upward mobility coupled with the failure of government-sponsored programs designed to alleviate poverty may make crime an attractive solution to socially deprived but economically enterprising people.

Sociology's stress on intergroup and interpersonal transactions also promotes it as a source for criminological study. Criminologists believe that understanding the dynamics of personal interactions between individuals and their families, their peers, their schools, their jobs, the criminal justice agencies, and the like is important for understanding the cause of crime.[4] The relationship of one social class or group to another or to the existing power structure that controls the nation's legal and economic system may also be closely related to criminality. Sociology is concerned with the benefits of positive human interactions and the costs of negative ones. Crime is itself an interaction and therefore should not be studied without considering the interactions of all participants in a criminal act—the law violator, the victim, the law enforcers, the lawmakers, and society in general. Individual-oriented theory often neglects to consider these important factors.

To summarize, concern about the ecological distribution of crime, the effect of social change and differentiation on criminality, and the interactive nature of crime itself has made sociology the foundation of modern criminology.

Historical Foundations of Sociological Criminology

Chapter 5 reviewed the development of classical theory in the works of Bentham and Beccaria; chapter 6, the development of biological and psychological theories in the works of Lombroso and Freud. Among the pioneering contributors to the development of sociologically based theory, two stand out for closer attention—Lambert A. J. Quetelet (1796–1874) and Emil Durkheim (1858–1917).

L. A. J. QUETELET

Lambert Quetelet was a Belgian mathematician who began (along with a Frenchman, Andre-Michel Guerry) what is known as the **cartographic school of criminology**.[5] Quetelet, who made use of statistics developed in France in the early nineteenth century (called the *Comptes generaux de l'administration de la justice*), was one of the first social scientists to use objective mathematical techniques to investigate the influence of social factors such as season, climate, sex, and age on the propensity to commit crime.

Some of Quetelet's most important findings are summarized below.

- *Age*—Age is the factor Quetelet found to have the greatest influence on crime. Crime appears to be proportionate to the "physical power and passions" of people. At twenty-five, a man reaches his physical peak and therefore is most likely to commit crime.[6]
- *Sex*—Sex contributes to the propensity to commit crime. Only one woman goes before the court for every four men. Crime usually manifests itself later in women—at thirty—than in men. Women are more likely to be property offenders than violent criminals. When women wish to harm others, they usually use poison.[7]
- *Season*—Season exercises a marked influence on crime. During the summer, the greatest number of crimes against persons are committed; during the winter, property crimes predominate.
- *Climate*—Southern climates promote crimes against the person; severe climates have higher property crime rates.
- *Heterogeneity*—"The countries where frequent mixture of the people takes place; those in which industry and trade collect many persons and things together, and possess the greatest activity; finally, those where the in-

equality of fortune is most felt, all things being equal, are those which give rise to the greatest number of crimes."[8]

- *Education*—"[Education] is far from having so much innocence on the propensity to crime as is generally supposed. Moreover, moral instruction is very often confounded with instruction in reading and writing alone, and which is most frequently an accessory instrument to crime."

- *Poverty*—"Several of the departments of France, considered to be the poorest, are at the same time the most moral. Man is not driven to crime because he is poor, but more generally because he passes rapidly from a state of comfort to one of misery, and an inadequacy to supply the artifical wants which he has created.

    The higher we go in the ranks of society, and consequently in the degrees of education, we find a smaller and smaller proportion of guilty women to men; descending to the lowest orders, the habits of both sexes resemble each other more and more."[9]

- *Drink*—Drink in a four-year period accounted for 446 of 1,129 murders.[10]

Quetelet was a pioneer of sociologically oriented criminology. He identified many of the relationships between crime and social phenomena that still serve as a basis for criminology today.

EMIL DURKHEIM

There is little question that Durkheim has been for three-quarters of a century, and remains today, the preeminent theorist in the sociological treatment of deviant behavior.[11]

Emil Durkheim is one of the founders of sociology and a significant contributor to criminology. In fact, it is probably accurate to claim that his presentation of crime has been more influential on modern criminology than any other.

Durkheim's most significant contribution was his conclusion that crime is a normal and necessary social behavior. Since it has existed in every age, in both poverty and prosperity, it seems part of human nature.[12]

According to Durkheim, the inevitability of crime is linked to the differences (heterogeneity) within society. Since people are so different from one another and employ such a variety of methods and forms of behavior to meet their needs, it is not surprising that some will resort to criminality. Thus, as long as human differences exist, crime is inevitable and one of the fundamental conditions of social life.

Crime, argued Durkheim, can also be useful, and on occasion even healthy, for a society to experience. The existence of crime implies that a way is open for social change and that the social structure is not rigid or inflexible. Put another way, if crime did not exist, it would mean that everyone behaved the same way and agreed totally on what is right and wrong. Such universal conformity would stifle creativity and independent thinking.

To illustrate this concept, Durkheim offered the example of the Greek philosopher Socrates, who was considered a criminal and put to death for corrupting the morals of youth. Durkheim distinguished this *altruistic criminal* type from the *common criminal* by analyzing the motivation and reason behind the deviant behavior of each. The common criminal rejects all discipline, makes destruction or law violation an end unto itself, and manifests little interest in moral conduct.

The altruistic criminal is offended by the rules of society and seeks social change and an improved moral climate through his or her acts.

In addition, Durkheim argued that crime is beneficial because it calls attention to social ills. A rising crime rate can signal the need for social change and promote a variety of programs designed to relieve the human suffering that may have caused crime in the first place.

Social Structure Theories

People in the United States live in a stratified society. Social strata are created by the unequal distribution of wealth, power, and prestige. Social classes are segments of the population whose members have a relatively similar share of desirable things and who share attitudes, values, norms, and an identifiable lifestyle. In U.S. society, it is common to identify people as upper-, middle-, and lower-class citizens, with a broad range of economic variations existing within each group. The upper-upper class is reserved for a small number of exceptionally well-to-do families who maintain enormous financial and social resources.

The Internal Revenue Service estimates that in 1984 about 21,500 people had assets in excess of $5 million. In contrast, the lower class is made up of the chronically poor who are dependent on government supplements, such as welfare, to survive. While the richest 2.8 percent of U.S. families hold more than 28 percent of the nation's wealth, the poorest 20 percent have only 5 percent. Education, health, nutrition, occupational prestige, and social activities are also closely correlated with class membership.[13]

Members of the lower class also suffer in other ways. They are more prone to depression, less likely to have achievement motivation, and less likely to put off immediate gratification for future gain. Lower-class citizens are constantly bombarded with a flood of media advertisements linking material possessions to self-worth, but they are often unable to attain desired goods and services through conventional means. Thus, though they are members of a society that extols material success above all other, they are unable to satisfactorily compete for such success with members of the upper classes.

The disabilities suffered by the lower-class citizen are particularly acute for racial minorities. Black citizens, for example, have a mean income level almost half that of whites, an unemployment rate almost twice as high, and a male high-school dropout rate 50 percent higher.[14] Though blacks comprise about 12 percent of the U.S. population, approximately 50 percent of the inmates in prisons and jails are black; and the black crime rate for many major crimes is significantly higher than the white crime rate.

PROBLEMS OF LOWER-CLASS CULTURE

Lower-class slum areas are the scene of inadequate housing and health care, disrupted family lives, underemployment, and despair. More than half the families are fatherless and husbandless, headed by a female who is the sole breadwinner and who is often aided by welfare and ADC (Aid to Dependent Children). Though it is estimated that two-thirds to three-quarters of the urban poor are white, minorities are overrepresented within the poverty classes; children under 18 make up about 40 percent of the urban poor.[15]

Social scientists such as Oscar Lewis argue that the crushing lifestyle of slum areas produces a **culture of poverty** passed from one generation to the next.[16] The culture of poverty is marked by apathy, cynicism, helplessness, and mistrust of social institutions such as schools, government agencies, and the police. This mistrust prevents slum dwellers from taking advantage of the meager opportunities available to them. In 1970 Gunnar Myrdal described a worldwide underclass cut off from society, its members lacking the education and skills needed to be effectively in demand in modern society[17]; in 1982 Ken Auletta described an American **under class** in much the same terms.[18] Despite all our technological success, the fact that a significant percentage of U.S. citizens live in poverty and suffer its consequences remains an important social problem.

SOCIAL STRUCTURE AND CRIME

Considering the deprivations suffered by the lower class, it is not surprising that a disadvantaged economic class position has been viewed by twentieth-century criminologists as a primary cause of crime. This view is referred to as **social structure theory.** As a group, social structure theories suggest that forces operating in the lower-class areas of the environment push many of their residents into criminal behavior patterns. They consider the existence of unsupervised teenage gangs, high crime rates, and social disorder in slum areas as major social problems.

Lower-class crime is often the violent, destructive product of youth gangs and marginally employed young adults. Although members of the middle and upper classes also engage in crime, social structure theorists view middle-class crime as being of relatively lower frequency, seriousness, and danger to the general public. Thus, social structure theory views the real crime problem as essentially a lower-class phenomenon, beginning in youth and continuing into young adulthood.

Most social structure theories focus on the law-violating behavior of youth. They suggest that the social forces that cause crime begin to have effect on people while they are relatively young, and then continue their influence throughout a person's life. Though not all youthful offenders become adult criminals, many begin their training and learn criminal values while members of youth gangs and groups.

There are two main branches of thought within the social structure perspective—cultural deviance theory and strain theory.

Cultural deviance theory, also referred to as **cultural transmission** or **culture conflict theory**, suggests that criminal behavior is an expression of conformity to lower-class cultural values and traditions. Obedience to the informal rules of behavior existing in slum areas causes inevitable conflict with the laws of conventional society. By adhering to the values of people with whom they are in close personal contact, lower-class citizens are often put in a position in which they must violate the law. Furthermore, nonconventional lower-class values are handed from one generation of urban slum dwellers to the next; hence the term *cultural transmission.*

The second branch of social structure theory can be labeled **strain theory.** Strain theories are similar to cultural deviance theories when they portray the lower-class citizen as being more crime-prone than members of the middle and upper classes. Also, both strain and cultural deviance theories view crime as a collective response to culturally defined behavior demands. The two perspectives differ in their treatment of the distribution of social norms, values, and goals. Whereas the cultural deviance school views the lower-class culture as maintaining its own unique set of values and goals, strain theorists argue that similar sets of goals and values are common to all economic strata; the overwhelming majority of people in the United States desire wealth, personal possessions, education, power, prestige, and other life comforts. Nonetheless, because of their economic and social disadvantages, lower-class citizens are unable to achieve these symbols of success through the conventional means available to them. Consequently, they feel anger, frustration, and resentment toward a society that placed them, by birth, within a disadvantaged economic category. Criminologists refer to these feelings of frustration as **strain.** As a consequence of perceived strain, lower-class citizens have some choices to make. They can accept their lot in life and live out their days as socially responsible, if unrewarded, citizens. Or they can choose an alternative means of achieving success; gain through criminality is a popular choice.

Social structure theories refute the notion that crime is an individualistic expression of psychological imbalance, biological traits, or personal insensitivity to social controls. It says that links between people living in similar social environments cause them to behave in a similar, predictable fashion. If individuals acted independently, then it would be impossible that the mere fact of their social predicament could cause crime or that lower-class life could influence their behavior.

The second assumption is that a tangible relationship exists between social position and crime. As noted in chapter 3, official statistics almost uniformly support the contention that there is an inverse relationship between class and crime—the lower people are on the economic scale, the more likely they are to engage in criminal activities. Research using other measures of criminality—self-reports and victimization studies, for example—are less uniform but still seem consistent in direction. Moreover, it is alleged by social structure theorists that the most serious and violent crimes are for the most part committed by the lower classes.

Critics of the approach counter with the charge that lower-class crime rates are an artifact of bias in the criminal justice system. Lower-class citizens seem to have higher crime rates because they are arrested and prosecuted by agents of the justice system who, as members of the middle class, exhibit class bias. This pattern is particularly noticeable with respect to minority group members, who have long suffered at the hands of the justice system. We will examine this debate more fully later in the book. Let us now turn to a discussion of the most important social structure theories of crime.

Cultural Deviance Theory

Cultural deviance theory suggests that slum dwellers violate the law because they adhere to the unique, independent value system existing within lower-class areas— a value system that places them in conflict with middle-class norms and rules. Lower-class values applaud such behaviors as being tough and "cool," never showing fear, being disrespectful to authority, living for today and letting tomorrow take care of itself, and respecting "street smarts" and disparaging formal education. More importantly, these distinct lower-class values are passed down from one generation to the next. Therefore, to understand crime, one must focus on the developing careers of young teenage criminals as they mature into serious adult offenders.

THE CHICAGO SCHOOL

The Department of Sociology at the University of Chicago was the foundation of cultural deviance theory. Begun by Albion Woodbury Small in 1892, it was the home of such distinguished scholars as W. I. Thomas, Robert Ezra Park, and Ernest W. Burgess.

Crime and Unemployment

The social structure approach links crime to the economic deprivation experienced in ghetto areas. It follows that rates of unemployment are related to crime rates: If people don't hold jobs, they will be more likely to turn to crime as a means of support. Is this assumption valid? Is there a relationship between crime and unemployment?

Despite the logic of this proposition, little clear-cut evidence linking unemployment to high crime rates exists. For example, even during the economic prosperity of the 1960s the crime rate rose dramatically.

Richard Freeman reviewed the literature on the subject and found that crime and unemployment are only weakly related. Though Freeman found evidence that criminals have poorer work records than noncriminals, there was little indication that changing market conditions would cause them to choose legitimate earning opportunities. Though crime rates in cities and states are slightly linked to labor market conditions, the sanctions and criminal penalties employed in these areas have a greater effect on the crime rate than market factors.

More supportive of the unemployment/crime link are data on incarcerated inmates. Some of the important findings of a national survey of inmates were summarized in a report by the Federal Government's Bureau of Justice Statistics, described below.

UNEMPLOYMENT WAS EXPERIENCED BY MANY OFFENDERS

About 40 percent of all males in jail had been unemployed at the time they entered jail. Among the 60 percent who were working, 12 percent were working only part time. Compare this with an 84 percent employment rate for the U.S. male population age 18–54, and with only 3 percent limited to part-time work.

Many prison inmates were unemployed prior to arrest. The highest incarceration rate among U.S. males age 16–64 was among those who were unemployed:

	Incarceration rate per 100,000 U.S. population
In labor force	396
Employed	356
Unemployed	933
Not in labor force	442
Total	405

SOURCE. *Prisons and prisoners*, January 1982.

A HIGH PROPORTION OF ADULT FELONS LACKED STEADY EMPLOYMENT

Adult felons were more likely than the general population to have never worked at all or to have held a wide variety of short-term jobs. Some 40 percent of a group of prisoners in a Rand Corporation study were evenly divided between these two extremes. On the average, these felons committed more crimes, particularly more property crimes, than the 60 percent who had a more stable employment history.

As noted by Freeman, research shows some connection between crime and unemployment, but fails to

---

The *Chicago School*, as it is called, devoted a great deal of its attention to ecological studies of the city. In 1916, Robert Ezra Park called for anthropological methods of description and observation to be applied to urban life.[19] He was concerned about how neighborhood structure developed, how isolated pockets of poverty developed, and what social policies could be used to alleviate urban problems.

Over the next twenty years, Chicago School sociologists carried out an ambitious program of research and scholarship. Such works as Harvey Zorbaugh's *The Gold Coast and the Slum*,[20] Frederick Thrasher's *The Gang*,[21] and Louis Wirth's *The Ghetto*[22] are classic examples of objective, highly descriptive accounts of urban life.

The methods of the Chicago School were used by several of its resident scholars to study crime. Cultural deviance theory was popularized by the work of three Chicagoans—Henry McKay, Clifford R. Shaw, and Frederick Thrasher. They linked life in transitional slum areas to the inclination to commit crime. The following discussion will examine their work more closely.

show a well-defined, clearly quantifiable linkage. He adds that stronger evidence exists that shows criminal sanctions having a greater impact on crime than labor/market factors and that the widely different crime rates of cities and states are loosely linked to labor/market conditions. As with other characteristics, most unemployed people do not become criminals.

AVERAGE INMATE WAS AT THE POVERTY LEVEL BEFORE ENTERING JAIL OR PRISON

Almost half of all male inmates in jail in 1978 said they had incomes under $3,000 prior to arrest. Thus the median income (for those reporting any income at all) was roughly a third of that for the general population. The median income for both male and female jail inmates was near the "poverty level" as defined by the U.S. Government ($3,147 for persons age 14–64 in 1977).

Before their arrest, 40 percent of all prisoners who were working were employed outside what they considered to be their customary occupation. For many, this suggests their inability to find work in their chosen field, and it also suggests some degree of underemployment.

MANY INMATES HAD INCOME FROM NONTRADITIONAL SOURCES BEFORE ENTERING JAIL

Among jail inmates:
- 25 percent had no source of income prior to arrest or depended on welfare, Social Security, or unemployment benefits.
- Only 4 percent said that their main source of income was illegal.
- 70 percent said that their main source of income had been a wage or a salary.

Relatively more female than male inmates:
- Depended on welfare, unemployment benefits, or Social Security (30 percent vs. 11 percent); many received Aid to Families with Dependent Children.
- Depended on family, friends, or loans from third parties for their subsistence (25 percent vs. 14 percent).
- Admitted that their main income was from illegal activities (6 percent vs. 4 percent).

Almost twice as many black as white women had income other than wages or salaries, mainly unemployment and social welfare funds.

As indicators of a crime/employment link, these data must be interpreted with caution. They may be more a reflection of the relationship between economic status and judicial sentencing practices than between work force participation and crime. In other words, the unemployed may stand a greater likelihood of being sent to jail or prison for their crimes than do offenders who hold jobs.

As Samuel Walker points out, employment rates may have little to do with inner-city minority youth whose employment status is consistently way below average. Even if employment rates rose, opportunities may be in high-tech areas whose doors are open only to the college trained. Members of the underclass may find crime to be one of the few areas of opportunities—even in the midst of national plenty.

SOURCE. Richard Freeman, "Crime and Unemployment," in James Q. Wilson, ed. Crime and Public Policy (San Francisco: Institute for Contemporary Studies, 1983), pp. 89–106; Samuel Walker, Sense and Nonsense About Crime (Monterey, Calif.: Brooks Cole, 1985), pp. 212–20; Bureau of Justice Statistics, Report to the Nation on Crime and Justice (Washington, D.C.: National Institute of Justice, 1983), p. 38.

THE ECOLOGY OF CRIME

Clifford Shaw and Henry McKay began their pioneering work on crime in Chicago during the early 1920s.[23] This period in the city's history was typical of the transition taking place in many other urban areas. Chicago had experienced a mid-nineteenth century population expansion, fueled by a dramatic influx of foreign-born immigrants and, later, migrating southern black families. Congregating in the central city, the newcomers occupied the oldest housing and therefore faced numerous health and environmental hazards. Physically deteriorating sections of the city soon developed.

This condition prompted the city's wealthy, established citizens to become concerned about the moral fabric of Chicago society. There existed a widespread belief that foreign immigrants and blacks were crime-prone and morally dissolute. In fact, local groups were created with the very purpose of "saving" the children of poor families from moral decadence.[24] It was popular to view crime as the property of inferior racial and ethnic groups.

Though there is little evidence that unemployment causes crime, most prison inmates have had poor employment records.

Based in Chicago, Shaw and McKay sought to explain crime and delinquency within the context of the changing urban environment. They rejected the racial and cultural explanations of criminality then popular and instead viewed the ecological condition of the city itself as the real culprit in the creation of criminal behavior. They saw that Chicago had developed into distinct neighborhoods, some marked by wealth and luxury and others by overcrowding, poor health and sanitary conditions, and extreme poverty. These slum areas were believed to be the spawning grounds of young criminals.

Shaw and McKay viewed crime as a product of the decaying **transitional neighborhood,** which manifested social disorganization and maintained conflicting values and social systems. Below, Clifford Shaw describes the concept of **social disorganization:**

> *The successive changes in the composition of population, the disintegration of the alien cultures, the diffusion of divergent cultural standards, and the gradual industrialization of the area have resulted in a dissolution of the neighborhood culture and organization. The continuity of conventional neighborhood traditions and institutions is broken. Thus, the effectiveness of the neighborhood as a unit of control and as a medium for the transmission of the moral standards of society is greatly diminished. The boy who grows up in this area has little access to the cultural heritages of conventional society. For the most part, the organization of his behavior takes place through his participation in the spontaneous play groups and organized gangs with which he had contact outside of the home. . . . this area is an especially favorable habitat for the development of boys' gangs and organized criminal groups.*[25]

Shaw and McKay identified the places in Chicago where youthful delinquents were found. They noted that distinct ecological areas had developed in the city, comprising a series of five concentric circles, or zones, and that some of the zones had more delinquent behavior than others (see figure 6.1). The areas of heaviest concentration appeared to be the transitional inner-city zones, where large numbers of foreign-born citizens had recently settled.[26] The zones farthest from the city's center were less prone to delinquency. Analysis of these data indicated a surprisingly stable pattern of delinquent activity in the five ecological zones over a sixty-five year period.

Shaw and McKay concluded that in the transitional neighborhoods, deviant and conventional values compete side by side with one another. Boys exposed to both value systems are often forced to choose between them and may then align themselves with groups that share similar ideas and behavior. Thus, the development of teenage law-violating groups and gangs is an essential element of youthful misbehavior in slum areas.

Because of their deviant values, slum youths often come into conflict with existing middle-class norms, which demand strict obedience to the legal code. Consequently, a value conflict occurs that sets the delinquent boy and his peer group even farther apart from conventional society. The result is a fuller acceptance of deviant goals and behavior. Shut out of conventional society, neighborhood street gangs become fixed institutions, recruiting new members and passing on delinquent traditions from one generation to the next.

Shaw and McKay's statistical analysis confirmed their theoretical suspicions. They found that even though crime rates changed, the highest rates were always in zones I and II (central city and transitional area). Moreover, the areas with the highest crime rates retained high rates even when the ethnic composition of the zone changed from German and Irish to Italian and Polish.[27]

An Analysis of Shaw and McKay. Most prominent among Shaw and McKay's many achievements was their finding that the ecology of the city influences criminal behavior. The Shaw-McKay model was an alternative to the view that criminals were either biological throwbacks, intellectually impaired individuals, or psychologically damaged people. Moreover, their research refuted the assumption that criminality is a property of any one minority or ethnic group.

Since the basis of their theory was that neighborhood disintegration and slum conditions are the primary causes of criminal behavior, Shaw and McKay paved the way for the many community action and treatment programs developed in the last half-century. Shaw himself was the founder of one very influential community-based treatment program, the *Chicago Area Project*, which will be discussed later in this chapter.

Another important feature of Shaw and McKay's work is that it depicted both adult criminality and delinquent gang membership as a normal response to the adverse social conditions existing in urban slum areas. Their findings mirror Durkheim's concept that crime can be normal and useful.

Despite these noteworthy achievements, Shaw and McKay ignore some important methodological issues. This oversight seriously damages the potential value of their work. Most important, their heavy reliance on police and court records undermines the accuracy of the research findings. Many valid reasons exist to question the accuracy of official police and court statistics (see chapter 3). Even if they are accurate, official statistics may merely reflect the current law enforcement practices operating in the city's various ecological zones. That is, a zone's high crime rate may be a result of diligent and extensive police surveillance in selected areas of the city and therefore may not reflect actual rates of criminal activity.

Numerous studies indicate that police use extensive discretion when arresting people and that social status is one factor that influences their decisions. Thus, it is likely that people in middle-class neighborhoods commit many criminal acts that never show up in official statistics because of police practices in these areas. On the other hand, people in lower-class areas face a far greater chance of arrest and court adjudication.

These criticisms aside, the Shaw-McKay theory provides a valuable contribution to our understanding of the causes of criminal behavior. By introducing a new variable—the ecology of the city—into the study of crime, the authors paved the way for a whole generation of criminologists to focus on the social influences on criminal and delinquent behavior.

FIGURE 7.1

Shaw and McKay's concentric zone model

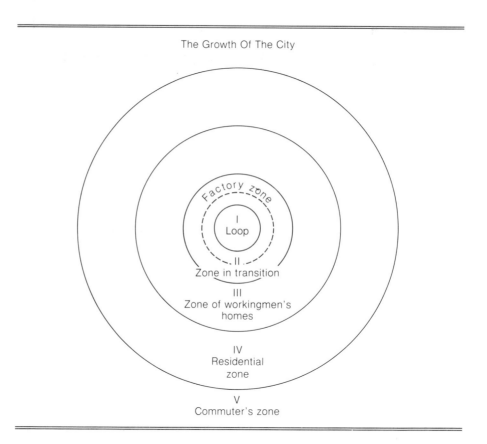

CULTURE CONFLICT

Thorsten Sellin's famous work, *Culture Conflict and Crime,* is a theoretical attempt to link cultural adaptation to criminality.[28] Sellin's main premise is that criminal law is an expression of the rules of the dominant culture. The content of the law, therefore, may create a clash between conventional, middle-class rules and splinter groups such as ethnic and racial minorities, who maintain their own set of **conduct norms**—rules governing the day-to-day living conditions within these subcultures.

Law is also a constantly changing concept; crimes of yesteryear may be legal conduct today, while crimes in one contemporary state may be legal conduct in another. Thus, to call persons deviant or criminal simply because they violate the rule of law is to neglect the diversity and heterogeneity that exists in society. To analyze crime, criminologists must be freed from dependence on law-oriented definitions.

Sellin instead focuses on conduct norms, which are the product of social life.[29] They reflect the restrictions social groups place on the activity of their members, restrictions aimed at protecting group norms. Violations of these norms might injure or harm the group. Each person belongs to social groups; and in a complex society, the number of groups they belong to—family, peer, occupation, and the like—is quite large. "A conflict of norms is said to exist when more or less divergent rules of conduct govern the specific life situation in which a person may find himself."[30] Thus, obedience to the norms of one group, such as friends, may violate the norms of another, such as society. Conduct norms are universal; they are not the product of one group, culture, or political structure.

Sellin goes on to describe how culture conflict has produced crime and delinquency. He points to the growth of a technological society that creates both a confusion of norms and a vast extension of impersonal control agencies designed to enforce rules. For many people living in such a culture, certain life situations are governed by conflicting norms, so that no matter how they behave, they will be violating the rules of one group or another. Sellin argues that the Chicago area studies of Clifford Shaw are examples of the problems of culture conflict. He also finds that immigrants who adhere to the norms of their cultural origin may find themselves in conflict with the rules of the U.S. community. For example, Sellin cites the case of a Sicilian father in New Jersey who killed the sixteen-year-old seducer of his daughter and then expressed surprise at being arrested, because he had "merely defended his family honor in a traditional way."[31]

MILLER'S THEORY OF LOWER-CLASS CULTURE CONFLICT

Walter Miller's theory of lower-class culture conflict is another important attempt to explain the criminal activity found in lower-class environments.[32] Instead of viewing crime as a psychological aberration or the product of a diseased personality, Miller, like Sellin, portrays criminal behavior as a normal reaction to the norms and values of a unique lower-class culture.

Miller generally takes a cultural deviance approach, but his work differs markedly from that of Shaw and McKay. Most notably, Miller views criminality as a product of the values and attitudes ingrained in all elements of lower-class culture. In contrast, Shaw and McKay suggest that (1) criminal behavior is a product of the unsupervised youth groups and gangs that form in lower-class areas to gain financial and social privileges, and (2) many families in lower-class areas actually espouse middle-class values. Both approaches, however, characterize crime as a neighborhood tradition passed from one generation to the next.

Characteristics of Lower-class Culture. Miller studied the daily activities of working-class citizens while conducting a delinquent gang control program in a major eastern city. He found that slum areas manifest a distinct cultural climate that remains stable over long periods of time. Citizens in these areas are on the fringe of the established economic system, with little chance for success within the legitimate social order. Consequently, they seek to achieve personal satisfaction in their own neighborhoods and culture.

According to Miller, a unique group of valuelike *focal concerns* dominates life among the lower class. These concerns do not necessarily represent a rebellion against middle-class values; rather, they have evolved specifically to fit conditions in slum areas. The major focal concerns that Miller identified are set out in more detail below.[33]

Trouble. Getting into and staying out of trouble is a major concern of lower-class citizens. Trouble includes such behavior as fighting, drinking, and sexual misconduct. In lower-class communities, people are evaluated by their actual or potential involvement in trouble-making activity. The attitude toward trouble is not always clear-cut. Sometimes it confers prestige—for example, when a man gets a reputation for being able to handle himself well in a fight. However, getting into trouble and having to pay the consequences can make a person look foolish and incompetent. In most instances, trouble-making escapades are designed with a goal in mind, such as stealing an automobile when the money to buy one is unobtainable. They are usually not examples of unplanned, destructive behavior.

Toughness. Lower-class males want local recognition of their physical and spiritual toughness. They refuse to be sentimental or soft and instead value physical strength, fighting ability, and athletic skill. Lower-class males who cannot meet these standards risk getting a reputation for being weak, inept, and effeminate.

Smartness. Another critical concern of lower-class citizens is maintaining an image of streetwise savvy, which carries with it the ability to outfox and outcon the opponent. This, of course, does not mean that intellectual brilliance is admired; in fact, ivory-tower types are disdained. Smartness, to the lower-class citizen, means knowing essential survival techniques like gambling, conning, and outsmarting the law.

Excitement. Another important feature of the lower-class lifestyle is the search for fun and excitement to enliven an otherwise drab existence. The search for excitement may lead to gambling, fighting, getting drunk, seeking sex, and so on. Going out on the town looking for excitement may eventually lead to that other focal concern, trouble. Excitement is not sought all the time. In between, the lower-class citizen may simply "hang out" and "be cool." Those who do not seek excitement are known as deadheads. They are safe and passive.

Fate. Lower-class citizens believe their lives are in the hands of strong spiritual forces that guide their destinies. Getting lucky, finding good fortune, and hitting the jackpot are all slum dwellers' daily dreams.

Autonomy. A general concern exists in lower-class cultures about personal freedom and autonomy. Being in the control of authority figures such as the police, teachers, and parents is an unacceptable weakness, incompatible with toughness. Conflicts arise when the lower-class citizen is confronted with rigidly controlled environments like schools, hospitals, the military, courts, and prisons. The usual manner of dealing with these authoritarian regimes is to actively disdain them, a behavior response that frequently results in a continuing relationship with them. For example, such behavior in youths can result in their being held back in school.

Focal Concerns and Crime. It seems evident that obedience to lower-class focal concerns will promote behavior that often runs afoul of the law. In this area, Miller's work is quite similar to Sellin's culture conflict approach. For example, proving one's toughness may demand that one never backs down from a fight. Displaying street smarts may lead to con games and other illegal schemes, while the search for excitement may result in drinking, gambling, or drug abuse. Thus, it is obedience to existing cultural demands that precipitates lower-class crime, and not a sense of frustration or alienation from the greater society.

An Analysis of Focal Concern Theory. Professor Miller's theoretical model has been praised as a sensitive attempt to view crime and delinquency from the perspective of the lower-class slum dweller. Instead of analyzing from the middle-class point of view, he reports his data from the orientations of the residents themselves.

Miller draws attention to the emergence of lower-class culture as a stable condition in U.S. life. He maintains that this culture contains its own unique rules, values, and norms—all quite different from those of upper- and middle-class societies. Crime is a functional response to these values rather than a violation of existing community rules. This statement, of course, is the key to the validity of Miller's view. If we believe that an isolated, unique lower-class culture exists, then it logically follows that the demands of this culture actually produce criminality. Yet, it is the necessity of maintaining this belief that presents the greatest challenge to the validity of Miller's theory. It is difficult to imagine that an isolated lower-class community exists that totally shuns generally held values and concerns such as education, religion, and family and instead substitutes excitement, toughness, and fate.

Miller's focal concerns may be elements of a lower-class culture, but they certainly do not seem to be the only ones operating in lower-class communities. Nor, considering the impact of the media, government agencies, and private charities, does it seem likely that lower-class citizens are insulated from at least a minimal awareness of middle-class values and goals. Yet Miller chooses to ignore the effect of middle-class values on lower-class communities and the possible influence this interaction can have.

Miller also ignores research evidence suggesting that lower-class youths' admiration of conventional values and behaviors is equal to that of middle-class adolescents. Several studies have found that gang boys and other lower-class youths have a high regard for such traditional behaviors as getting an education, working for grades at school, reading books, and saving money, and conversely, that they do not rate "being cool," using drugs, being a good fighter, or knowing how to steal any more highly than they rate traditional middle-class behaviors.[34] Thus, crime rates may be higher in lower-class areas, but there is little evidence that this is entirely the result of a unique and independent value orientation.

Strain Theories

Strain theories constitute the second branch of social structure theory. Collectively, they view crime and delinquency as a result of the frustration and anger people experience over their inability to achieve legitimate social and financial success. Strain theorists agree that most people originally share similar values and goals but that the ability to achieve them is stratified by socioeconomic class. In middle-

and upper-class communities, strain does not exist, since education and prestigious occupations are readily obtainable. In lower-class slum areas, strain occurs because legitimate avenues for success are all but closed. When no acceptable means for obtaining success exist, individuals may either use deviant methods to achieve their goals or reject socially accepted goals and substitute others for them.

This last point is quite important, because it distinguishes strain theories from cultural deviance theories. Strain theories hold that everyone desires middle-class goals but that the frustration of failing to achieve them causes lower-class people to substitute criminal behavior. Cultural deviance theories, on the other hand, maintain that many, if not all, lower-class people have a separate value system that places them in conflict with middle-class social control agents. The following subsections examine the most significant strain theories in greater detail.

MERTON'S THEORY OF ANOMIE

The best known strain theory is Robert Merton's **theory of anomie.**[35] Merton adapted Durkheim's concept of anomie to conditions in U.S. society. As initially developed by Durkheim, *anomie* was a condition of relative normlessness in a society or group. It referred to a property of the social structure, not to a property of the individual in relationship to society. Durkheim viewed an anomic condition as arising when the existing social structure could no longer establish and maintain control over individuals' wants and desires.

As originally conceived, anomie resulted from disruption in the social world resulting from natural or human-made catastrophes such as economic depression, war, famine, and so on. Durkheim also recognized an *anomie of prosperity,* which occurred when sudden good fortune disrupted a person's concept of norms, rules, and behavior.

Merton adapted Durkheim's abstract concept to fit the conditions of American society. He believes that two elements of all modern cultures interact to produce potentially anomic conditions—culturally defined **goals** and socially approved **means** for obtaining them. For example, U.S. society stresses the goals of acquiring wealth, success, and power. Socially permissible means include hard work, education, and thrift. Merton argues that every social system maintains a unique combination of goals and means.

Merton's position is that the legitimate means to acquire wealth are stratified across class and status lines. Those with little formal education and few economic resources soon find that they are denied the ability to legally acquire money and other success symbols. When socially mandated goals are uniform throughout society and access to legitimate means is bound by class and status, the resulting strain produces an anomic condition among those who are locked out of the legitimate opportunity structure. Consequently, they may develop criminal or delinquent solutions to the problem of attaining goals.

Social Adaptations. Merton argues that each person has his or her own concept of the goals of society and the means at his or her disposal to attain them. U.S. society, as mentioned, stresses the success goal above all others. Whereas some people have inadequate means of attaining success, others, who do have the means, reject societal goals as being unsuited to them.

TABLE 7.1
Typology of individual
modes of adaptation

Modes of adaptation	Cultural goals	Institutionalized means
I. Conformity	+	+
I. Innovation	+	−
II. Ritualism	−	+
V. Retreatism	−	−
V. Rebellion	±	±

SOURCE. Robert Merton, "Social Structure and Anomie" in *Social Theory and Social Structure* (Glencoe, Ill.: Free Press, 1957).

Table 7.1 shows Merton's diagram of the hypothetical relationship between social goals, the means for getting them, and the individual actor. The individual, as shown, can develop one of five adaptations to deal with the possibility of stress.

Conformity. Conformity occurs when individuals adopt social goals and also have the means at their disposal to attain them. In a balanced, stable society, this is the most common social adaptation. If a majority of its people did not practice conformity, the society would cease to exist.

Innovation. Innovation occurs when an individual accepts the goals of society but rejects or is incapable of using legitimate means to attain them. For example, when people want luxuries but lack money, the resulting conflict sometimes forces them to adopt an innovative solution to the problem—they steal.

Of the five adaptations, innovation is most closely associated with criminal behavior. The inescapable demand to succeed that pervades U.S. culture places such an enormous burden on those lacking economic opportunity that deviant modes of adaptation are not a surprising result. This condition accounts for the high rate of crime in poverty areas, where access to legitimate means is severely limited. However, innovative adaptations can occur in any social class when members perceive a lack of appropriate means to gain social success. For example, witness the stock frauds and tax evasion schemes of the rich.

Successful innovation has long-term effects. A continued frequency of successful deviance tends to lessen, and possibly eliminate, the perceived legitimacy of conventional norms for others in the social system. "The process thus enlarges the extent of anomie within the system," claims Merton, "so that others, who did not respond in the form of deviant behavior to the relatively slight anomie which first obtained, come to do so as anomie is spread and is intensified."[36] Thus, anomie causes an interactive effect in which people who observe the inability of society to control crime will resort to the law-violating means others have successfully used. This explains why crime is created and sustained in certain low-income ecological areas.

Ritualism. Ritualism results when goals are lowered in importance and means are at the same time rigidly adhered to. The maintenance of a strict set of manners and customs that serve no purpose is an example of ritualism. Such practices often exist in religious services, feudal societies, clubs, college fraternities, and other organizations. Ritualists gain pleasure from the practice of traditional ceremonies that have neither a real purpose nor a goal.

Manny: A Criminal-Addict's Story

This story is a first-person account of a gang boy who later evolved into a drug abuser. Here, he tells of his early life in teenage gangs similar to those described by Miller, Shaw, and McKay.

We used to have a lot of dances. That was during the time of Bill Haley and the Comets. Rock and roll was just starting to break through in the early fifties. We used to skip school and gather at people's houses. Their parents would be away working and we would throw big parties. But it was mostly dancing and fighting, with occasional making out. We'd drink a little, but there wasn't much booze around, and very little dope. We'd get all worked up dancing, and then it would feel good to go home and fight it out in the street with a rival gang member.

We used to have these dances in the school gym with four or five rival gangs. We're all supposed to go there; kind of a neighborhood integration thing. During the day we're trying to kill each other, but just 'cause it's nighttime we're supposed to be nice to each other? The chaperons would tell us that we couldn't wear sweaters to the dance. But we used to put our sweaters on under a white shirt and sport coat. So we had our front on until the shit started. At these dances there would always be an argument come up over something. There had to be arguments 'cause you had these rival gangs there. Anytime you got Young Stars and Hoods together, for example, you had an argument. It couldn't be any other way.

And pretty soon off the shirts would come and you'd see the different sweaters pop out. And we'd just get right down to the nitty-gritty right there. Kids would be busting heads; shivs would flash; tire irons and chains would start rapping. Before long there would be guys laying all over the dance floor bleeding. So they finally stopped having school dances trying to promote peace 'cause they just became another battlefield.

I remember, we used to roam the school halls looking for somebody to fight—anybody! I hear a lot of talk about race riots, and I know they are going on because I've been in a few; people getting killed for their color. But in those days it made no difference what color you were. If you were white, orange, blue, it made no difference. What mattered was the sweater you had on—what territory you were from—especially at night. And we never used to say that we were going out to fight all these "niggers," because a lot of gangs were made up of mixed groups. Even the Mau Maus over in Brooklyn were mixed, although they were mostly black guys. We used to ride the subways over into Nicky Cruz' area in Brook-

Retreatism. Retreatism entails a rejection of both the goals and the means of society. Merton suggests that people who adjust in this fashion are "in the society but not of it."

Included in this category are "psychotics, psychoneurotics, chronic autists, pariahs, outcasts, vagrants, vagabonds, tramps, chronic drunkards, and drug addicts." Often, this posture results when an individual accepts socially acceptable goals but is denied the means to attain them. Because such people are also morally or otherwise incapable of using illegitimate means, they attempt to escape their lack of success by withdrawing—either mentally or physically.

Rebellion. A rebellious adaptation involves the substitution of alternative sets of goals and means for the accepted ones of society. This adaptation is typical of revolutionaries, who wish to promote radical change in the existing social structure and who call for alternative lifestyles, goals, and beliefs. For many years, revolutionary groups have abounded in the United States, some espousing the violent overthrow of the existing social order and others advocating the use of nonviolent, passive resistance to change society. The revolutionary orientation can be used as a reaction against a corrupt and hated regime or as an effort to create alternate opportunities and lifestyles within the existing system.

It is evident that behaviors associated with retreatism, rebellion, and innovation are relevant to the production of criminal behavior. Considering the apparent inequality in U.S. society, it is not surprising that large segments of the population react to the resulting anomic condition with innovations such as theft

lyn. That was a bad thing to do, 'cause there were lots of warriors in the Mau Maus. All over the streets, and you could get caught short over in Brooklyn real easy. We just barely escaped with our lives once over there.

The gangs we rumble with mostly were the Hoods, of course, and then the Seven Crowns, the Scorpions, occasionally the Mau Maus, and then the Fordham Baldies. The Baldies were a group of guys made up of the sons of racketeers from the Fordham Road area. The Godfather up Fordham way used to be known as Baldie. So naturally the kids took the name. They were a pretty tough group so we mostly left them alone.

One all-black gang did emerge as a very powerful gang—like a couple that are going in LA right now. They must of had something like four thousand members. When they would get together they could down anybody. But we were in the upper Bronx and we had our territory. The Seven Crowns, the Mau Maus, and the Bishops were mostly from Brooklyn or Manhattan.

The Bishops used to have a guy called the Batman who walked around with a cape and all that regalia on all the time. He was a stone-cold killer. Everybody was scared shitless of the Batman. I mean, he was fourteen years old and he would kill just for the hell of it. One time Batman walked into a candy store over on Forty-fifth and sat down kind of behind some display cases. In walks this dude that had been making noises like he was looking to get the Batman. So, the Batman just takes this 12-gauge piece out from under his cape and blows the dude away. Killed him deader than a mackerel. He just walked up next to the guy, stuck the shotgun in his guts, pulled the trigger, and walked away. Just like that, no pain, no strain. The dude was dead before he hit the floor, and you know what? The Batman didn't give a shit. He just walked away.

Kids used to give the Batman contracts on other kids. For a few lousy bucks Batman would wipe out anybody. He threw a guy off the Third Avenue El one time for ten bucks. Just threw him off and killed him. They finally give him the electric chair. I don't know how many people Batman killed before that. But nobody thought much about it. That was the thing to do, in a way, for most of us. If you didn't like somebody, if they got in your way, kill them. So, in a sense we were all Batman. And the same way with appearance. We didn't look like most people think a "gang fighter" looks. If you'd have looked at Batman, you'd have never thought he was a stone-cold killer. I mean, he was really small and kind of pale looking. Always reading comic books. You guessed it; he was especially fond of Batman comics. That was his trip. Batman was the only dude I ever met who I was really scared of.

DISCUSSION QUESTIONS

1. How can a youth in a lower-class culture avoid gang membership?
2. How would you deal with a youth like Manny?

SOURCE. From Rettig-Torres-Garrett: *Manny: A Criminal Addict's Story*. Copyright © 1977 by Houghton Mifflin Company.

---

or extortion, with retreat into drugs or alcohol, or with rebellion exhibited by joining revolutionary or cultist groups.

An Analysis of Anomie Theory. Since its publication, Merton's theoretical model has received praise for its scope and precision. It is more sophisticated than the earlier cultural deviance approach, since it raises the possibility of differing types or styles of both deviant and nondeviant behavior and offers explanations for the existence of each. Furthermore, by linking deviant behavior to the success goals that control social behavior, anomie theory attempts to pinpoint the cause of the conflict that produces personal frustration and consequent criminality.

Merton's theory does not actually concern itself with the reason why any particular individual becomes deviant. Instead, it attempts to explain crime rates that exist in society. By acknowledging that society unfairly distributes the legitimate means to achieving success, anomie theory helps explain the existence of high crime areas and the apparent predominance of delinquent and criminal behavior among particular social and ethnic groups. By suggesting that social conditions, not individual personalities, produce crime, Merton—together with Shaw and McKay, Miller, and other social theorists—has greatly influenced the directions taken to reduce and control criminality during the latter half of the twentieth century.

The concept of anomie has also been linked to individual criminality. Scales have been created to measure an individual's perceptions of anomie by asking him or her to answer questions such as: "I feel depressed much of the time."[37] Research studies have shown that self-reported delinquents and incarcerated offenders are more likely to report feelings of anomie than members of the general public.[38] Yet, such data must be regarded with caution, since it is difficult to determine whether the perceptions of anomie preceded criminal activity or developed as a consequence of the law violations.

A number of questions are left unanswered by anomie theory.[39] Merton does not explain why people differ in their choice of behavior. Why does one person become a mugger and another enter a car-theft ring while another chooses school and a job? Anomie may be used to explain differences in crime rates, but it cannot explain why a particular individual in an anomie-susceptible area becomes a criminal while another remains a conformist, or why one chooses rebellion and another innovation.

Subcultural Strain Theories

Subcultural strain theories are extensions of Merton's earlier work on adaptations to deviance. Anomie theory predicts the formation of *subcultures*—groups of like-minded individuals who share similar ideas and values and who band together for support, defense, and mutual need. Subcultures are distinct elements within the larger culture; they share some of its features, but not all of them. Most importantly, they maintain distinct values and behaviors that may sometimes oppose the norms of the greater society.

Subcultural strain theories suggest that lower-class people, especially youths, are often alienated from approved means of attaining social success, such as education, family support, influential connections, and so on. To compensate, they develop their own subcultures in which they can feel important and successful. Often, membership in a criminal subculture stresses violence and criminality as means of attaining status, wealth, and pride.

This model seems similar to the previously discussed cultural deviance theories, but there is a major distinction between the two approaches: Whereas the cultural deviance school suggests that people living in lower-class, high-crime areas develop their own set of values and norms, subcultural strain theories suggest that citizens in lower-, middle-, and upper-class areas all share the same values and norms. Crime develops because lower-class citizens find that their opportunity to gain success through legitimate means is blocked or impeded. The strain between upper-class goals and lower-class means eventually produces an independent lower-class subculture that provides the ghetto youth with avenues for obtaining alternate forms of success and self-esteem. Members of this subculture engage in a mutual support system, in which teenage gangs form to prey upon victims; to provide members with a sense of belonging, camaraderie, and esteem; and to prepare members for a life of adult crime. Thus, subcultural strain theories focus on the development of teenage lower-class delinquents as they develop into career criminals.

COHEN'S THEORY OF DELINQUENT SUBCULTURES

Albert Cohen first articulated the theory of delinquent subculture in his 1955 book, *Delinquent Boys*.[40] Cohen's main purpose was to explain the disproportionate amount of officially recognized delinquent behavior found in lower-class slum neighborhoods. His central position was that delinquent behavior of lower-class youths is actually a protest against the norms and values of the middle-class U.S. culture. Because social conditions make them incapable of achieving success legitimately, lower-class youths experience a form of culture conflict that Cohen labels **status frustration.**[41] As a result, many of them join together in teenage gangs and engage in behavior that is "nonutilitarian, malicious, and negativistic."[42] Cohen views delinquents as forming a separate subculture and possessing a value system directly in opposition to that of the larger society. He describes the subculture as one that takes "its norms from the larger culture but turns them upside down. The delinquent's conduct is right by the standards of his subculture precisely because it is wrong by the norms of the larger cultures."[43]

Causes of Delinquency. According to Cohen, the development of the delinquent subculture is a function of the social and familial conditions children experience as they mature in the ghetto or slum environment. Delinquency is not a product of inherent class inferiority. Rather, it is a result of the social and economic limitations suffered by members of the less fortunate groups in society. The numbing burden of poverty is the real villain in the creation of delinquent careers.

A critical element of lower-class life, one that directly influences later delinquent behavior, is the nature of the child's family structure. Cohen argues that the relative position of a child's family in the social structure determines the quality of experiences and problems that the child will encounter later in life. By implication, Cohen suggests that lower-class families are incapable of teaching their offspring proper socialization techniques for entry into the dominant middle-class culture. Lower-class families, permanently cut off from the middle-class way of life, produce children who lack the basic skills necessary to achieve social and economic success in the demanding U.S. society. Developmental handicaps produced by a lower-class upbringing include lack of educational training, poor speech and communication skills, and inability to delay gratification.

Middle-Class Measuring Rods. One significant handicap that lower-class children face is the inability to positively impress authority figures such as teachers, employers, or supervisors. In U.S. society, these positions tend to be held by members of the middle or upper class, who have difficulty relating to the lower-class youngster. Cohen calls the standards set by these authority figures **middle-class measuring rods.** The conflict lower-class youths feel when they fail to meet these standards is a primary cause of delinquency.

In U.S. culture, people are constantly being evaluated on their performance in institutional settings—work, school, the military, the justice system—all controlled by representatives of the middle class. Negative evaluations become part of a permanent file that follows an individual for the rest of his or her life. When he or she wants to improve, earlier failure to adjust to middle-class standards may be used to discourage advancement. For example, a school record may be reviewed by juvenile court authorities, a juvenile court record may be opened by the military, a military record can influence the securing of a job. Lower-class youths who have difficulty adjusting to the middle-class measuring rods of one institution may find themselves prejudged by others. As criminologist Clarence Schrag puts it:

> *The ratings are reviewed, revised, magnified, or deprecated by the periodic updating of records and by the informal exchanges of information that commonly occur among the leaders of institutions, who frequently are also the pillars and the decision-makers of the community. From this we may conclude that a person's status and esteem in the community are largely determined by the judgements of his elders, which judgements reflect the traditional values of American society and are therefore*

regarded as binding on the middle class and on "respectable" members of the lower class as well.[44]

Reactions to Middle-Class Measuring Rods. Cohen believes lower-class boys who suffer rejection of middle-class decision makers become deeply affected by their lack of social recognition. They usually elect to adopt one of three alternative behaviors: the *corner boy* role, the *college boy* role, or the *delinquent boy* role.

The corner boy role is the most common response to middle-class rejection. The corner boy is not overtly delinquent but behaves in a way that is sometimes defined as delinquent. For example, he is a truant. He hangs out in the neighborhood; engages in gambling, athletics, and other group activities; and eventually obtains a menial job. His main loyalty is to his peer group, on which he depends for support, motivation, and interest. His values, therefore, are those of the group with which he is in close personal contact. The corner boy, well aware of his failure to achieve the standards of the American dream, retreats into the comforting world of his lower-class peers and eventually becomes a stable member of his society.

The college boy embraces the cultural and social values of the middle class. Rather than scorning middle-class measuring rods, he actively strives to be successful by middle-class standards. Cohen views this type of youth as one who is embarking on an almost hopeless path, since he is ill-equipped academically, socially, and linguistically to achieve the rewards of middle-class life.

The delinquent boy adopts a set of norms and principles in direct opposition to middle-class society's. Cohen describes some general properties of the delinquent subculture. For one thing, its members often manifest **short-run hedonism.**[45] That is, they live for today and let tomorrow take care of itself. Although Cohen believes short-run hedonism is a characteristic of lower-class culture as a whole, he finds it especially applicable to delinquent groups.

Members of the delinquent subculture are also careful to maintain **group autonomy.** They resist efforts by family, school, or other sources of authority to control their behavior. Although some individual delinquents may respond to direction from others, the gang itself is autonomous, independent, and the focus of "attraction, loyalty, and solidarity."[46]

Though members of the delinquent subculture often manifest negativistic and malicious behavior, Cohen believes they are still controlled to some degree by the norms and values of the generalized culture. They really want to be successful at school, jobs, and so on. To deal with the conflict inherent in this frustrating dilemma, the delinquent resorts to a process Cohen calls **reaction formation.** Symptoms of reaction formation include overly intense responses that seem disproportionate to the stimuli that trigger them. For the delinquent boy, this takes the form of "irrational, malicious, unaccountable hostility to the enemy within the gates as well as without—the norms of respectable middle-class society."[47] Reaction formation causes the delinquent boy to overreact to any perceived threat or slight. Consequently, the delinquent boy establishes himself as being quite distinct from middle-class society. Whereas the college boy and corner boy may be viewed as inferior to their middle-class counterparts, the delinquent's nonconformity to middle-class standards sets him, in his view, above the most exemplary college boy.

An Analysis of Cohen's Theory of Delinquent Subcultures. Cohen carries the work of cultural transmission theorists a step further by explaining the factors that promote and sustain a delinquent subculture. By introducing the concepts of status frustration, failure to meet middle-class measuring rods, and family disability, Cohen makes a clear presentation of factors that cause lower-class delinquency. Furthermore, by introducing the corner boy–college boy–delinquent boy triad, he attempts to explain why some lower-class youths are able to avoid entry into the delinquent subculture.

Despite its merits, Cohen's work is also subject to significant criticisms. For one thing, he presents no rigorous empirical evidence to support his contentions; and, as you saw in chapter 4, self-report studies have uncovered data indicating that delinquent behavior may be unrelated to social status or status frustration. Thus, although Cohen's theory seems plausible, he does not present enough evidence to unequivocally support its validity.

The internal consistency of Cohen's theory has also been brought into question. In a much-cited article, John Kitsuse and David Detrick note some ambiguities that run through Cohen's statements.[48] For example, at some points Cohen claims that delinquent boys value the opinion of middle-class persons; at others he says that they care little for middle-class opinions. Kitsuse and Detrick also question Cohen's concept of *reaction formation* and suggest that it is impossible to test the validity of this concept scientifically. Kitsuse and Detrick object to the categorization of delinquent behavior as nonutilitarian, malicious, and negativistic. They point to evidence that delinquent behavior is often rational, calculated, and utilitarian. It is, they conclude, a serious mistake to categorize all delinquents as being similarly engaged in destructive and thoughtless behavior.

Responding to these and other criticisms, Cohen (in conjunction with James Short) presented a refined version of his original theory.[49] Cohen and Short acknowledged that the original formulation of the delinquent subculture may have been too simplistic and that a more complex model may be called for.

Results of studies specifically designed to test Cohen's theory have been inconclusive. Albert Reiss and Lewis Rhodes found little relationship between status deprivation and criminality.[50] Their findings were supported in a recent study by Marvin Krohn and his associates.[51] However, two relatively recent studies, one by J. Johnstone[52] and another by Joseph Harry,[53] found that status perceptions were related to criminality. Thus, although Cohen's view seems plausible enough, research conducted to test its validity has not yielded conclusive results.

CLOWARD AND OHLIN'S THEORY OF DIFFERENTIAL OPPORTUNITY

In their well-known work *Delinquency and Opportunity*, Richard Cloward and Lloyd Ohlin add significantly to our knowledge of the development of criminal subcultures.[54]

Cloward and Ohlin propose that independent delinquent subcultures exist within society. "A delinquent subculture is one in which certain forms of delinquent activity are essential requirements for the performance of the dominant roles supported by the subculture."[55] Not all illegal acts are committed by youths who are part of this subculture; but the most serious, sustained, and costly ones are.

Delinquent subcultures spring up in areas where youths lack the opportunity to gain success through conventional means. True to strain theory principles, Cloward and Ohlin portray delinquents as individuals who want to conform to middle-class values but lack the means to do so: "Reaching out for socially approved goals under conditions that preclude their legitimate achievement may become a prelude to deviance."[56]

Differential Opportunities. The centerpeice of the Cloward-Ohlin theory is the concept of **differential opportunity.** The authors agree with Merton that people who perceive themselves as failures within conventional society will seek innovative ways to gain success; some will question the legitimacy of conventional codes of conduct as an appropriate guide for their own behavior and instead begin to use illegal means. The person who sees little hope for advancement by legitimate means may join with like-minded people to form a criminal subculture. Group support helps them handle the shame, fear, or guilt they may develop from engaging in illegal acts. Their participation in a delinquent subculture also gives them the opportunity to achieve personal success and satisfaction through the approval afforded them by their peers.

Now the concept of differential opportunity comes into play. If the ecological area in which a person resides provides the opportunity for personal success through crime-related activities—theft, organized crime, and the like—then the person may make use of these illegitimate opportunities to achieve financial gain. For example, such a person may join a successful car theft ring, become a member of organized crime, get involved in gambling, and so on. However, not all lower-class areas are stable enough to provide even illegal opportunities.

Put another way, not only are conventional opportunities stratified unequally in the social structure, but so too are illegal opportunities. Cloward and Ohlin propose the existence of three types of collective responses to blocked legitimate opportunities—criminal gangs, which seek monetary gain through crime; conflict gangs, which specialize in violence; and retreatist gangs, which are drug-related. The response taken depends on the means available.

Criminal Gangs. Youths join criminal gangs as a training ground for adult criminal careers. The dominant feature of group membership involves learning the knowledge and skills needed for success in criminal activities. The gang member starts by learning to look up to older criminals, as a middle-class youth might admire athletes or rock stars. Delinquent experiences help the gang boy to learn the techniques and orientation of the criminal world and to "cooperate successfully with others in criminal enterprises."[57] The gang boy learns to regard the world with suspicion—everyone has a "racket." However, he must prove himself reliable and dependable in his contacts with his criminal associates and be a "right guy."

A youth can best pursue a dependable criminal career by cultivating connections with successful older offenders who can help him "learn the ropes." Older offenders introduce aspiring delinquents to the *middlemen* of the crime business—fences, pawn shop operators—and also to legal connections—crooked police officers, shady lawyers, grafting politicians—who can insure their freedom of movement in a world made safe for crime.

The criminal subculture is likely to arise in an area characterized by close connections among young, young adult, and adult offenders. It creates a new opportunity structure that provides "alternative avenues to success goals."[58] Furthermore, the subculture controls youths' behavior, limiting activities that would otherwise lessen the probability of their receiving illegal gain—for example, engaging in nonfunctional, irrational violence.

Teenage gangs form in lower-class areas where conventional opportunities are unavailable.

Conflict Gangs. The stereotype of the conflict gang member is the "bopper" who swaggers with his gang, fights with weapons to win respect from rivals, and engages in unpredictable and destructive assaults on persons and property.

The conflict gang member must be ready to fight to protect his own and his gang's integrity and honor. By doing so, he develops a "rep," which provides him with a means for acquiring admiration from his peers and consequently helps him develop his own self-image. Conflict gangs "represent a way of securing access to the scarce resources for adolescent pleasure and opportunity in underprivileged areas."[59]

Conflict gangs develop in communities unable to provide either legitimate or illegitimate opportunities. These highly disorganized areas are marked by transient residents and physical deterioration. Crime in this area is "individualistic, unorganized, petty, poorly paid and unprotected."[60] There are no successful adult criminal role models from whom youths can learn criminal skills. Thus, when severe limitations on both criminal and conventional opportunity intensify frustrations of the young, it is likely they will turn to violence as a means of gaining status.

Retreatist Gangs. Members of the retreatist subculture are in constant search of ways of getting high—alcohol, pot, heroin, unusual sexual experiences, music. They are always "cool," detached from relationships with the conventional world. To feed their habits, retreatists develop a "hustle"—pimping, conning, selling drugs, and committing other nonviolent crimes. Personal status derives from the respect retreatists get from the society of which they are members—they want to be the "coolest" people around.

Many retreatists are double failures, unable to gain success through legitimate means and unwilling to do so through illegal ones. Others have tried to use illegal or violent tactics but have failed to gain proficiency in these adaptations. Not all double failures become retreatists; some may choose to be the law-abiding, low-economic-status corner boys previously identified by Albert Cohen.

An Analysis of Differential Opportunity Theory. Cloward and Ohlin's theory has the distinct advantage of avoiding the pitfalls of previous theoretical models. It is neither so broad as to lack precision nor so narrow as to be unimportant. Their recognition of the existence of different types of delinquent gang cultures—conflict, retreatist, and criminal—seems to be a more realistic reflection of the actual world of the delinquent than Cohen's original view of purely negativistic, destructive delinquent youths who oppose all social values. It is difficult to believe, as Cohen originally had it, that the majority of delinquent acts are purposeless and destructive, when statistics show that teenagers engage in many profit-related offenses, such as burglaries and robberies. Cloward and Ohlin's model seems to fit existing data more closely.

Cloward and Ohlin's tripartite model of urban delinquency also relates directly to the treatment and rehabilitation of delinquents. While other theorists, such as Cohen, Miller, Shaw, and McKay, see delinquent youths maintaining values and attitudes in opposition to middle-class culture, Cloward and Ohlin suggest that many delinquents share the goals and values of the general society but lack the means to obtain them. This position is an argument for rehabilitation programs, because it suggests that preventing delinquency does not involve changing basic attitudes and beliefs of delinquent youth. Rather, such programs have the somewhat simpler task of providing youths with the means for obtaining the success they truly desire. Later discussions will describe how Cloward and Ohlin's conceptualizations have influenced social policy and crime prevention programs.

Several studies have been conducted to test Cloward and Ohlin's model. Judson Landis and Frank Scarpitti surveyed a group of incarcerated boys and a high school control group and found that the delinquent youths perceived more limited opportunities than the nondelinquent youths.[61] These findings were supported by James Short, Ramon Rivera, and Ray Tennyson, who found in a study of gang delinquents that the perception of limited access to legitimate opportunity was more likely to be associated with delinquency than the perception of access to illegitimate opportunity.[62]

Despite this evidence, some research has produced results that conflict with opportunity theory. For example, when testing samples of lower- and middle-class delinquents, Leon Fannin and Marshall Clinard found that subjects differed in their attitudes and values:

> Lower class boys felt themselves to be . . . tougher, more powerful, fierce, fearless, and dangerous than middle-class boys. Middle-class delinquents . . . conceived of themselves as being more loyal, clever, smart, smooth and bad. . . . The lower class would like to be [ideal self] tougher, harder and more violent than the middle class, while the latter would like to be more loyal, lucky and firm.[63]

Fannin and Clinard's findings were supported by a similar study of peer associations conducted by Maynard Erikson and Lamar Empey.[64]

Some recent surveys of gang delinquency have also called into question Cloward and Ohlin's conclusions. They suggest that gangs are more pervasive than was previously expected, that more than one type of gang (conflict, criminal, and so on) exists in a particular area, and that the commitment of gang boys to one another is less intense than opportunity theory would suggest. Moreover, gangs do not seem to specialize in any particular type of behavior.

Thus, while some empirical evidence supports Cloward and Ohlin, an equal amount seems to contradict their approach.

Juvenile Gangs

An integral part of social structure theory involves the widespread existence of teenage gangs in lower-class areas. Shaw and McKay, Miller, Cohen, and Cloward and Ohlin all maintain that gangs are an essential part of the lower-class crime problem.

Much of what we know about the gang problem comes from Walter Miller's recent survey of gang behavior. According to Miller, gang delinquency is most serious in six cities: Chicago, New York, Los Angeles, Philadelphia, Detroit, and San Francisco. Using data from police, courts, and other agencies, Miller estimates that these cities contain between 760 and 2,700 gangs at any one time, with total memberships of 28,450 to 81,500 youths. The wide range of these statistics gives evidence of the difficulty in accurately estimating the extent of the gang problem.

In a subsequent analysis of his survey data, Miller reported on information gathered in 24 cities throughout the United States, which he grouped into separate categories based on population. In one analysis of gang problems in a group of 15 large cities, Miller discovered the existence of 1,300 gangs. Five of the cities—Boston, Philadelphia, New York, Chicago, and Los Angeles—reported having had at least 100 gangs in operation between 1973 and 1977. For the total group of 15 cities, the number of gang members was estimated at 52,000 (or about 25 members per gang). Gang size ranged from 60 members in New York and Los Angeles to 10 to 15 in Boston and San Francisco. Furthermore, it was estimated that 3.5 percent of all males between the ages of 10 and 19 were active gang members.

In another analysis of his data, Miller examined the presence of law-violating youth groups in 13 medium-sized cities, ranging from St. Paul, with a population of 287,000, to Dallas, with a population of 816,000. More than 8,000 youth groups were found in these cities—an average of 615 per city. They ranged in size from 23 members in Miami to 9 in Cleveland and St. Louis, with a national average of 15 members.

Miller extrapolates from these findings to estimate the existence of 120,000 law-violating youth group members in the 13 cities, making up 19 percent of the male population aged 10 to 19. In the 900 U.S. cities with populations of more than 25,000, Miller projects the existence of 105,000 youth groups with a combined membership of 1.6 million. Nationally, he estimates the existence of 80 groups for every gang in his data and 30 group members for every gang member.

Miller found evidence that gang-related killings are extremely frequent. The five largest cities with gang problems (New York, Chicago, Los Angeles, Philadelphia, and San Francisco) have almost 200 gang-related killings a year. In addition, gangs such as the Brotherhood in Detroit, Savage Skulls in New York, and Hwa Ching in San Francisco are using greater numbers of sophisticated weapons than ever before.

In his analysis of gang behavior between 1973 and 1977, Miller found little evidence that the gang problem is abating. In the three cities that take special notice of gang members arrested by police—New York, Los Angeles, and Chicago—13,000 yearly arrests occurred, 6,000 of them for serious crimes. During the six-year period from 1972 to 1977, approximately 1,000 gang-related killings were reported in the six largest cities. Miller also found that gangs and other law-violating youth groups committed over half of all youth crimes, or 1.6 million criminal acts.

DISCUSSION QUESTIONS

1. Are there gangs in your neighborhood? Have you had contact with them?

2. Does the extent of the gang problem support or contradict Cloward and Ohlin's model of lower-class crime?

SOURCE. Walter Miller, *Violence by Youth Gangs and Youth Groups as a Crime Problem in Major American Cities* (Washington, D.C.: Government Printing Office, 1975); Walter Miller, "Gangs, Groups and Serious Youth Crime," in *Critical Issues in Juvenile Delinquency*, ed. David Schichor and Delos Kelly (Lexington, Mass.: Lexington Books, 1980).

Routine Activities

A new social structure approach, routine activities theory, attempts to explain the crime patterns uncovered by both official and victimization crime surveys. According to Laurence Cohen and Marcus Felson and their associates, predatory crime is a function of three events: an offender motivated to commit the violation; a suitable target to be victimized by the offender; the absence of crime prevention or control influences.[70] The routine activities approach would suggest that people risk criminal behavior in proportion to their daily activities (for example, whether or not they stay close to home) and their personal characteristics which control these activities (for example, blacks have higher victim rates because of a high unemployment rate which controls their activities). The routine activities approach seems a promising way of understanding crime and victimization patterns and predicting the probability of victim risk.

Evaluation of Social Structure Theories

The social structure approach has had a tremendous influence on both criminological theory and crime prevention strategy. Both branches of social structure theory—cultural deviance theory and strain theory—seem to make sense when we view the deteriorated inner-city slum areas of the nation's largest cities and the high crime and delinquency rates occurring within them. Most people's image of the slum includes roaming bands of violent teenage gangs, drug users, prostitutes, muggers, and similar frightening examples of criminality.

Despite such images, we cannot be sure that it is lower-class culture itself that promotes crime and not some other force operating in society. For example, the preceding chapter reviewed theories suggesting that biological or psychological factors promote criminality. Another issue is whether a real delinquent subculture or lower-class culture actually exists. As previously mentioned, several researchers have found that gang boys and other delinquent youths seem to value middle-class concepts such as sharing, earning money, and respecting the law as highly as middle-class youths. Similarly, criminologists contend that lower-class youths value education as highly as middle-class students.

Some studies have found that delinquency is affected far more strongly by educational achievement than by social status. Kenneth Polk and F. Lynn Richmond compared students' academic achievement with their delinquent behavior and found that among both poor and wealthy youths, delinquency was low where students had earned good grades and grew progressively higher as grade point averages decreased.[65]

Similarly, criminological research has indicated that boys with high aspirations (even if they don't expect to achieve them) are less likely to be delinquent than youths with low aspirations, a finding that surely contradicts strain theory.

Opinion polls can also be used as evidence that a majority of lower-class citizens maintain middle-class values. For example, a recent national survey found that people earning under $5,000 were more likely to consider teenage gangs and crime in general a severe problem than citizens who earned $30,000 and more. Similarly, more than half the citizens earning less than $5,000 rated police protection in their neighborhood fairly good and said it would be acceptable for a police officer to strike a fleeing suspect.[66] These opinions seem similar to conventional middle-class values rather than representative of an independent, deviant subculture.

The most telling criticism of social structure theory, though, is that it ignores the criminality of the middle and upper classes. Chapter 1 noted, and chapter 10 will reemphasize, that white-collar crime accounts for billions of dollars each year. Whatever forces are pushing businesspeople to steal are not coming from the strain of lower-class life. Thus, most social structure theories must be viewed as explanations of lower-class street crime and not crime in the broadest sense.

Social Structure Theory and Social Policy

Social structure theory has profoundly affected social policy. If the cause of criminality is viewed as a separation between lower-class individuals and conventional goals, norms, and rules, it seems logical that alternatives to criminal behavior can be provided by giving slum dwellers opportunities to share in the goals and benefits of society.

Crime prevention efforts based on social structure precepts can be traced back to the Chicago Area Project, supervised by Clifford R. Shaw. This program attempted to organize existing community structures in slum areas to develop social stability in otherwise disorganized slums. The project sponsored recreation programs for children in the neighborhoods, including summer camping. It campaigned for community improvement in such areas as education, sanitation, traffic safety, physical conservation, and law enforcement. Project members also worked with police and court agencies to supervise and treat gang youth and adult offenders. In a twenty-five year assessment of the project, Solomon Kobrin found that it was successful in demonstrating the feasibility of creating youth welfare organizations in high-delinquency areas.[67] Kobrin also discovered that the project made a distinct contribution to ending the isolation of urban males from the mainstream of society.

Social structure concepts, especially the views of Cloward and Ohlin, were a critical ingredient in the Kennedy and Johnson administrations' "War on Poverty," begun in the early 1960s. Rather than organizing existing community structures, as Shaw's Chicago Area Project had done, this later effort called for an all-out attack on the crime-producing structures of slum areas.

The cornerstone of the War on Poverty's crime prevention effort was called Mobilization for Youth (MFY). This New York City-based program was funded for over $12 million. It was designed to serve multiple purposes: it provided teacher training and education to help educators deal with problem youth, created work opportunities through a youth job center, organized neighborhood councils and associations, provided street workers to deal with teen gangs, and set up counseling services and assistance to neighborhood families. Subsequent War on Poverty programs included the Job Corps; VISTA (the urban Peace Corps); Head Start and Upward Bound (educational enrichment programs); Neighborhood Legal Services; and the largest community organizing effort, the Community Action Program (CAP).[68]

War on Poverty programs such as MFY were sweeping efforts to change the social structure of the slum area. They sought to reduce crime by developing a sense of community pride and solidarity in poverty areas and providing educational and job opportunities for crime-prone youths. As history tells us, the programs failed. Federal and state funding often fell into the hands of middle-class managers and community developers and not the people it was designed to help. Managers were accused of graft and corruption. Some community organizers engineered rent strikes, lawsuits, protests and the like, which angered government officials and convinced them that financial backing of such programs should be ended. Rather than appeal to the political power structure, program administrators alienated them. Still later, the mood of the country began to change. The more conservative political climate under the Nixon, Ford, Carter, and Reagan administrations did not favor federal sponsorship of radical change in U.S. cities. Instead of a total community approach to solve the crime problem, a more selective crime prevention policy was adopted (see chapters 5 and 8). Some War on Poverty programs—Head Start, Neighborhood Legal Services, and the Community Action Program—have

TABLE 7.2 Social structure theories

Theory	Major premise	Strengths	Unanswered questions and other weaknesses
Cultural deviance theories			
Shaw and McKay's Ecological Theory	Crime is a product of transitional neighborhoods that manifest social disorganization and value conflict.	Identifies why crime rates are highest in slum areas. Points out the factors that produce crime. Suggests programs to help reduce crime.	Why does middle-class crime occur? Why are some youths insulated from a delinquent career? What causes gang members to forego criminality as adults? How accurate are official statistics?
Sellin's Culture Conflict Theory	Obedience to the norms of their lower-class culture puts people in conflict with the norms of the dominant culture.	Identifies the aspects of lower-class life that produce street crime. Adds to Shaw and McKay's analysis. Creates the concept of culture conflict.	Ignores middle-class crime. Does not provide an adequate means of testing theoretical premises. Uses vague terms (e.g., *conduct norms*).
Miller's Lower-Class Culture Conflict Theory	Citizens who obey the street rules of lower-class life (focal concerns) find themselves in conflict with the dominant culture.	Identifies more coherently the elements of lower-class culture that push people into committing street crimes.	Does not provide empirical support for the existence of a lower-class culture. Does not account for middle-class influence. Does not explain upper-class crime.
Strain theories			
Merton's Theory of Anomie	People who adopt the goals of society but lack the means to attain them seek alternatives such as crime.	Points out how success goal creates conflict and crime. Suggests that social conditions and not personality can account for crime. Can explain middle- and upper-class crime.	Does not explain why people choose the crime patterns they do. Does not account for violent and senseless acts.
Cohen's Theory of Delinquent Subcultures	Status frustration of lower-class boys, created by their failure to achieve middle-class success, causes them to join gangs.	Shows how the conditions of lower-class life produce crime. Explains violence and destructive acts. Identifies conflict of lower class with middle class.	Does not account for middle-class crime. Has not been empirically tested. Research efforts have been inconclusive. Ignores delinquency that is rational and profitable.
Cloward and Ohlin's Theory of Differential Opportunity	Blockage of conventional opportunities causes lower-class youths to join criminal, conflict, or retreatist gangs.	Shows that even illegal opportunities are structured in society. Indicates why people become involved in a particular type of criminal activity. Presents a way of preventing crime.	Does not account for middle-class crime. Assumes that lower-class citizens have the same values as the middle class. Gang surveys indicate that delinquent gang boys do not specialize in one type of crime.

continued to give people aid; nonetheless, this attempt to change the very structure of society must be judged a noble failure.

Summary

Sociological theory links crime to social institutions and processes. There are three main areas of sociological criminology: social structure theory, social process theory, and social conflict theory. (Table 7.2 reviews some of these theories.) Sociology has been the main orientation of criminologists because they know that crime rates vary among elements of the social structure, that society goes through changes that affect crime, and that social interaction relates to criminality.

Social structure theories suggest that people's places in the socioeconomic structure of society influence their chances of becoming criminal. Poor people are more likely to commit crimes because they are unable to achieve monetary or social success in any other way.

Social structure theory has two schools of thought—cultural deviance theory and strain theory. Cultural deviance theory suggests that slum dwellers violate the law because they adhere to a unique value system existing within their environment. Lower-class values approve of such behaviors as being tough, never showing fear, and defying authority. The origin of cultural deviance theory can be traced to the Chicago School. Clifford R. Shaw and Henry D. McKay made ecological maps of Chicago showing the concentration of delinquents in certain inner-city areas that were among the most decayed and poverty-stricken sections of the city. Shaw and McKay concluded that disorganized areas marked by divergent values and transitional populations produced criminality.

Thorsten Sellin's theory of culture conflict is similar to the Shaw-McKay model of crime. Sellin suggests that conduct norms that reflect the rules of small social groups are the key to crime causation. When persons adhere to the conduct norms of one group, they may find themselves in conflict with the rules of conventional society. In a similar vein, Walter Miller's theory of lower-class culture conflict suggests that lower-class citizens maintain a unique group of focal concerns—for example, being tough, being smart, looking for trouble—that result in their committing law violations.

Strain theories comprise the second branch of the social structure approach. They view crime as a result of the anger people experience over their inability to achieve legitimate social and economic success. Strain theories hold that most people share common values and beliefs but that the ability to achieve them is differentiated throughout the social structure. The best-known strain theory is Robert Merton's theory of anomie, which describes what happens when the means people have at their disposal are not adequate to satisfy their goals.

Subcultural strain theories are an extension of Merton's work. They suggest that people perceiving strain will bond together in their own groups or subcultures for support and recognition. Albert Cohen links the formation of subcultures to the failure of lower-class citizens to achieve recognition from middle-class decision makers such as teachers, employers, police officers, and the like. He calls their decisions middle-class measuring rods. Similarly, Richard Cloward and Lloyd Ohlin have argued that crime results from lower-class people's perception that their opportunity for success is limited. Consequently, youths in low-income areas may join criminal, conflict, or retreatist gangs.

Empirical research on social structure theory has not provided clear-cut evidence that it is a valid explanation of the cause of crime. Some studies show that crime is prevalent in the middle and upper classes as well as in lower-class culture; this may be interpreted as being in opposition to the social structure approach. On the other hand, recent studies have differentiated between lower- and middle-class crime. Research has also indicated that, though gangs do exist in lower-class areas, they may not take the format predicted by social structure theorists.

Social structure theories have been influential in shaping social policy. In the 1960s, community action and delinquency prevention programs were based on concepts of Cloward and Ohlin's differential opportunity theory.

Notes

1 Ferdinand Tonnies, *Community and Society*, trans. and ed. Charles P. Loomis (East Lansing: Michigan State University Press, 1957).

2 Emil Durkheim, *The Division of Labor in Society* (New York: Free Press, 1964).

3 Daniel Bell, *The Coming of Post-Industrial Society* (New York: Basic Books, 1973).

4 Edwin Lemert, *Human Deviance, Social Problems and Social Control* (Englewood Cliffs, N.J.: Prentice-Hall, 1967).

5 L. A. J. Quetelet, *A Treatise on Man and the Development of His Faculties* (Gainesville, Fla.: Scholars' Facsimilies and Reprints, 1969), pp. 82–96.

6 Ibid., p. 95.

7 Ibid.

8 Ibid.

9 Ibid.

10 Ibid., p. 82.

11 Robert Nisbet, *The Sociology of Emil Durkheim* (New York: Oxford University Press, 1974), p. 209.

12 Emil Durkheim, *Rules of the Sociological Method*, trans. S. A. Solvay and J. H. Mueller, ed. G. Catlin (New York: Free Press, 1966), pp. 65–73.

13 "28 Percent of Wealth Held by 2.8 Percent of Population," *Omaha World Herald*, 8 March 1985, p. 48.

14 Jon Shepherd, *Sociology* (St. Paul, Minn.: West Publishing Co., 1981), p. 202.

15 "1 in 5 Children Live in Poverty," *Omaha World Herald*, 1 March 1984, p. 17A.

16 Oscar Lewis, "The Culture of Poverty," *Scientific American* 215 (1966):19-25.

17 Gunnar Myrdal, *The Challenge of World Poverty* (New York: Vintage Books, 1970).

18 Ken Auletta, *The Under Class* (New York: Random House, 1982).

19 Robert E. Park, "The City: Suggestions for the Investigation of Human Behavior in the Urban Environment," in *Human Communities*, ed. Robert E. Park (New York: Free Press, 1952), pp. 13–51.

20 Harvey Zorbaugh, *The Gold Coast and the Slum* (Chicago: University of Chicago Press, 1929).

21 Frederick Thrasher, *The Gang* (Chicago: University of Chicago Press, 1927).

22 Louis Wirth, *The Ghetto* (Chicago: University of Chicago Press, 1928).

23 Clifford R. Shaw and Henry D. McKay, *Juvenile Delinquency and Urban Areas*, rev. ed. (Chicago: University of Chicago Press, 1972).

24 Anthony Platt, *The Child Savers: The Invention of Delinquency* (Chicago: University of Chicago Press, 1968).

25 Clifford Shaw, *The Natural History of a Delinquent Career* (Philadelphia: Albert Saifer, 1951), p. 15.

26 Shaw and McKay, *Juvenile Delinquency and Urban Areas*, p. 52.

27 Ibid., p. 171.

28 Thorsten Sellin, *Culture Conflict and Crime*, bulletin no. 41 (New York: Social Science Research Council, 1938).

29 Ibid., p. 22.

30 Ibid., p. 29.

31 Ibid., p. 68.

32 Walter Miller, "Lower-Class Culture as a Generating Milieu of Gang Delinquency," *Journal of Social Issues* 14 (1958):5–19.

33 Ibid., pp. 14–17.

34 James Short and Fred Strodtbeck, *Group Process and Gang Delinquency* (Chicago: University of Chicago Press, 1965), p. 59.

35 Robert Merton, *Social Theory and Social Structure*, enlarged ed. (New York: Free Press, 1968).

36 Ibid., p. 234.

37 Leo Srole, "Social Integration and Certain Corollaries," *American Sociological Review* 21 (1956):709–16.

38 For a general review, see M. Rosenberg, *Society and the Adolescent Self-Image* (Princeton, N.J.: Princeton University Press, 1965).

39 Albert Cohen, "The Sociology of the Deviant Act: Anomie Theory and Beyond," *American Sociological Review* 30 (1965):5–14.

40 Albert Cohen, *Delinquent Boys* (New York: Free Press, 1955).

41 Ibid., p. 25.

42 Ibid., p. 28.

43 Ibid.

44 Clarence Schrag, *Crime and Justice American Style* (Washington, D.C.: Government Printing Office, 1971), p. 74.

45 Cohen, *Delinquent Boys,* p. 30.

46 Ibid., p. 31.

47 Ibid., p. 133.

48 John Kitsuse and David Detrick, "Delinquent Boys: A Critique," *American Sociological Review* 24 (1958):20.

49 Albert Cohen and James Short, "Research on Delinquent Subcultures," *Journal of Social Issues* 14 (1958):20.

50 Albert Reiss and H. Lewis Rhodes, "The Distribution of Delinquency in the Social Class Structure," *American Sociological Review* 26 (1961):720–32.

51 M. Krohn, R. Akers, M. Radosovich, and L. Lanza-Kaduce, "Social Status and Deviance," *Criminology* 18 (1980):303–17.

52 J. Johnstone, "Social Class, Social Areas, and Delinquency," *Sociology and Social Research* 63 (1978):49–72.

53 Joseph Harry, "Social Class and Delinquency: One More Time," *Sociological Quarterly* 15 (1974):294–301.

54 Richard Cloward and Lloyd Ohlin, *Delinquency and Opportunity* (New York: Free Press, 1960).

55 Ibid., p. 7.

56 Ibid., p. 85.

57 Ibid., p. 23.

58 Ibid., p. 171.

59 Ibid., p. 24.

60 Ibid., p. 73.

61 Judson Landis and Frank Scarpitti, "Perceptions Regarding Value Orientation and Legitimate Opportunity: Delinquents and Non-delinquents," *Social Forces* 84 (1965):57–61.

62 James Short, Ramon Rivera, and Ray Tennyson, "Perceived Opportunities, Gang Membership and Delinquency," *American Sociological Review* 30 (1965):56–57.

63 Leon Fannin and Marshall Clinard, "Differences in the Conception of Self as a Male among Lower- and Middle-Class Delinquents," *Social Problems* 13 (1965):205–15.

64 LaMar Empey and Maynard Erickson, "Class Position, Peers, and Delinquency," *Sociology and Social Research* 49 (1965):268–82.

65 Kenneth Polk and F. Lynn Richmond, "Those Who Fail," in *Schools and Delinquency,* ed. Kenneth Polk and Walter Schafer (Englewood Cliffs, N.J.: Prentice-Hall, 1974), p. 67.

66 Hindelang, Gottfredson, and Flanagan, *Sourcebook of Criminal Justice Statistics—1980,* p. 188.

67 Solomon Kobrin, "The Chicago Area Project—25-Year Assessment," *Annals of the American Academy of Political and Social Science* 322 (1959):20–29.

68 See Barry Krisberg and James Austin, *Children of Ishmael* (Palo Alto, Calif.: Mayfield Publishing, 1978), p. 37.

69 Laurence Cohen and Marcus Felson, "Social Change and Crime Rate Trends: A Routine Activities Approach," *American Sociological Review* 44(1979):588–608; Laurence Cohen, James Kleugel, and Kenneth Land, "Social Inequality and Predatory Criminal Victimization: An Exposition and Test of a Formal Theory," *American Sociological Review* 46(1981):505–24; Steven Messner and Kenneth Tardiff, "The Social Ecology of Urban Homicide: An Application of the 'Routine Activities' Approach," *Criminology* 23(1985):241–67.

70 Ibid.

8 Sociological Approaches: Social Process Theories

CHAPTER OUTLINE

KEY TERMS

self-fulfilling prophecy

social process theories

social learning theories

control theory

labeling perspective

Edwin H. Sutherland

Donald Cressey

operant conditioning

differential reinforcement

differential association

David Matza

Gresham Sykes

drift

subterranean values

Travis Hirschi

commitment to conformity

Walter Reckless

containment

stigma

retrospective reading

dramatization of evil

primary deviance

secondary deviance

deviance amplification

diversion

restitution

Introduction

Social process theories hold that criminality is a function of the social-psychological interactions people have with the various organizations, institutions, and processes of society. For example, people may be influenced toward criminal behavior by poor familial relationships, peer group pressure, lack of educational success, or negative reactions by agents of the justice system. They may have differences of opinion, but all social process theorists share one basis concept: *people in all walks of life have the potential to become delinquents or criminals.* Although lower-class citizens may have added burden of poverty, racism, and low status, even middle- or upper-class citizens may turn to crime if their socialization is poor or destructive. As was the case for the social structure theories discussed in chapter 7, social process theories usually focus on the early development of young offenders. Though most delinquents do not evolve into adult criminals, those who do are believed to become enmeshed in criminal activities, learn criminal values and skills, and identify themselves as law violators while still in their teens.

The social process view reached prominence in the 1960s and 1970s, though some models had existed since the 1930s, because social structure theory seemed inadequate as an explanation of existing crime patterns. First, self-report studies made it clear that many youths from middle-class backgrounds engaged in frequent and serious criminal behavior. Even college students seemed to be engaged in the widespread use of drugs. The social structure view, with its emphasis on lower-class street crime, failed to address this issue adequately.

Second, social structure theories failed to explain why youthful offenders are able to forego deviant behavior when they reach maturity. If lower-class culture causes crime, that should not occur. There is no reason for social and economic forces operating in lower-class culture to lose their crimogenic influence on people as they mature. Process theorists have argued that people with high aspirations do not usually become criminals and that many delinquents and criminals do not feel deprived in the ways suggested by strain or cultural deviance theorists.[1]

A third factor prompting the development of social process theories was a growing realization that lower-class people could not be lumped together as a homogeneous group. Certainly not all people who lack financial resources are linked together in an unconventional deviant subculture. Because so many people in the lower end of the social and economic scale employ conventional means to get ahead—saving money, going to college, applying for small business loans, and so on—it is evident that differences in value orientations exist among the lower class. Conversely, many middle-class people have been found who reject conventional goals, drop out, use drugs, and so on. Thus, forces associated with crime seem to be operating at all levels of the social structure.

Social Processes and Crime

Criminologists have long studied the critical elements of socialization to determine how they contribute to the development of a criminal career. Prominent among these elements are the family, peer group, school, and society in general.

The family has long been considered a major determinant of criminal or conventional behavior.[2] It is alleged that youths who grow up in a household characterized by conflict and tension, where parents are absent or separated, or where there is a lack of familial love and support, will be susceptible to the crime promoting forces in the environment. Conversely, some criminologists maintain that even those children living in so-called high crime areas will be better able to resist the temptations of the streets if they receive fair discipline, care, and support from parents who provide them with strong, positive role models.[3]

Numerous studies have suggested a relationship between experiences in the family and crime. At one time growing up in a broken home was considered a primary cause of criminal behavior. More recent research has debunked that notion.[4] Factors now considered to have greater predictive value include inconsistent discipline, poor supervision, and lack of a warm, loving, supportive parent-child relationship. Intrafamily conflict and parental deviance have also been linked to a child's criminal behavior. Of recent interest has been the link between child abuse, neglect, sexual abuse, and crime.[5] A growing number of studies are finding that people who were abused as children are likely to engage in violent crime themselves when they mature into adulthood.[6] (See the following Close-Up entitled "Socialization and Crime").

A person's relationship with their school and the educational process have also been linked to criminality. Studies show that children who do poorly in school, lack educational motivation, and feel alienated are the most likely to engage in criminal acts.[7] Schools help contribute to criminality when they set problem youths apart from conventional society by creating a track system that identifies some students as college-bound and others as academic underachievers or potential dropouts; recent research by Terence Thornberry, Melanie Moore and R.L. Christenson indicates that school drop-outs face a significant chance of entering a criminal career.[8] It is not surprising that the U.S. school system has been the subject of recent criticism concerning its methods, goals, and objectives.[9] Most importantly, surveys indicate an extraordinary amount of serious criminal behavior occurs within the schools themselves.[10]

Peer group and peer relations have also been the focus of significant criminological inquiry. It is believed that much adolescent criminal activity begins as a group process and that the delinquent gang is the spawning ground of adult criminals. Surveys indicate that possibly over a million youths belong to delinquent gangs and law-violating youth groups.[11] Delinquent peers exert tremendous influence on a person's behavior, attitudes, and beliefs. In every element of the social structure, those youths who fall in with a "bad crowd" become more susceptible to delinquent, and later criminal, behavior patterns.

Finally, some criminologists believe that youths labeled by the agents of society as outsiders, delinquents, criminals, or deviants will incorporate these labels within their own personality structure and accept them as fitting portrayals of their character. For example, the person who teachers consider unmanageable, or in need of special education, will perceive these views as accurate since they come from those in power.[12] After the label is bestowed, such students may feel conventional modes of success are closed to them and subsequently seek illegal modes of gaining respect or achievement; this is referred to as a **self-fulfilling prophecy.** The bestowal of negative social labels and self-fulfilling prophecy is part of the ongoing social process.

SOCIAL PROCESS THEORIES

To many criminologists these social processes are the chief determinants of criminal behavior. They believe that even people living in the most deteriorated areas can successfully survive inducements to crime if they have positive experiences with the agents of socialization. They point to studies showing an absence of a clear-cut relationship between social class and crime rates (see chapter 4) as proof that forces other than economic ones influence criminal behavior. Even if it can be

Socialization and Crime

Social process theory holds that a turbulent home life, poor school relations, lack of family ties, and other personal problems are at the root of the crime problem. It therefore follows that people who have been involved in crime should manifest a significant amount of these problems. In order to test this assumption, the federal government sponsored a survey of the nation's prison inmates. Some of the survey findings are reprinted below.

MANY OFFENDERS COME FROM UNSTABLE HOMES

Research shows a higher incidence of unstable homes among delinquents than among nondelinquents. State prison inmates were more likely to have grown up in a home with only one parent present or to have been raised by relatives. Forty-seven percent of all inmates grew up in a two-percent household; in contrast, 77 percent of all children under age 18 in 1979 were living with two-parent families.

Because criminal careers typically begin at a young age, the identification of characteristics that distinguish delinquents from nondelinquents has been given considerable attention and has focused largely on what researchers term *under-the-roof culture*—the interactions of love, discipline, and supervision that occur between parents and children in the home.

VIOLENT BEHAVIOR IS LINKED TO ABUSE AS CHILDREN AND TO NEUROLOGICAL ABNORMALITIES

Violent behavior and physical and psychological abnormalities often appear among children and adolescents subjected to extreme abuse and violence in their families. D. O. Lewis and others, in a study comparing an extremely violent group of delinquent boys with a group of less violent delinquent boys, found striking psychological and neurological differences between the two groups. The more violent group exhibited a wide range of neurological abnormalities, were significantly more likely to have paranoid symptoms, and were more likely to have suffered and to have witnessed physical abuse. They also had far more severe verbal deficiencies.

PRISON INMATES WERE LIKELY TO HAVE RELATIVES WHO SERVED TIME

Forty percent of prison inmates had an immediate family member (father, mother, brother, or sister) who had served time in jail or prison. Similar data are not available for noncriminals, but it is highly unlikely that the proportion is as great.

MOST OFFENDERS WERE NOT MARRIED

Among jail and prison inmates:

- About half had never been married and another 20 percent were divorced or separated (vs. about half unmarried and 4 percent divorced or separated among U.S. males age 20–29).
- 20 percent were married (vs. 47 percent of the comparable U.S. population).

shown that crime rates are actually higher in lower-class areas, the presence of significant amounts of middle- and upper-class crime indicates that the crime problem cannot be explained solely by one's position in the social class structure.

Criminologists who hold these views have produced theoretical models dependent on social psychological, social development, and social interaction variables; as a group they are referred to here as **social process theories.**

Like social structure theories, the social process approach has several independent branches (see figure 8.1). The first branch, **social learning theories,** suggests that people learn the techniques of crime from close and intimate relationships with criminal peers. The second, **control theory,** maintains that everyone has the potential to become a criminal but that most people are controlled by their bond to society. The third branch, the **labeling perspective,** says people become criminals when significant members of society label them as such and they accept those labels as a personal identity.

The proportion of divorced and separated whites was much higher in jails and prisons than in the U.S. population; the marital status of black inmates was closer to that of blacks in the U.S. population.

MOST INMATES HAD DEPENDENT CHILDREN

Despite the high proportion of unmarried inmates, more than half had children, almost all of them under age 18. More than a third had three or more children. In most cases, children were cared for by the inmate's immediate family while the inmate was in jail or prison.

THE LEVEL OF EDUCATION REACHED BY JAIL AND PRISON INMATES WAS FAR BELOW THE NATIONAL AVERAGE

These data overrepresent street criminals as opposed to white-collar criminals; only about 40 percent of all jail and prison inmates had completed high school (vs. 85 percent of 20- to 29-year-old males in the U.S. population):

• The proportion of high school dropouts (those who started but did not complete high school) was about three times larger among the incarcerated.

Education level	Incarceration rate (per 1,000 U.S. males age 20-29)
No school/kindergarten	259
1–7 years	83
8th grade	70
9–11 years	46
12th grade	11
13–15 years	6
16 or more years	1

• Fully 6 percent of all prisoners had no schooling or only kindergarten. Their rate of incarceration was more than three times that of high school dropouts, the group with the next highest incarceration rate.
• College graduates had an extremely low incarceration rate.

EDUCATIONAL LEVEL WAS CLOSELY RELATED TO TYPE OF OFFENSE

• For whites, drug offenses and property crimes such as forgery, fraud, and embezzlement were more characteristic of those with at least twelve years of formal schooling than of those with less than eight years.
• Confinement for public-order crimes or for burglary was more apt to be associated with the lower educational levels.
• Imprisonment for drug offenses or for robbery was more commonly associated with high school graduates.
• Prisoners who had some college prior to incarceration were more likely than those with less education to have been convicted of a nonviolent offense and less likely to have a past record.

DISCUSSION QUESTIONS

1. Do these findings support the crime-socialization link?
2. What policy implications can be derived from these findings?

SOURCE. Bureau of Justice Statistics, *Report to The Nation on Crime and Justice*, p. 37.

Social Learning Theories

The social learning branch of social process theory suggests that crime is a product of learning the norms, values, and behaviors associated with criminal activity. Social learning can involve the actual techniques of crime—how to hotwire a car, how to "roll a joint"—as well as the psychological aspects of criminality—how to deal with the guilty feelings created by illegal activities, how to feel like a drug user.

The psychological social learning theories discussed in chapter 6 can be distinguished from the sociological social learning theories discussed here. Whereas the former rely on principles of behavioral psychology and do not rely heavily on interpersonal growth and interaction, the latter posit that social learning is a function of a long-term process of growth and development in which the significant others in a person's life control and direct their behavior.

Historically, the social learning perspective can be traced to the late nineteenth century and Gabriel Tarde's *theory of imitation*.[13] Tarde proposed three laws of

FIGURE 8.1

Social process theories

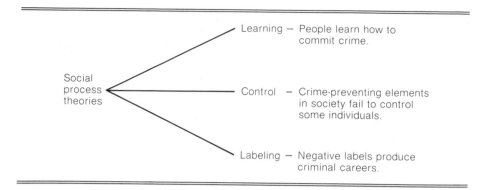

imitation to describe why people engage in crime: First, individuals in close and intimate contact with one another imitate each other's behavior. Second, imitation spreads from the top down; consequently, youngsters imitate older individuals, paupers imitate the rich, peasants imitate royalty, and so on. Crime among young, poor, or low-status people is really their effort to imitate wealthy, older, high-status people (for example, by gambling, drunkenness, accumulation of wealth).

Tarde's third law is the law of *insertion*. New acts and behaviors are superimposed on old ones and subsequently act either to reinforce or to discourage previous customs. For example, drug taking may be a popular fad among college students who previously used alcohol. However, students may find that a combination of both substances provides even greater stimulation, causing the use of both drugs and alcohol to increase. Or, a new criminal custom can develop that eliminates an older one—for example, train robbing has been replaced by truck hijacking.

This section briefly reviews the three prominent forms of social learning theory—differential association theory, differential reinforcement theory, and neutralization theory—that are the theoretical heirs to Tarde's laws of imitation.

DIFFERENTIAL ASSOCIATION THEORY

Edwin H. Sutherland, long considered the preeminent U.S. criminologist, first put forth the theory of differential association in 1939 in his text *Principles of Criminology*.[14] The final form of the theory appeared in 1947. In this form, differential association was applied to all criminal and delinquent behavior patterns; and its form has remained unchanged. Since Sutherland's death in 1950, his work has been continued by his long-time associate **Donald Cressey**. Cressey has been so successful in explaining and popularizing his mentor's efforts that differential association remains one of the most enduring explanations of criminal behavior.

Sutherland's research on white-collar crime, professional theft, and intelligence (as defined by IQ) led him to dispute the notion that crime was a function of the inadequacy of people in the lower classes.[15] To Sutherland, crime resulted from the learning of deviant values, which can occur in any culture.

A few ideas are basic to the theory of differential association:[16] Crime is a politically defined construct. It is defined by government authorities who are in political control of a particular jurisdiction. In societies characterized by culture conflict, the definition may be inconsistent and therefore may be rejected by some groups of people. Put another way, people may vary in their relative attachments to criminal and noncriminal definitions. The acquisition of behavior is a social learning process, not a political/legal process. Skills and motives conducive to crime are learned as a result of contacts with pro-crime values, attitudes, and definitions, and other patterns of criminal behavior.

Principles of Differential Association. The basic principles of differential association are explained in the statements below.[17]

- *Criminal behavior is learned.* This statement differentiates Sutherland's theory from prior attempts to classify criminal behavior as an inherent characteristic of born criminals. By suggesting that delinquent and criminal behavior is actually learned, Sutherland implied that it can be classified in the same manner as any other learned behavior, such as writing, painting, or reading.
- *Criminal behavior is learned in interaction with other persons in a process of communication.* Sutherland believed that illegal behavior is learned actively. An individual does not become a law violator simply by living in a crimogenic environment or by manifesting personal characteristics, such as low IQ or family problems, associated with criminality. Instead, criminal and other deviant behavior patterns are learned. People actively participate in the process with other individuals who serve as teachers and guides to crime. Thus, criminality cannot occur without the aid of others.
- *The principal part of the learning of criminal behavior occurs within intimate personal groups.* People's contacts with their most intimate social companions—family, friends, and peers—have the greatest influence on their learning of deviant behavior and attitudes. Relationships with these individuals color and control the interpretation of everyday events. Consequently, they help people to overcome social controls so that they can embrace criminal values and behaviors. The intimacy of these associations far outweighs the importance of any other form of communication—for example, movies or television. Even on those rare occasions when violent motion pictures seem to provoke mass criminal episodes, these outbreaks can be more readily explained as a reaction to peer group pressure than as a reaction to the films themselves.
- *Learning criminal behavior includes (a) learning the techniques of committing the crime, which are sometimes very complicated, sometimes very simple, and (b) learning the specific direction of motives, drives, rationalizations, and attitudes.* Since criminal behavior is similar to other learned behavior, it follows that the actual techniques of criminality must be acquired and learned. For example, young delinquents learn from their associates the proper way to pick a lock, shoplift, and obtain and use narcotics. In addition, novice criminals must learn to use the proper terminology for their acts and then acquire the proper personal reactions to them. For example, getting high on marijuana and learning the proper way to "smoke a joint" are behavior patterns usually acquired from more experienced companions. Moreover, criminals must learn how to react properly to their illegal acts—when to defend them, rationalize them, show remorse for them.
- *The specific direction of motives and drives is learned from perceptions of various aspects of the legal code as being favorable or unfavorable.* Since the reaction to social rules and laws is not uniform across society, people constantly come into contact with others who maintain different views on the utility

of obeying the legal code. When definitions of right and wrong are extremely varied, people experience what Sutherland calls *culture conflict*. The attitudes toward criminal behavior of the important people in an individual's life influence the attitudes that individual develops. The conflict of social attitudes is the basis for the concept of differential association.

- *A person becomes delinquent when he or she perceives more favorable than unfavorable consequences to violating the law.* According to Sutherland's theory, individuals become law violators when they are in contact with persons, groups, or events that produce an excess of definitions favorable toward criminality and are isolated from counteracting forces.

    A definition favorable toward criminality occurs, for example, when a person is exposed to friends sneaking into a theater to avoid paying for a ticket or friends talking about the virtues of getting high. A definition unfavorable toward crime occurs when friends or parents demonstrate their disapproval of crime. Of course, neutral behavior, such as reading a book, exists. It is neither positive nor negative with respect to law violation. Cressey argues that this behavior is important, "especially as an occupier of the time of a child so that he is not in contact with criminal behaviors during the time he is so engaged in the neutral behavior."[18]

- *Differential associations may vary in frequency, duration, priority, and intensity.* Whether a person learns to obey the law or to disregard it is influenced by the quality of social interactions. Those of lasting duration have greater influence than those that are briefer. Similarly, frequent contacts have greater effect than rare and haphazard contacts. Sutherland did not specify what he meant by priority, but Cressey and others have interpreted the term to mean the age of children when they first encounter definitions of criminality. Contacts made early in life probably have a greater and more far-reaching influence than those developed later on. Finally, intensity is generally interpreted to mean the importance and prestige attributed to the individual or groups from whom the definitions are learned. For example, the influence of a father, mother, or trusted friend far outweighs the effect of more socially distant figures.

- *The process of learning criminal behavior by association with criminal and anticriminal patterns involves all of the mechanisms that are involved in any other learning.* This statement suggests that the learning of criminal behavior patterns is similar to the learning of nearly all other patterns and is not a matter of mere imitation.

- *While criminal behavior is an expression of general needs and values, it is not excused by those general needs and values, since noncriminal behavior is also an expression of the same needs and values.* This principle suggests that the motives for criminal behavior cannot logically be the same as those for conventional behavior. Sutherland rules out such motives as desire to accumulate money or social status, personal frustration, or low self-concept as causes of crime, since they are just as likely to produce noncriminal behavior, such as getting a better education or working harder on a job. It is only the learning of deviant norms through contact with an excess of definitions favorable toward criminality that produces illegal behavior.

Empirical Research on Differential Association. Despite the importance of differential association theory, research devoted to testing its assumptions has been less than adequate. It is difficult to conceptualize the principles of the theory in a way that lends itself to empirical measurement. For example, social scientists find it difficult to evaluate such vague concepts as "definition toward criminality." However, several notable research efforts have been undertaken to test the validity of Sutherland's approach.

James Short tested a sample of 176 institutionalized boys and girls and found that a consistent relationship existed between delinquent behavior and prior associations with delinquent youths.[19] Similarly, Albert Reiss and A. Lewis Rhodes found an association between delinquent friendship patterns and the probability that a youth would commit a criminal act.[20] Travis Hirschi's 1969 study also found that attachment to delinquent peers was related to criminal behavior.[21] However, none of these studies presented findings sufficient to show that the differential association preceded or caused the onset of delinquency or that perceptions of criminal definitions were sufficient to cause delinquency.

Charles Tittle surveyed almost two thousand adults in New Jersey, Oregon, and Iowa. His survey instrument included both a differential association scale and self-report items.[22] Questions measuring differential association included questions about the number of people the respondent knew personally who had engaged in deviance, the number of people the respondent knew who often got in trouble, and the frequency with which the respondent attended church (the sermon was assumed to supply definitions against criminality). Tittle found that his differential association scale correlated significantly with such criminal activity as income tax cheating, theft of amounts over $5, theft of amounts over $50, gambling, and assault.[23]

In general, attempts to measure the validity of differential association have proved inconclusive and inadequate and have been marked by ineffective methodologies. This has led critics such as Robert Burgess and Ronald Akers to state: "The attempts to subject the theory to empirical test are marked by inconsistent findings both within the same study and between studies, as well as by highly circumscribed and qualified findings and conclusions."[24]

An Analysis of Differential Association Theory. As mentioned, since Sutherland's death the leading advocate and interpreter of differential association theory has been his associate Donald Cressey. Cressey has attempted to reply to critics of the theory and has compiled a list of the most severe criticisms directed against it.[25] Cressey suggests that some misconceptions about differential association theory exist. For example, some criminologists mistakenly claim that the theory is solely concerned with the number of personal contacts and associations a delinquent has with other criminal or delinquent offenders. If this assumption were true, those most likely to become criminals would be police officers, judges, and correctional authorities, since they are constantly associating with criminals. Cressey argues that Sutherland stressed the importance of "excess definitions toward criminality," not mere association with criminals. Personnel of the criminal justice system do have extensive associations with criminals, but these associations are more than counterbalanced by their associations with law-abiding citizens.

Another misconception is that law-violating behavior is learned only by contact with delinquents and criminals. Cressey claims that even though differential association theory stresses the importance of an excess of definitions favorable toward criminality, it does not specify that they must come solely from criminal sources. For example, seemingly law-abiding parents can encourage delinquent behavior by telling their children that it is acceptable to cheat on a test if that's the only way to get ahead. Another example of this phenomenon is society's seeming admiration of law violators who consistently flaunt social norms yet remain immune to legal sanctions—gamblers, white-collar criminals, organized crime chieftains, and so on.

Cressey does acknowledge that Sutherland's theory fails to explain why one person who is exposed to criminal definitions eventually succumbs to them while another, living under the same conditions, avoids them. According to Cressey, however, the validity of differential association theory does not rest on why particular individuals have the associations they do. He argues that many human personality traits have yet to be explored in their entirety and that this complex endeavor is an independent concern for future research.

These matters aside, Cressey recognizes some legitimate criticisms that can be directed at differential association theory. For one thing, the fourth principle listed above, which discusses the learning of criminal techniques, fails to account for the origin of these techniques. How did the first "teacher" learn criminal techniques and definitions? Another apparently valid criticism of differential association theory is that it assumes criminal and delinquent acts to be rational and systematic. This ignores spontaneous and wanton acts of violence and damage that appear to have little utility or purpose, such as the isolated psychopathic killing, which is virtually unsolvable because of the killer's anonymity and lack of criminal associations.

Perhaps the most serious criticism of differential association theory concerns the vagueness of its terms, which makes it very difficult to test its assumptions. For example, what constitutes an "excess of definitions toward criminality"? How can we determine whether an individual actually has a pro-criminal imbalance of these definitions? It is simplistic to assume that, by definition, all criminals have experienced a majority of definitions favorable toward criminality, and all non-criminals a minority of them. Unless the terms employed in the theory can be defined more precisely, its validity remains a matter of guesswork.

Despite these criticisms, differential association theory maintains an important place in the study of delinquent and criminal behavior. For one thing, it provides a consistent explanation of all types of such behavior. Unlike the social structure theories discussed previously, it is not limited to the explanation of a single facet of antisocial activity—for example, lower-class gang activity. The theory can account for the extensive criminal behavior found in middle- and upper-class areas. Even in these cultures, people can be exposed to a variety of pro-criminal definitions from such sources as overly opportunistic parents and friends. Thus, differential association theory has greater application than the subcultural strain theory discussed earlier.

DIFFERENTIAL REINFORCEMENT THEORY

Differential reinforcement theory is another attempt to explain crime as a type of learned behavior. It is a revision of Sutherland's work that incorporates elements of the learning theory popularized by B. F. Skinner and Albert Bandura (discussed in chapter 6).[26] The description of the theory is summarized in Ronald Akers's 1977 work, *Deviant Behavior: A Social Learning Approach.*[27]

According to Akers, people learn social behavior by **operant conditioning**, behavior controlled by stimuli that follow the behavior. Social behavior is acquired through direct conditioning and modeling of others' behavior. Behavior is reinforced when positive rewards are gained or punishment is avoided (negative reinforcement). It is weakened by negative stimuli (punishment) and loss of reward (negative punishment). Whether deviant or criminal behavior is begun or persists depends on the degree to which it has been rewarded or punished and the rewards or punishments attached to its alternatives. This is the theory of **differential reinforcement**.

According to Akers, people learn to evaluate their own behavior through interaction with significant others and groups in their lives. This process makes use of such devices as norms, attitudes, and orientations. The more individuals learn to define their behavior as good or at least as justified, rather than as undesirable, the more likely they are to engage in it.

Akers's theory posits that the principal influence on behavior comes from "those groups which control individuals' major sources of reinforcement and punishment and expose them to behavioral models and normative definitions."[28] The important groups are the ones with which a person is in **differential association**—peer and friendship groups, schools, churches, and similar institutions. Behavior results when an individual perceives an excess of reinforcements over punishments for certain acts or their alternatives. Definitions conducive to deviant behavior occur when positive or neutralizing definitions of that behavior offset negative definitions of it. Subsequently, "deviant behavior can be expected to the extent that it has been differentially reinforced over alternative behavior . . . and is defined as desirable or justified."[29]

Once people are initiated into crime-related activities, their behavior is influenced by a variety of factors—social reinforcement; exposure to deviant behavior models; association with deviant peers; and lack of negative sanctions from parents, peers, and so on. The deviant behavior, originated by imitation, is sustained by social support.

In a recent test of his theory, Akers and his associates surveyed 3,065 male and female adolescents on drug- and alcohol-related activities and their perception of variables related to social learning and differential reinforcement. Items in the scale included the respondents' perception of the attitudes toward drug and alcohol use of the adults and peers they admired; the number of people they admired who actually used controlled substances; and whether people they admired would reward or punish them for substance abuse. Akers found a strong association between drug and alcohol abuse and the social learning variables, with particular emphasis on differential association.[30]

Though not as influential as Sutherland's differential association theory, Akers's work is an important contribution linking sociological and psychological variables. Moreover, it relates classical criminology (discussed in chapter 5) to sociological theory by suggesting that punishment for criminal acts should reinforce conventional behaviors.[31]

NEUTRALIZATION THEORY

A third social learning theory is referred to as neutralization, or drift, theory and is identified with the writings of **David Matza** and his associate, **Gresham Sykes**.[32] Like Sutherland and Akers before them, Sykes and Matza view the process of becoming a criminal as a learning experience. However, their approach differs on some critical issues. Sutherland and Akers dwell on the learning of techniques, values, and attitudes necessary for performing criminal acts. In contrast, Sykes and Matza maintain that most delinquents and criminals hold conventional values and attitudes; however, they learn techniques that enable them to neutralize these values and drift back and forth between illegitimate and conventional behavior. Since neutralization theory focuses on young people's learning of crime-producing rationalizations, it has been primarily used as an explanation of youth crime and delinquency.

In his major work, *Delinquency and Drift,* Matza explains his position more fully. He suggests that most individuals spend their lives behaving on a continuum somewhere between total freedom and total restraint. **Drift** is the process by which an individual moves from one extreme of behavior to another, behaving sometimes in an unconventional, free, or deviant manner, and at other times with constraint and sobriety.[33]

The existence of a subculture of delinquency, in which criminal behavior is regularly supported, encourages drift among young people. Matza views the subculture as relatively amorphous, without formal rules or values (except those bestowed upon it by sociologists). He characterizes it as an informal, relatively inarticulate oral tradition. Members of the subculture infer the behavior they are to follow from their comrades' behavior cues, including words and actions.

Subsequently, writing with Gresham Sykes, Matza rejected the notion that the subculture of delinquency maintains an independent set of values and attitudes that place the delinquent in direct opposition to the values of the dominant culture. Rather, Matza and Sykes point to the existence in U.S. society of a complex, pluralistic culture that is both deviant and ethical. Juveniles are particularly susceptible to **subterranean values** (those in opposition to middle-class values) because society does not provide them with specific goals or role orientations.[34]

In a later paper, Matza, writing alone, further defined his concept of the teenage subculture as a version of the delinquent's traditional behavior. It emphasizes fun and adventure, and its members are persistently involved in juvenile offenses like smoking, drinking, gambling, and making out. They disdain school work and scholars and are overly concerned with proving masculinity or femininity.[35]

Techniques of Neutralization. Sykes and Matza suggest that juveniles develop a distinct set of justifications for their behavior when it violates accepted social norms. These neutralization techniques allow youths to temporarily drift away from the rules of the normative society and participate in subterranean behaviors. Sykes and Matza base their theoretical model on several observations.[36]

First, delinquents sometimes voice a sense of guilt over their illegal acts. If a stable delinquent value system existed in opposition to generally held values and rules, it would be unlikely that delinquents would exhibit any remorse for their acts other than regret at being apprehended.

Second, juvenile offenders frequently respect and admire honest, law-abiding persons. Really honest persons are often revered; and if for some reason such persons are accused of misbehavior, the delinquent is quick to defend their integrity. Those admired may include sports figures, priests and other clergy, parents, teachers, and neighbors.

Third, delinquents draw a line between those whom they can victimize and those whom they cannot. Members of similar ethnic groups, churches, or neighborhoods often are off limits. This practice implies that delinquents are aware of the wrongfulness of their acts. Why else limit them?

Finally, delinquents are not immune to the demands of conformity. Most delinquents frequently participate in many of the same social functions as law-abiding youths—for example, in school, church, and family activities.

Sykes and Matza argue that the evidence stated above substantiates that delinquents operate as part of the normative culture and adhere to its values and standards. How, then, do these theorists account for delinquency? They suggest that delinquency is a result of the neutralization of accepted social values through the employment of a standard set of rationalizations for illegal behavior. Thus, most youths generally adhere to the rules of society but learn techniques to temporarily release themselves from these moral constraints. Specifically, the techniques are as follows:[37]

- *Denial of responsibility*—Young offenders sometimes claim their unlawful acts were simply not their fault. Criminals' acts resulted from forces beyond their control or were accidents.
- *Denial of injury*—By denying the wrongfulness of an act, criminals are able to rationalize their illegal behavior. For example, stealing is viewed as borrowing; vandalism is considered mischief that has gotten out of hand. Society often agrees with delinquents, labeling their illegal behavior as pranks and thereby reaffirming the delinquents' view that crime can be socially acceptable.
- *Denial of victim*—Juveniles sometimes rationalize their behavior by maintaining that the victim of crime "had it coming." Thus, vandalism may be directed against a disliked teacher or neighbor; or homosexuals may be beaten up by a gang because their behavior is considered offensive. Denying the victim may also take the form of ignoring the rights of an absent or unknown victim—for example, the unseen owner of a department store. It becomes morally acceptable for delinquents to commit crimes such as vandalism, when the victims, because of their absence, cannot be sympathized with or respected.
- *Condemnation of the condemners*—The youthful offender views the world as a corrupt place with a dog-eat-dog code. Since police and judges are on the take, teachers show favoritism, and parents take out their frustrations on their kids, it is ironic and unfair for these authorities to condemn youthful misconduct. By shifting the blame to others, delinquents are able to repress the feeling that their own acts are wrong.
- *Appeal to higher loyalties*—Novice criminals often argue that they are caught in the dilemma of being loyal to their own peer group while at the same time attempting to abide by the rules of the larger society. The needs of the group take precedence over the rules of society because the demands of the former are immediate and localized.

In sum, the theory of neutralization presupposes a condition in which such slogans as "I didn't mean to do it," "I didn't really hurt anybody," "They had it coming to them," "Everybody's picking on me," and "I didn't do it for myself" are used by youths to rationalize unconventional norms and values so they can drift into delinquent modes of behavior.

Empirical Research on Neutralization Theory. Several attempts have been made to empirically verify the assumptions of neutralization theory. Robert Ball's study of institutionalized youths showed that they accepted excuses for deviant behavior to a significantly greater degree than control subjects.[38] Similar findings were achieved by Robert Regoli and Eric Poole.[39]

In contrast to these views, Michael Hindelang's self-report study found that delinquents and nondelinquents had different moral values, a finding that contradicts basic principles of the neutralization approach.[40]

Even studies that support Matza's approach have failed to show that the neutralization of moral restraints precedes the onset of criminality. A valid test of neutralization theory would have to be able to show that a person first neutralized his or her moral beliefs and then drifted into delinquency. Otherwise, any data that showed an association between crime and neutralization could be interpreted as suggesting that people who commit crime later make an attempt at rationalizing their behavior. The validity of Matza's model depends on showing that the neutralizations come first, causing the criminal behavior to follow. So far such data are unavailable.

An Analysis of Neutralization Theory. The theory of neutralization is a major contribution to the literature of crime and delinquency. As a theoretical model, it avoids many of the pitfalls that beset earlier attempts to explain delinquent behavior.

One important feature of the theory is that it accounts for the fact that many teenage criminals do not evolve into adult criminals. Neutralization theory implies that youths can forego criminal behavior when they reach their majority because in reality they never rejected the morality of conventional society. Once the needs and pressures of the post-teenage world exert themselves—marriage, family, and job—delinquents are more likely to drift into legitimate modes of behavior.

Second, unlike social structure theories, neutralization theory does not suppose that criminals reject most middle-class attitudes, beliefs, and values. It is difficult to believe, and harder to prove, that delinquent youths do not share at least some of the values and attitudes of other citizens. After all, they belong to the same churches, attend the same schools, and share other facilities.

Finally, the concept of neutralization provides a logical explanation of many criminal activities that defy other theoretical explanations. For example, the use of soft drugs such as marijuana, LSD and cocaine seems particularly amenable to neutralization techniques embodied in the slogans "everybody's doing it," "no one is really hurt," and so on.

Neutralization theory also has its drawbacks. Do delinquents neutralize law-violating behavior before or after they engage in it? If in fact they neutralize their guilt after engaging in illegal activity, then neutralization theory loses its power as an explanation of the cause of delinquency and becomes a theory describing the reactions of juveniles to their misdeeds.

Even if neutralization techniques are actually used before the commission of delinquent acts, the theory fails to distinguish why some youths consistently drift into delinquency and others do not. Unless we can understand why drift occurs, the theory will remain too abstract and vague to be of practical use.

Control Theories

The second branch of the social process perspective is control theory. Control theories maintain that all people have the potential to violate the law and that modern society presents many opportunities for illegal activity. The question control theory asks, then, is "Why do people obey the rules of society?" To a classical theorist, the answer would be "fear of punishment, the most basic element of social control." Yet control criminologists, using a sociological perspective, view fear as only one element of the ties that bind people to the social order. People refrain from committing crime because they have a stake in conformity—a real, present, and logical reason to obey the rules of society. Perhaps they believe that getting caught at criminal activity will hurt a dearly loved parent or jeopardize their chance at a college scholarship, or perhaps they feel that their jobs will soon allow them to save enough to obtain what they want without resorting to illegitimate means.

Why do some people choose to forego criminal activity even though they may not have achieved, and may be unable even to hope to achieve, what they aspire to? A control theorist would suggest that there is variation in people's belief in the moral code. For some people, considerations of morality are quite important; for others, they are not. Put another way, it seems foolish to conjecture that all people believe and value the same things. Variations among humans create a state of affairs in which a certain percentage of people will disagree with and violate the rules of society. Travis Hirschi has stated this position as follows:

> In the end, then, control theory remains what it always has been; a theory in which deviation is not problematic. The question, "Why do they do it?" is simply not the question the theory is designed to answer. The question is, "Why don't they do it?" There is much evidence that we would if we dared.[41]

This section will briefly focus on four prominent examples of control theory—Hirschi's social bond theory,[42] Briar and Piliavin's commitment to conformity,[43] Reckless's containment theory,[44] and Glazer's differential anticipation theory.[45]

HIRSCHI'S SOCIAL BOND THEORY

Travis Hirschi put forth the most widely read sociologically based control theory in his 1969 book, *Causes of Delinquency.*[46]

Hirschi links the onset of criminality to the weakening, in a person's youth, of the ties that bind him or her to society. Hirschi assumes that all individuals are potential law violators but are kept under control by their fear that illegal behavior may lead to irreparable harm in their relationships with friends, parents, neighbors, and important social institutions such as schools, jobs, and the like. Without social bonds, and in the absence of sensitivity to and interest in others, a person is free to commit criminal acts.

Like most social process theorists, Hirschi does not believe that different elements of society maintain separate and unique value systems that reject conventional norms and behaviors. Rather, he suggests that in all elements of society there exists variation in the way people respond to social rules and values. Thus, even in the middle and upper classes, a person whose bond to society is weak may fall prey to crimogenic behavior patterns.

Elements of the Social Bond. Hirschi argues that the social bond a person maintains with society is divided into four main elements: attachment, commitment, involvement, and belief.

Attachment. Attachment refers to a person's sensitivity to and interest in others.[47] Psychologists believe that without a sense of attachment, a person becomes a psychopath and loses the ability to relate coherently to the world. The acceptance

According to Hirsch's control theory, a close family life in which children are attached to their parents can prevent criminal behavior.

of social norms and the development of a social conscience depend on attachment to and caring for other human beings. Hirschi views parents, peers, and schools as the important social institutions with which a person should maintain ties. Attachment to parents is the most important. Even if a family is shattered by divorce and separation, a child must retain a strong attachment to one or both parents. Without attachment to family, it is unlikely that feelings of respect for others in authority will develop.

Commitment. Commitment involves the time, energy, and effort expended in conventional lines of action. It embraces such activities as getting an education and saving money for the future. Social bond theory holds that if people build up a strong involvement in life, property, and reputation, they will be less likely to engage in acts that will jeopardize their positions. Conversely, lack of commitment to conventional values may foreshadow a condition in which risk-taking behavior, such as crime, becomes a reasonable behavior alternative.

Involvement. Heavy involvement in conventional activities leaves little time for illegal behavior. Hirschi believes that involvement—in school, recreation, and family—insulates a person from the potential lure of criminal behavior, while idleness enhances it.

Belief. People who live in the same social setting often share common moral beliefs; they may adhere to such values as sharing, sensitivity to the rights of others, and admiration for the legal code. If these beliefs are absent or weakened, individuals are more likely to participate in antisocial acts.

Hirschi further suggests that the interrelationship of elements of the social bond influences whether an individual pursues illegal or conventional activities.

For example, people who feel kinship and sensitivity to parents and friends should be more likely to adopt and work toward legitimate goals. On the other hand, a person who rejects social relationships probably lacks commitment to conventional goals. Similarly, people who are highly committed to conventional acts and beliefs are more likely to be involved in conventional activities.

Empirical Research on Social Bond Theory. One of Hirschi's most significant contributions to criminological research was his attempt to test the principal hypotheses of control theory. He administered a complex self-report survey to a sample of over four thousand junior and senior high school students in Contra Costa County, California.[48] In a detailed analysis of the data, Hirschi found considerable evidence to support the control theory model.

Among Hirschi's more important findings are the following:

- Youths who were strongly attached to their parents were less likely to commit criminal acts.
- Commitment to conventional values such as striving to get a good education and refusing to drink and "cruise around" was also related to conventional behavior.
- Youths involved in conventional activity such as homework were less likely to engage in criminal behavior. Youths involved in unconventional behavior such as smoking and drinking were more delinquency-prone.
- Delinquent youths maintained weak and distant relationships with people. Nondelinquents were attached to their peers.
- Delinquents and nondelinquents shared similar beliefs about society.

Hirschi's data lent important support to the validity of social bond theory. The statistical significance of his findings was sometimes less than he expected, but his research data were extremely consistent. Only in very rare instances did his findings contradict the theory's most critical assumptions.

There have been other attempts to corroborate Hirschi's findings, most notably a 1973 study by Michael Hindelang. Using subjects in the sixth through twelfth grades in a rural New York State school system, Hindelang replicated several of Hirschi's most important results. With few exceptions, Hindelang's evidence supported Hirschi's control theory principles. The major difference between the two studies was in the area of attachment to peers. Hindelang found that close identification with peers was directly related to delinquent activity, while Hirschi's research produced the opposite result. Further support for Hirschi's theory was established by the research of Joseph Rankin, Marvin Krohn and James Massey; Stephen Cernkovich, Michael Wiatrowski, David Griswold and Mary Roberts; and Randy LaGrange and Helene Raskin White, to name a few. Robert Agnew, however, found little support for social bond theory in his recent longitudinal analysis.[49]

Unlike many other theoretical models, social bond theory has for the most part stood the test of rigorous empirical research designed to evaluate its most significant assertions. It therefore presents an important arena for future research designed to validate its assumptions.

THEORY OF COMMITMENT TO CONFORMITY

Scott Briar and Irving Piliavin's version of control theory is based on two assumptions.[50] First, people are often exposed to stimuli of relatively short duration that can affect, to varying extents, their values and behaviors. For example, a young student who lacks the financial resources to purchase a desired record may find that advertisements for the record displayed in a neighborhood hi-fi store are so appealing that they cause him to overcome moral compunctions he has against stealing. Once exposure to these short-term inducements is over, he will return to his normal behavior and value patterns.

Second, persons have varying degrees of **commitment to conformity**. This commitment comprises not only fear of the punishment that might come from being discovered as an offender but also apprehension about the effect of being caught in a criminal act on self-image, valued relationships, and current and future status and activities.

Given equal situational motives, a person with strong commitments to conformity is less likely to engage in a criminal act than a person with minimal commitments. However, given enough inducement and a good chance of success, even a high-commitment person may succumb to the lure of crime.

How are commitments to conformity constructed? One way involves maintaining positive relationships with people and obtaining the approval of those whose love and protection a person regards as important, such as parents, teachers, and peers. Further, people's stakes in conformity influence their choice of friends—people seek out others with similar commitments to conventional values and behaviors. Thus, the probability of their experiencing situational inducements to deviance because of peer activity is reduced.

How do Briar and Piliavin explain the development of conventional bonds? Important factors include belief in God, affection for conventionally behaving peers, occupational aspirations, ties to parents, desire to perform well in school, and fear of the material deprivations and punishments associated with arrest. Of these, the early relationship a person develops with parents is probably the most important. The parent/child relationship is productive when discipline is used to promote and reinforce socially approved behaviors. However, "the punitive parent who does not reward conformity with affection thereby may undermine the basis for voluntary compliance by his child."[51] Furthermore, parents who ignore their children, who fail in their own conventional commitment, or who lack the economic means to provide adequate role models may also impede desired social bonding.

Briar and Piliavin's work has not received the wide notice and interest that has been given Hirschi's bond theory, but we can see many of the same theoretical themes running through both efforts.

CONTAINMENT THEORY

Containment theory is a clear departure from sociological theories that fail to devote attention to the individual characteristics of criminals. It is directed at answering the questions "How is it possible for a person living in a high-crime poverty area to resist engaging in criminal activity?" and "What personal properties insulate a person from crime-producing influences?" **Walter Reckless**, the criminologist who developed containment theory, argues that sociological theories that ignore individual characteristics of offenders are insufficient as explanations of individual or group criminality.[52]

Briefly, containment theory contends that society produces a series of pushes and pulls toward criminality. These in turn are counteracted by internal and external **containments**, which help insulate the individual from criminality. The elements of the theory are discussed in greater detail below.[53]

- *Inner Containments*—Inner containments consist of the inner strength of an individual personality—for example, good self-concept, strong ego, high frustration tolerance, goal orientation, and tension-reducing capabilities.
- *Outer Containments*—Outer containments are the normative constraints that societies and social groups ordinarily use to control their members. They provide such factors as a sense of belonging; a consistent moral front; reinforcement of norms, goals, and values; effective supervision and discipline; and a meaningful social role.
- *Internal Pushes*—Internal pushes involve such personal factors as restlessness, discontent, hostility, rebellion, mental conflict, anxieties, and need for immediate gratification.
- *External Pressures*—External pressures are adverse living conditions that influence deviant behavior. They include relative deprivation, poverty, unemployment, insecurity, minority status, limited opportunities, and inequalities.
- *External Pulls*—External pulls are represented by deviant companions, membership in criminal subcultures or other deviant groups, and influences such as mass media and pornography.

Simply put, containment theory suggests that the two containments act as a defense against potential deviation from legal and social norms and work to insulate a person from the pressures and pulls of crimogenic influences. If, in fact, social causes of crime exist, the containments act as buffers against them. Reckless suggests that of the two types of containment, inner containment is the more important in U.S. society, because individuals spend much of their time away from the family and other supportive groups that can contain them.[54] They must therefore rely on their internal strengths to control their criminal urges. Nevertheless, people operating under both containments are less likely to become criminals than those under only one. Those with weak inner and external containments are the most prone to criminality.

Empirical Research on Containment Theory. Walter Reckless has made an extensive effort to validate the principles of containment theory. In one early study, Reckless and his associates asked high school teachers in a high-crime area to nominate boys who in their opinion would neither commit delinquent acts nor experience police and juvenile court contact.[55] The 125 boys included in Reckless's final sample of "good boys" scored very high on social responsibility scales and very low on delinquency proneness scales. On self-evaluation items, the good boys reported themselves to be rather law-abiding and obedient. They attempted to avoid trouble at all costs and conformed to expectations of parents and teachers. In addition, their home lives and relationships with parents were excellent. These findings led the researchers to conclude that insulation against delinquency is an ongoing process reflecting an "internalization of non-delinquent values and conformity to the expectations of significant others."[56] Whether nondelinquent boys are able to maintain their conventional status depends on their ability to maintain their positive self-image in the face of environmental pressures toward delinquency.

In a follow-up study, Reckless and his associates compared "insulated" boys with those nominated as potential delinquents by their teachers.[57] When the two groups were compared, significant differences in parental relations, self-image, and social responsibility were found. The good boys did better in each category. Four years later, Simon Dinitz, Frank Scarpitti, Walter Reckless, and Ellen Murray followed up the original sample to measure any changes that had occurred.[58] The researchers found remarkable stability in self-image and personal behavior. Good boys maintained their superiority in self-image, behavior, and optimism.

The research efforts of Reckless and his associates have been criticized for lack of methodological rigor. Questions have been raised about the adequacy of Reckless's measurements, sampling techniques, and definitions of delinquency.[59]

DIFFERENTIAL ANTICIPATION THEORY

Daniel Glazer's theory of differential anticipation is an attempt to combine social control theory with differential association concepts.[60] Glazer's version asserts: "A person's crime or restraint from crime is determined by the consequences he anticipates from it."[61] These expectations are based on the following factors:

- The social bonds a person develops in life. These bonds create stakes in conformity to the conduct standards of others; conformity allows the person to please rather than alienate others.
- "Differential learning by which we acquire tastes, skills, and rationalizations that determine whether gratification is achieved in criminal or in alternative activities."[62]
- "Perceived opportunities, reflecting a person's observations of circumstances and assessments of prospects and risks in law-violating or conforming behavior."[63]

According to Glazer, people try to commit crimes whenever and wherever the expectations of gain from them exceed expectations of losses with respect to social bonds, relationships with others, and prior learning experiences. The basic assumption is that expectations determine conduct. However, a person who has acquired the knowledge and desire to commit crime will be more likely to engage in criminality than a person who has not come into contact with criminal definitions. Hence, Glazer's view of criminality combines elements of differential association with classical criminology and control theory.[64]

SOCIAL DEVELOPMENT THEORY—AN INTEGRATED VIEW

Joseph Weis and his associates have attempted to integrate the social control approach with the social structure models discussed earlier.[65] Weis recognizes that factors related to a person's place in the social structure—sex, race, and economic status—do in fact exert powerful forces on their behavioral choices. At the same time, social psychological processes also help explain whether an individual will engage in criminal or conventional behavior.

Weis, working with J. David Hawkins and John Sederstrom, developed the model of criminality illustrated in figure 8.2.

Weis's model uses elements of both control and social structure theories. In a low-income, disorganized community, the influences of front-line socializing institutions are weak. Families are under great stress; educational facilities are inadequate; there are fewer material goods; respect for the law is weak. Because

FIGURE 8.2

A general model of
delinquency: integration
of control and cultural
deviance theories

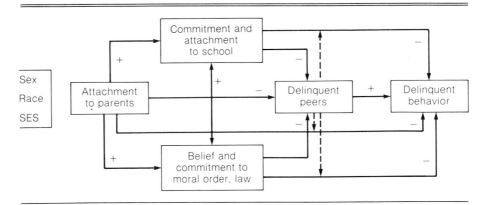

*SES = Socioeconomic status.

SOURCE. Joseph Weis and John Sederstrom, *Reports of the National Juvenile Justice Assessment Centers, The Prevention of Serious Delinquency: What to Do* (Washington, D.C.: U.S. Department of Justice, 1981), p.35.

existing crime rates are high, there are greater opportunities for law violation, putting even greater strain on the agencies of social control.

Within this context of weak social control and community disorganization, legitimate social institutions are incapable of combatting the lure of criminal groups and gangs. The family remains the front-line defense to a criminal career. Positive familial relationships are related to developing a commitment and attachment to school and the educational process. Concomitantly, those whose educational experience is a meaningful one marked by academic success and commitment to educational achievement will be more likely to develop conventional beliefs and values, become committed to conventional activities, and seek out and be influenced by noncriminal peers. But if a person does not find participation in school and family activities rewarding, they will be likely to seek associations with those who are equally disillusioned and consequently engage in deviant activities that hold the promise of alternative rewards.

Weis's theoretical model has not been given the empirical attention it deserves. Its power rests in its accounting both for the high crime rates found in lower-class areas as well as for the influence of critical agents of the social order on criminal behavior.

AN ANALYSIS OF CONTROL THEORY

Control theory is a broad, far-reaching approach to the study of criminal behavior. It avoids the narrow focus of sociocultural theories, since it is applicable to people in high, middle, and low socioeconomic groups. For example, in lower-class settings, the social bond may weaken because of limitations on access to legitimate activities; lack of attachment to the school system, which may be a poor one; and impairment in commitment to goals, which may be seen as unattainable. Middle- and upper-class people may find that their bonds to their parents and friends are weak, that their academic abilities fall below what is expected of people in their cultural circumstances, or that their relatively secure financial status interferes with a true commitment to long-term goals.

Another strength of control theory is its adaptability to empirical measurement. Many of the theoretical models discussed previously rely heavily on ambiguous concepts such as anomie, definitions toward crime, and drift; but control theorists define elements of the bond in simple, straightforward terms. For example, a person's involvement can be measured by actual participation in cultural activities, community programs, and religious services. And their attachment to and belief in conventional goals, values, and institutions can be operationalized by research using standard attitude and personality measures.

Despite their merits, control theories fail to explain some important issues. Why do some youths who lack commitment to conventional values and behavior refrain from participating in crime? Conversely, why do some highly committed individuals commit crimes? Can we honestly say, as Briar and Piliavin suggest, that youths commit less crime as they become older because of fewer situational inducements to deviance? Would not the financial pressure of maintaining a family create even more pressure to commit crime? How are commitments created? How are they weakened? What determines self-concept? Are delinquents truly lacking in feelings of self-worth?

Labeling Theory

Labeling theory reached prominence in the mid-seventies as an *interactionist* explanation of criminal careerism. Using the interactionist concept of crime and deviance discussed in chapter 1, labeling theorists attempt to show how crime is a product of social interactions and encounters. People are portrayed as becoming deviant and criminal when significant others—teachers, police, neighbors, parents, friends—label them as such. Labeling theory seems to place the blame for criminal career formation on the agencies of social control operating in society. Often mistrustful of institutions such as schools, mental hospitals, police, court, and correctional agencies, labeling advocates find it logical to say that these institutions can produce stigma harmful to the very people they are trying to help, treat, or correct.

Members of the labeling school view negative labels such as "dummy," "poor reader," "mentally unstable person," "criminal," and "delinquent," as causing permanent harm to the people on whom they are bestowed.

The way labels are applied, and the nature of the labels themselves, is likely to have important future consequences for the offender. For example, the degree to which a person is perceived a criminal may affect his or her treatment at home, at work, at school, and in other social situations. Young offenders may find that their parents consider them a negative influence on younger brothers and sisters. School officials may limit them to classes reserved for people with behavior problems. Adults who have been given official labels such as "criminal," "ex-con," "mental patient," or "addict" may find their eligibility for employment severely restricted. And, of course, if the label is bestowed as the result of conviction for a criminal offense, the labeled person may be subject to official sanctions ranging from a mild reprimand to incarceration.

Beyond these immediate results, labeling advocates maintain that, depending on the visibility of the label and the manner and severity with which it is applied, a person will have an increasing commitment to a deviant career. "Thereafter he may be watched; he may be suspect . . . he may be excluded more and more from legitimate opportunities."[66] Consequently, labeled persons may find themselves turning to other similarly labeled for support. At the conclusion of the labeling process, stigmatized persons may find themselves isolated from conventional society and locked into deviant careers and thereafter may identify themselves as members of an outcast group.

Though the labeling perspective has been used to describe a variety of deviant identities—homosexual, mental patient, alcoholic—this discussion limits its application to crime and delinquency.

CRIME AND LABELING THEORY

Labeling theorists use an interactionist definition of crime. "Deviance is not a property inherent in certain forms of behavior," argues sociologist Kai Erikson, "it is a property conferred upon those forms by the audience which directly or indirectly witnesses them."[67] This definition has been amplified by Edwin Schur, who states:

> *Human behavior is deviant to the extent that it comes to be viewed as involving a personally discreditable departure from a group's normative expectation, and it elicits interpersonal and collective reactions that serve to "isolate," "treat," "correct" or "punish" individuals engaged in such behavior.*[68]

Crime and deviance, therefore, are defined by the social audience's reaction to people and their behavior and the subsequent effects of that reaction; they are not defined by the moral content of the illegal act itself. In its purest form, labeling theory argues that crimes such as murder, rape, and assault are only bad or evil because people label them as such. After all, the difference between an excusable act and a criminal one is often a matter of legal definition, which changes from place to place and from year to year. Labeling theorists would argue that acts such as abortion, use of marijuana, possession of a hand gun, and gambling have been legal at some points and places in history and illegal at others. As you may recall, Howard Becker refers to people who create rules as *moral entrepreneurs*. He sums up their effect as follows:

> *Social groups create deviance by making rules whose infractions constitute deviance, and by applying those rules to particular people and labeling them as outsiders. From this point of view, deviance is not a quality of the act a person commits, but rather a consequence of the application by others of rules and sanctions to an "offender." The deviant is one to whom the label has successfully been applied; deviant behavior is behavior that people so label.*[69]

DIFFERENTIAL ENFORCEMENT

An important principle of labeling theory is that the law is differentially applied, benefitting those who hold economic and social power and penalizing the powerless. In this respect, labeling theory is similar to the social conflict theories that will be discussed in chapter 9.

Labeling theorists argue that the probability of being brought under the control of legal authority is a function of a person's race, wealth, sex, and social standing. They point to studies indicating that police officers are more likely to formally arrest males, minority group members, and those in the lower class, and to use their discretionary powers to give beneficial treatment to more favored groups.[70] Similarly, labeling advocates cite evidence that minorities and the poor are more likely to be prosecuted for criminal offenses and receive harsher punishments when convicted.[71] This evidence is used to support the labeling concept that personal characteristics and social interactions are actually more important variables in the criminal career formation process than the mere violation of the criminal law.

Labeling theorists also argue that the content of the law reflects power relationships in society. They point to the evidence that white-collar crimes are most often punished by a relatively small fine and rarely result in prison sentences, and contrast this treatment with the long prison sentences given to those convicted of "street crimes" such as burglary or car theft.[72]

In sum, a major premise of labeling theory is that the law is differentially constructed and applied. It favors the powerful members of society who direct its content and penalizes people whose actions represent a threat to those in control.[73]

BECOMING LABELED

Labeling theorists are not especially concerned with explaining why people originally engage in acts that result in their being labeled. Walter Gove has listed some reasons why persons may participate in outlawed behavior: (1) they may belong to minority groups or subcultures whose values and expected behaviors may lead to violations of the rules of the dominant group; (2) they may have conflicting personal responsibilities, so that adequately performing one task produces violations in a second role; (3) their desire for personal gain coupled with their belief that they will not be caught may lead them into law violations; (4) they may simply be unaware of the rules and may violate them unintentionally.[74] Gove concludes that the forces that initiate participation in deviant acts may be traced to inconsistencies in the social structure, to hedonistic variables (the desire for wealth and luxury), or to ignorance.[75] Labeling theorists would not dispute any of the previously discussed theories of the onset of criminality. Their concern is with criminal career formation and not the origin of criminal acts.

It is consistent with the labeling approach to suggest that social factors influence the likelihood of a person's engaging in label-producing acts: an individual's place in the social structure may influence both (1) the probability that he or she will engage in disapproved behavior and (2) the chance that he or she will be sanctioned for these actions. For example, the poor or minority-group teenager may run a greater chance of being officially processed for delinquent acts by police, court, and correctional agencies than the wealthy white youth. In the labeling view, a person is labeled deviant primarily as a consequence of societal characteristics—most specifically, the power and resources of the individual, the social distance between the labeler and the person labeled, the tolerance level in the community, and the visibility of the individual's deviant behavior.

Of course, not all labeled people have chosen to engage in label-producing activities such as crime. Some labels are bestowed on people for behaviors over which they have little control. Negative labels of this sort include "homosexual," "mentally ill," "alien," and "mentally deficient" persons. In these categories, too, the probability of being labeled may depend on the visibility of the person in the community, the tolerance of the community for unusual behavior, and the person's own power to combat labels.

CONSEQUENCES OF LABELING

Criminologists are most concerned with two effects of labeling: the creation of stigma and the effect on self-image.

People are often labeled deviant because of their lifestyles or appearances. Describe the personalities of the people in this picture.

Labels are believed to produce **stigma**. The labeled deviant becomes a social outcast who may be prevented from enjoying higher education, well-paying jobs, and other social benefits. Labeling theorists consider public condemnation an important part of the label-producing process. It may be accomplished in such "ceremonies" as a hearing in which a person is found to be mentally ill or a trial in which an individual is convicted of crime. Public record of the deviant acts causes the denounced person to be ritually separated from a place in the legitimate order and placed outside the world occupied by citizens of good standing. Harold Garfinkle has called transactions that produce irreversible, permanent labels *successful degradation ceremonies.*[76]

Beyond these immediate results, the label tends to redefine the whole person. For example, the label "ex-con" may create in people's imaginations a whole series of behavior descriptions—tough, mean, dangerous, aggressive, untrustworthy, sneaky—that a person who has been in prison may or may not possess. People begin to react to the content of the label and what the label signifies, and not to the actual behavior of the person who bears it. This is referred to as **retrospective reading**, a process in which the past of the labeled person is reviewed and reevaluated to fit his or her current outcast status. For example, boyhood friends of an assassin or killer are interviewed by the media and report that the suspect was withdrawn, suspicious, and negativistic as a youth. Now we can understand what prompted his current behavior; the label must certainly be accurate.[77]

The second important consequence of being labeled is the acceptance of the label as a personal identity. As the negative feedback of law enforcement agencies, parents, friends, teachers, and other figures amplifies the force of the original label, stigmatized offenders may begin to reevaluate their own identities. If they are not really evil or bad, they may ask themselves, why is everyone making such a fuss about them? Frank Tannenbaum referred to this process as the **dramatization of evil**. With respect to the consequences of labeling delinquent behavior, Tannenbaum states:

> *The process of making the criminal, therefore, is a process of tagging, defining, identifying, making conscious and self-conscious; it becomes a way of stimulating, suggesting and evoking the very traits that are complained of. If the theory of relation of response to stimulus has any meaning, the entire process of dealing with the young delinquent is mischievous insofar as it identifies him to himself or to the environment as a delinquent person. The person becomes the thing he is described as being.* [78]

PRIMARY AND SECONDARY DEVIANCE

One of the more well known views on the consequences of becoming labeled is Edwin Lemert's concept of **primary and secondary deviance**.[79] According to Lemert, primary deviations are initial acts of norm violations or crimes that have very little influence on the actor and can be quickly forgotten; for example, a college student taking a "five-finger discount" at the campus bookstore.

In contrast, **secondary deviance** occurs when the actor reorganizes his or her personality around the consequences of the deviant act. The drug experimenter becomes an addict; the recreational drinker an alcoholic; the joy rider a car thief. As society begins to recognize and sanction these roles, a **deviance amplification** effect occurs. The offenders feel isolated from the mainstream of society and become firmly locked within their deviant roles. They may seek out others similarly labeled in order to form deviant subcultures or groups. Secondary deviance is a product of resocialization in which the deviant role becomes the central fact of existence and the person is transformed into one who "employs his behavior or a role based upon it as a means of defense, attack, or adjustment to the overt and covert problems created by the consequent social reaction to him."

Lemert's concept of secondary deviance expresses the core of labeling theory: Deviance is a process in which one's identity is transformed. Efforts to control the offenders, whether by treatment or punishment, simply help lock them in their deviant role.

RESEARCH ON LABELING THEORY

Research on labeling theory can be classified into two distinct categories. The first focuses on the characteristics of offenders who are chosen for labels. Labeling theory maintains that these offenders should be relatively powerless people who are unable to defend themselves against the negative labeling. The second type of research attempts to discover the effects of being labeled. Labeling theorists predict that people who are labeled should (1) view themselves as deviant and (2) commit increasing amounts of criminal behavior.

With regard to the first category, research results seem inconclusive. Some studies (such as those mentioned earlier in the chapter) do in fact show that poor and powerless people are victimized by the law and justice system, and that labels are not equally distributed across class and racial lines. However, other research indicates that the justice system operates more fairly than labeling theorists would have us believe. That is, such procedures as arrest, prosecution, and sentencing may actually be based on behaviors, past and present, rather than personal characteristics. Nonetheless, enough evidence exists to suggest that class and racial bias exist (for example, see chapter 6 on racial factors and the death penalty) to convince labeling theorists that the probability of receiving labels is unequally distributed. For example, The National Minority Advisory Council on Criminal Justice states:

> *Although substantive and procedural laws govern almost every aspect of the American criminal justice system, discretionary decision making controls its operation at every level. From the police officer's decision on whom to arrest; to the prosecutor's decisions on whom to charge and for how many and what kind of charges; to the court's decision on whom to release or on whom to pyramid bail; to the Grand Jury decision on indictment; to the judge's decision on how long to sentence, discretion that works to the detriment of minority people is a source of concern to black, Hispanic, Asian-American and Indian-American peoples.*[80]

Conditions such as these would help explain racial and class differences in the crime rate.

With regard to the second category, support has been inconsistent for the proposition that becoming labeled actually has a dramatic and negative influence on the self-image of offenders. Research studies indicate that the effects of stigma-generating encounters have a relatively minor effect.[81]

In an in-depth analysis of research on the crime-producing effects of labels, Charles Tittle found little evidence that stigma produces crime. He states that "studies of recidivism do not confirm labeling expectations that more than half will be recidivists, and case materials provide many exceptions to labeling predictions."[82] Tittle also claimed that case materials challenge labeling hypotheses by showing that many criminal careers occur without labeling, that labeling often comes after rather than before adoption of a criminal career, and that criminal careers may not follow even when labeling takes place.

Despite the negative evidence, research studies have indicated that processing by agencies of the justice system does influence self-perception. Susan Ageton and Delbert Elliott found in a longitudinal study of 2,616 youths in California that the self-concept of white youths who had contact with police declined.[83] This was not the case with peers who had avoided police contact. Ageton and Elliott discovered, however, that police contact was not a significant factor in changing the self-concept of Hispanic, black, or other minority youths. Also, lower-class youths were more likely to be negatively affected by their experience with the law than were middle- or upper-class youths. Nonetheless, Ageton and Elliott concluded that, in general, police contact was more important in measuring decreasing self-concept than factors such as self-reported delinquent behavior and the influence of a deviant peer group.

Of course, there is considerable evidence that both youths and adults who are labeled by being arrested and punished by the justice system stand a good chance of continuing in their deviant careers. Wolfgang's cohort studies certainly support a deviance amplification model. However, the question remains whether the mere fact of being labeled accounts for criminal career formation or whether it can be better explained by other personal and social factors. For example, those who believe in the deterrence model dispute deviance amplification and counter that the significant relationship between official labels and future deviance results from the inadequacy of sanctions rather than their severity. In the 1980s, attention has shifted from concern over the effect of negative labels to concern over how labels and sanctions can be efficiently and uniformly applied.

AN EVALUATION OF LABELING THEORY

The validity of labeling theory is widely, but not unanimously, accepted. Not enough studies have been conducted for conclusions about its properties to be reached. Among the theoretical failures of the approach is its inability to distinguish between deviance and nondeviance—that is, to specify the conditions that must exist before an act or individual is labeled deviant.[84] Critics also charge that labeling theory is too narrow, fails to explain differences in crime rates,[85] ignores the onset of deviant behavior (that is, fails to ask why people commit the initial deviant act), and does not deal with personal decision making in the deviance process.[86]

One sociologist, Charles Wellford, questions the validity of several premises essential to the labeling approach. He takes particular issue with the labeling assumption that no act is intrinsically criminal. Wellford points to the fact that some crimes, such as rape and homicide, are almost universally sanctioned. He says: "Serious violations of the law are universally understood and are, therefore, in that sense, intrinsically criminal."[87] Furthermore, he suggests, the labeling theory proposition that almost all law enforcement is biased against the poor and minorities is equally spurious: "I contend that the overwhelming evidence is in the direction of minimal differential law enforcement, determination of guilt and application of sanction."[88]

According to Wellford, this means that law enforcement officials most often base their arrest decisions on such factors as the seriousness of the offense and pay less attention to such issues as the race, class, and demeanor of the offender—factors that labeling theorists often link to the labeling decision.

Finally, Wellford challenges the theory's ideas about self-labeling. Though labeling may indeed affect offenders' attitudes about themselves, there is little evidence that attitude changes are related to actual behavior changes. Wellford believes instead that criminal behavior is situationally motivated and depends on ecological and personal conditions.[89]

Following Wellford, Charles Tittle has concluded: "Neither of the major propositions of labeling theory find much support in the available data concerning crime."[90] Because of these criticisms, criminologists who once valued its premises now reject labeling theory. Some charge that it all too often focuses on "nuts, sluts, and perverts" and ignores the root causes of crime.[91] As we shall see in the following chapter, several of these critics have embraced more radical explanations of crime.

An Evaluation of Social Process Theory

The three branches of social process theory—social learning, control, and labeling—are compatible because they suggest that criminal behavior is an ongoing social psychological process in which the actor is influenced by the people and institutions surrounding them. Though the three branches disagree about the relative importance of those influences and the form the influence takes, there seems to be little question that social process theories involve perception of outside influences that shape and control the beliefs, values, and self-image of the offender. And the person who has been negatively influenced—either by learning deviant social values, finding themselves detached from conventional others, or being negatively labeled by them—will be the most likely to fall prey to the attractions of criminal behavior. These negative influences can influence people in all walks of life, beginning in their youth and continuing through their majority.

Process theories answer some important questions about the onset of criminality, but they ignore many others. For example, as noted previously, learning theories have not met with unqualified empirical support; and it does not seem possible, considering the vagueness of their chief concepts, that they ever can be adequately tested. Control theories do not adequately explain why a person loses his or her commitment to society. By suggesting that it is a result of poor socialization in the school, home, or neighborhood, control theorists create an unanswerable question: What causes poor socialization in the first place? Labeling theory seems a good explanation of criminal careers until we review the existing research literature which, unfortunately, rarely supports its major propositions. It is for these reasons that some modern criminologists have moved from the positivist social process orientation to the broader conflict orientation to be discussed in chapter 9 and the more individualized approaches discussed in chapters 4 and 5.

Social Process Theory and Social Policy

Social process theories have had a great influence on social policy making from the 1950s through the 1980s. However, because of the divergent viewpoints existing within the perspective, policies influenced by social process theory often seem to oppose one another.

Learning theories have greatly influenced concepts of treatment of the criminal offender. Their effect has mainly been felt by young offenders, who are viewed as being more salvageable than "hardened" criminals. Advocates of the social learning approach argue that if people become criminal by learning definitions and attitudes toward criminality, they can "unlearn" them by being exposed to definitions toward conventional behavior. This philosophy was used in numerous treatment facilities throughout the United States, the most famous being the Highfields Project in New Jersey and the Silverlake Program in Los Angeles. These residential treatment programs for young male offenders used group interaction sessions to attack the criminal behavior orientations held by residents (being tough, using alcohol and drugs, believing that school was for "sissies"), while promoting conventional lines of behavior (going straight, saving money, giving up drugs). Nonresidential programs offering a similar treatment orientation were experimented with in Provo, Utah, and Essex County, New Jersey, and more recently in Boston and in Boulder, Colorado. Though small in scale, these programs have been promoted by their originators as significant contributions to rehabilitation strategies. (See the following Close-Up entitled "A Social Process Approach to Crime Prevention".)

Control theories have also indirectly influenced criminal justice and other social policy making. Programs have been developed to improve people's commitments to conventional lines of action. Examples of this approach are the career, work furlough, and educational opportunity programs being developed in the nation's prisons. These programs are designed to help inmates maintain a stake in society so they will be less willing to resort to criminal activity on their release. Lack of funding and the generally overcrowded condition of the prison system has seriously impeded these efforts (see chapter 17).

The educational system has been the scene of numerous programs designed to improve basic skills and create an atmosphere in which youths will develop a bond

A Social Process Approach to Crime Prevention

Many programs incorporate social process concepts as a means of preventing crime. The program described below is typical of one that focuses on the interpersonal needs of the offender and attempts to help them fit into the mainstream of society.

NEW DIRECTIONS FOR YOUNG WOMEN
(Tucson, Arizona)

Strategies: Education, role development, power enhancement, abandonment of legal control

Causes of the Problem: Female adolescents, particularly those who have been in contact with the juvenile justice system, experience many problems while growing up. These problems may include an inability to communicate with their parents, lack of skills, and the social and economic consequences of running away from home. Although all youths may encounter these problems, young women also experience unique problems because of their sex. For example, they may be unable to attend school because of pregnancy or childrearing responsibilities; they may be unable to express their needs due to inexperience in being assertive; or, as a result of sex role stereotyping, they may be unaware of the opportunities available to them. These factors can contribute to a young woman's commission of delinquent acts and to involvement with the juvenile justice system.

Program Rationale: By removing young women from secure facilities and offering them opportunities for positive personal growth, the problems they experience which may contribute to delinquency can be avoided and juvenile delinquency among teenage women can be prevented or reduced.

Target Population: The program serves young women between the ages of twelve and twenty-one in Tucson and in the rural areas of Pima County, Arizona, including the Papago Indian Reservation.

Program Description: New Directions for Young Women (NDYW) advocates change in the juvenile justice system and other social institutions (such as the school, the family, and the labor market) with respect to their treatment of young women. Its focus has been advocacy for the deinstitutionalization of female status offenders in Pima County and the provision of technical assistance to other agencies to establish new programs as alternatives to incarceration. These new programs include "Creative Teen Power," a collaborative project with the YWCA and the Tucson Urban League which provides practical on-site work experience for females in nontraditional job areas (carpentry, construction, and other trades); the establishment of a Teenage Women's Task Force as part of the Tucson Women's Commission with a young women's column inserted in the commission's

to their schools. At the same time, the nation's social service agencies have made a concerted effort to help people adjust to middle-class society's rules and values.

Labeling theorists have suggested that an opposite tack be taken. Rather than ask social agencies to attempt to rehabilitate people who may be manifesting problems with the law, they argue that less is better. Put another way, the more institutions try to "help" people, the more these people will be stigmatized and labeled. For example, a special education program designed to help problem readers may cause them to be labeled by themselves and others as slow or stupid; a mental health rehabilitation program created with the best intentions may cause clients to be labeled crazy or dangerous.

The influence of labeling theory can be viewed in the development of diversion and restitution programs.

Diversion programs are designed to remove both juvenile and adult offenders from the normal channels of the criminal justice process by placing them in programs designed for rehabilitation. For example, a college student whose careless drunken driving causes injury to a pedestrian may, before a trial takes place, be placed for six months in an alcohol treatment program. If he successfully completes the program, charges against him will be dismissed. Thus, he avoids the stigma of a criminal label. Such programs are common throughout the nation. Often, they newspaper; and advocacy efforts which have resulted in the prioritization of the needs of female status offenders by the Arizona League of Women Voters and the American Association of University Women.

NDYW has sponsored two national conferences entitled "Changing Values: Teenage Women in the Juvenile Justice System" and has published a book on the first conference to heighten public concern regarding female status offenders. Other training/education efforts have included workshops with the Arizona State Department of Education, the U.S. Army, and personnel of the Tucson Unified School District. NDYW has also developed a Sex-Role Stereotyping Awareness Tool for use with junior and senior high school students. Tucson teachers have used the tool and other materials to help break down sex-role stereotyping with their students.

In addition to its advocacy function, NDYW provides a number of direct services to young women who are in need of support, information, and guidance rather than intensive therapy. Individual and family counseling are offered on an appointment or drop-in basis at the Center, in school, or at the client's home. All services are free. The counselor seeks to provide support and a positive atmosphere for the client and to act as a resource to the young woman and her family, particularly with regard to birth control, rape, sexuality, the job market, and local cultural and educational opportunities.

An alternative education program is available to women sixteen years old or over. Free day care is provided for those with children. Coursework emphasizes the basic educational requirements needed to obtain a GED, as well as independent living skills such as parental effectiveness, job preparation skills, budgeting,

and the like. Informational and support groups are available to all young women, who are encouraged to make their own decisions, resolve conflicts, and be independent and self-confident. Assertiveness training, sex-role stereotyping awareness, women's sexuality awareness, parent readiness and single parent training, and a general communications group are offered.

A nine-week parent study group, Systematic Training for Effective Parenting, is provided to parents to help them live with their children as equals. NDYW also offers a two-day camping trip/retreat program which combines recreation with many of the training and awareness programs the agency sponsors. The retreat seeks to provide young women with nonthreatening ways of dealing with problems and building communication skills. Supervised by NDYW staff and other agency personnel who volunteer to participate, the retreats are usually held in camping sites in the nearby mountains.

Originally funded by the federal government, NDYW is now part of the Family Counseling Agency of Arizona and is supported by the United Way.

DISCUSSION QUESTIONS

1. Is it reasonable to expect such programs to help offenders fit into society?

2. Should we focus on changing society rather than the offender?

SOURCE. J. Wall, J. D. Hawkins, D. Lishner, and M. Fraser, *Reports of the National Juvenile Justice Assessment Centers, Juvenile Delinquency Prevention: A Compendium of 36 Program Models* (Washington, D.C.: U.S. Government Printing Office, 1981). Updated with material supplied by NDYW, 1985.

---

offer counseling; vocational, educational, and family services; and medical advice.

Another label-avoiding innovation that has gained popularity is **restitution**. Rather than face the stigma of a formal trial, an offender is asked to either (1) pay back the victim of the crime for any loss incurred or (2) do some useful work in the community in lieu of receiving a court-ordered sentence.

Despite their good intentions, stigma-reducing programs have not met with great success. Critics charge that they substitute one kind of stigma for another—for instance, attending a mental health program in lieu of a criminal trial. In addition, diversion and restitution programs usually screen out violent offenders and repeat offenders. Finally, there is little hard evidence that the recidivism rate of people who have attended alternative programs represents an improvement over the rate shown by people who have been involved in the traditional criminal justice process.

Summary

Social process theories view criminality as a function of people's interaction with various organizations, institutions, and processes in society. People in all walks of life have the potential to become criminals if they maintain destructive social relationships. Social process theory has three main branches: the social learning

TABLE 8.1 Social process theories

Theories	Major premise	Strengths	Unanswered questions and other weaknesses
Social Learning Theories			
Differential Association Theory	People learn to commit crime from exposure to antisocial definitions.	Explains onset of criminality. Explains the presence of crime in all elements of social structure. Explains why some people in high-crime areas refrain from criminality. Can apply to adults and juveniles.	Where do antisocial definitions originate? How can we measure antisocial definitions or prove that someone has been exposed to an excess of them? Fails to explain illogical acts of violence and destruction. Fails to discuss how to test theory adequately.
Differential Reinforcement Theory	Criminal behavior depends on the person's experiences with rewards for conventional behaviors and punishments for deviant ones. Being rewarded for deviance leads to crime.	Adds learning theory principles to differential association. Links sociological and psychological principles.	Fails to explain why those rewarded for conventional behavior, such as middle-class youths, commit crimes. Fails to explain why some delinquent youths do not become adult criminals despite their having been rewarded for crime.
Neutralization Theory	Youths learn ways of neutralizing moral restraints and periodically drift in and out of criminal behavior patterns.	Explains why many delinquents do not become adult criminals. Explains why youthful law violators can participate in conventional behavior.	Fails to show whether neutralizations occur before or after law violations. Does not explain why some youths drift and others do not. Cannot explain self-destructive acts such as heroin addiction.
Control Theories			
Social Bond Theory	A person's bond to society prevents him or her from violating social rules. If the bond weakens, the person is free to commit crime.	Explains onset of crime; can apply to both middle- and lower-class crime. Explains its theoretical constructs adequately so they can be measured. Has been empirically tested.	Fails to explain differences in crime rates. Fails to show whether a weakened bond can be strengthened. Does not distinguish the importance of different elements of the social bond—for example, is attachment more important than commitment?

continued

The social learning branch of social process theory suggests that people learn criminal behaviors much as they learn conventional behavior. Differential association theory, formulated by Edwin Sutherland, holds that criminality is a result of a person's perceiving an excess of definitions in favor of crime over definitions that uphold conventional values. Ronald Akers has reformulated Sutherland's work stresses that people learn how to commit crimes; social control theory analyzes the failure of society to control the criminal tendencies of certain people; and labeling theory maintains that negative labels produce criminal careers. These theories are summarized in table 8.1.

using psychological learning theory. He calls his approach differential reinforcement theory. David Matza's theory of neutralization stresses youths' learning of behavior

TABLE 8.1 Social process theories—cont'd

Theories	Major premise	Strengths	Unanswered questions and other weaknesses
Theory of Commitment to Conformity	Short-term stimuli influence behavior. Their influence is controlled by a person's commitment to conventional society. Commitment helps people resist temptations.	Can explain middle- and lower-class crime. Shows how control is manifested over middle-class youths.	Fails to explain variations in crime rates. Fails to explain why some children develop commitments and others do not. Fails to explain variations in crime rates.
Containment Theory	Society produces pushes and pulls toward crime. In some people, they are counteracted by internal and external containments such as a good self-concept and group cohesiveness.	Brings together psychological and sociological principles. Can explain why some people are able to resist the strongest social pressures to commit crime.	The methodology used to support the theory has been heavily criticized. Does low self-concept cause delinquency, or are delinquent youths subject to social conditions and destroy their self-images?
Differential Anticipation Theory	People commit crimes whenever and wherever expectations of gain from crime exceed expectations of losses with respect to social bonds. Expectations determine conduct.	Combines principles of social bond, differential association, and classical theories.	Has not been subject to extensive empirical testing. Does not explain why expectations vary. Does not explain crime rate variations.
Social Development Theory	Weak social controls produce crime. A person's place in the social structure influences his or her bond to society.	Combines elements of social structural and social process theories. Accounts for variations in the crime rate.	Has not been subject to rigorous empirical testing.
Labeling Theories	People enter into law-violating careers when they are labeled for their acts and organize their personalities around the labels.	Explains the role of society in creating deviance. Explains why some juvenile offenders do not become adult criminals. Develops concepts of criminal careers.	Does not explain the original reason why a person commits a crime. Places too much emphasis on society's role in the labeling process. Empirical verification is inconsistent.

rationalizations that enable them to overcome societal values and norms and engage in illegal behavior.

Control theory is the second branch of the social process approach. Control theories maintain that all people have the potential to become criminals but that their bonds to conventional society prevent them from violating the law. Travis Hirschi describes the social bond as containing the elements of belief, commitment, attachment, and involvement. Briar and Piliavin describe a person's commitment to conformity and how situational inducements can overcome it. Walter Reckless's containment theory suggests that a person's self-concept aids his or her commitment to conventional action. Daniel Glazer has also formulated a control theory, called differential anticipation theory.

Labeling theory argues that a person's criminality is promoted by his or her being negatively labeled by significant others. Labels such as criminal, ex-con, and junkie serve to isolate people from society and lock them into lives of crime. Labels create expectations that the labeled person will act in a certain way; so labeled people are always watched and suspected. Eventually, these people begin to accept their labels as personal identities, locking them further into lives of crime and deviance. Edwin Lemert has said that people who accept labels are involved in secondary deviance. Unfortunately, research on labeling has not supported its major premises. Consequently, critics have charged that it lacks credibility as a description of crime causation.

Social process theories have had a great influence on social policy. They have controlled treatment orientations as well as community action policies.

Notes

1 Travis Hirschi, *Causes of Delinquency* (Berkeley, Calif.: University of California Press, 1969), p. 7.

2 Sheldon and Eleanor Glueck, *Unraveling Juvenile Delinquency* (Cambridge, Mass.: Harvard University Press, 1950); Ashley Weeks, "Predicting Juvenile Delinquency," *American Sociological Review* 8 (1943):40–46.

3 Joseph Weis, Katherine Worsley, and Carol Zeiss, "The Family and Delinquency: Organizing the Conceptual Chaos," Center for Law and Justice, University of Washington, 1982 (monograph).

4 Lawrence Rosen and Kathleen Neilson, "Broken Homes," in *Contemporary Criminology*, ed. Leonard Savitz and Norman Johnston (New York: Wiley, 1982), pp. 126–35.

5 Richard Smith and James Walters, "Delinquent and Non-delinquent Males' Perceptions of Their Fathers," *Adolescence* 13 (1978):21–28; Paul Robinson, "Parents of 'Beyond Control' Adolescents," *Adolsecence* 13 (1978):116–19.

6 Ruth Inglis, *Sins of Fathers: A Study of the Physical and Emotional Abuse of Children* (New York: St. Martin's Press, 1978).

7 Delos Kelly and William Pink, "School Crime and Individual Responsibility: The Perpetuation of a Myth," *The Urban Review* 14 (1982):47–63.

8 Walter E. Schafer, Carol Olexa, and Kenneth Polk, "Programmed for Social Class: Tracking in High School," in Kenneth Polk and Walter E. Schafer, eds., *Schools and Delinquency* (Englewood Cliffs, N.J.: Prentice-Hall, 1972), pp. 34–54; Terence Thornberry, Melanie Moore and R.L. Christenson, "The Effect of Dropping Out of High School on Subsequent Criminal Behavior," *Criminology* 23((1985):3–18.

9 National Commission on Excellence in Education, *A Nation at Risk* (Washington, D.C.: U.S. Government Printing Office, 1982).

10 U.S. Department of Justice, *Disorder in Our Public Schools* (Washington, D.C.: U.S. Government Printing Office, 1984).

11 Walter Miller, *Violence by Youth Gangs and Youth Groups as a Crime Problem in Major American Cities* (Washington, D.C.: U.S. Government Printing Office, 1975).

12 Delos Kelly, *Creating School Failure, Youth Crime, and Deviance* (Los Angeles: Trident Shop, 1982); Delos Kelly and W. Grove, "Teachers' Nominations and the Production of Academic Misfits," *Education* 101 (1981):246–63.

13 Gabriel Tarde, *The Laws of Imitation* (1903; reprint ed. Gloucester, Mass.: Peter Smith, 1962).

14 Edwin Sutherland, *Principles of Criminology* (Philadelphia: Lippincott, 1939).

15 See, for example Edwin Sutherland, "White-Collar Criminality," *American Sociological Review* 5 (1940):2–10.

16 This section is adapted from Clarence Schrag, *Crime and Justice: American Style* (Washington, D.C.: Government Printing Office, 1971), p. 46.

17 See Edwin Sutherland and Donald Cressey, *Criminology*, 8th ed. (Philadelphia: Lippin-cott, 1970), pp. 77–79.

18 Ibid.

19 James Short, "Differential Association as a Hypothesis: Problems of Empirical Testing," *Social Problems* 8 (1960):14–25.

20 Albert Reiss and A. Lewis Rhodes, "The Distribution of Delinquency in the Social Class Structure," *American Sociological Research* 26 (1961):732.

21 Hirschi, *Causes of Delinquency*, p. 95.

22 Charles Tittle, *Sanctions and Social Deviance* (New York: Praeger, 1980).

23 Ibid., p. 188.

24 Robert Burgess and Ronald Akers, "A Differential Association—Reinforcement Theory of Criminal Behavior," *Social Problems* 14 (1966):128–47.

25 Donald Cressey, "Epidemiologies and Individual Conduct: a Case from Criminology," *Pacific Sociological Review* 3 (1960):128–47.

26 See, for example, Albert Bandura, *Social Learning and Personality Development* (New York: Holt, Rinehart and Winston, 1963).

27 Ronald Akers, *Deviant Behavior: A Social Learning Approach*, 2d ed. (Belmont, Mass.: Wadsworth, 1977).

28 Ronald Akers, Marvin Krohn, Lonn Lonza-Kaduce, and Marcia Radosevich, "Social Learning and Deviant Behavior: A Specific Test of a General Theory," *American Sociological Review* 44 (1979):638.

29 Ibid.

30 Ibid., pp. 636–55.

31 For an opposing view, see C. Ray Jeffery, "Criminal Law and Learning Theory," *Journal of Criminal Law, Criminology, and Police Science* 56 (1965):300.

32 Gresham Sykes and David Matza, "Techniques of Neutralization: A Theory of Delin-quency," *American Sociological Review* 22 (1957):664–70; David Matza, *Delinquency and Drift* (New York: John Wiley, 1964).

33 Matza, *Delinquency and Drift*, p. 51.

34 Sykes and Matza, "Techniques of Neutralization," pp. 664–70.

35 David Matza, "Subterranean Traditions of Youths," *Annals of the American Academy of Political and Social Science* 378 (1961):116.

36 Sykes and Matza, "Techniques of Neutralization," pp. 664–70.

37 Ibid.

38 Robert Ball, "An Empirical Exploration of Neutralization Theory," *Criminologica* 4 (1966):22–32. For a similar view, see M. William Minor, "The Neutralization of Crim-inal Offense," *Criminology* 18 (1980):103–20.

39 Robert Regoli and Eric Poole, "The Commitment of Delinquents to Their Misdeeds: A Reexamination," *Journal of Criminal Justice* 6 (1978):261–69.

40 Michael Hindelang, "The Commitment of Delinquents to Their Misdeeds: Do Delin-quents Drift?" *Social Problems* 17 (1970):509.

41 Hirschi, *Causes of Delinquency*, p. 34.

42 Ibid., see generally.

43 Scott Briar and Irving Piliavin, "Delinquency, Situational Inducements and Commit-ment to Conformity," *Social Problems* 13 (1965–1966):35–45.

44 Walter Reckless, *The Crime Problem* (New York: Appleton Century Crofts, 1967).

45 Daniel Glazer, "Differential Association and Criminological Prediction," *Social Problems* 8 (1960):13–19.

46 Hirschi, *Causes of Delinquency*.

47 Ibid., p. 231.

48 Ibid., pp. 66–74.

49 Michael Hindelang, "Causes of Delinquency: A Partial Replication and Extension," *Social Problems* 21 (1973):471–87; Joseph Rankin, "Investigating the Interrelations Among Social Control Variables and Conformity," *Journal of Criminal Law and Crimi-*

nology 69 (1977):470–480; Marvin Krohn and James Massey, "Social Control and Delinquent Behavior: An Examination of the Elements of the Social Bond," *Sociological Quarterly* 21 (1980):529–544; Stephen Cernkovich, "Evaluating Two Models of Delinquency Causation," *Criminology* 16 (1978):335–352; Michael Wiatrowski, David Griswold and Mary Roberts, "Social Control Theory and Delinquency," *American Sociological Review* 46 (1981):525–541; Randy LaGrange and Helene Raskin White, "Age Differences in Delinquency: A Test of Theory," *Criminology* 23 (1985):19–45; Robert Agnew, "Social Control Theory and Delinquency: A Longitudinal Analysis," *Criminology* 23 (1985):47–61.

50 Briar and Piliavin, "Delinquency, Situational Inducements and Commitment to Conformity."

51 Ibid., p. 41.

52 Among the many research reports by Walter Reckless and his colleagues are: W. Reckless, S. Dinitz, and E. Murray, "Self-Concept as an Insulator against Delinquency," *American Sociological Review* 21 (1956):744–46; Walter Reckless, Simon Dinitz, and Ellen Murray, "The Good Boy in a High Delinquency Area," *Journal of Criminal Law, Criminology, and Police Science* 48 (1957):1826; Walter Reckless, Simon Dinitz, and Barbara Kay, "The Self-Component in Potential Delinquency and Potential Non-delinquency," *American Sociological Review* 22 (1957):566–70; W. Reckless and S. Dinitz, "Pioneering with Self-Concept as a Vulnerability Factor in Delinquency," *Journal of Criminal Law, Criminology, and Police Science* 58 (1967):515–23.

53 The description of inner and outer containments is from Schrag, *Crime and Justice: American Style*, p. 85.

54 Walter Reckless, "Containment Theory," in *The Sociology of Crime and Delinquency*, ed. Marvin Wolfgang, Leonard Savitz, and Norman Johnston, 2d ed. (New York: John Wiley, 1970), p. 402.

55 Reckless, Dinitz, and Murray, "Self-Concept as an Insulator."

56 Ibid., p. 746.

57 Reckless, Dinitz, and Kay, "The Self-Component in Potential Delinquency."

58 Frank Scarpitti, Ellen Murray, Simon Dinitz, and Walter Reckless, "The Good Boy in a High Delinquency Area: Four Years Later," *American Sociological Review* 23 (1960):555–58.

59 Michael Schwartz and Sandra Tangri, "A Note on Self-Concept as an Insulator against Delinquency," *American Sociological Review* 30 (1965):922–26.

60 Daniel Glazer, *Crime in Our Changing Society* (New York: Holt, Rinehart and Winston, 1978).

61 Ibid., p. 125.

62 Ibid., p. 126.

63 Ibid.

64 Ibid.

65 Joseph Weis and J. David Hawkins, *Reports of the National Juvenile Justice Assessment Centers, Preventing Delinquency* (Washington, D.C.: U.S. Department of Justice, 1981); Joseph Weis and John Sederstrom, *Reports of the National Juvenile Justice Assessment Centers, The Prevention of Serious Delinquency: What to Do* (Washington, D.C.: U.S. Department of Justice, 1981).

66 President's Commission on Law Enforcement and the Administration of Youth Crime, *Task Force Report: Juvenile Delinquency and Youth Crime* (Washington, D.C.: Government Printing Office, 1967), p. 43.

67 Kai Erickson, "Notes on the Sociology of Deviance," *Social Problems* 9 (1962):397–414.

68 Edwin Schur, *Labeling Deviant Behavior* (New York: Harper & Row, 1972), p. 21.

69 Howard Becker, *Outsiders, Studies in the Sociology of Deviance* (New York: Macmillan, 1963), p. 9.

70 Christy Visher, "Gender, Police Arrest Decisions, and Notions of Chivalry," *Criminology* 21 (1983):5–28.

71 Marjorie Zatz, "Race, Ethnicity and Determinate Sentencing," *Criminology* 22 (1984):147–71.

72 Roland Chilton and Jim Galvin, "Race, Crime and Criminal Justice," *Crime and Delinquency* 31 (1985):3–14.

73 Joan Petersilia, "Racial Disparities in the Criminal Justice System: A Summary," *Crime and Delinquency* 31 (1985):15–34.

74 Walter Gove, ed., *The Labeling of Deviance: Evaluating a Perspective* (New York: John Wiley, 1975), p. 5.

75 Ibid., p. 9.

76 Harold Garfinkle, "Conditions of Successful Degradation Ceremonies," *American Journal of Sociology* 61 (1956):420–24.

77 John Lofland, *Deviance and Identity* (Englewood Cliffs, N. J.: Prentice-Hall, 1969).

78 Frank Tannenbaum, *Crime and the Community* (New York: Columbia University Press, 1938), pp. 19–20.

79 Edwin Lemert, *Social Pathology* (New York: McGraw-Hill, 1951).

80 National Minority Advisory Council on Criminal Justice, *The Inequality of Justice* (Washington, D.C.: National Minority Advisory Council on Criminal Justice, 1981), p. 200.

81 Paul Lipsett, "The Juvenile Offender's Perception," *Crime and Delinquency* 14 (1968):49; Jack Foster, Simon Dinitz, and Walter Reckless, "Perception of Stigma Following Public Intervention for Delinquent Behavior," *Social Problems* 20 (1972):202.

82 Charles Tittle, "Labeling and Crime: An Empirical Evaluation," in *The Labeling of Deviance: Evaluating a Perspective,* ed. Walter Gove (New York: John Wiley, 1975), pp. 157–79.

83 Susan Ageton and Delbert Elliott, "The Effect of Legal Processing on Self-Concept," (Boulder, Colo.: Institute of Behavioral Science, 1973).

84 Jack Gibbs, "Conceptions of Deviant Behavior: The Old and the New," *Pacific Sociological Review* 9 (1966):11–13.

85 Schur, *Labeling Deviant Behavior,* p. 14.

86 Ronald Akers, "Problems in the Sociology of Deviance," *Social Problems* 46 (1968):463.

87 Charles Wellford, "Labeling Theory and Criminology: An Assessment," *Social Problems* 22 (1975):335.

88 Ibid.

89 Ibid., p. 107.

90 Tittle, "Labeling and Crime," p. 174.

91 Alexander Liazos, "The Poverty of the Sociology of Deviance: Nuts, Sluts, and Perverts," *Social Problems* 20 (1971):103–120.

9 Sociological Approaches: Social Conflict Theory

CHAPTER OUTLINE

KEY TERMS

conflict theory
Karl Marx
Friedrich Engels
critical criminology
radical criminology
Marxist criminology
new criminology
productive forces

productive relations
capitalist bourgeoisie
proletariat
class
lumpen proletariat
dialectic
Ralf Dahrendorf
George Vold

Richard Quinney
Austin Turk
power
the social reality of crime
behavior pattern
Willem Bonger
privilege
class interest

Introduction

It would be unusual to pick up the morning paper without seeing headlines loudly proclaiming renewed strife between the United States and her overseas adversaries, between union negotiators and management attorneys, between citizens and police authorities, or between Republicans and Democrats. The world is filled with conflict. Conflict can be destructive when it leads to war, violence, and death; it can be functional when it results in positive social change.

This chapter will review theories that allege that crime is a function of the conflict existing in almost every society. As you may recall, theorists who hold a conflict orientation see the criminal law as an expression of the beliefs and values of the ruling class and the criminal justice system as its social control mechanism. In contrast to the consensus/positivist position, which holds that crime is a violation of socially acceptable legal rules and norms, the conflict position views crime as a reaction to the unfair distribution of wealth and power existing in society.

Conflict theorists are concerned with such issues as the role the government plays in creating a crimogenic environment; the relationship of personal or group power to controlling and shaping the criminal law; the role of bias in the operations of the justice system; and the relationship between a capitalist free enterprise economy and crime rates. Conflict theorists see struggles everywhere—between two students competing for a scholarship; between the poor and the wealthy; between the police and the public. "How can you suggest that the existing law represents a consensus of values and beliefs," a conflict theorist would ask, "when so much antagonism and disagreement exists among rival groups and individuals?" Conflict works to promote crime by creating a social atmosphere in which the law is a mechanism for controlling dissatisfied, "have-not" members of society while maintaining the position of the powerful.

Social conflict theory has several independent branches. The first assumes that crime is caused by the conflict which, historically, has existed in every society. This approach will be referred to simply as **conflict theory.** The second branch is based on the writings of the economic philosopher **Karl Marx** and his colleague **Friedrich Engels.** Criminologists of this school focus on the crime-producing conflict unique to capitalist society. This approach will be referred to as **critical criminology, radical criminology, Marxist criminology,** or the **new criminology.**

The theoretical models contained within the social conflict perspective are usually less formal than those constructed by positivist criminologists (chapters 6, 7, and 8). In fact, critics have argued that the lack of theoretical precision is a major drawback to conflict theory. Nevertheless, social conflict theorists have on occasion attempted to systematically articulate their ideas; and wherever possible, this chapter will present their more formal statements in some detail.

Before reviewing theoretical models of the two branches of the conflict approach, it might be helpful to go over some of the basic elements of Marxist theory. An understanding of Marxist thought is essential for analyzing conflict theory concepts, since even conflict criminologists who reject Marx's economic and social philosophy have certainly been influenced by it.

Marxist Thought

The foundation of conflict theory can be traced to the political and economic philosophy of Karl Marx (1818–1883) and his colleague Friedrich Engels (1820–1895).[1] Marx believed that the character of every civilization is determined by its mode of production—the way its people develop and produce material goods.

Karl Marx, German political philosopher and author of *Das Kapital,* provided the foundation for radical criminology.

Production has two components: (1) **productive forces,** which include such things as technology, energy sources, and material resources; and (2) **productive relations,** which are the relationships that exist among the people producing goods and services. The most important relationship in industrial culture is between the owners of the means of production, the **capitalist bourgeoisie,** and the people who do the actual labor, the **proletariat.** Throughout history, society has been organized this way—master-slave, lord-serf, and now capitalist-proletarian.

According to Marx and Engels, capitalist society is subject to the development of a rigid **class** structure. At the top is the capitalist bourgeoisie. Next comes the working proletariat who actually produce goods and services. At the bottom of society are the fringe members who produce nothing and live, parasitically, off the work of others—the **lumpen proletariat.**

In Marxist theory, the term *class* does not refer to an attribute or characteristic of a person or a group; rather, it denotes position in relation to others. Thus, it is not necessary to have a particular amount of wealth or prestige to be a member of the capitalist class; it is more important to have the power to exploit others economically, legally, and socially.

The political and economic philosophy of the dominant class influences all aspects of life. Consciously or unconsciously, artists, writers, and teachers bend their work to the whims of the capitalist system. Thus, the economic system controls all facets of human life; and consequently, people's lives revolve around the means of production. As Marx says in *Grundrisse:*

> In all forms of society there is one specific kind of production which predominates over the rest, whose relations thus assign rank and influence to the others. It is a general illumination which bathes all the other colours and modifies their particularity. It is a particular ether which determines the specific gravity of every being which has materialized within it.[2]

Marx believed that societies and their structures were not stable but could change through slow evolution or sudden violence. Historically, such change occurs because of contradictions present in a society. These contradictions are antagonisms or conflicts between elements in the existing social arrangement that in the long run are incompatible with one another. If these social conflicts are not resolved, they tend to destabilize society, leading to social change.

How could social change occur in capitalist society? Marx holds that the laboring class produces goods that exceed wages in value. The excess value then goes into the hands of the capitalists as profit. Though some of this profit is spent on personal luxuries, most is spent on acquiring an ever-expanding capitalist base that relies on advanced technology for efficiency. Thus, capitalists are in constant competition with each other to maintain market position. To compete, they must produce goods more efficiently and cheaply, a necessity that requires them either to pay workers the lowest possible wages or to replace them with labor-saving machinery. Soon the supply of efficiently made goods outstrips the ability of the laboring classes to purchase them, a condition that precipitates an economic crisis. During this period, weaker enterprises go under and are consequently incorporated into ever-expanding, monopolistic megacorporations strong enough to further exploit the workers. Marx believed that in the ebb and flow of the business cycle, the capitalist system contained the seeds of its own destruction and that from its ashes would grow a socialist state in which the workers themselves would own the means of production.

In his analysis, Marx used the **dialectic** method, based on the analysis developed by the philosopher Georg Hegel (1770–1831). Hegel argues that for every idea, or *thesis*, there exists an opposing argument, or *antithesis*. Since neither position can ever be truly accepted, the result is a merger of the two ideas, a *synthesis*. Marx adapted this analytic method for his study of class struggle. History, argues Marx, is replete with examples of two opposing forces whose conflict promotes social change. When conditions are bad enough, the oppressed will rise up to fight the owners and eventually replace them. Thus, in the end, the capitalist system will destroy itself.

MARX AND ENGELS ON CRIME

Marx and Engels did not write a great deal on the subject of crime. Engels did spend some time on the subject in his work, *The Condition of the Working Class in England in 1844.*[3] Here, he portrayed crime as a function of social demoralization—a collapse of people's humanity reflecting a decline in society. Workers, demoralized by capitalist society, are caught up in a process that leads to crime and violence.

Marx paid even less attention to crime. His most famous statement on the subject seems almost tongue-in-cheek:

> *A philosopher produces ideas, a poet poems, a clergyman sermons, a professor compendia and so on. A criminal produces crimes. If we look a little closer at the connection between this latter branch of production and society as a whole, we shall rid ourselves of many prejudices. The criminal produces not only crimes but also criminal law, and with this also the professor who gives lectures on criminal law and in addition to this the inevitable compendium in which this same professor throws his lectures onto the general market as "commodities" . . .*

The criminal moreover produces the whole of the police and of criminal justice, constables, judges, hangmen, juries, etc.; and all these different lines of business, which form equally many categories of the social division of labour, develop different capacities of the human spirit, create new needs and new ways of satisfying them. Torture alone has given rise to the most ingenious mechanical inventions, and employed many honourable craftsmen in the production of instruments.[4]

Marx seems to be implying that there are benefits to crime and its role in producing social institutions—police, courts, law, and law professors. Criminologists Ian Taylor, Paul Walton, and Jock Young interpret Marx's passage as emphasizing the criminal nature of the capitalist system.[5] They argue that Marx is suggesting the possibility of a crime-free society by showing that capitalist economic and social relationships produce crime. Moreover, these authors believe Marx is ridiculing the consensus/functionalist theorists, who maintain that all behavior serves a function or reflects a consensus of societal viewpoints. So long as capitalism exists, it is foolish to think that people obey the law because it is "right"; they do so because the law represents the will of those who hold power.

Marxist thought provides a point of departure from which crime and deviance can be understood. It points out the relationship between economic conditions and the decision to violate the law. Theorists who use Marxian analysis reject the notion that law is designed to maintain a tranquil and fair society and that criminals are malevolent people who wish to trample the rights of others. By focusing on the capitalist state's role in producing a crimogenic society, Marxist thought serves as the basis for all conflict theory.

Conflict Theory

The conflict perspective has had a long history in sociological thought; yet its popularity as an explanation of crime, law, and justice is a relatively recent phenomenon. How can its rise in popularity be explained? One root can be traced to the self-report studies developed in the 1960s and 1970s, which yielded data suggesting that crime and delinquency were much more evenly distributed through the social structure than had been indicated by the official statistics. If middle-class participation in crime goes unrecorded, this fact may easily be interpreted to mean that the lower class is the subject of bias and discrimination by the criminal justice system. Criminologists began to view the justice system as a mechanism to control the lower class and maintain the status quo rather than as a device to serve and protect all honest citizens.

The popularity of the labeling perspective (described in chapter 8) in the late 1960s and early 1970s also contributed to the development of the conflict model. Labeling theorists such as Howard Becker rejected the notion that crime is morally wrong and called for the analysis of the interaction among crime, criminal, victim, and labeling authority. Yet some criminologists charged that labeling theory did not go far enough in analyzing the important relationships in society—that it dwelled on "nuts, sluts and perverts."[6] Consequently, a group of criminologists led by Richard Quinney, Austin Turk, and William Chambliss began to produce scholarship and research directed at (1) identifying "real" crimes in U.S. society, such as profiteering, sexism, and racism; (2) evaluating how the criminal law is used as a mechanism of social control; and (3) turning the attention of citizens to the inequities in U.S. society.[7] One sociologist, David Greenberg, comments:

The theme that dominated much of the work in this area was the contention that criminal legislation was determined not by moral consensus or the common interests of the entire society, but by relative power of groups determined to use the criminal law to advance their own special interests or to impose their moral preferences on others.[8]

Adding impetus to this movement was the general and widespread social and political upheaval of the late sixties and early seventies. These forces included Vietnam War protests, counterculture movements, and various forms of political protest. Conflict theory flourished within this framework, since it provided a systematic basis for challenging the legitimacy of the government's creation and application of law. The crackdown on political dissidents by agents of the federal government, the prosecution of draft resistors, and the like all seemed designed to maintain control in the hands of political power brokers.

In formulating their perceptions of people and crime, modern conflict theorists rely heavily on the writings of pioneering social thinkers. This section will now review the work of two such influential critical thinkers—Ralf Dahrendorf and George Vold.

RALF DAHRENDORF

Ralf Dahrendorf is considered one of the major contributors to the modern conflict perspective. His work has been described as assuming "the status of a catechism."[9]

Dahrendorf charges that the consensus/functionalist model of society is utopian and without basis in the real world. He views society as being organized into *imperatively coordinated associations.* These relationships comprise two groups—those who dominate (possess authority) and those who are subject to authority. However, since dominating one section of society—for example, industry—does not mean dominating another—such as government—society is a plurality of competing interest groups.

Dahrendorf rejects the Marxian approach when describing social conflict. In his classic work *Class and Class Conflict in Industrial Society,* Dahrendorf attempts to show how society has changed since Marx formulated his concepts of class, state, and conflict.[10] Dahrendorf argues that Marx did not foresee the changes that have occurred in the laboring classes. "The working class of today," he states, "far from being a homogeneous group of equally unskilled and impoverished people, is in fact a stratum differentiated by numerous subtle and not so subtle distinctions."[11] Today, workers are divided into the unskilled, semiskilled, and skilled; and the interests of one group may not match the needs of the others. Consequently, Marx's concept of a cohesive proletarian class has proved inaccurate.

Theory of Conflict. Dahrendorf proposes a unified conflict theory of human behavior, which can be summarized in the following statements:

- Every society is at every point subject to processes of change; social change is everywhere.
- Every society displays at every point dissent and conflict; social conflict is everywhere.
- Every element in a society renders a contribution to its disintegration and change.
- Every society is based on the coercion of some of its members by others.[12]

Dahrendorf argues that it is not consensus, cohesion, or cooperation that binds society together, but the enforced constraint of citizens. In every society—capitalist, socialist, feudal, and so on—there exists a differential distribution of power and authority; those who have power and authority exercise control over others. Wherever such conditions exist, group conflicts are to be expected.

The social class structure consists of conflict groups arising out of the unequal distribution of authority. However, conflict is not necessarily evil. It can be destructive if it is evidence of a breakdown of social stability. However, it can also be functional; from the seeds of conflict may develop a more efficient, fair, and effective social order.

Dahrendorf does not speak directly to the issue of crime, but his model of conflict serves as a pillar of modern conflict criminology.

GEORGE VOLD: CONFLICT AND CRIME

Though Dahrendorf contributed its theoretical underpinnings, conflict theory was actually adapted to criminology by **George Vold.** It cannot be said that Vold individually "pioneered" conflict criminology, but his writings are among the earliest and most influential. His basic ideas can be expressed in a few simple concepts.[13]

People are inherently social animals whose lives are bound up in group processes. People join groups because of mutual interests and needs that can best be furthered through collective action. Groups must serve their members or face extinction. New groups are constantly being formed to replace weak or ineffective ones.

People constantly struggle to further the interests of their group and improve its standing among the totality of social groups. The end result is a continuous state of social struggle. "Conflict is viewed, therefore, as one of the principal and essential social processes upon which the continuing ongoing of society depends."[14]

Conflict arises when groups compete in the same general field of interaction. Since each group tries to defend its social position and maintain its supremacy, intergroup conflict is the result. We can see examples of this in the continuous conflicts between union members and management, landlords and tenants, inmates and guards, and taxpayers and the government.

Conflict can bring out the best in people. During war and calamity, heroes emerge and people show their mettle through self-sacrifice and loyalty. Conflict can inspire people to serve their compatriots and not merely their own selfish ends.

Social Conflict and Crime. Vold argued that crime can also be explained by social conflict. Laws are created by politically oriented groups who seek the assistance of the government to help them defend their rights and protect their interests. If a group can marshal enough support, a law will be created to hamper and curb the interests of some opposition group. As Vold says, "the whole political process of law making, law breaking and law enforcement becomes a direct reflection of deep-seated and fundamental conflicts between interest groups and their more general struggles for the control of the police power of the state."[15] Every stage of the process—from the passage of the law, to the prosecution of the case, to the relationships between inmate and guard and parole agent and parolee—is marked by conflict.

Vold finds that criminal acts are a consequence of direct contact between forces struggling to control society. Though their criminal content may mask their political meaning, closer examination of even the most basic violent acts often reveals political undertones.

Vold's model cannot be used to explain all types of crime. It is limited to situations in which rival group loyalties collide. It cannot explain impulsive, irrational acts unrelated to any group's interest. Despite this limitation, Vold finds that a great deal of criminal activity results from intergroup clashes.

Conflict Criminology

In the early 1970s, conflict theory began to significantly affect criminological studies. Several important scholars switched their allegiance from a positivist/consensus to a conflict orientation. For example, William Chambliss and Robert Seidman wrote the well-respected treatise *Law, Order and Power,* which documents the power relations in law enforcement and describes how the justice system operates to protect the rich and powerful. After closely observing the reality of justice, Chambliss and Seidman drew this conclusion:

> In America it is frequently argued that to have "freedom" is to have a system which allows one group to make a profit over another. To maintain the existing legal system requires a choice. On this argument that choice is between maintaining a legal system that serves to support the existing economic system with its power structure and developing an equitable legal system accompanied by the loss of "personal freedom." But the old question comes back to plague us: Freedom for whom? Is the black man who provides such a ready source of cases for the welfare workers, the mental hospitals, and the prisons "free"? Are the slum dwellers who are arrested night after night for "loitering," "drunkenness," or being "suspicious" free? The freedom protected by the system of law is the freedom of those who can afford it. The law serves their interests, but they are not "society"; they are one element of society. They may in some complex societies even be a majority (though this is very rare), but the myth that the law serves the interests of "society" misrepresents the facts.[16]

Chambliss and Seidman's work reflects the goal of modern conflict theorists: to describe how power and control affect criminal behavior and the administration of criminal justice. The writing of two other leading scholars of this period, **Richard Quinney** and **Austin Turk,** also stands out as vital to the development of conflict theory. Because of the importance of their work, this section will examine their efforts in some detail.

RICHARD QUINNEY AND THE SOCIAL REALITY OF CRIME

In his early formulation of conflict criminology, Richard Quinney sought to explain the emergence of criminal behavior from a conflict perspective. "In any society," he claimed, "conflicts between persons, social units, or cultural elements are inevitable, the normal consequences of social life."[17] Conflict is intertwined with **power**—the ability of persons and groups to determine and control the behavior of others. The differential distribution of power produces conflict; conflict is rooted in the competition for power. Power is the means by which people shape public opinion to meet their personal interests. Quinney believes human behavior is intentional, has a particular meaning for the actors involved in it, and is goal-oriented; moreover, he believes people are aware of the consequences of their behavior.

Quinney weaves his beliefs about power, society, and criminality into a theory he calls **the social reality of crime.** The theory contains six propositions, which are discussed below.

1. (Definition of Crime):[18] *Crime is a definition of human conduct that is created by authorized agents in a politically organized society.*

    Employing a neointeractionist definition of crime, Quinney claims that criminality is a definition of behavior that is conferred on some persons by others. People and their behaviors are viewed as criminal because of the formulation and application of criminal definitions; crime is created. It follows, then, that the greater the number of criminal definitions formulated and applied, the greater the amount of crime.

2. (Formulation of Criminal Definitions): *Criminal definitions describe behaviors that conflict with the interests of the segments of society that have the power to shape public policy.*

    Quinney states here the essential conflict theory proposition: criminal definitions (law) represent the interests of those who hold power in society. Where there is conflict between social groups—for example, the wealthy and the poor—those who hold power will create laws to benefit themselves and hold rivals in check. Thus, property laws are designed to help those who have wealth keep it in their possession. Quinney believes that the formulation of criminal definitions is based on such factors as (1) changing social conditions; (2) emerging interests; (3) increasing demands that political, economic, and religious interests be protected; and (4) changing conceptions of public interest.

3. (Application of Criminal Definitions): *Criminal definitions are applied by the segments of society that have the power to shape the enforcement and administration of criminal law.*

    The interests of powerful groups are involved not only when law is defined but also when it is administered. Law enforcement activities and judicial administration are designed to protect the interests of the powerful. The probability that criminal sanctions will be applied is influenced by such issues as (1) the community's expectations about law enforcement and administration, (2) the visibility and public reporting of offenses, and (3) the occupational ideology and actions of law enforcement agencies. The more legal agents evaluate behaviors and persons as being worthy of criminal labels, the greater the probability that such definitions will be applied.

4. (Development of Behavior Patterns in Relation to Criminal Definitions): *Behavior patterns are structured in segmentally organized society in relation to criminal definitions, and within this context persons engage in actions that have relative probabilities of being defined as criminal.*

    All behaviors are similar in that they represent the behavior patterns of segments of society. **Behavior patterns** represent the norms people learn in their own cultural settings. People who are not members of the power structure are more likely to develop behaviors that will have criminal labels applied to them. The probability that people will develop behavior patterns likely to be labeled depends on such social variables as their opportunities for legitimate success, their learning experiences, their interpersonal associations and identifications, and their self-conceptions. Quinney embraces labeling theory doctrine when he states that those who have

been defined as criminal will eventually conceive of themselves as criminal. Furthermore, as they adjust to the label, they will (1) learn to play the role of criminal and (2) increase the probability of their behavior's being defined as criminal. Thus, crime is an interactive process—the behavior of both the definers and the defined is shaped by their common, continued, and related experiences.

5. (Construction of Criminal Conceptions): *Conceptions of crime are constructed and diffused in the segments of society by various means of communication.*

People create their own reality based on the kind of knowledge they develop, the ideas to which they are exposed, the manner in which they select information, and the way in which they interpret these inputs. Crime fits this pattern. People's attitudes toward crimes and criminals develop and spread through mass communications. Those in power are able to spread their reality to others; they can shape public opinion so that it agrees with their definitions of crime. Thus, the conceptions held by those in power become the social reality of crime.

6. (The Social Reality of Crime): *The social reality of crime is constructed by the formulation and application of criminal definitions, the development of behavior patterns to criminal definitions, and the construction of criminal conceptions.*

In the sixth statement, Quinney pulls together the ideas he developed in the preceding five. According to his formulation, people's concepts of crime are controlled by the powerful; and the criminal justice system works to secure the needs of the powerful. When people develop behavior patterns that conflict with these needs, the agents of the rich—the justice system— defines them as criminals.

Quinney's theoretical model blends the interactionist (labeling) approach popularized by Becker and Lemert (discussed in chapter 8) with the conflict concepts of Dahrendorf and Vold. Quinney views crime and the laws defining it as a constantly changing set of concepts that mirrors the political organization of society. Law is not an abstract body of rules that represents an absolute moral code. Law is an integral part of society, a force that represents a way of life and a method of doing things. Quinney's model is valuable for its identification of the power relations in the criminal defining process.

AUSTIN TURK

Austin Turk, another well-respected conflict criminologist, rejects the notion that social conflict is inherently ideological and can be used only to explain why capitalism is evil. He is concerned with the power conflicts that emerge in any form of economic system. Turk offers a nonpartisan conflict theory that attempts to be as value-free as possible. The basic premises of his work are set out below.

- Individuals differ in their perceptions, understanding of social phenomena, and commitment to conventional or unconventional lines of action.
- Divergence and disagreement lead people to be in conflict with one another.
- Each conflicting party or person tries to promote his or her own way of thinking and acting as the most appropriate one.

- The result is a conscious struggle over the distribution of available resources and the opportunity to succeed in life goals.
- People with similar understanding, beliefs, and commitments tend to join forces; people who join forces tend to develop and strengthen their mutual beliefs and understandings.
- Continuing conflicts tend to become institutionalized in the form of stratification systems. Conflict groups tend to become a fixed, independent part of the social structure.
- Such systems are characterized by economic exploitation sustained by political domination in all forms—from the most clearly violent to the most subtle forms of political persuasion.
- Power is the single most important attribute determining a group's position in the social structure. Changes in the position a social group manifests in society reflect only changes in the distribution of power.
- Group members share experiences in dealing with group members, group antagonists, and the environment in which people live.
- Human interrelationships are essentially dynamic and subject to constant changes. Hence, the basic social process is one of conflict.[19]

Though Turk's ideas are highly abstract and theoretical, he does link them to actual social practice. He states:

There are indications that some authorities are beginning to understand that such norm violations as juvenile misconduct, family disorganization, indifference to hygiene, personality disorder, and lack of usable work skills constitute insoluble problems until and unless a total, determined attempt is made to destroy the structures of values and social relationships—the cultural and social structures—creating and perpetuating the unwanted patterns of language and behavior, and to force people into the structures that lead to "good".[20]

Turk's ideas seem utopian; and as you will see later in this chapter, conflict theory in general has been criticized for calling for sweeping, and therefore impractical, social changes.

RESEARCH ON CONFLICT THEORY

Research efforts designed to test conflict theory seem quite different from those evaluating consensus models. Similar methodologies are often used, but conflict-centered research places less emphasis on testing hypotheses of a particular theory and instead attempts to show that conflict principles hold up under empirical scrutiny. Topics of interest include such issues as comparing the crime rates of members of powerless groups with those of members of the elite classes. Conflict researchers examine the operation of the justice system to uncover bias and discrimination. They also attempt to chart the historical development of criminal law, and to identify laws created with the intent of preserving the power of the elite classes at the expense of the poor.

In general, research efforts have achieved mixed results. For example, as reviewed in chapter 4, whereas some studies do show that the privileged classes are as delinquent and criminal as the lower classes, other research efforts reach the opposite conclusion. Thus, the position that lower-class citizens have higher official crime rates owing to class bias of justice system members has not actually been proven.[21] Also, though some criminologists support the contention that the poor are driven to crime for survival in a world in which they lack the power to better their lives by conventional means, others view crime as a selfish act motivated by greed.[22]

Similarly, studies of the criminal justice system often fail to prove conclusively that it is generally biased and unfair. Studies in the area of police discretion, criminal court sentencing, and correctional policy have mixed conclusions. While some show bias and unfairness, others seem to indicate that the system is fair to all groups or at least that it does not exclusively discriminate against the poor and minority group members.[23]

For example, criminologists David Jacobs and David Britt examined the relationship between police officers' use of deadly force, the percentage of minority group members in the population, and other relevant variables such as the number of violent crimes, the geographic area (south, north, and so on), the percentage of the population living in large cities, and the percentage of population change.[24]

The authors found that states with greater increases in population and more violence were likely to have more killings by police officers. Moreover, states with the greatest differences among citizens' economic levels were most likely to have the largest number of police-caused homicides. However, the percentage of blacks in the population did not significantly influence police officers' use of force. The authors concluded that their data support conflict theory with respect to economic discrimination but not racial discrimination.

Alan Lizotte used 816 criminal cases processed by the Chicago criminal courts during a one-year period to test the conflict theory assumption that members of powerless, disenfranchised groups are the most likely to receive prejudicial sentences in criminal courts.[25] More specifically, he wished to determine the effects of legal variables (prior arrests, evidence, seriousness of case, not making bail, bail amount, and legal counsel's degree of success in sentencing) and status variables (occupation and race) on the length of prison sentences.

Using a complex statistical model, Lizotte found that his data lent plausibility to the conflict model. Gross inequality in sentencing was found to be associated with race and occupation. Both black and white laborers received longer prison sentences than white-collar workers and, all other things being equal, were more than twice as likely to remain in jail.[26]

Lizotte's findings are disputed by a study conducted by Theodore Chiricos and Gordon Waldo, who examined the prison sentences of 10,488 inmates in three southeastern states.[27] After analyzing the relationship between a defendant's socioeconomic status and the sentence he or she received, the authors found no support for conflict theory. They concluded:

> *What the data suggest, rather conclusively, is that the socioeconomic status of convicted criminal offenders is unrelated to the severity of the state's official sanction, as reflected in the length of prison terms assigned by the courts. Such a conclusion, which strongly contradicts common folklore, and the general expectations of conflict criminology is given added credence by the fact that it is true for a total of seventeen different criminal offenses and for three separate states. Furthermore, that conclusion is sustained (for Florida) regardless of the age, race, number of prior arrests, felony convictions or juvenile commitments.*[28]

In general, the only area of criminal sanctioning policy that does consistently reflect theory propositions is the use of capital punishment. As discussed in chapter

5, this most serious punishment has been reserved for the poor and minority group members, and there are indications of racial bias in the prosecutors' decision to seek the death penalty.

A CRITIQUE OF CONFLICT THEORY

Conflict theories attempt to identify the power relations in society and draw attention to their role in promoting criminal behavior. Conflict criminologists adopt the labeling/interactionist approach but push it beyond the study of deviant groups. Their aims are more global. They wish to describe how class differentials produce an ecology of human behavior that favors the wealthy and powerful over the poor and weak. To believe their view, we must reject the consensus view that law is designed to create a just society and that criminals are predators who violate the rights of others.

Whereas the conflict approach has merit as an explanation of certain criminal behaviors, as Vold suggests, it does not seem an adequate explanation of the many varieties of illegal acts. For example, it is difficult to understand how laws forbidding rape or child molesting are designed to keep the "haves" in power at the expense of the "have-nots." This confusion is compounded when we consider that lower-class citizens are more often the victims of violence than people in the middle and upper classes. To suggest that the penalties of law are applied solely to maintain class boundaries seems to ignore these proven facts.

Conflict theorists also have trouble explaining the many studies showing that the justice system may operate with less bias against the working class than previously believed. Little hard data, with the exception of studies evaluating capital punishment (see chapter 5), exist to support the conflict hypothesis.

Marxist Criminology

The second branch of social conflict theory is known as Marxist, critical, or new criminology.[29] As mentioned previously, it views crime as a function of the capitalist mode of production—capitalism produces haves and have-nots, each engaging in a particular brand of criminality. The poor and destitute commit street crimes—rape, murder, mugging—since those are the only crimes available to them; members of the middle class cheat on their taxes and engage in petty corporate crime (employee theft); the wealthy are involved in acts that should be described as crimes but are not—racism, sexism, profiteering. And, of course, the law is constructed to punish the poor and protect the wealthy.

The birth of modern Marxist criminology can be traced to the publication in 1973 of *The New Criminology* by Ian Taylor, Paul Walton, and Jock Young.[30] This brilliant work was a widespread critique of existing concepts in criminology and a call for development of new criminological methods. However, their work had an antecedent in the National Deviancy Conference (NDC), formed in 1968 by a group of British sociologists. Numbering about three hundred, this organization sponsored several national symposiums and dialogues. Members of the group came from all walks of life, but at its core was a group of academics who were critical of the positivist criminology being taught in English and American universities. More specifically, they rejected the conservative stance of criminologists and their close financial relationship with government funding agencies.

Originally, the NDC was not a Marxist-oriented group, but rather investigated the concept of deviance from a labeling perspective. They called attention to ways in which social control might actually be a cause of deviance rather than a response

The Differences Between Conflict Theory and Marxist Theory

In a recent paper, a criminologist, Thomas Bernard, attempted to clearly differentiate between the major principles of Marxist criminology and conflict theory. The following passages represent an effort to summarize the core principles of these two views.

CONFLICT THEORY

- One's "web of life" or the conditions of one's life affect one's values and interests.
- Complex societies are composed of groups with widely different life conditions.
- Therefore, complex societies are composed of groups with disparate and conflicting sets of values and interests.
- The behavior of individuals is generally consistent with their values and interests.
- Because values and interests tend to remain stable over time, groups tend to develop relatively stable behavior patterns that differ in varying degrees from the behavior patterns of other groups.
- The enactment of laws is the result of a conflict and compromise process in which different groups attempt to promote their own values and interests.
- Individual laws usually represent a combination of the values and interests of many groups, rather than the specific values and interests of any one particular group. Nevertheless, the higher a group's political and economic position, the more the law in general tends to represent the values and interests of that group.

- Therefore, in general, the higher a group's political and economic position, the less likely it is that the behavior patterns characteristic of the group (behaviors consistent with their values and interests) will violate the law, and vice versa.
- In general, the higher the political and economic position of an individual, the more difficult it is for official law enforcement agencies to process him when his behavior violates the law. This may be because the types of violations are more subtle and complex, or because the individual has greater resources to conceal the violation, to legally defend himself against official action, or to exert influence extralegally on the law enforcement process.
- As bureaucrats, law enforcement agencies will generally process easier rather than more difficult cases.
- Therefore, in general, law enforcement agencies will process individuals from lower rather than higher political and economic groups.
- Because of the processes of law enactment and enforcement described above, the official crime rates of groups will tend to be inversely proportional to their political and economic position, independent of any other factors (such as social or biological

to it. However, by 1973, many conference members became concerned about the political nature of social control. A schism developed within the NDC, with one group clinging to the now-conservative interactionist/labeling perspective while the second embraced Marxist thought.

While these events were transpiring in Britain, a small group of scholars in the United States began to follow a new radical approach to criminology. The locus of the radical school was the criminology program at the University of California at Berkeley. The most noted Marxist scholars at that institution were Anthony Platt, Paul Takagi, and Herman and Julia Schwendinger. Marxist scholars at other U.S. academic institutions included Richard Quinney, William Chambliss, and Barry Krisberg. The U.S. radicals were influenced by the widespread social ferment occurring during the late 1960s and early 1970s. The war in Vietnam, prison struggles, and the civil rights and feminist movements produced a climate in which criticism of the ruling class seemed a natural by-product. Rehabilitation-oriented, positivist criminologists were criticized as being overtly conservative, progovernment, and antihuman. Critical criminologists scoffed when their fellow scholars used statistical analysis of computerized data to describe criminal and delinquent behavior. As Barry Krisberg has written:

ones) that might also influence the distribution of crime rates.

MARXIST CRIMINOLOGY

- No consensus exists in society on the basic values and interests of individuals, and on the contrary, society is characterized by conflict on these issues.

- Society in general is divided into classes whose members have similar values and interests, the principal classes being those who own the means of production (the ruling class) and those who are employed in production (the working class). The principal conflict in society is between the ruling class and the working class.

- Crimes are defined as socially harmful actions that violate basic human rights. That includes both "street" crimes in which the lower class preys on itself and on others, and ruling class crimes in which the lower class is victimized through unemployment, pollution, and exploitation. Because the law is a tool of the ruling class in its conflict with the working class, the socially harmful actions of the ruling class are generally not defined as crimes by the official criminal justice system.

- Conventional criminologists accept the definitions of crime provided by the law, and so assume a technocratic role in the social control of the working class. They do this through "correctionalism," which attempts to reconcile the working class to the structure imposed by the ruling class, and through "reformism," which attempts to improve the operation of the criminal justice system and increase its effectiveness in controlling the working class.

- Radical criminologists reject the definitions of crime provided by the law and study all socially harmful behaviors that violate basic human rights. They argue that contradictions in the capitalist economic system are the underlying causes of these behaviors.

- The crime problem can be solved only by the overthrow of the capitalist economic system and the establishment of a socialist state. Once capitalism is overthrown, the law in its present form will eventually become unnecessary, for the conflicts between classes will have been resolved.

- The principal task of radical criminology is to promote the overthrow of the capitalist economic system, and thus radicals must guard against the danger of "co-optation," that is, having specific points of radical criminology accepted by mainstream criminology and placed in a context that does not promote the overthrow of capitalism.

DISCUSSION QUESTIONS

1. Do you believe all crimes are linked to the means of production? If not, which are? Which are not?

2. Do the wealthy and powerful enjoy privileges from the criminal justice system that the poor are deprived of?

3. Does it make sense to consider racism, sexism, and profiteering as crimes?

SOURCE. Excerpted from Thomas Bernard, "The Distinction between Conflict and Radical Criminology." Reprinted by Special Permission of The Journal of Criminal Law and Criminology, vol. 72 no. 1, pp. 366–67, 369–70. © 1981 by Northwestern University School of Law. Footnotes omitted.

Many of our scientific heroes of the past, upon rereading, turned out to be racists or, more generally, apologists for social injustice. In response to the widespread protests on campuses and throughout society, many of the contemporary giants of social science emerged as defenders of the status quo and vocally dismissed the claims of the oppressed for social justice.[31]

Many of the new Marxist criminologists had enjoyed distinguished careers as positivist criminologists. Some, such as William Chambliss and Richard Quinney, were moved by career interests from positivism to social conflict theory to a more radical, Marxist approach to crime. Marxists did not meet widespread approval at major universities. Rumors of purges were common during the 1970s, and the criminology school at Berkeley was eventually closed for what many believe were political reasons.

ROOTS OF MARXIST CRIMINOLOGY

Marxist criminologists are influenced by numerous historically important sources. Of course, the writings of Marx and Engels have had the greatest influence on their thinking. A later work by George Rusche and Otto Kircheimer, *Punishment and Social Structure,* which traces the influence of capitalism on concepts of law and justice, has also been quite influential.[32] Another critical perspective is contained in the writings of **Willem Bonger.** Because of the importance of his ideas, they are discussed in detail below.

Willem Bonger. Willem Bonger was born in 1876 in Holland, and committed suicide in 1940 rather than submit to Nazi rule. He is famous for his Marxist socialist concepts of crime causation. Bonger's criminological thoughts can be summarized as follows:[33]

- The abnormal element of crime is of social and not biological origin. With the exception of a few special cases, crime lies within the boundaries of normal human behavior.
- The response to crime is punishment—the application of penalties considered more severe than spontaneous moral condemnation. It is administered by those in political control—that is, by the state.
- No act is naturally immoral or criminal. Crimes are antisocial acts that reflect current morality. Since the social structure is changing continually, ideas of what is moral and what is not change continually. The tension between rapidly changing morality, which is common in modern society, and a comparatively static, predominantly bourgeois criminal law can become very great. Attempts to control law violations through force are a sign of a weak society.
- Crimes are antisocial acts harmful to those who have the power at their command to control society.
- In every society divided into a ruling class and an inferior class, penal law serves the will of the former. Even though criminal laws may appear to protect members of both classes, hardly any act is punished that does not injure the interests of the dominant class.
- Society is divided into have and have-not groups, not on the basis of people's innate ability but because of the system of production that is in force.
- The capitalist system, characterized by extreme competition, is held together by force rather than consensus. The social order is maintained for the benefit of the capitalists at the expense of the population as a whole.
- The desire for pleasure is innate in everyone. Unfortunately, in capitalist society, people can enjoy luxuries and advantages only if they possess large amounts of capital. Nonetheless, the present society exhorts all people to obtain pleasure in general and money in particular. People are encouraged by capitalist society to be egotistical, caring only for their own lives and pleasures and ignoring the plight of the disadvantaged. As a consequence of the present environment, Bonger claims, man has become very egoistic and more capable of crime than if the environment had developed under a socialist philosophy.
- Though the environment makes both the proletariat and the bourgeoisie crime-prone, only the former are likely to become officially recognized criminals. The key to this problem is that the legal system discriminates against the poor by legalizing the egoistic actions of the wealthy.
- Upper-class individuals, the bourgeoisie, will commit crime if (a) they have

an opportunity to gain an illegal advantage and (b) their lack of moral sense enables them to violate social rules. It is the drive toward success at any price that pushes wealthier individuals toward criminality.

- Crime is a function of poverty. The relationship can be direct, as when a person steals to survive, or indirect, as when poverty kills the social sentiments in each person and destroys the sentiments between people. It is not the absolute amount of wealth that affects crime, but its distribution. If wealth is distributed unequally through the social structure and people are taught to equate economic advantage with superiority, then those who are poor and therefore inferior will be crime-prone.

- The economic system will intensify any personal disadvantage people have—for example, psychological problems—and increase their propensity to commit crime.

- Almost all crime will disappear if society progresses from competitive capitalism, to monopoly capitalism, to having the means of production held in common, to the ultimate state of society, the redistribution of property according to the maxim "each according to his needs." If this stage of society cannot be reached, a residue of crime will always occur. If socialism can be achieved, then remaining crimes will be of the irrational psychopathic type caused by individual mental problems.

MARXIST CRIMINOLOGY TODAY

No single theoretical pronouncement defines Marxist criminology today. Several scholars have made important contributions to the existing body of theory.

As articulated by Gresham Sykes, Marxist theory views the criminal law and criminal justice system as a vehicle for controlling the poor, have-not members of society.[34] It helps the powerful and rich to:

- Impose their morality and standards of good behavior on the entire society.
- Protect their property and physical safety from the depredations of the have-nots, even though the cost may be high in terms of the legal rights of those it perceives as a threat.
- Extend the definition of illegal or criminal behavior to encompass those who might threaten the status quo.

Sykes further asserts that the ruling elite draws the middle class into this pattern of control, leading it to believe that it also has a stake in maintaining the status quo.

The poor, according to conflict theory, may or may not commit more crimes than the rich; but they certainly are arrested and punished more often. Sykes argues that the poor are driven to crime for the following reasons:

- The rules imposed from above have little relationship to the dictates of the cultural norms of the poor.
- A natural frustration exists in a society in which affluence is well publicized but unattainable.
- A deep-rooted hostility is generated among members of the lower class toward a social order they are not allowed to shape or participate in.

According to the conflict perspective, capitalism exploits the poor, minorities and workers.

Herman Schwendinger and Julia Schwendinger suggest that the nature of the conflict view of society, law, and deviant behavior can be summarized in the following way:

- Legal relations in the United States secure an economic infrastructure that centers around a capitalist mode of production. The legal system is designed to guard the position of the owners (bourgeoisie) at the expense of the workers (proletariat).
- Legal relations maintain the family and school structure so as to secure the labor force. Even common-law crimes such as murder and rape are implemented to protect capitalism.
- The capitalist state is made up of a civil society in which the dominance of the bourgeoisie is challenged by the antagonistic rural and urban proletariat.
- The class interests that underlie the basic laws of the land (such as constitutional laws) are based on the conditions that reproduce the class system as a whole. Laws are aimed at securing the domination of the capitalist system.
- Legal relations in the capitalist system may at times secure the interests of the working class, for example, laws protecting collective bargaining and personal income.
- Due to the inherent antagonisms built into the capitalist system, all laws generally contradict their stated purpose of producing justice. Legal relations maintain patterns of individualism and selfishness and in so doing perpetuate a class system characterized by anarchy, oppression, and crime.[35]

In a highly regarded article, Stephen Spitzer has attempted to articulate a Marxian theory of deviance.[36] He finds that law in the capitalist system defines as deviant (or criminal) any person who disturbs, hinders, or calls into question any of the following:

- Capitalist modes of appropriating the product of human labor (for example, when the poor "steal" from the rich).

- The social conditions under which capitalist production takes place (for example, when some persons refuse or are unable to perform wage labor).
- Patterns of distribution and consumption in capitalist society (for example, when persons use drugs for escape and transcendence rather than sociability and adjustment).
- The process of socialization for productive and nonproductive roles (for example, when youths refuse to be schooled or deny the validity of "family life").
- The ideology that supports the functioning of capitalist society (for example, when people become proponents of alternative forms of social organization).

Among the many important points Spitzer makes is that capitalist societies have special ways of dealing with troublesome numbers of deviants. One mechanism is to *normalize* formerly deviant or illegal acts by absorbing them into the mainstream of society—for example, through legalization of abortions. *Conversion* involves co-opting deviants by making them part of the system—for example, a gang leader may be recruited to work with younger delinquents. *Containment* involves segregation of deviants into isolated geographic areas so that they can easily be controlled—for example, by creating a ghetto. Finally, Spitzer believes that capitalist society actively supports some criminal enterprises, such as organized crime, so that they can provide a means of support for groups who might otherwise become a burden on the state.

The work of another well-known Marxist theorist, Richard Quinney, has evolved from a conflict ideology (as described earlier in this chapter) to a Marxist orientation. Quinney argues that the purpose of criminology is to expose the real purpose of law in capitalist society—the preservation of the ruling class. Quinney's Marxist approach can be summarized in the following statements:

- American society is based on an advanced capitalist economy.
- The state is organized to serve the interests of the dominant economic class, the capitalist ruling class.
- Criminal law is an instrument of the state and ruling class to maintain and perpetuate the existing social and economic order.
- Crime control in capitalist society is accomplished through a variety of institutions and agencies established and administered by a governmental elite, representing ruling class interests for the purpose of establishing domestic order.
- The contradictions of advanced capitalism—the disjunction between existence and essence—require that the subordinate classes remain oppressed by whatever means necessary, especially through the coercion and violence of the legal system.
- Only with the collapse of capitalist society and the creation of a new society, based on socialistic principles, will there be a solution to the crime problem.[37]

Other Marxist scholars have called for a review of the role of the professional criminologist. For example, Anthony Platt has charged that criminologists have helped support state repression with their focus on poor and minority criminals·

We are just beginning to realize that criminology has serviced domestic repression in the same way that economics, political science, and anthropology have greased

*the wheels and even manufactured some of the important parts of modern impe-
rialism. Given the ways in which this system has been used to repress and maintain
the powerlessness of poor people, workers, people of color, and young people, it is
not too far-fetched to characterize many criminologists as domestic war criminals.* [38]

Platt goes on to suggest that criminology must redefine its goals and definitions:

*In the past we have been constrained by a legal definition of crime which restricts
us to studying and ultimately helping to control only legally defined "criminals."
We need a more humanistic definition of crime, one which reflects the reality of a
legal system based on power and privilege. To accept the legal definition of crime
is to accept the fiction of neutral law. A human rights definition of crime frees us
to examine imperialism, racism, sexism, capitalism, exploitation and other political
or economic systems which contribute to human misery and deprive people of their
potentialities.* [39]

In a well-received work, Barry Krisberg has linked crime to the differentials
in privilege that exist in capitalist society. According to Krisberg, crime is a function
of **privilege**. Crimes are created by the powerful to further their domination. They
deflect attention from the violence and social injustice the rich inflict upon the
masses to keep them subordinate and oppressed.

Krisberg is concerned with how privilege influences criminality. He defines
privilege as the possession of that which is valued by a particular social group in
a given historical period. Privilege includes rights such as life, liberty, and happiness; traits such as intelligence, sensitivity, and humanity; and material goods
such as monetary wealth, luxuries, land, and the like. The privilege system is also
concerned with the distribution and preservation of privilege. Krisberg argues that
force—the effective use of violence and coercion—is the major factor in determining which social group ascends to the position of defining and holding privilege. [40]

RESEARCH ON MARXIST CRIMINOLOGY

Marxist criminologists rarely use standard social science methodologies to test their
constructs. They consider the traditional approach of measuring research subjects
as being antihuman and insensitive. Marxists believe that the research conducted
by mainstream liberal/positivist criminologists is designed to unmask the weak and
powerless members of society so they can be better dealt with by the legal system—
a process called correctionalism. They are particularly offended by purely empirical
studies such as those showing that minority group members have lower IQs than
the white majority or that the inner city is the site of the most serious crime while
middle-class areas are relatively crime-free.

Marxist research is historical and analytical. Social trends are interpreted in
order to understand how capitalism has affected human interaction. Marxists investigate both macro-level issues, such as how the accumulation of wealth affects
crime rates, and micro-level issues, such as the effect of criminal interactions on
the lives of individuals living in a capitalist society. Of particular importance to
Marxist critical thinkers is analysis of the historical development of capitalist social
control institutions such as criminal law, police agencies, courts, and prison systems.

Although there is not space here to evaluate the vast number of these research
efforts, a few representative studies are mentioned below.

How Capitalism Influences Rape

Herman and Julia Schwendinger's study of rape provides an excellent example of Marxian critical analysis.

The Schwendingers' goal is to find out why women who are raped often feel guilty about their role in the rape experience. The Schwendingers believe that a rape victim frequently experiences guilt because she has been raised in a sexist society and has internalized discriminatory norms.

Women are viewed as the weaker sex, dependent on persons in authority such as parents or husbands. The Schwendingers postulate that dependency originates historically in socioeconomic conditions that are often directly related to family life in capitalist society. During the early stages of capitalism, families underwent strain when industry demanded a labor force of men, only infrequently supplemented by single women. The role of father was strained as men were separated from their households. Woman's role became more narrowly defined as childbearer and child raiser. The limited economic role of women helped to define them as dependents. Married women, especially, were viewed as nonproductive, since they did not participate in commodity markets, where people earn money.

In reality, women's household productivity must be viewed as an essential contribution to working-class life; yet, theirs is an unpaid contribution that often goes unappreciated by husbands and the rest of society. Since the housewife only produces for family use, her labor is necessarily unpayable; and while her needs are partly supported by the husband's wage, she is totally dependent on that wage for access to the commodities necessary for the family's existence.

Because she has been socialized into dependency by the capitalist system, a woman's sense of self-worth may be more responsive to the evaluations of other persons. Furthermore, negative evaluations, such as those created by a rape experience, are likely to be turned inward by the woman herself, creating unwarranted self-recrimination and remorse.

The family is not the only culprit in this transaction.

Schools and mass media further reinforce dependency by teaching boys and girls in school to "look down on women." Textbooks stereotype the woman's role; girls are depicted as helpless and frightened. Vocational tests provide fewer opportunities for girls. In media presentations, women are usually depicted as housewives and mothers. When women are portrayed on television commercials, they seem "concerned mainly with clean floors and clean hair—housework and their personal appearance."

Though women have made strides in the job market, their labor is often in low-paid, low-mobility occupations such as secretary or piece worker. Consequently, their appearance in the labor force often does little to improve their economic dependency.

It is for these reasons that women often blame themselves for being raped. The Schwendingers imply that women feel they have "let down" the people they depend on when they allow themselves to be trapped in a rape encounter. A woman's own sense of inadequacy leads to self-blame for the attack and prevents her from focusing on the true culprits: the rapist and the capitalist system whose economic structure results in a rape-producing climate.

We can see in the Schwendingers' research approach the Marxian stress on analysis and interpretation of social process and their disdain for quantitative statistical evidence.

DISCUSSION QUESTIONS

1. What can society do to help women who are the victims of rape?
2. Does the Schwendingers' portrayal of a rape victim seem accurate?

SOURCE. Herman and Julia Schwendinger, "Rape Victims and the False Sense of Guilt," *Crime and Social Justice* 13 (1980):4–17.

Crime, the Individual, and the State. Marxists devote considerable attention to the study of the relationships between crime, victims, the criminal, and the state. Two common themes emerge: (1) crime and its control are a function of capitalism, and (2) the justice system is biased against the working class and favors upper-class interests. Marxian analysis of the criminal justice system is designed to identify the often hidden processes that exert control over people's lives. It seeks an understanding of how conditions, processes, and structures became as they are today.

For example, William Chambliss analyzed the process by which deviant behavior is defined as criminal or delinquent in U.S. society.[41] In a similar vein,

Timothy Carter and Donald Clelland used a Marxist approach to test whether dispositions in a juvenile court were a function of social class.[42] David Greenberg also studied the association between social class and sentencing and later, with Drew Humphries, evaluated how power relationships help undermine any benefit the lower class gets from sentencing reforms.[43] In general, Marxist research efforts have not yielded conclusive evidence linking operations of the justice system to class bias.[44]

In addition to conducting studies showing the relationship between crime and the state, some critical researchers have attempted to show how capitalism intervenes throughout the entire spectrum of crime-related phenomena. Research by Herman and Julia Schwendinger attempts to show how capitalist social expectations affect women in the aftermath of a rape experience. Described in the accompanying Close-Up, the Schwendinger's effort is a good example of Marxist analytical research.[45]

Critical research of this sort is designed to reinterpret commonly held beliefs about society within the framework of Marxist social and economic ideas. The goal is not to prove statistically that capitalism causes crime but rather to show that it creates an environment in which crime is inevitable. Marxist research is humanistic, situational, descriptive, and analytical rather than statistical, rigid, and methodological.

Historical Analyses. A second type of Marxist research focuses on the historical background of commonly held institutional beliefs and practices. One aim is to show how changes in the criminal law corresponded to the development of capitalist economy. For example, Michael Rustigan analyzed historical records to show that law reform in nineteenth-century England was largely a response to pressure from the business community to make the punishment for property law violations more acceptable.[46]

In a similar vein, Rosalind Petchesky has explained how the relationship between prison industries and capitalism evolved during the nineteenth century, while Paul Takagi has described the rise of state prisons as an element of centralized state control over deviants.[47]

Another topic of importance to Marxist critical thinkers is the development of modern police agencies. Since police often play an active role in putting down labor disputes and controlling the activities of political dissidents, their interrelationship with capitalist economics is of particular importance to Marxists. Prominent examples of research in this area include Stephen Spitzer and A. T. Scull's discussion of the history of private police and Dennis Hoffman's historical analysis of police excesses in the repression of an early union, the International Workers of the World (popularly known as the Wobblies).[48] Sidney Harring has provided one of the more important analyses of the development of modern policing; his work is described in the accompanying close-up to provide an example of Marxist historical research.[49]

CRITIQUES OF MARXIST CRIMINOLOGY

Marxist criminology has met with a great deal of criticism from members of the criminological establishment. Rumors of purges of Marxist theorists have cropped up; lawsuits involving the denial of academic tenure to Marxists have not been

A Marxist Analysis of Police

Sidney Harring has attempted to show how police forces developed as an instrument of the capitalist state. In one study, Harring sets out to prove that police played an important role in eighteenth- and nineteenth-century capitalism by working repeatedly to break working-class resistance to corporate power, to socialize new immigrants to the demands of monopoly capitalism, to provide protection to strike-bound companies and those threatened with strikes, to control rebellious segments of the working-class population, and to gather intelligence in working-class communities.

Harring takes the nontraditional position that during the 1880s the police were transformed into a far more efficient, better organized, and better disciplined system than ever before. For example, Buffalo, New York's police force went from 200 to 900 men in the space of 20 years. The strikes and labor movements of the 1870s and 1880s brought demands for increased police power to control workers. Larger, more efficient police departments meant that long-term antistrike campaigns could be carried out. Increased size was matched by improved technology—patrol wagons and signal alarm systems were placed throughout larger cities; and police used them to get information, request help, and so on. "Reputable" citizens were given access to the call boxes so that they would have greater access to police services. Harring attributes the use of these measures directly to the police establishment's role in controlling strikes and labor unrest.

During this period, police departments became more stable and efficient. At the same time, control of police departments fell into the hands of industrialists, who began to see the value of police officers as strike breakers. The police aided industrialists like Cyrus McCormick when their plants were closed by strikes.

Officers suspected of prolabor sentiments were disciplined or removed. (During a 1913 strike, thirty-three Indianapolis police officers were suspended for refusing to ride on subway cars driven by "scabs," or workers hired to replace strikers.) Though police work was not financially rewarding, it provided secure work at pay somewhat higher than a laborer's, creating a class distinction between the police and the laboring classes.

Harring concludes that police agencies in the late nineteenth and early twentieth centuries were violently antilabor. He states that though labor activists were sometimes violent, "since police and scabs provided considerable violence, police repression must be seen as more than simple defense."

DISCUSSION QUESTIONS

1. How does Harring's view that police were agents of the capitalist system jibe with the low pay and poor working conditions of turn-of-the-century police officers?

2. Are police "agents of the capitalist state" today?

SOURCE. Sidney Harring, "Policing a Class Society: The Expansion of the Urban Police in the Late Nineteenth and Early Twentieth Century," in *Crime and Capitalism*, ed. David Greenberg (Palo Alto, Calif.: Mayfield Publishing, 1981), pp. 292–313.

---

uncommon. Liberal criminologists sometimes view Marxists as dangerous to the continued existence of their means of livelihood. After all, Marxists call for the dissolution of the state, expose the relationship between big universities and big government, and analyze the control that corporations and other capitalist institutions have over the legal system—they are not the colleagues who will encourage government or private foundations to award the research grants so prized by university administrators. As previously mentioned, Marxists, such as Anthony Platt, have accused mainstream criminologists of being culprits in the development of state control over individual lives; in so doing, these theorists have caused disturbance in the halls of academia.

However, positivist consensus criminologists have also attacked the substance of Marxist thought. For example, Jackson Toby argues that Marxist theory is a simple rehash of the old tradition of helping the underdog. He likens the ideas behind Marxist criminology to the ideas in such traditional and literary works as *Robin Hood* and Victor Hugo's *Les Miserables*, in which the poor stole from the rich to survive.[50] In reality, Toby claims, most theft is for luxury, not survival. Moreover, he disputes the idea that the crimes of the rich are more reprehensible and less understandable than those of the poor. Criminality and immoral behavior occur at every social level, but Toby believes that the relatively disadvantaged contribute disproportionately to crime and delinquency rates.

Richard Sparks's thorough critique of Marxist criminology leads him to conclude that the quality of research efforts made to test its assumptions are faulty.[51] He believes it unlikely that Marxist criminology will ever have a great effect on criminological thought.

The most stunning and controversial critique of Marxist criminology has been rendered by a sociologist, Carl Klockars.[52] Klockars finds that the core issue for Marxist criminologists is class. Marxists assume that class conflict, created by the unequal distribution of wealth, is the cause of most of society's evils—war, racism, sexism, poverty, and crime. Klockars debates this point. He claims that class differences may actually have a beneficial effect on society. During periods of great artistic and cultural achievements, class differences serve to protect innovators from the power of the state and the jealousy and envy of the masses. Historically, class differences performed the important function of creating, maintaining, and perpetuating a set of standards that carried authority and inspired the rest of society. Further, in today's American culture, the poverty classes enjoy more luxuries and benefits than ever before, so the concept of poverty has lost much of its meaning.

Klockars further asserts that Marxists mistakenly equate ownership of production with control of production. The former is open to anyone who is willing to buy a share of stock or participate in a job-related pension fund. But owners do not necessarily control the means of production. This is left to managers and bureaucrats, who may or may not own the institutions and agencies they control (a conclusion similar to those of Ralf Dahrendorf, discussed earlier).

Klockars also focuses on Marxist criminologists' concern for **class interest** as a dominant factor in U.S. life. He charges that Marxists ignore all the varied prestige and interest groups that exist in a pluralistic society and focus almost unilaterally on class differentials. Moreover, their claim that capitalism is the root of all evil is untestable by research. Klockars scoffs, for example, at critical thinkers who charge that legal reforms are really disguised means of placating the masses. Is it logical to believe that giving people more rights is a trick to allow greater control to be exerted over them? "People are more powerful with the right to a jury than without it. . . . The rights of free speech, free press, free association, public trial, habeas corpus and governmental petition extended substantial power to colonials . . . who had previously been denied them."[53]

Klockars's views of the problems of Marxist theory are summarized in the following statements:

- Marxist criminology as a social movement is untrustworthy. Marxists refuse to confront the problems and conflicts of socialist countries, such as the Gulags and purges of Stalinist Russia.
- Marxist criminology is predictable. Capitalism is blamed for every human vice. "After class explains everything, after the whole legal order is critiqued, after all predatory and personal crime is attributed to the conditions and reproduction of capitalism, there is nothing more to say—except more of the same."[54]
- Marxism does little to explain the criminality existing in states that have abolished the private ownership of the means of production (Cuba, China, Russia).

- Marxists ignore objective reality. For example, they overlook empirical evidence of distinctions that exist between people in different classes. Such tactics will eventually destroy the foundation for a new postrevolutionary social science, should one be needed.
- Marxists attempt to explicate issues which, for most people, need no explanation. The revelation that politicians are corrupt and businesspeople greedy comes as a shock to no one.
- The evil that Marxists consistently discover and dramatize is seen from a moral ground set so high that it loses meaning and perspective. Every aspect of capitalist society is suspect, including practices and freedoms most people cherish as the cornerstones of democracy (right to trial, free press, religion, and so on).
- By presenting itself as a mystical, religionlike entity, Marxist criminology is relieved of the responsibility for the exploitation, corruption, crime, and human abuse that has been and continues to be perpetrated in socialist countries.

In general, criticism of Marxist theory has undercut its utopianism. To blame the state for all evil seems to ignore the great variety of human differences. Not all people react in the same way to social and economic conditions. Why is it that many people suffering the pains of capitalist existence refrain from committing crime? In this sense, Marxist theory suffers the same inconsistency as do positivist/sociological theories of crime causation. However, in recent years Marxists, responding to criticism, have tried to reorient their approach to criminology. In the following Close-Up Anthony Platt, a leading Marxist theorist, discusses the changes in radical criminology and provides an agenda for the 1980s.

Summary

Social conflict theorists view crime as a function of the conflict that exists in society. It has its theoretical basis in the works of Karl Marx.

Pure conflict theorists suggest that crime in any society is caused by class conflict. Laws are created by those in power to protect their rights and interests. All criminal acts have political undertones. Richard Quinney has called this concept the social reality of crime. Unfortunately, research efforts to validate the conflict approach have not produced significant findings. One of conflict theory's most important premises is that the justice system is biased and designed to protect the wealthy. Research has not been unanimous in supporting this point.

The second division of social conflict theory is Marxist criminology. Marxists view the competitive nature of the capitalist system as a major cause of crime. The poor commit crimes because of their frustration, anger, and need. The wealthy engage in illegal acts because they are used to competition and also because they must do so to keep their positions in society. Marxist scholars such as Richard Quinney, Anthony Platt, and Barry Krisberg have attempted to show that the law is designed to protect the wealthy and powerful and to control the poor, have-not members of society.

Research on Marxist theory focuses on how the system of justice was designed and how it currently operates to further class interests. Quite often, it uses historical analysis to show how the capitalist classes have exerted their control over police, court, and correctional agencies.

Radical Criminology in the 1980s: An Alternative to "Law and Order"

The conservative tide in the 1980s has put radical criminologists on the defensive. Their influence has been threatened by the public's acceptance of the right wing's law-and-order, get-tough policies. The post-Watergate era's mistrust of the government has given way to attitudes and policies supportive of what the left would consider repression.

In an important analysis, influential left-wing theorist Tony Platt summarizes the major problems facing the left, and offers some direction for the future. According to Platt, left-wing policy makers have identified the following critical issues:

• *Failure of the Left and Progressives to Provide Alternatives to the Right.* In the 1980s, the left has failed to take law and order seriously. They have failed to offer politically persuasive programs to combat violent crime. The radical critique of the criminal justice system was generally "moralistic, atheoretical, and utopian."

• *Ideological Combat.* The left has failed to engage right-wing thinkers in debate. They have thus been unable to make public their view that get-tough policies are ineffective—they will not lessen crime, make communities safer, nor provide assistance to victims. Moreover, the expense of crime control is exorbitant and the money would be better spent elsewhere. The left must show that the rise of right-wing criminology is related to the ideological shift toward "authoritarian populism," which the left must counter with alternative world views.

• *Short-term Reforms in Criminal Justice.* The left has been so preoccupied with a "hypothetical socialist future" and utopian change that it has failed to address the real problem of street crime. Various progressive programs can be suggested to serve the need of short-term intervention in the criminal justice system:

rape crisis centers, escort services for the elderly, community patrols, aid for victims. At the same time, radicals agree that these neo-liberal reforms are not enough. An anticrime program that incorporates "liberal bromides," but goes beyond them, is needed.

• *Long-term Structural Changes in the Political Economy.* Long-term structural changes in the political economy must be achieved to produce real improvement in the crime problem. These include: achieving full employment (especially as a means of reducing the prison population); redefining criminal justice priorities to target violence against women, corporate crime, government corruption, health and safety violations, racist violence, etc.; decentralizing the economic and political system to increase local control; reforming the tax system; increasing the minimum wage, etc.

• *Community Control.* The left believes that power must be returned to the people in one form or another. Such terms as "neighborhood control" or "local control" are commonly used to express the direction of justice reform. "Popular justice" can include community self-help and protection such as that provided by the Guardian Angels and similar groups.

Considering these issues, Platt believes it is time for progressives, liberals, and radicals to bury the hatchet and join forces to fight the right wing. The idealism of the sixties and seventies must give way to the practicalities of the real world. Sloganeering must be tempered by an assessment of strategies to create real

Both Marxist and conflict criminology have been heavily criticized by consensus criminologists. Richard Sparks finds the research of Marxists faulty. Jackson Toby sees Marxists as being sentimental and unwilling to face reality. Carl Klockars's criticism suggests Marxists make fundamental errors in their concepts of ownership and class interest. As Tony Platt suggests, Marxists must reorient their thinking in the 1980s.

Notes

1 See, for example, Karl Marx and Friedrich Engels, *Capital: A Critique of Political Economy,* trans. E. Aveling (Chicago: Charles Kern, 1906); Karl Marx, *Selected Writings in Sociology and Social Philosophy,* trans. P. B. Bottomore (New York: McGraw Hill, 1956).

2 Karl Marx, *Grundrisse: Introduction to the Critique of Political Economy,* trans. Martin Nicolaus (New York: Vintage, 1973), pp. 106–107.

change. For example, all too often radicals call for mobilization on the community level through a coalition of organized labor, community organizations, and political leaders. However, these target groups are neither representative of nor accountable to the majority of the population. In fact, a compelling argument could be made that their politics and practice since World War II have been antagonistic to working class interests—examine, for example, the failure of organized labor to organize the unorganized, the role of "community leaders" in cooling out dissent and resistance in the 1960s, the collaboration of "community organizations" with the federal government's so-called war on poverty, and the upward mobility of self-appointed community leaders. There is no reason to believe that these forces, as presently constituted, will fight for neighborhood interests.

Finally, the left wing has failed to deal with the crime problem in socialist countries. This contradiction to radical thought is usually explained away by saying it is a vestige of capitalism and that it will eventually wither away. This "lazy" view ignores the dynamic nature of crime in socialist nations and allows the right wing to claim that crime in socialist countries verifies either the failure of socialism or the universality of crime.

In conclusion, Platt identifies five areas of importance that need to be discussed and studied by radical criminologists in the future:

1. They need to understand much more clearly why criminal justice is resistant to even the most modest kind of reforms, why attempts to democratize the content and governance of criminal justice are so fiercely opposed.

2. Many proposals exist for reforming different aspects of the criminal justice system. Radicals need to discuss and debate what issues to target. They need to discuss how they can strategically and tactically mobilize a broad base of support while challenging the criminal justice apparatus itself.

3. Radical criminologists need to explore how they can mobilize a broad, cross-class base of progressive activism that includes but is not dominated by professionals. They also need to examine why it is difficult to activate professionals in the fight for social justice.

4. They need to look more closely at the organizational context and forms of struggle. What kinds of political and community organizations are required to wage a successful battle for even the most minimal reforms? Why do spontaneous and localized struggles disintegrate so quickly?

5. The focus on immediate reforms cannot obviate the need for macroscopic analysis of global developments in crime and criminal justice. It is legitimate for people to ask about the experience of socialist nations, about the lessons learned from the socialist reconstruction of criminal justice. Radicals need a theoretical framework that addresses how "capitalist" relations within "socialist" nations continue to generate inequalities and the conditions for criminality.

Platt's analysis is an important blueprint for radical criminology in the eighties. It is important because it represents a shift in direction of radical thinking, toward a "real politik" view of changing the justice system. It signifies the dominance of the right wing of criminology and the recognition by the left that they must gain the initiative if they are to remain an important force in influencing justice policies.

DISCUSSION QUESTIONS

1. Will the public accept radical/liberal reforms or are they sold on law and order?

2. Is crime universal? Can an ideal economic system remove the need to commit crimes?

SOURCE. Tony Platt, "Criminology in the 1980s: Progressive Alternatives to 'Law and Order'," Crime and Social Justice 21-22 (1985):191–99. Quotes from pp. 194, 196, 199.

3 Friedrich Engels, *The Condition of the Working Class in England in 1844* (London: Allen and Unwin, 1950).

4 Karl Marx, *Theories of Surplus Value*, vol. 1 (London: Lawrence and Wishart, 1969), pp. 387–88.

5 Ian Taylor, Paul Walton, and Jock Young, *The New Criminology: For a Social Theory of Deviance* (London: Routledge and Kegan Paul, 1973), p. 212.

6 Alexander Liazos, "The Poverty of the Sociology of Deviance: Nuts, Sluts and Perverts," *Social Problems* 20 (1972):103–20.

7 See generally Robert Meier, "The New Criminology: Continuity in Criminological Theory," *Journal of Criminal Law and Criminology* 67 (1977):461–69.

8 David Greenberg, ed., *Crime and Capitalism* (Palo Alto, Calif.: Mayfield Publishing, 1981), p. 3.

9 Taylor, Walton, and Young, *The New Criminology*, p. 240.

10 Ralf Dahrendorf, *Class and Class Conflict in Industrial Society* (Stanford, Conn.: Stanford University Press, 1959).

11 Ibid., p. 6.

12 Ibid., p. 48.

13 George Vold, *Theoretical Criminology* (New York: Oxford University Press, 1958).

14 Ibid., p. 204.

15 Ibid., p. 209.

16 William Chambliss and Robert Seidman, *Law, Order and Power* (Reading, Mass.: Addison-Wesley, 1971), p. 503.

17 Richard Quinney, *The Social Reality of Crime* (Boston, Mass.: Little, Brown, 1970), p. 9.

18 Ibid., pp. 15–23.

19 Austin Turk, "Analyzing Official Deviance: For Nonpartisan Conflict Analyses in Criminology," in *Radical Criminology: The Coming Crisis,* ed. J. Inciardi (Beverly Hills, Calif.: Sage Publications, 1980), pp. 78–91.

20 Austin Turk, *Criminality and Legal Order* (Chicago: Rand McNally, 1969), p. 58.

21 See, for example, Michael Hindelang, "Race and Involvement in Common Law Personal Crimes," *American Sociological Review* 43 (1978):109–25.

22 Jackson Toby, "The New Criminology is the Old Sentimentality," *Criminology* 16 (1979):513–26.

23 Charles Wellford, "Labeling Theory and Criminology: An Assessment," *Social Problems* 22 (1975):332–45.

24 David Jacobs and David Britt, "Inequality and Police Use of Deadly Force: An Empirical Assessment of a Conflict Hypothesis," *Social Problems* 26 (1979):403–12.

25 Alan Lizotte, "Extra-Legal Factors in Chicago's Criminal Courts: Testing the Conflict Model of Criminal Justice," *Social Problems* 25 (1978):564–80.

26 Ibid., p. 577.

27 Theodore Chiricos and Gordon Waldo, "Socioeconomic Status and Criminal Sentencing: An Empirical Assessment of a Conflict Proposition," *American Sociological Review* 40 (1975):753–72.

28 Ibid., p. 767.

29 This section borrows heavily from Richard Sparks, "A Critique of Marxist Criminology," in *Crime and Justice,* vol. 2, ed. Norval Morris and Michael Tonry (Chicago: University of Chicago Press, 1980), pp. 159–208.

30 Taylor, Walton, and Young, *The New Criminology.*

31 Barry Krisberg, *Crime and Privilege: Toward a New Criminology* (Englewood Cliffs, N.J.: Prentice-Hall, 1975), p. 167.

32 George Rusche and Otto Kircheimer, *Punishment and Social Structure* (New York: Columbia University Press, 1939).

33 Adapted from Austin Turk introductory notes to Willem Bonger, *Criminality and Economic Conditions,* abridged ed. (Bloomington, Ind.: Indiana University Press, 1969).

34 Gresham Sykes, "The Rise of Critical Criminology," *Journal of Criminal Law and Criminology* 65 (1974):211.

35 Herman Schwendinger and Julia Schwendinger, "Delinquency and Social Reform: A Radical Perspective," in *Juvenile Justice,* ed. Lamar Empey (Charlottesville: University of Virginia Press, 1979), pp. 246–90.

36 Stephen Spitzer, "Toward a Marxian Theory of Deviance," *Social Problems* 22 (1975):638–51.

37 Richard Quinney, "Crime Control in Capitalist Society," in *Critical Criminology,* Taylor, Walton and Young, eds., (London: Routledge and Kegan Paul, 1975), p. 199.

38 Elliott Currie, "A Dialogue with Anthony M. Platt," *Issues in Criminology* 8 (1973):28.

39 Ibid., p. 29.

40 Krisberg, *Crime and Privilege.*

41 William Chambliss, "The State, the Law and the Definition of Behavior as Criminal

or Delinquent," in *Handbook of Criminology*, ed. D. Glazer (Chicago: Rand McNally, 1974), pp. 7–44.

42 Timothy Carter and Donald Clelland, "A Neo-Marxian Critique, Formulation and Test of Juvenile Dispositions as a Function of Social Class," *Social Problems* 27 (1979):96–108.

43 David Greenberg, "Socio-Economic Status and Criminal Sentences: Is There an Association?" *American Sociological Review* 42 (1977):174–75; David Greenberg and Drew Humphries, "The Co-optation of Fixed Sentencing Reform," *Crime and Delinquency* 26 (1980):206–25.

44 Franklin Williams, "Conflict Theory and Differential Processing: An Analysis of the Research Literature," in *Radical Criminology: The Coming Crisis*, ed. J. Inciardi (Beverly Hills, Calif.: Sage Publications, 1980), pp. 213–31.

45 Herman Schwendinger and Julia Schwendinger, "Rape Victims and the False Sense of Guilt," *Crime and Social Justice* 13 (1980):4–17.

46 Michael Rustigan, "A Reinterpretation of Criminal Law Reform in Nineteenth Century England," in *Crime and Capitalism*, ed. D. Greenberg (Palo Alto, Calif.: Mayfield Publishing, 1981), pp. 255–78.

47 Rosalind Petchesky, "At Hard Labor: Penal Confinement and Production in Nineteenth Century America," in *Crime and Capitalism*, ed. D. Greenberg (Palo Alto, Calif.: Mayfield Publishing, 1981), pp. 341–57; Paul Takagi, "The Walnut Street Jail: A Penal Reform to Centralize the Powers of the State," *Federal Probation* 49 (1975):18–26.

48 S. Spitzer and A. T. Scull, "Privatization and Capitalist Development: The Case of the Private Police," *Social Problems* 25 (1977):18–29; Dennis Hoffman, "Cops and Wobblies" (Ph.D. diss., Portland State University, 1977).

49 Sidney Harring, "Policing a Class Society: The Expansion of the Urban Police in the Late Nineteenth and Early Twentieth Centuries," in *Crime and Capitalism*, ed. D. Greenberg (Palo Alto, Calif.: Mayfield Publishing, 1981), pp. 292–313.

50 Toby, "The New Criminology is the Old Sentimentality."

51 Sparks, "A Critique of Marxist Criminology," pp. 198–99.

52 Carl Klockars, "The Contemporary Crises of Marxist Criminology," in *Radical Criminology: The Coming Crisis*, ed. J. Inciardi (Beverly Hills, Calif.: Sage Publications, 1980), pp. 92–123.

53 Ibid., pp. 112–14.

54 Ibid.

III Crime Typologies

REGARDLESS OF WHY PEOPLE commit crime in the first place, their actions are defined by law as falling into particular crime categories, or *typologies*. Criminologists often seek to link individual criminal offenders or behaviors together so they may be more easily studied and understood. These are referred to as crime or offender typologies.

In this section, crime patterns are clustered into four typologies: violent crime (chapter 10); economic crimes involving common theft offenses (chapter 11); economic crimes involving criminal organizations (chapter 12); and public-order crimes, such as prostitution and drug abuse (chapter 13). This format groups criminal behaviors by their focuses and consequences: bringing physical harm to others; misappropriating other people's property; and violating laws designed to protect public morals.

Typologies can be useful in classifying large numbers of criminal offenses or offenders into easily understood categories. This text has grouped offenses and offenders on the basis of their (1) legal definitions and (2) collective goals, objectives, and consequences.

10 Violent Crime

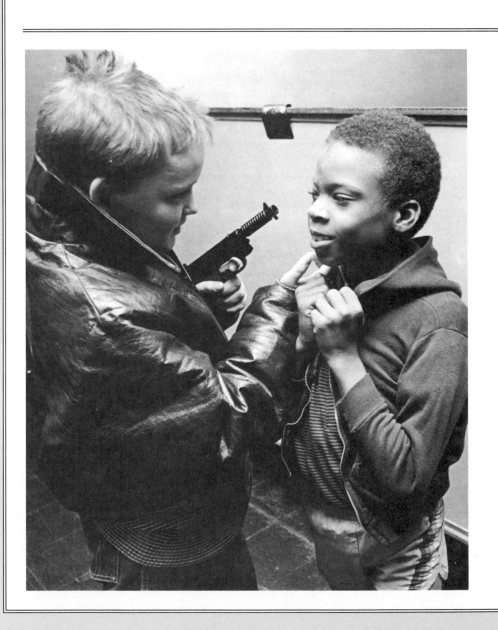

CHAPTER OUTLINE

KEY TERMS

instinctual drive
eros
thanatos
subculture of violence
economic inequality
date rapes
virility mystique
consent
corroboration
shield laws
marital exemption

express malice
implied malice
murder in the first degree
premeditation
deliberation
voluntary manslaughter
involuntary manslaughter
justifiable homicide
excusable homicide
victim-precipitated

serial murder
mass murder
aggravated assault
child abuse
neglect
sexual abuse
guardian ad litem
defensible space
convictional criminal
terrorism

Introduction

U.S. society has at various times been called violent, sick, and diseased. Violence has been described as being as "American as apple pie."[1] People's daily lives have been influenced by fear of violent crime. When asked "In general, have you limited or changed your activities in the past few years because of crime?" 49 percent of people living in the largest U.S. cities replied that they had.[2]

Many people have personally experienced violence or have a friend who has been victimized; everyone has heard about someone's being robbed, beaten, or killed. Riots and mass disturbances plague urban areas. Assassination has claimed the lives of political, religious, and social leaders all over the world. One commentator notes:

> During the crises that follow assassinations and riots, the speculation about violence reaches feverish proportions. Violence becomes the monomania of the press, the core substance of politics, the mainstay of the cocktail party, and the obsession of the public. Violence is promiscuously viewed, and it is seen everywhere. Historically, it becomes the theme of evolution; psychologically, the corollary of human nature; educationally, the enemy of learning; socially, the wrong road to change.[3]

Much debate surrounds the question of what can be done to prevent violent acts. Some experts suggest that the problem is created by a small number of inherently violence-prone individuals who must be kept out of circulation if society is to be protected. Others consider violence a situationally motivated phenomenon that can infect any person at any time. Still others view violence as being caused by cultural phenomena that increase the probability that people in particular ethnic, racial, economic, or environmental groups will commit violent acts.

Criminologists are also uncertain about what to do to prevent and control violent acts: Increase penalties? Decrease penalties and increase rehabilitation efforts? Execute violent criminals? Whereas some advocate compassion for the criminal and a return to the treatment ideal, others react to stories such as that of rape victim Cheryl Bess, a fifteen-year-old whose attacker poured industrial solvent on her face and left her to die in the California desert. Blinded and near death, Cheryl had burns that eroded the skin to the bones of her face, skull, shoulders, neck, hands, and forearms. Her attacker had previously served sixteen years in prison for the rape of a nine-year-old girl.[4] Such accounts produce cries for the death penalty and long, mandatory prison sentences for violent crime.

People today seem to be reacting to violence with violent measures of their own and applauding others who take the initiative in violent encounters. When Bernard Goetz shot four assailants on a New York subway in 1984, many in the city cheered his efforts. A rock group wrote a song in his honor, which said in part:

> I'm not going to give you my pay
> Try and take it away
> Come on make my day
> They call him the vigilante.

T-shirts went on sale with a "Thug Buster" logo.[5]

Thus, despite crime statistics telling us the violence rate has stabilized, declined, or both, Americans see violence as an established part of their daily lives.

This chapter will survey the nature and extent of violent crime. First, it will briefly review some of the patterns and causes of violence. Then it will turn its attention to specific types of interpersonal violence—rape, assault, homicide, robbery, and domestic violence. Then it will examine violence against the state—terrorism.

The Roots of Violence

There seems to be no question that people in the United States live in a violence-prone society. For example, Graeme Newman has assembled the following facts about violence:

- Since 1900, guns have been used to kill over 100,000 people in the United States. Total casualties exceed those from all wars from the Revolution to Vietnam.
- Someone is shot on the average of once every twenty-five minutes.
- It is estimated that there are anywhere from 100 million to 200 million privately owned guns in the United States.
- Many more people have used guns than other methods to kill themselves.
- The rate of gun homicide is thirty-five times higher in the United States than in England, Germany, or Denmark.[6]

What causes people to behave so violently? It seems reasonable to believe that destructive, inhumane violence is the handiwork of the mentally ill or deranged. Yet, as noted in chapter 6, little evidence exists that the mentally ill are any more violence-prone than the rest of us. Some violence-prone criminals may suffer from mental illness, but there are many others whose emotional problems manifest themselves in anything but violent behavior—passivity, delusion, depression, and so on.

Another view is that violent responses and emotions are actually ingrained within all humans, needing the right spark to trigger them off. For example, among the concepts introduced by Sigmund Freud was the belief that human aggression and violence were produced by **instinctual drives**.[7] Freud maintained that humans possess two opposing instinctual drives whose interrelationship controls behavior: **eros**, the life instinct, which drives people to self-fulfillment and enjoyment; **thanatos**, the death instinct, which operates to produce self-destruction. Thanatos can be expressed externally (as violence and sadism) or internally (as suicide, alcoholism, or other self-destructive habits). Because aggression was instinctual, Freud saw little hope in treating it.

A few biologists have also speculated that instinctual violence promoting traits may be common to the human species as a whole. One view is that aggression and violence are results of instincts inborn in all animals, including human beings. A leading proponent of this view, Konrad Lorenz, developed this theory in his famous book, *On Aggression*.[8] Lorenz argues that aggressive energy is produced by inbred instincts that are independent of environmental forces. In the animal kingdom, aggression usually serves a productive purpose—for example, it leads members of grazing species to spread out over available territory to insure an ample food supply and the survival of the fittest.

Lorenz believes that humans possess some of the same aggressive instincts as animals, but without the inhibitions against fatal violence that members of lower species usually maintain. That is, among lower species, aggression is rarely fatal; when a conflict occurs, the winner is determined through a test of skill or endurance. This inhibition against killing members of their own species protects animals from self-extinction. Humans, lacking this inhibition against fatal violence, are thor-

Causes of Violent Crime

Some disagreement exists among criminologists about the cause of violent crime. Each of the main criminological perspectives maintains its own unique position on the root causes of violence. Some possibilities are listed below.

Perspective	Cause	Solution
Classical	People who do not fear social sanctions, disapproval, and punishment will use violence to achieve their goals or vent frustrations.	Increase fear of legal sanctions; improve efficiency of criminal justice system; use the death penalty more often.
Individual		
Biological	Unique physical characteristics coupled with environmental stress and triggering mechanisms cause violence. Cause may be biochemical, neurological, or genetic.	Physical evaluation of offenders; treatment of individual problems; diet; environmental control.
Psychological Behaviorist	Seeing people receive rewards for violent actions may increase arousal levels and cause aggression.	Teach people that violence is often punished; reward conventional behavior; provide nonviolent role models.
Psychoanalytic	Unresolved conflicts produced by early childhood trauma result in personality disorders and aggressive behavior; weak ego control also plays a part.	Use psychotherapy, which unlocks the personality conflicts related to violent episodes. Use mood-altering drugs.
Cognitive	Some people's moral development has not progressed to the point at which they can understand the destructiveness of their actions.	Increase offenders' moral level by placing them in a setting in which moral values are stressed and rewarded.

oughly capable of killing their own kind; and as technology develops and more lethal weapons are produced, the extinction of the human species becomes a significant possibility.

In a similar vein, Robert Ardrey, an anthropologist, has argued that humans' evolution and development are due to their innate aggressiveness, their ability to kill, and their love of weapons—from the crude weapons of early people to the guns of modern criminals.[9]

The works of Lorenz and Ardrey have been disputed on two significant points. First, they neglect to determine whether the varied ecological and environmental conditions under which humans exist today influence their behavior. Second, they disregard the human capacity to learn from mistakes and the effect of this capacity on the development of aggression inhibitors. According to another anthropologist, Ashley Montagu—one of Lorenz's staunchest critics, people's ability to adapt and control their environment makes the human species actually better equipped to survive than lower species.[10]

The Subculture of Violence

Explanations of the cause of violent behavior that focus on the individual offender fail to account for the patterns of violence in the United States. The various sources of crime statistics tell us that interpersonal violence is more common in certain areas (large, urban communities), at certain times of year (July, August), and

Perspective	Cause	Solution
Sociological		
Social Structure	The strain and frustration of living in lower-class slum areas can trigger violent acts. Lower-class values stress toughness and strength, which lead to conflict with authorities.	Provide economic, educational, and social opportunities for the lower class; reduce feelings of anomie and frustration.
Social Process	Some people are alienated from conventional institutions such as schools, jobs, and families. They may learn to react violently to stress. Stigma for transgressions reinforce their violent nature.	Create opportunities to strengthen people's bond to conventional society, such as through educational enrichment or job training programs; provide conventional role models; avoid labeling.
Social Conflict	Violence is a function of the conflict between haves and have-nots. The capitalist system produces violence through its stress of materialism and competition. The crimes of the upper class go unpunished.	Restructure society; end capitalist domination; increase humans' concern for one another.

DISCUSSION QUESTIONS

1. Can one theory explain violence, or is it possible that people are violent for a variety of reasons?

2. What would you do with extremely violent people? Do you favor treatment? Incarceration? The death penalty?

among certain groups (young males). Because such predictable patterns exist, it seems evident that social forces must be operating when people engage in violent behavior.

To explain the existence of areas and groups in U.S. society with disproportionately high violence rates, Marvin Wolfgang and Franco Ferracuti have suggested that a **subculture of violence** exists.[11] The subculture's norms are separate from the central, dominant value system. In this subculture, a potent theme of violence influences lifestyles, the socialization process, and interpersonal relationships. Even though the subculture's members share some of the values of the dominant culture, they expect that violence will be used to solve social conflicts and dilemmas. In fact, members who act nonviolently will be rejected by their peer group.

According to Wolfgang and Ferracuti, violence can become part of one's daily lifestyle, the theme for solving difficult problems and problem situations. Within the subculture, violent individuals will not be burdened by guilt. After all, they will be attacking people of similar age, race, and economic status, who also share their cultural values. Even law-abiding citizens within the subculture of violence do not view violence as menacing or immoral. When attacked they see their assailants as agents of the same kind of aggression they themselves represent. Violence is legitimized by custom, norms; it is "appropriate" behavior within culturally defined situations.

The subculture of violence thesis is supported by the distribution of violent

Blaus claims that violence is prevalent in areas where the rich and poor live in close proximity.

crime in American society. An analysis of violence trends in the United States conducted by Neil Alan Weiner and Marvin Wolfgang found that between 1969 and 1982, violence plagued larger cities and that young, male, minority group members were disproportionately involved in crimes such as rape, robbery, and homicide.[12] Similarly, the victims of violent crime are concentrated among young, poor, minority citizens. In fact, the personal characteristics of the victims of violent crimes were much like those of their assailants. Except for the crime of robbery, violence tended to be intraracial; and except for rape, intrasexual.

In sum, for the past decade or so the demographic characteristics of violent crime support Wolfgang and Ferracuti's subculture of violence concept. There seem to be pockets of violence within our society that contain both the violent criminal and victims who may actually share the criminal's values.

SOCIAL INEQUALITY AND VIOLENCE

Wolfgang's subculture of violence seems to be located in ghetto areas of large urban cities. What is it about these areas that produces violent conditions? A growing body of literature suggests that it is not simply the grinding poverty that exists in these areas, nor their racial or ethnic composition. That is, violence cannot be explained solely by the concept of subcultural values. What seems to produce violence is the relative economic deprivation suffered by ghetto residents—**economic inequality**—which produces the anger, rage, and frustration leading to violence.

In one well-respected study Judith and Peter Blau compared crime, race, and economic patterns in America's 125 largest cities and found that socioeconomic inequality between races as well as general inequality increases the rates of violent crime. The Blaus conclude that if there is a violent culture in U.S. society, its "roots are pronounced economic inequalities, especially if associated with ascribed position," such as race. They go on to state:

> *High rates of criminal violence are apparently the price of racial and economic inequalities. In a society founded on the principle "that all men are created equal" economic inequalities rooted in ascribed positions violate the spirit of democracy and are likely to create alienation, despair, and conflict. The hypothesis derived from this assumption, which is also deducible from a general sociological theory, is that racial socioeconomic inequalities are a major source of much criminal violence.* [13]

Similar research has been conducted by Leo Carroll and Pamela Jackson, and by John Braithwaite. [14] This view is also supported by Richard Block's analysis of violent crime in Chicago. Block found that neighborhoods in which very poor and middle-class people live in close proximity are the ones experiencing the highest crime rates. [15] Though both Block's and the Blau's work can be criticized because they rely on official crime data, their findings seem comparable in part to similar research that uses victimization data (NCS) as the means of analysis. [16]

In the following sections, some major forms of interpersonal violence produced by social inequality and other factors will be discussed in detail.

Forcible Rape

Rape—defined by the common law as "the carnal knowledge of a female forcibly and against her will"—is one of the most loathed, misunderstood, and frightening of crimes. Under traditional common-law definitions, rape involved nonconsensual sexual intercourse performed by a male against a female he was neither married to nor cohabitating with. Excluded from the crime of rape are sexual acts which, though illegal, are usually included in other crime categories; for example:

- Forced participation in fellatio, cunnilingus, and, in many states, anal intercourse;
- Coerced participation of a male in intercourse or other sexual activity by a female or by another male, or of a female by another female;
- Coerced sexual intercourse or other sexual abuse within marriage or between cohabitants; and
- Coerced sexual intercourse induced by the threat of social, economic, or vocational harm rather than of physical injury. [17]

Within this framework rape can take many different forms: stranger-to-stranger rapes; **date rapes**; "acquaintance rapes" involving friends and family members; rapes involving alcohol or drug abuse; marital rapes, and so on. Though crime data indicate that most rapists and victims were strangers to one another, there is a disturbing trend for rapes to involve people who knew each other beforehand. For example, the date rape is believed to occur frequently on college campuses. It has been estimated that 20 percent of all college women are the victims of rape or attempted rape. [18] Similarly, one survey conducted on a midwestern campus found that 100 percent of all self-reported rapists knew their victim beforehand. Well-publicized gang rapes have occurred at Duke, Florida State, and Pennsylvania State universities and at Siena Heights College.[19] The Alpha Tau Omega Fraternity at Penn State was suspended after a 1983 gang rape.

Despite their prevalence, less than one in ten date rapes may be reported to police. Some victims do not even view their experiences as a real rape, which they believe involves a strange man jumping out of the bushes. Coercive sexual encounters have become a disturbingly common occurrence in our culture.

Because of its content, rape was often viewed as a sexual offense in the traditional criminological literature. In recent times, the violent, coercive nature of rape has become fully appreciated and it is today considered more an expression of anger and aggression against women than a forceful expression of sexuality. Women's groups have mounted a national campaign designed to alert the public about the seriousness of rape, initiate help for victims, and change legal definitions to facilitate prosecution of rape offenders. Such efforts have been only marginally effective in reducing rape rates, but there has been significant change in liberalizing rape laws and a vast social service network to aid victims has been developed.

HISTORY OF RAPE

Rape has been known throughout history. It has been the subject of art, literature, film, and theatre. Paintings such as the "Rape of the Sabine Women," novels such as *Clarissa* by Samuel Richardson, poems such as "The Rape of Lucrece" by William Shakespeare, and films such as "Anatomy of a Murder" and "Roshomon" have as their central themes sexual violence.

In early civilization, rape was a common occurrence. Men staked a claim of ownership on a woman by forcibly abducting and raping her. This practice, claims Susan Brownmiller, led to males' solidification of power and their historical domination of women.[20] In fact, in her oft-cited book, *Against Our Will,* Brownmiller charges that the criminalization of rape occurred only after the development of a monetary economy. Thereafter, the violation of a virgin caused an economic hardship on her family, who expected a significant dowry for her hand. According to Brownmiller, further proof of the sexist basis of rape law can be seen in Babylonian and Hebraic law. These ancient peoples considered a married rape victim and her attacker as being of equal blame and sentenced the victim to death for adultery.

During the middle ages, Brownmiller says, forcible sex was first outlawed only if the victim was high-born, and later for all classes of females; married women were not considered rape victims until the fourteenth century. The Christian condemnation of sex during this period was also a denunciation of women as evil, with lust in their hearts, redeemable only by motherhood. A woman who was raped was almost automatically suspected of contributing to her attack.

Throughout recorded history, rape has also been associated with warfare. Soldiers of conquering armies have considered sexual possession of their enemies' women one of the spoils of war. Among the ancient Greeks, rape was socially acceptable and well within the rules of warfare. During the Crusades, even knights and pilgrims, ostensibly bound by vows of chivalry and Christian piety, took time off to rape as they marched toward Constantinople. The belief that women are part of the spoils of war has continued through the ages, from the Crusades to the war in Vietnam.

OFFICIAL RAPE STATISTICS

Most of what we know today about the scope of the rape problem comes from two national statistical sources: the Uniform Crime Report and the National Crime Survey (see chapter 3).[21]

The Uniform Crime Report uses the common-law definition of rape (the carnal knowledge of a female forcibly and against her will). Additionally, the UCR includes in its computations assaults or attempts to commit rape.

The 1983 data show that 78,918 rapes or attempted rapes were reported to police in 1983, a slight increase over 1982's figure of 78,898. This amounted to a rape rate of 66 per 100,000 females for 1983, a 2-percent increase over the year before. In 1984, the rape rate increased about 6 percent (84,233 reported rapes).

Geographical and ecological conditions influenced the probability that a woman would be raped. Though the most rapes occurred in the south (35 percent) and the least in the northeast (16 percent), the western states had the highest rape rate (86 per 100,000 females). Population density also influenced the rape rate; metropolitan areas had a rate of 76 per 100,000; smaller cities, 41; rural areas, 29.

The police cleared 52 percent of all reported rape offenses by arrest. Of those arrested, 50 percent were under twenty-five years of age, and 25 percent were aged eighteen to twenty-two. Whites comprised 50 percent of those arrested, while 49 percent were black; the racial pattern of rape arrests has been fairly consistent for some time. Finally, rape is a warm-weather crime—most occur during July and August, with the lowest rates occurring during December, January, and February.

VICTIM ACCOUNTS

The National Crime Survey has also been used to tell us something about rapists and their victims. A 10-year study of rape released by the Justice Department in 1985 found that between 1972 and 1982, 1.5 million rapes or attempted rapes took place in the United States. In 1983, for example, 154,000 rapes and attempted rapes occurred. About 1 in every 600 women over twelve years old was a rape victim in 1983. Though 81 percent of all victims were white, black women are overrepresented in rape statistics. Other relevant findings include:

- More than 70 percent of the victims were unmarried women.
- A woman was twice as likely to be attacked by a stranger as by someone she knew.
- Half the female victims reported a family income of less than $10,000; more than 90 percent reported income below $25,000.
- Two of every three cases involved victims from sixteen to twenty-four years old.
- About 15 percent of the incidents involved more than one assailant.
- Victims reported $72 million in medical expenses related to the attacks from 1973 through 1982.
- An estimated 123,000 rapes in the ten-year period involved male victims.
- Rape accounts for 3 percent of all violent crime in the United States.[22]

The NCS also tells us something about the rape offender.[23] Victims who were able to describe their attacker described them as being usually over twenty-one years of age; although when more than one offender was involved in rape, both victim and offenders seemed somewhat younger. Rapes were described as being intraracial—blacks raped blacks, whites raped whites. However, the chance of a black offender raping a white victim was greater than that of a black victim being raped by a white offender.

Rapes tended to occur in the evening hours (about two-thirds) and most took place in an open place such as a street or park (about two-thirds). Most were committed by a single offender and involved a single victim. Though only half of all rapists were armed, use of a weapon dramatically affected the completion of a rape attack.

The NCS indicates that only half of all victims reported their crimes to police; those not reporting claimed it was a "private matter" or that "nothing could be done."

Finally, most rape victims tried to protect themselves from their attackers. Those who did tended to be more seriously injured than those who complied with the attack; however, resisters were also more likely to fight off the attack than those who complied with it.

The picture of the rape victim that emerges from the data is of a younger, single, lower-class woman who frequents public places during the evening hours and is raped by an assailant who is generally of the same age and racial group. In contrast, older women, married or widowed, who stayed home, especially during the evening and summer months, were more likely to avoid sexual attacks.

REPORTING RAPE

One significant problem confounding the study and control of rape is that only half of all rapes are reported to police. Women who do not report rape usually believe that nothing can be done about the crime, that it is a private matter; or perhaps they are embarrassed about having friends and relatives hear about the attack. The well-publicized rape that occurred in "Big Dan's Bar" in New Bedford, Massachusetts illustrates the potential embarrassment caused by a rape trial. In that incident a woman reported being raped by six attackers on the bar's pool table. At first the news media reported to a shocked nation that a large group of bar patrons actually cheered the proceedings. But later, during a televised trial, what actually took place seemed markedly different: Only a few people were in the bar during the attack, and some witnesses had attempted to call police.[24] Though the rapists were convicted at trial, the sensationalism and publicity generated by the case are believed to have inhibited some women from reporting similar attacks.[25]

What factors prompt women to report rapes to the police? Criminologist Alan Lizotte studied NCS data and found that the major reporting factors were seriousness of the crime and the probability that the offender would eventually be convicted if brought to trial.[26] For example, if a rapist robs or assaults his victim in addition to raping them, the victim will be more likely to report the rape to police because the crime seems more serious.

The familiarity of the offender to the victim is another important predictor of rape reporting. If the offender had the right to be present when the attack occurred, such as during a date rape, women are less likely to call the police. Perhaps they fear their stories will not be believed if their attacker is a personal friend or relative. However, a married woman is more likely to report rapes since her marital status implies that the actions against her were forced and unwarranted.

Although Lizotte's findings show that crime seriousness and convictability were related to reporting rapes, there were some exceptions. For example, interracial rapes, rapes involving multiple victims, rapes involving the use of a weapon by the offender, and rapes involving victims who were highly educated were less likely to be reported. With regard to the last factor, Lizotte believes it possible that college-educated women, knowing full well the limitations of the criminal justice system, refrain from reporting their sexual assaults to the police.

CAUSES OF RAPE

What factors predispose some men to commit rape? The answers formulated by criminologists to this question are almost as varied as the varieties of the crime of rape itself. However, most explanations can be grouped into a few consistent categories.

One type of explanation focuses on the biological aspects of the male sexual drive. It is suggested that rape may be an instinctual male drive, developed over the ages as a means of perpetuating the species. In more primitive times, forcible sexual contact may have served the purpose of spreading the gene pool and maximizing offspring. Some believe that these prehistoric drives remain in modern man. Biologist Donald Symons suggests that males still have a built-in sexual drive that encourages them to have intimate relations with as many women as possible.[27] Symons champions the sociobiological view that the sexual urge is correlated with the need to preserve the species by spreading the gene pool as widely as possible. Symons argues that rape is bound up with sexuality as well as violence.

In contrast to the biological view, some researchers argue that rape is a function of male socialization in modern society. In her book *The Politics of Rape*, Diana Russell suggests that rape is actually not a deviant act but one conforming to the qualities regarded as masculine in U.S. society.[28] From an early age boys are taught to be aggressive, forceful, tough and dominating. Men are taught to dominate at the same time that they are led to believe that women want to be dominated. Russell's view conforms to Susan Brownmiller's portrait of the male as a predatory animal and the female as the victim of his sexual aggression. Russell describes the **virility mystique**—the belief that males learn to separate their sexual feelings from needs for love, respect and affection. She believes that men are socialized to be the aggressors and expect to be sexually active with many women; male virginity and sexual inexperience are marks of shame. Similarly, sexually aggressive women frighten some men and cause them to doubt their own masculinity. Sexual insecurity may lead some men to commit rape in order to bolster their self-image and masculine identity. Rape, argues Russell, helps keep women in their place.

Rape and the Subculture of Violence. Russell's virility mystique conforms to the subculture of violence concept. It holds that men who are socialized in a highly violent environment, and whose peers hold similar views, will be the most likely to use violence to obtain sex. In these areas traditional sex roles stress that males are expected to seduce and females to be seduced.[29] The more strongly some men are socialized into traditional sex role stereotypes, the more likely they are to be sexually aggressive. In fact, the sexually aggressive male may view the female as a legitimate victim of sexual violence. Women, they believe, may want to be knocked around or dominated. Or victims may be perceived as teasers, who deserve what's coming to them. Sexual aggression may help increase the offender's status among peers, proving that he is a "man's man." Christine Adler's self-report study of sexual aggression among prison inmates found that perceptions of peers' sexual

Who is the Rapist?

People have varied visions of the rapist—the psychopath who can't control his sexual urges, the college boy who gets drunk and forces his will on a young coed, the gang member who participates in a rape to prove his manhood.

A leading expert on the personality and behavior of rapists, Dr. A. Nicholas Groth, has disputed the idea that rapists are oversexed people or, indeed, that rape is a sexual act. Dr. Groth maintains that rape is always a symptom of some psychological dysfunction, either temporary and transient or chronic and repetitive. Furthermore, it is usually a desperate act that results when an emotionally weak and insecure individual is unable to handle the stresses and demands of his life.

After observing five hundred convicted rapists in his role as director of the sex offenders program for Connecticut's department of corrections, Groth found that in every act of rape, both aggression and sexuality were involved but that sexuality became the means of expressing the aggressive needs and feelings that underlay the assault.

Groth identifies three patterns, or typologies, of rape offenders; these typologies help explain the hostility, control, and dominance associated with the act.

The *anger rape* occurs when sexuality becomes a means of expressing and discharging pent-up anger and rage. The rapist uses far more brutality than would have been necessary if his real objective had been simply to have sexual relations with his victim. His aim is to hurt his victim as much as possible; the sexual aspect of rape may have been an afterthought. Often the anger rapist acts on the spur of the moment after an upsetting incident has caused him conflict, irritation, or aggravation. Surprisingly, anger rapes are less psychologically traumatic for the victim than might be expected. Since a woman is usually physically beaten, she is more likely to receive sympathy from her peers, relatives, and the justice system and consequently be immune from any suggestion that she complied with the attack.

The *power rape* involves an attacker who does not want to harm his victim as much as he wants to possess her sexually. His goal is sexual conquest, and he uses only the amount of force necessary to achieve his objective. The power rapist wants to be in control, to be able to dominate women and have them at his mercy. Yet it is not sexual gratification that drives the power rapist; in fact, he often has consenting relationships with his wife or girlfriend. Rape is instead a way of putting personal insecurities to rest, of asserting heterosexuality and preserving a sense of manhood. The power rape's victim usually is a woman equal in age to or younger than the rapist. The lack of physical violence may reduce the support given the victim by family and friends. Therefore, the victim's personal guilt over her rape experience is increased—perhaps, she thinks, she could have done something to get away.

In some rape cases, both sexuality and aggression are fused into a single psychological trait that Groth calls *sadism*. The *sadistic rapist* is bound up in ritual—he may torment his victim, bind her, torture her. Victims are usually related in the rapist's view by a personal characteristic that he wants to harm or destroy. The rape experience is intensely exciting to the sadist; he gets satisfaction from abusing, degrading, or humiliating his captive. This type of rape is particularly traumatic for the victim; Groth found that victims of such crimes need psychiatric care long after their physical wounds have healed.

In his treatment of rape offenders, Groth found that about 55 percent were of the power type; about 40 percent, the anger type; and about 5 percent, the sadistic type. Groth's major contribution has been his recognition that rape is generally a crime of violence and not a sexual act.

DISCUSSION QUESTIONS

1. Can rape be motivated by sexual drive or by aggression?

2. What do you think is an appropriate penalty for rape?

SOURCE. A. Nicholas Groth and Jean Birnbaum, *Men Who Rape* (New York: Plenum Press, 1979).

---

aggression was the most significant predictor of personal aggression.[30] Thus, the socialization view holds that all men are brought up in an environment that supports rape, whereas the subculture of violence theory suggests that environmental and peer pressure will increase the likelihood of violent sexual relations.

Psychological Views. An alternative view is that rapists are suffering from some type of personality disorder or mental illness. Paul Gebhard and his associates concluded that a significant percentage of incarcerated rapists exhibits psychotic tendencies, while many others have hostile and sadistic feelings toward women.[31] Similarly, Richard Rada found that many rapists were psychotics, others could be classified as sociopaths, and a large group suffered from a masculine identity crisis that made them oblivious to the sufferings of their victims.[32]

One of the best known attempts to classify the personality of rapists was made by psychologist A. Nicholas Groth. According to Dr. Groth, every rape encounter contains three elements: anger, power, and sexuality. Consequently, rapists can be classified according to one of these dimensions. Groth's views on rape are presented in the following Close-Up, entitled "Who is the Rapist?"

Another psychologically based viewpoint is that men learn to commit rapes much as they learn any other behavior. This view conforms to the psychological learning theory models discussed in chapter 6. For example, A. Nicholas Groth found that 40 percent of the rapists he studied were sexually victimized themselves as adolescents.[33] A growing body of literature links personal sexual trauma with the desire to inflict sexual trauma on others.

In a similar vein, evidence is mounting that some men are influenced by observing films and books with both violent and sexual content.[34] In other words, watching violent or pornographic films featuring women who are beaten, raped, or tortured has been linked to sexually aggressive behavior in men. In one startling case, a twelve-year-old Providence, Rhode Island boy sexually assaulted a ten-year-old girl on a pool table after watching trial coverage of a similar event on television. The link between sexually explicit material and violence will be discussed further in chapter 13's analysis of pornography.[35]

In sum, criminologists are at odds over the precise cause of rape. It seems evident that within the universe of rapists a number of social, cultural, and psychological forces are at work. Though some experts view rape as a normal response to an abnormal environment, others view rape as the product of a disturbed mind and deviant life experiences.

RAPE AND THE LAW

Of all violent crimes, none has created such conflict in the legal system as rape. Women who are sexually assaulted are reluctant to report the crime to the police because of the discriminatory provisions built into rape laws; the sexist treatment given women by police, prosecutors, and court personnel; and the legal technicalities that authorize invasion of women's privacy when a rape case is tried in court. Some state laws have made rape so difficult to prove that women believe that the slim chance their attacker will be convicted is not sufficient to warrant their participation in the prosecutorial process.

There are a number of reasons why rape represents a major legal challenge to the criminal justice system.[36] One issue involves the concept of **consent**. In most jurisdictions, it is essential to prove that the attack was forced and that the victim did not give voluntary consent to her attacker. In a sense, the burden of proof is on the victim to prove that her character is beyond question and that she in no way encouraged, enticed, or misled the accused rapist. In most jurisdictions, evidence of the victim's character can be introduced by her attacker's attorney, who tries to create a reasonable doubt about the woman's credibility. Unfortunately, it may be relatively easy for a defense attorney to create in the minds of a jury suspicion that the woman may have consented to the sexual act and later regretted her decision. Conversely, it is difficult for a prosecuting attorney to establish that a woman's character is so impeccable that the absence of consent is a certainty. Such distinctions are important in rape cases, because male jurors may be sympathetic to the accused if the victim is portrayed as unchaste. Simply referring to the woman as sexually liberated may be enough to result in exoneration of the accused, even if violence and brutality were used in the attack.

In addition to requiring evidence that consent was not given, some states require **corroboration** that the crime of rape actually took place. This involves evidence that the accused is actually the person who committed the crime, that sexual penetration took place, and that force was present and consent absent. A few states require an innocent third-party eyewitness to corroborate that a rape occurred. Often this testimony can come from a third party, such as a police officer, to whom the rape was reported shortly after it occurred. Even when corroboration by others is not required, it is essential that the victim establish her intimate and detailed knowledge of the act in order for her testimony to be believed in court. This may include searching questions about her assailant's appearance, the location in which the crime took place, and the nature of the physical assault itself. Embarrassing questions of this sort are partially responsible for the low number of rapes reported to police.

Proving a rape case often also involves convincing a jury that penetration of the woman's sex organs actually took place. This usually involves the medical evidence supplied by the doctors who examined the victim, the condition of the woman's clothing and effects when she reported the crime, whether semen or blood was found on the victim or the accused rapist, the woman's testimony backed by the absence of any motive to falsify evidence, and so on. Though medical evidence is often critical, proving the case hinges on the information given to police soon after the act occurs. One of the greatest traumas associated with the rape experience involves the often embarrassing questions police ask the victim. The reluctance of women to discuss the humiliating details of a rape soon after it has occurred is yet another reason why many rape cases are not reported to the criminal justice system.

Stringent proof is required in rape cases, for several reasons. First, some male psychiatrists and therapists still maintain that women fantasize rape and therefore may falsely accuse their alleged attackers. Some judges also fear that women may charge men with rape because of jealousy, revenge, false proposals of marriage, or pregnancy.

Second, the stigma associated with a conviction for rape and the severity of the criminal penalties that accompany it make it imperative that the defendant be given every opportunity to prove his innocence. Third, it is assumed that the jury will have a natural sympathy toward the victim, who has been so severely hurt; therefore, the law makes proof of rape especially rigorous. Fourth, the sexism that exists in U.S. society has resulted in a cultural suspiciousness toward women, who are often seen as provocateurs in any sexual encounter with men. Consequently, the burden is shifted to the woman to prove she has not provoked or condoned the rape. Although the law does not recognize it, jurors are sometimes swayed by the insinuation that the rape was victim-precipitated; thus, the blame is shifted from rapist to victim. To get a conviction, it becomes essential for prosecutors to establish that the act was forced and violent and that no question of voluntary compliance exists. Thus, the legal consequences of rape often reflect archaic legal traditions along with inherent male prejudices and suspicions.

The need for stringent proof in rape cases was given national attention in March of 1985 when Cathleen Webb, alleged rape victim, stepped forward and claimed that Gary Dotson, convicted of raping her in Illinois six years earlier, had actually been falsely accused.[37] Ms. Webb stated before a national audience that her fear of a teenage pregnancy led her to accuse Dotson of a crime that never actually occurred. The news that an innocent man had spent six years in prison shocked the nation's conscience. Ironically, despite Ms. Webb's recantation, the judge who originally presided in the case returned Dotson to prison, letting stand his earlier conviction. Dotson's case was then brought before the Illinois governor, who issued a pardon.

CHANGES IN RAPE LAWS

The law of rape has been changing around the country. States have developed **shield laws**, which protect women from being questioned about their sexual history unless it is judged to have a direct bearing on the case. In addition, the **marital exemption** has been under attack. Traditionally a legally married husband could not be charged with raping his own wife. However, about ten state courts, including those in New York, have convicted husbands of marital rapes, making compulsive sex a crime even among married couples.[38]

Some state jurisdictions have abolished the legal category of rape and have substituted the sexually neutral concept of sexual assault.[39] Sexual assault laws outlaw any type of forcible sex, including homosexual rape. Martin Schwartz and Todd Clear go one step further by suggesting that rape laws be blended with existing assault statutes.[40] The creation of a special status for assaulted women, they argue, is one of the barriers that prevents them from being the political equals of men.

Several states, among them Nebraska and Michigan, have already substituted sexual assault statutes for traditional rape laws in an effort to remove the barriers from rape convictions. Have these changes proved effective? A recent study by Susan Caringella-MacDonald compared the processing of sexual assault cases with nonsexual assault cases in Michigan. There was some similarity, but the credibility of sexual assault victims was more likely to be challenged in court; concomitantly, offenders were more likely to receive significant sentence reductions when they plea bargained. Caringella-MacDonald concludes that "the historic difficulties in adjudicating sexual assault offenses cannot be erased by the stroke of a pen."[41]

Similar reforms have been tried in other states. For example, California's new rape law prevents defense attorneys from using a victim's prior sexual history in proving consent.[42] The law also created mandatory prison terms of up to eight years for more serious rape cases. If the offender was sent to prison in the absence of mitigating circumstances, the mandatory sentence would be six years. Although rape reform in California has not significantly increased the number of crimes reported to the police, the probability of arrest, or the percentage of convictions, it has substantially increased the probability of a convicted offender's receiving a prison sentence—from 58 percent in 1975 to 81 percent in 1982.[43]

In addition to these reforms, feminist groups have lobbied hard for reform of rape laws. Changes advocated by the antirape movement and legislated in some jurisdictions include:

(1) *Eliminating corroboration requirements that necessitate evidence—in addition to the victim's testimony—that the alleged offense did, in fact, occur;*

(2) *Limiting the defense attorney's ability to make the victim's past sexual conduct an issue at trial;*

(3) *Repealing provisions requiring corroborating evidence of resistance on the part of the victim;*

(4) *Eliminating "spousal immunity" to the charge of rape;*

(5) *Making rape a "sex-neutral" offense, thereby providing for prosecution as rape of cases in which the victims are males and/or the offenders are females;*

(6) *Broadening the legal definition of forcible rape to include coerced sexual acts in addition to intercourse; and*

(7) *Broadening the concept of "coercion" to include psychological, economic, and vocational coercion.*[44]

RAPE AND THE COMMUNITY TODAY

In the past few years, a greater sensitivity to the plight of rape victims has developed. An antirape philosophy has been incorporated in feminine consciousness. Rape crisis centers have been opened around the country; these centers typically feature twenty-four-hour-a-day emergency phone lines and information on police, medical, and court procedures. Some provide volunteers to assist the victim as her case is processed through the justice system. The growth of these services—which began with the Washington, D.C., Rape Crisis Center's phone line in 1972—has been so explosive that services are available in almost all major cities and college communities. Today there are over a thousand rape-related programs in the United States.[45]

Most rape programs provide two types of services.[46] According to Janet Gornick and her associates, *direct services* involve interaction between center staff and clients:

(1) *Emergency assistance: including information, referral, and some support, usually provided over the telephone, and available 24 hours a day;*

(2) *Face-to-face crisis intervention, or accompaniment: usually provided in the hospital, police station, courts, or other public location, also available 24 hours a day; and*

(3) *Counseling: either one-on-one or in groups, a varying number of sessions, often provided at the center, usually scheduled, and limited to business hours and evenings.*[47]

In addition, *indirect services* involve prevention and community education efforts.

The much more controversial side of rape crisis center work is the community education and action, also called "indirect services," "community services," or simply, "prevention." This kind of work has four relatively distinct components:

(1) *Public education: usually to lay audiences, most frequently to business and professional groups, schools, women's groups, civic associations, and other community organizations;*

(2) *Organization, training, and monitoring of other professional agencies: including medical, law enforcement, criminal justice agencies, and, less often, mental health professionals;*

(3) *Lobbying: usually at the state level, for legislative changes relevant to rape and other forms of violence against women; and*

(4) *Political action work: including sponsoring or supporting demonstrations, rallies, marches, protests, boycotts, and other types of actions aimed at bringing about change, either in the activities of individuals or agencies or general changes in the attitudes or awareness of the community.* [48]

Murder

Murder is defined in the common law as "the unlawful killing of a human being with malice aforethought."[49] In most state jurisdictions, in order for a person to be legally responsible for killing another, that person must intentionally and with malice have desired the death of the person killed. Two types of malice are recognized in law: **Express malice** is the state of mind assumed to exist when someone kills another person in the absence of any apparent provocation. **Implied malice** is considered to exist when a death results from negligent or unthinking behavior, even though the intention to kill was absent—for example, when a drunk driver kills a pedestrian or when a bystander is killed during the course of a robbery. Even though the perpetrator did not wish to kill the victim, the killing was the result of an inherently dangerous act and therefore is considered murder.

There are gradations of homicide. **Murder in the first degree**, usually punishable by death or imprisonment for life, occurs when a person kills another after premeditation and deliberation. **Premeditation** means that the killing was considered beforehand and suggests that it was motivated by more than a simple desire to engage in an act of violence. **Deliberation** means the killing was planned and decided on after careful thought rather than carried out on impulse. "To constitute a deliberate and premeditated killing, the slayer must weigh and consider the question of killing and the reasons for and against such a choice; having in mind the consequences, he decides to and does kill."[50] The planning implied by this definition need not involve a long, drawn-out process but rather may involve an almost instantaneous decision to take another's life. Also, a killing accompanying a felony such as robbery or rape usually constitutes first-degree murder.

In contrast, second-degree murder requires the actor to have malice aforethought but not premeditation or deliberation. A second-degree murder occurs when a person's wanton disregard for the victim's life and his or her desire to inflict serious bodily harm on the victim results in the loss of human life.

An unlawful homicide without malice is called manslaughter and is usually punished by anywhere between one and fifteen years in prison. **Voluntary manslaughter** refers to a killing committed in the heat of passion or during a sudden quarrel considered to have provided sufficient provocation to produce violence; while intent may be present, malice is not. **Involuntary manslaughter** refers to a killing that occurs during the commission of a minor criminal act or misdemeanor, such as when a drunk driver causes the death of a pedestrian.

These definitions are illustrated in the following example: If during a bar fight, one person punched another and the blow caused the victim's death, the act would probably be considered manslaughter, since the violent act was intentional but the death could not be foreseen and was not intended. If in the heat of the fight, one person pulled out a knife and subsequently killed another, it might be construed a second-degree murder, since the act was performed with malice but the actual killing probably was not planned or thought out. On the other hand, if after the fight one of the combatants went home, got a gun and loaded it, returned to the bar an hour later, and killed his opponent, he would probably be charged with first-degree murder, since after he had had a chance to cool off, he planned and carried out the death of another.

A homicide can also be **justifiable homicide** and therefore unpunished if it is performed in self-defense or is allowed by law, such as when a police officer shoots a dangerous fleeing felon. To qualify as self-defense, the offense must be proven unavoidable and justifiable in light of the perceived threat. For example, if an attacker uses only his fists, it would not be justifiable homicide to shoot him in self-defense (see chapter 2).

Excusable homicide results from an unintentional killing, or accident. For a killing to be ruled an accident, it must be proven in court that the behavior that led to the death was not the product of negligence and that the accused acted as any reasonable and prudent person would have under the same set of circumstances.

MURDER STATISTICS

After 20 years of increase, as you may recall from chapter 3, the murder rate began declining in 1980. From a rate of 10.2 murders per 100,000 persons in 1980, the rate declined to about 8 per 100,000 in 1984, or about 18 percent in a four-year period. The decline came as a surprise to alarmists who predicted that the sharp increase between 1960 and 1980, when the murder rate doubled, would continue indefinitely.

How can this pattern be explained? The 1960–1980 period was marked by economic instability and inequality, social unrest, the war in Vietnam, and a surge in the under-twenty population—all factors that have been linked to crime and violence.[51] The 1980s have seen a dramatic "aging" of the population coupled with a reliance on conservative law enforcement policies. It is not lost on policy makers that the murder rate has declined at a time when the prison population has increased markedly and the death penalty has been reinstated. Nonetheless, almost 20,000 murders were committed in 1984.

What do the statistics tell us about murder today? Murder, like rape, tends to be an intraracial crime. For example, 94 percent of the black murder victims were slain by black offenders and 88 percent of whites by white offenders. Similarly, people arrested for murder were disproportionately male (87 percent), racial and ethnic minorities (66 percent), and young (41 percent were under 25).

The environmental pattern of murder was also similar to that of rape. Murder rates are highest in large cities, in the South, and during the summer months and holiday seasons. In contrast, rural counties and the midwestern states have relatively low murder rates.

Today, few would deny that some relationship exists between social and ecological factors and murder. This section will explore some of the more important issues related to these factors.

RELATIONSHIPS BETWEEN VICTIMS AND CRIMINALS

One factor that has received a great deal of attention from criminologists is the relationship that allegedly exists between the murderer and the victim. Unlike most other criminals, murderers usually know their victims and have had some sort of personal relationship with them. For example, in 1983, in only 15 percent of the murders in which the police were able to determine the relationship between criminal and victim were the actors strangers to one another.[52] In most instances, the victim and criminal were either related (husband, wife, brother, son, or the like) or acquainted (friend, boyfriend, girlfriend, neighbor, and so on).

This relationship pattern underscores one of the most important concepts in criminology, the view that murder can be **victim-precipitated**. This position is most closely associated with Marvin Wolfgang, the criminologist who first used the term in his study of criminal homicide patterns.[53] He defined the term as follows:

> The term "victim-precipitated" is applied to those criminal homicides in which the victim is a direct, positive precipitator in the crime. The role of the victim is characterized by his having been the first in the homicide drama to use physical force directed against his subsequent slayer. The victim-precipitated cases are those in which the victim was the first to show and use a deadly weapon, to strike a blow in an altercation—in short, the first to commence the interplay or resort to physical violence.[54]

Examples of a victim-precipitated homicide include the death of an aggressor in a barroom brawl, or a wife who kills her husband after he attacks and threatens to kill her.

Wolfgang found that 150, or 26 percent, of the 588 homicides in his sample could be classified as victim-precipitated.

Since Wolfgang's work was published, over twenty years ago, the concept of victim precipitation has remained somewhat controversial. For example, Menachim Amir's suggestion that rape is victim-precipitated has been viewed as a sexist concept implying that some women deserve to be raped.[55] Others have argued that the incidence of victim precipitation may be declining. In a recent analysis, a sociologist, Margaret Zahn, found that homicide in the 1960s and 1970s was primarily intraracial (whites killing whites and blacks killing blacks) and intrasexual (males killing males and females killing females).[56] There was also an increase in murders by strangers (and an increase in cases in which the offender simply remained unknown), although this increase was much more pronounced in northern cities. In southern and southwestern cities, domestic violence remains the most significant category, whereas in northern areas, homicides by strangers or unknown assailants now represent a dominant (if not the dominant) murder pattern.

Despite the controversy, the concept of victim precipitation is important because it helps focus attention on the transactional nature of murder, which will now be discussed in more detail.

MURDER TRANSACTIONS

At one time it was popular to view murderers as mentally unstable persons who killed because they were driven by psychotic personalities or were so deeply disturbed that they did not know what they were doing. Although it is true that some convicted murderers suffer from mental illnesses such as schizophrenia or paranoia, it is also probably true that the incidence of psychosis among murderers is no greater than the incidence of psychosis in the total population.

Today, criminologists have revised their concepts of murder. Attempts have been made to classify criminal homicide by its cause and the relationship between the actors involved in it. For example, James Boudouris classifies murder interaction as follows: Domestic relations (husband-wife); lovers' affairs; relations between friends and acquaintances; business relations (landlord-tenant, doctor-patient, employer-employee); criminal transactions (holdup man-store owner, drug user-pusher); noncriminal homicide (police officer-holdup man); cultural recreation-causal (bar fight, quarrel over car accident); subcultural recreation-causal (two gamblers fight over card game); psychiatric (murder by a mentally disturbed person); suicide-murder (the killer immediately kills himself or herself); incidental (a peacemaker in a fight is accidentally killed); unknown cause. In a study of homicides occurring in Detroit between 1926 and 1968, Boudouris found that an overwhelming number were related to domestic and family quarrels and relatively few murders were caused by psychiatrically disturbed persons.[57]

David Luckenbill studied murder transactions to determine whether particular patterns of behavior are common to the transaction between killer and victim.[58] Luckenbill found that many homicides take a sequential form: The victim made what the offender considered an offensive move; the offender typically retaliated in a verbal or physical manner; an agreement to end things violently was forged with the victim's response; the battle ensued, leaving the victim dead or dying; the offender's escape was shaped by his relationship to the victim or the reaction of the audience, if any.

Thus, whereas some murders may be the result of wanton violence by a stranger, the typical homicide seems to involve a social interaction between two or more people who know each other and whose destructive social interaction leads to the death of one party. If anything, recent research seems to support Wolfgang's victim precipitation model.

GEOGRAPHIC ISSUES

One issue often debated by criminologists is whether the southern part of the United States is significantly more homicide-prone than other parts of the country. In a well-known paper, Raymond Gastil found that a significant relationship existed between murder rates and residence in the South; that these differences predated the Civil War; and that in states outside the South, homicide rates increased when southerners had moved into that state.[59] Gastil attributed high homicide rates to the culture of the South, which stresses a "frontier" mentality, mob violence, night riders, the acceptance of personal vengeance by the legal system, and the widespread availability of firearms.

In a follow-up study, Colin Lofton and Robert Hill introduced economic variables into the study of southern homicide rates and concluded that any argument pointing to a southern culture of lethal violence and murder was fallacious.[60] The Lofton-Hill study did not put this debate to rest, however. Further analyses, using different data, by Howard Erlanger and later by William Doerner, also disputed the idea that southerners are more violence-prone than others.[61] However, the debate over this issue still rages; and Gastil himself replied to his critics by stating that they missed his real view—that southern culture promotes lethal violence, not just the approval of violence.[62]

SERIAL MURDER

Christopher Bernard Wilder was an Australian-born multimillionaire and Grand Prix auto racer.[63] He owned land and houses valued at $1 million, a home with a pool, sheep dogs, and was an accomplished amateur photographer. What Wilder's neighbors and friends didn't know was that he had a long history of sexual assault and had recently forfeited $400,000 bail to an Australian court after absconding from charges that he attacked two fifteen-year-old girls. Returning to the United States, Wilder went on a cross-country killing spree, between 28 February and 13 April 1984, which left eight girls dead. Posing as a fashion photographer, Wilder lured girls for "interviews," then raped, tortured, and murdered them. He was killed during a struggle with New Hampshire state police who were attempting to take him into custody.

Christopher Wilder's murderous actions fall within a frightening pattern referred to as **serial murder**. Some serial murderers, such as Theodore Bundy, roam the country killing at random. Others terrorize a city, such as the Los Angeles based Night Stalker, the still uncaught Green River Killer, who at the time of this writing is believed to have slain twenty-seven young women in Seattle; and the Hillside Strangler(s), Kenneth Bianchi and Angelo Buono who tortured and killed ten women in the Los Angeles area.[64]

There is no distinct type of serial killer. Some seem to be monsters—such as Edmund Kemper who, in addition to killing six young female hitchhikers, killed his mother, cut off her head, and used it as a dartboard. Others—like Bianchi, Wilder, and Bundy—were suave lady's men whose murderous actions surprised even close friends. Consequently, the cause of serial murder eludes criminologists. Such widely disparate factors as mental illness, sexual frustration, neurological damage, child abuse and neglect, smothering relationships with mother (David Berkowitz, the Son of Sam, slept in his parents' bed until he was ten), and childhood anxiety have been suggested as possible causes. However, most experts view the serial killers as sociopaths who enjoy killing, are immune to their victims' suffering, and when caught bask in the media limelight. Wayne Henley, Jr., who along with Dean Corril killed twenty-seven boys in Houston, offered to help prosecutors find the bodies of additional victims so he could break Chicago killer Wayne Gacy's record of 33 murders.[65]

Serial killers come from diverse backgrounds. They have been described by Ann Rule, an expert of **mass murder**, as follows:

> Most of them are very intelligent; if they're not intelligent, they are very conniving and clever. The dumb ones are caught early on; they can't run up a string of 35 murders. Now the street-smarts may make up for a lack of IQ, but most of them are very bright.
>
> A lot of them are handsome. I think lay women particularly expect a serial killer to look like Frankenstein, but he doesn't. Most of them have relationships with women, pretty women who love them. That's not why they're killing.
>
> Most of these serial killers have tremendous egos, and when they're caught and they're backed into a corner, they like to brag about what they've done.
>
> A lot of them are very attracted to law enforcement. They're either police groupies, where they hang around the cops, or they serve as reserve officers, or they may use police uniforms as a disguise. Kenneth Bianchi, the Hillside Strangler, wore a police uniform, and when he was finally caught in Washington he was working for a security service, and was just about ready to be appointed a reserve deputy sheriff.
>
> They travel continually. Where we might put 10,000 to 20,000 miles a year on our cars, a serial killer will put on 100,000 miles a year. They're always trolling for victims. They will pick certain types of victims—like Ted (Bundy) chose college

girls with long dark hair parted in the middle. Historically victims of serial killers are young women, prostitutes, homosexuals, children, vagrants and old people, people who are very vulnerable. I have yet to find a serial killer that has gone after body-builders.

They usually will stick within their victim pattern, they usually kill within their own race. Therefore a white serial killer kills whites. Actually you rarely find a black serial killer. Often they lead such double lives that when they're arrested finally, they're utterly shocked. [66]

So far law enforcement officials have been at a loss to control random killers who leave few clues, constantly change their whereabouts, and have little connection to their victims. Catching serial killers is often a matter of luck. To help local law enforcement officials the FBI has developed a profiling system to identify potential suspects. In addition, the Justice Department's Violent Criminal Apprehension Program (VI-CAP) is a computerized information service that gathers information and matches offense characteristics on violent crimes around the country.[67] This way crimes can be linked to determine if they are the product of a single culprit. The following Close-Up, entitled "Mass Murder," further discusses this issue.

Serious Assault

The FBI defines serious assault, or **aggravated assault**, as "an unlawful attack by one person upon another for the purpose of inflicting severe or aggravated bodily injury"; this definition is similar to the one used in most state jurisdictions.[68] The pattern of criminal assault is quite similar to that of homicide—one could say that the only difference between the two is the lack of a death. In 1983, the FBI recorded 639,532 assaults, a decline of 2.4 percent from the year before. Similarly, the assault rate declined 3.4 percent to 273 per 100,000. Unfortunately, in 1984 there was a 4-percent rise in the volume of aggravated assaults (685,349 crimes).

The pattern of assault is quite similar to that of both rape and murder. People arrested for assault and those identified by victims seem to be young, male, disproportionately minority group members. Similarly, assault rates were highest in urban areas, during the summer months, and in southern regions. Interestingly, the use of firearms in assault cases declined 4 percent between 1979 and 1983, while the use of other weapons such as knives increased about 10 percent.

ASSAULT IN THE HOME

One of the most frightening aspects of assaultive behavior today is the incidence of violent attacks in the home. Criminologists are now aware that intrafamily violence is an enduring social problem in the United States.

One arena of intrafamily violence that has received a great deal of media attention is **child abuse**. This term describes any physical or emotional trauma to a child for which no reasonable explanation, such as an accident or ordinary disciplinary practices, can be found.[69] Child abuse can result from actual physical beatings being administered to a child by hands, feet, weapons, belts, sticks, burnings, and so on. Another form of abuse results from **neglect**—not providing a child with the care and shelter to which it is entitled. Another aspect of the abuse syndrome is **sexual abuse**—the exploitation of children through rape, incest, and molestation by parents and guardians.

Mass Murder

In a recent book, sociologists Jack Levin and James Fox analyze one of the most frightening aspects of modern violence—mass murder.

According to Levin and Fox, about thirty-five mass murderers are active across the United States today. They include serial killers, who wander the country killing at random as they go. Other serial killers stay in their hometown and lure victims to their death. Theodore Bundy, convicted killer of three girls and suspected killer of many others, roamed the country killing as he went, while Wayne Gacy killed over thirty young boys without leaving Chicago. Mass murder can also be part of a single, uncontrollable outburst called simultaneous killing. Examples of simultaneous mass murderers include Charles Whitman, who killed fourteen people and wounded thirty others from atop the 307-foot tower on the University of Texas campus on 1 August 1966; and James Huberty, who killed twenty-one people in a MacDonald's in San Ysidro, California on 18 July 1984.

Levin and Fox dispute the notion that all mass murderers have some form of biological or psychological problems such as genetic anomalies or schizophrenia. They contend that mass murderers are actually ordinary citizens driven to extreme acts. They reached this conclusion by intensively studying 156 cases of mass murder involving 675 victims.

Levin and Fox found that even the most sadistic mass murderers are more "evil than crazy." Few are mentally ill and driven by delusions or hallucinations. Instead, they typically exhibit a sociopathic personality that deprives them of feelings of conscience or guilt to guide their behavior. They maintain the need to control and dominate their victims without concern about the victims' feelings.

Mass murderers are often motivated by profit and expediency: to get rid of witnesses, to stifle troubling family members, to eliminate snitches. There is usually a reason for the attack; rarely are total strangers victimized. Even serial killers look for particular physical or emotional features in their victims. They usually prey on people vulnerable to attack—prostitutes, hitchhikers, runaways. However, some sadistic types kill because they enjoy their victim's sufferings or get sexual gratification from them.

No one can predict who will turn out to be a mass murderer. Many are the "boy next door," whose neighbors are astonished to find out about their murderous rampages. Some are motivated by overwhelming personal problems that trigger an emotional bombshell. Others, like San Francisco's Zebra killers who executed fourteen people in 1973–74, may be part of a cult or group that espouses murder.

So far police have been successful in capturing simultaneous killers whose outburst is directed at family members or friends. The serial killer has proven a more elusive target. Today the U.S. Justice Department is coordinating efforts to gather information on unsolved murders in different jurisdictions in order to find patterns linking the crimes. Unfortunately, when a serial murderer is caught, it is often the work of luck—or a snitch—and not investigative skill.

DISCUSSION QUESTIONS

1. Can a mass murderer be legally sane?
2. Should there be a mandatory death sentence for all serial killers?

SOURCE. Jack Levin and James Alan Fox, *Mass Murder* (New York: Plenum Press, 1985), p. 47.

It is difficult to estimate the actual number of child abuse cases, since so many incidents are never reported to the police. Nonetheless, child abuse and neglect appear to have reached epidemic proportions in recent years. In Illinois, reported abuse cases have doubled since 1976; similar increases have occurred in other states.

Douglas J. Besharov, director of the National Center on Child Abuse and Neglect, estimates that approximately one million children are maltreated each year. Of these, as many as 100,000 to 200,000 are physically abused, 60,000 to 100,000 are sexually abused, and the rest are neglected.[70] A national survey conducted by two sociologists, Richard Gelles and Murray Straus, greatly expands these figures.[71] Gelles and Straus found that between 1.4 and 1.9 million children in the United States are subject in a given year to physical abuse from their parents. Moreover, physical abuse was found to be rarely a one-time event. The average number of assaults per year was 10.5; the median, 4.5. Children of all ages suffer abuse. In general, boys are more frequently abused than girls until age twelve. Among teenagers, girls are more frequently the object of abuse. Finally, the American Humane Society, which collects data on reported child abuse, estimates that one million cases are discovered by authorities each year.[72]

Though it is difficult to estimate incidence of sexual abuse, Diana Russell's survey of women in the San Francisco area found that 38 percent had experienced intra- or extrafamilial sexual abuse by the time they reached 18.[73]

CAUSES OF CHILD ABUSE

Why do parents physically assault their children? Such maltreatment is a highly complex problem with neither a single cause nor a readily available solution. It cuts across ethnic, religious, and socioeconomic backgrounds. Abusive parents cannot be categorized by sex, age, or educational level; they are persons from all walks of life. Some general factors do seem to be present with some frequency in families in which abuse and neglect take place. One factor is familial stress. Abusive parents are unable to cope with life crises—divorce, financial problems, alcohol and drug abuse, poor housing conditions. This inability leads them to maltreat their children.

Statistics also show that a high rate of assault on children occurs among the lower economic classes. This had led to the misconception that lower-class parents are more abusive than those in the upper class. However, two conditions may account for this discrepancy. First, low-income people are often subject to greater levels of environmental stress and have fewer resources available to deal with such stress. Second, cases of abuse among poor families are more likely to be dealt with by public agencies and therefore are more frequently counted in official statistics.[74]

Two other factors have a direct correlation with abuse and neglect. First, parents who themselves suffered abuse as children tend to abuse their own children; second, isolated and alienated families tend to become abusive. A cyclical pattern of family violence seems to be perpetuated from one generation to another within families. Evidence indicates that a large number of abused and neglected children grow into adolescence and adulthood with a tendency to engage in violent behavior. The behavior of abusive parents can often be traced to negative experiences in their own childhood—physical abuse, lack of love, emotional neglect, incest, and so on. These parents become unable to separate their own childhood traumas from their relationships with their children. They also often have unrealistic perceptions of the appropriate stages of childhood development. Thus, when their children are unable to act "appropriately"—when they cry, throw food, or strike their parents— the parents may react in an abusive manner. For parents such as these, "the axiom about not being able to love when you have not known love yourself is painfully borne out in their case histories. . . . They spend their days going around the house, ticking away like unexploded bombs. A fussy baby can be the lighted match."[75]

Parents also become abusive if they are isolated from friends, neighbors, or relatives who can provide a lifeline in times of crisis:

> Potentially or actually abusing parents are those who live in states of alienation from society, couples who have carried the concept of the shrinking nuclear family to its most extreme form, cut off as they are from ties of kinship and contact with other people in the neighborhood.[76]

Many abusive and neglectful parents describe themselves as highly alienated from their families and lacking close relationships with persons who could provide help and support in stressful situations.

It would be misleading to pinpoint any one factor as a definitive explanation of why abuse and neglect occur. It does seem, however, that a combination of the following elements is likely to result in parental maltreatment of children:

- The parents have a history of having been abused, neglected, or deprived as children.
- The parents are isolated, with no lifeline for help in a crisis.
- The parents perceive their child as disappointing in some way.
- A crisis precipitates the abuse.[77]

CHILD PROTECTION

Parents who assault their children are subject to prosecution in criminal courts under the traditional statutes against assault and battery. Though special abuse laws exist in each state, they are generally more concerned with the care and protection of children than the punishment of parents.

Abuse cases are referred to family or juvenile courts. Children are represented by a court-appointed attorney called a **guardian ad litem**. If parents are found to be abusive, the child can be removed from the home while treatment is provided. In severe cases, the court has the right to terminate the rights of parents over their children and place battered children in permanent foster care. This is actually a rare occurrence, since courts are reluctant to destroy intact families.

Although an increased awareness of the child abuse syndrome has led to the development of programs designed to treat assaultive parents, the fact that most abuse occurs behind closed doors makes it difficult to eliminate this social problem. The reporting of child abuse by doctors, social workers, and other such persons is mandated by law. Nonetheless, it is difficult to isolate child abuse from accidents or other unintentional physical harm.

SPOUSE ABUSE

Spouse abuse, which involves the physical assault of a wife by a husband (though husband abuse is not unknown), has occurred throughout recorded history. During the Roman era, men had the legal right to beat their wives for minor acts such as attending public games without permission, drinking wine, or walking outdoors with their faces uncovered.[78] More serious transgressions, such as adultery, were punishable by death. During the later stages of the Roman Empire, the practice of wife beating abated; and by the fourth century A.D., excessive violence on the part of husband or wife could be used as sufficient grounds for divorce.[79]

Later, during the early Middle Ages, there was a separation between love and marriage.[80] The ideal woman was protected and cherished. The wife, with whom marriage had been arranged by family ties, was guarded jealously and could be punished severely for violations of duty. A husband was expected to beat his wife for "misbehaviors" and might himself be punished by neighbors if he failed to do so.[81] Through the later Middle Ages and into modern times—that is, from 1400 to 1900—there was little objection within the community to a man's using force against his wife as long as the assaults did not exceed certain limits, usually construed as death or disfigurement. By the mid-nineteenth century, severe wife beating fell into disfavor; and accused wife beaters were subject to public ridicule. Nonetheless, limited chastisement was still the rule.

By the close of the nineteenth century, laws had been passed in England and the United States outlawing wife beating. Yet the long history of husbands' domination of their wives' lives made physical coercion hard to control. Until recent times, the subordinate position of women in the family was believed to give husbands the legal and moral obligation to manage their wives' behavior. These ideas form the foundation of men's traditional physical control of women and have led to severe cases of spousal assault.

The Nature and Extent of Spouse Abuse. It is difficult to estimate the extent of spouse abuse today; however, some statistics give indications of the extent of the problem. In their national survey of family violence, Gelles and Straus found that 16 percent of surveyed families had experienced husband/wife assaults. In police departments around the country, 60 to 70 percent of evening calls involve domestic disputes. In a one-year period, the New York City police recorded 14,167 complaints involving wife abuse.

What are the characteristics of the wife assaulter? After a careful analysis of the factors correlated with spouse abuse, a criminologist, Graeme Newman, has identified the following traits:[82]

- Presence of alcohol. Excessive alcohol use may turn otherwise docile husbands into wife assaulters.
- Hostility dependency. Some husbands who appear docile and passive may resent their dependency on their wives and react with rage and violence; this factor has been linked to sexual inadequacy.
- Excessive brooding. Obsession with a wife's behavior, however trivial, can result in violent assaults.
- Social approval. Some husbands believe that society approves of wife assault and use these beliefs to justify their violent behavior.
- Socioeconomic factors. Men who fail as providers and are under economic stress may take their frustrations out on their wives.
- Flash of anger. Research shows that a significant amount of family violence resulted from a sudden burst of anger after a verbal dispute.
- Military service. Spouse abuse among men who have seen military service is extremely high. Similarly, those currently serving in the military are more likely to assault their wives than civilian husbands. The reasons for this phenomenon may be (a) the violence promoted by military training and (b) the close proximity of military families to one another.
- Having been battered children. Husbands who assault their wives were battered as children.

A growing amount of support is being given to battered women. Shelters for assaulted wives are springing up around the country, and laws are being passed to protect a wife's interests. It is essential that this problem be brought to public light and controlled.

Efforts to help victims of domestic violence are being increased.

The following Close-Up reports on a recent federal survey on the extent of violence within the family.

Robbery

The common-law definition of robbery, and the one used by the FBI, is "the taking or attempting to take anything of value from the care, custody or control of a person or persons by force or threat of force or violence and/or by putting the victim in fear."[83] A robbery is a crime of violence because it involves the use of force to obtain money or goods. Robbery is punished severely because the victim's life is put in jeopardy; the value of the items taken has nothing to do with the punishment meted out.

Like other violent crimes, the robbery rate has declined in recent years. In 1983, 500,221 robberies were reported, a rate of 213 per 100,000 population. These figures reflect a decline of 8 percent in volume and 9 percent in rate from the year before. In 1984, robberies declined an additional 5 percent (485,000 crimes).

The ecologic pattern for robbery is similar to that of other violent crimes, with two major discrepancies. First, northeastern states have by far the highest robbery rate (314 per 100,000) while the South, which has high rates for other violent crimes, reported 171 robberies per 100,000 population. Second, minorities made up an even more significant portion of all persons arrested for robbery (63 percent) than they did for other violent crimes.

NCS data indicate that robbery is more of a problem than the FBI data show; according to the NCS, about 1.3 million robberies are committed each year. The two data sources agree, however, on the age, race, and sexual makeup of the offenders—they are disproportionately young, male, and minority.

Family Violence

Patsy Klaus and Michael Rand, two researchers at the Federal Government's Bureau of Justice Statistics, used National Crime Survey data collected between 1973 and 1981 to create a profile of family violence in the United States. The following are the most significant of their findings.

Overall, the National Crime Survey shows:

• Crimes by spouses or ex-spouses make up the majority—57 percent—of all crimes committed by relatives measured by the survey (table A). The NCS questionnaire does not separate spouse and ex-spouse offenders, so these categories must remain combined in this analysis.

the previous six months. Such serial victimization occurs at the hands of parents, siblings, or "other" relatives to a somewhat lesser degree (15 percent, 13 percent and 11 percent, respectively). By contrast, persons violently victimized by nonrelatives (i.e., ac-

TABLE A. Estimated family violence reported to NCS, by relationship of offender to victim

Relationship	1973-81 Total	Yearly average
Total by all relatives	4,108,000	456,000
Spouses or ex-spouses	2,333,000	259,000
Parents	263,000	29,000
Children	173,000	19,000
Brothers or sisters	351,000	39,000
Other relatives	988,000	110,000

All estimates rounded to nearest thousand.

• Of the crimes committed by relatives measured by the NCS, 88 percent were assaults, 10 percent were robberies, and 2 percent were rapes. Of the assaults, about a third were aggravated, indicating use of a weapon, a serious injury, or both. The remaining two-thirds were simple assaults, indicating either a minor injury or a threat of harm.
• About a quarter of the victims of attack by their spouses or ex-spouses reported that they had been the victim of a series of similar crimes (at least three) within

quaintances or strangers) were victims of a series of similar crimes in only 9 percent of all victimizations.

CHARACTERISTICS OF VICTIMS OF FAMILY VIOLENCE

• NCS data show that women were victims of family violence at a rate three times that of men. In fact, violent crimes between siblings was the only category for which males and females were victimized about

THE ECOLOGY OF ROBBERY

Most robberies committed in the United States were accompanied by the use of some kind of weapon. In 1983, about 37 percent of all robberies involved the use of firearms; 40 percent, "strong-arm tactics" (hands, fist, feet, and the like); 13 percent, knives or cutting instruments; and 9 percent, other weapons.[84]

Robbery is most often a street crime—that is, fewer robberies occur in the home than in public places such as parks, streets, and alleys. For example, 25 percent of rapes reported by victims to NCS researchers occurred in the home, but only 13 percent of reported robberies. About 56 percent of robberies occurred in streets, parks, and fields.

The public nature of robbery has had a great influence on people's behavior. Most people believe that large cities suffer the most serious instances of violent equally. Interestingly, while males appear to attack other male relatives about as often as they do females, females attack other female relatives about three times as often as they do other male relatives.

- Of all spousal violent crimes reported to NCS, 91 percent were victimizations of women by their husbands or ex-husbands, who acted alone while committing the offense. Five percent were victimizations by wives or ex-wives alone; the remainder were primarily victimizations by a spouse or ex-spouse in concert with another offender.
- About half of the victims of family violence (49 percent) reported being injured in the attack, though 80 percent of the injured said that they suffered no worse than cuts and bruises. Persons victimized by all other related (nonspouse) persons or unrelated persons suffered injury in a lesser percentage of victimizations (38 percent and 27 percent, respectively). In 20 percent of all spousal violent crime, the victim needed or obtained medical attention: 8 percent from a doctor, 9 percent from a hospital emergency room, and 3 percent from overnight hospital care.
- Victims resisted about 75 percent of attacks by their relatives, but this resistance usually took a passive form, such as trying to reason with the offender or trying to get away or obtain help. Victims of attacks by relatives offered active resistance (using or trying to use physical force or a weapon) about half as often as passive resistance.
- Judging from incidents reported to interviewers, lower income persons and those in the twenty to thirty-four age range were more likely than other age or income groups to be victims of family violence. No difference was detected in the victimization rates of blacks and whites for violent crimes by spouses or ex-spouses; however, blacks reported violence by relatives other than spouses to a higher degree than did whites.
- Although divorced and separated people make up only 7 percent of the population age twelve and over, about 75 percent of the spousal violence reported in the survey involved persons who were divorced or separated. Because limitations in the data make it impossible to determine whether the incidents occurred before or after a marital separation, this finding is open to several interpretations. It is possible that women who were still married at the time of the interview were either much more reluctant than divorced or separated women to report violence committed by their spouses or else less likely to consider such violence a criminal act. A related theory is that divorced or separated women feel more free than married women living with their spouses to discuss violence by their ex-spouses that preceded their separation or divorce. Alternatively, it may be that after a separation or divorce, men commit more violence against their ex-spouses than they did while still married. Another possibility is that divorced or separated women perceive actions to be criminal that they did not view in that way while living with their husbands.

CHARACTERISTICS OF FAMILY VIOLENT CRIME

- Crimes by spouses and ex-spouses are almost always committed by the offender acting alone; however, crimes by siblings and by other relatives are committed by two or more offenders a significant part of the time (18 percent and 15 percent, respectively).
- About 57 percent of the spousal assaults reported to the NCS were actual attacks; the rest were attempted attacks or threats of violence. In contrast, only about 38 percent of all other victimizations by relatives were completed assaults.

DISCUSSION QUESTIONS

1. Do you know of families that experience violence? Are the police aware of the problem?
2. Is it better to remove children from violence-prone families?

SOURCE. Patsy Klaus and Michael Rand, *Family Violence* (Washington, D.C.: U.S. Department of Justice, Bureau of Justice Statistics, 1984).

crimes such as robbery; and, not surprisingly, many people have moved out of inner-city areas into suburban communities.

ROBBER TYPOLOGIES

Attempts have been made to classify and explain the nature and dynamics of robbery. In a study conducted in London, F. H. McClintock and Evelyn Gibson found that robbery follows one of five patterns:[85]

1. Robbery of persons who, as part of their employment, are in charge of money or goods. This category includes robberies in jewelry stores, banks, offices, and other places in which money changes hands. In recent years, the rate of this category of robbery has dramatically increased. For example,

robberies of convenience and grocery stores increased 47 percent between 1976 and 1980, while bank robbery was up 71 percent, commercial house robbery up 20 percent, and gas station robbery up 5 percent.

2. **Robbery in an open area.** These robberies include street offenses, muggings, purse snatchings, and other attacks. In urban areas, this type of robbery constitutes about 60 percent of reported totals; and nationally, street robberies have increased 45 percent in the past four years. Street robbery is most closely associated with *mugging* or *yoking*—grabbing victims from behind and threatening them with a weapon.

3. **Robbery on private premises.** This type of robbery involves robbing people after breaking into homes. FBI records indicate that this type of robbery accounts for about 10 percent of offenses.

4. **Robbery after preliminary association of short duration.** This type of robbery comes in the aftermath of a chance encounter—in a bar, at a party, or after a sexual encounter.

5. **Robbery after previous association of some duration between the victim and offender.** Incidents in patterns 4 and 5 are substantially less common than stranger-to-stranger robberies, which account for more than 75 percent of the total.

Another well-known robbery typology has been created by John Conklin. Instead of focusing on the nature of robbery incidents, Conklin categorizes robber types into the following various specialties.[86]

Professional Robber. Professionals are those who "manifest a long-term commitment to crime as a source of livelihood, who plan and organize their crimes prior to committing them, and who seek money to support a particular lifestyle that may be called hedonistic." Some professionals are exclusively robbers, while others may engage in other types of crimes. Professionals are committed to robbing because it is direct, fast, and very profitable. They hold no other steady job and plan three or four "big scores" a year to support themselves. Planning and skill are the trademark of the professional robber. Operating in groups in which assigned roles are the rule, professionals usually steal large amounts from commercial establishments. After a score, they may take a few weeks off until "things cool off."

Opportunist Robber. Opportunists steal to obtain small amounts of money when an accessible and vulnerable target presents itself. They are not committed to robbery but will steal from cab drivers, drunks, the elderly, and other such persons if they need some extra spending money for clothes or other elements of their lifestyle. Opportunists are usually young minority group members who do not plan their crimes. Although they operate within the milieu of the juvenile gang, they are seldom organized and spend little time discussing weapon use, getaway plans, or other strategies.

Addict Robber. Addict robbers steal to support their drug habits. They have a low commitment to robbery because of its danger but a high commitment to theft because it supplies needed funds. The addict is less likely to plan crime or use weapons than the professional robber but is more cautious than the opportunist. Addicts choose targets that present a minimum of risk; however, when desperate for funds, they are sometimes careless in selecting the victim and executing the crime. They rarely think in terms of the big score; they only want enough money to get their next fix.

Alcoholic Robber. Many robbers steal for reasons related to their excessive consumption of alcohol. Alcoholic robbers steal (1) when, in a disoriented state, they attempt to get some money to buy liquor or (2) when their condition makes them unemployable and they need funds. Alcoholic robbers have no real commitment to robbery as a way of life. They plan their crimes randomly and give little thought to victim, circumstances, or escape; for that reason, they are the most likely to be caught.

Controlling Interpersonal Violence

Despite a recent respite in the crime rate (though rape and assault rates increased in 1984), interpersonal violence continues to provoke fear in the American public. How can it be controlled? The most common approach is to deter crime through fear of the law and, if deterrence fails, incapacitate known offenders in prison. Yet the nature of violent crime itself often defeats these social control measures. For example, violence may result from an emotion-laden personal experience, difficult to control by conventional means. As you may recall, many murderers knew their victims beforehand and their actions may have been precipitated through some sort of interpersonal transaction. Or violence can be triggered by a personality disturbance whose very nature makes the threat of punishment ineffective.

What alternatives have been suggested, then, to reduce violence? Certainly one approach is to reduce the root causes of crime—poverty, social inequality, racism, and so on. Yet to be effective such measures must be carried out on a scale that heretofore has seemed impossible.

A more conservative approach has been to encourage community cooperation with police, improve police effectiveness, create longer prison sentences for repeat or violent offenders, discourage plea bargaining, use the death penalty, and so on. With this approach we may not be able to control or prevent violence before it occurs, but we can lower violence rates if the most violence-prone people can be removed from society. Though it is in vogue today, this policy has had the unfortunate side effect of creating an overcrowded prison system whose clientele are actively recruited for terror groups such as the Aryan Nation and Black Liberation Army.

The physical environment has also been the focus of violence-control efforts. In the 1970s Oscar Newman's concept of **defensible space** was in vogue. Newman argued that "targets" could be hardened or protected, street lighting improved, surveillance made easier, and people given a sense of belonging or territoriality.[87] However, attempts to operationalize Newman's ideas did not meet with any clear-cut success.[88]

Today in the mid-1980s, the emphasis in controlling violence is on identifying chronic violent offenders (the chronic 6 percent) and tailoring long prison sentences for them. Such measures may work in an era of declining crime rates, but the economic costs may be staggering if the crime rate escalates as predicted in the 1990s (see chapter 4).

GUN CONTROL

One method long advocated for controlling interpersonal violence has been handgun control. The FBI usually finds that about half of all murders and a third of all rapes and robberies are committed with a handgun. Handguns were the cause of death for two-thirds of all police killed in the line of duty. Considering the estimated 30-50 million illegal handguns in the United States today, these findings should certainly not be surprising![89]

Efforts to control handguns have many different sources. Each state and many local jurisdictions have laws banning or restricting sales or possession of guns. Others regulate dealers who sell guns. For example, the Federal Gun Control Act of 1968 prohibits dealers from selling guns to minors, ex-felons, drug users, and so on. In addition, each dealer must keep detailed records of who purchases guns. Unfortunately, the resources available to enforce this law are meager.[90]

Do strict gun control laws make a difference in the violent crime rate? The jury is still out on this issue. The most famous attempt to regulate handguns is the Massachusetts Bartley-Fox Law, which provides a mandatory one-year prison term for possession of a handgun (outside the home) without a permit. A detailed analysis of violent crime in Boston in the years after the law's passage found that the use of handguns in robberies and murders did decline substantially (robbery 35 percent, and murder 55 percent in a two-year period). However, these optimistic results must be tempered by two facts: rates for similar crimes dropped significantly in comparable cities that did not have gun control laws; the use of other weapons, such as knives, increased.[91]

Another gun control method is to add an extra punishment for any crime involving a handgun. A well-known example is Michigan's Felony Firearm Statute, which requires that anyone convicted of a crime in which a handgun was used receive an additional two years tacked on to their sentence. An analysis by Colin Loftin and his associates found that the Michigan law had (1) little effect on the sentence given to convicted offenders, and (2) little effect on violent crime in Detroit.[92]

Similarly, in a study evaluating the handgun laws of all fifty states, David Lester found little evidence that strict handgun laws influence homicide rates.[93]

The use of handguns in political crimes, such as the Robert Kennedy assassination, has spurred a majority of Americans to advocate controls of the sale of handguns, and a ban on cheap "Saturday Night Specials." Some conservatives view gun control as a threat to personal liberty and call instead for severe punishment of criminals rather than control of handguns. In either event, gun control efforts may have little effect on violence.[94] There are so many guns in the United States that banning their manufacture would have a relatively small effect for years to come. And if they are made more valuable by banning their manufacture or sale, illegal overseas importation of guns might increase, as it has for another controlled substance—narcotics. Increasing penalties for gun-related crimes has also met with limited success, since judges may be reluctant to alter their sentencing policies to accommodate legislators. Regulating dealers is difficult and would only encourage private sales and bartering. Nonetheless, some combination of control and penalty may prove useful and efforts should be made to discover, if at all possible, whether handgun control could indeed reduce violent crime rates.

Political Violence

While interpersonal violence and street crime have been on most people's minds, many people are also very concerned about violence against the state, or political violence. Every day seems to bring news of terrorist plots, bombings, and assassinations. Yet these activities represent only a small aspect of the entire range of activity engaged in by political criminals.

Political crime has been with us throughout history. Stephen Schafer maintains that it is virtually impossible to find a history book of any society that does not record the existence of political criminals, "those craftsmen of dreams who possess a gigantic reservoir of creative energy as well as destructive force."[95]

Political crime can be defined in various ways. Barton Ingraham suggests that it can be divided into two broad categories: (1) acts that are seen as involving betrayal of allegiance to principles or persons that bind the political order, and (2) acts that are viewed as involving a challenge to or hindrance of political authority.[96]

Ernest Van Den Haag views political crimes as law violations used to (1) acquire power, (2) exercise power, (3) challenge authority, and (4) enforce authority.[97]

It is often difficult to separate violent political crimes from interpersonal crimes of violence. For example, if a group robs a bank in order to obtain funds for its revolutionary struggles, should the act be treated as a political crime or a common bank robbery? In this instance, the definition of a crime as political depends on the kind of legal response the act evokes from those in power. To be a political crime, an act must carry with it the intent to disrupt and change the government and must not merely be a simple common-law crime committed for reasons of greed or egotism. Schafer refers to those who violate the law because they believe their actions will ultimately benefit society as **convictional criminals**. They are constantly caught in the dilemma of knowing their actions may be wrong and harmful but also believing these actions are necessary to create the changes they fervently desire. "A member of the Second World War Resistance," Schafer argues, "may have condemned violence, yet his own conviction overshadowed any sense of repugnance and induced him to engage in violent crimes in an effort to expel the invader from his Fatherland."[98]

TERRORISM

One aspect of political violence that is of great concern to criminologists is **terrorism**.[99] Terrorism has been defined by the National Advisory Commission on Criminal Justice as "a tactic or technique by means of which a violent act or the threat thereof is used for the prime purpose of creating overwhelming fear for coercive purposes."[100] Terrorism is a type of political crime that emphasizes violence as a mechanism to promote change. Whereas other political criminals may engage in acts such as demonstrating, counterfeiting, selling secrets, spying, and the like, terrorists make systematic use of murder and destruction or the threat of such violence to terrorize individuals, groups, communities, or governments into conceding to the terrorists' political demands.[101]

The term *terrorist* is often used interchangeably with the term *guerrilla*. The latter term, meaning "little war," developed out of the rebellion directed against French troops by Spanish rebels after Napoleon's invasion of the Iberian peninsula in 1808.[102] Daniel Georges-Abeyie distinguishes between the two terms by suggesting that terrorists have an urban focus; that the objects of their attacks include the property and persons of civilians; and that they operate in small bands, or cadres, of three to five members.[103] Guerrillas are located in rural areas; the objects of their attacks include the military, the police, and government officials; and their organization can grow quite large and eventually take the form of a conventional military force. However, guerrillas can infiltrate urban areas in small bands, while terrorists can make forays into the countryside; consequently, the terms have come to be used interchangeably.[104]

Today, terrorism is used to promote political goals. Terrorists use violence as a tool to invoke fear in those in power and in those who support authority. Terrorist actions—kidnapping, assassination, bombing—are used to draw repressive responses from governments trying to defend themselves. These responses help revolutionaries to expose, through the skilled use of media coverage, the governments' antihuman nature. The original reason for the governments' harsh response may be lost as the effect of counterterrorist activities is felt by noninvolved people.

HISTORICAL PERSPECTIVE

Acts of terrorism have been known throughout history. The assassination of Julius Caesar on 15 March, 44 B.C. can be considered an act of terrorism. Terrorism became widespread at the end of the Middle Ages, when political leaders were subject to assassination by their enemies. The word *assassin* was derived from an Arabic term meaning "hashish-eater"; it referred to members of a drug-using Moslem terrorist organization that carried out plots against prominent Christians and other religious enemies.[105] At a time when rulers were absolute despots, terrorist acts were viewed as one of the only means of gaining political rights. At times, European states encouraged terrorist acts against their enemies. For example, Queen Elizabeth I empowered her "sea-dogs," John Hawkins and Francis Drake, to carry out attacks against the Spanish Fleet. These privateers would have been considered pirates had they not operated with government approval. American privateers operated against the British during the Revolution and the War of 1812. As you can see, history can turn terrorists into heroes, depending on whose side wins.

The term *terrorist* became popular during the French Revolution. From the fall of the Bastille on 14 July 1789, until July 1794, thousands suspected of counterrevolutionary activity went to their deaths on the guillotine. Here again the relative nature of political crime is documented: while most victims of the French terror were revolutionaries who had been denounced by rival factions, thousands of members of the hated nobility lived their lives in relative tranquility. The end of the terror was signaled by the death of its prime mover, Maximilien Robespierre, on 28 July 1794, as the result of a successful plot to end his rule; he was executed on the same guillotine to which he sent almost 20,000 people to their deaths. In the hundred years after the French Revolution, terrorism continued around the world. The Hur Brotherhood in India was made up of religious fanatics who carried out terrorist acts.[106] In Eastern Europe, the Internal Macedonian Revolutionary Organization (IMRO) campaigned against the Turkish government, which controlled its homeland (Macedonia is now part of Yugoslavia). Similarly, the protest of the Union of Death Society, or Black Hand, against the Austro-Hungarian empire's control of Serbia led to the group's assassination of Archduke Franz Ferdinand, an act that signalled the beginning of World War I. The Irish Republic Army (IRA) developed around 1916 and kept up a steady battle with British forces from 1919 to 1923, culminating in the southern part of Ireland's gaining independence.

Between the world wars, right-wing terrorism existed in Germany, Spain, and Italy, while Russia was the scene of left-wing revolutionary activity leading to the death of the czar and the rise of the Marxist state. During World War II, resistance to the Germans was common throughout Europe; these terrorists are now, of course, considered heroes. In Palestine, Jewish terrorist groups—the Haganah, Irgun, and Stern Gang, whose leaders included Menachim Begin—waged war against the

British to force them to allow Jewish survivors of the Holocaust to settle in their traditional homeland.

U.S. TERRORISM TODAY

It is difficult to provide an up-to-date assessment of terrorist activity in modern times, since the national and international scene has been changing so rapidly. However, some general observations can be made about the nature and extent of terrorist activity today.

In the United States, terrorist activities are being carried out by several groups. The Armed Forces of National Liberation for Pureto Rico (FALN) has supported the goal of independence for Puerto Rico and the Puerto Rican Socialist Party. It has claimed responsibility for more than a hundred bomb attacks in New York, Washington, and Chicago. On the West Coast, the New World Liberation Front (NWLF), a Marxist/Leninist group that advocates the overthrow of the U.S. government and corporate interests, has been active since 1974. It has claimed to be responsible for more than forty bombings, including one that caused $1 million worth of damage at the Hearst Castle at San Simeon, California. The NWLF has been closely associated with other groups, including the Friends and Neighbors of the Poor (FNP), the People's Light Brigade (PLB), and the Johnathon Jackson Brigade; these groups have claimed responsibility for bombings of stores, government offices, and power stations on the West Coast.[107]

During the 1960s and early 1970s, terrorist groups grew up around the dual themes of racial conflict and antiimperialism. Fueled by antiwar sentiment, the Revolutionary Action Movement (RAM), the Black Liberation Army (BLA), and the Weather Underground were quite active. After the riots at the 1968 Democratic convention in Chicago, commonly called the "Days of Rage," many of these groups went underground—that is, they submerged from public view. Years later, one clique of the Weather Underground, the best-known radical group, split off from the main organization and formed the above-ground Prairie Fire Organizing Committee in order to better recruit new members. The organization's leaders were arrested in 1977 on the charge of recruiting members for an underground group whose primary objective was the assassination of public figures and bombing of public buildings. These arrests caused the demise of Prairie Fire.[108] However, other members of the Weather Underground, led by Bernadine Dohrn, continued their antigovernment activities. When Dohrn surrendered to authorities after ten years as a fugitive, the Weather Underground appeared defunct. Then, in October 1981, a series of robberies and killings in New York linked the Weather Underground with elements of the Black Liberation Army, the Black Panthers, and several European groups, including the Irish Republican Army (IRA). Kathy Boudin, another Weather Underground leader, who had been a fugitive for eleven years, was arrested in connection with a robbery and killing of two police officers. By December 1981, the FBI was able to state: "The Weather Underground is not a viable organization. There is no evidence that such an organization is functioning."[109] However, other groups such as the Sam Melville-Jonathon Jackson unit continue to operate despite arrests of their leaders. The following Close-Up describes the activities of two such groups.

Right-Wing Terrorism. Whereas the above-mentioned groups have a left-wing orientation, there is growing awareness of political violence associated with ultra-

Terrorist Groups

The activities and motives of two U.S.-based terrorist groups are described below.

RED GUERRILLA RESISTANCE

This group was responsible for a total of three incidents in 1984.

The Red Guerrilla Resistance (RGR) became known on 5 April 1984, when it claimed credit for a bombing at Israeli Aircraft Industries, New York, New York. Since then, the group has also claimed credit for two additional bombings. The motivations for the bombings, according to communiqués received, included protest against American and Israeli imperialism and militarism in the Middle East, Central and Latin America, Puerto Rico, and the Caribbean; and against South African apartheid policies.

On 5 April 1984, two bombs detonated at the office of Israeli Aircraft International, Inc. (IAII)—a non-Israeli government company—in New York, New York, causing extensive damage. A warning call was received at United Press International from an unknown male who identified himself as a member of the RGR and stated, "We bombed the IAII Office, free Palestinians, down with Zionism . . ."

Killed: 0   Injured: 0

On 20 April 1984 at approximately 1:55 A.M., an improvised explosive device detonated at the Washington Navy Yard, Officer's Club, Washington, D.C., causing extensive damage. The United Press International and the *Washington Post* newspaper received recorded telephone calls, during which the called stated, "The Guerrilla Resistance (inaudible) at 2 A.M. bombed the Officer's Club at the Washington Navy Yard to protest the (inaudible) war games, the United States Imperialist War in Central America, and the Caribbean." Also mentioned was the Frente Farabundo Marti de Liberacion Nacional, Frente Democratio Revolucionario, and the Puerto Rico Independence Movement.

Killed: 0   Injured: 0

On 26 September 1984 at approximately 12:23 A.M., a bomb detonated in the twelfth-floor stairway of the thirty-three-floor structure housing the South African Consulate, located at 425 Park Avenue, New York, New York, causing extensive damage. No injuries were reported. The bombing was preceded by a warning call to the building's security guard. The Associated Press received a recorded telephone call in which the Red

conservative right-wing groups. These tend to be heavily armed groups organized around such themes as white supremacy, Nazism, militant tax resistance, and religious revisionism. Identified groups include the Aryan Nation, the Order, the Brotherhood, Posse Comitatus, Silent Brotherhood, and the White American Bastion, as well as the traditional Ku Klux Klan organizations. Some of these groups have formed their own churches; for example, the Church of Jesus Christ Christian, which claims that Jesus was born an Aryan rather than a Jew and that white Anglo-Saxons are the true "chosen people."[110]

Right-wing political violence first became national news when in 1983 Posse Comitatus member Gordon Kahl murdered two federal marshalls in North Dakota and was later slain in a gun battle with federal agents in Arkansas. On 9 December 1984, Robert Matthews, leader of The Order, was killed in a shootout on Whidby Island off Seattle, Washington. The government's interest in right-wing groups is heightened since some have declared war on the United States and made officials and federal agents top enemies.[111]

INTERNATIONAL TERRORISM

On the international scene, terrorism for political purposes has been much more extensive than in the United States.[112] In many instances, Marxist terrorist groups have been pitted against capitalist governments. In Germany, the Marxist Baader-Meinhoff group conducted a series of robberies, bombings, and kidnappings; in Italy, the Red Brigade succeeded in kidnapping and executing a former Italian president, Albert Moro.

Guerrilla Resistance claimed responsibility, stating that the bombing was to show solidarity with the South African Human Rights Movement. A Red Guerrilla Resistance communiqué was also located.

Killed: 0   Injured: 0

MAY 19TH COMMUNIST ORGANIZATION

The May 19th Communist Organization (M19CO) is a Marxist-Leninist group which openly advocates the overthrow of the U.S. government through armed struggle and the use of violence. Its members have been linked with other known domestic terrorist organizations such as the Fuerzas Armadas de Liberacion Nacional (FALN), Republic of New Afrika, and remnants of the Weather Underground Organization and the Black Liberation Army.

On 29 November 1984, Susan Lisa Rosenberg and Timothy A. Blunk, reputed M19CO members, were arrested by local authorities and subsequently indicted on Federal charges.

At the time of their arrests, Rosenberg and Blunk were in possession of a huge cache of explosives* and numerous weapons. Rosenberg had been a Federal fugitive since 1982, on charges in connection with the November 1979 prison escape of the alleged leader of the Black Liberation Army, Joanne Chesimard, who is currently an FBI fugitive, as well as the 20 October 1981 Brink's robbery and slayings in Nanuet, New York. Rosenberg has been charged with participation in the planning of this holdup and subsequent shootout, which left a guard and two police officers dead.

FBI investigation indicates that Blunk and another M19CO member, Alan Berkman, also an FBI fugitive wanted as an accessory in the aforementioned 1981 Brink's robbery and slayings in Nanuet, New York, were involved in the 2 September 1984 robbery of a Stop and Shop Supermarket in Cromwell, Connecticut.

Killed: 0   Injured: 0

*Experts determined that part of the explosives seized were from a cache stolen in Austin, Texas in 1980.

DISCUSSION QUESTIONS

1. Do you think the United States will be subject to increased numbers of terrorist attacks in the future?
2. Should terrorist demands ever be given in to?

SOURCE. Federal Bureau of Investigation, "FBI Analysis of Terrorist Incidents and Terrorist-Related Activities in the United States, 1984," 31 December 1984. Mimeo.

When the Red Brigade kidnapped James Dozier, a U.S. general, in Italy during December 1981, it issued a communiqué that sums up the Marxist group's goals for Europe: To wage war against the Western powers; to prevent a buildup of nuclear arms by NATO (North Atlantic Treaty Organization) in Europe; and to cause dissension in chief NATO countries such as Italy, Germany, and Spain.[113] The recapture of General Dozier by Italian police temporarily interrupted the power of terrorists in Italy. Yet in November 1984, the Italian secret service was barely able to disrupt a plot to blow up the U.S. embassy in Rome. The plot was hatched by a new terrorist threat—agents of Islamic Jihad, the group claiming responsibility for the 1983 bombing of the U.S. Marine compound in Beirut, in which 241 Americans died.[114] A few weeks later, Italian authorities were not so lucky: On December 23 the Naples-Milan train was bombed, killing 15 and wounding 80 others.[115]

It has become common to link left-wing terrorism abroad with the Libyan government's efforts to sponsor terrorist groups. The "Libyan Connection" has been linked to numerous Middle East and European organizations. The shoot-out in London in April 1984 in front of the Libyan embassy brought to a head the subversive activities of so-called diplomats acting as political assassins.[116] Though a British policewoman was killed, the British government's reaction was merely to expel the embassy staff. Such reaction is markedly different from that of another target of Libyan-sponsored terrorism—Israel—whose "Iron Fist" policy demands retribution in blood for any terrorist act.[117]

Not all terrorist activity abroad is left-oriented. Many nationalist groups such as the Irish Republican Army, the Palestine Liberation Organization (PLO), and

Sikh radicals use violence for the purpose of recovering what they believe to be lost homelands. Sikh militants, you may recall, were responsible for Indian leader Indira Gandhi's assassination on 6 November 1984 in retaliation for the government's storming of their Golden Temple religious shrine (and revolutionary base) in June 1984.[118]

THE EXTENT OF TERRORISM

It is difficult to estimate the total number of violent terrorist acts around the world. In West Germany, for example, about 150–200 terrorist acts are committed each year. In the United States, the government estimates that 60,000 left-wing and 22,000 right-wing terrorists are operating. The U.S. State Department counted 401 incidents against U.S. citizens and property in 1982, and 393 in 1983.[119]

In 1983, 274 U.S. citizens were killed and 118 wounded (most of them in the Beirut bombing). In addition, the FBI found that 38 bombings were claimed by terrorist groups in the United States in 1982, and 22 in 1983.[120] In 1984, the number of domestic terrorist attacks declined to 13.[121]

During the past decade, between 13 and 120 terrorist acts have taken place in the United States each year. However, with the intensified activity of both right- and left-wing groups, this number may soon rise. Similarly, international terrorism is growing by leaps and bounds. The events of the week of 20 June 1985 are an example of heightened terrorist activity: Shiite Moslems kidnapped 40 Americans from a TWA flight[122]; guerrillas in El Salvador gunned down five Americans in a cafe; Sikhs claimed to have blown up a plane containing over 300 Indian passengers; bombs went off in a terminal in Japan, killing two. Terrorism on an international scale has reached epidemic proportions.

WHO IS THE TERRORIST?

Terrorists engage in criminal activities such as bombings, shootings, and kidnappings. What motivates these individuals to risk their lives and those of the innocent people who may fall victim to their activities. M. Cherif Bassiouni describes the process by which ideological terrorists become enmeshed in their activities as follows:

- Heightened perception of oppressive conditions—whether real or imaginary
- Recognition that such conditions are not the immutable order of things, but are amenable to active reform
- That action designed to promote change is not forthcoming
- That one must at last resort to violence
- That such action need not be successful, but only contribute to setting in motion a series of events enlisting others and leading to change (a realization that dissemination of the cause is more important than success of the action)
- That the individual's self-sacrifice outweighs the guilt borne by committing a violent act (thus, violence without guilt)
- That the cause transcends the need to rationalize the act of violence (the self-gratification merges with the higher purpose)[123]

According to Austin Turk, terrorists tend to come from upper- rather than lower-class backgrounds.[124] This may be because the upper classes can produce people who are more politically sensitive, articulate, and focused in their resentments. Since their position in the class structure gives them the feeling that they can influence or change society, upper-class citizens are more likely to seek confrontations with the authorities.

Class differences are also manifested in different approaches to political violence. The violence of the lower class is more often associated with spontaneous expressions of dissatisfaction, manifested in collective riots and rampages and politically inconsequential acts. Higher-class violence tends to be more calculated and organized and uses elaborate strategies of resistance. Revolutionary cells; campaigns of terror and assassination; logically complex and expensive assaults; and writing and disseminating formal critiques, manifestos, and theories are typically acts of the socially elite.

GOVERNMENTS' RESPONSES TO TERRORISM

Governments have attempted numerous responses to terrorism. Law enforcement agencies have infiltrated terrorist groups and turned members over to police.[125] Rewards have been given for information leading to the arrest of terrorists. "Democratic" elections have been held to discredit terrorists' complaints that the state is oppressive. Counterterrorism laws have been passed to increase penalties and decrease political rights. For example, Israel has passed the Administrative Detention Law, which allows searches and detention of suspected terrorists. The West German Contract Ban Law, passed in 1977, deals with terrorists as follows:

- Permits complete isolation of a terrorist inmate who is suspected of involvement in outside terrorist activities. This applies especially to his or her attorney.
- Provides for acceleration of court proceedings.
- Tightens the law on illegal possession of weapons.
- Introduces regulations for theft-proof license plates, plate numbers, and automobile papers.

In the United States, antiterrorist legislation and activities have not been closely coordinated. While the threat of skyjacking has been reduced by better airport security, other efforts have not been as successful.

The U.S. federal government entered into counterterrorist activities in 1972, when President Nixon formed the cabinet-level Committee to Combat Terrorism. However, no federal law has been passed to unify efforts against terrorists; and strict behavior codes have limited the activities of the FBI and the Central Intelligence Agency (CIA) in infiltrating terrorist groups. The United Nations has passed numerous resolutions condemning terrorism but has refrained from taking an active antiterrorist stance. Cooperation among countries has tended to be on an individual basis. For example, the United States and Cuba signed an antihijacking agreement on 15 February 1973.

Although the U.S. has stated a policy prohibiting violence or assassination attempts against suspected terrorists, both federal law enforcement agencies and the U.S. military have specially trained antiterrorist squads. The military, for example, has created the renowned Delta Force, made up of members from the four service areas.[126] Delta Force activities are generally secret, but it is known that the force saw action in Iran (1980), Honduras (1982), and Sudan (1983), and during the Grenada invasion (1983), and was prepared to take action against the hijacking of the ship the Achille Lauro (1985).

Despite the U.S. government's efforts to control terrorism, any attempts to meet force with force are fraught with danger. If the government's response is retaliation in kind, it could provoke increased terrorist activity—for revenge or to gain the release of captured comrades. Of course, a weak response may be interpreted as a license for terrorists to operate with impunity. The alternative is a prevention model. For example, the U.S. Congress is now considering such measures as putting U.S. Sky Marshalls on overseas flights, monitoring security at overseas airports, and so on. Nonetheless, preventing terrorism is a task that so far has stymied the governments of most of the world's nations.

Summary

People in the United States live in an extremely violent society. Among the various explanations for violent crimes, one postulates the existence of a subculture of violence that stresses violent solutions to interpersonal problems. Another view holds that humans may be instinctually violent. Still another claims that violence is related to economic inequality.

There are many types of interpersonal violent crime. Rape is defined as the carnal knowledge of a female forcibly and against her will. Rape has been known throughout history; at one time, it was believed that a woman was as guilty as her attacker for her rape. At present, 80,000 rapes are reported to police each year; but the true number is probably much higher. Rape is an extremely difficult charge to prove in court. The victim's lack of consent must be proven; therefore, it almost seems that the victim is on trial. Consequently, rape crisis centers to aid victims have been developed and changes in rape law and procedure are ongoing.

Murder is the unlawful killing of a human being with malice aforethought. There are different degrees of murder, and punishments vary accordingly. The murder rate has declined in the past few years to about eight per 100,000 people. One important characteristic of murder is that the victim and criminal often know each other. This has caused some criminologists to believe that murder is a victim-precipitated crime. Murder victims and offenders tend to be young, black, and male. There is also a tendency for the South to have a higher murder rate than other parts of the country.

Assault is another serious interpersonal violent crime. One important type of assault is that occuring in the home, including child abuse and spouse abuse. It has been estimated that almost 2 million children are abused by their parents each year and that 16 percent of families report husband/wife violence. It even appears there is a trend toward violence between dating couples on college campuses.

Robbery involves theft by force, usually in a public place. Types of offenders include professional, opportunist, addict, and alcoholic robbers.

Political violence is another serious problem. Many terrorist groups exist, both at the national and the international level. Hundreds of terrorist acts are reported each year in the United States alone. Terrorists may be motivated by criminal gain, psychosis, grievance against the state, or ideology.

Notes

1 Graeme Newman, *Understanding Violence* (New York: Lippincott, 1979), p. 89.

2 M. Hindelang, M. Gottfredson, and T. Flanagan, *Sourcebook of Criminal Justice Statistics, 1980* (Washington, D.C.: Government Printing Office, 1981), p. 171.

3 Hans Toch, *Violent Men* (Chicago: Aldine, 1969), p. 1.

4 Associated Press, "Girl Battles Burns Inflicted by Would-Be Rapist," *Omaha World Herald,* 15 November 1984, p. 4A.

5 John Leo, "Low Profile for a Legend," *Time,* 21 January 1985.

6 See Newman, *Understanding Violence,* p. 229.

7 Sigmund Freud, *Beyond the Pleasure Principle* (London: Inter-Psychoanalytic Press, 1922).

8 Konrad Lorenz, *On Aggression* (New York: Harcourt, Brace, Jovanovich, 1966).

9 Robert Ardrey, *African Genesis* (New York: Atheneum, 1963).

10 Ashley Montagu, *Man and Aggression* (New York: Oxford University Press, 1968).

11 Marvin Wolfgang and Franco Ferracuti, *The Subculture of Violence* (London: Tavistock, 1967).

12 Neil Alan Weiner and Marvin Wolfgang, "The Extent and Character of Violent Crime in America, 1969–1982," in Lynn Curtis, ed. *American Violence and Public Policy* (New Haven, Conn.: Yale University Press, 1985), pp. 17–39.

13 Judith Blau and Peter Blau, "The Cost of Inequality: Metropolitan Structure and Violent Crime," *American Sociological Review* 47 (1982):114–29.

14 Leo Carroll and Pamela Irving Jackson, "Inequality, Opportunity and Crime Rates in Central Cities," *Criminology* 21 (1983):178–93; John Braithwaite, *Inequality, Crime and Public Policy* (London: Routledge and Kegan Paul, 1979).

15 Richard Block, "Community, Environment and Violent Crime," *Criminology* 17 (1979):46–57.

16 Robert O'Brien, "Metropolitan Structure and Violent Crime: Which Measure of Crime," *American Sociological Review* 48 (1983):434–37.

17 Susan Randall and Vicki McNickle Rose, *Forcible Rape,* in Robert Meyer, ed. (Beverly Hills, Calif.: Sage Publications, 1984), p. 47.

18 Thomas Meyer, "Date Rape: A Serious Campus Problem that Few Talk About," *Chronicle of Higher Education* 29 (5 December 1984):15.

19 Ibid.

20 Susan Brownmiller, *Against Our Will: Men, Women and Rape* (New York: Simon & Schuster, 1975).

21 Edmund McGarrell and Timothy Flanagan, *Sourcebook, 1980,* p. 240; FBI, *Crime in the United States, 1983* (Washington, D.C.: Government Printing Office, 1984), p. 14.

22 Summarized in "U.S. Report on Rape Cases Cites Victims' Frustration with Law," *New York Times,* Monday, 25 March 1985, p. A17.

23 Patsy Klaus and Marshall DeBerry, *The Crime of Rape* (Washington, D.C.: Bureau of Justice Statistics, 1985); see also M. Joan McDermott, *Rape Victimization in 26 American Cities* (Washington, D.C.: Government Printing Office, 1979).

24 Barry Siegel, "Rape Case May Have Been Distorted by Rush to Judgement," *Omaha World Herald,* 25 March 1984, p. 18A.

25 UPI, "Officials Say Women Alarmed by Questions," *Omaha World Herald,* 19 March 1984, p. 8; "The Crime that Tarnished a Town," *Time,* 5 March 1984, p. 19.

26 Alan Lizotte, "The Uniqueness of Rape: Reporting Assaultive Violence to Police," *Crime and Delinquency* 31 (1985):169–91.

27 Donald Symons, *The Evolution of Human Sexuality* (Oxford, England: Oxford University Press, 1979).

28 Diana Russell, *The Politics of Rape* (New York: Stein and Day, 1975).

29 Charles McCaghy, *Deviant Behavior Crime, Conflict and Interest Groups* (New York: MacMillan, 1976).

30 Christine Adler, "An Exploration of Self-Reported Sexually Aggressive Behavior," *Crime and Delinquency* 31 (1985):306–31.

31 Paul Gebhard, John Gagnon, Wardell Pomeroy, and Cornelia Christenson, *Sex Offenders: An Analysis of Types* (New York: Harper & Row, 1965), pp. 198–205.

32 Richard Rada, ed. *Clinical Aspects of the Rapist* (New York: Grune & Stratton, 1978), pp. 122–30.

33 A. Nicholas Groth and Jean Birnbaum, *Men Who Rape* (New York: Plenum, 1979), p. 101.

34 Diana Russell, *Sexual Exploitation* (Beverly Hills, Calif.: Sage Publications, 1985), pp. 115–16.

35 Associated Press, "Trial of TV May Have Influenced Boy Facing Sexual-Assault Count," *Omaha World Herald,* 18 April 1984, p. 50.

36 This section relies heavily on Gerald Robin, "Forcible Rape: Institutionalized Sexism in the Criminal Justice System," *Crime and Delinquency* 23 (1977):136–53.

37 "Woman Urges Dotson's Release," *Omaha World Herald,* 25 April 1985, p. 3.

38 Associated Press, "New York Judge Rules Husbands May Be Convicted of Rape," *Omaha World Herald,* 21 December 1984, p. 28.

39 See, for example, Mich. Comp. Laws Ann § 750.5200-(1); Florida Statutes Annotated, Sec. 794.011. See generally Gary LaFree, "Official Reactions to Rape," *American Sociological Review* 45 (1980):842–54.

40 Martin Schwartz and Todd Clear, "Toward a New Law on Rape," *Crime and Delinquency* 26 (1980):129–51.

41 Susan Caringella-MacDonald, "The Comparability in Sexual and Nonsexual Assault Case Treatment: Did Statute Change Meet the Objective," *Crime and Delinquency* 31 (1985):206–23.

42 West's Ann. Cal. Penal Code Sec. 261, 1978.

43 Kenneth Polk, "Rape Reform and Criminal Justice Processing," *Crime and Delinquency* 31 (1985):191–206.

44 Randall and McNickle Rose, "Forcible Rape," p. 48.

45 Vicki McNickle Rose, "Rape as a Social Problem: A By-product of the Feminist Movement," *Social Problems* 25 (1977):75–89.

46 Janet Gornick, Martha Burt, and Karen Pittman, "Structure and Activities of Rape Crises Centers in the Early 1980s," *Crime and Delinquency* 31 (1985):247–68.

47 Ibid., p. 252.

48 Ibid.

49 Donald Lunde, *Murder and Madness* (San Francisco: San Francisco Book Co., 1977), p. 3.

50 Ibid.

51 See generally Harrington Brearly, *Homicide in the United States* (Montclair, N.J.: Patterson Smith, 1969); Dane Archer and Rosemary Gartner, "Violent Acts and Violent Times: A Comparative Approach to Postwar Homicide Rates," *American Sociological Review* 41 (1976):937–63.

52 FBI, *Crime in the United States, 1983,* p. 12.

53 Marvin Wolfgang, *Patterns in Criminal Homicide* (New York: John Wiley, 1966), p. 253.

54 Ibid., p. 252.

55 Menachim Amir, *Patterns in Forcible Rape* (Chicago: University of Chicago Press, 1971).

56 Margaret Zahn, "Homicide in the Twentieth Century, United States" (Unpublished manuscript, Temple University, 1980).

57 James Boudouris, "A Classification of Homicide," *Criminology* 11 (1974):525–40.

58 David Luckenbill, "Criminal Homicide as a Situational Transaction," *Social Problems* 25 (1977):176–86.

59 Raymond Gastil, "Homicide and the Regional Culture of Violence," *American Sociological Review* 36 (1971):412–27.

60 Colin Loftin and Robert Hill, "Regional Subculture of Violence: An Examination of the Gastil-Hackney Thesis," *American Sociological Review* 39 (1974):714–24.

61 Howard Erlanger, "Is There a Subculture of Violence in the South," *Journal of Criminal Law and Criminology* 66 (1976):483–90.

62 Raymond Gastil, "Comments," *Criminology* 16 (1975):60–64.

63 "Police Suspect 'Something Snapped' to Ignite Wilder's Crime Spree," *Omaha World Herald,* 15 April 1984, p. 21A.

64 Mark Starr, "The Random Killers," *Newsweek*, 26 November 1984, pp. 100–106.

65 Ibid., p. 106.

66 Jennifer Browdy, "Interview with Ann Rule," *Law Enforcement News*, 21 May 1984, p. 12.

67 Jennifer Browdy, "VI-CAP System to be Operational This Summer," *Law Enforcement News*, 21 May 1984, p. 1.

68 *Uniform Crime Reports, 1983*, p. 21.

69 See generally Ruth S. Kempe and C. Henry Kempe, *Child Abuse* (Cambridge, Mass.: Harvard University Press, 1978).

70 Douglas J. Besharov, "The Legal Aspects of Reporting Known and Suspected Child Abuse and Neglect," *Villanova Law Review* 23 (1978):458.

71 Richard Gelles and Murray Straus, "Violence in the American Family," *Journal of Social Issues* 35 (1979):15–39.

72 The American Humane Society, *Highlights of Official Child Neglect and Abuse Reporting* (Denver, 1984).

73 Diana Russell, "The Incidence and Prevalence of Intrafamilial and Extrafamilial Sexual Abuse of Female Children," *Child Abuse and Neglect* 7 (1983):133–46; see also David Finkelhor, *Sexually Victimized Children* (New York: Free Press, 1979), p. 88.

74 Brandt Steele, "Violence within the Family," in *Child Abuse and Neglect: The Family and the Community*, ed. R. Helfer and C. H. Kempe (Cambridge, Mass.: Ballinger Publishing, 1976), p. 12.

75 Ruth Inglis, *Sins of the Fathers: A Study of the Physical and Emotional Abuse of Children* (New York: St. Martin's Press, 1978), p. 68.

76 Ibid., p. 53.

77 Kempe and Kempe, *Child Abuse*, p. 24.

78 R. Emerson Dobash and Russel Dobash, *Violence against Wives* (New York: Free Press, 1979).

79 Julia O'Faolain and Laura Martines, eds., *Not in God's Image: Women in History* (Glasglow, Scotland: Fontana/Collins, 1974).

80 Laurence Stone, "The Rise of the Nuclear Family in Modern England: The Patriarchal Stage," in *The Family in History*, ed. Charles Rosenberg (Philadelphia: University of Pennsylvania Press, 1975), p. 53.

81 Dobash and Dobash, *Violence against Wives*, p. 46.

82 Newman, *Understanding Violence*, pp. 145–46.

83 FBI, *Crime in the United States, 1983*, p. 16.

84 Ibid., p. 18.

85 F. H. McClintock and Evelyn Gibson, *Robbery in London* (London: Macmillan, 1961), p. 15.

86 John Conklin, *Robbery and the Criminal Justice System* (New York: Lippincott, 1972), pp. 1–80.

87 Oscar Newman, *Defensible Space: Crime Prevention through Urban Design* (New York: MacMillan, 1972).

88 Charles Murray, "The Physical Environment and Community Control of Crime," in James Q. Wilson, ed. *Crime and Public Policy* (San Francisco: ICS Press, 1983), pp. 107–25.

89 Samuel Walker, *Sense and Nonsense about Crime* (Monterey, Calif.: Brooks/Cole, 1985), p. 152.

90 Franklin Zimring, "Firearms and Federal Law: The Gun Control Act of 1968," *Journal of Legal Studies* 4 (1975):133–98.

91 Glenn Pierce and William Bowers, "The Bartley-Fox Gun Law's Short-Term Impact on Crime," *The Annals* 455 (1981):120–37; Walker, *Sense and Nonsense*, pp. 70–71.

92 Colin Loftin, Milton Heumann, and David McDowall, "Mandatory Sentencing and Firearms Violence: Evaluating An Alternative to Gun Control," *Law and Society Review* 17 (1983):287–319.

93 David Lester, *Gun Control* (Springfield, Ill.: Charles Thomas, 1984).

94 See generally James Wright, Peter Rossi, and Kathleen Daly, *Under the Gun: Weapons, Crime and Violence in America* (New York: Aldine, 1983).

95 Stephen Schafer, *The Political Criminal* (New York: Free Press, 1974), p. 1.

96 Barton Ingraham, *Political Crime in Europe* (Berkeley: University of California Press, 1979), pp. vi–viii.

97 Ernest Van Den Haag, *Political Violence and Civil Disobedience* (New York: Harper & Row, 1972).

98 Schafer, *The Political Criminal*, p. 150.

99 Robert Friedlander, *Terrorism* (Dobbs Ferry, N.Y.: Oceana Publishers, 1979).

100 National Advisory Commission on Criminal Justice Standards and Goals, *Report of the Task Force on Disorders and Terrorism* (Washington, D.C.: Government Printing Office, 1976), p. 3.

101 Paul Wilkinson, *Terrorism and the Liberal State* (New York: John Wiley, 1977), p. 49.

102 Friedlander, *Terrorism*, p. 14.

103 Daniel Georges-Abeyie, "Political Crime and Terrorism," in *Crime and Deviance: A Comparative Perspective*, ed. Graeme Newman (Beverly Hills, Calif.: Sage Publications, 1980), pp. 313–33.

104 Ibid., p. 319.

105 This section relies heavily on Friedlander, *Terrorism*, pp. 8–20.

106 See Friedlander, *Terrorism*, p. 16.

107 See Generally John Wolf, "Domestic Terrorist Movements," in *Political Terrorism and Business*, ed. Yonah Alexander and Robert Kilmark (New York: Praeger, 1979), pp. 12–33.

108 "5 Held in Plot to Bomb California Aide's Office," *New York Times*, 21 November 1977, p. 6.

109 "FBI: Gang May Be Tied to the IRA," *Omaha World Herald*, 25 October 1981, p. 18A; "FBI Chief: Terrorism Up, No U.S. Political Focus Seen," *Omaha World Herald*, 30 December 1981, p. 15.

110 Robert Zint, "Dreams of a Bigots Revolution," *Time*, 18 February 1985, p. 42.

111 Ibid.

112 M. Cherif Bassiouni, "Terrorism, Law Enforcement, and Mass Media: Perspectives, Problems and Proposals," *Journal of Criminal Law and Criminology* 72 (1981):1–51.

113 Claire Sterling, "Gen. Dozier and the International Terror Network," *Wall Street Journal*, 29 December 1981, p. 12.

114 "Disaster Averted," *Time*, 10 December 1984, p. 45.

115 "Tunnel of Death," *Time*, 7 January 1985, p. 71.

116 William Smith, "Libya's Ministry of Fear," *Time*, 30 April 1984, pp. 36–38.

117 *Grave Doubts*, 30 April 1984, p. 38.

118 William Smith, "Death in the Garden," *Time*, 12 November 1984, pp. 42–48.

119 Associated Press, "Terrorist Groups Gained in Strength," *Omaha World Herald*, 10 May 1985, p. 5.

120 David Ignatius, "U.S. Readies Anti-Terrorism Policy," *Wall Street Journal*, 12 March 1984, p. 30.

121 "FBI Analysis of Terrorist Incidents and Terror Related Activities in the United States, 1984," Internal Memo, 31 December 1984.

122 Associated Press, Shiite Militia is Put on Alert Around Hijacked TWA Jet," *Omaha World Herald*, 17 June 1985, p. 1.

123 Bassiouni, "Terrorism, Law Enforcement, and Mass Media," p. 10.

124 Austin Turk, "Political Crime," in R. Meier, ed. *Major Forms of Crime*, pp. 119–35.

125 C. Allen Graves, "The U.S. Government's Response to Terrorism," in *Political Terrorism and Business* ed. Yonah Alexander and Robert Kilmark (New York: Praeger, 1979), pp. 175–83.

126 Ignatius, "U.S. Readies Anti-Terrorism Policy."

11 Economic Crimes: Street Crime

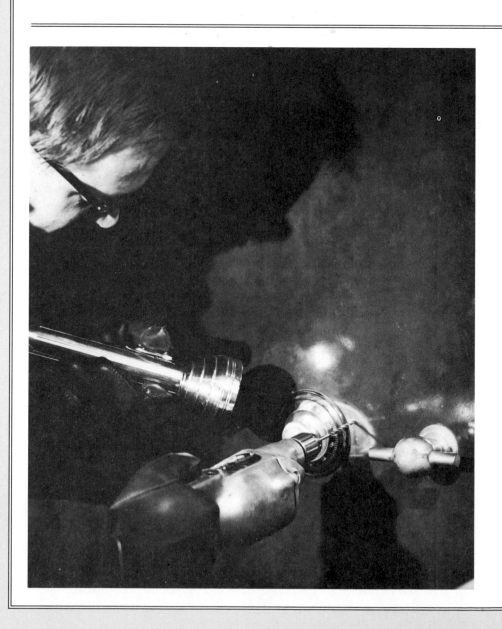

CHAPTER OUTLINE

Introduction

Professional vs. Amateur
Occasional Criminals
Professional Crime
Sutherland's Professional Criminal
Fencing and Professional Crime

Common Theft Offenses: Street Crimes
Larceny/Theft
False Pretenses/Fraud
Embezzlement
Modern Theft Categories
Burglary

Arson

Summary

KEY TERMS

professional crime
fence
commercial thieves
street crime
burglary
occasional criminals
situational inducement
flash house
smuggler

poacher
constructive possession
false pretenses
fraud
naive check forger
closure
systematic forger
pigeon drop

booster
heel
snitch
joyriding
good burglar
arson for profit
arson fraud
torch

Introduction

As a group, economic crimes can be defined as acts in violation of the criminal law designed to bring financial reward to an offender. In U. S. society, the range and scope of criminal activity motivated by financial gain is tremendous: self-report studies show that property crime among the young of every social class is widespread; national surveys of criminal behavior indicate that more than 30 million personal and household thefts occur annually; corporate and other white-collar crimes are accepted as commonplace; political scandals such as ABSCAM indicate that bribery and corruption reach even the highest levels of government.

Though average citizens may be puzzled and enraged by violent crimes, believing them to be both senseless and cruel, these citizens often view economic crimes with a great deal more ambivalence. While it is true that society generally disapproves of crimes involving theft and corruption, the public seems quite tolerant of the "gentleman bandit," even to the point of admiring such figures. They pop up as characters in popular myths and legends—Robin Hood, Jesse James, Bonnie and Clyde, D. B. Cooper. They are the heroic subjects of books and films such as *Lassiter* and *48 Hours.* How can such ambivalence be explained? For one thing, national tolerance toward economic criminals may be prompted by the fact that, if criminological studies are to be belived, almost every U. S. citizen has at some time been involved in economic crime. Even those among us who would never consider themselves criminals may have at one time engaged in petty theft or cheated on their income tax or stolen a textbook from a college bookstore or pilfered from their place of employment. Consequently, it may be difficult for society to condemn economic criminals without feeling somewhat hypocritical.

People may also be somewhat more tolerant of economic crimes because they never seem to seriously hurt anyone—banks are insured; large businesses pass along losses to consumers; stolen cars can be easily replaced; and so on. The true pain of economic crime often goes unappreciated. It is not uncommon for convicted offenders, especially businesspeople who commit white-collar crimes involving millions of dollars, to be punished rather lightly.

This chapter is the first of two that review the nature and extent of economic crime in the United States. It is divided into two principal sections. The first deals with the concept of **professional crime** and focuses on two types of professional criminals—the **fence** (a buyer and seller of stolen merchandise), and **commercial thieves** who steal from business establishments. Then the chapter turns to a discussion of common theft-related offenses, often referred to by criminologists as **street crimes.** These crimes include the major forms of common theft: larceny, embezzlement, and theft by false pretenses. Included within these general offense categories are such common crimes as auto theft, shoplifting, and credit card fraud. Then the chapter discusses a more serious form of theft—**burglary**—which involves forcible entry into a person's home or place of work for the purpose of theft. Finally, the crime of arson is discussed briefly. In the following chapter, attention will be given to economic crimes that involve organizations devoted to criminal enterprise.

Professional vs. Amateur

As you may recall, millions of property and theft-related crimes occur each year. Many are committed by **occasional criminals** who do not define themselves by a criminal role or view themselves as committed career criminals; other theft-offenders are in fact skilled, professional criminals. The following sections review these two orientations toward property crime.

OCCASIONAL CRIMINALS

Though criminologists are not certain, they suspect that the great majority of economic crimes are the work of amateur criminals whose decision to steal is spontaneous and whose acts are unskilled, unplanned, and haphazard. As noted in chapter 3, millions of theft-related crimes occur each year, and most are not reported to police agencies. Many of these theft offenses are committed by school-age youths who are unlikely to enter into a criminal career and whose behavior has been described as drifting between conventional and criminal behavior. Added to the pool of amateur thieves are the millions of adults whose behavior may occasionally violate the criminal law—shoplifters, pilferers, tax cheats—but whose main source of income comes from conventional means and whose self-identity is noncriminal. Added together, their behaviors form the bulk of theft crimes.

According to John Hepburn, occasional property crime occurs when there is an opportunity or **situational inducement** to commit crime.[1] Opportunities are available to members of all classes, but members of the upper class have the opportunity to engage in the more lucrative business-related crimes of price-fixing, bribery and embezzlement, etc., which are closed to the lower classes. Hence, lower-class individuals are overrepresented in street crime.

Situational inducements are short-run influences on a person's behavior that increase risk taking. These include psychological factors, such as stress; physiological factors, such as intoxication; economic factors, such as financial problems; and social factors, such as peer pressure.

According to Hepburn, opportunity and situational inducements are not the cause of crime; rather, they are the *occasion* for crime; hence the term occasional criminal. It seems evident that opportunity and inducements are not randomly situated. Consequently, the frequency of occasional property crime varies according to age, class, sex, and so on.

Occasional offenders are not professional criminals, nor do they make crime their occupation. They do not rely on skills or knowledge to commit their crimes, they do not organize their daily activities around crime, and they are not committed to crime as a way of life.

Occasional criminals have little group support for their acts. Unlike professionals, they do not receive informal, peer group support for their crimes. In fact, they will deny any connection to a criminal lifestyle and instead view their transgressions as being "out of character." They may see their crimes as being motivated by necessity. For example, they were only "borrowing" the car the police caught them with; they were going to pay back the store they stole merchandise from. Because of the lack of commitment, occasional offenders may be the most likely to respond to the general deterrent effect of the law.

PROFESSIONAL CRIME

In contrast, *professional criminals* make a significant portion of their income from crime. Professionals do not delude themselves with the belief that their acts are impulsive, one-time efforts, nor do they employ elaborate rationalizations to excuse the harmfulness of their action ("shoplifting doesn't really hurt anyone"). Consequently, professionals pursue their craft with vigor, attempting to learn from older, experienced criminals the techniques that will earn them the most money with the least risk. Though their numbers are relatively small, professionals engage in crimes that produce the greater losses to society and perhaps cause the more significant social harm.

Professional theft traditionally refers to nonviolent forms of criminal behavior that are undertaken with a high degree of skill, for monetary gain, and that exploit interests tending to maximize financial opportunities and minimize the possibilities of apprehension. The most typical forms include pocket picking, burglary, shoplifting, forgery and counterfeiting, extortion, sneak theft, and confidence swindling.[2]

Relatively little is known about the career patterns of professional thieves and criminals. From the literature on crime and delinquency, three patterns emerge: youths come under the influence of older, experienced criminals who teach them the trade; juvenile gang members continue their illegal activities at a time when most of their peers have "dropped out" to marry, raise families, and take conventional jobs; youths sent to prison for minor offenses learn the techniques of crime from more experienced thieves. For example, Harry King, a professional thief, relates this story about his entry into crime after being placed in a shelter-care home by his recently divorced mother:

> It was while I was at this parental school that I learned that some of the kids had been committed there by the court for stealing bikes. They taught me how to steal and where to steal them and where to sell them. Incidentally, some of the "nicer people" were the ones who bought bikes from the kids. They would dismantle the bike and use the parts: the wheels, chains, handle bars and so forth.[3]

There is some debate in the criminological literature over who may be defined as a professional criminal. Some criminologists, such as Edwin Sutherland, use the term to refer only to thieves who do not use force or physical violence in their crimes and live solely by their wits and skill.[4] However, some criminologists use the term to refer to any criminal who identifies with a criminal subculture, who makes the bulk of his or her living from crime, and who possesses a degree of skill in his or her chosen trade.[5] Thus, one can become a professional safecracker, burglar, car thief, or fence. However, drug addicts who steal to support their habit would not be considered professionals; they lack skill and therefore are amateur opportunists rather than professional technicians.

SUTHERLAND'S PROFESSIONAL CRIMINAL

What we know about the lives of professionals criminals has come to us through their journals, diaries, and autobiographies, or the first-person accounts they have given to criminologists. The best-known account of professional theft is Edwin Sutherland's recording of the life of a professional thief or con man, Chic Conwell, in his classic book, *The Professional Thief.*[6]

Conwell and Sutherland's concept of professional theft has two critical dimensions. First, professional thieves engage in limited types of crimes. They can be described by the following labels:

- Pickpocket (cannon)
- Sneak thief from stores, banks, and offices (heel)
- Shoplifter (booster)
- Jewel thief who substitutes fake gems for real ones (pennyweighter)
- Thief who steals from hotel rooms (hotel prowl)
- Confidence game artist

- Thief in rackets related to confidence games
- Forger
- Extortionist from those engaging in illegal acts (shakedown artist)[7]

Professionals depend solely on their wit and skill. Thieves who use force or commit crimes that require little expertise are not considered worthy of the title professional. Their areas of activity include such "heavy rackets" as bank robbery, car theft, burglary, and safecracking. You can see that the Conwell/Sutherland criteria for professionalism are weighted heavily toward con games and trickery and give little attention to common street crimes.

The second requirement to establish professionalism as a thief is the exclusive use of wits, *front* (a believable demeanor), and talking ability. Manual dexterity and physical force are of little importance. Moreover, professional thieves must acquire status in their profession. Status is based on their technical skill, financial standing, connections, power, dress, manners, and wide knowledge. In their world, *thief* is a title worn with pride.

Conwell and Sutherland also argue that professional thieves share feelings, sentiments, and behaviors. Of these, none is more important than the code of honor of the underworld; even under threat of the most severe punishment, a professional thief must never inform (squeal) on his or her fellows.

Sutherland and Conwell view professional theft as an occupation with much the same internal organization as that characterizing such legitimate professions as advertising, teaching, or police work. They conclude:

A person can be a professional thief only if he is recognized and received as such by other professional thieves. Professional theft is a group way of life. One can get into the group and remain in it only by the consent of those previously in the group. Recognition as a professional thief by other professional thieves is the absolutely necessary, universal and definitive characteristic of the professional thief.[8]

FENCING AND PROFESSIONAL CRIME

Nowhere is the concept of professional theft better illustrated than in the crime of buying and reselling stolen merchandise, or fencing.

Professional fences play an important role in the thief's working world. They provide an outlet for stolen merchandise—ranging from diamonds to auto hubcaps—that would never be open to the average street criminal. The fence's critical role in criminal transactions has long been appreciated. As early as 1795, Patrick Colquhoun stated in his book, A *Treatise on the Police of the Metropolis*:

In contemplating the characters of all these different classes of delinquents (that is Thieves, Robbers, Cheats and Swindlers), there can be little hesitation in pronouncing the Receivers to be the most mischievous of the whole: inasmuch as without the aid they afford, in purchasing and concealing every species of property stolen or fraudulently obtained, Thieves, Robbers and Swindlers, . . . must quit the trade, as unproductive and hazardous in the extreme.

Nothing therefore can be more just than the old observation, "that if there were no Receivers there would be no Thieves".—Deprive a thief of a safe and ready market for his goods and he is undone.[9]

Despite its importance, little is known about professional fencing. Much of what is known comes from first-person accounts, the best-known being Carl Klockars's highly respected work, *The Professional Fence*.[10] Klockars examined the life

Causes of Economic Crime

There is great debate over the cause of economic crime. Each of the major criminological cal perspectives maintains its own position on the root causes and possible solutions to theft-related offenses. These positions are presented below.

Perspective	Cause	Solution
Classical	Economic crime is caused by greed, lack of fear of possible punishments, ineffectiveness of criminal justice system to deter crime.	Increase criminal penalties; increase efficiency of justice system; incapacitate known criminals.
Individual		
Biological	Unique physical characteristics make some people unable to control their behavior. Possible factors include low IQ, psychopathy, blood-chemistry disorders, brain dysfunction. Under certain environmental conditions, these factors promote illegal behavior solutions.	Physically evaluate offenders; treat individual physical problems; improve environmental conditions.
Psychological Behaviorist	Offenders learn that theft is appropriate under certain circumstances. They receive rewards for illegal acts.	Change learning patterns; reward conventional behavior; provide proper role models.
Psychoanalytic	Offenders' behavior is an impulsive manifestation of their early childhood frustrations. Weak ego development causes frustration and aggression.	Provide psychiatric evaluation and treatment of offenders to help them uncover the root causes of their behavior and effectively control it.
Cognitive	Offenders' moral development is impaired.	Help offenders improve moral development; provide a treatment milieu in which higher moral standards are rewarded.

and times of one successful fence, Vincent Swaggi. Through four hundred hours of listening to and observing Vincent, Klockars found that this highly professional criminal had developed techniques that made him almost immune to prosecution. Consequently, during the course of a long and profitable career in crime, Vincent spent only four months in prison. He stayed in business in part because of his sophisticated knowledge of the law of stolen property: To convict someone of receiving stolen goods, the prosecution must prove that the accused was in possession of the goods and knew that they had been stolen. Vincent had the skills to make sure that these elements could never be proven.

Also helping Vincent stay out of the law's grasp were the close working associations he maintained with society's upper classes, including influential members of the justice system. Vincent helped them purchase items at below-cost, bargain prices. He also helped authorities recover stolen goods and therefore remained in

Perspective	Cause	Solution
Sociological		
Social Structure	Individuals' positions in the social structure determine their behavior. Those in the lower economic classes lack the opportunity and skill to earn money through conventional means. Consequently, they seek criminal solutions to their financial problems. Poverty causes crime.	Provide economic opportunities for lower-class citizens; create job, education, welfare, and child-care programs.
Social Process	Individuals' relationships with social institutions determine their behavior. Some people learn to steal in interaction with others. Some feel alienated from society and therefore feel free to violate its rules.	Provide counseling and outreach for potential criminals; make them feel part of conventional society; help them establish bonds, strengthen family ties.
Social Conflict	Economic crime is a function of the conflict between the haves and have-nots. For the poor, theft is a means of survival. For the wealthy, it is a means of maintaining or increasing social position. In capitalist societies, the wealthy use their positions to "steal" through legal means such as profiteering, stock market manipulation, price-fixing, monopolies.	Marxists would restructure society; end the capitalist system; create a world in which people are concerned with each other's welfare. Pure conflict theorists would limit the economic gulf between rich and poor; and enforce laws against the economic crimes of the wealthy.

DISCUSSION QUESTIONS

1. Which of the criminological perspectives do you think provides the most reasonable explanation of economic crime?

2. If each position has some merit, what does this mean for crime control?

their good graces. Klockars's work strongly suggests that fences customarily cheat their thief-clients and at the same time cooperate with the law.

In another study of fencing, Marilyn Walsh draws this picture of the professional fence: he is a white male in his middle to late forties, owns and operates a legitimate retail establishment, probably never has been arrested, and looks very much like a totally legitimate manager or business administrator.[11] Walsh found that fences handle a tremendous number of products—televisions, cigarettes, stereo equipment, watches, autos, cameras. In dealing their merchandise, fences operate through many legitimate fronts, including art dealerships, antique stores, furniture and appliance retailers, remodeling companies, salvage companies, trucking companies, and jewelry stores. When deciding what to pay the thief for goods, the fence uses a complex pricing policy: professional thieves who steal high-priced items are usually given the highest amounts—about 30 to 50 percent of the whole-

Life in the Fast Lane: Commercial Thieves

Another type of professional criminal is the commercial thief. The Center for the Study of Crime and Gain at Rutgers University's School of Criminal Justice has been conducting an ongoing study of this phenomenon by intensively interviewing small numbers of incarcerated men whose career patterns involved commercial theft.

The researchers, John Gibbs and Peggy Shelly, found that professionals commercial thieves could be classified into two categories: (1) commercial burglars and (2) hijackers.

Burglars' main goal is to acquire cash. They specialize in victimizing establishments that primarily do a cash rather than credit business: supermarkets, bars, restaurants. Between two to six men form the burglary team. Each may specialize in a different skill: opening safes, using torches, handling explosives, bypassing alarms, etc.

When possible, the commercial burglar will carefully choose a site, waiting for a day when the maximum amount of money will be on hand. The vulnerability of the site has an important influence on the decision to steal. For example, a freestanding building is more dangerous than a shopping center because the center cannot be easily surrounded by police. As one subject said:

. . . it's a lot more difficult for them to surround a shopping center than it would be to surround one single building. . . . I just go out the back. There's no way he can get around that building fast enough. If the car pulls in around the back, I go out the front. You know, so the chances are good that I'll get away,

especially with the doors locked. They're not positive that somebody's in there yet because they haven't seen anybody, you know, so usually they'll check the doors and call the manager, and they wait until the manager comes, and then they go inside the building. By that time, I'm long gone.

Commercial burglars differ in their approach from household thieves. They have more information about the content of their target, whereas the household burglar usually chooses a target at random. More skill is required in commercial theft since few houses have protective security devices.

The second broad occupational classification of commercial theft is *hijackers*, who steal goods in transit from trucks. These targets are selected because (1) they contain large quantities of goods, (2) the goods are ready for transport, and (3) the merchandise is less well protected than it would be in a warehouse.

The most common method of theft is to just take trucks away when left unattended. As one pro remarked:

There were certain areas, right, certain days of the week, you know, certain areas that would get deliveries, we'd go in that area, we'd walk up and down the street and we'd spot a truck, mostly we'd spot a truck as it pulls up; like standing on the corner or sitting on the stoop and watch them take off what they're going to deliver and watch them go into the building or apartment. . . . By the time they go in the building I usually jump in the truck. It don't take more

sale price. For example, furs valued at $5,000 may be bought for $1,200. However, the amateur thief or drug addict who is not in a good bargaining position may receive only ten cents on the dollar.

Fencing seems to contain many of the elements of professional theft as described by Sutherland: fences live by their wits, never engage in violence, depend on their skill in negotiating, maintain community standing based on connections and power, and share the sentiments and behaviors of their fellows. The only divergence between Sutherland's thief and the fence is the code of honor; it seems likely that the fence is much more willing to cooperate with authorities than most other professional criminals.

In the following Close-Up, another type of professional criminal—commercial thieves—is examined in some detail.

Common Theft Offenses: Street Crimes

Theft offenses are frequent occurrences. Millions of auto thefts, shoplifting incidents, embezzlements, burglaries, and larcenies are recorded each year. National surveys indicate that almost 15 percent of the U.S. population are victims of theft offenses each year.

than 3 or 4 seconds, more like 10 seconds. . . . You use what you call a pulley, some people call it a slap hammer, it's a rod about so long, you got a screw at the end, and you got like a weight in the middle that you slide up and down, slide it up and down the bar, screw that into the ignition and you just hit it and it comes up and you can stick anything in there and it starts.

Some thieves work in collusion with the truck driver, while others stop trucks and kidnap drivers before making off with the merchandise.

The secret to successful hijacking is to be able to distribute stolen goods. This is almost always done through a fence. Later in their careers, many thieves make a career move up to the less risky work of a fence.

CAREERS OF COMMERCIAL THIEVES

Gibbs and Shelly found that most commercial thieves did not specialize in one type of crime their whole lives. Though they may have preferred one type of theft, when opportunities arose in other areas of crime the thieves would not be reluctant to take advantage of them.

Why did these men enter into professional crime? Some saw themselves as "born criminals," others attributed their life to a disorganized environment, a few blamed economic problems and the need to make a "fast buck." Most, however, considered that they learned to become seasoned professional thieves after an early jail experience:

Well, you might say, everything I've learned, I've learned in jail. That's where it comes from really. I didn't learn it on the street. Most of my thing was

when I was in county jail, I think on my first bit, let me see, I went to the county jail when I was 16. In jail, in the county jail a lot of guys meet there and you have bull sessions and they explain how to do it, "This is how you rob a safe, how you do this," and you go by things that they told you. And you did it yourself, tried it out, and it worked. You know what to look for, how to break an alarm system, how to wire, everything, and people would explain, this is right down the line, everything would be explained.

Most thieves felt that their illegal gains gave them the opportunity to live in the "fast lane." They spent their ill-gotten gains as fast as they earned them on luxuries: wine, women, clothes, and cars. The excitement of making deals, of meeting and wooing fences and other professionals all added to the glamour of being a professional criminal. Though most made in excess of $75,000 a year, few thought of saving for the future. Being realists, professional thieves assumed they would eventually get caught; so why live for tomorrow, when tomorrow you might be in Joliet or Attica?

DISCUSSION QUESTIONS

1. What legitimate professions are similar to that of commercial thief?
2. What theoretical models are supported by the lifestyle of professional thieves?

SOURCE. John Gibbs and Peggy Shelly, "Life in the Fast Lane: A Retrospective View by Commercial Thieves," *Journal of Research in Crime and Delinquency* 19 (1982):229–330. Quotes from pp. 309, 314, 321.

Theft is not a phenomenon unique to modern times; the theft of personal property has been known throughout recorded history. The Crusades of the eleventh century inspired peasants and downtrodden noblemen to leave the shelter of their estates to prey upon passing pilgrims.[12] Not surprisingly, Crusaders felt it within their rights to appropriate the possessions of any infidels—Greeks, Jews, or Moslems—they happened to encounter during their travels. By the thirteenth century, returning pilgrims, not content to live as serfs on feudal estates, gathered in the forests of England and the Continent to poach game that was the rightful property of their lord or king and, when possible, to steal from passing strangers. By the fourteenth century, many of such highwaymen and poachers were full-time livestock thieves, stealing great numbers of cattle and sheep.[13]

The fifteenth and sixteenth centuries brought the onset of hostilities between England and France in what has come to be known as the Hundred Years' War. Foreign mercenary troops fighting for both sides roamed the countryside; loot and pillage were viewed as a rightful part of their pay.

Theft became more professional with the rise of the city and the establishment of a permanent class of propertyless urban poor.[14] By the eighteenth century, three separate groups of property criminals were active. In the larger cities, such as

London and Paris, groups of skilled thieves, pickpockets, forgers, and counterfeiters operated freely. They congregated in **flash houses**—public meeting places, often taverns, that served as headquarters for gangs. Here, deals were made, crimes plotted, and the sale of stolen goods negotiated.[15]

The second group of thieves were the **smugglers**, who moved freely in sparsely populated areas and transported goods without bothering to pay tax or duty. The third group were the **poachers**, who lived in the country and supplemented their diet and income with game that belonged to a landlord.

By the eighteenth century, professional thieves in the larger cities had banded together into gangs to protect themselves, to increase the scope of their activities, and to help dispose of stolen goods. Jack Wild, perhaps London's most famous thief, perfected the process of buying and selling stolen goods and gave himself the title of "Thief-Taker General of Great Britain and Ireland." Before he was hanged, Wild controlled numerous gangs and dealt harshly with any thief who violated his strict code of conduct.[16]

During this period, individual theft-related crimes began to be defined by the common law. The most important of these categories are still in use today.

LARCENY/THEFT

Larceny/theft was one of the earliest common-law crimes created by English judges to define acts in which one person took for his or her own use the property of another.[17] At common law, larceny was defined as "the trespassory taking and carrying away of the personal property of another with intent to steal."[18] Most state jurisdictions have incorporated the common-law crime of larceny in their legal codes. Today, definitions of larceny often include such familiar acts as shoplifting, auto theft, passing bad checks, and other theft offenses that do not involve using force or threats on the victim or forcibly breaking into a person's home or place of work. (The former is robbery; the latter, burglary).

As originally construed, larceny involved only taking property that was in the possession of the rightful owners. For example, it would have been considered larceny for someone to go secretly into a farmer's field and steal his cow. Thus, the original common-law definition required a "trespass in the taking"; this meant that for an act to be considered larceny, goods must have been taken from the physical possession of the rightful owner.

In creating this definition of larceny, English judges were more concerned with disturbance of the peace than they were with thefts. They reasoned that if someone tried to steal property from another's possession, the act could eventually lead to a physical confrontation and possibly the death of one party or the other. Consequently, the original definition of larceny did not include crimes in which the thief had come into the possession of the stolen property by trickery or deceit. For example, if someone entrusted with another person's property decided to keep it, it was not considered larceny.

The growth of manufacturing and the development of the free enterprise system required that greater protection be given private property. The pursuit of commercial enterprise often required that one person's legal property be entrusted to a second party; therefore, larceny evolved to include the theft of goods that had come into the thief's possession through legitimate means.

To get around the element of "trespass in the taking," English judges created the concept of **constructive possession**. This legal fiction applied to situations in which persons voluntarily and temporarily gave up custody of their property but

Theft of another's possessions is larceny.

still believed that the property was legally theirs. For example, if a person gave a jeweler her watch for repair, she would still believe she owned the watch, although she had handed it over to the jeweler. Similarly, when a person misplaces his wallet and someone else finds it and keeps it—although identification of the owner can be plainly seen—the concept of constructive possession makes the person who has kept the wallet guilty of larceny.

Larceny Today. Most state jurisdictions have, as mentioned, incorporated larceny in their criminal codes. Larceny is usually separated by state statute into petit (or petty) larceny and grand larceny. The former involves small amounts of money or property; it is punished as a misdemeanor. Grand larceny, involving merchandise of greater value, is considered a felony and is punished by a sentence in the state prison. Each state sets its own boundary between grand larceny and petty larceny but $50 or $100 is not unusual.

This distinction often presents a serious problem for the justice system. Car thefts and other larcenies involving high-priced merchandise are easily classified, but it is often difficult to decide whether a particular theft should be considered petty or grand larceny. For example, if a ten-year-old watch that originally cost $500 is stolen, should its value be based on its original cost; on its current worth, say, $50, or on its replacement cost, say, $1,000? As most statutes are worded, the current market value of the property governs its worth. Thus, the theft of the watch would be considered petty larceny, since its worth today is only $50. However, if a painting originally bought for $25 has a current market value of $500, its theft would be considered grand larceny.

Larceny/theft is probably the most common criminal offense. Self-report studies, discussed in chapter 2, indicate that a significant number of youths have engaged in theft-related activities. The FBI recorded over 6.7 millions acts of larceny in 1983, a rate of 2,866 per 100,000 persons; in 1984 the larceny rate declined about 3 percent, to 2,791 crimes per 100,000 people.[19]

FALSE PRETENSES/FRAUD

False pretenses, or **fraud**, involves a wrongdoer's misrepresenting a fact to cause a victim to willingly give his or her property to the wrongdoer, who keeps it.[20]

The definition of false pretenses was created by the English Parliament in 1757 to cover an area of law left untouched by larceny statutes. The first false pretenses law punished people who "knowingly and designedly by false pretense or pretenses, [obtained] from any person or persons, money, goods, wares or merchandises with intent to cheat or defraud any person or persons of the same."[21] False pretenses differs from traditional larceny because the victims willingly give their possessions to the offender; and the crime does not, as does larceny, involve a "trespass in the taking."

An example of false pretenses would occur if an unscrupulous merchant sold someone a chair, claiming it was an antique but knowing all the while it was a cheap copy. Another example would occur if a phony healer sold a victim a bottle of colored sugar water and called it an "elixir" that would cure a disease.

Some states retain the crime of false pretenses in their criminal code; others have combined it with larceny into a general theft category.

EMBEZZLEMENT

The crime of embezzlement was created by the English Parliament during the sixteenth century to fill a gap in the larceny law.[22] Until then, to be guilty of theft, a person had to take goods from the physical possession of another (trespass in the taking). However, as explained earlier, this definition did not cover instances in which one person trusted another and willfully gave that person temporary custody of his or her property. For example, in everyday commerce, store clerks, bank tellers, brokers, and merchants gain lawful possession *but not legal ownership* of other people's money. Embezzlement occurs when someone who is so trusted with property *fraudulently converts* it—that is, keeps it for his or her own use or the use of others.

Most U.S. courts require that a serious breach of trust have occurred before a person can be convicted of embezzlement. The mere act of moving property without the owner's consent, or damaging it, or using it, is not considered embezzlement. However, using it up, selling it, pledging it, giving it away, or holding it against the owner's will is considered embezzlement.[23]

Although it is impossible to know how many embezzlement incidents occur annually, the FBI found that only 8,100 people were arrested for embezzlement in 1984—probably an extremely small percentage of all embezzlers (see the section in chapter 12 on white-collar crime for more on embezzlement).

MODERN THEFT CATEGORIES

Many state jurisdictions have found it necessary to create additional theft-related offenses to meet the conditions created by changing social mores. This section will review some representative examples of modern theft offenses.

Bad Checks. Most state jurisdictions have passed laws making it a criminal act to obtain money or property in exchange for a check that is knowingly and intentionally drawn on a nonexistent or underfunded bank account. In general, for a person to be guilty of passing a bad check, the bank the check is drawn on must refuse payment and the check casher must fail to make the check good within ten days after finding out the check was not honored.

The best-known study of check forgers was conducted by Edwin Lemert.[24] Lemert found that the majority of check forgers—he calls them **naive check forgers**—are amateurs who don't believe their actions will hurt anyone. Most naive check forgers come from middle-class backgrounds and have little identification with a criminal subculture. They cash bad checks because of a financial crisis that demands an immediate resolution—perhaps they have lost money at the horse track and have some pressing bills to pay. Lemert refers to this condition as **closure**. Naive check forgers are often socially isolated people who have been unsuccessful in their personal relationships. They are risk-prone when faced with a situation that is unusually stressful to them. The willingness of stores and other commercial establishments to cash checks with a minimum of fuss in order to promote business encourages the check forger to risk committing a criminal act.

Not all check forgers are amateurs. Lemert found that a few professionals—whom he calls **systematic forgers**—make a substantial living by passing bad checks. However, professionals constitute a relatively small segment of the total population of check forgers.

It is difficult to estimate the number of check forgeries committed each year, or the amounts involved. Stores and banks may choose not to press charges, since the effort to collect the money due them is often not worth their while. It is also difficult to separate the true check forger from the neglectful shopper. However, FBI figures indicate that about 270,000 people in the United States are arrested on fraud charges annually.[25]

Confidence Games. Many state jurisdictions have created criminal laws to protect people from swindlers whose goal is to separate a victim (or sucker) from his or her hard-earned money. "Con games" usually involve getting a "mark" interested in some get-rich-quick scheme, which may have illegal overtones. The criminal's hope is that when victims lose their money they will either be too embarrassed or too afraid to call the police.

There are hundreds of varieties of con games. The most common is called the **pigeon drop**.[26] Here, a package or wallet containing money is "found" by a con man or woman. A passing victim is stopped and asked for advice about what to do, since no identification can be found. Another "stranger," who is part of the con, approaches and enters the discussion. The three decide to split the money; but first, to make sure everything is legal, one of the swindlers goes off to consult a lawyer. Upon returning, he or she says that the lawyer claims the money can be split up; first, however, each party must prove he or she has the means to reimburse the original owner, should one ever show up. The victim then is asked to give some good-faith money for the lawyer to hold. When the victim goes to the lawyer's office to pick up a share of the loot, he or she finds the address bogus and the money gone.

It is difficult to estimate the extent of con games, since many victims will not report their involvement to the authorities. However, as you will see in chapter 12, swindles involving business-related crimes can run into the billions of dollars.

Credit Card Theft. The use of stolen credit cards has become a major problem in U.S. society. It has been estimated that a billion-dollar loss through fraud has been experienced by credit card companies. In New York City, police officials estimate that five thousand credit cards are stolen each month.[27]

Most credit card abuse is the work of amateurs who acquire stolen cards through theft or mugging and then use them for two or three days. However, professional credit card rings may be getting into the act. For example, in Los Angeles, members of a credit card gang got jobs as clerks in several stores, where they collected the names and credit card numbers of customers. Gang members bought plain plastic cards and had the names and numbers of the customers embossed on them. The gang created a fictitious wholesale jewelry company and applied for and received authorization to accept credit cards from the "customers." The thieves then used the phony cards to run up charges for nonexistent jewelry purchases on the accounts of the people whose names and card numbers they had collected. The banks that issued the original cards honored over $200,000 in payments before the thieves withdrew the money from their business account and left town.[28]

To combat losses from credit card theft, Congress passed a law in 1971 limiting a person's liability to $50 per stolen card. Similarly, some states, such as California, have passed specific statutes making it a misdemeanor to obtain property or services by means of stolen, forged, cancelled, or revoked credit cards, or cards whose use is for any reason unauthorized.[29]

Shoplifting. Shoplifting is a common form of larceny involving the theft of goods from retail stores. Usually shoplifters try to snatch goods—jewelry, clothes, records, appliances—when store personnel are otherwise occupied and hide the goods on their person. The "five-finger discount" is an extremely common form of crime; losses from shoplifting are measured in the billions of dollars each year.[30] Retail security measures add to the already high cost of this crime, all of which is passed on to the consumer.

Shoplifting incidents have increased dramatically in the past twenty years, and retailers now expect an annual increase of from 10 to 15 percent. Some studies estimate that about one in every nine shoppers steal from department stores. Moreover, the increasingly popular discount stores, such as K-Mart, Target, and Penney's have a minimum of sales help and depend on highly visible merchandise displays to attract purchasers, all of which makes them particularly vulnerable to shoplifters.

The classic study of shoplifting was conducted by Mary Owen Cameron.[31] In her pioneering effort, Ms. Cameron found that about 10 percent of all shoplifters were professionals who derived the majority of their income from shoplifting. Sometimes called **boosters** or **heels**, professional shoplifters intend to resell stolen merchandise to pawnshops or fences, usually at half the original price.[32]

According to Cameron's study, most shoplifters are pilferers, called **snitches** in thieves' argot. Snitches are usually respectable persons who don't conceive of themselves as thieves. Nonetheless, they are systematic shoplifters who steal merchandise for their own use. They are not simply taken by an uncontrollable urge to take something that attracts them; they come equipped to steal. Usually, snitches who are arrested are first offenders who have never been apprehended before. For the most part, they are people who lack the kinds of criminal experience that suggest extensive association with a criminal subculture.

Controlling Shoplifting. One major problem associated with combatting shoplifting is that many customers who observe pilferage are reluctant to report it to security agents. Store employees themselves are often reluctant to get involved in apprehending a shoplifter. For example, in a controlled experiment, Donald Hartman and his associates found that customers observed only 28 percent of staged shoplifting incidents that had been designed to get their attention.[33] Furthermore, only 28 percent of people who said they had observed an incident reported it to store employees.

In another controlled experiment using staged shoplifting incidents, Erhard Blankenburg found that less than 10 percent of shoplifting was detected by store employees and that customers appeared unwilling to report even serious cases.[34] Even in stores with an announced policy of full reporting and prosecution, only 70 percent of the shoplifting detected by employees was actually reported to managers; and only 5 percent was prosecuted. According to Blankenburg, foreigners, adults, and blue-collar workers were disproportionately represented among those officially punished.

In a study that reached a different conclusion, Michael Hindelang found that the decision of store owners to refer shoplifters to the police was more closely related to the value of the goods stolen, the nature of the goods stolen, and the manner of the theft than to the race, sex, or age of the offender.[35] For example, shoplifters who had used an apparatus such as a bag pinned to the inside of their clothing were more apt to be prosecuted than those who had impulsively put merchandise into their pockets.

In general, criminologists view shoplifters as people who are likely to reform if apprehended. Mary Owen Cameron reasons that snitches are not part of a criminal subculture and do not think of themselves as criminals. Consequently, being arrested has a traumatic effect on them, and they will not risk a second offense. Findings of a similar nature were uncovered in a study by Laurence Cohen and Rodney Stark.[36] However, in a recent study of juvenile shoplifters, Lloyd Klemke found that youths who had been previously apprehended for shoplifting reported more current shoplifting activity than unapprehended youths and that apprehended youths who had been processed by police authorities were more likely to recidivate than those handled by store personnel alone; these findings were generated in support of labeling theory (see chapter 8).[37] Though Klemke's work contradicts that of Cameron and of Cohen and Starke, his sample consisted solely of juvenile offenders, who may react quite differently to apprehension than middle-aged, middle-class adults.

As stated earlier, shoplifting continues to be a serious problem. FBI data indicate that shoplifting comprises about 13 percent of all larceny cases—about 870,000 cases in 1984, or 372 per 100,000 population. This represents an increase of 25 percent between 1979 and 1984.[38] Many stores have installed elaborate security devices to combat shoplifting, but the growth of this type of larceny has continued.

Auto Theft. Motor vehicle theft is another common larceny offense. The FBI estimates that over a million auto thefts occur annually, accounting for a total loss of over $4.6 billion.

Auto theft is usually considered the pastime of relatively affluent, white, middle-class teenagers looking for excitement through **joyriding**.[39] This belief is supported by the fact that 36 percent of people arrested for auto theft in 1984 were under eighteen, and 56 percent were twenty-one or younger. Moreover, of the people arrested for auto theft, 68 percent were white and 91 percent male.

In an effort to shed some light on the true nature of auto theft, Charles McCaghy and his associates examined data from police and court files in several state jurisdictions.[40] The researchers uncovered five categories of auto theft transactions:

1. *Joyriding*—Many car thefts are motivated by teenagers' desire to acquire the power, prestige, sexual potency, and recognition associated with an automobile. Joyriders do not steal cars for profit or gain but to experience, even briefly, the benefits associated with owning an automobile.

2. *Short-term transportation*—Auto theft for short-term transportation is most similar to joyriding. It involves the theft of a car simply to go from one place to another. In more serious cases, the thief may drive to another city or state and then steal another car to continue the journey.

3. *Long-term transportation*—Thieves who steal cars for long-term transportation intend to keep the cars for their personal use. Usually older than joyriders and from a lower-class background, these auto thieves may repaint and otherwise disguise cars to avoid detection.

4. *Profit*—Auto theft for profit is, of course, motivated by hope for monetary gain. At one extreme are highly organized professionals who resell expensive cars after altering their identification numbers and falsifying their registration papers. At the other end of the scale are amateur auto strippers who steal batteries, tires, and wheel covers in order to sell them or reequip their own cars.

5. *Commission of another crime*—A small portion of auto thieves steal cars so they can be used in other crimes, such as robberies and thefts. This type of auto thief desires both mobility and anonymity.

The various categories of motor vehicle theft constitute a large percentage of the index crimes committed in the United States. In 1983, the FBI reported 1,004,372 offenses, a rate of 429 per 100,000. In 1984, auto thefts increased 1.5 percent to 437 per 100,000.[41]

FBI data on auto theft are quite similar to the projections of the National Crime Survey (1.3 million thefts annually). The similarity of data between these sources is because, since almost every state jurisdiction requires car owners to insure their vehicles, auto theft is one of the most highly reported of all major crimes (89 percent of completed auto thefts are reported to police).

BURGLARY

At common law, you may recall, the crime of burglary is defined as "the breaking and entering of a dwelling house of another in the nighttime with the intent to commit a felony within."[42]

Burglary is considered a much more serious crime than larceny/theft, since it involves entering another's home, a situation in which the threat of harm to occupants is great. Even though at the time of the burglary the home may be unoccupied, the potential for harm to the family is so significant that most state jurisdictions punish burglary as a felony.

The legal definition of burglary has undergone considerable change since its common-law origins. When first created by English judges during the late Middle Ages, laws against burglary were designed to protect a family whose home might be set upon by wandering criminals. Including the phrase "breaking and entering" in the definition protected people from unwarranted intrusions; if an invited guest stole something, it would not be considered a burglary. Similarly, the requirement that the crime be committed at nighttime was added because evening was considered the time when honest people might fall prey to criminals.[43]

In more recent times, state jurisdictions have changed the legal requirements of burglary; and most have discarded the necessity of forced entry. Many now protect all structures, and not just dwelling houses. A majority of states have removed the nighttime element from burglary definitions as well.

It is quite common for states to enact laws creating different degrees of burglary. In this instance, the more serious and heavily punished crimes involve a nighttime forced entry into the home; the least serious involve a daytime entry into a non-residence by an unarmed offender. Several gradations of the offense may be found between these extremes.

Careers in Burglary. Great variety exists within the ranks of burglars. Many are crude thieves who, with little finesse, will smash a window and enter a vacant home or structure with minimal preparation. However, because it involves planning, risk, and skill, burglary has been a crime long associated with professional thieves.

To become a skilled practitioner of burglary, the would-be burglar must learn the craft by the side of an experienced burglar. For example, Francis Hoheimer, an experienced professional burglar, has described his education in the craft of burglary by Oklahoma Smith when the two were serving time in the Illinois State Penitentiary. Among Smith's recommendations:

> Never wear deodorant or shaving lotion, the strange scent might wake someone up. The more people there are in a house, the safer you are. If someone hears you moving around, they will think it's someone else. . . . If they call answer in a muffled, sleepy voice. . . . Never be afraid of dogs, they can sense fear. Most dogs are friendly, snap your finger, they come right to you. . . .[44]

When he was released from prison, Hoheimer formed a criminal gang that specialized in burglary. Hoheimer and his associates would check into a motel near the home of their intended victim. Registering under assumed names and giving false addresses, they would correctly describe their cars but mix up license plate numbers. Checking out of the motel before the burglary, they would enter the victim's home between two o'clock and five o'clock in the morning. If the owners were present, they would be tied, hand and foot, with surgical tape. Hoheimer and his gang concentrated on taking jewelry, furs, and money. The victims would be asked for the location of wall safes and valuables. While on the job, Hoheimer carried a hand gun as well as an attache case containing such items as ski masks, work gloves, pen-type flashlights, a propane fuel tank with torch head, a pry bar, a screwdriver, a pair of lock pliers, a pair of wirecutters, a glass cutter, and six rolls of surgical tape. Despite his elaborate preparations, Hoheimer spent many years confined for his acts.

The Good Burglar. Neal Shover has studied the careers of professional burglars and uncovered the existence of a particularly successful type—the **good burglar**.[45] This is a characterization applied by professional burglars to colleagues who have distinguished themselves as burglars. Characteristics of the good burglar include:

The Professional Burglar

The reading below describes the methods and operations of a professional burglar.

Greg is a jewelry and fur specialist who has taken a gemology course in order to evaluate and learn about the property he steals. He has jewelers' tools and removes stones from their settings to weigh and safely secure them. His main targets are the homes of wealthy persons who, he takes pains to discover, have such property in their homes rather than in a bank vault. Greg spends considerable time, before contemplating a theft, researching possible victims to build a profile of them. He searches the social register, the social and financial pages of the newspapers, the city directory, and the directories of corporate officials. He visits the neighborhoods of the wealthy at different times and days to get a feel for their living patterns. When satisfied that an individual not only is likely to possess property he might be interested in, but also maintains a lifestyle that includes substantial periods away from home, Greg will add him to a list of *possible* targets. This list includes the name, address, and phone number of that individual as well as a notation about any item that he may have heard about or seen worn by one of the occupants (in a news photo, for example) that particularly interests him.

When he is ready to pull a job, he has a group of three or four other burglars with whom he works. They begin by calling individuals on Greg's list until they find a home with no one answering. Next they proceed toward the target, stopping at a phone booth to try the residence again. If still no one answers, the drama begins.

They are equipped with two police radios and a walkie-talkie. One of them is designated as the driver and he lets the others out of the car somewhere near the preferred approach to the house. The driver then proceeds to a phone booth and, giving his cohorts approximately 10 minutes, he calls the home once more. If no one or someone unfamiliar answers, he proceeds immediately to a predetermined pick-up point. If his friends answer, he gives them his number and begins waiting at the booth, monitoring police calls and phoning them intermittently to be advised of their progress.

In the house the thieves again divide the labors. One of them waits for the phone call and mans the walkie-talkie if it becomes necessary for them to be separated on different floors of the house. The first step is to find the luggage owned by the occupants, for they will be using this to transport the property from the house. This done, they proceed to steal what they will, opening a safe if that is necessary or merely lifting what is around of value. Their ease of operation will depend on what they have calculated to be the maximum time they will have to operate inside. Thus, if they know the occupants to be at a social function, they will use the luxury of several hours to do a thorough job. If, however, they have determined that their victims are out dining, they may allow themselves less time to complete the job and execute their exit.

When they have finished, they notify their driver, with whom they have been in intermittent contact, and proceed to the arranged pick-up point, leaving as they came, through a side door or a back window with suitcases in hand. Anything they decide is of little value, for example costume jewelry picked up by mistake, is put back in the suitcases and, bag and baggage, is taken to another predetermined safe place and disposed of. (Their preference was a desolated wharf area, where they would drop the merchandise they didn't want into a swift-flowing channel.)

DISCUSSION QUESTIONS

1. How do Greg's preparations compare with those of other professionals, such as a lawyer preparing a case or a surgeon preparing for an operation?
2. Can thieves like Greg be deterred?

SOURCE. Excerpted from Marilyn Walsh, *The Fence* (Westport, Conn.: Greenwood Press, 1977), pp. 164–66.

---

(1) technical competence, (2) maintenance of personal integrity, (3) specialization in burglary, (4) financial success at crime, and (5) ability to avoid prison sentences.

Shover found that to receive recognition as good burglars, novices must learn to overcome four problems of the trade. First, they must learn the many skills needed to commit lucrative burglaries. This process may include learning such techniques as how to gain entry into homes and apartment houses, how to select targets with high potential payoffs, how to choose items with a high resale value, how to properly open safes without damaging their contents, and how to use the proper equipment, including cutting torches, electric saws, explosives, and metal bars.

Second, the good burglar must be able to team up to form a criminal gang. Choosing trustworthy companions is essential if the obstacles to completing a successful job—police, alarms, secure safes—are to be overcome.

Third, the good burglar must have inside information. Without knowledge of what awaits them inside, burglars can spend a tremendous amount of time and effort on empty safes and jewelry boxes.

Finally, the good burglar must cultivate fences or buyers for stolen wares. Once the burglar gains access to people who buy and sell stolen goods, he or she must also learn how to successfully sell these goods for a reasonable profit.

Shover finds that the process of becoming a professional burglar is similar to the process Sutherland described in his theory of differential association (described in chapter 8). According to Shover, a person becomes a good burglar through learning the techniques of the trade from older, more experienced burglars. During this process, the older burglar teaches the novice about such tricks of the trade as dealing with defense attorneys, bail bondsmen, and other agents of the justice system. Consequently, the opportunity to become a good burglar is not open to everyone. Apprentices must be known to have the appropriate character before they are taken under the wing of the "old pro." Usually the opportunity to learn burglary comes as a reward for being a highly respected juvenile gang member; from knowing someone in the neighborhood who has made a living at burglary; or more often, from having built a reputation for being solid while serving time in prison.

Other attempts have been made to analyze and classify the characteristics of burglars. H. A. Scarr distinguishes between professional burglars and high-school-age, drug-abusing "casual" burglars.[46] Thomas Repetto investigated burglary in the Boston area and found that the typical burglar was a young, nonwhite male who was not skilled at his trade (not a professional, good burglar).[47] Using a complex statistical analysis of burglary incidents in California, Carl Pope found there was no relationship between the racial or criminal backgrounds of offenders and the patterns of their burglary offenses. Pope concluded: "unlike violent crimes . . . burglary, and other property crimes as well, may reflect more opportunity than choice."[48]

The Extent of Burglary. The FBI's definition of burglary is not restricted to burglary from a person's home; it includes any unlawful entry of a structure to commit theft or felony. Burglary is further categorized into three subclasses: forcible entry, unlawful entry where no force is used, and attempted forcible entry.[49]

According to the UCR, 3,120,842 burglaries occurred in 1983, a decline of about 9 percent from the preceding year. Similarly, the burglary rate declined about 10 percent to 1,333 per 100,000 population. In 1984 the rate dropped another 6 percent to 1263 per 100,000 (2,984,434 crimes). Most burglaries (66 percent) were of private residences; the remainder were business-related. Victims suffered a loss of $2.7 billion due to burglary.

The Bureau of Justice Statistics has analyzed burglary trends from 1973 to 1982 in order to provide a picture of burglary victimization. Some highlights of the survey are listed below:

- Between 1973 and 1982, 73,308,000 household burglaries occurred in the United States.

The Professional Torch

The following selection describes the activities of "torches"—professional criminals who make their living from setting fires.

In arson-for-profit, individuals hired to start fires, "torches," range from amateurs to professionals. Torches are the most familiar criminal specialists, but they are often the most difficult to apprehend. One reason for this difficulty is that many torches are recruited from the ranks of burglars and other petty thieves who know how to case a neighborhood and building, and how to enter and exit at night without being noticed. Another reason is that the "technology" required to set incendiary fires is very basic, and the use of gasoline or other available accelerants leaves few traces that automatically point to a particular torch. A third reason is that the requirements of proof under most arson statutes involve a showing of exclusive opportunity to set the fire, and when the owner-insured has contracted out the arson to a torch (amateur or professional), the question of who had exclusive opportunity to set the fire becomes very difficult to answer.

Torches often specialize in the types of structures they burn. This seems to be largely a function of their familiarity with a certain section of a city or with certain types of housing or commercial establishments. A further distinction can be drawn among amateur, semi-professional, and professional torches based on their use of timing devices, accelerants, or explosives.

The professional torch is knowledgeable in the sophisticated use of timing devices, chemicals that do not leave an easily traceable accelerant pattern (as does gasoline), and explosives used in burning commercial structures. The semiprofessional torch is adept in the proper and relatively safe use of gasoline and paint thinner as accelerants, probably with the use of trailers. He has some basic knowledge as to the necessity of proper ventilation if a building is to burn successfully. The amateur torch can be a one-time or occasionally an experienced torch who simply uses a relatively small quantity of gasoline and immediate ignition devices, such as matches or railroad flares. The amateur lacks knowledge as to the true burning characteristics of fire, ignition devices, chemicals, and explosives; the amateur is also unsophisticated in terms of the evidence left behind and the relative dangers in immediate ignition of an incendiary fire. It is not uncommon for amateurs to kill or burn themselves in the act.

While most torches are known to boast about their professional expertise, the handiwork of those who are more amateur than professional can be seen in cases where adjacent buildings were badly damaged or fire fighters were injured or killed. Very often, the use of extraordinary quantities of accelerant, seriously endangering fire fighters and occupants, is a sign of an amateur. One hallmark of a true professional is the total engagement of the target premises (and no damage to another) by the time the fire service arrives. What may be deceiving is the first try of a torch experienced at setting multifamily residential fires who tries his hand at an industrial facility and comes wide of the mark through the use of too much gasoline or explosives improperly placed. Such a torch is not really a rank amateur, but one who has gone beyond the range of his particular expertise.

As torches progress in their criminal careers, many graduate into planning and supervisory roles. These individuals may be termed "master torches." Usually they act as prime contractors for the owner or fire broker and procure others to commit the actual incendiarism. Because their experience builds over the years, proficient master torches generally know just how much accelerant to use and whether an explosive device may be needed. Because they act as prime contractors, they frequently serve as middlemen between the actual torches who set the fires and fire brokers and/or owners. It is also not uncommon to find a fire broker whose fascination with incendiary crime leads him to assume the additional role of master torch. In so doing, the fire broker brings increased specialization to his task without the added cost of a separate specialist. However, he also increases his vulnerability because of additional interactions with

- About 40 percent of all burglaries were committed by family or acquaintances of the victim.
- Black homes were victimized much more frequently than white homes.
- Families with the lowest (under $7,500) and highest (over $25,000) incomes experienced the most burglaries.
- Homeowners and single-family residences had lower burglary rates than renters and multiple-family dwellings.
- Urban areas had significantly higher burglary rates than rural areas.
- Burglary occurs more often in warm summer months.

torches, owners, and others who are involved to discuss specific plans for the fire. If a master torch is at all active in a jurisdiction, his role in a conspiracy probably will be central enough to implicate the others.

The torch is usually paid a flat fee, rather than a percentage of the insurance, for his service. Professional torches, especially the very good ones, normally command between $1000 and $5000 per arson fire. The fee for semiprofessional torches will normally range from $500 to $1000, and amateurs usually receive between $100 and $500. In contrast to the fortunes that other fraud schemers make in arson frauds, the torch, certainly a specialist, may seem in comparison to be underpaid. This phenomenon has several explanations. First, the torch is usually paid in cash, with a "good faith" down payment prior to the fire, and the remainder afterwards. Second, the amount paid to a torch is controlled by the simple law of supply and demand. In any jurisdiction there are enough freelance torches so that the availability of this essentially cheap, semiskilled labor has the effect of driving down the price any one torch can command. If the price for a commercial business is $1000, and a torch who is asked to set that fire refuses, demanding $2000, the owner merely says, "Ridiculous—too high; see you around," and proceeds to find one of the many other equally competent and trustworthy torches who will set the fire for the prevailing wage. Third, torches are basically freelance underworld fringe figures, handling perhaps a burglary here, a fire there. While many of them do not exactly live hand-to-mouth, the irregular and often unpredictable demand for their services makes almost any arson offer attractive, especially because it carries the promise of quick payment.

There have been instances of a torch reportedly being paid upwards of $5000 for a fire, or possibly 10 percent of the insurance settlement. Such apparent exceptions to the rule can be explained. Basically, the deal that a torch strikes alone with an owner is a bargain between the two of them. When there is no organized market for the services of a torch, or when the owner is naive and does not check prevailing torch fees, negotiations often turn to the advantage of the torch. One reason for the attractiveness of pigeons and fire brokers to owners is that these specialists, who market the commodity of information, help the owner understand what he will have to do to execute an arson fraud, and how much he can expect to pay for "quality" workmanship. Just like the upperworld of legitimate business, the owner pays the broker or pigeon a consideration for making him privy to this valuable, highly technical information on prices and quality of workmanship. However, the isolated owner may not know how to find such expertise, or may be too frightened even to look. Hence, he ends up being "gouged" by the torch who may be a cunning businessman in his own right.

Torches come from many underworld quarters, but they are mainly fringe figures in crime who perform a variety of usually dirty, manual tasks. Many either double as drug user/dealers or burglars or got their start earlier in burglary or other petty thieving. Others became torches because they were seasonally unemployed as lower-level fringe figures in white-collar or organized crime or in a legitimate business (such as contracting) where they rubbed shoulders with financial schemers always looking for torches to do the hazardous, dirty work of setting fires. There are reports that many torches have a violent streak that causes them to enjoy the damage done by incendiary fires. Those who describe such torches also point to their frequent eagerness to serve as underworld enforcers, suggesting that they especially enjoy such tasks as threatening or beating loan shark clients who are in default. Altogether, too few torches have been caught to permit an objective study of their psychological motivation. Clearly, their economic motivation, of which considerably more is known, goes a considerable length in explaining this criminal behavior.

DISCUSSION QUESTIONS

1. Which is the most serious criminal—the torch or the businessperson who hires him?

2. Should arson for profit be punished more severely than crimes such as robbery, rape or burglary?

SOURCE. Leigh Edward Somers, *Economic Crimes* (New York: Clark Boardman, 1984), pp. 158–68.

• During the ten-year period, 2.8 million acts of violence were committed during an act of burglary.[50]

Arson

Arson is the willful and malicious burning of a home, public building, vehicle, or commercial building of another. The FBI found that 101,947 arsons were committed in 1983—about 48.7 per 100,000. The arson rate did not change substantially in 1984 when 101,836 arsons were reported.[51]

Arson is a young man's crime. Of the 19,000 people arrested in 1983, about 64 percent were under twenty-five, 43 percent were eighteen and under, and 28 percent were fifteen and under. The percentage of young teens arrested for the crime of arson was higher than it was for any other Part I crime and most Part II crimes (except vandalism, runaways, and curfew violations). Also, arson is primarily a white (78 percent), male (88 percent) crime.

There are several motives for arson; some stem from personal psychological problems, others are the work of a deranged person bent on revenge, still others are simply teenagers out to vandalize property. But a growing phenomenon is **arson for profit**, or **arson fraud**, which involves a business owner burning his or her property, or hiring someone to do it for them, to escape from financial problems.[52] Over the years, investigators have found that businesspeople are willing to become involved in arson to collect fire insurance or for various other reasons, including but not limited to:

- Obtaining money during a period of financial crisis
- Getting rid of outdated or slow-moving inventory
- Destroying outmoded machines and technology
- Paying off legal and illegal debt
- Relocating or remodeling a business; for example, when a "theme" restaurant has not been accepted by customers
- Taking advantage of government funds available for redevelopment
- Applying for government building money, pocketing it without making repairs, and then claiming that fire destroyed the "rehabilitated" building
- Planning bankruptcies to eliminate debts from creditors, after the merchandise supposedly destroyed was secretly sold before the fire
- Eliminating business competition by burning out rivals
- Employing extortion schemes that demand pay-up or the rest of the victim's holdings will be burned
- Solving labor/management problems; arson may be committed by a disgruntled employee
- Concealing another crime, for example, embezzlement

The following Close-Up describes the activities of an important participant in the crime of arson for profit, the professional **torch**.

Summary

Economic crimes are designed to bring financial reward to the offender. The majority of economic crimes are committed by opportunistic amateurs. However, economic crime has also attracted professional criminals. Professionals earn the bulk of their income from crime, view themselves as criminals, and possess skills that aid them in their law breaking.

Edwin Sutherland's classic book, *The Professional Thief*, is perhaps the most famous portrayal of professional crime. According to Sutherland and his informant Chic Conwell, professionals live by their wits and never resort to violence. A good example of the professional criminal is the fence who buys and sells stolen merchandise.

Common theft offenses include larceny, embezzlement, fraud, and burglary. These are common-law crimes, created by English judges to meet existing social needs. Larceny involves taking the legal possession of another. Petty larceny is theft of amounts under $100; grand larceny, of amounts usually over $100. The crime of false pretenses, or fraud, is similar to larceny because it involves the theft of goods or money; but it differs because the criminal tricks victims into voluntarily giving up their possessions. Embezzlement is another larceny crime. It involves people's taking something that was temporarily entrusted to them, such as bank tellers' taking money out of the cash drawer and keeping it for themselves. Most states have codified these common-law crimes in their state codes. New larceny crimes have also been defined to keep abreast of changing social conditions: passing bad checks, stealing or illegally using credit cards, shoplifting, stealing autos.

Burglary, a more serious theft offense, was defined in the common law as the "breaking and entering of a dwelling house of another in the nighttime with the intent to commit a felony within." Today, most states have modified their definitions of burglary to include theft from any structure at any time of day. Because burglary involves planning and risk, it attracts professional thieves. The most competent are known as good burglars. Good burglars have technical competence and personal integrity, specialize in burglary, are financially successful, and avoid prison sentences.

Arson is another serious property crime. Though most arsonists are teenage vandals, there are professional arsonists who specialize in burning commercial buildings for profit.

Notes

1 John Hepburn, "Occasional Criminals," in Robert Meier, ed. *Major Forms of Crime* (Beverly Hills, Calif.: Sage Publications, 1984), pp. 73–94.

2 James Inciardi, "Professional Crime," in Meier, *Major Forms of Crime*, p. 223.

3 Harry King and William Chambliss, *Box Man: A Professional Thief's Journal* (New York: Harper & Row, 1972), p. 24.

4 Edwin Sutherland, "White-Collar Criminality," *American Sociological Review* 5 (1940): 2–10.

5 Gilbert Geis, "Avocational Crime," in *Handbook of Criminology*, ed. D. Glazer (Chicago: Rand McNally, 1974), p. 284.

6 Edwin Sutherland and Chic Conwell, *The Professional Thief* (Chicago: University of Chicago Press, 1937).

7 Ibid., pp. 197–98.

8 Ibid., p. 212.

9 Cited in Marilyn Walsh, *The Fence* (Westport, Conn.: Greenwood Press, 1977), p. 1.

10 Carl Klockars, *The Professional Fence* (New York: Free Press, 1976).

11 Walsh, *The Fence*.

12 Andrew McCall, *The Medieval Underworld* (London: Hamish Hamilton, 1979), p. 86.

13 Ibid., p. 104.

14 J. J. Tobias, *Crime and Police in England 1700–1900* (London: Gill and Macmillan, 1979).

15 Ibid., p. 9.

16 Walsh, *The Fence*, pp. 18–25.

17 This section depends heavily on a classic book: Wayne La Fave and Austin Scott, *Handbook on Criminal Law* (St. Paul, Minn.: West Publishing Company, 1972).

18 Ibid., p. 622.

19 FBI, *Crime in the United States, 1984* (Washington, D.C.: Government Printing Office, 1985), p. 27.

20 La Fave and Scott, *Handbook on Criminal Law*, p. 655.

21 30 Geo. III, C.24 (1757).

22 La Fave and Scott, *Handbook on Criminal Law*, p. 644.

23 Ibid., p. 649.

24 Edwin Lemert, "An Isolation and Closure Theory of Naive Check Forgery," *Journal of Criminal Law, Criminology and Police Science* 44 (1953):297–98.

25 FBI, *Crime in the United States, 1983*, p. 170.

26 As described in Charles McCaghy, *Deviant Behavior* (New York: Macmillan, 1976), pp. 230–31.

27 "Credit Card Fraud Toll 1 Billion," *Omaha World Herald*, 16 March 1982, p. 16.

28 Ibid.

29 La Fave and Scott, *Handbook on Criminal Law*, p. 672.

30 D. Hartmann, D. Gelfand, B. Page, and P. Walder, "Rates of Bystander Observation and Reporting of Contrived Shoplifting Incidents," *Criminology* 10 (1972):248.

31 Mary Owen Cameron, *The Booster and the Snitch* (New York: Free Press, 1964).

32 Ibid., p. 57.

33 Hartmann et al., "Rates of Bystander Observation and Reporting," p. 267.

34 Erhard Blankenburg, "The Selectivity of Legal Sanctions: An Empirical Investigation of Shoplifting," *Law and Society Review* 11 (1976):109–29.

35 Michael Hindelang, "Decisions of Shoplifting Victims to Invoke the Criminal Justice Process," *Social Problems* 21 (1974):580–95.

36 Laurence Cohen and Rodney Stark, "Discriminatory Labeling and the Five-Finger Discount: An Empirical Analysis of Differential Shoplifting Dispositions," *Journal of Research on Crime and Delinquency* 11 (1974):25–35.

37 Lloyd Klemke, "Does Apprehension for Shoplifting Amplify or Terminate Shoplifting Activity," *Law and Society Review* 12 (1978):390–403.

38 FBI, *Crime in the United States, 1984*, p. 29–31.

39 Donald Gibbons, *Society, Crime and Criminal Careers* (Englewood Cliffs, N.J.: Prentice-Hall, 1977), p. 310.

40 Charles McCaghy, Peggy Giordano, and Trudy Knicely Henson, "Auto Theft," *Criminology* 15 (1977):367–81.

41 FBI, *Crime in the United States, 1984*, p. 32. Updated.

42 La Fave and Scott, *Handbook on Criminal Law*, p. 708.

43 E. Blackstone, *Commentaries on the Laws of England* (London: 1769), p. 224.

44 Frank Hoheimer, *The Home Invaders: Confessions of a Cat Burglar* (Chicago: Chicago Review, 1975). Cited in J. Macdonald, *Burglary and Theft* (Springfield, Ill.: Charles C. Thomas, 1980), p. 21.

45 See Generally, Neal Shover, "Structures and Careers in Burglary," *Journal of Criminal Law, Criminology and Police Science* 63 (1972):540–49.

46 H. A. Scarr, *Patterns of Burglary* (Washington, D.C.: Government Printing Office, 1973).

47 Thomas Repetto, *Residential Crime* (Cambridge, Mass.: Ballinger, 1974).

48 Carl Pope, "Patterns in Burglary: An Empirical Examination of Offense and Offender Characteristics," *Journal of Criminal Justice* 8 (1980):39–51.

49 See generally FBI, *Crime in the United States, 1984*, p. 24–26.

50 Bureau of Justice Statistics, *Household Burglary* (Washington, D.C.: National Institute of Justice, 1985).

51 FBI, *Uniform Crime Reports, 1984*, pp. 37–41.

52 Leigh Edward Somers, *Economic Crimes* (New York: Clark Boardman, 1984), pp. 158–68.

12 | Economic Crimes: Organizational Criminality

CHAPTER OUTLINE

Introduction

White-Collar Crime

The White-Collar Crime Problem

Components of White-Collar Crime

Why Do They Do It?

Controlling White-Collar Crime

White-Collar Law Enforcement

White-Collar Law Enforcement Systems

Organized Crime

Activities of Organized Crime

The Concept of Organized Crime

Characteristics of Organized Crime

History of Organized Crime

Organized Crime Today

Controlling Organized Crime

Summary

KEY TERMS

white-collar crime

organized crime

enterprise

churning

pilferage

Knapp Commission

Operation Greylord

tying arrangement

compliance

deterrence

technical violation

economism

Mafia

La Cosa Nostra

alien conspiracy theory

enterprise syndicates

power syndicates

Kefauver Committee

RICO

Introduction

Economic crimes are not committed solely by lower-class people striving to make up for financial deficiencies. A significant portion of all economic crimes are illegal practices involving existing organizations and institutions. In this chapter, we divide these crimes into two distinct categories—**white-collar crimes** and **organized crime**. The first category, white-collar crime, involves the *illegal* activities of people and institutions whose acknowledged purpose is profit and gain through *legitimate* business transactions. The second category, organized crime, involves the *illegal* activity of people and organizations whose acknowledged purpose is *illegitimate* gain through *illegal* enterprise.

Organized crime and white-collar crime are linked together here because, as criminologist Dwight Smith argues, **enterprise** and not crime is the governing characteristic of both phenomena:

> . . . white-collar crime is not simply a dysfunctional aberration. Organized crime is not something ominously alien to the American economic system. Both are made criminal by laws declaring that certain ways of doing business, or certain products of business, are illegal. In other words, criminality is not an inherent characteristic either of certain persons or of certain business activities but rather, an externally imposed evaluation of alternative modes of behavior and action.[1]

According to Smith, the concept of business enterprise can be viewed as flowing through a spectrum of acts ranging from the most saintly to the most sinful.[2] Any business transaction, be it legitimate or illegitimate, can be located within the range of behavior. And, regardless whether "sinful" organizational practices may be desirable (e.g., sale of narcotics) or efficient (e.g., dumping of hazardous wastes), society has seen fit to regulate or outlaw these behaviors. Consequently, organized crime and the crimes of business are the results of a process by which "political, value-based, constraints are based on economic activity."[3] In other words, organizational crimes occur when people or institutions find that their entrepreneurial objectives are blunted by restrictions placed against the product they wish to merchandise or the process they use to obtain, create, or distribute it. Organized crime occurs because of restrictions placed against a desired product (drugs, sex, gambling, loan sharking, and so on), whereas white-collar crimes involve the use of illegal processes (embezzlement, price-fixing, bribery, etc.) to merchandise a legitimate product. Both acts involve human enterprise and attempts by society to control its abuses.

White-Collar Crime

In the late 1930s, the distinguished criminologist Edwin Sutherland first used the phrase *white-collar crime* to describe the criminal activities of the rich and powerful. As Sutherland saw it, white-collar crime involved conspiracies by members of the wealthy classes to use their position in commerce and industry for personal gain without regard to the law. All too often these actions were handled by civil courts, since injured parties were more concerned with getting back their losses than seeing the offenders punished criminally. Consequently, Sutherland believed that the great majority of white-collar criminals did not become the subject of criminological study. Yet their crimes were very costly:

> The financial cost of white-collar crime is probably several times as great as the financial cost of all the crimes which are customarily regarded as the "crime

problem." . . . *the financial loss from white-collar crime, great as it is, is less important than the damage to social relations. White-collar crimes violate trust and therefore create distrust, which lowers social morale and produces disorganization on a large scale. Other crimes produce relatively little effect on social institutions or social organization.*[4]

Though Sutherland's work is considered a milestone in criminological history, his focus was on corporate criminality. Today, there exists some debate among criminologists over what actually constitutes white-collar crime. Sutherland's major concern was the crimes of the rich and powerful. Modern criminologists have broadened their definition of white-collar crime so that it now includes a wide variety of situations.[5] For example, today's definition of white-collar criminals can include people acting as individuals who use the marketplace for the purpose of their criminal activity. This category of crime includes such acts as income tax evasion, credit card fraud, and bankruptcy fraud. Other white-collar criminals use their positions of trust in business or government to commit crimes. Their activities might include pilfering, soliciting bribes or kickbacks, and embezzlement. Some white-collar criminals set up businesses for the sole purpose of victimizing the general public. They engage in land swindles (representing swamps as choice building sites), securities thefts, medical or health frauds, and so on.

In addition to acting as individuals, some white-collar criminals become involved in criminal conspiracies designed to improve the market share or profitability of their corporations. This type of white-collar crime, which includes antitrust violations, price-fixing, and false advertising, is also known as *corporate crime.*

It is evident that Sutherland's original concept of the upper-class, white-collar criminal has been expanded by these later formulations. Today, as a general rule, criminologists use the term white-collar crime to refer to almost any occupationally oriented law violation. "White-collar crimes can be committed by persons in all social classes," claims one sociologist, Gilbert Geis; this perspective has been accepted by most mainstream criminologists.[6]

THE WHITE-COLLAR CRIME PROBLEM

It is difficult to estimate the extent and influence of white-collar crime. Some experts place its total monetary value in the hundreds of billions of dollars, far outstripping the expense of any other type of crime. Beyond their monetary cost, white-collar crimes often involve damage to property and loss of human life. Violations of safety standards, pollution of the environment, and industrial accidents due to negligence can be classified as corporate violence. Laura Schrager and James Short suggest that corporate crime annually results in 20 million serious injuries, including 110,000 people who become permanently disabled and 30,000 deaths.[7] They say that "the potential impact ranges from acute environmental catastrophies such as the collapse of a dam to the chronic effects of diseases resulting from industrial pollution."[8]

In a similar vein, sociologist Gilbert Geis charges that white-collar crime is actually likely to be much more serious than street crimes:

It destroys confidence, saps the integrity of commercial life and has the potential for devastating destruction. Think of the possible results if nuclear regulatory rules are flouted or if toxic wastes are dumped into a community's drinking water supply.[9]

The public has begun to recognize the seriousness of white-collar crimes and demand that they be controlled. The national survey of crime seriousness reported on in chapter 1 found that some white-collar crimes—such as a county judge taking a bribe to give a light sentence (15.7), a doctor cheating on Medicare forms (14.1), and a factory knowingly getting rid of waste in a way that pollutes the water supply (13.0)—are given higher seriousness scores than a person stabbing another with a knife (11.8) and a person stealing property worth $10,000 from outside a building (10.9).[10]

Nonetheless, the prosecution of white-collar criminals remains a relatively rare event and their imprisonment occurs even less often. Frequently, monetary fines and not prison sentences are the choice of judges and prosecutors who are loath to incarcerate offenders who do not fit the image of "common criminals."

The leniency afforded white-collar criminals is illustrated by two incidents involving big business, which received widespread national attention.[11] In one case, stockbroker E.F. Hutton pleaded guilty to 2,000 counts of fraud arising from a multibillion-dollar bad check scheme. More than 20 Hutton executives defrauded 400 banks out of millions of dollars in interest. The penalty: a fine of $2.75 million and an order to repay the banks. In the second case, General Electric was found guilty of defrauding the Air Force of $800,000 on a nuclear warhead contract. Their penalty: $1.84 million. To multibillion-dollar companies, these penalties are a slap on the wrist. No company officers went to prison, nor were they personally penalized. A Senate investigating committee looking into these cases made note of a concurrent incident in which a woman who shoplifted four sweaters received a thirty-day jail sentence; society still punishes nonviolent street crimes more severely than multimillion-dollar white-collar crimes, and all too often the perpetrators are immune from prosecution.

COMPONENTS OF WHITE-COLLAR CRIME

As noted, white-collar crimes today represent a range of behaviors involving individuals acting alone and also within the context of a business structure. The victims of white-collar crime can be the general public, the organization that employs the criminal, or another organization.

Numerous attempts have been made to create subcategories or typologies of white-collar criminality. One of the most well known was presented by Herbert Edelhertz over a decade ago.[12] Edelhertz divided white-collar criminality into four distinct categories:

1. *Ad-hoc violations.* Committed for personal profit on an episodic basis. For example, welfare fraud, tax cheating.
2. *Abuses of trust.* Committed by a person in a place of trust in an organization against the organization. For example, embezzlement, bribery, or taking kickbacks.
3. *Collateral business crimes.* Committed by organizations to further their business interests. For example, antitrust violations, use of false weights and measures, concealment of environmental crimes.
4. *Con games.* Committed for the sole purpose of cheating clients. For example, fraudulent land sales, sales of bogus securities, sales of questionable tax shelters.

Edelhertz's typology captures the diverse nature of white-collar criminality and illustrates how both individuals and institutions can be the victims/offenders of a white-collar crime.

In the present text, a typology created by criminologist Mark Moore serves as a means of organizing the discussion of white-collar crime. Moore's typology contains seven elements, ranging from an individual using a business enterprise to commit theft-related crimes, to an individual using their place within a business enterprise for illegal gain, to business enterprises themselves collectively engaging in illegitimate activity.

Stings and Swindles. Moore's first category of white-collar crime involves stealing through deception by individuals who have no continuing institutional or business position and whose entire purpose is to bilk people out of their money.[13]

Offenses in this category range from frauds involving the door-to-door sale of faulty merchandise to the passing of millions of dollars in counterfeit stock certificates to an established brokerage firm. If caught, white-collar swindlers are usually charged with common-law crimes such as embezzlement or fraud.

Swindles can run into millions of dollars. In one well-known case, Gary Lewellyn misappropriated almost $18 million, most of it from an Iowa bank his father managed. He used the money to manipulate and drive up the price of stock he purchased in Safeguard Scientific, Inc. When his scheme was uncovered the stock's price plummeted, wiping Lewellyn out. As a final gesture, he withdrew $500,000 of embezzled money and flew to Las Vegas, where he played blackjack sixteen hours a day to recoup his losses; he lost $300,000 more. After his father's bank went bankrupt, Lewellyn received a twenty-year prison sentence.[14]

The extent of Lewellyn's actions are staggering, but they pale in comparison with the case of the Equity Funding Corporation of America, whose officers bilked the public out of an estimated $2 billion in 1973. The directors of this firm, a life insurance company, claimed to have 90,000 policy holders. However, more than 60,000 of them existed as fictitious entries in the company's computer banks. Equity sold ownership and management of these bogus policies to reinsurance companies, and corporate officers pocketed the profit. The $2 billion loss probably is the greatest of all time from a white-collar crime.[15]

Although scams such as these have received widespread publicity, the public seems quite willing to continue to be fleeced by business-related cons. For example, a task force in securities fraud formed in the State of Utah estimated that 12,000 investors lost at least $215 million in phony stock deals in a five-year period ending in 1985.[16]

The Close-Up entitled "Stings and Swindles" illustrates some common schemes still used to bilk people.

Chiseling. Chiseling, the second category of white-collar crime, involves cheating consumers on a regular basis. This can involve charging for bogus auto repairs, cheating customers on home repairs, or short-weighting in supermarkets or dairies. The offenders may be individuals looking to make quick profits in their own businesses, or employees of large organizations who decide to cheat on obligations to customers or clients by doing something contrary to company policy.

Investigators at the Stanford Research Institute found that chiseling from the federal government may cost taxpayers as much as $25 billion a year. Among the various schemes uncovered were the following:

Stings and Swindles: Real Estate and Land Crimes

This type of economic crime usually involves the purported *developers, or perpetrators, misrepresenting the investment and development of land and real estate*. Perpetrators often make false and misleading investment claims concerning the land's or real estate's profit potential, quality as an investment, time frame for profitable sale, lack of risk, and ease of resale. This scheme usually includes promises by the perpetrators of improvement to the land, such as construction of roads or utilities, and misleading statements concerning the timing of future developments and the cost of improvements. Often, after substantial down payments are made by a large number of investors, they discover that there is no land or real estate and that the perpetrators have departed with the money.

The following is an example of a land sales fraud that is typical of many perpetrators' method of operation. This example is from testimony given before the House of Representatives Select Committee on Aging on 16 June 1982. The committee was investigating land investments and time-sharing abuses.

EXAMPLE

One of the largest fraud schemes perpetrated in the state of California began when several individuals formed Prebuilder Land Corporation (PBL). From the time of its formation until the conviction of its principal operators in November 1980, the scheme operated by PBL resulted in losses to investors, many of whom were elderly, in excess of $15 million. PBL advertised extensively in newspapers and business journals. Prospective customers were told that PBL was a land broker soliciting customers to purchase raw land that allegedly was being sold at below market value and was in the path of imminent development. Customers were promised that they would double their money within three to five years, and that the PBL would advise customers of the best time to sell their land. When customers contacted PBL to make arrangements to sell their land, they discovered that rather than doubling in value, their investment actually had little if any market value. Much of the land was located in a flood plain, which completely precluded any potential development and made the land unsalable at any price.

PBL told investors it had never owned the land it was selling and had acted only as a broker. In fact, the land was owned by PBL's principals through shell companies. PBL would purchase property and then resell it through a paper transaction one or two times from one PBL-controlled shell corporation to another at escalating prices. PBL would then sell parcels to investors at claimed "bargain prices," which were almost double the price at which PBL originally acquired the land. PBL sales techniques and presentations were so effective that many potential investors did not even visit the land they were buying. Three promoters were convicted of mail fraud and were sentenced to prison terms of from eighteen months to three years. All three will be on probation for three years following their release from prison.

DISCUSSION QUESTIONS

1. Should swindlers be punished with prison sentences, or be made to pay restitution plus fines?
2. Should the government closely monitor the sale of land and real estate as they do pharmaceuticals?

SOURCE. Leigh Edward Somers, *Economic Crimes* (New York: Clark Boardman, 1984), pp. 7–8.

- A doctor bills the government for unnecessary or duplicate Medicaid services.
- The government receives bills for medical treatments that were not performed.
- An individual applies for several welfare benefits under different names.
- A farming couple receives two crop loss loans at low interest rates, one under the husband's name and the other in the wife's maiden name.
- A store accepts food stamps for liquor, cigarettes, or television sets.
- The operator of a school lunch program overstates the number of children fed and the cost of their meals.[17]

Helping the chiselers were the facts that few government agencies keep reliable statistics and that each program uses different requirements and terminology.

Some people view chiseling as a lower-class phenomenon, but it is not uncommon for professionals to use their positions to commit this type of crime. For example, some physicians have been caught cheating the federal government out of Medicare or Medicaid payments. Abusive practices include such techniques as "ping-ponging" (referring patients to other physicians in the same office), "gang visits" (billing for multiple services), and "steering" (directing patients to particular pharmacies). Doctors who abuse their Medicaid/Medicare patients in this way are liable to civil suit.[18]

Of a more serious nature are fraudulent acts designed to cheat both the government and the consumer. Such Medicaid frauds generally involve billing for services not actually rendered, billing in excessive amounts, setting up kickback schemes, and providing false identification on reimbursement forms. Doctors involved in these schemes are liable to criminal prosecution under federal and state law.[19]

It has been estimated that the total cost of Medicaid fraud is $2.5 to $6.25 billion a year. Despite the magnitude of this abuse, the state and federal governments have been reluctant to prosecute Medicaid fraud. A study of enforcement practices found that eighteen states did not convict a single person of Medicaid abuse in 1980, and the national average over a seven-year period (1974–1980) was 1.5 convictions per state per year. One trend has been to establish Medicaid fraud investigation units. The thirty states that have employed such measures have already disallowed $86.5 million in faulty Medicaid bills.[20]

Physicians are not the only professionals who engage in chiseling. Pharmacists have been known to alter prescriptions or substitute low-cost generic drugs for more expensive name brands. In a study of prescription violations, Richard Quinney found that the professional orientation of individual pharmacists had a significant influence on their law-violating behavior.[21] Pharmacists who were business-oriented—and therefore stressed merchandising, inventory turnover, and sales rather than servicing the public—were more inclined to chisel customers. Quinney attributed their fraudulent acts to the pursuit of profit at the expense of professional ethics.

The legal profession has also come under fire because of the unscrupulous behavior of some of its members. The Watergate hearings, which revealed the unethical behavior of high-ranking government attorneys, prompted the American Bar Association to require that all law students take a course in legal ethics.

Another common chiseling crime involves **churning** of a client's account by an unscrupulous stockbroker. Churning refers to repeated, excessive, and unnecessary buying and selling of stock. In one recent case a broker for Drexel, Burnham Lambert, pleaded guilty to bilking elderly clients out of $570,000 in fees.[22] The broker covered up the crime by diverting the clients' brokerage statements to a post office box and mailing out false statements.

Individual Exploitation of Institutional Position. The third type of white-collar crime involves individuals' exploiting their power or position in organizations to take advantage of other individuals who have an interest in how that power is used. For example, a fire inspector who demands that the owner of a restaurant pay him in order to be granted an operating license is abusing his institutional position. In most cases, this type of offense occurs when the victim has a clear right to expect a service and the offender uses his or her power to ask for an additional payment or bribe.

Exploitation in Government. U.S. political and governmental figures have long been accused of using their positions to profit from bribes and kickbacks.[23] As early as the 1830s, New York's political leaders used their position to control and profit from the city's police force. In the early nineteenth century, New York City's police chief, George Matsell, was the subject of numerous charges of bribe taking and profiteering. Though no evidence of his wrongdoing was ever proven in court, it was revealed five years after he retired in 1851 that Matsell had "saved" enough on his modest salary to build a twenty-room mansion on a three-thousand-acre estate.

During the Civil War, corruption increased proportionately with the amount of money being spent on the war effort. After the war, the nation's largest cities were controlled by political machines that used their offices to buy and sell political favors. The most notorious of these corrupt politicians was William Marcy "Boss" Tweed, who ruled New York City's Democratic party (Tammany Hall) from 1857 to 1871. During Tweed's reign, every company doing business with the city had to give kickbacks. Crime flourished under the protection of Tweed's Tammany Hall political allies. Within three miles of city hall, 400 brothels employing 4,000 prostitutes survived by paying protection money directly to city officials.[24]

Tweed's ring was ultimately responsible for the theft of millions of dollars. It used the construction of the city's new courthouse building to pull off one of its most ambitious plots. Originally budgeted for $250,000, the building ultimately cost $13 million. Companies supplying material for the courthouse made payoffs to Tweed in order to secure contracts. The building's carpets and furniture alone cost $7.5 million at a time when the dollar bought far more than it does today. Time eventually caught up with Tweed. A special investigating committee obtained evidence that he had misappropriated over $6 million in city funds. Indicted, he fled to Europe, only to be recognized and returned for trial. Tweed offered to confess and give evidence about others in return for leniency. However, when his confession named leading politicians of the time, it was suppressed; and Tweed died in jail.[25]

The use of political office for economic gain has not subsided. It is common for scandals to emerge naming liquor license board members, food inspectors, and fire inspectors as bribe takers. It is not unusual for building inspectors to expect a payoff in return for approving a construction project. One survey of New York City workers who had contact with the building and construction trade found that all who responded to the survey had either been personally involved with corruption or heard of its existence.[26]

Exploitation in Business. Exploitation also occurs in private industry. It is common for purchasing agents in large industries to demand a piece of the action for awarding contracts to suppliers and distributors. Marshall Clinard and Peter Yeager report on many cases, such as the one involving a J.C. Penney company employee who received $1.4 million from a contractor who eventually did $23 million of business with the concern.[27] In another case, a purchasing agent for the American Chiclets division of Warner-Lamberg (makers of Dentyne, Chiclets, Trident, and Dyna-mints) received a $300,000 kickback from the makers of the wire racks on which the gum products are displayed in supermarkets.

Another twist on the exploitation of a business position involves using inside information to help influence stock purchases and sales. The Securities and Exchange Commission regularly polices the abuse of power. In one celebrated case, the writer of the influential "Heard on the Street" column in the *Wall Street Journal* was convicted on a fraud and conspiracy charge after he wrote favorably about stocks purchased previously by a co-conspirator and then sold for profits in which the writer shared.[28]

In sum, exploitation in the business world involves using one's position to secure illegal payments and profits. For many Americans this has almost become an accepted way of life.

Embezzlement and Employee Fraud. The fourth type of white-collar crime involves individuals' use of their positions to embezzle company funds or appropriate company property for themselves. Here, the company or organization that employs the criminal, rather than an outsider, is the victim of white-collar crime.

Employee theft can reach all levels of the organizational structure. One significant problem has been widespread theft of company property or profits by employees, commonly called **pilferage**. It is difficult to determine the value of goods taken by employees, but it has been estimated that pilferage accounted for 30 to 75 percent of all shrinkage and amounts to losses of $5–10 billion annually.[29]

The techniques of employee theft are quite varied. Charles McCaghy reports on different methods used to steal from employers:

- Piece workers zip up completed garments into their clothing and take them home.
- Cashiers ring up lower prices on single-item purchases and pocket the difference. Some will work with an accomplice and ring up low prices as [the accomplice goes] through the line.
- Clerks do not tag sale merchandise and then [they] sell it at its original cost, pocketing the difference.
- Receiving clerks obtain duplicate keys to storage facilities and then return after hours to steal.
- Truck drivers make fictitious purchases of fuel and repairs and then split the gains with truck stop owners. Truckers have been known to cooperate with the receiving staff of department stores to cheat employers. In one instance, truckers would keep 20 cases of goods out of every 100 delivered. The store receiving staff would sign a bill of lading for all 100, and the two groups split the profits after the stolen goods were sold to a fence.
- Some employees simply hide items in garbage pails, incinerators, or under trash heaps until they can be retrieved later.[30]

Blue-collar workers are not the only employees who commit corporate theft. Management-level fraud is also quite common. Such acts include: (1) converting company assets for personal benefit; (2) fraudulently receiving increases in compensation (such as raises or bonuses); (3) fraudulently increasing personal holdings of company stock; (4) retaining one's present position within the company by manipulating accounts; (5) concealing unacceptable performance from stockholders.[31]

In their study of workplace theft, John Clark and Richard Hollinger found that about 35 percent of employees reported involvement in pilferage.[32] Clark and Hollinger's data indicate that employee theft is most accurately explained by factors relevant to the work setting such as job dissatisfaction and the workers' feeling that they were being exploited by employers or supervisors. In contrast, economic problems played a relatively small role in the decision to pilfer. Even though economic and community variables can help explain street crime, they have relatively little effect on employee crime.

Computer Crime. Computer-related thefts are a new trend in employee theft and embezzlement. The widespread use of computers to record business transactions has encouraged some people to use them for illegal purposes. Computer crimes generally fall into one of four categories: (1) theft of services, in which the criminal uses the computer for unauthorized purposes or an unauthorized user penetrates the computer system; (2) use of data in a computer system for personal gain; (3) unauthorized use of computers employed for various types of financial processing to obtain assets; and (4) theft of property by computer for personal use or conversion to profit.[33]

Several common techniques are used by computer criminals. In fact, computer theft has become so common that experts have created their own jargon to describe theft styles and methods:

- *The trojan horse.* One computer is used to reprogram another for illicit purposes. In a recent incident, two high-school-age computer users reprogrammed the computer at DePaul University, preventing that institution from using its own processing facilities. The youths were convicted of a misdemeanor.

- *The salami slice.* An employee sets up a dummy account in the company's computerized records. A small amount—even a few pennies—is subtracted from customers' accounts and added to the account of the thief. Even if they detect the loss, the customers don't complain, since a few cents is an insignificant amount to them. The pennies picked up here and there eventually amount to thousands of dollars in losses.

- *Super-zapping.* Most computer programs used in business have built-in antitheft safeguards. However, employees can use a repair or maintenance program to supersede the antitheft program. Some tinkering with the program is required, but the "super-zapper" is soon able to order the system to issue checks to his or her private account.

- *The logic bomb.* A program is secretly attached to the company's computer system. The new program monitors the company's work and waits for a sign of error to appear, some illogic that was designed for the computer to follow. Illogic causes the logic bomb to kick into action and exploit the weakness. The way the thief exploits the situation depends on his or her original intent—theft of money, theft of defense secrets, sabotage, and so on.

- *Impersonation.* An unauthorized person uses the identity of an authorized computer user in order to use the computer in his or her stead.

- *Data leakage.* A person illegally obtains data from a computer system by leaking it out in small amounts.

Several well-publicized cases have involved computer theft. A federal grand jury indicted a boxing promoter and two bank officials on charges of embezzling more than $21 million by computer from the Wells Fargo Bank. The bank officials knew how to submit false credits and debits to the computer in time to prevent the bank's internal security system from detecting the fraud. In a similar case, Jerry Schneider, an employee of Pacific Telephone and Telegraph, gained access to the company's computers and authorized them to make daily deliveries of equipment to a warehouse he rented.[34] After he had stolen $1 million worth of telephone parts, his crimes were detected; Schneider was sentenced to sixty days in jail. Upon his release, he was hired as a computer security consultant. In Baltimore, a Social Security department worker was convicted on charges of ordering the office computer to send unauthorized disability payments to confederates in Philadelphia and

Washington; over $500,000 was stolen before the crime was detected. The Equity Funding case, discussed earlier, involved the use of falsified computer records to steal an estimated $2 billion.[35]

An accurate accounting of computer crime will probably never be made, since so many offenses go unreported. One computer consultant, Robert H. Courtney, claims that the likelihood of prosecution is inversely proportional to the amount of money involved. "The bigger the theft, the greater the embarrassment to the company." Though one of Courtney's clients, an insurance company, lost $38.1 million to a senior officer, management refused to report the crime to police lest they display their managerial incompetence to stockholders and competitors.[36]

It is likely that computer-related crime will blossom as business becomes more computer-dependent. For example, such recent advances as automatic bank teller machines have been a source of illegal gain. Bank employees have used returned or unused bank cards to make withdrawals after electronically transferring funds to the nonexistent account. Similarly, computer culprits have benefited from the increased use of computerized phone networks like Sprint and MCI; in California, "hackers" made $60,000 worth of illegal charges on the Sprint account of a man whose access number they obtained.[37] Thus, as computer applications become more varied, so too will the use of computers for illegal purposes.

The growth of computer-related crimes prompted Congress in 1984 to enact the Counterfeit Active Device and Computer Fraud and Abuse Act. This statute makes it a felony for a person to use illegal entry to a computer to make a gain of $5,000, or cause another to incur a loss of $5,000, or to access data affecting the national interest. Violation of this act can bring up to ten years in prison and a $10,000 fine. Repeat offenders can receive twenty-year prison sentences and $100,000 fines.[38]

Client Frauds. A fifth component of white-collar crime is theft by an economic client from an organization that advances credit to its clients. Included in this category are insurance fraud, credit card fraud, fraud related to welfare and Medicare programs, and tax evasion. These offenses are linked together because they involve theft from organizations that have many individual clients, who may take advantage of their positions of trust to steal from the organizations.

One important aspect of client fraud is tax evasion. This is a particularly challenging area for criminological study, since (1) so many U.S. citizens regularly underreport their income and (2) it is often difficult to separate honest error from deliberate tax evasion.

The basic law on tax evasion is contained in the Federal Internal Revenue Code, section 7201, which states:

> Any person who wilfully attempts in any manner to evade or defeat any tax imposed by this title or the payment thereof shall, in addition to other penalties provided by law, be guilty of a felony and, upon conviction thereof, shall be fined not more than $10,000 or imprisoned not more than 5 years, or both, together with the costs of prosecution.

To prove tax fraud the government must find that the taxpayer either underreported his or her income or did not report taxable income. No minimum dollar amount of fraud must exist before the government takes action. Theoretically, a person can be prosecuted for underreporting even one dollar. In practice, the government usually takes legal action when there is a "substantial underpayment of tax" and when the evader either deposits unreported money in a bank or spends it.

A second element of tax fraud is "willfulness" on the part of the tax evader. In the major case on this issue, willfulness was defined as a "voluntary, intentional violation of a known legal duty and not the careless disregard for the truth."[39]

Finally, to prove tax fraud, the government must show that the taxpayer has purposely attempted to evade or defeat a tax payment. If the offender is guilty of passive neglect, the offense is a misdemeanor. Passive neglect means simply not paying taxes, not reporting income, or not paying taxes when due. On the other hand, affirmative tax evasion, such as keeping double books, making false entries, destroying books or records, concealing assets, or covering up sources of income, constitutes a felony.

Tax evaision is a difficult crime to prosecute. Since legal tax avoidance is a favorite U.S. pastime, it is often difficult to prove the difference between the careless, unintentional nonreporting of income and willful fraud. The line between legal and fraudulent behavior is often so fine that many people are willing to step over it. In fact, in a statement on the subject, Ronald Reagan estimated that about $450 billion of income goes unreported every year, amounting to tax evasion of $95 billion per year.[40] The Internal Revenue Service recently said that about $100 billion went uncollected in 1983 because individuals failed to report all their income.[41] It was estimated that nearly a third of that amount was from self-employed workers, including professionals, laborers, and door-to-door salespeople.

The IRS may be losing its battle against tax cheats. The number of audits it conducts is actually declining. In 1983 it audited 1.5 percent of all returns, in 1984 the number declined to 1.36 percent; in the 1960s, 5 percent of all returns were audited. One reason for the decline has been the growth of complex tax shelters that require extensive IRS auditing time.[42] Consider the following legal tax scheme:

> In 1982 Bear, Stearns, a New York brokerage firm, acted as agent for the sale of 45,000 billboards to 534 wealthy investors for $485 million, nearly all of it borrowed. The investors promptly leased them back to the original owner, Broadcaster Metromedia. They are now in the process of rapidly writing off the costs of the billboards. At the end of five years, the plan is to resell them to Metromedia for $645 million, a 33-percent profit. The outcome: for individual cash investments of $150,000, each investor stands to gain a return in tax savings of $169,550, plus $355,000 in cash. And Metromedia can start writing off the billboards all over again as newly acquired assets.[43]

The IRS prosecuted only 1,800 people in 1984—only two out of every 100,000 who filed returns. And when penalties are exacted, they are usually relatively light. Rare are such instances as financier Marck Rich's 1984 IRS prosecution, which resulted in a $200 million settlement; the largest amount of money ever recovered by the United States in a criminal tax evasion case.[44] Various schemes to eliminate tax cheating have been proposed, such as flat taxes or taxes automatically deducted on bank, bond, and stock interest and dividends.

Influence Peddling and Bribery. The sixth component of white-collar crime involves the situation in which an individual with an important institutional position sells power, influence, and information to outsiders who have an interest in influencing or predicting the activities of the institution. Offenses within this category include government employees' taking kickbacks from contractors in return for awarding them contracts they could not have won on merit; or outsiders' bribing government officials, such as those in the Securities and Exchange Commission, who might sell information about future government activities.

One major difference distinguishes influence peddling from the previously discussed exploitation of an institutional position. Exploitation involves forcing victims to pay for services to which they have a clear right. In contrast, influence peddlers and bribe takers use their institutional positions to grant favors and sell information to which their co-conspirators are not entitled. Thus, in crimes of institutional exploitation, the victim is the person forced to pay, whereas the victim of influence peddling is the organization compromised by its own employees for their own interests.

Influence Peddling in Government. The seriousness of bribery was dramatically brought home to U.S. citizens by the ABSCAM case. Here, FBI agents, working with a convicted swindler, Melvin Weinberg, posed as wealthy Arabs looking for favorable treatment from high-ranking politicians. The pseudo-Arabs said they wished to obtain U.S. citizenship and receive favorable treatment in business ventures. Several office holders were indicted, including a U.S. senator from New Jersey, Harrison Williams.[45] Senator Williams was convicted of accepting an interest in an Arab-backed mining venture in return for promising to use his influence to obtain government contracts. The senator also promised to use his influence to help the "Arab sheik" enter and stay in the United States. At Williams's trial, the prosecution played tapes showing Williams meeting with federal undercover agents, boasting of his influence in the government, and saying he could "with great pleasure talk to the president of the United States" about the business venture; a later tape showed the senator promising to seek immigration help for the bogus sheik and agreeing to take part in the mining operation.

It has also been common for police officers to be accused of using their positions of power to coerce citizens into making payoffs. The best-known instance of police corruption was brought to light when a former New York mayor, John Lindsay, appointed a commission under the direction of Judge Whitman Knapp to investigate allegations of police corruption. The **Knapp Commission** found that police corruption was widespread, ranging from patrol officers' accepting small gratuities from local business people to senior officers' receiving payoffs in the thousands from gamblers and narcotics violators.[46]

The commission found that construction firms made payoffs to have police ignore violations of city ordinances such as double parking, obstruction of sidewalks, and noise pollution. Bar owners paid police to allow them to operate after hours or to give free reign to the prostitutes, drug pushers, and gamblers operating on their premises. Drug dealers allowed police to keep money and narcotics confiscated during raids in return for their freedom. Police also gave confiscated narcotics to informers for their own use or sale to others. Gamblers made regular payoffs to keep their operations going. The average individual share was $400 to $1,500 per month.

The Knapp Commission Report and other public scandals have not deterred incidents of government agents' exploiting their positions for gain. Recently Federal prosecutors mounted **Operation Greylord** to expose corruption in the Cook County (Illinois) court system.[47] They uncovered examples of judges selling favors to corrupt attorneys for up to $50,000 in under-the-table payments; one culprit received a fifteen-year sentence. In another recent scandal, twenty Philadelphia police officers were indicted on charges of extorting money from bar owners and poker-machine video game vendors. James Martin, the former second-in-command of the Philadelphia police department, was sentenced to eighteen years in the case.[48] These cases illustrate that the exploitation of one's position in government is far from over.

Influence Peddling in Business.   Politicians are not the only ones accused of bribery; business has had its share of scandals. In the 1970s, revelations were made that multinational corporations regularly made payoffs to foreign officials and businesspeople in order to secure business contracts: Gulf Oil executives admitted paying $4 million to the South Korean ruling party; Burroughs Corporation admitted paying $1.5 million to foreign officials; Lockheed Aircraft admitted paying $202 million. In a more recent case, McDonnell-Douglas Aircraft Corporation was indicted for paying $1 million in bribes to officials of Pakistani International Airlines in order to secure orders.[49]

Despite recognition of these offenses, bribery has not abated. For example, in 1984 the Justice Department began an investigation of the Bechtel Corporation's alleged bribing of South Korean officials.[50]

In response to these revelations, Congress in 1977 passed the Foreign Corrupt Practices Act (FCPA), which makes it a criminal offense to pay bribes to foreign officials or make other questionable overseas payments. Violations of the FCPA draw strict penalties for both the defendant company and its officers.[51] Moreover, all fines imposed on corporate officers are paid by them and not absorbed by the company. For example, for violation of the antibribery provisions of the FCPA, a domestic corporation can be fined up to $1 million. Moreover, company officers, employees, or stockholders who are convicted of bribery may have to serve a prison sentence of up to five years and pay a $10,000 fine. Congressional dissatisfaction with the harshness and ambiguity of the bill has caused numerous revisions to be considered; these revisions are currently being reviewed by Congress.

Despite the penalties imposed by the FCPA, corporations that deal in foreign trade have continued to give bribes to secure favorable trade agreements.[52] They have come up with a variety of schemes to defeat the federal law. One way is to join with a foreign company that is not controlled by U.S. law and let it negotiate the contracts.

So bribery continues to flourish. The typical case involves a large project in an industry made up of highly competitive companies whose products differ little from one another. The large amounts of money involved allow the parties to hide the payoffs in the price without drawing the attention of auditors. The likelihood of bribery is also usually affected by the number of competitors—the greater the competition, the more likely bribery will occur. These conditions are most likely to be found in the sale of telecommunications equipment, aircraft, and large-scale construction work. For example, it has been reported that leading European electric companies paid as much as $140 million in payoffs and kickbacks to win shares of the construction of a $10 billion dam being built jointly by Brazil and Paraguay.[53]

Not surprisingly, U.S. businesses have complained that stiff penalties for bribery give foreign competitors the edge over domestic corporations. In European countries such as Italy and France, giving bribes to secure contracts is perfectly legal; and in West Germany, bribes are actually tax-deductible. Consequently, it is possible that any future changes in the FCPA will decriminalize some forms of bribery.[54]

Wilful Noncompliance with Rules Regulating the Conduct of Economic, Political, and Governmental Institutions. The final component of white-collar crime involves situations in which powerful institutions or their representatives willfully violate the laws that restrain these institutions from doing social harm or require them to do social good. This is also known as *corporate crime.*

Corporate crime is probably what Sutherland had most in mind when he coined the term *white-collar crime.* These illegal acts are committed by the wealthy and powerful to further their business interests. They include such acts as price-fixing and illegal restraint of trade, false advertising, and the use of company practices that violate environmental protection statutes. The variety of crimes contained within this category is great, and the damage they cause vast. The following subsections will examine some of the most important offenses individually.

Illegal Restraint of Trade/Price-Fixing. A restraint of trade involves a contract or conspiracy designed to stifle competition, create a monopoly, artificially maintain prices, or otherwise interfere with free market competition.

The control of restraint of trade violations has its legal basis in the Sherman Antitrust Act. For violations of its provisions, this federal law created criminal penalties of up to three years imprisonment and up to $100,000 in fines for individuals and $1 million in fines for corporations.[55]

The Sherman Antitrust Act outlaws conspiracies between corporations designed to control the marketplace. In most instances, the act leaves to the presiding court's judgment the determination of whether corporations have conspired to "unreasonably restrain competition." However, four types of market conditions are considered so inherently anticompetitive that federal courts, through the Sherman Antitrust Act, have defined them as illegal per se, without regard to the facts or circumstances of the case. The first is *division of markets;* here, firms divide a region into territories, and each firm agrees not to compete in the others' territories.[56] The second is the **tying arrangement**, in which a corporation requires customers of one of its services to use other services it offers. For example, in the case of *Northern Pacific Railway Co.* versus *United States,* a federal court ruled that the railroad's requirement that all tenants of its lands use the railroad to ship all goods produced on the land was an illegal restraint of trade.[57]

A third type of absolute Sherman Act violation is the *group boycotts,* in which an organization or company boycotts retail stores that do not comply with its rules or desires.

Finally, *price-fixing*—a conspiracy to set and control the price of a necessary commodity—is considered an absolute violation of the act. Of all criminal violations associated with restraint of trade, none, perhaps, is as important as price-fixing. Michael Maltz and Stephen Pollock have described the four forms this act usually takes.[58] The first is *predation,* in which large firms agree among themselves to bid below market prices to drive out weaker firms. The goal is to reduce competition and permit the remaining firms to raise their prices with relative impunity.

A second scheme is *identical bidding.* Here, all competitors agree to submit identical bids for each contract, although they may vary bids from contract to contract. The price is well above what would have been expected if collusion had not occurred. Purchasing agents use their discretion to choose among bidders.

However, identical bidding usually assures all vendors of getting a share of the marketplace without losing any profitability.

Geographical market sharing involves dividing the potential market into territories within which only one member of the conspiring group is permitted a low bid. The remaining conspirators either refrain from bidding or give artificially high bids.

Rotational bidding involves a conspiracy in which the opportunity to submit a winning bid for a government or business contract is rotated among the institutional bidders. The conspirators meet in advance and determine who will give the low bid. The winning bid is, of course, higher than it should be, since the losers have all submitted abnormally high bids. Close coordination among the bidders is essential; therefore, these schemes usually involve only a few large firms.

Despite enforcement efforts, restraint-of-trade conspiracies are quite common. The best-known case involved some of the largest members of the electrical equipment industry.[59] In 1961, twenty-one corporations, including the industry leaders, Westinghouse and General Electric, were successfully prosecuted; forty-five executives were found guilty of criminal violations of the Sherman Antitrust Act. Company executives met secretly—they referred to their meetings as "choir practice"—and arranged the setting of prices on sales of equipment, the allocation of markets and territories, and the rigging of bids. At the sentencing, fines amounting to $1,924,500 were levied against the defendants, including fines of $437,500 against General Electric and $372,500 against Westinghouse. Although these fines meant little to the giant corporations, subsequent civil suits cost General Electric $160 million. Even more significant was that seven defendants, all high-ranking executives, were sentenced to jail terms.

In subsequent cases, American Cyanamid, Charles Pfizer, and Bristol Myers, all pharmaceutical companies, were convicted of price-fixing and monopolistic practices. In the case of one drug produced by the firms, tetracycline, the government found that the conspirators had guaranteed themselves a markup of 3,350 percent. In another case, American Standard and fourteen other firms were found guilty of conspiring to set artificially high prices in the billion-dollar-a-year plumbing fixture market.[60] And, in California, the state government brought action against seven major oil firms—including Mobil, Arco, and Shell—to recover $256 million they underpaid the state for crude oil taken from public lands.[61]

False Claims and Advertising. Executives in even the largest corporations are sometimes caught in the position in which stockholders' expectations of ever-increasing company profits seem to demand that sales be increased at any cost. At times, executives respond to this challenge by making claims about their product that cannot be justified by its actual performance. However, the line between clever, aggressive sales techniques and fraudulent claims is a fine one. It is traditional to show a product in its best light, even if that involves resorting to fantasy. Thus, we cannot really say it is fraudulent to show a crown suddenly appearing on the head of a person eating a certain brand of margarine, nor is it fraudulent to imply that taking one sip of iced tea will make people feel they have just jumped into a swimming pool. However, it is illegal to knowingly and purposely advertise a product as possessing qualities that the manufacturer realizes it does not have.

Charges stemming from false and misleading claims have been common in several U.S. industries. For example, the Federal Trade Commission reviewed and disallowed advertising by the three major U.S. car companies; the advertising alleged that new cars got higher gas mileage than buyers actually could expect. The Warner-Lambert Drug Company was prohibited from claiming that Listerine mouthwash could prevent or cure colds. Sterling Drug was prohibited from claiming that Lysol disinfectant killed germs associated with colds and flu. The A&P food company was sanctioned for mispricing and for advertising unavailable products. An administrative judge ruled that the American Home Products Company falsely advertised Anacin as a tension reliever. The list seems to go on endlessly.[62]

In the pharmaceutical industry, false advertising has a long history. It has been common for medicines to be advertised as cure-alls for previously incurable diseases. Such medicines include alleged cures for cancer and arthritis and drugs advertised to give energy and sexual potency. Recent, a well-publicized debate has surrounded the drug Laetrille—a derivative of apricot pits—and its alleged ability to cure some forms of cancer.

How can we explain the frequency of false advertising by drug manufacturers? Often the problem arises because several competing companies market similar products, and the key to successful sales is believed to be convincing the public that one of these products is far superior to the rest. Sometimes the intense drive for profits leads to falsification of data and unethical and illegal sales promotions. For example, when the Richardson-Merrill pharmaceutical company launched a highly aggressive advertising campaign for an anticholesterol drug, Mer-29, it downplayed efforts to warn the public about the drug's harmful side effects, such as sexual dysfunction, loss of hair, and development of eye cataracts.[63] Even after the company learned of these problems, it issued a memorandum to its salespeople warning them to avoid mentioning the problems. When warnings were finally issued, their purpose was to protect the company against damage suits rather than to aid customers. Eventually, permission to market the drug was withdrawn by the Food and Drug Administration. Though no criminal charges were filed, one commentator has stated: "here we see a company in a highly competitive and highly profitable industry resorting to unethical and probably illegal tactics to sell its products."[64]

The Merrill-Richardson case is certainly not the end of such matters. In 1984 the Smith Kline Beckman Corporation pleaded guilty to failing to make timely reports on a drug, Selacryn, which was linked to twenty-five deaths before being removed from the market. Despite the legal action in U.S. courts, the drug continues to be sold in France.[65]

It has been difficult for authorities to police such violations of the public trust. Often, the most serious consequence to the corporation is an order that they refrain from using the advertising or withdraw the advertising claims. Criminal penalties for false claims are rarely given. However, the offending parties can be sued civilly by their competitors for loss of revenue. In one case, U-Haul received a $40 million judgment against Jartran, a rival truck rental outfit, when the latter company's ad campaign photographically reduced a larger U-Haul truck so it looked the same size as a smaller Jartran truck.[66]

Environmental Crimes. Much attention has been called to the intentional or negligent environmental pollution caused by many large corporations. The numerous allegations in this area involve almost every aspect of U.S. business.

There are many different types of environmental crimes. Some corporations have endangered the lives of their own workers by maintaining unsafe conditions in their plants and mines. It has been estimated that 21 million workers have been exposed to hazardous materials while on the job. The National Institute of Occupational Safety and Health estimated that it would cost about $40 million just to alert these workers to the danger of their exposure to hazardous waste, and $54 billion to watch them and keep track of whether they developed occupationally related disease.[67]

Some industries have been particularly hard-hit by complaints and allegations. The asbestos industry was the target of a flood of lawsuits after environmental scientists found a close association between exposure to asbestos and development of cancer. Over 25,000 people have filed 12,000 lawsuits against 260 asbestos manufacturers. The Johns-Mansville Company alone has been sued about 400 times a month and is currently defending itself against 5,000 different claims. In all, some insurance company officials estimate, asbestos-related lawsuits could amount to $120 to $150 billion. Similarly, some 100,000 cotton mill workers suffer from some form of respiratory disease linked to prolonged exposure to cotton dust. About one-third of the workers are seriously disabled by brown lung disease, an illness similar to emphysema.[68]

The control of workers' safety has been the province of the Occupational Safety and Health Administration (OSHA). OSHA provides industry standards for the proper use of such chemicals as benzene, arsenic, lead, and coke. Intentional violation of OSHA standards can eventually involve criminal penalties.

Environmental Pollution. A second type of environmental crime committed by large corporations is the illegal pollution of the environment. Sometimes pollution involves individual acts caused by negligence on the part of the polluter. For example, in 1981 a leak of the chemical hexane into the sewers of Louisville, Kentucky, caused three miles of that city's streets, sidewalks, and sewers to explode. The company responsible for the leak, Ralston-Purina, gladly paid the $62,000 fine for environmental pollution; however, the company still faced millions in damage charges.[69]

The most striking pollution case so far, albeit one that has not been decided by the courts, involved the leaking of methyl isocynate from a Union Carbide plant in Bhopal, India on December 3, 1984. Estimates of the death toll range from 1,400 to 10,000 people; another 60,000 were injured. Union Carbide later reported that the plant had not been operating safely and should have been closed. They blamed the negligence, however, on local officials who were running the plant in India. The Bhopal incident may prove to be one of the largest settlements in U.S. legal history.[70]

Equally serious is the prolonged, intentional pollution of the environment. A case in point is the illegal dumping of the substance polychlorinated biphenyl (PCB).[71] This compound has been used since 1929 in power transformers, electric typewriters, and electrical capacitators. However, scientists have recently linked PCB to cancer and birth defects in laboratory animals. In Japan, people who ate rice oil contaminated with PCB suffered a variety of health problems. Chemical companies have been ordered not to use PCB; however, a serious problem exists with regard to disposing of the chemical. The Environmental Protection Agency (EPA) estimates that 20 million pounds await disposal and that 750 million pounds must eventually be destroyed. Some chemical companies have dumped their PCB stocks along public highways and in remote, illegal dumpsites. In some areas, illegally dumped PCB has proven extremely hazardous. When it has been carelessly dropped in landfills, pits, and lagoons, PCB has contaminated waters, fish, and wildlife. Because of PCB contamination, fishing has been restricted in the Housatonic and Hudson rivers in New York, Connecticut, Michigan, and other states.

The EPA has estimated that the cost of cleaning up the 1,500 to 2,500 hazardous waste dumpsites scattered around the United States ranges from $7.6 billion to $22.7 billion; their best overall estimate is $11.7 billion. Although the cleanup is expected to be supported by taxes on petrochemicals, which go into a "superfund," some experts believe that it is unrealistic to believe that private industry will pay for even half the costs.[72]

Controlling Environmental Pollution. The nature and scope of environmental crimes have prompted the federal government to pass a series of control measures designed to outlaw the worst abuses. These measures are described below.

Clean Air Act (CAA). The CAA provides sanctions for companies that do not comply with the air quality standards established by the EPA.[73] The CAA can impose penalties on any person or institution that, for example, knowingly violates EPA plan requirements or emission standards, tampers with EPA monitoring devices, or makes false statements to EPA officials.

Clean Water Act (CWA). The CWA punishes the knowing or negligent discharge of a pollutant into navigable waters.[74] According to the CWA, a *pollutant* is any "man-made or man-induced alteration of the chemical, physical, biological, and radiological integrity of the water."

Rivers and Harbors Act of 1899 (Refuse Act). The Refuse Act punishes any discharge of waste materials that damages natural water quality.[75]

Resource Conservation and Recovery Act of 1976 (RCRA). The RCRA provides criminal penalties for four acts involving illegal treatment of solid wastes: (1) the knowing transportation of any hazardous waste to a facility that does not have a legal permit for solid waste disposal; (2) the knowing treatment, storage, or disposal of any hazardous waste without a government permit or in violation of the provisions of the permit; (3) the deliberate making of any false statement or representation in a report filed in compliance with the RCRA; (4) the destruction or alteration of records required to be maintained by the RCRA.[76]

Toxic Substance Control Act (TSCA). The TSCA prohibits the following: manufacturing, processing, or distributing chemical mixtures or substances in a manner not in accordance with established testing or manufacturing requirements; commercial use of a chemical substance or mixture that the commercial user knew was manufactured, processed, or distributed in violation of TSCA requirements; and noncompliance with the reporting and inspection requirements of the TSCA.[77]

Considering the uncertainties of federal budget allocations, there is some question whether these acts can effectively deter environmental crime.

WHY DO THEY DO IT?

There probably are as many explanations for white-collar crime as there are white-collar crimes themselves. Herbert Edelhertz, an expert on the white-collar crime phenomenon, suggests that many offenders feel free to engage in business crime because they can easily rationalize its effects. Some convince themselves that their actions are not really crimes, because the acts involved do not resemble street crimes. For example, a banker who uses his position of trust to lend his institution's assets to a company he secretly controls may see himself as a shrewd businessman, not as a criminal. Or a pharmacist who chisels customers on prescription drugs may rationalize by telling himself his behavior doesn't really hurt anyone.

Further, some businesspeople feel justified in committing white-collar crimes because they believe that government regulators do not really understand the business world or the problems of competing in the free enterprise system. Even when caught, many white-collar criminals cannot see the error of their ways. For example, one offender who was convicted in the electrical industry price-fixing conspiracy discussed earlier categorically denied the illegality of his actions. "We did not fix prices," he said, "I am telling you that all we did was recover costs."[78]

Some white-collar criminals believe that everyone violates business laws and that it therefore is not so bad if they do so themselves. We can see the "everyone is doing it" rationale operating in such crimes as income tax evasion and bribe taking by government employees. White-collar crimes are viewed as morally neutral.

Need also plays an important role in all levels of white-collar crime. Executives may tamper with company books because they feel the need to keep or improve their jobs, satisfy their egos, or support their children. Blue-collar workers may pilfer because they need to keep pace with inflation or buy a new car.

A well-known study of embezzlers by Donald Cressey illustrates the important role need plays in white-collar crime.[79] According to Cressey, embezzlement is caused by what he calls a "nonshareable financial problem." This condition may be the result of offenders' living beyond their means, perhaps piling up gambling debts; offenders feel they can't let anyone know about such financial problems without ruining their reputations. Cressey claims that the door to solving personal financial problems through criminal means is opened by the rationalizations society has developed for white-collar crime: "Some of our most respectable citizens got their start in life by using other people's money temporarily." "In the real estate business, there is nothing wrong about using deposits before the deal is closed." "All people steal when they get in a tight spot."[80] Offenders make use of these and other rationalizations to resolve the conflict they experience over engaging in illegal behavior. Rationalizations allow offenders' financial needs to be met without compromising their values. In many ways, Cressey's concepts are similar to the techniques of neutralization discussed in chapter 8.

Beyond personal need and greed, the structure of business organizations themselves promotes white-collar criminality. Some managers, feeling the pressure of stockholders' demands, cut corners simply to keep their positions. Ronald Kramer argues that explanations of organizational or corporate crime involve three structural factors:

1. *Business organizations as institutions committed to goal attainment will engage in criminal behavior if they encounter serious difficulties in attaining their goals, especially profits. In addition product-goals play a role in the decision to violate rules, for example, when a car company tries to design a low-cost competitive model and sacrifices safety features.*

2. *The internal structure of an organization can also influence decisions to violate the law. Structure can have a significant influence on corporate goals. For example it can translate the overall quest for profit into sub-goals such as cost reductions which foster criminality. In some organizations law breaking and corner cutting becomes a norm which is passed on to employees; "This is the way things are done here, don't worry about it."*

3. *Organizational environment influences criminality. The economic, political, cultural, legal, technological, and interorganizational factors influence corporate behavior. For example, if market conditions are weak, competition intense, law enforcement lax, and the existing social norms stress success at any cost, the conditions for corporate crime are maximized.*[81]

CONTROLLING WHITE-COLLAR CRIME

Conflict theorists are quick to point out that, unlike lower-class street criminals, white-collar criminals are rarely prosecuted; and when convicted, receive relatively light sentences. This claim is supported by studies of white-collar criminality that show it is rare for a corporate or white-collar criminal to receive a serious criminal penalty.[82] For example, Marshall Clinard and Peter Yeager's analysis of 477 corporations found that only one in ten serious corporate violations and one in twenty moderate violations resulted in sanctions.[83] Similarly, a Bureau of National Affairs study of 307 white-collar defendants found that of the 138 (45 percent) who were sentenced, 26.8 percent received only fines, suspended sentences, or probation—although their crimes averaged $21.6 million in cost. Of defendants sentenced in cases involving an average loss of $23.6 million, 16.7 percent were sentenced to an average of a year or less in prison.[84]

There are a number of reasons for the leniency afforded white-collar criminals. Though white-collar criminals may produce millions of dollars of losses and endanger human life, some judges believe they are not "real criminals," but businesspeople just trying to make a living.[85] Similarly, as Clinard and Yeager report, businesspeople often seek legal advice and are well aware of the loopholes in the law. If caught, they can always claim that they had sought legal advice and believed they were in compliance with the law.[86]

White-collar criminals are often considered nondangerous offenders, usually respectable older citizens who have families to support. These "pillars of the community" are not seen in the same light as a teenager who breaks into a drugstore to steal a few dollars. Their public humiliation at being caught is usually deemed punishment enough; a prison sentence seems unnecessarily cruel. Still another factor complicating white-collar crime enforcement is that many legal business acts seem as morally tinged as those made illegal by government regulation. Consider *greenmail,* a common event in the 1980s. Here a speculator buys up stock in a company, threatening to take it over and replace management. To save their jobs, company executives eventually give in and repurchase the stock with company funds. Of course the repurchase price is considerably higher than the speculator paid originally. One greenmail expert, T. Boone Pickens of Mesa Petroleum, made $900 million for his partners and himself between 1982 and 1985 using takeover tactics and threats.[87] Despite its questionable ethics, greenmail is not a crime, but rather a clever business ploy that can have the potential for huge legitimate profits. Yet when it is compared to other business practices made illegal by government regulation, such as price-fixing, the distinctions are hard to see. It may seem unfair to prosecutors and judges to penalize some businessperson for actions not too dissimilar from those applauded in the *Wall Street Journal.*

WHITE-COLLAR LAW ENFORCEMENT

White-collar crime activity is controlled by law enforcement agencies such as the FBI or regulatory agencies such as the Federal Communications Commission (FCC).

In general, there are two types of enforcement strategies—**compliance** and **deterrence**—available to control organizational deviance.[88] Compliance aims for law conformity without the necessity of detecting, processing, or penalizing violators. Compliance systems attempt to create conformity by providing incentives, or by using administrative efforts to prevent unwanted conditions before they occur. The core violation in a compliance system is often referred to as a **technical violation**. For example, the Securities and Exchange Commission has a host of regulations, relating to bookkeeping and reporting of stock transactions, in which failure to report is a technical violation. There the incentive is to abide by the rules in order to remain in the good graces of the industry's licensing agency and forego any chance of criminal prosecution.

In contrast, deterrence strategies secure law conformity by detecting violations of the law, determining who is responsible, and penalizing them to deter future violations.[89] Punishment serves as a warning to potential violators who might break rules if other violators had not already been penalized. Deterrence systems are oriented toward apprehending violators and punishing them rather than creating conditions that induce conformity as compliance systems do. The core violation in a deterrence system is the immediately harmful behavior, rather than the long-term behaviors that compliance systems seek to control.

Many organizations that pursue white-collar crime use a mix of strategies, depending on the circumstance. Compliance is generally used when the concern is with the *violation* and not the *violator*. Rather than punishing individuals for their specific crimes, as in the case of deterrence, compliance is concerned with insuring that laws are obeyed and in obtaining future conformity once they are broken. Deterrence systems seek to penalize persons or organizations for the harms they have caused; compliance systems seek to avoid harms and their consequences.

An example of the compliance approach to controlling white-collar crime can be found in the area of environmental crimes such as pollution. Compliance (also referred to as **economism**) involves controlling wrongdoing through economic incentives, such as levying heavy taxes on the quantity and quality of pollution released into the environment.[90] Compliance strategies attempt to create a marketplace incentive to obey the law—the more a company pollutes, the more costly and unprofitable that pollution becomes. Compliance/economism has become the favored method of enforcement since criminal sanctions against corporations are often difficult to achieve.

Compliance systems are not applauded by all criminologists. Some experts point out that economic sanctions have limited value in controlling white-collar crime because economic penalties are imposed only after crimes have occurred, require careful governmental regulation, and often amount to only a slap on the wrist.[91] In contrast, more punitive deterrent strategies should—and have—worked, since white-collar crime by its nature is a rational act whose perpetrators are extremely sensitive to the threat of criminal sanctions. Gilbert Geis cites numerous instances in which prison sentences for corporate crimes have produced a significant decline in white-collar activity.[92] However, the favored method of controlling white-collar crimes remains economic. For example, in April 1985 the Pentagon decided to withhold all payments to General Dynamics Corporation until $124 million in contract overruns were repaid. Though this amount seems large, it would take only a few days for the company to recoup since General Dynamics regularly bills the government $700 million a month![93]

Despite the prevalence of economism, dramatic deterrence strategies have been used to prevent white-collar crime. In the 1970s, a local prosecutor failed in an attempt to indict Ford executives on charges of homicide in crashes involving Pintos, as a result of deaths due to known dangers in the car's design.[94] However, on 16 June 1985, an Illinois judge found three officials of the Film Recovery Systems corporation guilty of murder in the death of a worker.[95] The employee died after inhaling cyanide poison under "totally unsafe" work conditions. During the trial, evidence was presented showing that employees were not warned that they were working with dangerous substances, that company officials ignored complaints of illness, and that safety precautions had been deliberately ignored. A first of its kind, this decision indicates that the tide may be turning against corporate criminals. Nonetheless, the Film Recovery case does not in itself diminish the fact that white-collar criminals are treated more leniently than their blue-collar brethren.

WHITE-COLLAR LAW ENFORCEMENT SYSTEMS

On the federal level, detection of white-collar crime is primarily in the hands of administrative departments and agencies.[96] Any evidence of criminal activity is then sent to the Department of Justice or the FBI for investigation. Some other Federal agencies, such as the Securities and Exchange Commission and Postal Service, have their own investigative arms. Usually enforcement is reactive (generated by complaints) rather than proactive (involving ongoing investigations or the monitoring of activities).

Investigations are carried out by the various federal agencies and the FBI. The FBI has established enforcement of white-collar laws as one of its three top priorities (along with foreign counterintelligence and organized crime).

If criminal prosecution is called for, the case will be handled by attorneys from the Criminal, Tax, Antitrust, and Civil Rights Divisions of the Justice Department. If insufficient evidence is available to warrant a criminal prosecution, the case will be handled civilly or administratively by some other federal agency. For example, the Federal Trade Commission can issue a cease and desist order in antitrust or merchandising fraud cases.

On the state and local level, enforcement of white-collar laws is often disorganized and inefficient. Confusion may exist over the jurisdiction of the state attorney general and local prosecutors. The technical expertise of the federal government is often lacking on the state level. One area the states have made progress in is the control of consumer fraud. Similarly, there is a clear movement toward state-funded technical assistance offices to help local prosecutors; more than forty states offer such services.

White-collar crime law enforcement is often left to business organizations themselves. Corporations spend hundreds of millions of dollars each year on internal audits that help unearth white-collar offenses. Local chambers of commerce, the insurance industry, and other elements of the business community have mounted campaigns against white-collar crime.

Aiding the investigation of white-collar offenses is a movement toward protecting employees who "blow the whistle" on their firm's violations. Five states, including Michigan, Connecticut, Maine, California, and New York, has passed laws protecting workers from being fired if they testify about violations.[97] Without such help, the hands of justice are tied.

Despite these advances, control of white-collar crime remains problematic.

Charles "Lucky" Luciano was a powerful figure in organized crime in the 1930s.

Organized Crime

The second branch of organizational criminality involves criminal enterprise groups whose ultimate purpose is economic gain through illegitimate means. Here an enterprise system is set up to supply consumers with merchandise and services banned by the existing criminal law but for which a ready market exists. The demand for illegal goods and services—prostitution, pornography, gambling, narcotics—has produced an economic condition in which fantastic profits can be made in the black market: the illegal supply of contraband. It is not surprising that a diverse and far-flung criminal network has developed to supply desired, but legally unobtainable, commodities. That wide-ranging illegal supply network is referred to in total as organized crime.

Because of its secrecy and shadowy existence, a great mystique has grown up about organized crime. Its legendary leaders—Al Capone, Meyer Lansky, Lucky Luciano—are the subjects of books and films. The famous *Godfather* series popularized and humanized organized crime figures. Most citizens believe that organized criminals are capable of taking over legitimate business enterprises if the opportunity presents itself. Almost everyone is familiar with terms like *the mob*, *underworld*, **Mafia**, *racketeers*, *syndicate*, or **La Cosa Nostra** to refer to organized crime. Though most of us have neither met nor seen members of organized crime, we feel sure that they exist, and most certainly we fear them.

This section will briefly define *organized crime*, review its history, and discuss its economic effect and control.

ACTIVITIES OF ORGANIZED CRIME

What are the main activities of organized crime? The traditional sources of income are derived from providing illicit materials: gambling, pornography, prostitution, narcotics. Organized criminals also profit from loansharking—lending money at exorbitant rates to people desperate for money and later enforcing the loan repayments with violence or death. Organized criminals have infiltrated labor unions, taking control of their pension funds and dues. Hijacking of shipments and cargo theft are other sources of income. One study found that the annual losses due to theft of air cargo amount to $400 million, rail cargo $600 million, trucking $1.2 billion, and maritime shipment $300 million.[98]

Underworld figures engage in fencing of high-value items and maintain international sales territories. In recent years they have branched into computer crime and other white-collar activities.

Organized criminals are also responsible for a significant percentage of the U.S. drug trade. Alan Block and William Chambliss estimate the gross sale of heroin in the United States to be $30 billion, while cocaine sales amount to about $20 billion.[99]

Beyond these common crime patterns, organized criminals have used extortion and threat to attach themselves to many legitimate business enterprises. Merry Morash lists five ways that organized criminals today become involved in legitimate enterprise:

(1) business activity that supports illegal enterprises—for example, providing a front; (2) predatory or parasitic exploitation—for example, demanding protection money; (3) organization of monopolies or cartels to limit competition; (4) unfair advantages gained by practices such as manipulation of labor unions and corruption of public officials; and (5) illegal manipulation of legal vehicles, particularly stocks and bonds[100]

Organized criminals have specialized in infiltrating unions in order to borrow from their large pension funds and control the direction of their investments. Alan Block has described mob control of the New York waterfront and its influence on the use of union funds to buy insurance, health care, and so on from mob-controlled companies.[101]

Merry Morash claims that mob control of legitimate enterprise today is influenced by market conditions. Businesses most likely to be affected are low-technology, have uniform products, and operate in rigid markets where increases in price will not result in reduced demand. In addition, industries most affected by labor racketeering are ones subject to labor pressure because a work stoppage would destroy a product or delay meeting deadlines.

THE CONCEPT OF ORGANIZED CRIME

The term *organized crime* conjures up images of strong men in dark suits, machine-gun-toting bodyguards, rituals of allegiance to secret organizations, professional "gangland" killings, and meetings of "family" leaders who chart the course of crime much like the board members at General Motors decide on the country's transportation needs. These images have become part of what criminologists refer to as the **alien conspiracy theory** concept of organized crime. This is the belief, adhered to by the federal government and many respected criminologists, that organized crime is a direct offshoot of a criminal society—the Mafia—that first originated in Italy and Sicily and now controls racketeering in major American cities.

According to this view, the American Mafia, also called *La Cosa Nostra,* is made up of twenty-seven or so criminal syndicates, or families, which control crime

FIGURE 12.1

Organization of the
mafia "Family"

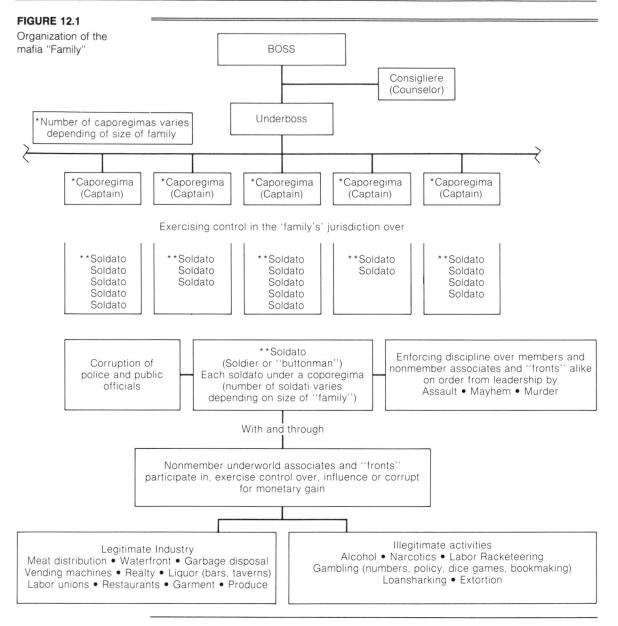

SOURCE. U. S., Senate, Permanent Subcommittee on Investigations, Committee on Governmental Affairs, *Hearings on Organized Crime and Use of Violence,* 96th Cong., 2d Sess., April 1980, p. 117.

in distinct geographic areas (see figure 12.1). New York City, the most important organized crime area, contains five families. The families are believed to be ruled by a "Commission," made up of a few of the most respected crime bosses, which settles personal problems, jurisdictional conflicts, and enforces rules that allow members to gain huge profits through manufacture and sale of illegal goods and services (see figure 12.2).[102]

The national crime syndicate demands absolute loyalty from its members, who may number over 50,000 nationwide. Membership is usually limited to Italians,

FIGURE 12.2

Sites of La Cosa Nostra
headquarter cities

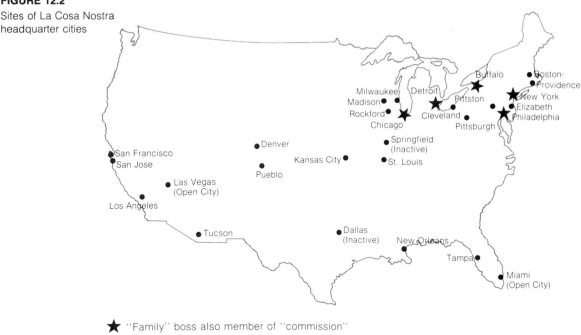

★ "Family" boss also member of "commission"

● Other "families"

SOURCE. U. S., Senate, Permanent Subcommittee on Investigations, Committee on Governmental Affairs, *Hearings on Organized Crime and Use of Violence*, 96th Cong., 2d Sess., April 1980, p. 116.

though non-Italians may be accepted. Indeed, early in the history of organized crime, many top leaders were of Jewish and Irish descent.

Alternative Explanations. Some scholars challenge this version of organized crime as being fanciful. They argue that the alien conspiracy theory is too heavily influenced by media accounts and by the testimony of a single person, mobster Joseph Valachi, before a U.S. Senate investigation committee headed by Senator John McClellan. Valachi's description of the Cosa Nostra was relied upon by conspiracy theorists as an accurate portrayal of mob activities. Yet critics question its authenticity and direction. For example, criminologist Jay Albanese compared Valachi's statements to those of another mob informer, Jimmy Frantianno, and found major discrepancies with respect to the location and size of organized criminal activity.[103]

The challenges to the alien conspiracy theory have produced alternative views of organized crime. Among them is Alan Block's well-known argument that organized crime is both a loosely constructed social system and a social world that reflects the existing American system, and not a tightly organized national criminal syndicate. The system is composed of "relationships binding professional criminals, politicians, law enforcers, and various entrepreneurs."[104] In contrast, the social world of organized crime is often chaotic because of the constant power struggle between competing groups. Block rejects the view that an all-powerful organized crime commission exists and instead views the world of professional criminals as one shaped by the political economy. He finds that independent crime organizations can be characterized as either **enterprise syndicates** or **power syndicates**. The former are involved in providing services and include madams, drug distributors, bookmakers, and so on. These are "workers in the world of illegal enterprise." They have set positions in an illegal enterprise system, with special tasks to perform if the enterprise is to function.

In contrast, power syndicates perform no set task except to extort or terrorize. Their leaders can operate against legitimate business or against fellow criminals who operate enterprise syndicates. Through coercion, buy-outs, and other similar means, power syndicates graft themselves onto enterprise systems, legal businesses, trade unions, and so on.

Block's view of organized crime is revisionist since it portrays mob activity as a quasi-economic enterprise system swayed by social forces and not a tightly knit, unified cartel dominated by ethnic minorities carrying out European traditions. His world of organized crime is dominated by business leaders, politicians, and union leaders who work hand in hand with criminals. Moreover, the violent, chaotic social world of power syndicates does not lend itself to a tightly controlled syndicate.

It is difficult to assess the accuracy of either view of organized crime. Certainly homogeneous ethnic groups flourished at one time in the nation's history. Yet to speak about organized crime as a national syndicate that controls all illegitimate rackets in an orderly fashion seems to ignore the variety of gangs and groups, their membership, and their relationship to the outside world. Mafia-type groups may play a major role in organized crime, but they are by no means the only ones that can be considered organized criminals.[105]

Thus, organized crime may be viewed as a loose confederation of ethnic and regional crime groups, bound together by a commonality of economic and political objectives. Some of these groups are located in fixed geographical areas. For example, the so-called Dixie Mafia operates in the South. Chicano crime families are found in areas with significant Hispanic populations, such as California and Arizona. However, Italian, Irish, and Jewish crime organizations are found across the nation. Some Mafia and Cuban groups operate internationally. Some have preserved their past identity, while others are constantly changing organizations.

CHARACTERISTICS OF ORGANIZED CRIME

A precise description of the characteristics of organized crime is difficult to formulate, but some of its general traits are included here:[106]

- Organized crime is a conspiratorial activity, involving the coordination of numerous persons in the planning and execution of illegal acts or in the pursuit of a legitimate objective by unlawful means (for example, threatening businesses in order to get a stake in a legitimate corporation). Organized crime involves continuous commitment by primary members, although individuals with specialized skills may be brought in when the need arises. Organized crime organizations are usually structured along hierarchical lines—a chieftain supported by close advisers, lower subordinates, and so on.
- Organized crime has economic gain as its primary goal, though achievement of power or status may also be a motivating factor. Economic gain is achieved

through maintenance of a near monopoly on illegal goods and services, including drugs, gambling, pornography, and prostitution.

- Organized crime activities are not limited to providing illicit services. They include such sophisticated activities as laundering illegal money through legitimate businesses, land fraud, and computer crimes.
- Organized crime employs predatory tactics such as intimidation, violence, and corruption. It appeals to greed to accomplish its objectives and preserve its gains.
- By experience, custom, and practice, organized crime's conspiratorial groups are usually very quick and effective in controlling and disciplining their members, associates, and victims. The individuals involved know that any deviation from the rules of the organization will evoke a prompt response from the other participants. This response may range from a reduction in rank and responsibility to a death sentence.
- Organized crime is not synonymous with the Mafia (or La Cosa Nostra— "Our Thing"), the most experienced, most diversified, and possibly best-disciplined of these groups. The Mafia is actually a common stereotype of organized crime. Although several families in the organization called La Cosa Nostra are important components of organized crime activities, they do not hold a monopoly on underworld activities.
- Organized crime does not include terrorists dedicated to political change. Although violent acts are a major tactic of organized crime, the use of violence does not mean that a group is part of a confederacy of organized criminals.

HISTORY OF ORGANIZED CRIME

The earliest organized urban groups made their home in the slum districts of New York City.[107] For the most part they were made up of Irish immigrants. The "Forty Thieves," considered the first New York gang with a definite acknowledged leadership, were muggers, thieves, and pickpockets on the lower east side of Manhattan from the 1820s to just before the Civil War. Other New York gangs included the "Roach Guards," "Dead Rabbits," "Plug Uglies," and "Shirt Tails." These early gangs often included hundreds of men and boys led by a chieftain. Gang members were regularly dispatched by their leaders to nearby areas to steal, rob, and kill, or wage fierce battles against rival gangs. The most notorious gang was the "Whyos," numbering five hundred criminals. The Whyos would accept a new member only after he had killed at least once. The gang passed out handbills advertising its services:

- Punching—$2
- Both eyes blackened—$4
- Nose and jaw broke—$10
- Blackjacked—$15
- Ear chawed off—$15
- Leg or arm broke—$19
- Shot in leg—$25
- Stabbing—$25
- Murder—$100 +

Around 1890, Italian immigrants began forming gangs modeled after the Sicilian crime organization known as the Mafia; these gangs were called the "Black Hand."

Around 1900, Johnny Torrio, a leader of New York's "Five Points" gang, moved to Chicago and helped his uncle, Big Jim Colosimo, organize the dominant gang in the Chicago area. Other gangs also flourished in Chicago, including those of Hymie Weiss and "Bugs" Moran. A later leader was the infamous Al "Scarface" Capone.

The turning point of organized crime was the onset of prohibition and the Volstead Act. This created a multimillion-dollar bootlegging industry overnight. Gangs vied for a share of the business, and bloody wars for control of rackets and profits became common. However, the problems of supplying liquor to thousands of illegal drinking establishments (speakeasies) required organization and an end to open warfare.

In the late 1920s, several events helped create the structure of organized crime. First, Johnny Torrio became leader of the Unione Siciliano, an ethnic self-help group that had begun as a legitimate enterprise but had been taken over by racketeers. This event helped bring together the Chicago and New York crime groups; and since Torrio was Italian, it also brought the beginnings of detente between Italians and Sicilians, who heretofore had been at odds with one another.

In December 1925, gang leaders from across the nation met in Cleveland to discuss strategies for mediating their differences in a nonviolent manner and for maximizing profits. A similar meeting took place in Atlantic City in 1929, and was attended by twenty gang leaders including Lucky Luciano, Al Capone, and "Dutch" Schultz.

Despite such efforts, however, gang wars continued into the 1930s. In 1934, according to some accounts, another meeting in New York, called by Johnny Torrio and Lucky Luciano, led to the formation of a national crime commission and acknowledged the territorial claims of twenty-four crime families around the country. This was considered the beginning of La Cosa Nostra.

Under the leadership of the national crime commission, organized crime began to expand in a more orderly fashion. Bugsy Siegel was dispatched to California to oversee West Coast operations. The end of prohibition required a new source of profits, and narcotic sales became the mainstay of gangland business. Al Polizzi, a Cleveland crime boss, formed a news service that provided information on horse racing, thereby helping create a national network of gang-dominated bookmakers.

After World War II, organized crime families began using their vast profits from liquor, gambling, and narcotics to buy into legitimate businesses, such as entertainment, legal gambling in Cuba and Las Vegas, hotel chains, jukebox concerns, restaurants, and taverns. By paying off politicians, police, and judges, and by using blackmail and coercion, organized criminals became almost immune to prosecution. The machine-gun-toting gangster had given way to the businessman/racketeer.

In the 1950s, cooperation among gangland figures reached its zenith. Gang control over unions became widespread, and many legitimate businesses made payoffs to promote labor peace. New gang organizations arose in Los Angeles, Kansas City, and Dallas.

Post-1950 Developments. In 1950, the Senate Special Committee to Investigate Organized Crime in Interstate Commerce, better known as the **Kefauver Com-**

mittee (after its chairman), was formed to look into organized crime. It reported the existence of a national crime cartel, whose members cooperated to make a profit and engaged in joint ventures to eliminate enemies. The Kefauver Committee also made public the syndicate's enforcement arm, Murder Inc., which, under the leadership of Albert Anastasia, disposed of enemies for a price.

The Kefauver Committee also found that corruption and bribery of local political officials was widespread. This theme was revived by the Senate Subcommittee on Investigations, better known as the McClellan Committee, in its investigation of the role organized crime played in labor racketeering. The committee and its chief counsel, Robert Kennedy, uncovered a close relationship between gang activity and the Teamsters Union, then led by Jimmy Hoffa. Hoffa's eventual death has been linked to his gangland connections.

Later investigations by the committee produced the testimony of Joseph Valachi, former underworld "soldier" who, as you recall, detailed the inner workings of La Cosa Nostra. The leaders of the national crime cartel at this time were Frank Costello, Vito Genovese, Carlo Gambino, Joe Bonnano, and Joe Profaci, all of New York; Sam Giancana of Chicago; and Angelo Bruno of Philadelphia.

During the next fifteen years, gang activity expanded further into legitimate businesses. Nonetheless, gangland jealousy, competition, and questions of succession produced an occasional flare-up of violence. The most well publicized conflict occurred between the Gallo brothers of Brooklyn—Albert, Larry, and Crazy Joe—and the Profaci crime family. The feud continued through the 1960s, uninterrupted by the death of Joe Profaci and the new leadership of his group by Joe Colombo. Eventually Colombo was severely injured by a Gallo hired assassin, and in return Joey Gallo was killed in a New York restaurant, Umberto's Clam House. Gallo's death once again brought peace in the underworld. Emerging as the most powerful syndicate boss was Carlo Gambino, who held this position until his death by natural causes in 1976.

ORGANIZED CRIME TODAY

Organized criminal activity exists today in larger cities throughout the country. In the Northeast, organized criminal groups are involved in numerous enterprises, including nightclubs, travel agencies, and real estate businesses. Principal income in this area comes from gambling, drug trafficking, and pornography.

In the Southeast, law enforcement officials now believe that organized crime is expanding into white-collar crime. Examples include illegal financial investments and infiltration of legitimate businesses. In the meantime, traditional "family businesses"—prostitution, gambling, and drug trafficking—are flourishing. For example, about half the cocaine and marijuana seized in the United States comes from one southeastern city—Miami, Florida. It has been estimated that it costs about $20,000 to bring in three tons of marijuana from Colombia; ten days later it can be sold for $1.4 million on the street.

In the Midwest, organized crime activities also remain at a high level. In one state in the region, the illegal gambling operations compete directly with the state's own legal lotteries; officials estimate that the syndicate's operation nets about $500 million to $700 million a year. In the Far West, there is more cooperation between independent "crime families" than in the East; however, tactics and sources of income remain similar.

One important recent change in organized crime is the interweaving, at least

Various groups practice organized crime today; for example, the Hells Angels have been active in the narcotics trade.

at its lowest levels, of new ethnic groups into the traditional structure. Blacks, Puerto Ricans, and Cubans now work side by side with Italian, Irish, and Jewish racketeers. In black or Hispanic areas these "new" ethnics oversee the distribution of drugs, prostitution, and gambling in a symbiotic relationship with old-line racketeers. As the traditional organized crime families drift into legitimate businesses, the distribution of contraband on the street is handled by newcomers, characterized by Francis Ianni as urban social bandits.[108] For example, the "Hell's Angels" motorcycle club is now believed to be one of the leading distributors of narcotics in the United States.

The prevalence of organized crime today and its relationship to big business can be viewed in the 1985 scandal that rocked the prestigious First National Bank of Boston. Federal prosecutors charged that the bank made unreported cash shipments of $1.2 million. They received $529,000 in small bills and sent $690,000 in bills of $100 or more. The bank was fined $500,000 for violating a law which requires that banks report any cash transaction of $10,000 or more. The bank's transaction came under scrutiny during an FBI investigation of the Angiulo crime family, which bought more than $1.7 million in cashier's checks from the bank.[109]

The First National scandal illustrates that organized crime today involves a cooperative relationship beteeen big businessmen, politicians, and racketeers. As Alan Block suggests, modern organized crimes involve cooperative enterprise systems. The distinction between organized and traditional white-collar crimes seems to be disappearing.

Because of the public's demand for illegal goods and services, its willingness to pay exhorbitant prices to obtain them, and the ability of organized crime to monopolize markets, underworld profits continue to grow. Thus the public has come to depend on organized crime, and vice versa. This symbiotic relationship is probably the single most important reason that organized crime can defy the efforts of law enforcement officials.

CONTROLLING ORGANIZED CRIME

Traditionally, law enforcement efforts to control organized crime have been rather sporadic and ineffective. George Vold has argued that the development of organized crime parallels early capitalist enterprises. It employs ruthless and monopolistic tactics to maximize profits. It is also secretive and protective of its operations and defensive against any outside intrusion.[110]

The federal and state governments actually did little to combat organized crime until fairly recently. One of the first directly anti-organized-crime measures was the Interstate and Foreign Travel or Transportation in Aid of Racketeering Enterprises Act (Travel Act)[111] The Travel Act prohibits travel in interstate commerce or use of interstate facilities with the intent to promote, manage, establish, carry on, or facilitate an unlawful activity; it also prohibits the actual or attempted engagement in these activities.

In 1970, Congress passed the Organized Crime Control Act (see Close-Up for some of the provisions). Title IX of the act, and probably its most effective measure, has been the Racketeer Influenced and Corrupt Organization Act (**RICO**).[112] RICO did not create new categories of crimes, but it did create new categories of offenses in racketeering activity, which it defined as involvement in two or more acts prohibited by twenty-four existing federal and eight state statutes.[113] The offenses listed in RICO include state-defined crimes such as murder, kidnapping, gambling, arson, robbery, bribery, extortion, and narcotic violations; and federally defined crimes such as bribery, counterfeiting, transmission of gambling information, prostitution, and mail fraud.

RICO is designed to limit "patterns" of organized criminal activity by defining racketeering as an act intended to:

- Derive income from racketeering or the unlawful collection of debts and to use or invest such income.
- Acquire through racketeering an interest in or control over any enterprise engaged in interstate or foreign commerce.
- Conduct business enterprises through a pattern of racketeering.
- Conspire to use racketeering as a means of making income, collecting loans, or conducting business.

An individual convicted under RICO is subject to twenty years in prison and a $25,000 fine. Additionally, the accused must forfeit to the U.S. government any interest in a business in violation of RICO. These penalties are much more potent than simple conviction and imprisonment.

To enforce these policy initiatives, the federal government created the Strike Force Program. This program, operating in eighteen cities, brings together various state and federal law enforcement officers and prosecutors to work as a team against racketeering. Several states, including New York, Illinois, New Jersey, and New Mexico, have created their own special investigative teams devoted to organized criminal activity.

These efforts began to pay off in 1984 when 3,118 RICO indictments were issued and 2,194 convictions resulted. In April 1985, a New-York-based strike force was successful in indicting members of the Zucchese, Genovese, and Bonnano

Highlights of the Organized Crime Control Act of 1970

The Organized Crime Control Act:

- Provides for the establishment of special grand juries in localities where there are major organized crime operations. These grand juries have expanded power to control the duration of their terms and the right to appeal any arbitrary termination. They also may issue reports recommending removal of any public officer or employee for noncriminal misconduct involving organized criminal activity and reports concerning organized crime conditions generally in their districts.
- Establishes a general federal immunity statute under which witnesses can be ordered by a court to testify in return for immunity from prosecution, and can be jailed for up to eighteen months if they refuse to do so. Witnesses are given "use immunity" rather than the "transactional immunity" provided for in legislation that the 1970 act supersedes. Use immunity forbids the use of information derived from witnesses while they are under court order to testify but does not protect them from prosecution for those acts about which they testified if evidence is developed entirely independently.
- Provides protection for witnesses in organized crime cases and for members of their families. Federal officials are authorized to provide secure housing and otherwise insure the safety of witnesses.
- Provides for perjury prosecution when a witness knowingly makes a false statement under oath or makes

two sworn statements that are completely contradictory. The law eliminates previous requirements of two witnesses and direct evidence for proof of perjury.
- Provides for the taking and use of pretrial depositions "whenever due to exceptional circumstances it is in the interest of justice."
- Expands federal jurisdiction over illegal gambling operation because it "involves widespread use of, and has an effect upon, interstate commerce. . . ."
- Prohibits persons who engage in a "pattern of racketeering activity" from using their illegal profits for the purpose of penetrating and taking over legitimate businesses and unions.
- Provides for extended sentences for persons convicted of participation in continuing illegal businesses, or who are habitual criminals, chief participants in conspiracies, or repeat offenders.

DISCUSSION QUESTIONS

1. Can these measures deter organized crime?
2. What policies would you implement if you were in charge of antiracketeering legislation?

SOURCE. Committee on Criminal Justice Standards and Goals, *Organized Crime* (Washington, D.C.: Government Printing Office, 1976), p. 18.

families.[114] The investigation also uncovered evidence to support the national crime cartel concept. Similar sweeps were conducted in Boston, Chicago, and Miami. These actions may put a dent in some organized crime cartels, but they are unlikely to stifle criminal entrepreneurship: many groups stand ready to fill the gaps and reap the profits of providing illegal goods and services.

Summary

White-collar and organized criminals are similar because they both use ongoing illegal business enterprise to make personal profits. There are various types of white-collar crime. Stings and swindles involve the use of deception to bilk people out of their money. Chiseling customers, businesses, or the government on a regular basis is a second common type of white-collar crime. Surprisingly, many professionals engage in chiseling offenses.

Other white-collar criminals use their positions in business and the marketplace to commit economic crimes. Their crimes include exploitation of position in a company or the government to secure illegal payments; embezzlement and employee pilferage and fraud; client fraud; and influence peddling and bribery. Further, corporate officers sometimes violate the law to improve the position and profitability of their businesses. Their crimes include price fixing, false advertising, and environmental crimes.

So far, little has been done to combat white-collar crimes. Most offenders do not view themselves as criminals and therefore do not seem to be deterred by criminal statutes. Though thousands of white-collar criminals are prosecuted each year, their numbers are insignificant compared with the magnitude of the problem.

The government has used various law enforcement strategies to combat white-collar crime. Some involve deterrence, which uses punishment to frighten potential abusers. Others involve economism or compliance strategies, which create economic incentives to obey the law.

The demand for illegal goods and services has produced a symbiotic relationship between the public and an organized criminal network. Though criminal gangs have existed since the early nineteenth century, their power and size were spurred by the Volstead Act and prohibition in the 1920s. Organized crime supplies alcohol, gambling, drugs, prostitutes, and pornography to the public. It is immune from prosecution because of public apathy and because of its own strong political connections. Though organized criminals used to be white ethnics—Jews, Italians, and Irish—today blacks, Hispanics, and other groups have become included in organized crime activities. The old-line "families" are more likely to use their criminal wealth and power to buy into legitimate businesses.

There is debate over the control of organized crime. Some experts believe there is a national crime cartel that controls all activities. Others view organized crime as a group of disorganized, competing gangs dedicated to extortion or to providing illegal goods and services.

Efforts to control organized crime have been stepped up. The federal government has used antiracketeering statutes to arrest syndicate leaders. But as long as there are vast profits to be made, illegal enterprise should continue to flourish.

Notes

1 Dwight Smith, "White-Collar Crime, Organized Crime and the Business Establishment: Resolving a Crisis in Criminological Theory," in *White Collar and Economic Crime: A Multidisciplinary and Crossnational Perspective*, P. Wickman and T. Dailey, eds. (Lexington, Mass.: Lexington Books, 1982), p. 53.

2 See generally Dwight C. Smith, Jr., "Organized Crime and Entrepreneurship," *International Journal of Criminology and Penology* 6 (1978):161–77; Dwight C. Smith, Jr., "Paragons, Pariahs, and Pirates: A Spectrum-Based Theory of Enterprise," *Crime and Delinquency* 26 (1980):358–86; Dwight C. Smith, Jr. and Richard S. Alba, "Organized Crime and American Life," *Society* 16 (1979):32–38.

3 Smith, "White-Collar Crime, Organized Crime and the Business Establishment," p. 33.

4 Edwin Sutherland, "White-Collar Criminality," *American Sociological Review* 5 (1940):2–10.

5 See generally Herbert Edelhertz, *The Nature, Impact and Prosecution of White-Collar Crime* (Washington, D.C.: Government Printing Office, 1970), pp. 73–75.

6 Gilbert Geis, "Avocational Crime," in *Handbook of Criminology*, ed. Daniel Glazer (Chicago: Rand McNally, 1974), p. 284.

7 Laura Schrager and James Short, "Toward a Sociology of Organizational Crime," *Social Problems* 25 (1978):415–25.

8 Ibid., p. 415.

9 Gilbert Geis, "White-Collar and Corporate Crime," in *Major Forms of Crime*, Robert Meier, ed. (Beverly Hills, Calif.: Sage Publications, 1984), p. 145.

10 Bureau of Justice Statistics, *The Severity of Crime* (Washington, D.C.: U.S. Government Printing Office, 1984).

11 Knight-Rider Inc., Washington Bureau, "Senators Say GE, Hutton Cases Follow Dual Standard," *Omaha World Herald*, 16 May 1985, p. 14.

12 Edelhertz, "The Nature, Impact and Prosecution of White-Collar Crime," pp. 73–75.

13 Mark Moore, "Notes toward a National Strategy to Deal with White Collar Crime," in A *National Strategy for Containing White Collar Crime*, ed. Herbert Edelhertz and Charles Rogovin (Lexington, Mass.: Lexington Books, 1980), pp. 32–44.

14 "Catch Me If You Can," *Time*, 26 April 1982, p. 55.

15 Scott Paltrow, "Goldblum Now in Consulting and on Parole," *Wall Street Journal*, 22 March 1982, p. 25.

16 Bruce Ingersoll, "Utah Investors Said to Lose $215 Million in Securities Scam," *Wall Street Journal*, 6 December 1984, p. 36.

17 "Report: Fraud Costs Billions for Taxpayers," *Omaha World Herald*, 17 May 1982, p. 9.

18 This subsection and the following ones rely heavily on "White-Collar Crime: Second Annual Survey of Laws," *American Criminal Law Review* 19 (1981):173–520.

19 Medicare and Medicaid Anti-Fraud and Abuse Amendment of 1977, Title XVIII, Pub. Law No. 95–142, 91 Stat. 1175.

20 Robert Pear, "Panel Says Most States Fail on Policing Medicaid Fraud," *New York Times*, 27 March 1982, p. 7.

21 Richard Quinney, "Occupational Structure and Criminal Behavior: Prescription Violation of Retail Pharmacists," *Social Problems* 11 (1963):179–85; see also John Braithwaite, *Corporate Crime in the Pharmaceutical Industry* (London: Routledge and Kegan Paul, 1984).

22 "Former Broker to Plead Guilty to Defrauding $570,000 from Clients," *Wall Street Journal*, 8 October 1984, p. 35.

23 This section depends heavily on Frank Browning and John Gerassi, *The American Way of Crime* (New York: Putnam, 1980), p. 151.

24 Ibid., p. 293.

25 Ibid.

26 Edward Ranzal, "City Report Finds Building Industry Infested by Graft," *New York Times*, 8 November 1974, p. 1.

27 Marshall Clinard and Peter Yeager, *Corporate Crime* (New York: Free Press, 1980), pp. 166–67.

28 John Boland, "The SEC Trims the First Amendment," *Wall Street Journal*, 4 December 1984, p. 28; "Winans Testifies He Didn't Tamper with Stock Column," *Wall Street Journal*, 20 March 1985, p. 10.

29 Charles McCaghy, *Deviant Behavior* (New York: MacMillan, 1976), p. 178.

30 Ibid., p. 168.

31 J. Sorenson, H. Grove, and T. Sorenson, "Detecting Management Fraud: The Role of the Independent Auditor," in *White-Collar Crime, Theory and Research*, ed. G. Geis and E. Stotland (Beverly Hills, Calif.: Sage Publications, 1980), pp. 221–51.

32 John Clark and Richard Hollinger, *Theft by Employees in Work Organizations* (Washington, D.C.: U.S. Government Printing Office, 1983), pp. 2–3.

33 M. Swanson and J. Territo, "Computer Crime: Dimensions, Types, Causes and Investigations," *Journal of Political Science and Administration* 8 (1980):305–306; see Donn Parker, "Computer Related White Collar Crime," in *White Collar Crime, Theory and Research*, ed. G. Geis and E. Stotland (Beverly Hills, Calif.: Sage Publications, 1980), p. 199–220.

34 Tom Nugent, "Security Experts Say Thefts Exceed $100 Million a Year," *Omaha World Herald*, 13 May 1982, p. 35.

35 Parker, "Computer Related White Collar Crime," p. 213.

36 Erik Larson, "Computers Turn Out to be Valuable Aid in Employee Crime," *Wall Street Journal*, 14 January 1985, p. 1.

37 "Computer Hackers Charge $60,000 to Sprint Number," *Omaha World Herald*, 6 February 1985, p. 1.

38 Comprehensive Crime Control Act of 1984, Pub. L. No. 98-473 §§2101-03, 98 Stat. 1837, 2190 (1984) (adding 18 USC § 1030 (1984)).

39 U.S. v. Bishop 412 U.S. 346 (1973).

40 "Reagan: Lower Interest Rates End Tax Cheats," *Omaha World Herald*, 25 April 1982, p. A–5.

41 Alan Murray, "IRS in Losing Battle Against Tax Evaders Despite Its New Gear," *Wall Street Journal*, 10 April 1984, p. 1.

42 Ibid.

43 Jay Branegan, "Of Windmills, Cattle and Form 1040," *Time*, 13 May 1984, p. 48.

44 Stephen Koepp, "Rich is Poorer," *Time*, 22 October 1984, p. 78.

45 "Now Williams—Last, Not Least of ABSCAM Trials," *New York Times*, 5 April 1982, p. E–7.

46 *The Knapp Commission Report on Police Corruption* (New York: George Braziller, 1973), pp. 1–3, 170–82.

47 "Greylord Term for Ex-Judge is Harshest Yet," *Omaha World Herald*, 19 December 1984, p. 8.

48 "Police Official Sentenced to 18 Years for Extortion," *Wall Street Journal*, 25 September 1984, p. 6.

49 Cited in Hugh Barlow, *Introduction to Criminology*, 2d ed. (Boston: Little, Brown, 1984).

50 Robert Taylor, "Bechtel Is Said to be Linked to Bid-Rigging, Bribes in Getting Contracts in South Korea," *Wall Street Journal*, 25 April 1984, p. 2.

51 Pub. Law. No. 95-213, 101-104, 91 Stat. 1494.

52 Christopher Bryon, "Big Profits in Big Bribery," *Time*, 16 March 1981, pp. 58–67.

53 Ibid., p. 59.

54 Ibid., p. 67.

55 15 U.S.C. 1-7 (1976).

56 See U.S. v. Sealy, Inc., 383 U.S. 350.

57 Northern Pacific Railways v. U.S., 356 U.S. 1 (1958).

58 M. Maltz and S. Pollock, "Suspected Collusion among Bidders," in *White Collar Crime, Theory and Research*, ed. G. Geis and E. Stotland (Beverly Hills, Calif.: Sage Publications, 1980), pp. 174–98.

59 Gilbert Geis, "White Collar Crime: The Heavy Electrical Equipment Antitrust Cases of 1961," in *Corporate and Governmental Deviance*, ed. M. Ermann and R. Lundman (New York: Oxford University Press, 1978), pp. 58–79.

60 Cited in Clinard and Yeager, *Corporate Crime.*

61 Brooks Jackson, "ARCO Will Pay $22.5 Million to Settle Its Part of Lawsuit Against Oil Firms," *Wall Street Journal*, 14 December 1983, p. 3.

62 Clinard and Yeager, *Corporate Crime.*

63 John Conklin, *Illegal but Not Criminal* (Englewood Cliffs, N.J.: Prentice-Hall, 1972), pp. 45–46.

64 Ibid.

65 Richard Koenig, "Smith/Kline Pleads Guilty to U.S. Charges It Was Slow to Report Drug's Side Effects," *Wall Street Journal*, 14 December 1984, p. 15.

66 "U-Haul is Awarded $40 Million in Civil Suit Against Hall's Jartran," *Wall Street Journal*, 30 November 1984, p. 56.

67 "Econotes," *Environmental Action* 13 (October 1981), p. 7.

68 "Econotes," *Environmental Action* 13 (September 1981), p. 5.

69 "Econotes," *Environmental Action* 13 (February 1982), p. 7.

70 "Union Carbide Says Bhopal Plant Should Have Been Closed," *Wall Street Journal*, 21 March 1985, p. 18.

71 See generally Paul Sweeney, "This Town's Not for Burning," *Environmental Action* 13 (February 1982), p. 9.

72 Robert Taylor, "EPA Says Cleanup of Sites Will Cost $11.7 Billion More," *Wall Street Journal*, 14 December 1984, p. 21.

73 42 USC 7413 (C) (Supp. III, 1979).

74 33 USC 1342 (1976); 33 USC 1362 (19).

75 33 USC 401-407 (1976).

76 42 USC 6901-87 (1976, Supp. III and Supp. IV, 1980).

77 15 USC 2601-29 (1976).

78 Herbert Edelhertz and Charles Rogovin, eds., *A National Strategy for Containing White Collar Crime* (Lexington, Mass.: Lexington Books, 1980), Appendix A, pp. 122–23.

79 Donald Cressey, *Other People's Money: A Study of the Social Psychology of Embezzlement* (Glencoe, Ill.: Free Press, 1972).

80 Ibid., p. 96.

81 Ronald Kramer, "Corporate Crime: An Organizational Perspective," in Wickman and Dailey, eds., *White Collar and Economic Crime*, pp. 75–94.

82 David Simon and D. Stanley Eitzen, *Elite Deviance* (Boston: Allyn and Bacon, 1982), p. 28.

83 Clinard and Yeager, *Corporate Crime*, p. 124.

84 Bureau of National Affairs, *White-Collar Justice: A BNA Special Report on White-Collar Crime* (Washington, D.C.: Bureau of National Affairs) cited in Clinard and Yeager, *Corporate Crime*, p. 286.

85 Geis, "Avocational Crime," p. 390.

86 Clinard and Yeager, *Corporate Crime*, p. 288.

87 *Time Magazine*, 4 March 1985, p. 55.

88 This section relies heavily on Albert Reiss, Jr., "Selecting Strategies of Social Control over Organizational Life," in Keith Hawkins and John M. Thomas, eds., *Enforcing Regulation* (Boston: Klowver Publications, 1984), pp. 25–37.

89 Ibid.

90 John Braithwaite, "The Limits of Economism in Controlling Harmful Corporate Conduct," *Law and Society Review* 16 (1981–1982):481–504.

91 John Braithwaite and Gilbert Geis, "On Theory and Action for Corporate Crime Control," *Crime and Delinquency* 28 (1982):292–314.

92 Geis, "White Collar and Corporate Crime," p. 154.

93 Tom Carrington, "Pay for General Dynamics Corporation to be Withheld," *Wall Street Journal*, 8 April 1985, p. 2.

94 Francis Cullen, William Maakestad, and Gary Cavender, "The Ford Pinto Case and Beyond: Corporate Crime, Moral Boundaries and the Criminal Sanction" in *Corporations as Criminals*, Ellen Hochstedler, ed. (Beverly Hills, Cal.: Sage Pub., 1984), pp. 107-130.

95 Bill Richards and Alex Kotlowitz, "Judge Finds 3 Corporate Officials Guilty of Murder in Cyanide Death of Worker," *Wall Street Journal*, 17 June 1985, p. 2.

96 This section relies heavily on Daniel Skoler, "White Collar Crime and the Criminal Justice System: Problems and Challenges," in Edelhertz and Rogovin, eds., *A National Strategy for Containing White Collar Crime*, pp. 57–76.

97 Alan Otten, "States Begin to Protect Employees Who Blow Whistle on Their Firms," *Wall Street Journal*, 31 December 1984, p. 11.

98 G. R. Blakey and M. Goldsmith, "Criminal Redistribution of Stolen Property: The Need for Law Reform," *Michigan Law Review* 81 (August 1976):45–46.

99 Alan Block and William Chambliss, *Organizing Crime* (New York: Elsevier, 1981).

100 Merry Morash, "Organized Crime," in Meier, ed., *Major Forms of Crime*, p. 198.

101 Alan Block, *East Side/West Side* (New Brunswick, N.J.: Transaction Books, 1983), p. VII, 10–11.

102 Robert Rhodes, *Organized Crime, Crime Control vs. Civil Liberties* (New York: Random House, 1984).

103 Jay Albanese, "God and the Mafia Revisited: From Valachi to Frantianno," paper presented at the Annual Meeting of the American Society of Criminology, Toronto, Ontario, 1982.

104 Block, *East Side/West Side*.

105 William Chambliss, *On the Take* (Bloomington, Indiana: Indiana University Press, 1978).

106 This section was adapted from Task Force on Organized Crime, *Organized Crime* (Washington, D.C.: Government Printing Office, 1976), pp. 7–8.

107 This section borrows heavily from Inciardi, *Reflections on Crime*, pp. 34–53; and F. Browning and J. Gerassi, *The American Way of Crime* (New York: Putnam, 1980), pp. 288–472; August Bequai, *Organized Crime* (Lexington, Mass.: Lexington Books, 1979).

108 Francis Ianni, *Black Mafia: Ethnic Succession in Organized Crime* (New York: Pocket Books, 1975).

109 Stephen Koepp, "Dirty Cash and Tarnished Vaults," *Time*, 25 February 1985, p. 65.

110 George Vold, *Theoretical Criminology*, 2d ed., rev. Thomas Bernard (New York: Oxford University Press, 1979).

111 18 USC 1952 (1976).

112 Pub. L. No. 91-452, Title IX, 84 Stat. 922 (1970) (codified at 18 USC 1961-68, 1976).

113 This section was adapted from "White-Collar Crime: Second Annual Review of Law," *American Criminal Law Review* 19 (1981):351.

114 Ed Magnuson, "Hard Days for the Mafia," *Time*, 4 March 1985.

Public Order Crime

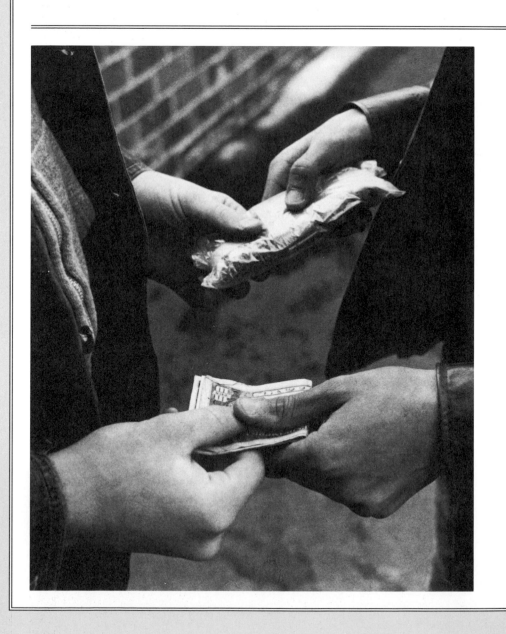

CHAPTER OUTLINE

Introduction

Law and Morality

Sex-related Offenses
Homosexuality
Prostitution
Pornography

Substance Abuse
Commonly Abused Drugs
Drug Use in the United States
Drugs and the Law
The Nature of Drug Abuse
The Extent of Drug Abuse
Drugs and Crime
Controlling the Drug Trade
Alcohol Abuse

Summary

KEY TERMS

mala in se
public order crimes
victimless crimes
mala prohibitum
pornography
prostitution
homosexual acts
moral entrepreneur

rule creator
homophobia
sodomy
watch queen
brothel
madam
call girls
massage parlor

baby pros
white slave act
kiddy porn
utterly without redeeming
 social importance
narcosis
addict

Introduction

The preceding three chapters discussed crimes of theft and violence. There is usually little question that, as a group, these acts are essentially harmful to their victims and should be eliminated from society. They are **mala in se** crimes—evil unto themselves. In this chapter, **public order crimes** will be the focus of our attention. They are often referred to as **victimless crimes**, though that title can be misleading.[1] Public order crimes involve acts that interfere with the operations of society and the ability of people to function efficiently. As a group, such crimes are **mala prohibitum**—outlawed because they conflict with social policy, accepted moral rules, and public opinion.

Statutes designed to uphold public order usually prohibit the distribution of morally questionable goods and services—erotic material, commercial sex, gambling, drugs. They are controversial in part because millions of otherwise law-abiding citizens—students, workers, professionals—often partake of these outlawed things and consequently become involved in criminal activity. They are also controversial because they represent the selective prohibition of desired goods and services; in other words, they outlaw sin and vice.

This chapter is divided into three main sections. The first briefly discusses the relationship of law and morality. The second deals with public order crimes of a sexual nature: **pornography**, **prostitution**, and **homosexual acts**. The third focuses on substance abuse: drugs and alcohol.

Law and Morality

Legislation of moral issues has always been debated. There is little question that the law should protect society and reduce social harm, but the question arises: Is harm really done by public order crimes, or any other acts made illegal because they violate prevailing moral standards?

When a store is robbed or a child assaulted, it is relatively easy to understand and condemn the social harm done the victim. However, it is more difficult to sympathize with or even identify the victim in a crime such as prostitution or pornography. Is the victim the prostitute? She may be a willing and successful entrepreneur, earning $75,000 or more a year. Is it her client? Hardly, since he has made a voluntary and determined effort to procure her services.

If public order crimes do not harm their participants, then perhaps society as a whole should be considered the "victim" of crime. Here is where the debate begins.

Some scholars argue that acts such as prostitution, pornography, and drug use erode the moral fabric of society and therefore should be punished by law. They are crimes, this argument goes, because " it is one of the functions of the criminal law to give expression to the collective feeling of revulsion toward certain acts, even when they are not very dangerous."[2]

In his classic statement on the function of morality in the law, Sir Patrick Devlin states:

> *Without shared ideas on politics, morals, and ethics no society can exist. . . . If men and women try to create a society in which there is no fundamental agreement about good and evil they will fail; if having based it on common agreement, the agreement goes, the society will disintegrate. For society is not something that is kept together physically; it is held by the invisible bonds of common thought. If the bonds were too far relaxed the members would drift apart. A common morality is part of the bondage. The bondage is part of the price of society; and mankind, which needs society, must pay its price.*[3]

In sum, society outlaws so-called victimless crimes because one of the functions of criminal law is to express public morality.[4]

However, opponents of this view reach a very different conclusion. Basing criminal definitions on moral beliefs, they argue, has always been a difficult decision: Who defines *deviance?* Are we not punishing differences rather than social harm? In the Puritan society of Salem, Massachusetts, were not women burnt at the stake as witches because their behavior seemed strange or different?

Some influential legal scholars have questioned the propriety of legislating morals. H. L. A. Hart states:

> It is fatally easy to confuse the democratic principle that power should be in the hands of the majority with the utterly different claim that the majority, with power in their hands, need respect no limits.
>
> Certainly there is a special risk in a democracy that the majority may dictate how all should live.[5]

Joseph Gussfield argues that the purpose of outlawing acts because they are immoral is to show the moral superiority of those who condemn the act over those who partake of them. The legislation of morality "enhances the social status of groups carrying the affirmed culture and degrades groups carrying that which is condemned as deviant."[6]

Howard Becker has labeled those who wish to control morality **moral entrepreneurs. Rule creators**, argues Becker, go on moral crusades to rid the world of evil. They operate with an absolute certainty that their way is right and that any means are justified to get their way; "the crusader is fervent and righteous, often self-righteous."[7]

Public order laws are usually created and enforced by rather small groups of individuals with a cause. Their efforts have produced a condition in which the criminal law is intertwined with existing moral concepts. However, concepts of morality are always changing, and they are subject to personal interpretation. Consequently, public order laws are unevenly enforced, they vary in content from jurisdiction to jurisdiction, and they carry a wide range of sanctions. For example, in some states possession of marijuana is punished by years in prison; in others by a small fine. The decriminalization of public order crimes is always a matter for great public debate.

Enforcement of morally tinged statutes is a great problem for law enforcement agencies. If police agencies enforce the law, they are branded reactionary and moralistic, and they are accused of wasting their time on petty issues (for example, why arrest prostitutes when murderers go free?). If police agencies ignore public order crimes, they are accused of condoning immorality, being lax, and being responsible for social degenerates. It has become fashionable for Hollywood to produce films showing the lone vigilante who gets rid of pushers and pimps when the police won't take action (for example, *Death Wish, Walking Tall, Fighting Back*).

Public order crimes are a good example of how conflict shapes law. There may be consensus in some areas of the legal code, but this is not one of them.

Sex-related Offenses

One type of public order crime bans deviant sexual practices. We will discuss three such practices: homosexuality, prostitution, and pornography. Laws controlling these acts have been the focus of much debate.

HOMOSEXUALITY

Homosexuality—the word derives from the Greek *homos,* meaning "same"—refers to erotic interest in members of one's own sex. However, to engage in homosexual behavior does not necessarily mean one is a homosexual. People may engage in homosexuality because heterosexual partners are unavailable (for example, in the armed services). Some may have sex forced on them by aggressive homosexual partners, a condition common to prison inmates. Some adolescents may experiment with partners of the same sex, though their sexual affiliation is heterosexual. Albert Reiss has described the behavior of delinquent youths, who engage in homosexual behavior for money but still regard themselves as heterosexuals, and who discontinue all homosexual activities as adults.[8] Finally, it is possible to be a homosexual but not to engage in sexual conduct with members of the same sex. To avoid this confusion it might be helpful to adopt the definition of a homosexual as one:

> *who is motivated in adult life by a definite preferential erotic attraction to members of the same sex and who usually (but not necessarily) engages in overt sexual relations with them.*[9]

In this section we will use the terms *gay* and *homosexual* to refer to people who engage in same-sex relations.[10]

Incidence of Homosexuality. Homosexual behavior has existed in most societies. Records of its presence can be found in prehistoric art and hieroglyphics. In their review of the literature on seventy-six preliterate societies, C. S. Ford and F. A. Beach found that male homosexuality was viewed as normal in forty-nine, female homosexuality in seventeen. Even when homosexuality was banned or sanctioned, it still persisted.[11]

There is some disagreement over the incidence of homosexual behavior in U.S. society. Alfred Kinsey and his associates surveyed five thousand white U.S. males and found that 10 percent were exclusively homosexual for at least three years between the ages of sixteen and sixty-five, 4 percent remained gay throughout their lives, and between 3 and 16 percent could be considered homosexual.[12] Kinsey also concluded that between 2 and 6 percent of unmarried females, but less than 1 percent of married ones, were exclusively homosexual. Furthermore, Kinsey reported that 37 percent of males and 13 percent of females had homosexual experiences. About 50 percent of men who remained single until age thirty-five had homosexual experiences.

Kinsey did not believe that human sexuality could simply be divided into the two groups of homosexual and heterosexual. He devised a seven-category rating scale that ranged from exclusively heterosexual (0) to equally homo- and heterosexual (3) to exclusively homosexual (7). People in the middle of Kinsey's scale respond sexually to both males and females and are known as bisexuals.

In a more recent survey, Morton Hunt estimates that about 3 percent of males are mainly or exclusively homosexual, as compared to Kinsey's estimate of 3 to 16 percent.[13] For women Hunt estimates that 1 to 3 percent are lesbians. Hunt estimates that about 3 million men and 2 million women in the United States are mainly or exclusively homosexual.

Attitudes Toward Homosexuality. Throughout Western history, homosexuals have been subject to sanction and punishment. The Bible expressly forbids homosexuality—Leviticus in the Old Testament, Paul's Epistles, Romans and Corinthians in the New Testament—and the prohibition has been the basis for repressing homosexual behavior.[14] Gays were brutalized and killed by the ancient Hebrews, a practice continued by the Christians who ruled Western Europe. Laws providing the death penalty for homosexuals existed until 1791 in France, until 1861 in England, and until 1889 in Scotland. Up until the Revolution, some American colonies punished homosexuality with death. In Hitler's Germany, fifty thousand homosexuals were put in concentration camps; up to 400 thousand more from occupied countries were killed.

Today, an extremely negative overreaction to homosexuals is referred to as **homophobia**. There are probably many reasons for it.[15] As already mentioned, some religious people believe that the Bible condemns same-sex relations and that this behavior is therefore a sin. Others develop a deep-rooted hatred of gays because they are insecure about their own sexual identity. Some are ignorant about the lifestyle of gays and fear that homosexuality is a disease that can be caught or that homosexuals will seduce their children.[16] Only recently, Anita Bryant's "Save Our Children" crusade was based on the homophobic belief that since gays cannot reproduce, they must seduce heterosexual children.

Are antigay attitudes changing? There is evidence that negative attitudes toward gays persist in our society. During the 1960s, 67 percent of people surveyed believed that homosexuality was obscene and vulgar. Fewer than 20 percent believed that laws banning homosexuality should be lifted.[17] Studies during the 1970s indicated that a majority of people viewed gays as sick, sinful, or dangerous.[18]

Even today there is some question about whether homosexuality is a disease, a mental illness, or an acceptable lifestyle. As late as 1973, the American Psychiatric Association (APA) removed homosexuality from its list of mental illnesses. However, in a 1978 survey of twenty-five hundred members of the APA, 69 percent reported the belief that homosexuality was an abnormal way of satisfying sexual needs, 60 percent saw homosexuals as less capable than heterosexuals of mature relationships, and 70 percent thought that homosexuals' problems were more likely to stem from inner conflicts than from prejudice.[19] These attitudes are reflected in the legal penalties suffered by gays. Recent fears about the disease AIDS has added to these tensions.

Homosexuality and the Law. Homosexuality, considered a legal and moral crime throughout most of Western history, is no longer a crime in the United States. In the case of *Robinson* v. *California*, the U.S. Supreme Court determined that people could not be criminally prosecuted because of their status (for example, drug addict or homosexual).[20]

However, in most states the lifestyle and activities of homosexuals are considered illegal. The United States actually has some of the harshest laws against homosexuality. For example, oral and anal sex and all other forms of nongenital heterosexual intercourse are usually banned under statutes prohibiting **sodomy**, deviant sexuality, or buggery. Maximum penalties range from three years to life imprisonment, with ten years being the most common sentence (see Close-Up).[21]

Influential legal bodies, such as the American Law Institute (ALI), have called for the abolition of statutes prohibiting nonheterosexual sex, unless force or coercion is used.[22] A few states, including Illinois, Connecticut and Nebraska, have adopted the ALI's Model Penal Code policy of legalizing any consensual sexual behavior between adults as long as it is conducted in private and is not forced.[23]

Because of the stigma still attached to homosexuality, many gays are forced into a life of brief sexual encounters, often conducted in public places such as

Homosexual Conduct

The following two statutes are typical of those designed to outlaw homosexual activity:

TEXAS

Section 21.01. Definitions
In this chapter:

(1) "Deviate sexual intercourse" means any contact between any part of the genitals of one person and the mouth or anus of another person.

Section 21.06. Homosexual Conduct

(a) A person commits an offense if he engages in deviate sexual intercourse with another individual of the same sex.

(b) An offense under this section is a Class C misdemeanor.

(Note: In Texas, Section 21.06 covers consensual behavior between adults in the privacy of their homes. Male-female "deviate sexual intercourse" is not considered a criminal act.)

MICHIGAN

Section 750.158. Penalty

Sec. 158. Any person who shall commit the abominable and detestable crime against nature either with

mankind or with any animal shall be guilty of a felony, punishable by imprisonment in the state prison not more than 15 years, or if such person was at the time of the said offense a sexually delinquent person, may be punishable by imprisonment in the state prison for an indeterminate term, the minimum of which shall be 1 day and the maximum of which shall be life. As amended P.A.1952, No. 73, § 1, Eff. Sept. 18.
(Note: Michigan retains the common-law concept of sodomy as "the abominable and destestable crime against nature"; notice how the statute does not say precisely what this term means.)

DISCUSSION QUESTION

1. Should these acts be punished as crimes?

SOURCE. *Vernon's Texas Code Annotated*, Chap. 21; *Michigan Compiles Laws Annotated*.

men's washrooms, parks, and theaters. In most larger cities, police vice squads stake out public places to catch homosexuals in the act. The men are then charged under statutes dealing with acts such as sodomy, solicitation, and lewd or lascivious behavior. Some departments limit their activities to arresting "hustlers," those who solicit other homosexuals for money. Laud Humphreys has described how homosexuals designate a lookout—a **watch queen**—to warn if police are in the vicinity.[24] However, Supreme Court cases upholding the right to privacy have eliminated most prosecutions of consenting homosexual activity between adults in the privacy of their homes.[25]

Homosexuals still suffer many legal disabilities. Although forty states have laws banning sexual discrimination, the movement had a setback when Miami repealed its gay rights ordinance in 1977. Similarly, in 1985 Houston voters rejected by a 4 to 1 margin a proposal to eliminate sexual preference in hiring, firing, and promoting city employees.[26] Though the federal government's Civil Service Commission found in 1975 that homosexuals could not be barred from federal employment, gays are still considered security risks and are not allowed to work in the CIA or FBI; they are also barred from military service. In the case of *Dronenburg v. Zech*, a U.S. Circuit Court of Appeals ruled that the Navy's policy of mandatory discharge for homosexuals does not violate their constitutional rights.[27]

Homosexuals may still be evicted from private housing at the landlord's discretion. With respect to public housing, the federal Department of Housing and Urban Development (HUD) proposed a regulation to allow homosexual couples to live in public housing projects: a month later the House of Representatives

Laws as well as acts of violence and oppression still attempt to control the activities of gay citizens.

nullified the proposal. Consequently, gays are prohibited from living together in public housing projects. In most areas, private employers may also discriminate against gay men and women. For example, a federal court upheld the right of an airline to fire a pilot who underwent a sex change operation.[28]

Though it is not a crime to be a homosexual, homosexual acts are still illegal in most states. However, most police agencies enforce laws banning homosexual practices only if they are forced to do so, if the acts occur in public places, or if the acts are done for financial consideration.

PROSTITUTION

Prostitution has been known for thousands of years. The term derives from the Latin *prostituere,* which means "to cause to stand in front of." By implication, the prostitute is viewed as publicly offering her body for sale. The earliest record of prostitution appears in ancient Mesopotamia, where priests engaged in sex to promote fertility in the community. All women were required to put in some time at temple duty, and passing strangers were expected to make donations to the temple after enjoying its services.[29]

Modern commercial sex appears to have its roots in ancient Greece, where Solon established licensed brothels in 550 B.C. The earnings of Greek prostitutes helped pay for the temple of Aphrodite. Famous men openly went to prostitutes to enjoy intellectual, aesthetic, and sexual stimulation.[30]

Today there are many variations of prostitution, but in general the term can be defined as the granting of nonmarital sexual access, established by mutual agreement of the prostitutes, their clients, and their employers, for remuneration. This definition is sexually neutral, since prostitutes can, of course, be straight or gay, male or female.[31]

A recent analysis has amplified the definition of prostitution by describing the conditions usually present in a commercial sexual transaction:

- Activity that has sexual significance for the customer. This includes the entire range of sexual behavior, from sexual intercourse to exhibitionism, sadism/masochism, oral sex, and so on.
- Economic transaction. Something of economic value, not necessarily money, is exchanged for the activity.
- Emotional indifference. The sexual exchange is simply for economic consideration. Though the participants may know one another, their interaction has nothing to do with affection for one another.[32]

In the following sections we will focus primarily on the nature and extent of heterosexual prostitution.

Incidence of Prostitution. It is difficult to assess the number of prostitutes operating in the United States. One estimate is one-quarter to one-half million full- or part-time prostitutes—one in two hundred to five hundred women.[33]

Kinsey's study of male sexuality found that nearly 50 percent of white males had visited a prostitute at least once. However, commercial sex was linked to social and educational standing. By age twenty-five, about two-thirds of non-college-educated men, but only about one-fourth of college-educated men, had visited a prostitute. Moreover, Kinsey found that about 20 percent of college men had been sexually initiated by prostitutes.[34]

It is likely that the number of men who hire prostitutes is declining. Hunt's 1974 study found that only 10 percent of college-educated men had been sexually initiated by prostitutes, half the number found by Kinsey in 1948. He states:

> A century ago, and even a generation ago, a considerable number of young males went to prostitutes for their sexual initiation, and some males—especially those in the lower social and educational levels—resorted to them often and regularly prior to marriage. The current wave of sexual liberation has made prostitution far more open and visible than ever before, as witness the burgeoning of "massage" and "body rub" establishments, commercially sponsored sex clubs, so-called dating bureaus, street-corner solicitation . . . and hooker traffic in singles bars. Yet our data show that, despite all this, there have been distinct decreases in the past generation in the percentage of American males who are sexually initiated by prostitutes, and in the average frequency with which they have such experiences.[35]

How can these changes be accounted for? One possibility is changing sexual mores brought about by the so-called sexual revolution. Men are less likely to engage prostitutes because legitimate alternatives for sexuality are more open to them.

Despite such supposed changes in sexual morality, arrests for prostitution have increased dramatically in the past decade. The Uniform Crime Reports indicate that such arrests increased 71 percent between 1974 and 1983 (from 51,000 to 88,000).[36] More alarming is the fact that about 1,500 arrests were of women under eighteen. In 1983, more than 270 recorded arrests were of children fifteen and under; some arrested prostitutes were under ten years old. The argument that the law should not interfere with sexual transactions because no one is harmed is undermined by these disturbing statistics.

Types of Prostitution. Several different types of prostitutes operate in the United States.

Streetwalkers. Working the streets in plain sight of police, citizens, and customers are streetwalkers. They are considered the least attractive, lowest paid, most vulnerable women in their profession.

Streetwalkers wear bright clothing, makeup, and jewelry to attract customers; they take their customers to hotels. However, the term *hooker* is not derived from the ability of streetwalkers to hook clients on their charms. The term actually stems from the popular name given women who followed Union General "Fighting Joe" Hooker's army during the Civil War.[37]

Because streetwalkers must openly display their occupation, they are very likely to be involved with the police. Studies indicate they are most likely to be members of ethnic or racial minorities who live in poverty. Of all prostitutes, streetwalkers have the highest incidence of drug abuse and larceny arrests, and they are the toughest.[38]

Bar girls. B-girls (bar girls) spend their time in bars, drinking and waiting to be picked up by customers. Though alcoholism may be a problem, B-girls usually work out an arrangement with the bartender so they are served diluted drinks or water colored with dye or tea, for which the customer is charged an exorbitant price. In some bars, the B-girl is given a credit for each drink she gets the customer to buy. It is common to find B-girls in towns with military bases and large transient populations, such as Boston and San Diego.[39]

Brothels. Also called bordellos, cathouses, sporting houses, and houses of ill repute, **brothels** flourished in the nineteenth and early twentieth centuries. They were large establishments, usually run by **madams**, that housed several prostitutes. The madam, often a retired prostitute, was the senior administrator and owner. She made arrangements for opening the place, attracted prostitutes and customers, worked out understandings with police authorities, and pacified neighbors.[40] The madam was part psychologist, part parent-figure, part business entrepreneur.

Some brothels and their madams have received national notoriety. Polly Adler wrote a highly publicized autobiography called *A House Is Not a Home.* Sally Stanford maintained a succession of luxuriously furnished brothels in San Francisco. Stanford never made a secret of her profession; she actually listed her phone number in the city directory. In 1962 and 1970 she ran for the San Francisco City Council. More recently, madam Xaviera Hollander made national headlines with the publication of her book *The Happy Hooker.*

Brothels declined in importance following World War II. The closing of the last brothel in Texas is chronicled in the play and movie *The Best Little Whorehouse in Texas.* Today the most well known brothels exist in Nevada, where prostitution is legal outside large population centers. Such houses as "Mustang Ranch," "Miss Kitty's," and "Pink Pussycat" service customers who are willing to drive out of Reno and Las Vegas to partake of their services.

In 1984, brothels made national news when socialite Sydney Biddle Barrows was arrested by New York police for operating a $1-million-per-year prostitution ring out of a bordello on West 74th Street.[41] Descended from a socially prominent family who traced their descendants to the Mayflower, Barrows ranked her twenty girls on looks and personality from A's ($125 per hour) to C's ($400 per hour) and kept 60 percent of their take. Her "black book" of clients was described by police as a mini *Who's Who.*

Call Girls. The aristocrats of prostitution are **call girls**. They charge customers up to $500 per night and may net up to $100,000 per year.

Many call girls come from middle-class backgrounds and service upper-class customers. Attempting to dispel the notion that their service is simply sex for money, they concentrate on making their clients feel important and attractive.

Working exclusively via telephone "dates," call girls get their clients by word of mouth or by making arrangements with local bellhops, cab drivers, and so on. They either entertain clients in their own apartments or do "outcalls" to clients' hotels and apartments. Upon retiring from "the life," a call girl can sell her datebook listing client names and sexual preferences for thousands of dollars. Despite the lucrative nature of their business, call girls suffer considerable risk by being alone and unprotected with strangers. It is common for them to request the business cards of their clients to make sure they are dealing with "upstanding citizens."

Circuit Travelers. Prostitutes known as circuit travelers travel in groups of two or three to lumber camps, labor camps, and railroad camps. They will ask the foremen for permission to ply their trade, service the whole crew in an evening, and then move on.

Rap Booths. A new phenomenon in commercial sex, rap booths are located in the adult entertainment zones of New York, Boston, and San Francisco.[42] The prostitute and her customer occupy separate booths, screened off by a glass wall. They talk via telephone for as long as the customer is willing to pay. The more money he spends, the more she engages in sexual banter and disrobing. There is no actual touching, and sex is through masturbation, with the prostitute serving as a masturbation aid similar in function to a pornographic magazine.

Other Varieties. Some "working girls" are based in **massage parlors**. Though it is unusual for a masseuse to offer all the services of prostitution, oral sex and manual stimulation are common. Most localities have attempted to limit commercial sex in massage parlors by passing ordinances specifying that the masseuse keep certain parts of her body covered and limiting the areas of the body that can be massaged.

Photography studios and model and escort services sometimes serve as covers for commercial sex. Some photo studios will allow customers to use body paint on models before the photo sessions start.

Stag party girls will service all-male parties and groups by putting on shows and having sex with participants.

In years past, many hotels had live-in prostitutes. Today's hotel prostitute makes a deal with the bell captain or manager to refer customers to her for a fee; some second-rate hotels still have resident prostitutes.

Becoming a Prostitute. Why does a woman turn to prostitution? Prostitutes often come from troubled homes marked by extreme conflict and hostility and from poor urban areas or rural communities. Hostility toward the father is common, as is incest and child molesting. Many prostitutes were initiated into sex by family members as early as ten to twelve years of age. Lower-class girls who get into "the life" report conflict with school authorities, poor grades, and an overly regimented school experience.[43]

In a similar vein, Charles Winick and Paul Kinsie provide this portrait of the girl who becomes a prostitute: She grew up in a slum neighborhood or broken home; was born out of wedlock; was a school dropout; is a minority group member; fantasizes about money and success; is a member of a "loose crowd"; had seen prostitutes in the neighborhood; father was absent, weak, or abusive; had unfortunate experiences with husband or boyfriend; had trouble keeping a job.[44]

However, there is no actual evidence that girls become prostitutes because of psychological problems or personality disturbances. In a study of white female prostitutes, Paul Gebhard found that very few (about 4 percent) were forced into the life; most reported entering prostitution voluntarily because they disliked the discipline of conventional work.[45] Also, Gebhard's study dispels the notion that prostitutes were seduced and abandoned as young girls, have insatiable sexual desires, or are drug addicts.

Jennifer James claims that the primary cause of women's becoming prostitutes is the supply and demand equation operating in society.[46] She contends that male clients are socialized to view sex as a commodity that can be purchased. The quantity of sex, rather than its quality, has the higher value for U.S. males. Women who are socialized to view themselves as sex objects may easily step over the line of propriety and accept money for their favors. These women view their bodies as salable commodities, and most prostitution does in fact pay better than other occupations available for women with limited education. Helping push the girl to take the final step into prostitution are the troubled personal circumstances described previously. James backs up her view with a research study that found that only 8 percent of prostitutes claim to have started because of dire economic necessity, while 57 percent were motivated by a desire for money and luxuries.

Pimps. A pimp derives part or all of his livelihood from the earnings of a prostitute. The pimp helps steer customers to the prostitute, stays on the alert for and deals with police, posts bail, and protects his girls from unruly customers.[47] To the prostitute, the pimp is a surrogate father, husband, and lover figure. She may sell her body to customers, but she reserves care and affection for her pimp.

Pimps can pick up established "working girls" or they can "turn out" young girls who have never been in "the life." Occasionally, but not as often as the media would like us to believe, they pick up young runaways, buy them clothes and jewelry, and turn them into **baby pros**.

What attracts men to the life of the pimp? One view is that many pimps originally worked on the fringes of prostitution as bellhops, elevator operators, or barmen and subsequently drifted into the profession. An opposing view is that pimps began as young men seduced by older prostitutes, who taught them how to succeed in "the life," how to behave, and how to control women.[48]

In the 1920s and 1930s most pimps were white ethnics. Today they are predominantly black, and the few whites who enter the profession adopt a black lifestyle. However, the decline of the brothel, the development of independent prostitutes, and the control of prostitution by organized crime has decreased the number of full-time pimps. In the last twenty years the terms *popcorn pimps, chili pimps,* and *coffee and cake pimps* have increasingly been used to describe the low esteem pimps are held in and their reduced importance to prostitutes.[49]

Prostitution and the Law. Although prostitution could not exist without a great deal of public support, it is currently illegal in all states except Nevada.

The federal government's Mann Act (1925) prohibits bringing women into the country or transporting them across state lines for the purposes of prostitution.

Often called the **white slave act**, it carries with it a $5,000 fine, five years in prison, or both.

Typically, prostitution is considered a misdemeanor, punishable by a fine or a short jail sentence. Consequently, even if arrested, most "working girls" are bailed out and are soon back on the street. Many streetwalkers have been arrested thirty or forty times. Of course, the longer their police record, the less likely they will be to enter conventional society.

Though police administrators may find the enforcement of solicitation laws a nuisance, they are often prodded into action by complaints of citizens and the news media. It is common for legitimate restaurant, theater, and store owners to pressure police officials to control streetwalkers, massage parlors, and B-girls who are disturbing customers in their area. Prostitution is also associated with other criminal acts and environments that demand police attention: drug use, larceny, the spread of venereal disease, and organized crime.

The classic confrontation between police and prostitutes occurs over the method of control. To prove solicitation, the police must be able to testify in court that they were approached and asked for payment for sexual services. Obviously, plainclothes officers are needed for this work. Most big-city police departments maintain vice squads whose members pose as customers and arrest prostitutes who solicit them. The line between legitimate police control and illegal entrapment of prostitutes is a fine one. Many cases get thrown out of court because police were too zealous in their jobs.[50]

To mitigate the conflict, some cities have set up areas where detente exists between prostitutes and law enforcement. In San Francisco it is the Tenderloin area, in New York it is 8th Avenue, and in Boston it is the Combat Zone. As long as pimps, streetwalkers, and B-girls stay in these areas, they are allowed to ply their trade with impunity. The concept of an adult entertainment zone is designed to limit the public's moral outrage, provide access to commercial sex for those adults who desire it, and reduce the costs to the criminal justice system of processing prostitutes.

Another legal ploy used to control prostitution is active enforcement of laws making it a crime to solicit prostitutes. Though clients are rarely arrested, some jurisdictions publish their names or license plate numbers in newspapers.

It is unlikely that the law will ever control prostitution. If the "oldest profession" is to end, it will probably be due to changing sexual morality and increased economic opportunities for women.

PORNOGRAPHY

Pornography is another moral/legal issue for criminological study. The term derives from the Greek *porne,* meaning "prostitute," and *graphein,* meaning "to write." In the heart of most major cities are stores devoted to the display and sale of books, magazines, and films that depict explicit sex acts of every imaginable kind. The purpose of this material is to provide sexual titillation and excitement for paying customers.

Though material depicting nudity and sex is legal, most federal, state, and city criminal codes prohibit the production, display, and sale of obscene material. *Obscenity,* the word derived from the Latin term *caenum* ("filth"), is currently defined by Webster's dictionary as "deeply offensive to morality or decency . . . designed to incite to lust or depravity."[51]

The problem of controlling pornography centers on this definition of obscenity.

Police and law enforcement officials can legally seize only material that is judged obscene. "But who," critics ask, "is to judge what is obscene?" At one time, such novels as *Tropic of Cancer*, by Henry Miller, *Ulysses*, by James Joyce, and *Lady Chatterley's Lover*, by D. H. Lawrence, were prohibited because they were considered obscene. Today they are considered works of great literary value. Thus, what is obscene today may be considered a work of art, or at least socially acceptable, at a future time. After all, *Playboy* and *Penthouse* magazines, sold openly on most college campuses, display nude men and women in all kinds of sexually explicit poses. Moreover, the First Amendment of the U.S. Constitution guarantees freedom of speech and expression. Allowing individual judgments on what is obscene makes the Constitution's guarantee of free speech unworkable. For example, what happens if a judge rules that books on Communism are obscene? Could not anti-obscenity statutes also be used to control political and social dissent?

Opponents of pornography argue that it degrades the men and women who are featured in "dirty pictures," customers, and members of the public who are sometimes forced to see obscene material. Pornographers also exploit women and children. The so-called **kiddy porn** industry is estimated to amount to over $1 billion of a total of $2.5 billion spent on pornography. In Houston, police uncovered a warehouse filled with fifteen thousand color slides of children, as well as thousands of pornographic magazines and reels of film. Each year, over a million children are used in pornography or prostitution, many of them runaways whose plight is exploited by adults. In New York City, Covenant House, a shelter care home for children, annually aids about five thousand runaways. Of these, two thousand have been involved in pornography and one thousand are under twelve years of age.[52]

Ann Wolbert Burgess studied fifty-five child pornography rings and found that the typical one contained between three and eleven children, predominantly males, some of nursery school age. The adults who controlled the ring used a position of trust to recruit the children and then continued to exploit them through a combination of material and psychological rewards. Burgess found that different types of child pornography rings exist. *Transition rings* are impromptu groups set up to sell and trade photos and sex. *Syndicated* rings have well-structured organizations that recruit children and create extensive networks of customers who desire sexual services.[53]

Critics of pornography also charge that it denigrates and exploits women. Laura Lederer cites the case of *Bondage* magazine, which regularly shows women being tied up and having scissors, hot irons, torches, and knives held to their breasts and vaginas.[54] Another magazine, *Brutal Trio*, in one issue shows three men kidnapping a young woman, a twelve-year-old girl, and a grandmother and beating them senseless, kicking them until they pass out, then raping them and beating them again. Even nationally distributed magazines such as *Playboy* are taken to task for their destructive view of women:

> *By socializing the view of women as unreal sex objects,* Playboy *and the magazines that have followed its lead have contributed to the increasing antagonism and subsequent violence between males and females, methodically helping break down the ability and need to care which . . . human beings are born with and which, as social animals, we need in order to survive.*[55]

Is Pornography Harmful? One issue critical to the debate over the legality of pornography is whether it is actually harmful to those who view it. Put another way, does viewing pornography produce sexual violence or assaultive behavior?

There is some evidence that viewing sexually explicit material actually has little effect on behavior. In 1970, the National Commission on Obscenity and Pornography reviewed all available material on the effects of pornography and commissioned independent research projects. The commission found little relationship between pornography and violence, and it recommended that federal, state and local legislation should not interefere with the rights of adults who wish to read, obtain, or view explicit sexual materials.[56]

Other research has backed the commission's finding. In a study conducted in Denmark, Berl Kutchinsky found that a steady drop-off in sex crimes occurred after pornography was decriminalized in 1967.[57] Kutchinsky attributes this trend to the fact that viewing erotic material may act as a safety valve for those whose impulses might otherwise lead them to violence.

On the other hand, Keith Davis and G. N. Braucht found a strong association between sex offenses and exposure to pornography. However, they also found a strong link between offenders' peer and family influences and both sex crimes and exposure to erotic material. When the social factors were mathematically controlled, the link between pornography and anitsocial behavior disappeared.[58]

In a similar vein, Michael Goldstein found that convicted rapists and sex offenders report less exposure to pornography than a control group of nonoffenders.[59]

These studies are typical of the many that indicate that there is little or no evidence of a relationship between exposure to pornography and violent crime. However, a few studies have shown that subjects exposed to erotic literature that portrays violence feel more sexually aggressive themselves. For example, Seymour Fishbach and Neal Malamuth found that exposure to violence in pornography influences erotic reactions to the portrayal of rape.[60]

The evidence suggests that violence and sexual aggression are not linked to erotic/pornographic films per se but that erotic films depicting violence, rape, brutality, and aggression may evoke similar feelings in viewers. This finding is especially distressing because the trend has been to portray increasing amounts of violence in pornographic films, movies, and cartoons. For example, Don Smith found that the theme of rape was common in adult-only books, that the frequency of depicting rape acts has increased since 1968, and that a dominant theme is that women really want to be raped.[61] Consequently, it seems apparent that further research is needed to measure the true relationship between sex crimes and pornography.

Pornography and the Law. The First Amendment of the Constitution protects free speech and prohibits police agencies from limiting the public's right of free expression. However, the U.S. Supreme Court held in the twin cases of *Roth* v. *United States* and *Alberts* v. *California* that obscenity was not covered by the First Amendment.[62] In deciding these cases, the Court stated that the First Amendment protects all "ideas with even the slightest redeeming social importance—unorthodox ideas, controversial ideas, even ideas hateful to the prevailing climate of opinion. . . . but implicit in the history of the First Amendment is the rejection of obscenity as **utterly without redeeming social importance**." (Boldface added.)

Though the Roth case settled the issue of whether obscenity is protected by the First Amendment, it still left unclear how obscenity is defined. A spate of movies after the decision alleged that they were educational or told a moral tale, so they could not be said to lack redeeming social importance. Many state obscenity

Some jurisdictions have attempted to curb pornography by giving it free rein in limited areas. Boston's Combat Zone and San Francisco's Tenderloin are examples.

cases were appealed to federal courts so judges could decide whether the films totally lacked redeeming social importance.

To rectify the situation, the Supreme Court redefined its concept of obscenity in the case of *Miller v. California*:

> *The basic guidelines for the trier of fact must be (a) whether the average person applying contemporary community standards would find that the work taken as a whole appeals to the prurient interest; (b) whether the work depicts or describes, in a patently offensive way, sexual conduct specifically defined by the applicable state law, and (c) whether the work, taken as a whole, lacks serious literary, artistic, political or scientific value.*[63]

To convict a person of obscenity under the *Miller* doctrine, the state or local jurisdiction must specifically define obscene conduct in its statute, and the pornographer must engage in that behavior. The Court gave some examples of what is considered obscene: "patently offensive representations or descriptions of masturbation, excretory functions and lewd exhibition of the genitals" (see Close-Up).

In subsequent cases the court overruled convictions for "offensive" or "immoral" behavior; these are not considered obscene.

Under existing Supreme Court guidelines, local police and prosecutors must obtain court orders to seize allegedly obscene material. It is then up to a jury to decide whether the material violates contemporary community standards. Of course, this definition varies, so what is obscene in Omaha might be acceptable in New York.

It is common practice for police to loosely enforce obscenity statutes. The difficulty of getting a conviction and the ambiguity of statutes often make enforcement difficult. Sometimes local antismut campaigns force police to take action, but the paying public's demand for pornography usually causes it to reemerge and, as is the case for prostitution, an adult entertainment area can be designated and pornographic material is sold there with impunity. In the case of *Young v. American Mini Theatres*, the Supreme Court permitted a zoning ordinance that restricted

Obscenity

Each local community, under current legal philosophy, must define its own standard of what material is considered obscene. The standard created for Council Bluffs, Iowa, is typical of local obscenity statutes:

43.101 Sale of obscene material to minors. It is unlawful to sell or display to minors with or without monetary consideration certain printed matter, photographs, motion picture film, and other similar visual representations depicting sexual conduct, nudity, or sado-masochistic abuse which is harmful to minors, or to exhibit, give, or sell admission tickets to premises wherein there are exhibited motion pictures depicting the same. (Chap 3897 1 (part), 1970).

43.020 Definitions. For the purposes of this chapter the following terms and phrases shall have the following meanings:

1. "Minor" means any person under the age of eighteen years;
2. "Nudity" means the showing of the human male or female genitals, pubic area, or buttocks with less than a full opaque covering, or the showing of the female breast with less than a fully opaque covering of any portion thereof below the top of the nipple, or the depiction of covered male genitals in a discernible turgid state;
3. "Sexual conduct" means acts of masturbation, homosexuality, sexual intercourse, or physical contact with a person's clothed or unclothed genitals, pubic area, buttocks, or, if the person be a female, breast;

4. "Sexual excitement" means the condition of human male or female genitals when in a state of sexual stimulation or arousal;
5. "Sado-masochistic abuse" means flagellation or torture by or upon a person clad in undergarments, a mask, or bizarre costume, or the condition of being fettered, bound, or otherwise physically restrained on the part of those clothed;
6. "Harmful to minors" means that quality of any description or representation, in whatever form, of nudity, sexual conduct, sexual excitement, or sado-masochistic abuse, when it:

   (a) predominantly appeals to the prurient, shameful, or morbid interest of minors, and

   (b) is patently offensive to prevailing standards in the adult community as a whole with respect to what is suitable material for minors.

DISCUSSION QUESTIONS

1. Does the legal definition of obscenity accurately and adequately define the term?
2. Do you agree with the legal definition of obscenity?

SOURCE. *Local Ordinances, Council Bluffs, Iowa*, Chap. 8, 43, Section 010, 020.

---

theaters showing erotic movies to one area of the city even though it did not find that any of the movies shown were obscene.[64] The state therefore has the right to regulate adult films as long as the public has the right to view them.

The landmark *New York* v. *Ferber case*, decided in July 1982, also seems to indicate the Supreme Court's willingness to allow the states to control pornography.[65] In this case, Paul Ferber, a Manhattan bookstore owner, was sentenced to forty-five days in jail for violating a New York statute banning material that portrays children in sexually explicit, though not necessarily obscene, conduct. He challenged the law as a violation of free speech. By unanimously upholding Ferber's conviction, the Supreme Court found that kiddy porn is damaging to the children it exploits and therefore can be legally banned. In his opinion, Justice Byron White said, "It has been found that sexually exploited children are unable to develop healthy affectionate relationships in later life, have sexual dysfunction and have a tendency to become sexual abusers as adults." The Court also found that the films were an invasion of the child's privacy that the child could not control.

Substance Abuse

The use of chemical substances to change reality and provide stimulation, relief, or relaxation has gone on for thousands of years. Mesopotamian writings indicate that opium was used centuries ago. The ancient Greeks knew and understood the problems of drug use. At the time of the Crusades, the Arabs were using marijuana. In the Americas, natives of Mexico and South America chewed coca leaves and used "magic mushrooms" in their religious ceremonies.[66]

In the United States, drug and alcohol abuse is often viewed as another type of victimless public order crime. There is great debate over the legalization of drugs and the control of alcohol. Some argue that their use is a private matter and that making it illegal is a matter of government intrusion into a person's private life. Others see them as dangerous, believing that the criminal activity of users makes the term *victimless* nonsensical. Still another position is that the possession and use of all drugs and alcohol should be legalized but that the sale and distribution of drugs should be heavily penalized. This would punish those profiting from drugs and would enable users to be helped without fear of criminal punishment.

A variety of substances are considered so harmful to society that their manufacture, sale, and possession are either illegal per se or strictly controlled. We will discuss them and their use in this section.

COMMONLY ABUSED DRUGS

A wide variety of drugs are sold and used by drug abusers. Some are addicting, others not. Some provide hallucinations; others cause a depressing, relaxing stupor; and a few give an immediate exhilarating uplift. This section will discuss some of the most widely used illegal drugs.[67]

Anesthetics. Anesthetic drugs are used as nervous system depressants. Local anesthetics block nervous system transmissions; general anesthetics act on the brain to produce a generalized loss of sensation, stupor, or unconsciousness (called **narcosis**).

The most widely abused anesthetic drug is phencyclidine (PCP), known on the street as "angel dust." PCP can be sprayed on marijuana or other plant leaves and smoked, drunk, or injected; the last two methods are extremely hazardous. Originally developed as an animal tranquilizer, PCP causes hallucinations and a spaced-out feeling. The effects of PCP can last up to two days; the danger of overdose is extremely high.

Narcotics. Narcotic drugs have the ability to produce insensibility to pain (analgesia) and to free the mind of anxiety and emotion (sedation). Users experience a rush of euphoria, relief from fear and apprehension, release of tension, and elevation of spirits. After experiencing this uplifting mood for a short period, the user becomes apathetic and drowsy and nods off. Narcotics can be injected under the skin or in a muscle (skin pop). Experienced users inject the drugs directly into the bloodstream (mainlining), which provides an immediate "fix."

The most common narcotics are derivatives of opium, a drug produced from the opium poppy flower. The Chinese popularized the habit of smoking or chewing opium extract to produce euphoric feelings. Morphine, a derivative of opium, is about ten times as strong and is used legally by physicians to relieve pain.

Heroin, the most commonly used narcotic in the United States, is produced from morphine but has an effect twenty-five times more powerful. Consequently, dealers cut it with neutral substances such as sugar (lactose). Street heroin is often only 1 to 4 percent pure. The danger of heroin is that users can rapidly build a tolerance for it. They constantly need more drugs to feel an effect and also will change the method of ingestion to get the desired "kick." At first heroin is usually sniffed or snorted; as tolerance builds, it is skin-popped and then finally mainlined. Through the process the user becomes an **addict**—a person with an overpowering physical and psychological need to continue taking the drug by any means possible. If addicts can't get a supply of heroin sufficient to meet their habit, they will suffer withdrawal symptoms. These include irritability, emotional depression, extreme nervousness, pain in the abdomen, and nausea. Heroin addiction will be discussed in subsequent sections.

Other opium derivatives used by drug abusers include codeine, dilaudid, percodan, and prinadol. It is also possible to create synthetic narcotics in the laboratory. Synthetics include demerol, methadone, nalline, and darvon. It is less likely that a user will become addicted to synthetic narcotics, but it is still possible, and withdrawal symptoms are similar to those experienced by users of natural narcotics.

Volatile Liquids. Volatile liquids are liquids that are easily vaporized. Some substance abusers inhale vapors from lighter fluid, paint thinner, cleaning fluid, and model airplane glue to reach a drowsy, dizzy state sometimes accompanied by hallucinations. The psychological effect produced by inhaling these substances is a short-term sense of excitement and euphoria followed by a period of disorientation, slurred speech, and drowsiness. Amyl nitrate ("poppers") is a commonly used volatile liquid that is sold in capsules that are broken and inhaled. Poppers allegedly increase sensation and are sometimes used during sexual activity to prolong and intensify the experience.

Barbiturates. The hypnotic-sedative drugs—barbiturates—are able to depress the central nervous system into a sleeplike condition. On the illegal market, barbiturates are called goofballs or downers or are known by the color of the capsules— reds (seconal), blue dragons (Amytal), and "rainbows" (tuinal).

Barbiturates can be prescribed by doctors as sleeping pills. In the illegal market they are used to create relaxed, sociable, and good-humored feelings. However, if dosages get too high, users become irritable and obnoxious, and finally they slump off into sleep. Barbiturate overdoses are probably the major source of drug overdose deaths.

Tranquilizers. Tranquilizers have the ability to relieve uncomfortable emotional feelings by reducing levels of anxiety. They relieve tension and promote a state of relaxation.

The major tranquilizers are used to control the behavior of the mentally ill who are suffering from psychoses, aggressiveness, and agitation. They are known by their brand names—Ampazine, Thorazine, Pacatal, Sparine, and so on.

The minor tranquilizers are used by the average citizen to combat anxiety, tension, fast heart rate, and headaches. The most common are valium, librium, miltown, and equanil. These mild tranquilizers are easily obtained by prescription. However, increased dosages can lead to addiction, and withdrawal can be painful and hazardous.

Cannabis (Marijuana). Commonly called "pot," "grass," "ganja," "maryjane," "dope," and a variety of other names, marijuana is produced from the leaves of *Cannabis sativa,* a plant grown throughout the world. Hashish (hash) is a concentrated form of Cannabis made from unadulterated resin from the female plant.

Smoking large amounts of pot or hash can cause drastic distortions in auditory and visual perception, even producing hallucinatory effects. Small doses produce an early excitement ("high") that gives way to a sedated effect and drowsiness. Pot use is also related to decreased physical activity, overestimation in time and space, and increased food consumption ("the munchies"). When the user is alone, marijuana produces a quiet, dreamy state. In a group, it is common for users to become giddy and lose perspective. Though marijuana is nonaddicting, its long-term effects have been the subject of much debate.

Hallucinogens. Hallucinogens are drugs, either natural or synthetic, that produce vivid distortions of the senses without greatly disturbing the viewer's consciousness. Some produce hallucinations, and others cause psychotic behavior in otherwise normal people.

One common hallucinogen is mescaline, named after the Mescalero Apaches, who first used it. Mescaline occurs naturally in the peyote, a small cactus that grows in Mexico and the southwestern United States. After initial discomfort, mescaline produces vivid hallucinations in all ranges of colors and geometric patterns, a feeling of depersonalization, and out-of-body sensations. A synthetic and highly dangerous form of mescaline used for a brief period in the 1960s was called STP. However, the danger of this drug made its use short-lived.

A second group of hallucinogens are alkaloid compounds. Alkaloids occur in nature or can be made in the laboratory. They include such familiar hallucinogens as DMT, morning-glory seeds, and psilocybin. These compounds can be transformed into a D-lysergic acid diethylamide-25, commonly called LSD. This powerful substance (eight hundred times more potent than mescaline) stimulates cerebral sensory centers to produce visual hallucinations in all ranges of colors, to intensify hearing, and to increase sensitivity. Users often report a scrambling of sensations; they may "hear colors" and "smell music." Users also report feeling euphoric and mentally superior, though to an observer they appear disoriented and confused. Unfortunately, anxiety and panic (a "bad trip") may occur during the LSD experience, and overdoses can produce psychotic episodes, flashbacks, and even death.

Cocaine. Cocaine is the principal ingredient of the South American coca plant. Though South American natives chew the plant's leaves to relieve fatigue and achieve a positive psychological effect, in the United States the coca plant is processed into an odorless, crystalline powder called cocaine, "snow," or "coke."

Cocaine is the most powerful natural stimulant. Its use produces euphoria, laughter, restlessness, and excitement. Overdoses can cause delirium, increased reflexes, violent manic behavior, and possible respiratory failure.

Cocaine can be sniffed, or "snorted," into the nostrils or injected. The immediate feeling of euphoria ("rush") is short-lived, and heavy users may snort coke as often as every ten minutes. Mixing cocaine and heroin is called "speedballing"; it is a practice that is highly dangerous and is alleged to have killed comedian John Belushi.

Amphetamines. Amphetamines ("uppers," "beans," "pep pills") are synthetic drugs that stimulate action in the central nervous system. They produce an intense physical reaction: increased blood pressure, increased breathing rate, increased bodily activity, and elevation of mood. Amphetamines also produce psychological effects such as increased confidence, euphoria, fearlessness, talkativeness, impulsive behavior, and loss of appetite.

The commonly used amphetamines are Benzedrine ("bennies"), Dexedrine ("dex"), Dexamyl, Biphetamine ("whites"), and Methedrine ("meth," "speed," "crystal meth").

Methedrine is probably the most widely used and most dangerous amphetamine. Some people swallow it; heavy users inject it for a quick rush. Long-term heavy use can result in exhaustion, anxiety, prolonged depression, and hallucinations.

DRUG USE IN THE UNITED STATES

In the early years of the United States, opium and its derivatives were easily obtained. Opium-based drugs were adopted for use in various patent medicine cure-alls. Morphine was used extensively to relieve the pain of wounded soldiers in the Civil War. By the turn of the century an estimated 1 million Americans were opiate users.[68]

Several factors precipitated the stringent drug laws that are in force today. Domestic issues include:

- The rural creeds of the nineteenth century—for example, Methodism, Presbyterianism, Baptism—emphasized individual human toil and self-sufficiency while designating the use of intoxicating substances as an unwholesome surrender to the evils of urban morality. Religious leaders were thoroughly opposed to the use and sale of narcotics.
- The medical literature of the late 1800s began to arbitrarily designate the use of morphine and opium as a vice, a habit, an appetite, and a disease.
- Nineteenth and early twentieth century police literature described drug users as habitual criminals.
- Moral crusaders in the nineteenth century defined drug use as evil and directed the actions of local and national rule creators to outlaw their sale and possession.
- Some well-publicized research efforts categorized drug use as highly dangerous.[69]

Another important factor leading to the control of drugs was their association with foreign immigrants. Immigrant groups recruited to work in factories and mines brought with them their national drug habits; Mexicans, for example, brought marijuana, and Chinese brought opium. Though narcotics were still widely used by many middle-class Americans, they came to be associated with these foreign groups. Consequently, early antidrug legislation appears tied to prejudice against ethnic minorities.[70]

After the Spanish-American War of 1898, the United States inherited Spain's opium monopoly in the Philippines. Concern over this international situation, plus the domestic issues outlined above, led the U.S. government to participate in the First International Drug Conference, held in Shanghai in 1908, and a second one at the Hague in 1912. Participants in these two conferences were asked to be strongly opposed to free trade in drugs. The international pressure coupled with a growing national concern led to the passage of the antidrug laws discussed here.

DRUGS AND THE LAW

The federal government first initiated legal action to curtail the use of some drugs early in the twentieth century.[71] In 1906 the Pure Food and Drug Act required manufacturers to list the amounts of habit-forming drugs in products on the labels but did not restrict their use. However, the act prohibited the importation and sale of opiates except for medicinal purposes.

In 1914 the Harrison Narcotics Act restricted the importation, manufacture, sale, and dispensing of narcotics. It defined *narcotics* as any drug that produces sleep and relieves pain, such as heroin, morphine, and opium. The act was revised in 1922 to allow the importation of opium and coca (cocaine) leaves for qualified medical practitioners.

The Marijuana Tax Act of 1937 required registration and payment of a tax by all persons who imported, sold, or manufactured marijuana. Since marijuana was classified as a narcotic, those registering would also be subject to criminal penalty.

In later years, other federal laws were passed to clarify existing drug statutes or revise penalties. For example, the Boggs Act of 1951 provided mandatory sentences for violating federal drug laws. The Durham-Humphrey Act of 1951 made it illegal to dispense barbiturates and amphetamines, without a prescription. The Narcotic Control Act of 1956 increased penalties for drug offenders.

In 1965 the Drug Abuse Control Amendment set up stringent guidelines for the legal use and sale of mood-modifying drugs such as barbiturates, amphetamines, LSD, and any other "dangerous drugs" except narcotics prescribed by doctors and pharmacists. Illegal possession was punished as a misdeameanor and manufacture or sale as a felony.

Then, in 1970, the Comprehensive Drug Abuse Prevention and Control Act set up unified categories of illegal drugs and the penalties associated with their sale, manufacture, or possession. The law gives the U.S. Attorney General discretion to decide in which category to place any new drug.

For the most part, state laws mirror federal statutes. Some, such as New York's, apply extremely heavy penalties for sale or distribution of dangerous drugs, involving long mandatory prison sentences.

THE NATURE OF DRUG ABUSE

Drug abusers in the United States can be seen as two distinct types. Hard drug users are involved in narcotics use, typically heroin, which leads to dependency and addiction; soft-drug users are involved in the recreational use of nonaddictive drugs. These two phenomena are discussed here.

Hard Drug Use. Hard drug use in the United States primarily involves heroin addiction. It has been estimated that there are anywhere between seven hundred thousand and eight hundred thousand practicing heroin addicts.[72] However, that estimate may be low. A national survey on drug abuse in the United States found that between 1 and 2 percent of respondents had tried heroin.[73] Projected over the national population, that could amount to between two and three million people.

Heroin abuse is generally considered a lower-class phenomenon, though a fair number of middle- and upper-class users exist. Even physicians are known to have serious narcotic abuse problems.[74] In the period between the 1950s and 1980s, however, heroin addiction was most prevalent among minority youths in lower-class inner-city neighborhoods.

The disproportionate number of heroin abusers found among black and Hispanic citizens has been tied to such factors as racial prejudice, "devalued identities" and low self-esteem, poor socioeconomic status, and the stress of living in the harsh urban environment.[75] Charles Winick attributes the relationship of drug addiction, race, and poverty to the high level of mistrust, negativism, and defiance found in lower socioeconomic areas.[76]

Residing in a high drug abuse neighborhood relates to contact with and entry into a drug subculture. There, feelings of alienation and hopelessness run high. Youths living in high drug use neighborhoods often come in contact with drug users who try to convince them that narcotics provide an answer to their feelings of personal inadequacy and stress.[77] Perhaps the youth will join with others to learn the techniques of drug use and receive social support for doing so. Shared feelings and a sense of intimacy lead the youth to become fully enmeshed in what has been described as the "drug-use subculture."[78]

But not all ghetto residents become drug addicts. Cloward and Ohlin have explained this as a function of some slum dwellers' having access to illegitimate sources of income or prestige. Those who cannot function as fighters or thieves may seek to lose themselves in the drug world.

Another explanation is that drug users come from the most unstable elements of the ghetto. An often encountered personal characteristic of lower-class heroin abusers is a poor family life and troubled adolescence. One study concluded that the majority of addicts led an unhappy childhood, which included harsh physical punishment and parental neglect and rejection.[79] It is also common to associate addiction with large families and parents who are divorced, separated, or absent.[80]

Personality disturbance is also associated with drug abuse. Research on the psychological characteristics of narcotic addicts reveals the presence of a significant degree of pathology. Personality testing of known users suggests that a significant percentage suffer from psychotic disorders, including various levels of schizophrenia. Studies have found that addicts suffer personality disorders characterized by a weak ego, low frustration tolerance, anxiety, and fantasies of omnipotence. Still another view is that addicts exhibit psychopathic or sociopathic behavior characteristics.[81]

In sum, the picture that emerges of the heroin addict is of a poor, disenfranchised, lower-class person living in a high drug use area, having a disturbed family life, and manifesting severe personality problems.

Some major changes seem to be occurring in the heroin subculture. It appears that heroin is now being "cut" with fillers much more significantly than in the past. Consequently, "true" addiction is less likely to occur than in the past. Also, studies seem to indicate that addicts can control their compulsion for drugs and can actually decrease or terminate drug usage for long time periods. Often, control is exerted before critical events such as committing a crime, and intensive usage resumed at a more appropriate time.[82]

Soft Drug Use. In the 1960s it became popular for middle-class people to use extensive amounts of soft drugs—defined here as marijuana, cocaine, amphetamines, and hallucinogens. A drug subculture or counterculture grew up on U.S. campuses. Marijuana and cocaine use had been the province of jazz musicians and lower-class slum dwellers; now it became a white middle-class youth phenomenon. The counterculture developed a separate set of rules and values and created its own language. Phrases such as "getting stoned after a couple of hits on a joint" became common in campus discussions.

Though soft drug use has become a stable element of U.S. culture, possession and sale of marijuana, cocaine, and hallucinogens are still illegal. Those who favor outlawing these drugs claim they may be dangerous and addicting and may lead to heavy drug abuse. Soft drug users argue that few ever go on to use hard drugs and that the use of soft drugs is more akin to alcohol consumption. A number of states, such as Oregon and Vermont, have decriminalized marijuana possession, making it, like a parking offense, subject to a small fine. However, a majority of states still restrict possession and sale of soft drugs and attach serious penalties for violation.

THE EXTENT OF DRUG ABUSE

How much substance abuse occurs in the United States? One indication is the annual self-report survey of drug abuse among high school seniors sponsored by the National Institute of Drug Abuse.[83] The most recent survey available indicates that while drug use is still frequent, it has leveled off in the past few years. Table 13.1 shows the prevalence rate among the almost seventeen thousand students who responded to the nationwide survey. The major findings of the survey are described below:

- This year's findings indicate that the gradual decline in overall *illicit drug use*, which began a couple of years ago, is still continuing. The adjusted measure of current use of an illicit drug (that is, some use in the past 30 days of one or more illicit drugs) is down from 31 percent in 1983 to 29 percent in 1984, following a drop in the earlier unadjusted measure from 39 percent in 1979 to 32 percent in 1983. Annual prevalence (the proportion reporting any use in the prior year), unadjusted, dropped from 54 percent to 49 percent between 1979 and 1983, and the new adjusted measure dropped another 1.6 percent this year. Lifetime prevalence is down less over that interval, suggesting that an increased rate of quitting is largely responsible for the decline.

TABLE 13.1
Prevalence (percent ever used) and recency of use of sixteen types of drugs (1984) (approx. N = 15900)

	Ever used	Past month	Past year, not past month	Not past year	Never used
Marijuana/Hashish	54.9	25.2	14.8	14.9	45.1
Inhalants	14.4	1.9	3.2	9.3	85.6
Inhalants	19.0	2.7	5.2	11.1	81.0
Amyl and Butyl Nitrites	8.1	1.4	2.6	4.1	91.9
Hallucinogens	10.7	2.6	3.9	4.2	89.3
LSD	8.0	1.5	3.2	3.3	92.0
PCP	5.0	1.0	1.3	2.7	95.0
Cocaine	16.1	5.8	5.8	4.5	83.9
Heroin	1.3	0.3	0.2	0.8	98.7
Other opiates	9.7	1.8	3.4	4.5	90.3
Stimulants	27.9	8.3	9.4	10.2	72.1
Sedatives	13.3	2.3	4.3	6.7	86.7
Barbiturates	9.9	1.7	3.2	5.0	90.1
Methaqualone	8.3	1.1	2.7	4.5	91.7
Tranquilizers	12.4	2.1	4.0	6.3	87.6
Alcohol	92.6	67.2	18.8	6.6	7.4
Cigarettes	69.7	29.3	———(40.4)———		30.3

SOURCE. "Use of Licit and Illicit Drugs By America's High School Students, 1975-1984" (Washington, D.C.: U.S. Government Printing Office, 1985), p. 21.

- Much of this decline is attributable to an ongoing drop in the use of the most popular of the illicit drugs, *marijuana*. Current use has dropped from 37 percent in 1979 to 25 percent in 1984; and annual prevalence has dropped from 51 percent to 40 percent over the same interval.

- In addition, the proportion of seniors reporting the use of *illicit drugs other than marijuana* has also been dropping gradually since 1981. Between 1981 and 1983 the unadjusted monthly prevalence for this class of behavior dropped from 22 percent to 18 percent.

- No given class of illicit drug exhibited a dramatic decline this year. Rather, a number continued their gradual longer-term decline. Among these are three of the major classes of psychotherapeutic drugs (*amphetamines, sedatives,* and *tranquilizers*) as well as *hallucinogens*.

- The psychotherapeutic drugs are quite different from one another in their recent histories of use among high school seniors. *Amphetamines* (prescription-controlled stimulants) are the second most prevalent of the illicitly used drugs, following marijuana. That, plus the fact that their use appeared to have been rising from 1975 through 1981, makes their decline from 20 percent annual prevalence (adjusted) in 1982 to 17.7 percent in 1984 particularly important. Current prevalence dropped even more, proportionately.

- The major hallucinogenic drug, *PCP*, showed a dramatic drop between 1979 and 1981, when annual and 30-day prevalence both dropped by more than two-thirds. Since 1981 there has been little further change. Annual prevalence now stands at only 2.3 percent nationwide, though it should be noted that press reports suggest that at least two cities in the country (Washington, D.C. and Los Angeles), may be experiencing higher levels of use.

- Not all drugs showed a decline in 1984. *Inhalant* use, for example, which declined some between 1979 (when first measured) and 1981 (adjusted annual prevalence fell from 9.2 percent to 6.0 percent), has shown some increase in the past three years (to 7.9 percent).

- The annual prevalence of heroin use dropped by one-half between 1975 and 1979 (from 1.0 percent to 0.5 percent) and has remained virtually constant since.

- The annual (and the 30-day) prevalence statistics for *cocaine* have likewise remained quite constant since 1979, but unlike heroin, this period of stability was preceded by one of sharp increase in use rather than a decline. Annual prevalence more than doubled between 1975 and 1979, rising from 5.7 percent to 12 percent.[84]

In sum, like crime rates in general, drug use has declined in recent years. Considering the alleged drug-crime link (see later in this chapter), the correlation may be more than coincidental.

DRUGS AND CRIME

One of the main reasons that narcotics are outlawed is the strong positive association believed to exist between drug abuse and crime. Research suggests that addicts do in fact commit an enormous amount of crime.[85] In a study sponsored by the National Institute on Drug Abuse, 243 opiate addicts in Baltimore were interviewed. The study found that the addicts spend two-thirds of their time addicted and one-third not addicted. Addiction time averaged eleven years per addict from the onset of addiction to the time of the interview. The onset of addiction usually occurred between fifteen and nineteen years of age.

During times of heroin use, the average addict commits one or more crimes during each of two thousand days. Addicts may have been responsible for committing more than five hundred thousand crimes during the eleven-year period. This figure is even more overwhelming than it seems initially because it does not include multiple offenses committed on a given day.

The study found that theft was the principal type of crime committed, followed by drug selling and then other crimes, including confidence games, forgery, gambling, and procuring (pimping). Drug addicts usually did not commit violent crimes.

In a similar vein, James Inciardi studied 356 addicts in Miami and found that they committed 118,134 criminal offenses during a twelve-month period; of these, 27,464 were index crimes.[86]

Such evidence of the vast criminal activity of narcotics users indicates that, at least for heroin abuse, narcotics use is truly not a "victimless crime."

The following Close-Up entitled "Drugs and Crime" explores this phenomenon further.

CONTROLLING THE DRUG TRADE

There has been a massive and concerted effort to control the flow of narcotics into the United States. The effort involves federal enforcement agencies, the military, Coast Guard, and so on. Foreign governments have cooperated by arresting drug smugglers and destroying supplies. For example, in December 1984, U.S. and Mexican officials destroyed nine thousand tons of marijuana, valued at $4 billion, on five plantations in Mexico's northern state of Chihuahua.[87] Similarly, "Operation Top Hat" pitted U.S. naval ships and jets against Caribbean drug smugglers, netting eighty tons of marijuana in twenty-five days.[88]

Despite massive law enforcement efforts, the fight against drugs has not proved successful. An estimated 4.2 million people in the United States are chronic cocaine users and another 500 thousand are addicted to heroin. As noted earlier, millions of citizens report taking marijuana and other soft drugs daily. Even more alarming is the connection between drug use and other crime. Though the fact that a significant portion of arrested and incarcerated offenders are drug users does not indicate that drug use causes crime, there seems little question that a close association exists between the two social problems, and that some drug users become chronic criminals.

The overwhelming problem associated with drug control is the enormous profits involved in the drug trade. A kilogram of cocaine can be bought in Columbia for $4,000 (1984 prices), wholesaled in Miami or elsewhere for $34,000, and sold on the street for $300,000. A drug dealer who can move 100 pounds of coke into the United States can make $1.5 million in one shipment. An estimated sixty-three tons of cocaine were imported into the country last year with a street value of $17 billion.[89] Government crackdowns simply serve to drive up the price of drugs and encourage more illegal entrepreneurs to enter the market. For example, the Hell's Angels motorcycle club has been accused by the federal government of now being one of the primary distributors of cocaine and amphetamines in the United States.[90] Movies like *Scarface*, which depicted the rise and fall of a cocaine dealer, may be

Drugs and Crime

A study sponsored by the National Institute on Drug Abuse indicates the extent of the relationship between drugs and crime. A research team from the New York State Division of Substance Abuse Services gathered data on the daily activities of 201 heroin users recruited in the Central and East Harlem areas of New York City. The subjects were divided according to their frequency of drug use into daily (six to seven days per week), regular (three to five days per week), or irregular (two days or less a week) users. The findings duplicated below provide a more detailed picture of street-level economics of drugs and crime than has previously been available.

Harlem heroin abusers committed a large number of nondrug crimes and an even larger number of drug distribution offenses. Daily heroin users reported the highest crime rates (figure A). They averaged 316 drug sales per year and participated in 564 more drug distribution offenses through "steering" (directing customers to sources of supply), "touting" (promoting a particular dealer's drugs), or "copping" (conveying drugs and money between buyers and sellers, who may not actually meet). Daily heroin users also committed more violent crimes (i.e., robberies), a quarter or more of which were committed against other drug users or dealers, drunks, and other street people.

Almost all tended to use a variety of other drugs in addition to heroin; 90 percent also used cocaine and alcohol, and 73 percent used marijuana. Some drug use occurred on 85 percent of the days—heroin on 54 percent of the days, alcohol on 51 percent, cocaine on 27 percent, and illicit methadone on 10 percent.

The daily heroin users each consumed more than $17,000 worth of drugs per year, compared to about $5,000 for the irregular users, with noncash arrangements covering about a third of their consumption. Daily heroin users also committed about twice as many robberies and burglaries as regular users, and about five times as many as the irregular users.

However, the daily users did not tend to commit more crimes per day than the other groups. Most of them had more criminal cash income during a year only because they were criminally active on more days (209 nondrug crimes per year, compared with 162 among regular and 116 among irregular users). The daily users did not tend to have significantly higher arrest or incarceration rates than the less intensive users, and may thus be considered more "successful" as criminals since they committed more crimes and used more drugs than the less regular users.

RELATIVELY MODEST RETURNS PER CRIME

The returns per crime proved to be relatively small, though they tended to be somewhat greater for the daily users ($41 per crime) than the $25 per crime netted by the irregular users. The average returns from robbery

viewed as a warning to potential drug dealers, but it also indicated the lavish lifestyles and unlimited cash supplies associated with life in the drug trade. The immense profit associated with the drug trade can even drive "respectable" businessmen like John DeLorean to get involved in drug trading as a quick cash fix for their ailing businesses (though of course DeLorean was acquitted on the defense of entrapment.)[91]

Though some South American and Asian governments have entered the fight against the drug trade, attempting to cut off the drug supply at its source, underdeveloped nations actually have an economic incentive to allow this lucrative cash crop to flourish. If drug crops are destroyed, their national economies will lose millions of dollars in foreign currency and their governments will face the displeasure of suddenly unemployed farmers. If the United States helps compensate for losses, other nations will be encouraged to get into the drug producing business to cash in on U.S. aid.

One approach to drug control has been to legalize or decriminalize controlled substances such as marijuana, and thereby remove them as a law enforcement issue. In the United States, *methadone maintenance* has been used to treat drug addicts. Methadone is a drug similar to heroin, and addicts can be treated at clinics where

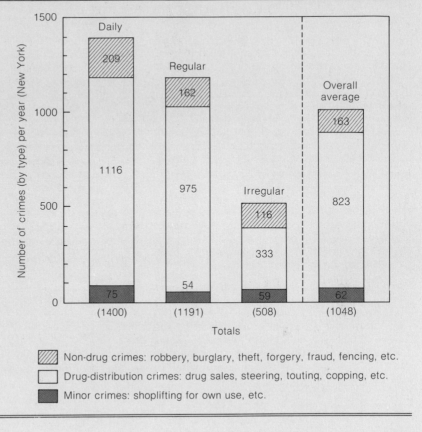

FIGURE A

Crime rates of street heroin abusers by level of drug usage (New York)

Number of crimes (by type) per year (New York)

Daily — 209 / 1116 / 75 — (1400)

Regular — 162 / 975 / 54 — (1191)

Irregular — 116 / 333 / 59 — (508)

Overall average — 163 / 823 / 62 — (1048)

Totals

Non-drug crimes: robbery, burglary, theft, forgery, fraud, fencing, etc.

Drug-distribution crimes: drug sales, steering, touting, copping, etc.

Minor crimes: shoplifting for own use, etc.

cont'd

they receive methadone under controlled conditions. However, methadone programs have been undermined because some users sell their methadone in the black market, while others supplement their dosages with illegally obtained heroin.

In the United States and elsewhere, the drug user is viewed more as a victim than a culprit of the drug trade. In Holland, for example, heroin users are allowed to enter methadone treatment programs though they still openly use heroin. The government then assumes that a certain percentage of the population will always be addicts and tries to accommodate and treat them rather than inflict criminal penalties. In fact, the city of Amsterdam is considering a program to give heroin to addicts in order to lessen their dependence on illegal supplies.[92]

ALCOHOL ABUSE

Though the purchase and sale of alcohol is legal today in most U.S. jurisdictions, alcohol abuse is a major criminological issue. There are two factors behind the crime-alcohol association. First, most jurisdictions maintain criminal laws prohibiting drunk driving, public intoxication, and the sale and use of liquor by minors.

Drugs and Crime—cont'd

($80) and burglary ($81) were modest compared with the risks. The typical drug sale or distribution offense provided $5 or less cash income.

The average daily heroin user gained more than $11,000 per year cash income from crime. This rose to more than $18,000 when the economic value of the drugs received without cash payment is included. In comparison, an irregular user netted only $6,000 total.

ECONOMIC EFFECT ON VICTIMS AND SOCIETY

These figures do not, of course, represent the full range of economic consequences that heroin users impose on other persons and on society. To provide a somewhat more extensive picture, the researchers developed estimates of 33 different types of economic harm imposed by such street heroin abusers. Among them were:

- *Nondrug crime.* The average street opiate user committed nondrug crimes (including burglary, robbery, and theft) from which victims suffered an economic loss of almost $14,000 annually, based on the retail value of stolen goods. The toll from such nondrug crimes by daily heroin users was nearly four times (almost $23,000) that due to the irregular users (almost $6,000).
- *Freeloading.* The public and relatives of friends of daily heroin users contributed more than $7,000 annually to them in the form of public transfer payments, evasion of taxes, cash "loans," and provision of shelter and meals.

- *Drug distribution crimes.* Street-level heroin abusers contribute substantially to the underground economy. In addition to being drug consumers, they function as low-level drug dealers and distributors. In this New York sample, the average daily heroin user distributed approximately $26,000 per year in illegal drugs. From this, they received about 40 percent in cash or drug "wages," while 60 percent went to higher-level dealers and others in the illegal drug distribution system.
- The combined costs imposed on society by the daily heroin users in this study totaled about $55,000 annually per offender. Regular heroin users cost society about $32,000, and irregular users about $15,000 each per year.
- The implications of this research are clear: reducing the number of daily heroin users could result in an enormous decrease in the crime rate and the economic costs of crime.

DISCUSSION QUESTIONS

1. Should heroin be legalized and distributed by the government for a nominal fee?
2. Should heroin addiction be considered a crime since heavy users are such a drain on society?

SOURCE. Bernard Gropper, "Probing the Links Between Drugs and Crime," *NIJ Reports*, National Criminal Justice Reference Service, November 1984, pp. 6–7. Research conducted by B. Johnson, P. Goldstein, E. Preble, J. Schmeidler, D. L. Pton, B. Spring, and T. Miller.

Second, there is a strong association between the use of alcohol and criminal activity.

The history of alcohol and the law in the United States has been controversial and dramatic. At the turn of the century, a drive was mustered to prohibit the sale of alcohol. The *temperance movement* was fueled by the belief that the purity of the U.S. agrarian culture was being destroyed by the growth of the city. Urbanism was viewed as a threat to the lifestyle of the majority of the nation's population, then living on farms and in villages.

The forces behind the temperance movement were lobbying groups such as the Anti-Saloon League, the Women's Temperance Union, and the Protestant clergy of the Baptist, Methodist, and Congregationalist faiths.[93] They viewed the growing city, filled with newly arriving Irish, Italian, and Eastern European immigrants, as centers of degradation and wickedness. The ethnics' propensity to drink heavily was viewed as the main force behind their degenerate lifestyle. The eventual prohibition of the sale of alcoholic beverages brought about by ratification of the Eighteenth Amendment in 1919 was viewed as a triumph of the morality of middle- and upper-class Protestants over the threat posed to their culture by the "new Americans."[94]

Prohibition turned out to be a failure. It was enforced by the Volstead Act, which defined intoxicating beverages as those containing one-half of 1 percent, or more, alcohol.[95] What doomed prohibition? One factor was the use of organized crime to supply illicit liquor. Also, the law made it illegal only to sell alcohol, not to purchase it; this factor cut into the law's deterrent capability. Finally, despite the work of Elliot Ness and his Untouchables, law enforcement agencies were inadequate, and officials were more than likely to be corrupted by wealthy boot-leggers.[96] Eventually, in 1933, the twenty-first amendment to the Constitution repealed prohibition, signaling the end of the "noble experiment."

Alcohol and the Law. Alcohol-related activities provide a serious problem for the criminal justice system. In 1983 the FBI reported that 1,921,000 people were arrested for driving under the influence of alcohol, another 1,115,000 for public drunkenness, and 498,000 for various liquor violations.[97] Furthermore, there is an alarming rate of alcohol abuse among young people. In a national survey of substance abuse, 65 percent of youths aged twelve to seventeen reported they had used alcohol.[98]

One of the more serious problems of widespread drinking is the alarming number of highway fatalities linked to drunk driving. In an average week, nearly five hundred people die in alcohol-related accidents, and twenty thousand are injured. On a yearly basis, that amounts to twenty-five thousand deaths, or about half of all auto fatalities. Spurred by groups like Mothers against Drunk Drivers (MADD), state legislatures are beginning to create more stringent penalties for drunk driving. For example, Florida recently enacted legislation creating a minimum fine of $250, fifty hours community service, and six months' loss of license for a first offense; a second offense brings a $500 fine and ten days in jail. In Quincy, Massachusetts, judges have agreed to put every drunk-driving offender in jail for three days.[99]

In California, legislation may be achieving positive results. Under a new law, a drunk driver faces a maximum of six months in jail, a $500 fine, suspension of operator's license for six months, and impounding of the vehicle. As a minimum penalty, the first offender could get four days in jail, a $375 fine, and loss of license for six months or three years' probation, a $375 fine, and either two days in jail or restricted driving privileges for ninety days. Preliminary reports indicate that the strict new policies may be working. Accidents and fatalities were down, and nearly nine hundred drunken drivers have had their licenses suspended, compared with seventy-two in a comparable period before the law was enacted.[100]

In New York, persons arrested for drunk driving now risk having their automobiles seized by the government under the state's new Civil Forfeiture Law. Originally designed to combat drug trafficking and racketeering, the new law will allow state prosecutors to confiscate cars involved in felony drunk driving cases, sell them at auction, and give the proceeds to the victims of crime; Texas enacted a similar law in 1984.[101]

More than thirty jurisdictions have now passed laws providing severe penalties for drunk drivers, including mandatory jail sentences. A study conducted by the federal government's National Institute of Justice in such cities as Seattle, Minneapolis, and Cincinnati found that such measures significantly reduced traffic fatalities in the target areas studied. However, there is a price to pay for get-tough policies. Arrest rates and court workload increased dramatically. Since fewer violators were ready to plead guilty, the number of jury trials increased—doubling in Seattle in the first two years after a mandatory confinement law was passed. Similarly, corrections departments have become overloaded, prompting the building of expensive new facilities exclusively to house drunk-driving offenders. The federal survey concluded that a feasible approach to paying for these programs is to require convicted offenders to reimburse the government for their confinement or treatment in alcohol abuse programs.[102]

Alcoholics are a serious problem, because treatment efforts to help chronic sufferers have not proved successful.[103] In addition, chronic alcoholics are arrested over and over again for public drunkenness and are therefore a burden on the justice system. To remedy this situation, a federal court in 1966 ruled that chronic alcoholism may be used as a defense to crime.[104] However, in a subsequent case, *Powell* v. *Texas*, the Supreme Court ruled that a chronic alcoholic could be convicted under state public drunkenness laws.[105] Nonetheless, the narrowness of the decision, 5–4, allowed those states desiring to excuse chronic alcoholics from criminal responsibility to do so. Thus, the trend has been to place arrested alcoholics in detoxification centers under a civil order rather than to treat them as part of the justice system.

Summary

Public order crimes are acts considered illegal because they conflict with social policy, accepted moral rules, and public opinion.

There is usually great debate over public order crimes. Some charge that they are not really crimes at all and that it is foolish to legislate morality. Others view such morally tinged acts as prostitution, gambling, and drug abuse as harmful and therefore subject to public control.

Many public order crimes are sex-related. Though homosexuality is not a crime per se, homosexual acts are subject to legal control. Some states still follow the archaic custom of long prison terms for consensual homosexual sex.

Prostitution is another sex-related public order crime. Though prostitution has been practiced for thousands of years and is legal in some areas, most states outlaw commercial sex. There are a variety of prostitutes, including streetwalkers, B-girls, and call girls. Studies indicate that prostitutes came from poor, troubled families and have abusive parents. However, there is little evidence that prostitutes are emotionally disturbed, addicted to drugs, or sexually abnormal. Though prostitution is illegal, some cities have set up adult entertainment areas where commercial sex is tolerated by law enforcement agents.

Pornography involves the sale of sexually explicit material intended to sexually excite paying customers.

The depiction of sex and nudity is not illegal, but it does violate the law when it is judged obscene. Obscene material is a legal term that today is defined as material offensive to community standards. Thus, each local jurisdiction must decide what pornographic material is obscene.

A growing problem is in the exploitation of children in obscenity—kiddy porn. Recently, the Supreme Court has ruled that local communities can pass statutes outlawing this practice. There is no hard evidence that pornography is related to crime or aggression, but data suggest that sexual material with a violent theme is related to sexual violence by those who view it.

Substance abuse is another type of public order crime. There is great debate over the legalization of drugs, usually centering around nonaddicting drugs such as marijuana and cocaine. However, most states and the federal government outlaw a wide variety of drugs they consider harmful, including narcotics, amphetamines, barbiturates, cocaine, hallucinogens, and marijuana. One of the main reasons for the continued ban on drugs is their relationship to crime. Numerous studies have found that drug addicts commit enormous amounts of property crime.

Alcohol is another commonly abused substance. Although alcohol is legal to possess, it too has been linked to crime. Drunk driving and highway deaths caused by drunk drivers are growing national problems.

Notes

1 Edwin Schur, *Crimes without Victims* (Englewood Cliffs, N.J.: Prentice-Hall, 1965).

2 M. Cohen, "Moral Aspects of the Criminal Law," *Yale Law Journal* 49 (1940):1017.

3 Sir Patrick Devlin, *The Enforcement of Morals* (New York: Oxford University Press, 1959), p. 20.

4 See Joel Feinberg, *Social Philosophy* (Englewood Cliffs, N.J.: Prentice-Hall, 1973), chap. 2, 3.

5 H. L. A. Hart, "Immorality and Treason," *Listener* 62 (1959):163.

6 J. Gussfield, "On Legislating Morals: The Symbolic Process of Designating Deviancy," *California Law Review* 56 (1968):58–59.

7 Howard Becker, *Outsiders* (New York: Macmillan, 1963), pp. 13–14.

8 Albert Reiss, "The Social Integration of Queers and Peers," *Social Problems* 9 (1961):102–20.

9 Judd Marmor, "The Multiple Roots of Homosexual Behavior," in *Homosexual Behavior*, ed. J. Marmor (New York: Basic Books, 1980), p. 5.

10 This section was produced with the help of Spencer Rathus. Refer to S. Rathus, *Human Sexuality* (New York: Holt, Rinehart and Winston, 1983).

11 C. S. Ford and F. A. Beach, *Patterns of Sexual Behavior* (New York: Harper & Bros., 1951).

12 A. Kinsey, W. Pomeroy, and C. Martin, *Sexual Behavior in the Human Male* (Philadelphia: W. B. Saunders, 1948); A. Kinsey et al., *Sexual Behavior in the Human Female* (Philadelphia: W. B. Saunders, 1953).

13 Morton Hunt, *Sexual Behavior in the 1970's* (New York: Dell Books, 1974), p. 317.

14 J. McNeil, *The Church and the Homosexual* (Kansas City, Mo.: Sheed, Andrews, and McNeel, 1976).

15 Marmor, "The Multiple Roots of Homosexual Behavior," pp. 18–19.

16 Ibid., p. 19.

17 M. Weinberg and C. J. Williams, *Male Homosexuals: Problems and Adaptations* (New York: Oxford Unviersity Press, 1974).

18 Rathus, *Human Sexuality*, p. 395.

19 Ibid., p. 409.

20 376 U.S. 660; 82 S.Ct. 1417; 8 L. Ed. 2d 758 (1962).

21 F. Inbau, J. Thompson, and J. Zagel, *Criminal Law and Its Administration* (Mineola, N.Y.: Foundation Press, 1974), p. 287.

22 American Law Institute, Model Penal Code, Section 207.5.

23 See, for example, Illinois Criminal Code, Article 11, Chap. 38, S.H.A.

24 Laud Humphreys, *Tearoom Trade: Impersonal Sex in Public Places* (Chicago: Aldine, 1970).

25 For example, the case of Stanley v. Georgia, 394 U.S. 557 (1969), upheld the right of people to possess obscene materials in their homes, though it would be illegal to display it in public places.

26 Associated Press, "Voters in Houston Defeat 'Sexual Orientations' Issues," *Omaha World Herald,* 20 January 1985, p. 1.

27 741 F. 2d 1388 (1984).

28 Associated Press, "Court Rules Against Transsexual Pilot," *Omaha World Herald*, 31 August 1984, p. 3.

29 See generally, V. Bullogh, *Sexual Variance in Society and History* (Chicago: University of Chicago Press, 1980).

30 Rathus, *Human Sexuality*, p. 463.

31 Loosely adapted from Charles Winick and Paul Kinsie, *The Lively Commerce* (Chicago: Quandrangle Books, 1971), p. 3.

32 Charles McCaghy, *Deviant Behavior* (New York: Macmillan, 1976), pp. 348–49.

33 Rathus, *Human Sexuality*, p. 463.

34 Ibid.

35 Hunt, *Sexual Behavior in the 1970's*, pp. 143–44.

36 Federal Bureau of Investigation, *Crime in the United States, 1983* (Washington, D.C.: Government Printing Office, 1981), p. 194.

37 Winick and Kinsie, *The Lively Commerce*, p. 58.

38 Jennifer James, "Prostitutes and Prostitution," in *Deviants: Voluntary Action in a Hostile World*, ed. E. Sagarin and F. Montanino (New York: Scott, Foresman, 1977), p. 384.

39 Winick and Kinsie, *The Lively Commerce*, pp. 172–73.

40 Ibid., p. 97.

41 Alessandra Stanley, "Case of the Classy Madam," *Time*, 29 October 1984, p. 39.

42 Described in Rathus, *Human Sexuality*, p. 468.

43 N. Jackman, Richard O'Toole, and Gilbert Geis, "The Self-Image of the Prostitute," in *Sexual Deviance* ed. J. Gagnon and W. Simon (New York: Harper and Row, 1967), pp. 152–53.

44 Winick and Kinsie, *The Lively Commerce*, p. 51.

45 Paul Gebhard, "Misconceptions about Female Prostitutes," *Medical Aspects of Human Sexuality* 3 (July 1969):28–30.

46 James, "Prostitutes and Prostitution," pp. 388–89.

47 Winick and Kinsie, *The Lively Commerce*, p. 109.

48 James, "Prostitutes and Prostitution," p. 419.

49 Winick and Kinsie, *The Lively Commerce*, p. 120.

50 Susan Hall, *Ladies of the Night* (New York: Trident Press, 1973).

51 *The Merriam-Webster Dictionary* (New York: Pocket Books, 1974), p. 484.

52 John Hurst, "Children—A Big Profit Item for the Smut Peddlers," *Los Angeles Times*, 26 May 1977, cited in Laura Lederer, ed., *Take Back the Night* (New York: William Morrow, 1980), pp. 77–78.

53 Ann Wolbert Burgess, *Child Pornography and Sex Rings* (Lexington, Mass.: Lexington Books, 1984).

54 Lederer, "Introduction" to *Take Back the Night*, p. 18.

55 Lederer, "Playboy Isn't Playing: An Interview with Judith Bat-Ada," in Lederer, *Take Back the Night*, p. 124.

56 *The Report of the Commission on Obscenity and Pornography* (Washington, D.C.: Government Printing Office, 1970).

57 Berl Kutchinsky, "The Effect of Easy Availability of Pornography on the Incidence of Sex Crimes," *Journal of Social Issues* 29 (1973):95–112.

58 Keith Davis and G. N. Braucht, "Exposure to Pornography, Character, and Sexual Deviance: A Retrospective Survey," *Journal of Social Issues* 29 (1973):183–96.

59 Michael Goldstein, "Exposure to Erotic Stimuli and Sexual Deviance," *Journal of Social Issues* 29 (1973):197–219.

60 Seymour Fishbach and Neal Malamuth, "Sex and Aggression: Proving the Link," *Psychology Today* 12 (1978):111–22.

61 Don Smith, "Sexual Aggression in American Pornography: The Stereotype of Rape," paper presented at the annual meeting of the American Sociological Association, 1976. Cited in Lederer, *Take Back the Night*, p. 213.

62 354 U.S. 476; 77 S.Ct. 1304 (1957).

63 413 U.S. 15 (1973).

64 427 U.S. 50 (1976).

65 New York v. Ferber, 50 L.W. 5077 (1982).

66 See generally, David Pittman, "Drug Addiction and Crime," in *Handbook of Criminology*, ed. D. Glazer (Chicago: Rand McNally, 1974), pp. 209–32; Board of Directors, National Council on Crime and Delinquency, "Drug Addiction: A Medical, Not a Law Enforcement, Problem," *Crime and Delinquency* 20 (1974):4–9.

67 This section relies heavily on the descriptions provided by Kenneth Jones, Louis Shainberg, and Curtin Byer, *Drugs and Alcohol* (New York: Harper & Row, 1979), pp. 57–114.

68 See Edwin Brecher, *Licit and Illicit Drugs* (Boston: Little, Brown, 1972).

69 James Inciardi, *Reflections on Crime* (New York: Holt, Rinehart and Winston, 1978), p. 15.

70 William Bates and Betty Crowther, "Drug Abuse," in *Deviants: Voluntary Actors in a Hostile World*, ed. E. Sagarin and F. Montanino (New York: Scott, Foresman and Co., 1977), p. 269.

71 See Jones, Shainberg, and Byer, *Drugs and Alcohol*, pp. 137–46.

72 Jerome Platt and Christina Platt, *Heroin Addiction* (New York: Wiley, 1976), p. 324.

73 P. Fishburne, H. Abelson, and I. Cisin, *National Survey on Drug Abuse: Main Findings 1979* (Washington, D.C.: Government Printing Office, 1980), pp. 32–34.

74 Charles Winick, "Physician Narcotics Addicts," *Social Problems* 9 (1961):174–86.

75 G. E. Vallant, "Parent-Child Disparity and Drug Addiction," *Journal of Nervous and Mental Disease* 142 (1966):534–39.

76 Charles Winick, "Epidemiology of Narcotics Use," in *Narcotics* ed. D. Wilner and G. Kassenbaum (New York: McGraw-Hill, 1965), pp. 3–18.

77 C. Bowden, "Determinants of Initial Use of Opiods," *Comprehensive Psychiatry* 12 (1971):136–40.

78 R. Cloward and L. Ohlin, *Delinquency and Opportunity: A Theory of Delinquent Gangs* (Glencoe, Ill.: Free Press, 1960).

79 D. Baer and J. Corrado, "Heroin Addict Relationships with Parents during Childhood and Early Adolescent Years," *Journal of Genetic Psychology* 124 (1974):99–103.

80 See S. F. Bucky, "The Relationship between Background and Extent of Heroin Use," *American Journal of Psychiatry* 130 (1973):709–10; I. Chien, D. L. Gerard, R. Lee, and E. Rosenfield, *The Road to H: Narcotics Delinquency and Social Policy* (New York: Basic Books, 1964).

81 Platt and Labate, *Heroin Addiction*, p. 127.

82 B. Johnson, E. Wish, and D. Huizinga, "The Concentration of Delinquent Offending: The Contribution of Serious Drug Involvement to High Rate of Delinquency," presented at the American Society of Criminology, Denver, 1983. Cited in Paul Gropper, "Probing the Links Between Drugs and Crime," *NIJ Reports*, (November 1984):5–8.

83 Lloyd Johnston, Patrick O'Malley, and Jerald Backman, *Use of Licit and Illicit Drugs By America's High School Students 1975-1984* (Washington, D.C.: U.S. Government Printing Office, 1985.

84 Ibid., pp. 8–10.

85 U.S. Department of Justice, "Addicts Commit Staggering Amount of Crime," *Justice Assistance News* 2 (May 1981):5.

86 James Inciardi, "Heroin Use and Street Crime," *Crime and Delinquency* 25 (1979):335–46. See also W. McGlothlin, M. Anglin, and B. Wilson, "Narcotic Addiction and Crime," *Criminology* 16 (1978):293–311.

87 Jacob Lamar, "The Best of the Century," *Time*, 3 December 1984.

88 Roger Lowenstein, "U.S. Anti-Drug Armada in Caribbean Has Limited Success Ending Shipments," *Wall Street Journal*, 26 November 1984, p. 38.

89 Robert Taylor and Gary Cohen, "War Against Narcotics by U.S. Government Isn't Slowing Influx," *Wall Street Journal*, 27 November 1984, p. 1.

90 Walter Shapiro, "Going After the Hell's Angels," *Newsweek*, 13 May 1985, p. 41.

91 "Red Handed?" *Time*, 19 March 1984.

92 L. Erik Calonius, "Controversy Surrounds the Way the Dutch Treat Heroin Addicts," *Wall Street Journal*, 5 December 1984, p. 1.

93 James Inciardi, *Reflections on Crime* (New York: Holt, Rinehart and Winston, 1978), pp. 8–10. See also A. Greeley, William McCready, and Gary Theisen, *Ethnic Drinking Subcultures* (New York: Praeger, 1980).

94 Joseph Gusfield, *Symbolic Crusade* (Urbana, Ill.: University of Illinois Press, 1963), Chap. 3.

95 McCaghy, *Deviant Behavior*, p. 280.

96 Ibid.

97 *Uniform Crime Reports, 1983*, p. 170.

98 Johnston, Bailman, and O'Malley, *Drugs and American High School Students, 1975–1983*.

99 Bennett Beach, "Is the Party Finally Over?" *Time*, 26 April 1982, p. 58.

100 "New Drunken Driver Law Shows Results in California," *Omaha World Herald*, 26 May 1982, p. 34.

101 Faye Silas, "Gimme the Keys," *ABA Journal* 71 (1985):36.

102 Fred Heinzelmann, *Jailing Drunk Drivers* (Washington, D.C.: National Institute of Justice, 1984).

103 Jones, Shainberg, and Byer, *Drugs and Alcohol*, pp. 190–93.

104 Easter v. District of Columbia, 361 F.2d 50 (D.C. Cir. 1966).

105 392 U.S. 514 (1968).

IV The Criminal Justice System

THE TEXT'S FINAL SECTION reviews the agencies and the process of justice designed to exert social control over criminal offenders. Chapter 14 provides an overview of the justice system and describes its major institutions and processes; chapter 15 looks at the police; chapters 16 and 17 analyze the court and correctional systems.

This vast array of people and institutions is beset by conflicting goals and values. Some view it as a mammoth agency of social control; others see it as a great social service dispensing therapy to those who cannot fit within the boundaries of society.

Consequently, a major goal of justice system policy makers is to formulate and disseminate effective models of crime prevention and control. Efforts are now being undertaken at all levels of the justice system to improve information flow, experiment with new program concepts, and evaluate current operating procedures.

There are many important links within the system, so we can study the agencies of justice on a cross-national level. For example, all agencies must obey the rule of law, and most use a common framework of operations in such everyday events as arrest, detention, bail, trial, and so on. However, the system fails to communicate effectively in getting out information on what works, what doesn't, and why.

These chapters will provide a good foundation for studying the justice system and its links to criminological thought.

14 | Overview of the Criminal Justice System

CHAPTER OUTLINE

Introduction

Components of Criminal Justice
Police
Courts
Corrections

Justice Agencies in the United States
Law Enforcement Agencies
Court-Related Agencies
Correctional Agencies

The Justice Process

Criminal Justice and the Rule of Law
Procedural Laws
Court Decision Making
Courts and Criminal Justice Policy
Due Process
The Exclusionary Rule
The Future of the Exclusionary Rule

Concepts of Justice
Crime Control Model
Rehabilitation Model
Due Process Model
Nonintervention Model
Radical Model
Justice Model

Criminal Justice and Victims

Criminal Justice in the 1980s

Summary

KEY TERMS

criminal justice
criminal justice nonsystem
police
discretion
courts
due process
fundamental fairness
United States Supreme Court
plea bargaining
probation
correctional system
penitentiaries

classification center
community-based
   correctional facility
parole
sheriff's departments
process
evidence
booking
lineup
confession
information
probable cause

grand jury
preliminary hearing
arraignment
hands-off doctrine
Earl Warren
Warren Burger
due process
exclusionary rule
praxis
flat sentencing
determinate sentencing

Introduction

Criminal justice refers to both the formal processes and the component agencies that have been established to apprehend, try, punish, and treat criminal offenders. In recent years it has become popular to refer to the components of justice as a system—the criminal justice system. This term implies that the major segments of justice—the various police, court, and correctional agencies—operate as a unified whole. Change in one area of the system should automatically produce a corresponding change in the others. In addition, the systems approach to criminal justice suggests that the planning and coordination of justice-related agencies could be carried out by a single policy-making body that could mandate rules, policies, and programs that would be uniformly beneficial to the agencies within the justice network.

Unfortunately, there is little actual "system" to justice in the United States. The various elements of the criminal justice system—police, courts, and corrections—are all related, but they are influenced by each other's policies and practices only to a degree. They have not yet become so well coordinated that they can be described as operating in unison. "Fragmented," "divided," and "splintered" continue to be the adjectives most commonly used to describe the U.S. system of criminal justice.[1] Critics have referred to the justice process as the **criminal justice nonsystem**.

In an article on the criminal justice nonsystem, Daniel Skoler cites the following as causing the system's fragmentation: (1) the constitutional separation of powers between the executive, legislative, and judicial branches of government; (2) the predominantly local character of police and prosecutorial agencies; (3) the elective nature of the attorney general's office in most jurisdictions; (4) the desire of the different components of the criminal justice system to enjoy cabinet-level status with one another; and (5) the tendency states have to group adult and juvenile services into human service rather than public service agencies.[2]

Similarly, Richter Moore suggests that each decision-maker in the justice system—the police chief, trial judge, state prosecutor, corrections administrator, and so on—views his or her effectiveness and mission differently.[3] Isolated within their own niche of the justice process, these people jealously promote their own service as the most crucial and compete with the others for public funds. This attitude, concludes Moore, reflects a lack of orientation toward a single, unified justice system.

Major efforts have been made by the federal and various state governments to unify the justice system. Yet the size of the problem and the resistance justice agencies must overcome have made this task difficult. Thus the goal of a truly unified system has not yet been met.

In this chapter, the various components and processes of criminal justice will be reviewed. Then the legal constraints on criminal justice agencies will be discussed. Some of the philosophical concepts that dominate the system will be mentioned, and the role of the government in aiding the victims of crime will be discussed.

Components of Criminal Justice

Criminal justice in the United States can be conceived of as a loosely aligned group of agencies organized around police agencies, the courts, and correctional agencies. In this section, the function of each of these major components will be briefly discussed.

POLICE

Traditionally, law enforcement (**police**) officers were concerned with maintaining public order, deterring potential criminals, and apprehending law violators.[4] As society became more complex, new and additional functions were required of the police. Today the police work actively with the community to prevent criminal behavior. They divert juveniles, alcoholics, and drug addicts from the criminal justice system; they participate in specialized areas such as the Juvenile Aid Bureau; they work with public prosecutors, court officials, correctional authorities, and criminal justice research and planning agencies; they resolve family conflicts; they facilitate the movement of people and vehicles; and they provide other services, such as preserving civil order during emergencies.[5]

Because of these expanded responsibilities, the role of the police officer has become highly complex. The officer must not only be technically competent to investigate crimes, but also must be aware of the rules and procedures associated with investigating criminal activity, arrests, and apprehending criminals.

By the nature of their functions and roles, police are the most visible agents of the justice process. Their reactions to victims and offenders are carefully scrutinized in the news media. On numerous occasions the police have been criticized for being too harsh or too lenient, too violent or too passive. Police control of such groups as minority citizens, youths, political dissidents, protestors, and union workers has been the topic of serious public debate. At the same time, police agencies have themselves been investigated for reasons of internal corruption, inefficiency, lack of effectiveness, and discriminatory hiring.[6] Consequently, at all levels of government the police have become defensive toward and suspicious of the public, resistant to change, and secretive in their activities.

Compounding the problem is the tremendous **discretion** afforded police officers. Though the officer sets the criminal justice system in motion by the authority to arrest, and though this authority is vested in the law, it is neither final nor absolute. The police officer's duty requires discretion on numerous matters dealing with various situations, victims, criminals, and citizens. The officer must determine when an argument becomes disorderly conduct or criminal assault, whether it is appropriate to arrest a juvenile or refer them to a social agency, and when to assume that probable cause exists to arrest a suspect for a crime. How police discretion is used—and how it can be controlled—are major problems for police administrators.[7] A more detailed analysis of this and other police-related issues is found in chapter 15.

COURTS

The criminal court is considered by many to be the core element in the administration of criminal justice. In the purest sense of justice, the court is responsible for determining the criminal liability of the offenders brought before it. Ideally, it is expected to convict and sentence those found guilty of crimes while insuring that the innocent are freed without any consequence or burden. The **courts** are formally required to seek the truth, to obtain justice for the individuals brought before their tribunals, and to maintain the integrity of the government's rule of law.

Once the truth has been determined, and in the event the defendant is found guilty, the criminal court is responsible for sentencing the offender. Whatever sentence is ordered by the court may serve not only to rehabilitate the offender but also to deter others from crime. Once sentencing is accomplished, the corrections component of criminal justice begins to function.

Hypothetically, the entire criminal court process is undertaken with the recognition that the rights of the individual should be protected at all times. These rights, determined by federal and state constitutional mandates, statutes, and case law, form the foundation for protection of the accused. They include such basic concepts as the right to an attorney, the right to a jury trial, and the right to a speedy trial. A defendant also has the right to **due process**, or the right to be treated with **fundamental fairness**. This includes the right to be present at trial, to be notified of the charges, to have an opportunity to confront hostile witnesses, and to have favorable witnesses appear. Such practices are an integral part of a system and process that seek to balance the interests of the individual and the state.

The court system administering the criminal process includes lower criminal courts, superior courts, and supreme courts. The states and the federal government have independent court structures unique to their particular jurisdictions. A crime that is a violation of state law is ordinarily prosecuted in the state court; offenses against federal laws are generally handled by the federal courts.

The lower criminal courts of any state, variously called police courts, district courts, or recorders courts, deal with the largest number of criminal offenses. Referred to as "people's courts," they are scattered throughout the state by county, town, or geographic district. They daily handle numerous minor criminal offenses, including assault and battery, disorderly conduct, breaking and entering, drug possession, petty larceny, traffic violations, and juvenile offenses. Many cases are disposed of without trial, either because the defendant pleads guilty or because the circumstances of the offense do not warrant further court action. When a trial is required in the lower courts, it often occurs before a judge rather than before a jury because the defendant often waives the constitutional right to a jury trial. Lower criminal courts, although primarily responsible for misdemeanor offenses, also process the first stage of felony offenses by holding preliminary hearings, making bail decisions, and conducting trials of certain felonies when they have jurisdiction as defined by statute.

In sum, the lower criminal courts often dispense routine and repetitious justice and are burdened with a heavy responsibility that they are not generally equipped to fulfill. Characterized by cramped courtrooms and limited personnel, they remain a critical problem area in criminal justice administration.

The superior courts, or major trial courts, have general jurisdiction over all criminal offenses but ordinarily concentrate on felony offenses. They conduct jury trials with much formality and strict adherence to the defendant's constitutional rights. In addition to conducting trials, these courts accept guilty pleas, generally give offenders longer sentences owing to the more serious nature of their crimes, and in certain instances review sentences originally imposed by lower courts.

The highest state court is a supreme or appeals court, whose functions are similar to those of the **United States Supreme Court** in the federal judicial system. State supreme courts, which are primarily appellate courts, do not conduct criminal trials; they receive and act upon appeals from the lower courts and settle controversies arising from lower-court decisions. Appellate courts deal with procedural errors arising in the lower courts, such as the use of illegal evidence, the applicability of statutes, or erroneously used technical motions. Questions of fact that were decided in the original trial are not ordinarily reviewed in the appellate process. The appellate court has the authority to affirm, modify, or reverse decisions of the lower criminal court.

Unfortunately, the ideal conditions of objectivity, fairness, and equal rights under which the nation's courts should operate are rarely matched by actual practice or procedure. While some well-publicized defendants, such as John Hinckley and Wayne Williams, receive their full share of rights and privileges, a significant number of defendants are herded through the court system with a minimum of interest or care. Court dockets are too crowded, and funds are insufficient to grant each defendant the full share of justice. Consequently, a system known as **plea bargaining** has developed; in it, defendants are asked to plead guilty as charged in return for consideration of leniency or mercy.[8] "Bargain justice" is estimated to occur in more than 90 percent of all criminal trials. Moreover, although the criminal court system is founded on the concept of equality before the law, there are unquestionably differences in the treatment that poor and wealthy citizens receive when they are accused of crimes. These concerns will be discussed more fully in chapter 16.

Probation. Probation is a judicial action or legal disposition that allows the convicted offender to remain in the community, subject to conditions imposed by court order under the supervision of a probation officer. It allows the offender to continue working and providing for the family and to avoid the debilitating effects of incarceration.

At the same time, social services are provided to help the offender adjust to the community. Counseling, assistance from social workers, group treatment, and the use of community resources to obtain employment, welfare, and housing are offered to the offender on probation. In providing these services, probation officers perform the dual functions of preparing presentencing reports for the court and supervising probationers in the community.

The origins of probation can be found in English common law, where such devices as benefit of clergy, judicial reprieve, and recognizance were used to mitigate harsh sentences and avoid capital punishment.[9] Subsequently, probation practices were established in the state of Massachusetts in 1841 by John Augustus, who is considered the father of probation in the United States.[10] His efforts resulted in the enactment in 1878 of the first statutory probation program in Massachusetts.[11] Since that time, probation as a court action and as a method of social service has been introduced into all the states and the federal government. Many experts believe that community treatment programs such as probation are of great significance in rehabilitating offenders and reducing recidivism rates.

CORRECTIONS

Following a criminal trial that results in conviction and sentencing, the offender enters the **correctional system**. Of the three major components of the criminal justice system, corrections has received the most attention in recent years. Public interest has become widespread as a result of well-publicized prison riots and the alleged inability of the system to rehabilitate offenders.

In the broadest sense, the corrections system involves community supervision, various types of incarceration (including jails, houses of correction, and state prisons), and parole programs for both juvenile and adult offenders. Corrections ordinarily represents the postadjudicatory care given to offenders when a sentence is imposed by the court and the offender is placed in the hands of the correctional agency.

A person given a sentence involving incarceration ordinarily is confined to a correctional institution for a specified period of time. Different types of institutions are used to hold offenders. Jails hold offenders convicted of misdemeanors and those awaiting trial or involved in other proceedings, such as grand jury deliberations, arraignments, or preliminary hearings. Jails are ordinarily operated by local governments and are referred to as detention facilities. They are often considered to be the worst of all penal institutions because of their poor physical conditions, lack of adequate staff, and custodial philosophy. The "Tombs" in New York City and the Suffolk County, or "Charles Street," jail in Boston are examples of facilities that have become notorious in recent years due to their inability to conform to adequate institutional detention standards. Both institutions were closed when judges ruled that their physical conditions were so poor that they violated the constitutional right of inmates to be free from cruel and unusual punishment.[12]

A second type of institution is ordinarily known as a house of correction. This facility holds sentenced prisoners who have committed less serious offenses. Normally, the minor offender is incarcerated in the house of correction for two years or less. Because the distinction between serious and less serious offenses is not always easy to establish, however, some jurisdictions admit felons as well as minor offenders to houses of correction. Many of these short-term institutions are administered by local county governments and suffer from the same shortcomings as jails. Little is done in the way of inmate treatment, principally because the personnel and institutions lack the qualifications, services, and resources.

The third type of correctional institution is the state and federally operated facilities that receive felony offenders sentenced by the criminal courts. These institutions are called prisons or **penitentiaries**. They are often divided into minimum, medium, and maximum security institutions. Prison facilities vary throughout the country. Some have high walls, cells, and large, heterogeneous inmate populations; others offer much freedom, good correctional programs, and small, homogeneous populations.

When an offender is sentenced by the court to a period of confinement, responsibility for custody and rehabilitation is transferred from the court to a correctional agency. A separate department of corrections, which is in the executive branch of each state's government and the federal government, ordinarily administers all the correctional institutions. Each institution is under the general supervision of a prison warden or superintendent.

Most new inmates are first sent to a reception and **classification center**, where they are given diagnostic evaluations and are assigned to institutions that meet individual needs as much as possible within the system's resources. The diagnostic process in the reception center may range from a physical examination and a single interview to an extensive series of psychiatric tests, orientation sessions, and numerous personal interviews. Classification is a way of evaluating inmates and assigning them to appropriate placements and activities within the state institutional system.

When entering the assigned institution, the offender is placed in an available program in accordance with the diagnostic evaluation. Most institutions offer varying degrees of programs and services, including health and medical care, counseling, education, religious study, and vocational training. However, the gap between what correctional programs promise to deliver and their actual performance is often significant. Some programs are understaffed and use antiquated equipment; others serve only a small percentage of the prison population. Consequently, the philosophy of correctional rehabilitation on which these programs are based has been attacked by critics, who charge that prisons are places of punishment, not treatment, and that rehabilitation is a doomed concept.

Many jurisdictions have therefore instituted a fourth type of confinement—**community-based correctional facilities**. The current trend is to deemphasize the use of large prisons and emphasize the use of smaller, community-based facilities, halfway houses, prerelease centers, and work-release and home-furlough programs. This movement results from the experts' belief that only a small percentage of prison inmates require maximum security and that most can be more effectively rehabilitated in community-based facilities. Rather than totally confining offenders to an impersonal and harsh prison experience, such programs offer the opportunity to maintain normal family and social relationships while giving access to rehabilitative services and resources at lower cost to taxpayers. Despite such efforts the prison population is at an all-time high of almost 500,000 people.

Parole. More than half of all offenders released from correctional institutions reenter the community via the parole system. **Parole** is a process whereby an inmate is selected for early release and serves the remainder of the sentence in the community under the supervision of a parole officer. It is the predominant form of release for prison inmates and exists in most states and in the federal government.[13] Other ways an offender may be released from an institution include mandatory release upon completion of the sentence, and the pardon, a form of executive clemency.

The main purpose of parole is to help the ex-inmate bridge the gap between institutional confinement and a positive adjustment within the community. Parole officers, usually employees of a state or federal correctional authority, first work with inmates to develop a work and living plan that they will implement upon their release. Later, the parole supervisor counsels inmates so they are better equipped to succeed on the job and in their personal and family relations. All parolees must adhere to a set of rules of behavior while they are "on the outside." If these rules are violated, the parole privilege can be terminated (revoked), and the parolee will be sent back to the institution to serve the remainder of the sentence.

The future of parole is undecided. Changes are being made in sentencing provisions throughout the country, and some thought is being given to eliminating parole altogether. Some states have recently implemented fixed sentencing statutes requiring offenders to serve their entire sentences in confinement.[14] If this movement expands, the future of parole in the criminal justice system will be in doubt.

Justice Agencies in the United States

The administration of criminal justice is a vast enterprise. Approximately 55,000 separate agencies can be classified as engaging in justice-related activities.[15] The overwhelming majority (81 percent) are part of local government structures, and the remainder are funded by state and federal jurisdictions. The estimated cost of the system of justice is from $25 to $30 billion annually.

LAW ENFORCEMENT AGENCIES

Approximately 20,000 law enforcement agencies are operating in the United States. Most are state and municipal general-purpose police forces, numbering about 13,000 in all. About 90 percent of all municipalities with populations over 2,500 maintain their own police forces. However, many of these forces are quite small; two-thirds have fewer than ten officers, and over one-third have fewer than five.

In addition, local jurisdictions maintain 1,122 special police units, including park rangers, harbor police, transit police, and campus security agencies at local universities.

At the county level of government there are approximately 3,028 **sheriff's departments**, or almost one for each of the 3,040 organized county governments in the United States. Sheriff's offices are multifunction agencies. They provide police protection in the unincorporated areas of the county. They also perform judicial functions such as serving subpoenas and maintaining order in courtrooms. Another significant function of most sheriff's departments (83 percent) is maintenance of the county jail and detention facilities.

In 1984, the FBI estimated that there were 449,730 state, county, and local police officers, and 136,580 civilian employees working in police agencies, for a total of 585,950 law enforcement employees.

There are also approximately 2,000 agencies that provide related services to law enforcement organizations. Of these, about 1,700 are county coroner or medical examiner agencies; the remainder include such agencies as bureaus of identification and investigation, departments of public safety, criminal justice information centers, training academies, forensic science laboratories, and police planning agencies. Chapter 15 will further discuss the role and function of the various federal, state, and local law enforcement agencies.

Finally, the federal government has its own law enforcement agencies, including the FBI and the Secret Service.

COURT-RELATED AGENCIES

There are approximately 25,000 court-related agencies in the United States. Of these, slightly over 8,000 are state and local prosecutors' offices, which represent the government in criminal and civil trials and appeals. Over half these offices are municipal, about one-third are county, and the remainder are state and federally affiliated. In addition, some 500 defender offices, which dispense free legal aid to indigent defendants, are in operation around the country.

There are also more than 17,000 courts in the United States. About 13,000 are courts of limited jurisdiction, 3,656 are general jurisdiction, and 207 are appellate courts.

CORRECTIONAL AGENCIES

There exist 9,000 agencies devoted to the correction and treatment of convicted offenders. Approximately 3,500 are adult and juvenile probation and parole agencies supervising offenders in the community.

There are also about 5,700 residential correctional facilities, divided into 3,500 jails, 800 prisons, and 1,100 juvenile institutions.

This complex array of agencies handles upward of 2 million offenders a year, employs more than 1.2 million people, and costs approximately $25 to $30 billion to operate (see table 14.1). About 600,000 people are employed by police agencies, 250,000 by the courts, and 285,000 by correctional agencies. Table 14.1 shows some of the costs involved in crime control: $13,000 per year to keep an inmate in a federal prison, $58,000 to build a prison cell, $39,000 for the annual salary of a state supreme court clerk, and so on. It is the size, diversity, and multiplicity of goals and values of justice agencies that have helped prevent the agencies from becoming a true system of justice.

The Justice Process

In addition to viewing the criminal justice system as a collection of agencies, it is also possible to see it as a series of decision points through which offenders flow. This **process** begins with an initial contact with police and ends with the offender's reentry into society (see figure 14.1). At any point in the process, the accused may be no longer considered to be an offender and allowed back into society without further penalty for such reasons as: (1) the case is considered unimportant or trivial; (2) legally admissible evidence is unavailable; (3) the accused is considered not to need further treatment, punishment, or attention; or (4) for personal reasons (discretion), those in power decide not to take further action in the case. Though each jurisdiction is somewhat different, a comprehensive view of the processing of a felony offender would probably contain the following decision points:

- *Initial contact.* The initial contact an offender has with the justice system is usually with police. Police officers may observe a criminal act during their patrol of city streets, parks, or highways. They may also find out about a crime through a citizen or victim complaint. Similarly, an informer can alert them about criminal activity in return for financial or other consideration. Sometimes political officials, such as the mayor or city council, will ask police to look into an ongoing criminal activity, such as gambling, and during their subsequent investigations, police officers will encounter an illegal act.
- *Investigation.* Regardless whether the police observe, hear of, or receive a complaint about crime, they may choose to conduct an investigation. The purpose of this procedure is to gather sufficient facts, or **evidence**, to identify the perpetrator, justify an arrest, and bring the offender to trial. An investigation may take a few minutes, as when police officers see a burglary in progress and apprehend the burglar at the scene of the crime. It may take months and involve hundreds of investigators, as was the case with the Atlanta murders investigation, which lasted from 1980 through 1981.
- *Arrest.* An arrest occurs when the police take a person into custody and deprive the person of freedom for allegedly committing a criminal act. An arrest is legal when all of the following conditions exist: (a) the police officer believes there is sufficient evidence (probable cause) that a crime is being or has been committed and intends to restrain the suspect; (b) the police officer deprives the individual of freedom; and (c) the suspect believes that he or she is in the custody of the police officer and cannot voluntarily leave. The police officer is not required to use the word *arrest* or any similar word to initiate an arrest; nor does the officer first have to bring the suspect to the police station. For all practical purposes, a person who has been

TABLE 14.1 Criminal justice costs: agencies and personnel

Agency function	Average annual expenses	Agency function—cont'd	Average annual expenses
Victim compensation		Average daily cost to the federal government to house an unsentenced federal prisoner in a local jail	$27
Average maximum award	$18,000		
Average award	$3,000		
Investigative and court costs		Average daily cost to the federal government to house a sentenced prisoner in a state or local:	
Average cost to return fugitive interstate	$600		
Average cost for a state or federal wiretap	$22,000	halfway house	$29
		prison or jail	$23
Average annual cost to protect a federal witness	$37,000–$56,000	Average daily cost to a state government to house a state prisoner in a local jail	$15
Daily payment for juror	$3–$30		
Average court cost per case-related minute:		Average hourly wage for inmate in prison industry	$0.21–$1.03
California Superior Court	$5	Average construction cost per bed in a:	
Florida Circuit Court	$4	maximum-security state prison	$58,000
Washington State Superior Court	$4	medium-security state prison	$46,000
U.S. District Courts	$9	minimum-security state prison	$26,000
Cost to arrest, prosecute, and try a robbery case in New York City:		"constitutional" jail	$43,000
		Typical new courthouse construction cost per square foot	$54–$65
with guilty plea and sentencing day after arrest	$851	Average purchase price for a police car	$8,000
with guilty plea after indictment and sentencing 68 days after arrest	$6,665	Average cost to equip a new police car with:	
with trial disposition and sentencing 250 days after arrest	$32,627	police radio	$2,000
		siren and light bar	$800
Most frequent assigned counsel hourly rate	$20–$30	other	$300
Corrections operations		Annual cost to maintain and operate a police car (not including patrol salary)	$6,000
Average annual cost for one adult offender:		Average resale value of a police car	$1,000
in a federal prison	$13,000		
in a state prison	$5,000–$23,000		
in a state "halfway house"	$12,000		
in a local community-based facility	$8,000		
in a local jail	$8,000		
on federal probation or parole	$1,300		
on non-federal probation or parole	$220–$1,700		

deprived of liberty is under arrest. Arrests can be made at the scene of a crime or upon a warrant being issued by a magistrate.

• *Custody.* After arrest, the suspect remains in police custody. The person may be taken to the police station to be fingerprinted and photographed and to have personal information recorded—a procedure popularly referred to as **booking**. Witnesses may be brought in to view the suspect (in a **lineup**), and further evidence may be gathered on the case. Suspects may be interrogated by police officers to get their side of the story, they may be asked to sign a **confession** of guilt, or they may be asked to identify others

Personnel	Average annual salaries	Personnel—cont'd	Average annual salaries
Law enforcement officers		U.S. magistrate	$63,600
City police officer	$16,000–$20,000	U.S. bankruptcy court judge	$63,600
County sheriff patrol officer (starting salary)	$13,000	U.S. court of claims judge	$65,200
		U.S. court of international trade judge	$73,100
State trooper	$13,000–$20,000	U.S. district (trial) court judge	$73,100
U.S. border patrol agent	$22,000	U.S. circuit (appellate) court judge	$77,300
U.S. immigration inspector	$22,000	U.S. Supreme Court Associate Justice	$96,700
Deputy U.S. marshal	$23,000	U.S. Supreme Court Chief Justice	$100,700
U.S. immigration agent	$29,000		
U.S. secret service agent	$29,000	Correctional Officers	
FBI agent	$36,000	County sheriff jail officer (starting salary)	$11,000
Federal drug agent	$36,000	State correctional officer	$15,000–$20,000
Prosecutors		State correctional sergeant	$17,000–$22,000
Local assistant prosecutor	$20,000	State superintendent of correction	$33,000–$44,000
Local chief prosecutor	$46,000	Federal correctional officer	$21,000
State assistant attorney general (entry level)	$20,000	Probation and parole officers	
State assistant attorney general	$32,000	Local probation officer	Not available
State deputy attorney general	$49,000	State probation and parole officer	$16,000–$22,000
State attorney general	$52,000	Senior state probation and parole officer	$21,000–$28,000
Federal prosecutor	$40,000	State director of probation and parole	$32,000–$42,000
Defenders		Federal probation officer	$16,559–$38,185
Staff state or local defender	$24,000	Supervisory federal probation officer	$34,930–$45,406
Chief state or local defender	$40,000	Deputy chief of a federal district probation office	$41,277–$53,661
Federal defender	$40,000	Chief of a federal district probation office	$41,277–$63,115
Court Personnel		Federal parole case analyst	$24,508–$38,185
State supreme court clerk	$39,000	Federal parole hearing examiner	$34,930–$53,661
State court administrator	$47,000	U.S. parole commissioner	$63,800
State general jurisdiction trial court judge	$48,000		
State intermediate appellate court justice	$54,000		
State supreme court justice	$55,000		

SOURCE. Bureau of Justice Statistics, *Report to The Nation on Crime and Justice*, pp. 92, 93, 95.

involved in the crime. The law allows suspects to have their lawyers present when police conduct in-custody interrogations.

- *Complaint.* After police turn evidence on a case over to the prosecutor, who is entrusted with representing the state at any criminal proceedings, a decision will be made whether to file a complaint, **information**, or bill of indictment with the court having jurisdiction over the case. Complaints are used in misdemeanors; information and indictment are employed in felonies. Each is a charging document asking the court to bring a case forward to be tried. The decision of whether to charge an offender

FIGURE 14.1 Flow chart of the criminal justice process

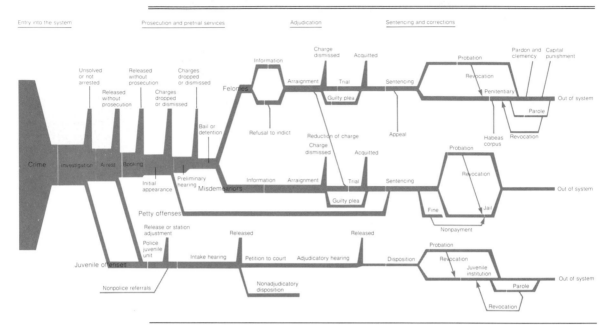

NOTE: This chart gives a simplified view of case flow through the criminal justice system. Procedures vary among jurisdictions. The weights of the lines are not intended to show the actual size of caseloads.

SOURCE. Adapted from *The Challenge of Crime in a Free Society*, President's Commission on Law Enforcement and Administration of Justice, 1967.

with a criminal offense is a complex one that will be discussed further in chapter 16.

- *Preliminary hearing–grand jury.* Since it is a tremendous personal and financial burden to stand trial for a serious felony crime, the U.S. Constitution provides that the state must first prove to an impartial hearing board that there is **probable cause** that the accused committed the crime and, therefore, that there is sufficient reason to try the person as charged. In about half the states and in the federal system, the decision on whether to bring a suspect to trial (indictment) is made by a group of citizens brought together to form a **grand jury**. The grand jury considers the case in a closed hearing, in which only the prosecutor presents evidence. In the remaining states an information is filed before an impartial lower-court judge, who decides whether the case should go forward. This is known as a **preliminary hearing** or probable cause hearing. The defendant may appear at a preliminary hearing and dispute the prosecutor's charges. During either procedure, if the prosecution's evidence is accepted as factual and sufficient, the suspect will be called to stand trial for the crime. These procedures are not used for misdemeanors because of their lesser importance and seriousness.
- *Arraignment.* An **arraignment** brings the accused before the court that will actually try the case. There, defendants are apprised of the formal charges and informed of their constitutional rights (such as the right to legal counsel). have their bail considered, and have the trial date set.

After arrest, suspects may be taken to police headquarters for identification and interrogation.

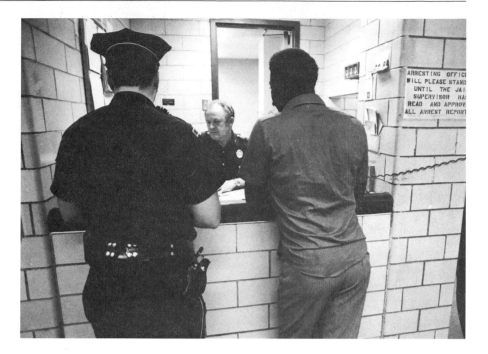

- *Bail/detention.* If the bail decision has not been considered previously, it will evaluated at arraignment. Bail is a money bond, the amount of which is set by judicial authority; it is intended to insure the presence of suspects at trial while allowing them their freedom until that time. Suspects who do not show up for trial forfeit their bail. Suspects who cannot afford bail or whose cases are so serious that a judge refuses them bail (usually restricted to capital cases) must remain in detention until trial. In most instances this means an extended stay in the county jail. In many jurisdictions, programs have been developed to allow defendants awaiting trial to be released on their own recognizance, without bail, if they are stable members of the community.
- *Plea bargaining.* After arraignment, it is common for the prosecutor to meet with the defendant and his or her attorney to discuss a possible guilty plea arrangement. If a bargain can be struck, the accused will plead guilty as charged, thus ending the criminal trial process. In return for the plea, the prosecutor may reduce charges, request a lenient sentence, or grant the defendant some other consideration.
- *Adjudication.* If a plea bargain cannot be arranged, a criminal trial will take place. This involves a full-scale formal inquiry into the facts of the case before a judge, a jury, or both. The defendant can be found guilty or not guilty, or the jury can fail to reach a decision (hung jury), thereby leaving the case unresolved and open for a possible retrial.
- *Disposition.* After a criminal trial, a defendant who is found guilty as charged will be sentenced by the presiding judge. Disposition usually involves either a fine, a term of community supervision (probation), a period of incarceration in a penal institution, or some combination of the above. In the most serious capital cases, it is possible to sentence the offender to death. Dispositions are usually made after a presentencing investigation is con-

Juvenile Justice

Independent of but interrelated with the adult criminal justice system, the juvenile justice system is primarily responsible for dealing with juveniles who commit crimes *(delinquents),* and those who are incorrigibles, truants, runaways, or unmanageables *(status offenders).*

The notion that juveniles who commit criminal acts should be treated separately from adults is a relatively new one. Until the late nineteenth century, youthful criminals were tried in adult courts and punished in adult institutions. However, in the 1890s, reformers, today known as "child savers," lobbied to separate young offenders from serious adult criminals. Their efforts were rewarded when the first separate juvenile court was set up in Chicago, Illinois, in 1899. Over the next twenty years, most other states created separate juvenile court and correctional systems.

At first the juvenile system was based on the philosophy of *parens patriae.* This meant that the state was acting in the best interests of children in trouble who could not care for themselves. Under the parens patriae doctrine, delinquents and status offenders (sometimes called "wayward minors" or "children in need of supervision") were adjudicated in an informal juvenile court hearing without the benefit of counsel or other procedural rights. The juvenile correctional system, designed

for treatment rather than punishment, was usually located in small institutions referred to as schools or camps (The first juvenile reform school was opened in 1847 in Massachusetts). However, after the separate juvenile justice system was developed, almost all incarcerated youths were maintained in separate juvenile institutions that stressed individualized treatment, education, and counseling.

In the 1960s the Supreme Court revolutionized the juvenile justice system when, in a series of cases, most importantly *In Re Gault,* it granted procedural and due process rights, such as the right to legal counsel, to juveniles at trial. The Court recognized that many youths were receiving long sentences without the benefit of counsel and other Fifth and Sixth Amendment rights and that many institutions did not carry out their treatment role. Consequently, the juvenile justice process became similar to the adult process.

In the 1970s the diversion movement once again changed juvenile justice. Every effort was made to remove youths from the official justice process and place them in alternative, community-based treatment programs. One state, Massachusetts, went so far as to close its secure correctional facilities and place all youths, no matter how serious their crimes, in community programs.

TABLE A. Similarities between juvenile and adult justice systems

- Discretion in decision making is used by police officers, judges, and correctional personnel in both adult and juvenile systems.
- Search and seizure law and the Fourth Amendment apply to juvenile and adult offenders.
- The right to receive *Miranda* warnings is applicable to juveniles as well as to adults.
- Juveniles are protected, as are adults, from prejudicial lineups or other identification procedures.
- Procedural safeguards similar to those of adults protect juveniles when they admit guilt.
- Prosecutors and defense attorneys play an equally critical role in juvenile and adult advocacy.
- Juveniles, like adults, have the right to counsel at most crucial stages of the court process.
- Pretrial motions are available in juvenile and criminal court proceedings.
- Negotiations and plea bargaining exist with juvenile and adult offenders.
- Both juveniles and adults have a right to trial and appeal.
- The standard of evidence in juvenile delinquency adjudications, as in adult criminal trials, is that of proof beyond a reasonable doubt.

ducted by the court's probation staff. After disposition, the defendant may appeal the conviction to a higher court.

- *Correctional treatment.* Offenders who are found guilty and are formally sentenced come under the jurisdiction of correctional authorities. They may serve a term of community supervision under control of the county probation department, they may have a term in a community correctional center, or they may be incarcerated in a large penal institution.

Today, concern over crime rates and juvenile violence has caused some critics to question the juvenile justice system's treatment philosophy. Some states, such as New York, have liberalized their procedures for trying serious juvenile offenders in the adult system, consequently making them eligible for incarceration in adult prisons. The general trend has been to remove as many nonviolent and status offenders as possible from secure placements in juvenile institutions and at the same time to lengthen the sentences of serious offenders or to move such offenders to the adult system.

Some of the similarities between the adult and juvenile justice systems are listed in table A. Some of the differences are listed in table B.

TABLE B. Differences between juvenile and adult justice systems

- The primary purpose of juvenile procedures is protection and treatment; with adults the aim is punishment of the guilty.
- The jurisdiction of the juvenile court is determined chiefly by age; in the adult system, jurisdiction is determined primarily by the offense.
- Juveniles can be held responsible for acts that would not be criminal if they were committed by an adult (status offenses).
- Juvenile proceedings are not considered criminal; adult proceedings are.
- Juvenile court procedures are generally informal and private; those of adult courts are more formal and are open to the public.
- Courts cannot release identifying information to the press concerning a juvenile, but must do so in cases dealing with adults.
- Parents are highly involved in the juvenile process; with adults, this is not the case.
- The standard of arrest is more stringent for adults than for juveniles.
- As a practical matter, juveniles are released into parental custody, while adults are generally given the opportunity for bail.
- Plea bargaining is used in most adult cases, while most juvenile cases are settled by open admission of guilt.
- Juveniles have no constitutional right to a jury trial; adults do have this right.
- Juvenile dispositional decisions are ordinarily based on indeterminate terms, while adults' sentences include proportionality and definiteness.
- The procedural rights of juveniles are based on the concept of fundamental fairness; those of adults are based on the constitutional right to due process under the Bill of Rights and the Fourteenth Amendment.
- Juveniles have the right to treatment under the Fourteenth Amendment; adult offenders have no such recognized right.
- A juvenile's record is sealed when the age of majority is reached; the record of an adult is permanent.
- The Supreme Court has said that a juvenile can be kept in preventive detention before trial. The Court has not ruled on adult preventive detention.

DISCUSSION QUESTIONS

1. Should serious juvenile offenders be treated like adults and tried in adult courts?
2. Should incorrigible and truant youths be given the same treatment as delinquents (criminal youths)?

SOURCE. Tables A and B are from Larry Siegel and Joseph Senna, *Juvenile Delinquency* (St. Paul, Minn.: West Publishing Company, 1985), pp. 316–17.

- *Release.* At the end of the correctional sentence, the offender is released into the community. Most incarcerated offenders are granted parole before the expiration of the maximum term given them by the court, and therefore finish their prison sentences in the community under supervision of the parole department. Offenders sentenced to community supervision, if successful, simply finish their terms and resume their lives unsupervised by court authorities.

Many cases are disposed of in this way; others are dealt with through more informal procedures such as diversion programs, withholding of prosecution, or dropping of the charges. Theoretically, nearly every part of the process requires that individual cases be disposed of as quickly as possible. However, the criminal justice process is slow and tedious because of congestion, inadequate facilities, limited resources, lack of knowledge, and the nature of government bureaucracy. When defendants are not processed smoothly, it is often because of the large caseloads and inadequate facilities that exist in many urban criminal courts. The procedure thus breaks down, the process within the system fails, and the ultimate goal of crime control in society is not achieved. Herbert Packer has described this process as follows:

> The image that comes to mind is an assembly line conveyor belt down which moves an endless stream of cases, never stopping, carrying them to workers who stand at fixed stations and who perform on each case as it comes by the same small but essential operation that brings it one step closer to being a finished product, or to exchange the metaphor for the reality, a closed file. The criminal process is seen as a screening process in which each successive stage—pre-arrest investigation, arrest, post-arrest investigation, preparation for trial, trial or entry of plea, conviction, disposition—involves a series of routinized operations whose success is gauged primarily by their tendency to pass the case along to a successful conclusion. [16]

Criminal Justice and the Rule of Law

For many years, U.S. courts exercised little control over the operations of criminal justice agencies, believing that their actions were not an area of judicial concern. This policy is referred to as the **hands-off doctrine**. However, in the 1960s, under the guidance of Chief Justice Earl Warren, the U.S. Supreme Court became more active in the affairs of the justice system, thereby lifting the hands-off doctrine. Today, each component of the justice system is closely supervised by state and federal courts. In this section we will review the influence of the rule of law on criminal justice agencies and discuss how it affects daily operations and decision making.

PROCEDURAL LAWS

The law of criminal procedure guarantees citizens certain rights and privileges when they are accused of crimes. Procedural laws control the action of the agencies of justice and define the rights of criminal defendants. They first come into play when people are suspected of committing crimes and the police wish to investigate them, search their property, interrogate them, and so on. Here the law answers such questions as: Can the police search my home if I don't want them to? Do I have to answer their questions even if I don't want to? If a formal charge is filed, procedural laws guide pretrial and trial activities. For example, they determine when and if people can obtain state-financed attorneys or when they can be released on bail. If, after a trial, a person is found guilty of committing a criminal offense, procedural laws guide the posttrial and correctional process. For example, they determine when a conviction can be appealed.

Procedural laws have several different sources. Most important are the first ten amendments of the U.S. Constitution, ratified in 1791 and generally called the *Bill of Rights*. The original Constitution, ratified in 1788, set up the structure of government and set out the rights and duties of its executive, legislative, and judicial branches. However, aware of the abuses people had been subjected to by royal decree in England and her colonies, the framers of the Constitution wanted to insure that the national government could not usurp the personal rights of citizens. Therefore, the Bill of Rights guaranteed, among other things, the right of the people to practice the religion of their choice, have freedom of speech and press, be secure in their homes from unwarranted intrusion by government agents, and be protected against cruel punishments, such as torture.

The guarantees of freedom contained in the Bill of Rights initially applied only to the federal government and did not affect the individual states. Then, in 1868, the Fourteenth Amendment made the first ten amendments to the Constitution binding on the state governments. However, it has remained the duty of state and federal court systems to interpret constitutional law and develop a body of case law that spells out the exact procedural rights a person is entitled to. For example, the Sixth Amendment states that a person has the right to be represented by legal counsel at a criminal trial. This right once had little meaning, because many criminal defendants were indigent and could not afford to pay for their legal defense. Then, in 1963, the U.S. Supreme Court interpreted the Sixth Amendment to mean that all people accused of felonies had the right to counsel; if they could not afford an attorney, the state had to provide the funds to hire one for them. Thus, it is the U.S. Supreme Court that interprets the Constitution and sets out the procedural laws that must be followed by the lower federal and state courts. If the Supreme Court has not ruled on a procedural issue, then the lower courts are free to interpret the Constitution as they see fit.

COURT DECISION MAKING

Until the passage of the Fourteenth Amendment, the rights and privileges made binding on the federal government by the first ten amendments did not apply to the states. However, ratification of the Fourteenth Amendment did not mean that the granting of rights and liberties was an automatic process. Instead, each right was decided upon when cases dealing with the particular issue came before the Supreme Court. Determining how to incorporate the rights into state criminal procedures became a topic of some debate. In the late 1930s the Supreme Court developed the concept of fundamental fairness and used it to guide its own decision making. Under this concept, if the Supreme Court decided that a particular guarantee in the Bill of Rights was fundamental to and implicit in the U.S. system of justice, it would hold that guarantee applicable to the states. This became the method by which states could be held to the same standards of criminal due process as the federal government.

With this formula, the provisions of the Bill of Rights were incorporated by the states, case by case. In 1953 Earl Warren became the Chief Justice of the U.S. Supreme Court; under his leadership, the due process movement reached its peak. Numerous landmark cases focusing on the rights of the accused were decided, and a revolution in the area of constitutional criminal procedure resulted. The Warren Court granted many new rights to those accused of crimes and went so far as to impose specific guidelines on the policies of police, courts, and correctional services to insure that due process of law would be maintained. Today the Supreme Court, under Chief Justice Warren Burger, has moved somewhat more cautiously in granting additional rights; and in some arenas, such as prisoners' rights, the Burger

Burger Court has reversed the trend toward liberalism established by the Warren Court.

COURTS AND CRIMINAL JUSTICE POLICY

Court decision making has had the effect of dictating policy within the criminal justice system. Most states and the federal government have codified judge-made procedural laws. In essence, state codes of criminal procedure contain the holdings of Supreme Court judgments plus additional rules of law covering issues the Supreme Court has so far ignored. For example, the New York State Code of Criminal Procedure lists the following restrictions on the police power to arrest:

> A peace officer may, without a warrant, arrest a person,
>
> 1. For an offense, committed or attempted in his presence, or where a police officer . . . has reasonable grounds for believing that an offense is being committed in his presence.
>
> 2. When the person arrested has committed a felony, although not in his presence;
>
> 3. When a felony has in fact been committed, and he has reasonable cause for believing the person to be arrested to have committed it;
>
> 4. When he has reasonable cause for believing that a felony has been committed, and that the person arrested has committed it, though it should afterward appear that no felony has been committed, or, if committed, that the person arrested did not commit it. [17]

Because the makeup of the Supreme Court can change, procedural laws are subject to different interpretations and can also change at any time. The Constitution and Bill of Rights are fairly abstract documents; hence there is much leeway as to the direction and content of procedural laws—what is law today may not be tomorrow.

The role courts play, especially the U.S. Supreme Court, in influencing the operations of the criminal justice system is quite controversial. When **Earl Warren** was Chief Justice of the Supreme Court, the court's rulings revolutionized criminal justice by liberalizing and enlarging the rights of people accused of crime. Under the present Chief Justice, **Warren Burger**, the Court has steered a more conservative course and consequently, the rights of criminal defendents have narrowed. Warren's court was accused by conservatives such as Richard Nixon and Gerald Ford of coddling criminals and eroding the rights of victims. In contrast, the Burger Court has been castigated by liberals for threatening civil rights and opening the door to a "police state."

Of the criminal justice issues the courts deal with, few are as important and have as much influence on the justice system as the concept of *due process* and the *exclusionary rule*. Therefore, these legal issues will be reviewed here in some detail.

DUE PROCESS

The concept of **due process** is mentioned in the Fifth (where it is applied to the federal government) and Fourteenth Amendments (where it is applied to the states) of the U.S. Constitution. It is usually divided into both substantive and procedural areas. The substantive aspects are generally used to determine whether a statute is fair, reasonable, and appropriate use of the legal power of the legislature. The concept of substantive due process was used extensively in the 1930s and 1940s to invalidate minimum-wage standards, price-fixing, and employment restriction statutes. Today it is used more sparingly; for example, it may be employed to hold that criminal statutes dealing with disorderly conduct, capital punishment, or a ban on pornography may be unconstitutional because they are arbitrary or unreasonable.

Much more important today are the procedural aspects of due process. In seeking to define the term, most legal experts indicate that it refers to the essential elements of fairness under law. An elaborate and complex definition of *due process* is found in *Black's Law Dictionary:*

> *Due process of law in each particular case means such an exercise of the powers of government as the settled maxims of law permit and sanction, and under such safeguards for the protection of individual rights as those maxims prescribe for the class of cases to which the one in question belongs.*[18]

This definition refers to the need for rules and procedures in the legal system to protect individual rights. The objectives of due process help define the term even more explicitly. Due process seeks to insure that no person will be deprived of life, liberty, or property without notice of charges, assistance from legal counsel, a hearing, and an opportunity to confront accusers. Basically, due process is intended to guarantee that functional fairness exists in each individual case. This doctrine of fairness as expressed in due process of the law is guaranteed under both the Fifth and Fourteenth Amendments.

Abstract definitions are only one aspect of due process. Much more significant are the procedures that give meaning to due process in the everyday practices of the criminal justice system. In this regard, due process provides numerous procedural safeguards for the offender, including:

- Notice of charges.
- A formal hearing.
- The right to counsel or some other representation.
- The opportunity to respond to charges.
- The opportunity to confront and cross-examine witnesses and accusers.
- The privilege to be free from self-incrimination.
- The opportunity to present one's own witnesses.
- A decision made on the basis of substantial evidence and facts produced at the hearing.
- A written statement of the reasons for the decision.
- An appellate review procedure.

Exactly what constitutes due process in a specific case depends on the facts of the case, the federal and state constitutional and statutory provisions, previous court decisions, and the ideas and principles that society considers important at a given time and in a given place.[19] Justice Felix Frankfurter emphasized this point in *Rochin v. California* (1952), when he wrote:

> *Due process of law requires an evaluation based on a disinterested inquiry, pursued in the spirit of science on a balanced order of facts, exactly and clearly stated, on the detached consideration of conflicting claims . . . on a judgement not ad hoc and episodic but duly mindful of reconciling the needs both of continuity and of change in a progressive society.*[20]

Both the elements and the definition of due process seem to be flexible and constantly changing. For example, due process at one time did not require a formal hearing for parole revocation, but today it does. Before 1968, juvenile offenders did not have the right to an attorney at their adjudication; counsel is now required in the juvenile court system. Thus, the interpretations of due process of law reflect what society deems fair and just at a particular time and in a particular place. The degree of loss suffered by the individual (victim or offender) balanced against the state's interest also determines which and how many due process requirements are ordinarily applied. When the accused's person's freedom is at stake in the criminal justice system, all applicable due process rights are usually granted; in other cases, due process may be modified.

Changing Concepts of Due Process. In the mid-1980s the concept of due process as applied by the courts seems to be changing. The balance of fairness is shifting away from the criminal and emphasis instead is being placed more squarely on the needs of the states to protect their citizens. The rights of both those accused of crime and those convicted of crime have been curtailed. For example, police have been given a freer hand in questioning suspects, searching for evidence, obtaining search warrants, and so on. Courts have resumed using the death penalty with fewer judicial restraints. Prison administrators have been given a freer hand to deal with inmates as they see fit. There seems little question that the Supreme Court has set the stage for a reevaluation of the due process concept.

Nonetheless, the concept of due process is securely held to in our legal system. Freedom from self-incrimination, the right to legal representation at all stages of the justice system, a fair hearing and trial, and sentencing review are rights that seem immutable. And while courts continue to redefine rights, they do so in the spirit of granting fairness to the criminal defendant without sacrificing the public interest.

In this context, focus has turned to the exclusionary rule, considered by some to be a cornerstone of individual freedom and by others to be a serious impediment to public safety. Discussion will now turn to this important aspect of fairness and liberty.

THE EXCLUSIONARY RULE

The foundation of the **exclusionary rule** is contained in the Fourth Amendment of the Constitution, which states that:

> *The right of the people to be secure in their persons, houses, papers, and effects, against unreasonable searches and seizures, shall not be violated and no warrant shall issue, but upon probable cause, supported by Oath or affirmation, and particularly describing the place to be searched, and the persons or things to be seized.*

The primary function of the Fourth Amendment is to protect the individual against an illegal arrest and prevent illegal searches and seizures of a person's possessions. This means that police must follow certain guidelines in arrests and searches; they cannot act arbitrarily. The standard as stated in the Fourth Amendment is that of reasonableness, and the Supreme Court has gone to great lengths to explain and interpret what this means. In doing so, the Court has balanced the individual's right to privacy, protected by the Fourth Amendment, with the right of the public to be protected against crime. Consequently, there exists a large body of case law describing how searches are to be conducted, when police can seize evidence, when search warrants are needed, and so on.

The Fourth Amendment clearly states that an individual's right against unreasonable searches and seizures is to be protected. However, for many years, evidence obtained in violation of the Fourth Amendment was admitted in criminal trials even though it should have been considered illegal.

In 1914 the Supreme Court rectified this injustice in the case of *Weeks v. United States.*[21] The defendant, Weeks, was accused of the federal violation of using the mails for illegal purposes. The evidence on which he was convicted was acquired through a search of his room without a valid search warrant. The Supreme Court ruled that, in a federal criminal trial, evidence acquired through an unreasonable search and seizure must be excluded. Thus the exclusionary rule was established.

However, the ruling in *Weeks* applied only to the federal government. The states were still free to admit evidence obtained by unreasonable searches and seizures. It was not until 1969, in the case of *Mapp v. Ohio*, that the Supreme Court made the exclusionary rule applicable to the states.[22] Thus, for the first time, the Supreme Court required that state law enforcement employees follow federal constitutional standards (see Close-Up).

In sum, the exclusionary rule means that evidence judged to be improperly obtained by police through illegal interrogation of suspects or searches of their person and property cannot be used (or even mentioned) against them in a court of law. It is as if it did not exist.

The exclusionary rule has been one of the most controversial aspects of justice system legal control. Its opponents argue that it permits the guilty to go free if the police err in the handling of a case. Thus, the rights of honest citizens and society as a whole are threatened because of arbitrary court rulings. Moreover, it weakens the power of the justice system to deter crime because victims and witnesses are reluctant to come forward for fear that an obviously guilty defendant will be released on a technicality.

In contrast, those in favor of the exclusionary rule find that it is one of the cornerstones of our freedom and that it protects us from becoming a police state in which law enforcement agents have a free hand to use any means at their disposal to investigate crime. Without the exclusionary rule, houses could be broken into, phones tapped, people searched, and cars stopped—with impunity. The exclusionary rule separates our society from those "evil" totalitarian regimes that we read about in the newspapers:

> *If constitutional rights are to be anything more than pious pronouncements, then some measurable consequence must be attached to their violation. It would be intolerable if the guarantee against unreasonable search and seizure could be violated without practical consequences.*[23]

THE FUTURE OF THE EXCLUSIONARY RULE

The exclusionary rule is under legal attack. For example, in two 1984 cases, *U.S. v. Leon*[24] and *Massachusetts v. Shepperd,*[25] the U.S. Supreme Court spelled out what is known as the *good faith exception* to the rule. The Court said that if a police officer acted in what they believed to be a proper manner in obtaining evidence, and it was discovered later that they or a magistrate had made an unintentional

Mapp v. Ohio

In the case of Mapp v. Ohio, *the Supreme Court extended the exclusionary rule to the states. Because of the importance of the case, it is set out here.*

FACTS:

On 23 May 1957, three police officers arrived at Dolree Mapp's residence pursuant to information that "a person (was) hiding out in the home, who was wanted for questioning in connection with a recent bombing, and that there was a large amount of police paraphernalia being hidden in the home." Mapp and her daughter by a former marriage lived on the top floor of the two-family dwelling. Upon their arrival at the house, the officers knocked on the door and demanded entrance but Mapp, after telephoning her attorney, refused to admit them without a search warrant.

The officers again sought entrance three hours later when four or more additional officers arrived on the scene. When Mapp did not immediately come to the door, the police forcibly opened one of the doors to the house and gained admittance. Meanwhile, Mapp's attorney arrived, but the officers would not permit him to see Mapp or to enter the house. Mapp was halfway down the stairs from the upper floor to the front door when the officers broke into the hall. She demanded to see the search warrant. A paper, claimed to be a search warrant, was held up by one of the officers. (It was later discovered that the warrant was not valid.) She grabbed the "warrant" and placed it in her bosom. A struggle ensued in which the officers recovered the piece of paper and handcuffed Mapp because she had ostensibly been belligerent.

Mapp was then forcibly taken upstairs to her bedroom, where the officials searched a dresser, a chest of drawers, a closet, and some suitcases. They also looked into a photo album and through personal papers belonging to her. The search spread to the rest of the second floor, including the child's bedroom, the living room, the kitchen, and the dinette. In the course of the search, the police officers found pornographic literature. Mapp was arrested and subsequently convicted in a Ohio court of possessing obscene materials.

legal or administrative error, the evidence might still be admitted in a court of law.

Critics believe that these and similar cases foretell a new era of a weakened exclusionary rule. There seems little doubt that the nation's courts are now granting the police and other agencies of justice greater leeway in conducting their business, even if it means restricting the rights of criminal suspects. But how much will these measures actually affect the justice system? Studies conducted by the federal government's National Institute of Justice, as well as by private researchers, all indicate that exclusionary rule violations occur rather infrequently.[26] In most of the jurisdictions studied, about 1 to 2 percent of all criminal cases were rejected because police made a technical legal error resulting in the invocation of the exclusionary rule. For violent crimes, the number was generally less than 1 percent. Of all crime types, only in narcotics-related offenses was a significant number of cases terminated because of exclusionary rule violations, and there again the percentages were smaller than might be expected—under 3 percent in the jurisdictions surveyed. Police appear more apt to illegally seize evidence in narcotics cases because there is usually no victim or complaining party to help them obtain proper search warrants.

Though abolishing or severely limiting the exclusionary rule might have relatively little effect on the justice system, the rule itself is of great symbolic value. It stands for the primacy of the individual over the state, and the right to privacy. Even if relatively few cases are thrown out of court on exclusionary rule violations, knowing of its existence places law enforcement agents on notice: obey constitutional limitations, respect the individual's right to privacy, or pay the consequences in court. The exclusionary rule must be evaluated not by those few cases that see the light of public scrutiny, but by the millions of others in which police power is limited by the rule's influence.

In the following chapters, the effect of the rule of law on the individual components of the justice system will be reviewed in greater detail. Table 14.2 summarizes some of the more important constitutional cases that define procedural law.

Concepts of Justice

Many justice system operations are controlled by the rule of law, but they are also influenced by the various philosophies or viewpoints held by its practitioners and policy makers. These in turn have been influenced by criminological theory and research. Knowledge about crime, its causes, and its control has significantly affected perceptions of how criminal justice should be managed.

Not surprisingly, many competing views of justice exist simultaneously in our culture. Those in favor of one position or another try to win public opinion to their side, hoping to influence legislative, judicial, or administrative decision making. Over the years, different philosophical viewpoints tend to predominate, only to fall into disfavor as programs based on their principles fail to prove effective.

Below, the most prominent concepts of criminal justice are briefly discussed.

CRIME CONTROL MODEL

Those espousing the crime control model believe that the overriding purpose of the justice system is protection of the public, deterrence of criminal behavior, and incapacitation of known criminals. Those who champion its principles view the

TABLE 14.2 Some leading constitutional cases and their findings

The Police Process

Chimel v. California, 395 U.S. 752 (1969)	In a search incident to an arrest the police are allowed to search only the defendant and the surroundings that are under the defendant's immediate control.
New York v. Belton, 453 U.S. 454 (1981)	The passenger compartment of a car is within the scope of a search when an arrest takes place after the car is stopped for a speeding violation.
Terry v. Ohio, 392 U.S. 1 (1968)	Even though there is no probable cause to arrest, the police have the power to stop an individual and conduct a pat-down search of outer clothing for weapons if the officer has reasonable belief that a threat to safety exists.
New York v. Quarles, 104 S. Ct. 2626 (1984)	A suspect's statements made without benefit of the Miranda Warning are admissible if "public safety" is at risk.
Illinois v. Gates, 103 S. Ct. 2317 (1983)	A judge may issue a search warrant based on the "totality of the circumstances" of the case.
United States v. Ross, 72 L. Ed. 2d 572 (1982)	Opening and searching without a warrant the closed opaque containers found in a car is legal if the officers have probable cause to believe that contraband is concealed somewhere in the car.
Bumper v. North Carolina, 391 U.S. 543 (1968)	In order for a consent search to be effective, the consent must be voluntary; threat or compulsion will invalidate the search.
Katz v. United States, 389 U.S. 347 (1967)	The Fourth Amendment protects a person's right to privacy at all times and is not limited to certain places or property. A search occurs whenever police activity violates a person's privacy.
U.S. v. Leon, 104 S. Ct. 3405 (1984)	Evidence may be admitted to trial even if a search warrant was faulty but the police officers acted on "good faith."
Steagald v. United States, 451 U.S. 204 (1981)	The Fourth Amendment privacy principle applies not only when searching a home for property but also when searching a home for a person.
Mapp v. Ohio, 367 U.S. 643 (1969)	When evidence is obtained in violation of the Fourth Amendment's right against unreasonable searches and seizures, it is not admissible in a state trial. This case made the exclusionary rule applicable to the states through the due process clause of the Fourteenth Amendment.
Miranda v. Arizona, 384 U.S. 436 (1966)	The police have a duty to warn a suspect in custody of the basic Fifth Amendment right against self-incrimination. If the warning is not given, any statement made by the defendant must be excluded from the evidence.
Nix v. Williams, 104 S. Ct. 2501 (1984)	Evidence can be seized without a warrant if it would have been "inevitably discovered by police officers."

The Trial Stage

Powell v. Alabama, 287 U.S. 45 (1932)	The state must provide counsel to an indigent defendant who is prosecuted for a capital offense.
Gideon v. Wainwright, 372 U.S. 335 (1963)	An indigent defendant subjected to a felony prosecution must have counsel provided by the state. This Sixth Amendment right was made applicable to the states through the due process clause of the Fourteenth Amendment.

justice system as a barrier between destructive criminal elements and conventional society. Quick, informal justice followed by punishment designed to fit the crime are the goals of advocates of the crime control model. Its disciples promote such policies as increasing the size of police forces, maximizing the use of discretion, building more prisons, using the death penalty, and reducing legal controls on the justice system.

Argersinger v. *Hamlin,* 407 U.S. 25 (1972)	The state must provide an indigent defendant with counsel in any case in which the sentence results in imprisonment, regardless whether the crime is classified as a misdeameanor or a felony.
Apodica v. *Oregon,* 406 U.S. 404 (1972)	A criminal conviction by less than a unanimous jury verdict in a non-first-degree murder case is constitutional under the Sixth and Fourteenth Amendments when a twelve-person jury is used.
Strickland v. *Washington,* 104 S. Ct. 2052 (1984)	Defendants have a right to effective, competent counsel in criminal cases.
Klopfer v. *North Carolina,* 387 U.S. 213 (1967)	The Sixth Amendment right to a speedy trial is applicable to the states through the due process clause of the Fourteenth Amendment.
Strunk v. *United States,* 412 U.S. 434 (1973)	When a person's right to a speedy trial is violated, the charges against the person must be dismissed.
Barker v. *Wingo,* 407 U.S. 514 (1972)	Four factors must be considered when determining whether a defendant's right to a speedy trial has been violated: (1) length of the delay, (2) reason for the delay, (3) defendant's assertion of the right, and (4) prejudice to the defendant.
Benton v. *Maryland,* 395 U.S. 784 (1969)	The Fifth Amendment protection against double jeopardy is applicable to the states through the due process clause of the Fourteenth Amendment.
Richmond Newspapers v. *Virginia,* 448 U.S. 555 (1980)	The press has the right to attend and report on trials.
Duncan v. *Louisiana,* 391 U.S. 145 (1968)	The Sixth Amendment right to a jury trial when the defendant is accused of a serious offense is applicable to the states through the due process clause of the Fourteenth Amendment.
Baldwin v. *New York,* 399 U.S. 66 (1970)	A defendant has a constitutional right to a jury trial under the Sixth and Fourteenth Amendments when the penalty is imprisonment for six months or more.
Williams v. *Florida,* 399 U.S. 78 (1970)	A six-person jury fulfills a defendant's Sixth amendment constitutional right to a jury trial.
North Carolina v. *Pearce,* 395 U.S. 711 (1969)	A judge who imposes a more severe sentence upon reconviction must state the reasons for the more severe sentence on the record.

Sentencing and Corrections

Gregg v. *Georgia,* 482 U.S. 153 (1976)	The death penalty may be applied when there exist aggravating circumstances in a murder case such as murder for profit.
Gagnon v. *Scarpelli,* 411 U.S. 778 (1973)	Probationers and parolees are entitled to limited representation of counsel at revocation hearings.
Rhodes v. *Chapman,* 452 U.S. 337 (1981)	Prisoners may be forced to share a cell if prison overcrowding exists.
Wolff v. *McDonnell,* 418 U.S. 539 (1974)	Prisoners who may face sanctions because of disciplinary problems are entitled to a hearing to defend their behavior.
Estelle v. *Gamble,* 429 U.S. 97 (1976)	An inmate is entitled to proper medical care.

The crime control model has its roots in classical theory. Fear of criminal sanctions is viewed as the primary deterrent to crime. Swift, sure, and efficient justice are considered essential elements of an orderly society.

The crime control philosophy emphasizes the protection of society and the compensation of victims. The criminal is someone who is responsible for his or her actions, who has broken faith with society and chosen to violate the law for

In the conservative '80s, the "get tough" approach to crime has wide support.

reasons of anger, greed, revenge, and so forth. Therefore money spent should be directed not at making criminals more comfortable, but on increasing the efficiency of police to apprehend them and the courts to effectively try them.

In the 1980s the crime control philosophy has become a dominant force in American justice. Fear of crime in the 1960s and 1970s, coupled with a growing skepticism about the effectiveness of rehabilitation efforts, has produced a climate in which conservative, hard-line solutions to the crime problem are being sought. The results of this swing to the right can be seen in such phenomena as the resumption of the death penalty, erosion of the exclusionary rule, prison over-crowding, and attack of the insanity defense. Crime control enthusiasts look on with glee, and their opponents with horror, as the crime rate continues to fall during a period of conservative justice.

REHABILITATION MODEL

The rehabilitation model embraces the notion that given the proper care and treatment, criminals can be changed into productive, law-abiding citizens. Influenced by positivist criminology, the rehabilitation school suggests that people commit crimes through no fault of their own. Instead, criminals themselves are the victims of social injustice, poverty, and racism; and their acts are a response to a society that has betrayed them. And, because of their disturbed and impoverished upbringing, they may be suffering psychological problems and personality disturbances that further enhance their crime committing capabilities.

To deal effectively with crime, its root causes must be attacked. First, funds must be devoted to equalize access to conventional means of success. This means supporting such programs as Aid to Dependent Children, educational opportunity, job training, and so on. If individuals run afoul of the law, efforts should be made to treat and not punish them. This means emphasizing counseling and psychological

Reaffirming Rehabilitation

The following excerpts from Francis Cullen and Karen Gilbert's book, Reaffirming Reha- bilitation, *are a clear call for the care and treatment of offenders. They also represent liberal thought and policy in the 1980s.*

. . . the ideology of rehabilitation disputes every facet of the conclusion that the constant escalation of punish- ment will mitigate the spectre of crime. To say that of- fenders are in need of rehabilitation is to reject the con- servatives' notion that individuals, regardless of their po- sition in the social order—whether black or white, rich or poor—exercise equal freedom in deciding whether to commit a crime. Instead, it is to reason that social and personal circumstances often constrain, if not compel, people to violate the law; and unless efforts are made to enable offenders to escape these criminogenic con- straints, little relief in the crime rate can be anticipated. Policies that insist on ignoring these realities by assum- ing a vengeful posture toward offenders promise to suc- ceed only in fostering hardships that will, if anything, deepen the resentment that many inmates find difficult to suppress upon their release back into society. . . .

In contrast to the justice model, it is instructive to note that the rehabilitative ideal has long provided lib- erals with a coherent framework which could be invoked to unmask repressive policies as both scientifically un- founded and non-humanistic in spirit. Whatever its fail- ings, criminal justice rehabilitation has thus persisted as a rationale for caring for offender needs and not for

making the wayward suffer. Without its humanizing in- fluence, it seems clear that the history of American cor- rections would be even bleaker than is now the case. Further, to the extent that liberals continue to contribute to the decline of rehabilitation, it is equally apparent that they will be left without a distinct ideological stance to draw upon in their urgent efforts to resist the ongoing and successful crusade by conservatives to introduce increasingly repressive crime control strategies. In the end, it is for this reason that we wish to persuade those with liberal leanings to reconsider the wisdom of ad- vocating a punishment response to crime and, alter- natively, to weigh the advantages of reaffirming reha- bilitation.

DISCUSSION QUESTIONS

1. Can criminals be successfully rehabilitated?
2. Does society owe a debt to its less fortunate mem- bers?

SOURCE. Francis Cullen and Karen Gilbert, *Reaffirming Re- habilitation* (Cincinnati, Ohio: Anderson Pub., 1982). Quotes from pp. 255 and XXIX.

care in community-based treatment programs. Whenever possible, offenders should be placed on probation in halfway houses or in other rehabilitation-oriented pro- grams.

This view of the justice system portrays it as a method for dispensing "treat- ment" to needy "patients." Also known as the "medical model," it portrays of- fenders as people who, because they have failed to exercise self-control, need the aid of the state. The medical model rejects the crime control philosophy on the ground that it ignores the needs of offenders, who are actually people whom society has failed to help. Similarly, it deprecates the due process approach for its emphasis on legal rights that ignores the needs of offenders. The popularity of the medical model reached its zenith in the 1950s and 1960s; enthusiasm for it waned in the conservative, crime-control-oriented 1970s and 1980s.

Yet rehabilitation still retains its enthusiasts. The following Close-up contains an excerpt from Francis Cullen and Karen Gilbert's book, *Reaffirming Rehabilitation*, which is considered a classic call for a return to a humanist approach to justice.

DUE PROCESS MODEL

In *The Limits of the Criminal Sanction*, Herbert Packer contrasted the crime control model with an opposing view that he referred to as the due process model.[27] According to Packer, the *due process model* combines elements of liberal/positivist criminology with the legal concept of procedural fairness for the accused. Those who adhere to due process principles believe in individualized justice, treatment, and rehabilitation of the offender. If discretion exists in the criminal justice system, it should be used to evaluate the treatment needs of the offender. Most importantly, the civil rights of the accused should be protected at all possible costs. This means practices such as strict scrutiny of police search and interrogation procedures, review of sentencing policies, and development of prisoners' rights.

The due process model has affected the trial stage of the criminal process by demanding defense counsel, jury trials, and other procedural safeguards. Further-more, this model tends to restrict the legal definition of criminal behavior by removing certain offenses, such as victimless crimes, juvenile delinquency, traffic offenses, and certain drug violations, from the criminal statutes. It has resulted in the elimination of a variety of vague laws, such as overly broad juvenile delinquency, abortion, vagrancy, and disorderly conduct statutes. Beyond this, the due process model has resulted in the establishment of various procedures to cover the ways that criminal justice agencies operate, particularly with regard to their discretionary power.

For obvious reasons, proponents of the due process philosophy are usually members of the legal profession who see themselves as protectors of civil rights. They view overzealous cops as violators of the basic constitutional rights that make our country great. Similarly, they are skeptical about the intentions of meddling social workers, whose "treatment" often entails greater confinement and penalties than punishment ever did. Due process is there to protect citizens—both from those who wish to punish them and those who wish to treat them without regard for legal and civil rights.

NONINTERVENTION MODEL

The fourth approach to justice was influenced by the popularity of the labeling theory in the late 1960s and 1970s. Both the rehabilitation ideal and the due process movement were viewed suspiciously by experts concerned with the stig-matization of offenders. Regardless of the purpose, the more the government in-tervenes in the lives of people, the greater the harm done to their future behavior patterns.

Noninterventionist philosophy was influenced by Edwin Lemert's call for *ju-dicious nonintervention*[28] and Edwin Schur's 1971 book, *Radical Nonintervention.*[29] These called for limitations on government intrusion into the lives of people, especially minors, who run afoul of the law. They advocated *deinstitutionalization* of nonserious offenders, *diversion* from formal court processes into informal treat-ment programs, and *decriminalization* of nonserious offenses such as the possession of small amounts of marijuana. Under this concept, the justice system should have as little interaction as possible with offenders. Police, courts, and correctional agencies would concentrate their efforts on diverting law violators out of the formal justice system, thereby helping them avoid the stigma of formal labels such as "delinquent" or "ex-con." Programs instituted under this model include diversion and community-based corrections.

The popularity of the noninterventionist philosophy has cooled in the 1980s. There has been little evidence that alternative programs actually reduce recidivism rates. Similarly, critics charge that alternative programs result in *widening the net.*[30] This refers to the process by which efforts to remove people from the justice system actually enmesh them further within it. For example, programs have been created around the United States to divert first-time misdemeanants (petty offenders) from the trial process into treatment-oriented counseling centers. However, many offenders spend more time in the alternative programs than they would have in the formal justice system. Whereas a fine or warning would have been the typical response in the past, the nonintervention approach now produces greater interaction with the justice system than does the formal legal process.

Despite such criticism, the nonintervention philosophy is alive and well. For example, the juvenile justice system has made a major effort to remove youths from adult jails and reduce the use of pretrial detention. In the adult system, pretrial release programs (alternatives to bail) are now the norm instead of an experimental innovation. And, though the prison population is rising, probation remains the model correctional treatment in the United States.

RADICAL MODEL

There is also a radical/conflict view of the justice system. Radicals reject the due process-crime control dichotomy. Instead they view the justice system as a "state-initiated and state-supported effort to rationalize mechanisms of social control."[31] The criminologist's role is to expose the aspects of the justice system that are designed to specifically control or exploit the laboring classes. Conflict criminologists call this **praxis**, the bringing about through writings, discussion, or social action a transformation of the current arrangements and relationships in society. It is difficult to see a direct connection between justice policy and conflict writing, but there is no question that greater sensitivity exists today than ever before about such issues as capitalist white-collar crime and the abuse of power. In the post-Watergate, post-ABSCAM society, where almost every political figure and business is suspected of bribery and tax evasion, and where police and correctional officials are subject to public scrutiny, it seems that some major conflict propositions are receiving ever-greater public interest.

JUSTICE MODEL

One of the newer models of criminal justice is known as the justice model.[32] First articulated by correctional expert David Fogel, the justice model contains elements of both liberal and conservative philosophies. Put another way, it is an essentially conservative view that is palatable to liberals because of its emphasis on fairness and due process.

Essentially, the justice model holds that it is futile to rehabilitate criminals because treatment programs are ineffective. Moreover, the needs of the rehabilitation models, which include individualized treatment and discretion, are basically an unfair violation of the constitutional right to equal protection. If two people commit the same crime but receive different sentences because one is receptive to treatment and the other not, the consequence is a sense of injustice in the criminal justice system and inmate anger at those who placed them in an institution. Beyond these problems, justice advocates find fault with both crime control and rehabilitation because they depend on predicting what an offender will do in the future when deciding what to do with them in the present.

As an alternative, the justice model calls for fairness in criminal procedure. This means **flat** or **determinate sentencing** models, in which all offenders in a particular crime category would receive the same prison sentence. Furthermore, prisons would be viewed as places of just and evenhanded punishment and not rehabilitation. Parole would be abolished to avoid the discretionary unfairness associated with that mechanism of early release.

The justice model has had an important influence on criminal justice policy making. Some states have adopted flat sentencing statutes and have limited the use of paroles. There is a trend toward giving prison sentences because people deserve punishment rather than because the sentence will deter or rehabilitate them.

Criminal Justice and Victims

One of the most significant criminal justice issues to surface in recent years is the concern for the victims of crime.[33] Within the last decade, criminal justice experts and legal commentators have pointed out that the crime victim often suffers as a result of the criminal action. Such harm generally revolves around financial problems, mental stress, and physical hardship. Assisting the victim in dealing with these problems has become the responsibility of society and, specifically, the criminal justice system. Law enforcement agencies, courts, and correctional systems have come to realize that due process and human rights exist both for the defendant and for the victim of criminal behavior.

During the mid-1960s the Department of Justice produced crime victim surveys which found that more crime exists than originally thought because much crime goes unreported. In addition, these surveys found that victims of crime had negative attitudes as a result of insensitive treatment received from the criminal justice process.[34] Consequently, the Justice Department provided research funds for victim-witness programs, which identified the needs of victims and witnesses who were involved in a criminal incident. The plight of the victim has thus been identified and has today become an even greater concern of the public and the justice system.

Because of concern over the effect of violent personal crime, President Ronald Reagan created a Task Force on Victims of Crime in 1982.[35] This group undertook an extensive study on crime victimization in America and determined how victims of crime could be given assistance. It found that crime victims had been transformed into a group of citizens burdened by a justice system that had been designed to protect them. Their participation both as victims and as witnesses was often overlooked, and concern for the defendant was given greater emphasis. The task force suggested that a balance be achieved between recognizing the rights of the victim and providing due process for the defendant. Its most significant recommendation was that the Sixth Amendment to the Constitution be augmented by a statement that says: "In every criminal prosecution, the victim shall have the right to be present and to be heard at all critical stages of the judicial proceedings."[36] Other recommendations involving victims and witnesses of crime included providing for protection of witnesses and victims from intimidation, requiring restitution in criminal cases, developing guidelines for fair treatment of crime victims and witnesses, and expanding programs of victim compensation.[37]

One primary concern of victim advocates has been for crime victim compensation programs created by legislation. In recent years, thirty-six states and the federal government have enacted crime victim compensation programs. As a result of such legislation, the victim ordinarily receives compensation from the state to pay for damages associated with the crime. Rarely are two compensation schemes alike, however, and many state programs suffer from lack of adequate funding and proper organization within the criminal justice system. However, the victim assistance projects that have been developed do seek to help the victim learn about victim compensation services and related programs.[38]

In addition to victim compensation and victim service programs, some criminal justice practitioners suggest that, under the Constitution, victims also have designated rights that are not being provided them. Frank Carrington suggests that the crime victim has rights that should insure basic services within the criminal justice system.[39] According to Carrington, just as the offender has the right to counsel and a fair trial, so society also has the obligation to ensure basic rights for law-abiding citizens. These rights range from adequate protection under the law from violent crimes to victim compensation and assistance from the criminal justice system.

In addition to relying on the justice system for aid and compensation, it has become common for victims to take matters into their own hands by bringing civil actions against those who victimized them. For example, the widow of the aspiring actor killed by Jack Henry Abbot, author of *In the Belly of the Beast,* sued to collect proceeds of his book sales under a New York law that prevents felons from cashing in on their crimes through book and movie sales (known as the Son of Sam law, it was created to prevent the mass murderer from collecting on his fame).[40] In a more recent incident, a Boston jury ordered a doctor to pay $4 million in civil damages to a woman he had raped.[41] Though most offenders do not have the financial ability to pay judgments, some victims simply want to feel they did their part to seek retribution and justice. Others will go after third parties indirectly responsible for the incident, such as a building security company that was negligent in its duties.

In sum, both government programs and individual initiatives have increased the protection and services given victims of crime.

Criminal Justice in the 1980s

The various philosophies of justice compete today for dominance in the criminal justice system. Each has supporters who lobby diligently for their positions. At the time of this writing, it seems apparent that the crime control/justice model views have captured the support of legislators and the general public. There is a growing emphasis on protection of the public, supplemented with fairness for the criminal.

But this is not to say that the other views of justice have been abandoned. Police, courts, and correctional agencies still supply a wide range of treatment alternatives to criminal offenders at all stages of the justice system. Whenever possible, especially in the juvenile system, offenders are given the least restrictive alternative, an offshoot of the noninterventionist view.

Similarly, the radical viewpoint has helped shift public focus onto corrupt practices and unfair procedures in the justice system. Are police too harsh in dealing with the underprivileged? Is there a disproportionate number of minorities in prison and on death row? These views also fit well with due process advocates, who are also determined to root out injustice in the justice system.

It is too easy to postulate that the justice system will continue to be dominated by conservative thinkers. If the crime rate continues to decline, there may be growing support for get-tough, firm-but-fair policies. On the other hand, the call for punitive treatment for serious, chronic offenders will open the door for greater reliance on treatment and limited intervention for nonviolent, nonchronic of-fenders. Consequently, rehabilitation efforts may actually increase in the years ahead.

Summary

Criminal justice refers to the formal processes and institutions that have been established to apprehend, try, punish, and treat law violators. The major com-ponents of the criminal justice system are the police, courts, and correctional agencies. Police maintain public order, deter crime, and apprehend law violators. The courts are charged with determining the criminal liability of accused offenders brought before them and dispensing fair and effective sanctions to those found guilty of crime. Corrections agencies provide postadjudicatory care to offenders who are sentenced by the courts to confinement or community supervision. Dis-satisfaction with traditional forms of corrections has spurred the development of community-based facilities and work-release and furlough programs. There are about 55,000 justice-related agencies in the United States. About 20,000 of them are police-related and 25,000 are court-related; 9,000 are correctional agencies. They employ about 1.2 million people and cost taxpayers about $30 billion per year.

Justice can also be conceived of as a process through which offenders flow. The justice process begins with an initial contact by a police agency and proceeds through investigation and police custody, early trial and trial stages, and correc-tional system processing. At any stage of the process, the offender can be excused because a lack of evidence exists, the case is trivial, or a decision maker simply decides to discontinue interest in the case.

Procedures, policies, and practices employed within the criminal justice system are scrutinized by the courts to make sure they do not violate the guidelines set down by the first ten amendments to the Constitution. If a violation occurs, the defendant can appeal the case and seek to overturn the conviction. Among the rights that must be honored are freedom from illegal searches and seizures and treatment with overall fairness and due process.

Several different philosophies or perspectives dominate the justice process. One is the crime control model, which asserts that the goals of justice are protection of the public and incapacitation of known offenders. In contrast, the due process model emphasizes liberal principles such as legal rights and procedural fairness for the offender. The rehabilitation model views the justice system as a wise and caring parent; the interactionist perspective calls for a minimum of interference in of-fenders' lives; the radical approach tries to expose the capitalist tendencies of the justice system; and the justice model calls for fair, equal treatment for all offenders.

Notes

1 National Advisory Commission on Criminal Justice Standards and Goals, *A National Strategy to Reduce Crime* (Washington, D.C.: Government Printing Office, 1973), p. 41.

2 Daniel Skoler, "Antidote for the Non-System: State Criminal Justice Superagencies," *State Government* 46 (1976): 2.

3 Richter Moore, "The Criminal Justice Non-System," in *Order under Law*, ed. B. Cul-bertson and M. Tezak (Prospect Heights, Ill.: Waveland Press, 1981), pp. 40–48.

4 See Albert Reiss, *Police and the Public* (New Haven, Conn.: Yale University Press, 1972).

5 American Bar Association, *Standards Relating to the Urban Police Function* (New York: Institute of Judicial Administration, 1973), Standard 2.2, p. 9.

6 See Peter Manning and John Van Mannen, eds., *Policing: A View from the Streets* (Santa Monica, Calif.: Goodyear Publishing, 1978).

7 Kenneth L. Davis, *Police Discretion* (St. Paul, Minn.: West Publishing Company, 1975).

8 See Donald Newman, *Conviction: The Determination of Guilt or Innocence without Trial* (Boston, Mass.: Little, Brown, 1966).

9 "The Legal Origins of Probation," *Probation and Related Measures* (New York: United Nations, Department of Social Affairs, 1951).

10 See Charles L. Chute and Marjorie Bell, *Crime, Courts and Probation* (New York: Macmillan, 1956).

11 Edwin Powers, *The Basic Structure of the Administration of Criminal Justice in Massachusetts* (Boston: Massachusetts Correctional Association, 1973), chap. 6.

12 "Inmates of Suffolk County Jail v. Eisenstadt," *Prison Law Reporter* 2 (July 1973):389–431.

13 National Advisory Commission on Criminal Justice Standards and Goals, *Corrections* (Washington, D.C.: Government Printing Office, 1973), p. 389.

14 Maine Revised Statistics Ann., Title 17-A, S. 1201.

15 This section is adapted from Department of Justice, *Justice Agencies in the United States* (Washington, D.C.: Government Printing Office, 1981), pp. vii–21.

16 Herbert L. Packer, *The Limits of the Criminal Sanction* (Stanford, Calif.: Stanford University Press, 1968), p. 159.

17 New York Criminal Code, Section 177, "Arrest by an Officer, Without a Warrant."

18 *Black's Law Dictionary*, 4th ed. rev. (St. Paul, Minn.: West Publishing Company, 1967), p. 590.

19 See Joseph J. Senna, "Changes in Due Process of Law," *Social Work* 19 (1974):319.

20 342 U.S. 165 (1952).

21 323 U.S. 383 (1914).

22 367 U.S. 643 (1969).

23 D. H. Oaks, "Studying the Exclusionary Rule in Search and Seizure," *University of Chicago Law Review* 37 (Summer 1970):756.

24 104 S.Ct. 3405 (1984).

25 104 S.Ct. 2424 (1984).

26 U.S. Department of Justice, *The Effects of the Exclusionary Rule: A Study in California* (Washington, D.C.: U.S. Government Printing Office, 1982); Sheldon Krantz, Bernard Gilman, Charles Benda, Carol Rogoff Halst and Gail Nadworny, *Police Policymaking* (Lexington, Mass.: Lexington Books, 1979); Brian Forst, Judith Lucianovic and Sarah Cox, *What Happens After Arrest* (Washington, D.C.: Inslaw, 1977).

27 Packer, *Limits of the Criminal Sanction*.

28 Edwin M. Lemert, "The Juvenile Court—Quest and Realities," in President's Commission on Law Enforcement and the Administration of Justice, *Task Force Report: Juvenile Delinquency and Youth Crime* (Washington, D.C.: U.S. Government Printing Office, 1967).

29 Edwin Schur, *Radical Nonintervention* (Englewood Cliffs, N.J.: Prentice-Hall, 1973).

30 James Austin and Barry Krisberg, "The Unmet Promise of Alternatives to Incarceration," *Crime and Delinquency* 28 (1982):3–19; for an alternative view, see Arnold Binder and Gilbert Geis, "Ad Populum Argumentation in Criminology: Juvenile Diversion as Rhetoric," *Criminology* 30 (1984):309–333.

31 I. Taylor, P. Walton and J. Young, *Critical Criminology* (London: Routledge and Kegan Paul, 1975), p. 24.

32 David Fogel, *. . . We Are the Living Proof* (Cincinnati, Ohio: Anderson, 1975). See also Fogel, *Justice as Fairness* (Cincinnati: Anderson, 1980).

33 See generally William F. McDonald, ed., *Criminal Justice and the Victim: An Introduction* (Beverly Hills, Calif.: Sage Publications, 1976); and American Bar Association, *Reducing Victim-Witness Compensation* (Chicago: American Bar Association, 1979).

34 Peter Finn and Beverly Lee, *Serving Two Masters: The Issue for Victim Assistance* (Cambridge, Mass.: Abt Associates, 1981).

35 U.S. Department of Justice, *Report of the President's Task Force on Victims of Crime* (Washington, D.C.: U.S. Government Printing Office, 1983).

36 Ibid., p. 115.

37 Ibid., pp. 2–10; and "Review on Victims—Witnesses of Crime," *Massachusetts Lawyers Weekly*, 25 April 1983, p. 26.

38 Randall Schmidt, "Crime Victim Compensation Legislation: A Comparative Study," *Victimology* (1980) 5:428–37.

39 See Frank Carrington, "Victim's Rights Litigation: A Wave of the Future," in *Perspectives on Crime Victims*, ed. Burt Galaway and Joe Hudson (St. Louis: C.V. Mosby Co., 1981).

40 Bennett Beach, "Getting Status and Getting Even," *Time*, 7 February 1983, p. 40.

41 United Press International, "Doctor is Told to Pay $4 Million in Rape Case," *Omaha World Herald*, 17 February 1985, p. 17A.

15 | The Police

CHAPTER OUTLINE

Introduction

History of Police

Eighteenth-Century Developments

The American Colonial Experience

Early Police Agencies

Reform Movements

Professionalism

Technological Changes

Law Enforcement Agencies

Federal Law Enforcement

County Law Enforcement

State Police

Local Police

Police Role

Police Functions

Patrol Function

Investigation Function

Other Police Functions

Police and the Rule of Law

Custodial Interrogation

Search and Seizure

Warrantless Search

What Constitutes a Search?

Current Issues in Policing

Police Personality and Subculture

Discretion

Police Discrimination?

Higher Education and Police Effectiveness

Women and Minority Police Officers

Police Violence

Summary

KEY TERMS

constable

shire reeve

watch system

justice of the peace

Sir Robert Peel

Wickersham Commission

August Vollmer

sheriff

patrol

walking the beat

aggressive preventive patrol

internal affairs division

Kansas City Study

team policing

foot patrol

detective

sting

selective enforcement

Miranda warning

inevitable discovery rule

probable cause

particularity

totality of the circumstances

stop and frisk

blue curtain

discretion

selective enforcement

Sherman Report

deadly force

Introduction

The police are the gatekeepers of the criminal justice process. They initiate contact with law violators and decide whether to formally arrest them and begin their journey through the criminal justice system, settle the issue in a nonformal way (such as by issuing a warning), or simply use their discretion and take no action at all. The strategic position of police agents, their visibility and contact with the public, and their use of weapons and arrest power have kept them in the forefront of public thought for most of the twentieth century.

In the late 1960s and early 1970s, great issue was taken with the existing political and social role of the police. Critics viewed police agencies as racially biased organizations that harassed minority citizens, controlled political dissidents, and generally seemed out of touch with the changing times. The major issue of the day appeared to be controlling the abuse of police power and making police agencies more responsible to public control.

During this period, major efforts were undertaken in the nation's largest cities to curb police power. In chapter 11, the work of the Knapp Commission, which investigated police corruption in New York, was discussed. Police review boards designed to allow members of the community to oversee police policies and operations and investigate citizen complaints were set up in cities such as Philadelphia, New York, and Detroit.

Since the mid-1970s, change has occurred in the overt relationship between police and the public. Police departments have become more sensitive about their public image. Internal programs have been created to improve relations between police and community and help police officers on the beat to be more sensitive to the needs of the public and deal better with the stress of their jobs.

Nonetheless, major city police departments continue to be the subject of public scrutiny. For example, scandals have shaken public confidence in three of the nation's top police departments: San Francisco, New York, and Philadelphia.[1] In San Francisco, the police department was embarrassed when it was revealed that a prostitute was hired to perform a sex act on a handcuffed, blindfolded recruit during a graduation party (an incident later depicted on the "Hill Street Blues" television show). A few months later, plainclothes officers roughed up fifty bar patrons during a search for evidence. An officer feloniously assaulted a homosexual after dragging him off a city bus.

The problems in New York were more serious and received greater national publicity. In October 1984, a police officer was indicted after the shotgun slaying of a sixty-six-year-old black woman whom he was trying to evict from her apartment. In February 1985, transit police officers were indicted for beating to death a young black man taken into custody for painting graffiti on the subway. Later, police in the 106th precinct were charged with using 50,000 volt electric stun guns to obtain confessions from three men accused of selling small amounts of marijuana. This final scandal rocked the police department, prompting the commissioner to suspend or dismiss several high-ranking officers. In each of the New York cases the victims were black and the police officers white, leaving the department open to charges of racism.

In Philadelphia, charges of corruption resulted in the firing of more than 20 officers in 1984. Then in May 1985, the country was startled to find that the Philadelphia police had used a bomb to root out a group of political extremists who had barricaded themselves in their headquarters. The resulting fire destroyed 53 other houses; left 240 people homeless; killed 11 people, including 4 children; and cost at least $8 million dollars.[2]

In the 1980s there is continuing concern over the police use of force and police treatment of citizens. At the same time, people are more concerned than ever with increasing police effectiveness—the public wants its police agencies to control the law-violating members of society. Consequently, questions are being asked about the type of officer employed in U.S. police agencies. Is a college education necessary? Should the hiring of members of minority groups and women be a top priority? Other important questions have been raised about what police officers actually do. Are they spending their time productively? How do they make decisions? How do they treat citizens? Another concern is police officers' personality and style. Is there a "cop personality," and if so, does it influence the way police officers carry out their daily activities? Thus, although areas of concern have changed somewhat, interest in policing has not abated.

This chapter reviews the function and role of police in U.S. society. First, the history of police will be briefly discussed. Then, the role and structure of police agencies will be discussed. Finally, some of the critical issues facing the police in society will be analyzed.

History of Police

As was the case with the criminal law, the origin of U.S. police agencies can be traced back to early English society.[3]

Before the Norman Conquest, there was no regular English police force. Every man living in the villages scattered throughout the countryside was responsible for aiding his neighbors and protecting the settlement from thieves and marauders. This was known as the *pledge system.* As reviewed in chapter 2, people were grouped into a collective of ten families called a *tithing* and entrusted with policing their own minor problems. Ten tithings were grouped into a *hundred,* whose affairs were supervised by a **constable** appointed by the local nobleman. The constable, who might be considered the first real police officer, dealt with more serious breaches of the law.[4]

Later, the hundreds were grouped into *shires* resembling the counties of today. The **shire reeve** was appointed by the crown to supervise a certain territory and assure the local nobleman that order would be kept. The shire reeve, forerunner of today's sheriff, soon began to pursue and apprehend law violators as part of his duties.

In the thirteenth century, during the reign of King Edward I, the **watch system** was created to help protect property in England's larger cities and towns. Watchmen patrolled at night and helped protect against robberies, fires, and disturbances. They reported to the area constable, who became the primary metropolitan law enforcement agent. In larger cities such as London, the watchmen were organized within church parishes; those applying for the job were usually members of the parish they protected.

In 1326, the office of **justice of the peace** was created to assist the shire reeve in controlling the county. Eventually, the justices took on judicial functions in addition to their primary duty as peacekeeper. A system developed in which the local constable became the operational assistant to the justice of the peace, supervising the night watchmen, investigating offenses, serving summonses, executing warrants, and securing prisoners. This working format helped delineate the relationship between police and the judiciary that has existed intact for five hundred years.

A turn-of-the-century Boston police force poses in a makeshift "motorized" machine gun carrier used during the May Day riots.

At first, the position of constable was an honorary one given to a respected person in the village or parish for a one-year period. Often, these men were wealthy merchants who had little time for their duties. It was common for them to hire assistants to help them fulfill their obligations, thereby creating another element of a paid police force. Thus, by the seventeenth century, the justice of the peace, the constable, his assistants, and the night watch formed the nucleus of the local metropolitan justice system. (The sheriff's duties lay outside the cities and towns.)

EIGHTEENTH-CENTURY DEVELOPMENTS

At the end of the eighteenth century, the industrial revolution lured thousands from the English countryside to work in the larger factory towns. The swelling population of urban poor, whose miniscule wages could hardly sustain them, heightened the need for police protection. In response to pressure from established citizens, the government passed statutes creating new police offices in London. These offices employed three justices of the peace who were each authorized to employ six paid constables. Law enforcement began to be more centralized and professional. However, many parishes still maintained their own foot patrols, horse patrols, and private investigators.

In 1829, **Sir Robert Peel**, England's Home Secretary, guided through Parliament an "Act for Improving the Police In and Near the Metropolis." The act established the first organized police force in London. Composed of over a thousand men, the London police force was structured along military lines. Its members wore a distinctive uniform and were led by two magistrates, who were later given the title of commissioner. However, the ultimate responsibility for the police fell to the Home Secretary and consequently the Parliament.

The London experiment proved so successful that the metropolitan police soon began sending aid to outlying areas that requested assistance in law enforcement matters. Another act of Parliament allowed justices of the peace to establish local police forces; by 1856, every borough and county in England was required to form its own police force.

THE AMERICAN COLONIAL EXPERIENCE

Law enforcement in colonial America paralleled the British model. In the colonies, the county sheriff became the most important law enforcement agent.[5] In addition to peacekeeping and crime fighting, these sheriffs collected taxes, supervised elections, and handled a great deal of other legal business.

The colonial sheriff did not patrol or seek out crime. Instead, he reacted to citizens' complaints and investigated crimes that had already occurred. His salary was related to his effectiveness. Sheriffs were paid by the fee system. They were given a fixed amount for every arrest made, subpoena served, or court appearance made. Unfortunately, their tax collecting chores were more lucrative than crime fighting; so law enforcement was not one of their primary concerns.

In the cities, law enforcement was the province of the town marshal, who was aided, often unwillingly, by a variety of constables, night watchmen, police justices, and city council members. However, local governments had little power of administration; and enforcement of the criminal law was largely an individual or community responsibility. Individual initiative was encouraged by the practice of offering rewards for the capture of felons.[6] If trouble arose, citizens might be called on to form a posse to chase offenders or break up an angry mob.

As the size of cities grew, it became exceedingly difficult for local leaders to step in and organize citizens' groups. Moreover, the early nineteenth century was an era of widespread urban unrest and mob violence. Local leaders began to realize that a more structured police function was needed to control demonstrators and keep peace.

EARLY POLICE AGENCIES

The modern police department was born out of urban mob violence, which wracked the nation's cities in the nineteenth century. Boston created the first formal U.S. police department in 1838. New York formed its police department in 1844; Philadelphia, in 1854. The new police departments replaced the night watch system and relegated constables and sheriffs to serving court orders and running the jail.

At first the urban police departments inherited the functions of the older institutions they replaced. For example, Boston police were charged with maintaining public health until 1853; in New York, the police were responsible for street sweeping until 1881.

Politics dominated the departments and determined the recruitment of new officers and promotion of supervisors. An individual with the right connections could be hired despite a lack of qualifications. "In addition to the pervasive brutality and corruption," writes one justice historian, Samuel Walker, "the police did little to effectively prevent crime or provide public services. . . . Officers were primarily tools of local politicians; they were not impartial and professional public servants."[7]

At mid-nineteenth century, the detective bureau was set up as part of the Boston police. Until then, "thief-taking" had been the province of amateur bounty hunters, who hired themselves out to victims for a price. When professional police departments replaced bounty hunters, the close working relationships that developed between police detectives and their underworld informants produced many scandals and consequently high personnel turnover.

Police during the nineteenth century were generally incompetent, corrupt, and disliked by the people they served. The police role was only minimally directed at law enforcement. Its primary function was serving as the enforcement arm of the reigning political power, protecting private property, and keeping control of the ever-rising numbers of foreign immigrants.

REFORM MOVEMENTS

Police agencies evolved slowly through the latter half of the nineteenth century. Uniforms were introduced in 1853 in New York. Technological innovations such as linking precincts to central headquarters by telegraph appeared in the 1850s; somewhat later, call boxes allowed patrolmen on the beat to communicate with their commanders. Nonpolice functions such as care of the streets began to be abandoned after the Civil War.

Despite any impetus toward improvement, big-city police were not respected by the public, were not successful in their role as crime stoppers, and were not involved in progressive activities. The control of police departments by local politicians impeded effective law enforcement and fostered an atmosphere of graft and corruption.

In an effort to control police corruption, civil leaders in some jurisdictions created police administrative boards to reduce the control over police exercised by local officials. These tribunals were given the responsibility to appoint police administrators and control police affairs. In many instances, these measures failed because the private citizens appointed to the review boards lacked expertise in the intricacies of police work.

Another reform movement was the takeover of some big-city police agencies by state legislators. Though police budgets were paid through local taxes, control of police was usurped by rural politicians in the state capitals. It was not until the first decades of the twentieth century that cities regained control of their police forces.

The Boston police strike of 1914 heightened interest in police reform. The strike was brought about by dissatisfaction with the status police officers held in society. While other professions were unionizing and increasing their standards of living, police salaries lagged behind. The Boston police officers' organization, the Boston Social Club, voted to become a union affiliated with the American Federation of Labor (AFL). The officers struck on 9 September 1914. Rioting and looting broke out, resulting in Governor Calvin Coolidge's mobilization of the state militia to take over the city. Public support turned against the police, and the strike was broken. Eventually, all the striking officers were fired and replaced by new recruits. The Boston police strike ended police unionism for decades and solidified power in the hands of reactionary, autocratic police administrators.

In the aftermath of the strike, crime commissions on the local, state, and national level began to investigate the extent of crime and the ability of the justice system to effectively deal with it. The **Wickersham Commission** was created by President Herbert Hoover to study police issues on a national scale. In its 1931 report, the commission found that the average police supervisor's term of office was too short and that his responsibility to political officials made his position insecure. The commission also disclosed a lack of effective, efficient, and honest patrolmen. It said that no intensive effort was being made to educate, train, and discipline prospective officers or to eliminate those who were incompetent. The Wickersham Commission found that, with few exceptions, police forces in cities with populations above 300,000 had neither adequate communications systems nor the equipment necessary to enforce the law effectively. The police task, according to the commission, was made much more difficult by the excessively rapid growth of U.S. cities in the past half-century and by the tendency of ethnic groups to retain their languages and customs in large cities. Finally, the commission said too many duties were cast upon each officer and patrolman.[8] The Missouri Crime Commission reported that in a typical U.S. city, the police were expected to be familiar with and enforce 30,000 federal, state, and local enactments.[9] However, with the onset of the Great Depression, justice reform became a less important issue than economic revival; and for many years, there was little change in the nature of policing.

PROFESSIONALISM

The onset of police professionalism might be traced to **August Vollmer**.[10] While serving as police chief of Berkeley, California, Vollmer instituted university training as an important part of his development of young officers. He also helped develop the School of Criminology at the University of California at Berkeley, which became the model of justice-related programs around the country.

Vollmer's disciples included O. W. Wilson, who pioneered the use of advanced training for officers when he took over and reformed the Wichita, Kansas, police department in 1928. Wilson also was instrumental in applying modern management and administrative techniques to policing. His text, *Police Administration*, became the single most influential work on the subject. Wilson eventually took over as dean of the Criminology School at Berkeley and ended his career in Chicago when Mayor Richard J. Daley asked him to take over and reform the Chicago police department in 1960.

Through the 1960s, police professionalism was interpreted as a tough, highly trained, rule-oriented law enforcement department organized along militaristic lines. The most respected department was in Los Angeles, under the leadership of its no-nonsense chief, William Parker. It is no mere coincidence that two of the most popular police television shows of the period, "Dragnet" and "Adam-12," stressed the high motivation, competence, and integrity of Los Angeles police officers.

The urban unrest of the late 1960s changed the course of police department development. Efforts were made to promote understanding between police and community, reduce police brutality, and recognize the stresses of police work. Efforts also were made, usually under court order, to add members of minority groups and women to police departments. The federal government's Law Enforcement Education Program (LEEP) encouraged officers to get college training. Rank-and-file patrol officers became dissatisfied with administration from the top down; consequently, local police unions were formed.

TECHNOLOGICAL CHANGES

Police agencies have also come to rely more heavily on technology. As a result of increasing professionalism, the ideal police officer came to be viewed as a product of the computer age, skilled in using the most advanced techniques to fight crime. A significant majority of funds went toward developing police hardware; in some quarters, technological advances were seen as the answer to the crime problem.[11]

Actually, the first technological breakthroughs in police operations came in the area of communications. In 1867 the first telegraph police boxes were installed; an officer could turn a key in a box and his location and number would automatically register at headquarters.

Additional technological advances were made in the area of transportation. The Detroit police department outfitted some of its patrol officers with bicycles in 1897. By 1913, the motorcycle was being employed by departments in the eastern part of the country. The first police car was used in Akron, Ohio, in 1910; the police wagon became popular in Cincinnati, Ohio, in 1912.

In recent years, the use of technology in police work has markedly increased, prompted in part by World War II scientific breakthroughs and discoveries and the infusion of federal support into scientific inquiry in the law enforcement field. In no area have these changes been more apparent than in electronic data processing. In 1964, for example, only one city, St. Louis, had a police computer system; by 1968, ten states and fifty cities had state-level criminal justice information systems. One example of computer use is the Police Information Network (PIN), which electronically links the ninety-three independent law enforcement agencies in the San Francisco area to enable them to share information. On a broader jurisdictional level, the FBI implemented the National Crime Information Center (NCIC) in 1967. This system makes possible the rapid collection and retrieval of data about persons wanted for crimes anywhere in the fifty states. In all, it is estimated that over four hundred computerized information systems dealing with criminal justice matters are operational in the United States; of these, 41 percent serve the needs of police agencies on both local and state levels.

An example of computer use can be found in Miami, Florida, where a computerized system is being used to electronically scan fingerprints found at the scenes of crimes and then cross-reference them with those on file. A similar system in Los Angeles helped capture the serial killer known as the "Night Stalker".

Despite technological and professional achievements, the effectiveness of the police is still questioned, their ability to control crime still considered problematic. Critics argue that plans to increase police professionalism place too much emphasis on hardware and not enough on police-citizen cooperation.

Law Enforcement Agencies

Law enforcement duties are distributed across local, county, state, and federal jurisdictions. This section discusses the role of each element of this complex system.

FEDERAL LAW ENFORCEMENT

The federal government maintains about fifty organizations that are involved in law enforcement duties. Some of the most important of these are discussed below.

The Federal Bureau of Investigation. In 1870, the U.S. Department of Justice became involved in actual policing when the Attorney General hired investigators to enforce the Mann Act (which prohibited white slavery). In 1908, this group of investigators was formally made a distinct branch of the government, the Bureau of Investigation; in the 1930s, the agency was reorganized into the Federal Bureau of Investigation (FBI) under the direction of J. Edgar Hoover.

Today's FBI is not a police agency but an investigative agency, with jurisdiction over all matters in which the United States is, or may be, an interested party. It limits its jurisdiction to federal laws, including all federal statutes not specifically assigned to other agencies.[12] These include statutes dealing with espionage, sabotage, treason, civil rights violations, the murder and assault of federal officers, mail fraud, robbery and burglary of federally insured (FDIC) banks, kidnapping, and interstate transportation of stolen vehicles and property.

The FBI offers important services to local law enforcement agencies. Its identification division, established in 1924, collects and maintains a vast fingerprint file that can be used for identification purposes by local police agencies. Its sophisticated crime laboratory, established in 1932, aids local police in testing and identifying evidence such as hairs, fibers, blood, tire tracks, and drugs.

The Uniform Crime Report is another service of the FBI. As discussed in chapter 3, the UCR is an annual compilation of data on crimes reported to local police agencies, arrests, police killed or wounded in action, and so on. Finally, the FBI's National Crime Information Center is a computerized network linked to local police departments by terminals. Information on stolen vehicles, wanted persons, stolen guns, and so on is made readily available to local law enforcement agencies.

For many years, the FBI was considered by many to be the elite U.S. law enforcement agency. Its agents were considered incorruptible, highly trained, and professional. FBI agents always got their man, whether it was gangsters of the 1930s such as John Dillinger, Nazi saboteurs during World War II, or Russian secret agents during the Cold War. However, during the era of political suspicion that followed the Watergate break-ins, information came to light that tarnished the agency's image. J. Edgar Hoover was portrayed as placing undue emphasis on controlling radical groups and harassing black civil rights leaders. One famous incident was the bugging of Martin Luther King's hotel rooms. The FBI's COINTELPRO (counterintelligence program) used wiretaps, opened mail, and burglarized the offices of radical political groups.[13] After a period of turmoil and internal unrest, the FBI, under the direction of William Webster, seems to have resumed its place as the nation's most respected law enforcement agency.

Other Federal Agencies. The U.S. government's interest in drug trafficking can be traced back to 1914, when the Harrison Act established federal jurisdiction over the supply and use of narcotics. Several drug enforcement units, including the Bureau of Narcotics and Dangerous drugs, were originally charged with enforcing drug laws. However, in 1973, these agencies were combined to form the Drug Enforcement Administration (DEA). Agents of the DEA assist local and state authorities in their investigation of illegal drug use and carry out independent surveillance and enforcement activities to control the importation of narcotics.

Federal law enforcement agencies under the direction of the Justice Department include the U.S. marshals, the Immigration and Naturalization Service, and the Organized Crime and Racketeering Unit. The U.S. marshals are court officers who help implement federal court rulings, transport prisoners, and enforce court orders. The Immigration and Naturalization Service is responsible for administration and deportation of illegal aliens and naturalization of aliens lawfully present in the

United States. This service also maintains border patrols to prevent illegal aliens from entering the United States. The Organized Crime and Racketeering Unit, under the direction of the U.S. Attorney General, has coordinated federal efforts to curtail organized crime and to contain members of the alleged national criminal syndicate.

The Treasury Department maintains the Alcohol, Tobacco, and Firearms Bureau, which has jurisdiction over sales and distribution of illegal firearms, explosives, and liquor and untaxed cigarettes.

The Internal Revenue Service, established in 1862, enforces violations of income, excise, stamp, and other tax laws. Its Intelligence Division actively pursues gamblers, narcotics dealers, and other violators who do not report their illegal financial gains as taxable income.

The Customs Bureau guards points of entry into the United States and prevents smuggling of contraband into (or out of) the country.

The Secret Service, an arm of the Treasury Department, was originally charged with enforcing laws against counterfeiting. Today the Secret Service is also accountable for the protection on the president and the vice-president and their families, presidential candidates, and former presidents.

COUNTY LAW ENFORCEMENT

The county police department is an independent agency whose senior officer, the **sheriff**, is usually an elected political official. The county sheriff's role has evolved from that of the early English shire reeve, whose main duty was to assist the royal judges in trying prisoners and enforcing the law outside of cities. From the time of U.S. westward expansion until municipal departments were developed, the sheriff often acted as the sole legal authority over vast territories.

The duties of a county sheriff's department vary according to the size and degree of development of the county where it is located. Officials within the department may serve as coroners, tax assessors, tax collectors, overseers of highways and bridges, custodians of the country treasury, keepers of the county jail, court attendants, and executors of criminal and civil processes; in years past, sheriffs' offices also conducted executions. Many of the sheriff's law enforcement functions today are carried out only in incorporated areas within a county or in response to city departments' requests for aid in such matters as patrol or investigation.

Probably the most extensive sheriff's department is located in Los Angeles county. This department provides services to over one million people and has service contracts with thirty-two cities.[14] It maintains a modern communication system and a police laboratory, in addition to performing standard enforcement functions.

STATE POLICE

The Texas Rangers, organized in 1835, are considered the first state police force. However, the Rangers were more a quasi-military force that supported the Texas state militia than a true law enforcement body. The first true state police forces emerged at the turn of the twentieth century, with Pennsylvania's leading the way.

The impetus for creating state police agencies can be traced both to the low regard of the public for crime fighting ability of local police agencies and the increasingly greater mobility of law violators. Using automobiles, thieves could strike at will and be out of the jurisdiction of local police before an investigation could be mounted. Therefore, a law enforcement agency with statewide jurisdiction was needed. Also, state police gave governors a powerful enforcement arm that was under their personal control and not that of city politicians.

Today the major role of state police is controlling traffic on the highway system, helping trace stolen automobiles, and aiding in disturbances and crowd control. In states with large and powerful county sheriff's departments, the state police function is usually restricted to highway patrol. In others, where the county sheriff's law enforcement role is limited, state police usually maintain a more active investigative and enforcement role.

LOCAL POLICE

Metropolitan police agencies make up the vast majority of the law enforcement community's members. They range in size from New York's, which employs around 23,000, to several rural departments, which maintain a staff of a single police officer.[15]

Most larger urban departments are independent agencies operating without specific administrative control from any higher governmental authority. They are organized at the executive level of government. It is therefore common for the city mayor (or the equivalent) to control the hiring and firing of the police chief and consequently determine departmental policies.

Most municipal departments are organized in a military way; they often use military terms to designate seniority (sergeant, lieutenant, captain).

The organization of a typical metropolitan police department is illustrated in figure 15.1. This complex structure is a function of the multiplicity of roles that police are entrusted with. Among the daily activities of police agencies are included:

- Identifying criminal suspects.
- Investigating crimes.
- Apprehending offenders and participating in their trials.
- Deterring crime through patrol.
- Aiding individuals in danger or in need of assistance; providing emergency services.
- Resolving conflict and keeping the peace.
- Maintaining a sense of community security.
- Keeping automobile traffic and pedestrian movement efficient.
- Promoting civil order.
- Operating and administering the police department.

POLICE ROLE

If you watch television and movies, it is easy to see why many people believe that the major police role is law enforcement. However, research conducted in the 1960s and 1970s showed that very little of a police officer's time was spent on "crime-fighting duties";[16] the great bulk of effort was devoted to what has been described as *order maintenance*, or peacekeeping.[17] James Q. Wilson's pioneering work, *Varieties of Police Behavior*, views the major police role to be "handling the situation."[18] Wilson believes that police encounter many troubling incidents that need some sort of "fixing up." Enforcing the law might be one tool a police officer

FIGURE 15.1

Organization of a
Metropolitan Police
Department

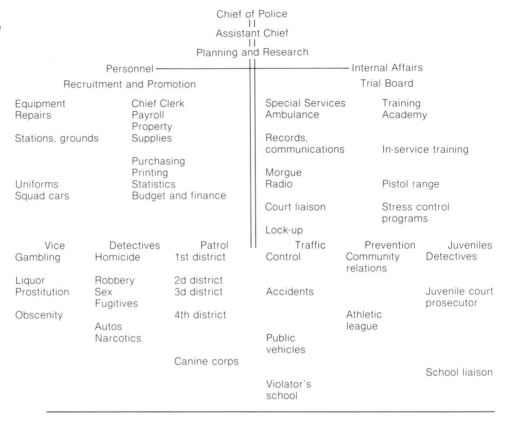

SOURCE. Adapted from Clarence Schrag, *Crime & Justice American Style,* National Institute of Mental Health (Washington, D.C.: U.S. Government Printing Office, 1971).

uses; threat, coercion, sympathy, understanding, and apathy might be others. Most important is "keeping things under control so that there are no complaints that he is doing nothing or that he is doing too much."

The peacekeeping role of the police has been documented by several different studies. For example, Richard Sykes and Edward Brent analyzed five thousand encounters between civilians and police in a mid-sized U.S. city. They focused on the dynamic nature of police/citizen encounters.[19] Their main conclusion is that police function essentially as order keeping, dispute settling agents of public health and safety. Just being there to handle the situation is the officers' main task; the better they are at it, the less likely they are to resort to violence. Unfortunately, police have a tendency to dominate actions and sometimes disregard the feelings of those who need their aid.

During the 1970s, considerable attention was paid to the conflict theory proposition—that the police are agents of the economic and social groups that control society. Writing in 1977, Peter Manning claimed:

> There is little question that public policy is everywhere shaped by economic elites and disproportionately reflects their political and social interests. The police, as an instrumentality of public policy, are no exception. Policing cannot be other than a

reflection of those interests that define the nature of the legitimacy on which they draw. [20]

Thus, the police officer's traditional role as law enforcer and protector of the public was challenged by various sources.

Today the police officer's role is recognized as being multidimensioned. Police officers are required to be keepers of the peace, investigators of crime, emergency medical technicians, traffic controllers, and symbols of public morality and stability. The burdens of police work have helped set law enforcement officers outside the mainstream of society and encouraged the development of a police subculture marked by insulation from the outside world and a code of secrecy. [21]

"Broken Windows." In a highly regarded article, James Q. Wilson and George Kelling call for a return to a nineteenth-century style of policing in which police maintained a presence in the community, walked beats, got to know citizens, and inspired feelings of public safety. [22] Wilson and Kelling ask police administrators to get their officers out of depersonalized patrol cars. Instead of deploying police on the basis of crime rates or in areas where citizens make the most calls for help, police administrators should station their men where they can do the most to promote public confidence and elicit citizen cooperation. Community preservation, public safety, and order maintenance—not crime fighting—should become the primary focus of police:

> *Just as physicians now recognize the importance of fostering health rather than simply treating illness, so the police—and the rest of us—ought to recognize the importance of maintaining intact communities without broken windows.* [23]

Of course, not all police experts agree that a return to the police officer of yesteryear—more a watchman than a crime fighter—is the panacea it is thought to be by Wilson and Kelling. For example, Samuel Walker disputes Wilson and Kelling's analysis on the grounds that they misread police history. [24] First, though the use of patrol cars may have produced some depersonalization of the police since the 1930s, this has been counteracted by the modern communication devices that have helped bring police and the community closer together. For example, use of the telephone allows the police to more easily "enter" people's residences and become involved in their personal problems. Second, the crime control orientation of the police has been exaggerated. In reality, police have acted as peacekeepers during most of the twentieth century. Third, there is little evidence that, in the "good old days," police enjoyed political legitimacy among the masses. Actually, they rarely enjoyed political acceptance during the nineteenth and early twentieth centuries. Finally, the watchman style proposed by Wilson and Kelling is essentially ineffective and does not serve neighborhood needs. Walker concludes that the police are actually incapable of improving the community's perceptions of public safety.

Despite such criticism, Wilson's call for a return to an earlier model of policing has had some effect on police managers. Later in this chapter we will review some recent foot patrol experiments, which are a response to a more personalized style of policing.

The Role of Police in the 1980s. The "broken windows" argument highlights the dilemma facing American police agencies in the 1980s. While the sixties and seventies could be described as an era of public mistrust of the police role, the eighties have seen public opinion shift toward a more sympathetic view of policing. But while crime rates decline, frustration grows over police ineffectiveness, police misuse of force, and so on. The public seems to want a return of the incorruptible, tough supercop; people, even presidents, cheer when Clint Eastwood's Lt. Harry Callahan tells the bad guy, "Make my day." Yet, police experts realize the limited capability police have to affect the crime rate. They are simply more effective at peacekeeping and maintaining order than at crime control.

So, to meet the public's need for safety and control, police agencies have turned to programs featuring greater visibility and citizen contact; that is, foot patrols. Even if the police cannot make the public safer, they can try to make them feel safer. This approach is a far cry from the 1960s, when liberal/radical thinkers decried police intrusion into their lives. Instead of depicting the police as agents of state control, influential criminologists like Wilson can portray them as benign public servants whose goal is community safety.

Police Functions

Numerous major functions are associated with the police role. This section will discuss a few of the most critical ones.

PATROL FUNCTION

Patrol entails police officers' visible presence on the streets and public places of their jurisdiction. The purpose of patrol is to deter crime, maintain order, enforce laws, and aid in service functions such as emergency medical care. There is a large variety of patrol techniques. In early police forces, foot patrol was almost exclusively used. Each officer had a particular area, or *beat,* to walk; the police officer was the symbol of state authority in that area. The beat officer dispensed "street justice," and some became infamous for their use of clubs or nightsticks.

When the old-style beat officer needed assistance, he would pound the pavement with his stick to summon his colleagues from nearby areas. Later, call boxes were introduced so the officer could communicate more easily with headquarters. Today, the introduction of patrol cars as well as motorcycles, helicopters, and other types of mechanized transportation has all but ended **walking the beat**. Though the patrol car allows the police to supervise more territory with fewer officers, it has removed and isolated patrol officers from the communities they serve. Some experts argue that this impersonal style of enforcement has worsened relations between police and community. In some communities, **aggressive preventive patrol**, designed to suppress crime before it occurs, has heightened tensions between the police and the minority community.

Considerable tension is involved in patrolling, especially in high-crime areas, where police feel they are open targets. The patrol officer must learn to work the street, taking whatever action is necessary to control the situation and no more.

When patrol officers take inappropriate action, or when their behavior results in violence or death, they are subject to intense scrutiny by public agencies and may be subject to disciplinary measures from the police department's **internal affairs division**. Thus, patrol officers are expected to make mature and reasoned decisions while facing a constant flow of people in emotional crisis.

A patrol officer's job, then, is extremely demanding; at the same time, it is often unrewarding and unappreciated. It is not surprising that the attitudes of police

On Patrol

Johnathan Rubenstein described the working habits, beliefs, and lifestyle of police offi-cers in his well-received book, City Police. *This excerpt describes the skills that go into patrol work.*

A patrolman approaches people in a variety of situa-tions. He comes upon them driving and walking; he sees them in places where he has responded to calls for help; he is approached by strangers for advice and aid, goes with them into houses to break up fights and settle ac-counts. He enters crowded public places and deserted private ones, looking for the source of trouble that has brought him there. Since he must constantly confront people under widely differing circumstances, he cannot develop a single approach to all situations. He behaves differently when he is working alone than when he is with a partner who understands his manner. If he is a fright-ened man unwilling to take the easy way out of his di-lemma by resigning or feigning work, he can allow the fears that assail even the bravest to control him. He may approach every situation with his holster unsnapped and his stick poised, but his colleagues will shun him and he cannot long remain on the job, although he may stay for enough time to cause pain and grief to himself, his colleagues, and whoever has the misfortune to cross his path.

He must learn to control his fears and anxiety by looking for signs of danger in the places and people he approaches; he must learn to examine people for signs of resistance, flight, and threat, to limit their chances of hurting him or creating situations he cannot control or can control only with the use of force which is inappro-priate to the circumstances. He must learn to use his body as a tool, positioning himself in an unobtrusive manner so that he is always able to retaliate with force

if attacked, while not giving a threatening and provoking appearance. He must learn to use the powerful weapons he carries, so they will do what they are supposed to do and no more. He must learn when to hit people and when not to hit them. He must also learn how to establish and express his authority by cajoling, requesting, threat-ening, "bullshitting them," as patrolmen say, to avoid using force. He must learn to use is body to express with his whole self the authority represented by the ap-pearance he presents; he must learn to use it as a weap-on when the occasion demands. He must learn when to mobilize his physical resources and when to let them slumber, allowing his legal power to act for him. In all of his actions he must learn to acquire a quickness, resolution, and decisiveness that urge him forward when others withdraw. He must accept and welcome the fact that, as a policeman, he must be in control of the situ-ation, lest it be in control of him.

DISCUSSION QUESTIONS

1. What personal qualities would qualify someone to be a superior patrol officer?
2. Should patrol officers live in the community they serve? Would that make them more accountable?

SOURCE. Reprinted by Permission of Farrar, Straus and Giroux, Inc. Excerpt from *City Police* by Jonathan Rubinstein, pp. 171–72. © 1973 by Jonathan Rubinstein.

officers toward the public have been characterized by ambivalence, cynicism, and tension.[25] The accompanying Close-Up discusses the dilemmas faced by the police officer on patrol.

How Effective Is Patrol? In most police departments, the majority of officers are assigned to patrol work; it can be stated that the patrol officer is the backbone of policing. Yet the question remains, "Does police patrol deter crime?" Put another way, should police spend so much time and resources keeping a visible presence on the street if their efforts have little effect on crime control?

The most comprehensive effort to evaluate the patrol function, the **Kansas City Study**, was conducted in Kansas City, Missouri, under sponsorship of the Police Foundation. To evaluate the effectiveness of patrol, fifteen independent police beats or districts were divided into three groups: one group retained normal police patrol; the second (proactive) set of districts was supplied with two to three times the normal amount of patrol forces; and the third (reactive) group had its preventive patrol entirely eliminated, and police officers responded only when summoned by citizens to the scene of a particular crime.

Surprisingly, data from the Kansas City Study indicated that these variations in patrol techniques had little effect on the crime patterns in the fifteen locales. The presence or absence of patrol did not seem to affect residential or business burglaries, auto thefts, larcenies involving auto accessories, robberies, vandalism, or other criminal behavior.[26]

Moreover, variations in police patrol techniques appeared to have little effect on citizens' attitudes toward the police, their satisfaction with police, or their fear of being victimized by criminal behavior.[27]

Other studies have indicated that patrol officers rarely invoke the criminal law. Albert Reiss found that the typical tour of duty does not involve a single arrest.[28] Egon Bittner concluded that patrol officers average about one arrest per month and only three index crime arrests per year.[29] Although arrests alone cannot be equated with effectiveness, they do give some indication of the relative value of patrol work.

Could patrol be a more effective crime control device if the number of police officers involved was expanded? Research has not shown this to be the case. In one study David Greenberg and his associates examined the relationship between police employment levels and crime in over five hundred jurisdictions.[30] Their conclusion: Although cities responded to violent crime rate increases by hiring more police, there is little evidence that police employment levels are related to crime rate reductions.

Police and Deterrence. Can we conclude that police presence has little to do with controlling crime? Police seem to have only a minimal general deterrent effect, but their actions have been shown to control recidivism among some offenders who fall into their grasp. In one important study, Larry Sherman and Richard Berk evaluated the effect of arrests on domestic dispute cases in Minneapolis. They found that the more formal the response of police (arrest versus warning), the less likely the perpetrators were to repeat their actions. The deterrent effect of arrest was present regardless of what later happened to the offender in court.[31]

Using data for drunken driving arrests in Sweden from 1976 to 1979, Perry Shapiro and Harold Votey found that an arrest experience reduces the probability that a person will drive while drunk.[32] An arrest increases a person's perceived probability of being re-arrested and also their perceptions of the unpleasantness of arrest, which lead to a reduced chance of drunk driving. Shapiro and Votey also found that violators could be classified into two groups: easily deterrable offenders, and those immune to the deterrent effect of an arrest. The authors say that the former are capable of learning from their mistakes, while the latter "persists in ignoring the law and the extent of penalties." These studies seem to suggest that although police patrol cannot reduce crime per se, aggressive formal actions by police can certainly have an effect on reducing the crime rate.

Patrol Innovations. Police departments have responded to the challenge of patrol ineffectiveness by attempting to implement innovations in patrol techniques. One approach has been to allocate staff on the basis of computer analysis of previous offense patterns. Another approach has been to use hidden cameras in areas where numerous crimes have occurred.

With today's communication gear, the foot patrol officer is not isolated on the street.

Another innovative approach that gained popularity in the 1970s was **team policing**.[33] In its most basic form, this concept brought together groups of junior officers and a supervisor, who were given jurisdiction over a designated neighborhood area on a twenty-four-hour-a-day basis. The supervisor had complete responsibility for the team area, and the team could patrol the area in the manner it believed would be most effective. The team determined its own deployment, working hours, assignments, and methods within broad policy guidelines established by the department. The purpose of the team was to create strong ties between the police officers and the community they served, and to involve the neighborhood in police operation. Team police models have not received widespread acceptance; where adopted, they have met with only intermittent success. Yet, they illustrate the efforts made by police agencies to improve patrol effectiveness.[34]

Foot Patrol. Still another approach to improving patrol effectiveness has been to reintroduce walking the beat, or **foot patrols**, in a limited number of jurisdictions. Returning to the early twentieth century practice of patrol in today's age of technology is believed to improve police/citizen cooperation and increase perceptions of public safety (see section entitled "Broken Windows"). The Police Foundation evaluated several of these programs in New Jersey and found that foot patrol had little effect on the crime rate, but it did help to improve citizen attitudes toward the police.[35]

Those in favor of foot patrol argue that it helps police monitor community concerns and control low-level drug selling, vandalism, and other misdemeanors associated with community decline. Officers on foot are more easily approachable and offer a comforting presence to citizens. And with today's mobile communication gear, the foot patrol officer is not isolated on the street. In many cities they carry the same communication gear that is used in patrol cars.

The foot patrol concept is growing. Begun in Flint, Michigan in 1978, foot patrol is seen as an effective means of improving police community relations by larger departments such as New York's. About 15 percent of San Francisco's police force is now devoted to foot patrol.

Not all supervisors agree that foot patrol is an ideal solution. Some do not want their officers to mingle in neighborhood problems, turning themselves into impromptu social workers. Similarly, they argue that it is difficult to manage foot patrol officers and monitor their whereabouts. Advocates counter that foot patrol can be a flexible supplement to motor patrol, producing increased community support and improved departmental morale.

INVESTIGATION FUNCTION

The second prominent police role is investigation and crime detection. The **detective** has been a figure of great romantic appeal since the first independent bureau was established by the London Metropolitan Police in 1841. The detective has been portrayed as the elite of the police force in such films and television shows as *Dirty Harry, Sudden Impact,* and *Miami Vice,* to name but a few.

Detective branches are organized on the individual precinct level or out of a central headquarters, and perform various functions.

Some jurisdictions maintain morals squads or vice squads, which are usually staffed by plainclothes officers or detectives specializing in victimless crimes such as prostitution or gambling. Vice squad officers may set themselves up as customers for illicit activities in order to make arrests. For example, undercover detectives may frequent public men's rooms and make advances toward men; those who respond are arrested for homosexual soliciting. In other instances, female police officers may pose as prostitutes. These covert police activities have often been criticized as violating the personal rights of citizens, and their appropriateness and fairness have been questioned.

Investigators most often enter a case after it has been reported to police and attempt to accumulate enough evidence to identify the perpetrator.[36] Detectives use various techniques in their investigatory function. Sometimes they obtain fingerprints from the scene of a crime and match them with those on file. Other cases demand the aid of informers to help identify perpetrators. In some instances, victims or witnesses are asked to identify offenders by viewing their pictures, or *mug shots,* or by pulling them out of lineups. It is also possible for detectives to solve a crime by being familiar with the working methods of particular offenders—their modus operandi, or MO. The detective identifies the criminal by matching the facts of the crime with the criminal's peculiar habits or actions. In some cases, stolen property is located and then the case is cleared. Either the suspect is arrested on another matter and subsequently found to be in possession of stolen merchandise, or during routine questioning a person confesses to criminal acts the police did not suspect him or her of in the first place.

Finally, detectives can use their own initiative to take special action in solving a case. For example, the **sting** type of operation has received widespread publicity.[37] Here, detectives pose as fences and conduct property transactions with thieves interested in selling stolen merchandise. Transactions are videotaped to provide prosecutors with extremely strong cases. A study of sting operations conducted in forty jurisdictions over a seven-year period found that 9,970 criminals were arrested and $300 million in stolen property recovered at a cost of $30 million.[38]

One of the more successful sting operations was conducted in Kansas City, Missouri. The Kansas City Police Department and the Bureau of Alcohol, Tobacco, and Firearms conducted a nine-month operation known as *Picaroon.* "A. Picaro Associates" (a *picaro* is a rogue or a vagabond) served as a front for an operation that recovered $1.5 million worth of property and obtained 124 indictments. Although most of the individuals indicted were street thieves, several were part of organized crime in Kansas City. Many were armed upon arrest (one answered the door holding a sawed-off shotgun). At the peak of activity, the operation recovered $168,000 worth of property in one day, including a stolen tractor trailer loaded with appliances, fifteen men's diamond rings, and two late-model cars valued at $16,000.[39]

Sting-type undercover operations are controversial since they involve a police officer's becoming involved in illegal activity and encouraging offenders to break the law. The ethics of these operations have been questioned, especially when the police actively recruit criminals as they did in the DeLorean case. Nonetheless, the sting operation seems to have found a permanent place in the law enforcement repertoire.

Are Investigations Effective? Although detectives in the movies and on television always capture the villain, research evidence indicates that real detectives are much less successful. The Rand Corporation, in a 1975 study of 153 detective bureaus, found that a great deal of detectives' time was spent in nonproductive work and that investigative expertise did little to help them solve cases.[40] In more than half of the cases cleared, the offender was identified at the time of reporting. In most of the other cases cleared, simple routine actions solved the case; there was little need for scientific, highly trained investigators. The Rand researchers estimated that half of all detectives could be removed without negatively influencing crime clearance rates.

The Rand findings have been replicated by other research efforts. For example, Mark Willman and John Snortum tracked 5,336 reported crimes and spent thousands of hours monitoring detective work in a suburban U.S. police department. They found that most crime clearances were accomplished when the suspect was identified before the case was assigned to a detective. When initial identification had not taken place at the scene of the crime, the perpetrator was usually identified through routine follow-up procedures. Nonetheless, Willman and Snortum agree that whereas detectives are not successful crime solvers, they make a valuable contribution in their skilled interrogation and processing of cases, which are essential to eventual convictions.[41]

Efforts have been made to revamp investigation procedures. One practice has been for patrol officers to be given greater responsibilities in conducting preliminary investigations at the scene of the crime. In addition, the precinct detective is being replaced by specialized units such as homicide or burglary squads, which operate over larger areas and can bring specific expertise to bear on a particular case.

Another trend has been the development of regional squads of local, state, and federal officers (called regional strike forces) who concentrate on major crimes such as narcotics offenses and organized crime and use their wider jurisdiction and expertise to provide services beyond the capability of a metropolitan police department.[42] Thus, in the coming years we may witness major changes in the organization and function of detective forces.

OTHER POLICE FUNCTIONS

Another important public contact police task is traffic control. It involves such activities as intersection control (directing traffic), traffic law enforcement, radar operations, parking law enforcement, and accident investigations.[43]

Traffic control is a complex daily task involving thousands, even millions, of motor vehicles within a single police jurisdiction. Consequently, police departments use **selective enforcement** in maintaining traffic laws. Police departments neither expect nor wish to punish all traffic violators. A department may set up traffic control units only at particular intersections, although its traffic coordinators know that many other areas of the city are experiencing violations. Manpower may be allocated to the traffic division based on prediction of accident or violation expectancy rates, determined by statistical analysis of previous patterns and incidents.

As the model of the typical police department in figure 15.1 indicates, various other roles are carried out by police agencies. For example, most departments take responsibility for the administration and control of their departmental budgets. This task involves purchasing equipment and services, planning for future expenditures, and managing the department's resources.

Many departments maintain separate units that keep records on offenders. Modern data management systems have been used to provide easy access to records for case investigations. Similarly, most larger departments have sophisticated communications networks, which process citizen complaints and police calls for assistance and dispatch vehicles to respond to them as efficiently as possible.

To promote citizen cooperation, many police departments maintain specialized community relations officers. Community relations teams perform such tasks as working with citizen groups, lecturing high school students on traffic safety, and creating neighborhood programs to prevent crime.

Some police agencies maintain (or have access to) forensic laboratories, which enable them to identify substances to be used as evidence, classify fingerprints, and augment investigations in other ways.

Another function often found in larger departments is planning and research. The planning and research division designs new programs to increase police efficiency and develops strategies to test programs' effectiveness. Police planners monitor recent technological developments and institute programs to adapt them to ongoing police services.

Police and the Rule of Law

Like other areas of criminal justice, police behavior is carefully controlled by court action. On the one hand, police want a free hand to enforce the law as they see fit. On the other hand, the courts must balance the needs of efficient law enforcement with the rights of citizens under the U.S. Constitution. Some important legal issues have emerged from this conflict, the most critical being citizen rights during a police interrogation and the right to be free from illegal searches and seizures by police officers.

CUSTODIAL INTERROGATION

The Fifth Amendment guarantees people the right to be free from self-incrimination. This has been interpreted as meaning that law enforcement agents cannot use physical or psychological coercion while interrogating suspects under their control in order to get them to confess or give information.

The federal government has long held that a confession must be made voluntarily if it is to be admissible as evidence in a criminal trial. Confessions obtained from defendants through coercion, force, trickery, or promises of leniency are inadmissible because their trustworthiness is questionable. The rule of voluntariness applies to confessions obtained at any time, whether the defendant was in police custody or not. In the past, one of the major drawbacks to determining the voluntariness of confessions was that the decision was made case by case, and was subjective in nature.

In 1966 the Supreme Court, in the case of *Miranda* v. *Arizona*, created objective standards for questioning by police after a defendant has been taken into custody.[44] Custody occurs when a person is not free to walk away, as when a person is arrested. The Court maintained that before the police can question a person who has been arrested or is in custody, they must inform the individual of the Fifth Amendment right to be free from self-incrimination. This is accomplished by the police issuing what is known as the **Miranda warning**. The warning informs the suspect that:

1. He or she has the right to remain silent.
2. If he or she makes a statement, it can be used against him or her in court.
3. He or she has the right to consult an attorney and to have the attorney present at the time of the interrogation.
4. If he or she cannot afford an attorney, one will be appointed by the state.

If the defendant is not given the Miranda warning prior to the interrogation, the evidence obtained from the interrogation cannot be admitted at the trial. Finally, the accused can waive the Miranda at any time. However, in order for the waiver to be effective, the state must first show that the defendant was aware of all the Miranda rights and must then prove that the waiver was made with the full knowledge of constitutional rights.

The Miranda Rule Today. Since its inception, the Supreme Court has used case law to define the boundaries of the Miranda warning. For instance, in the case of *Harris* v. *New York*, the Court agreed that evidence obtained in violation of the Miranda warning could be used by the government to impeach a defendant's testimony during trial.[45] In *Michigan* v. *Tucker*, the Court allowed the testimony of a witness whose identity was revealed by the suspect even though a violation of the Miranda rule occurred.[46] In the case of *Michigan* v. *Mosley*, the Court upheld the renewed questioning of a suspect who had already been given the Miranda warning and had refused to answer any questions, while in *California* v. *Prysock*, the court ruled that the Miranda warning given to a juvenile was valid even though the youth may have had trouble interpreting some of its provisions.[47]

Three recent cases have further narrowed the scope of Miranda. In *Nix* v. *Williams*, a murder suspect revealed the location of the body of his victim in violation of his right to remain silent. The Court ruled that the statement could be used against him because the body was bound to have been discovered by search parties anyway.[48] This is now referred to as the **inevitable discovery rule**.

In another case, *New York* v. *Quarles*, a rape suspect, believed by police to be armed, was taken into custody. When immediately asked where his weapon was, the suspect responded by pointing to where he had it hidden and saying, "It's over there." Though the question was asked before the Miranda warning had been given, the Supreme Court allowed that the gun and statements were admissible at trial on the grounds that the officers acted to protect public safety.[49]

In the case of *Oregon* v. *Elstad,* police in Oregon obtained a warrant to arrest Elstad, and after finding him at home, asked if he had been involved in a burglary. He responded, "Yes, I was there." Later, after being informed of his Miranda rights, he gave police a full confession. The Oregon courts overturned Elstad's conviction on the grounds that his pre-Miranda remarks tainted his post-Miranda statements. The Supreme Court reversed the decision, maintaining that the subsequent properly given Miranda warning "cured the condition" that had made the initial statements inadmissible.[50] In sum, original errors by police in getting statements do not make subsequent statements inadmissible.

In sum, though the Miranda warning controls police procedures in obtaining confessions, recent case law has narrowed its scope and given police greater leeway in their actions.

SEARCH AND SEIZURE

The second critical conflict between the police and courts involves Fourth Amendment rights and the exclusionary rule. As reviewed in chapter 13, if police officers violate the privacy of a citizen when obtaining evidence, it is possible to have that evidence excluded from trial by a court order. Thus, even if a suspect is caught with damaging contraband, such as narcotics, a police error in obtaining the evidence can make the suspect immune from prosecution. It is not surprising that most police officers view the exclusionary rule as a serious infringement on their effectiveness. The following sections will review the legal restraints placed on police investigations by the courts.

Search Warrant. As stated previously, the Fourth Amendment protects the individual against unreasonable searches and seizures. This means that, with some exceptions, police officers must have a *search warrant* in order to search a person and his or her possessions. A police officer must request the warrant from a court. The Fourth Amendment specifically states that before a warrant to search can be issued, it must be proven that there is **probable cause** to believe that a crime has been committed. The amendment further states that the belief that probable cause exists must be supported by "oath or affirmation." This means the police officer must testify before a judge as to the reasons he or she believed the warrant should be issued. If no good reason exists, then the warrant will not be issued and the police will be unable to interfere with the citizen's private possessions, home, or person.

The Fourth Amendment also protects citizens against unreasonable searches and seizures by demanding that the warrant meet the requirement of **particularity**. This means that the search warrant must specify the place to be searched and the property to be seized. Any search and seizure beyond that specified in the warrant would be considered unreasonable and therefore illegal.

Very often when the police try to obtain search warrants they rely on the word of informers. For many years, the courts required that before the police could obtain a search warrant based on an informer's information they had to prove that (1) the informer was reliable and (2) the informer had firsthand knowledge of the crime (known as *the two-pronged test*). In a dramatic move, the court abandoned this standard in the case of *Illinois* v. *Gates.*[51] In that case, police received the following anonymous letter and used it to get a warrant to search the Gates home:

This letter is to inform you that you have a couple in your town who strictly make their living on selling drugs. They are Sue and Lance Gates, they live on Greenway, off Bloomingdale Rd. in the condominiums. Most of their buys are done in Florida. Sue his wife drives their car to Florida, where she leaves it to be loaded up with drugs, then Lance flys down and drives it back. Sue flys back after she drops the car off in Florida. May 3 she is driving down there again and Lance will be flying down in a few days to drive it back. At the time Lance drives the car back he has the trunk loaded with over $100,000.00 in drugs. Presently they have over $100,000.00 worth of drugs in their basement.

They brag about the fact they never have to work, and make their entire living on pushers.

I guarantee if you watch them carefully you will make a big catch. They are friends with some big drugs dealers, who visit their house often:

Lance & Susan Gates

Greenway

in condominiums

Though the letter was anonymous and therefore the reliability of the informer could not be determined, the Court ruled that the evidence police obtained was admissible because the letter showed in-depth knowledge of the Gates's activities. The Court changed the standard of obtaining a warrant to what is known as the **totality of the circumstances** test. Loosely interpreted, if judges are presented with sufficient, knowledgeable evidence for issuing a warrant, they may do so even if the source of the information is unknown.

WARRANTLESS SEARCH

Under certain circumstances, a valid search may be conducted by police officers without a search warrant. The four major exceptions are: (1) search incident to a valid arrest, (2) threshold inquiry (stop and frisk), (3) automobile search, and (4) consent search.

Search Incident to a Valid Arrest. It has long been held that a warrantless search is valid if it is made incident to a lawful arrest. The reason for this exception is that the arresting officer must have the power to disarm the accused, protect himself, preserve evidence of the crime, and prevent the accused's escape from custody. Since the search is lawful, he retains what he finds if it is connected with a crime.[52] For example, if a police officer sees a person smoking marijuana and arrests him, the police officer can lawfully search the defendant without a warrant. The important thing to remember when dealing with search incident to arrest is that the arrest must be valid in order for the search to be lawful. An arrest is lawful if the officer witnessed the crime being committed or if he or she had probable cause to believe that the individual arrested committed the offense.

Certain restrictions are placed on a warrantless search incident to an arrest. First, to be valid, the search must occur immediately after the arrest. For example, in *United States* v. *Chadwick*, the Supreme Court maintained that searching a footlocker an hour and a half after an arrest was not a search incident to arrest. There was time to get a search warrant in that case.[53]

The second requirement deals with the area in which it is permissible to search. The reason for allowing a warrantless search after arrest is to allow the officer to search for weapons that might be harmful and to find evidence the defendant might destroy. With this in mind, the Supreme Court, in *Chimel v. California*, held that following an arrest an officer is permitted to search only the defendant's person and the areas in the defendant's immediate physical surroundings that are under his or her control.[54] This usually means an officer cannot search beyond an arm's length distance around the defendant. In *Chimel*, the search of the defendant's four-room house subsequent to his arrest was held invalid.

The Court further loosened the search-after-arrest doctrine during the 1985 term in the case of *United States v. Hensley*. In that case, the Court ruled that police may legally detain a suspect by relying on a "flyer" from another police department, even though arrest warrants had not been issued in the case.[55] Evidence uncovered during the detention is admissible in court if the department that issued the flyer had a reasonable suspicion that the suspect was involved in connection with a felony.

Threshold Inquiry (Stop and Frisk). The second exception to the search warrant requirement deals with a police officer's right to make a threshold inquiry, also known as the **stop and frisk** procedure. Threshold inquiry deals with the situation in which, although the officer does not have probable cause to arrest, his or her suspicions are raised concerning the behavior of an individual. In such a case, the officer has a right to stop and question the individual; if the officer has reason to believe that the person is carrying a concealed weapon, he or she may frisk the suspect. Unlike searching, frisking is a limited procedure; it is a patdown of the outer clothing for the purpose of finding a concealed weapon. If no weapon is found, the search must stop. However, if an illegal weapon is found, then an arrest can be made and a search incident to the arrest performed.

The stop-and-frisk exception was established by the Supreme Court in the case of *Terry v. Ohio*.[56] In this case, the police officer observed two men walking up and down in front of a store several times and then being joined by a third. Believing the men were casing the store for a burglary, the police officer approached the three and asked their names. When the officer was answered with a mumble, he turned Terry (the defendant) around, patted down his outer clothing, and found a pistol. The officer also found a revolver in the pocket of one of the other suspects. The defendants appealed to the Supreme Court, claiming that this was an illegal search and seizure. The Court maintained that "where a reasonably prudent officer is warranted in the circumstances of a given case in believing that his safety or that of others is endangered, he may make a reasonable search for weapons of the person believed by him to be armed and dangerous regardless of whether he has probable cause to arrest that individual for crime or the absolute certainty that the individual is armed." Thus, in a threshold inquiry situation, a police officer is permitted to conduct a limited search—that is, one confined to determining whether a suspect is armed.

Automobile Search. An automobile may be searched without a warrant in several situations. However, probable cause to believe that the car was involved in a crime must be present before such a search may be conducted.[57] The primary rationale in allowing a search of an automobile involves the inherent mobility of automobiles; there is a greater chance that the evidence will be lost if the search is not conducted immediately. A second reason for allowing a search of an automobile is the belief that people do not expect as much privacy in their cars as in their homes; thus, the Fourth Amendment protection for privacy in a car is minimal. Therefore, when police officers stop an automobile on the highway because they have probable cause to believe that it was involved in a recent robbery, they are justified in searching it immediately in an effort to find evidence. If a car involved in a crime is within the control and custody of the police, however, it is more likely that a warrant will be required before a search can be conducted, because there is little danger that the evidence will be lost or destroyed.

In June 1982, the Supreme Court decided the case of *United States v. Ross* and clarified the confusing law on automobile searches.[58] Acting on information obtained from an informant, the police searched the trunk of a car alleged to contain heroin. They opened the car's trunk and found a paper bag and, after opening the bag, discovered envelopes of heroin. They then drove the car to the stationhouse, where a second search uncovered a leather pouch containing money. The defendants were convicted on drug charges. On appeal, a federal court ordered the heroin and money excluded from trial, since the court considered the search of a closed bag in the trunk of a car to violate the defendants' right to privacy. The Supreme Court reversed this decision and said that police officers who have legitimately stopped an automobile and who have probable cause to believe that contraband is concealed somewhere within it may conduct a warrantless search of the vehicle that is as thorough as a magistrate could authorize by warrant.

Consent Search. In a consent search, individuals waive their constitutional rights; therefore, neither a warrant nor probable cause need exist. However, for the search to be effective, the consent must be given voluntarily; threat or compulsion invalidates the search. In the case of *Bumper v. North Carolina*, police officers falsely informed a woman that they had a warrant to search her home and asked her if they could search it.[59] The Court held that the consent they obtained was compulsory, not voluntarily given; therefore, the search was invalid.

Although it has been held that a voluntary consent is required, it has also been maintained that the police are under no obligation to inform individuals of their right to refuse the search.

WHAT CONSTITUTES A SEARCH?

Under certain circumstances there is no need for a search warrant, because the activity undertaken does not constitute a search as defined by the Fourth Amendment. As mentioned previously, the purpose of the Fourth Amendment is to protect an individual's right to privacy. Therefore, in situations in which there is no expectation of privacy, a search warrant is not required. Areas such as sidewalks, parks, and streets are not constitutionally protected. For example, a police officer can freely search an individual's garbage after it has been put out on the street for collection. Even when an object is in a house or automobile, areas involving an expectation of privacy, the object can be freely inspected if it can be seen by the general public. For example, if a police officer looks through the living room window of a house from the sidewalk and sees stolen property, then no search warrant is needed in order for the property to be inspected. The articles are considered to be in *plain view* and therefore are not the subject of a search as legally defined.

The plain-view doctrine also applies when the police have a search or arrest warrant and are lawfully on the premises of the defendant. In such a situation, the police have the authority to seize incriminating evidence if it is in plain view, even though the particular article was not specified in the search warrant. For example, the police have the right to confiscate a bag of marijuana lying on a kitchen table even though the search warrant that gave them access to the house was obtained for the purpose of finding gambling tickets.

In the important case of *Katz* v. *United States*, the Supreme Court addressed the issue that the Fourth Amendment protects people and not property.[60] In *Katz*, the FBI attached an electronic listening and recording device to a public telephone booth for the purpose of obtaining evidence that the defendant was transmitting wagering information in violation of a federal statute. The Court held that such action constituted an unreasonable search and seizure. The Court maintained that a search occurs whenever police activity violates a person's privacy. In this case, it was reasonable for the defendant to expect that he would have privacy in a phone booth.

In recent years the Court has given police greater latitude to search and seize evidence. It has allowed: extended on-the-spot detention of a suspect for preliminary questioning and investigation;[61] detention by mobile teams to take fingerprints from suspects on the street;[62] search of mobile homes without a warrant;[63] administrative searches in public school with less than probable cause;[64] and a search of sealed packages in a car three days after the car was seized.[65] The court's policy has reflected the legal orientation of its more conservative members. And concomitantly, it has provided the police with the leeway to conduct their operations in a less restrictive environment. The exclusionary rule (chapter 14), once a powerful control on police evidence gathering procedures, has been substantially weakened.

Current Issues In Policing

A number of important issues face police departments in the 1980s. Though an all-encompassing discussion of each is beyond the scope of this text, a few of the more important aspects of policing are discussed below.

POLICE PERSONALITY AND SUBCULTURE

It has become commonplace to argue that a majority of U.S. police officers maintain a unique set of personality traits that place them apart from the "average" citizen. The typical police personality is thought to include authoritarianism, suspicion, racism, hostility, insecurity, conservatism, and cynicism.[66] Maintenance of these negative values and attidues is believed to cause police officers to be secretive and isolated from the rest of society, producing what has been described by William Westly as the **blue curtain** subculture.[67]

There are two opposing viewpoints on the cause of this phenomenon: one position holds that police departments attract recruits who are by nature cynical, authoritarian, secretive, and so on; other experts maintain that socialization and experience on the police force cause these character traits to develop in police officers.[68] Since research evidence supportive of both viewpoints has been produced, neither position dominates on the issue of how the police personality develops; it is not even certain that one actually exists.

Research studies have attempted to describe the development of the police personality. One of the most influential authorities in this area is social psychologist Milton Rokeach.[69] In comparing the values of police officers in Lansing, Michigan with those of a national sample of private citizens, Rokeach and his associates found some significant differences: police officers seemed more oriented toward self-control and obedience than the average citizen; in addition, police were more interested in personal goals, such as "an exciting life," and less interested in social goals, such as "a world at peace." When comparing the values of veteran officers with those of recruits, Rokeach and his associates found evidence that police officers' on-the-job experience had not significantly influenced their personalities and that most police officers probably had had a unique value orientation and personality when they first embarked upon their careers in the police force.

Probably more evidence shows, however, that a police personality is developed through the ongoing process of doing police work. At first, police recruits become socialized into their roles in the police academy. Their field training officer (FTO) teaches them the ins and outs of police work, helping them through the "rites de passage" of becoming a "real cop."[70] The folklore, tales, myths, and legends surrounding the department are communicated to recruits. Soon, they begin to understand the rules of police work. John Van Maanen suggests that "the adjustment of a newcomer in police departments is one which follows the line of least resistance."[71] By becoming similar in sentiments and behavior to their peers, recruits avoid censure by their department, their supervisor, and, most importantly, their colleagues. Thus, young officers adapt their personality to that of the "ideal cop."

George Kirkham, a professor who also became a police officer, has described how the explosive and violent situations he faced as a police officer changed his own personality:

> As someone who had always regarded policemen as a "paranoid" lot, I discovered in the daily round of violence which became part of my life that chronic suspiciousness is something that a good cop cultivates in the interest of going home to his family each evening.[72]

Egon Bittner concludes that an "esprit de corps" develops in police work because of the dangerous and unpleasant tasks police officers are required to do. Police solidarity and a "one for all, and all for one" attitude are two of the most cherished aspects of the police occupation.[73]

Probably the best-known study of police personality is Arthur Niederhoffer's *Behind the Shield*.[74] Niederhoffer examined the assumption first popularized by William Westly that most police officers develop into cynics because of their daily duties.[75] Westly had maintained that police officers learn to mistrust the citizens they protect because they are constantly faced with keeping people in line and come to believe that most people are out to break the law or harm a police officer. Niederhoffer tested Westly's assumption by distributing a survey measuring attitudes and values to 220 New York City police officers. Among his most important findings were that cynicism did increase with length of service, that patrol officers with college educations became quite cynical if they were denied promotion, and that militarylike police academy training caused new recruits to quickly become cynical about themselves, the department, and the community. For example, Niederhoffer found that nearly 80 percent of first-day recruits believed that the police department was an "efficient, smoothly operating organization"; two months later, less than a third professed that belief. Similarly, half the new recruits believed that a police superior was "very interested in the welfare of his subordinates"; two months later, that number declined to 13 percent.[76]

It has been charged that the unique police personality causes most officers to band together in a police subculture characterized by clannishness, secrecy, and insulation from others in society. Police officers tend to socialize with each other and believe their occupation cuts them off from relationships with civilians. Joining the police subculture means having to support fellow officers against outsiders; maintain a tough, "macho" exterior personality; and mistrust the motives and behavior of outsiders.[77] The most serious consequences of the police subculture are police officers resistance to change and mistrust of the public they serve. Opening the police to change will be a prime task of police officials who seek professionalism and progress in their department.

DISCRETION

In one of the most important papers on a justice-related issue, Joseph Goldstein argued in 1960 that the law enforcement function of police is not merely a matter of enforcing the rule of law, but also involves an enormous amount of personal **discretion** as to whether to invoke the power of arrest.[78] Since then, police discretion has been recognized as a crucial force in all law enforcement decision making.

Richard Donnelly describes police discretion in these terms:

> *The policeman's lot is indeed a difficult one. He is charged with applying or enforcing a multitude of laws or ordinances in a degree or proportion and in a manner that maintains a delicate degree of social protection. His task requires a sensitive and wise discretion in deciding whether or not to invoke the criminal process. He must not only know whether certain behavior violates the law but also whether there is probable cause to believe that the law has been violated. He must enforce the law, yet he must determine whether a particular violation should be handled by warning or arrest. . . . He is not expected to arrest every violator. Some laws were never intended by the enactors to be enforced, and others condemn behavior that is not contrary to significant moral values. If he arrested all violators, the courts would find it impossible to do their work, and he would be in court so frequently that he could not perform his other professional duties. Consequently, the policeman must judge and informally settle more cases than he takes to court.*[79]

Thus, police discretion involves the **selective enforcement** of the law by duly authorized police agents. However, unlike members of almost every other criminal justice agency, police officers are neither regulated in their daily procedures by administrative scrutiny nor subjected to judicial review (except when their behavior clearly violates an offender's constitutional rights). As a result, the exercise of discretion may sometimes deteriorate into discrimination, violence, and other abusive practices on the part of police.[80]

Various factors have been associated with the exercise of police discretion. Some relate to the officers' working environment. Community attitudes and beliefs certainly influence the enforcement or nonenforcement of certain laws (for example, obscenity statutes), as do policies, practices, and customs of the local police department. An individual supervisor such as a sergeant or lieutenant can influence subordinates' decisions by making well known his or her personal preferences and attitudes.

Peer pressure from fellow officers also influences decision making. Fellow police officers dictate acceptable responses to street-level problems by displaying or withholding approval in office discussions. The officer who takes the job seriously and desires the respect and friendship of others will take their advice and abide by their norms and will seek out the most experienced and most influential patrol officers on the force and follow their behavior models.

A final environmental factor affecting the police officer's performance is his or her perception of community alternatives to police intervention or processing. A police officer may exercise discretion and arrest an individual in a particular circumstance if it seems that nothing else can be done, even if the officer does not believe that an arrest is the best possible example of good police work. In an environment in which a proliferation of social agencies exists—detoxification units, drug control centers, and child care services, for example—a police officer obviously has more alternatives from which to choose in the decision making process. In fact, referring cases to these alternative agencies saves the officer both time and effort—no records need be made out and court appearances can be avoided. Thus, social agencies provide for greater latitude in police decision making.

Studies have also shown that police officer's attitudes toward the suspects involved in a case and the circumstances of the crime influence their use of discretion. Some laws are more strictly enforced than others. Usually there is a positive relationship between the seriousness of the crime and the decision to arrest. Thus, a drunk and disorderly case involves much more discretion than a robbery.

Another discretionary influence is the way that a crime or situation is encountered. If, for example, a police officer stumbles on an altercation or a break-in, the discretionary response may be quite different than if the officer had been summoned by police radio. If official police recognition has been given to an act, action must be taken or an explanation made as to why it was not taken. If a matter is brought to an officer's attention by a citizen observer, the officer can ignore the request and risk a complaint, or take discretionary action. When an officer chooses to become involved in a situation without benefit of a summons or complaint, maximum discretion can be used. Even in this circumstance, however, the presence of a crowd or of witnesses may contribute to the officer's decision.

And, of course, the officer who acts alone is affected by personal matters—physical condition, mental state, whether there are other duties to perform, and so on.

Finally, the race, age, and sex of the offender may be considered when police officers decide to invoke their arrest powers. This issue is open to some debate, but empirical studies indicate that police discretion works against the young, the poor, and members of minority groups; and may often favor the wealthy, the politically well connected, and members of the majority group.[81] (See below for more on the issue.)

Numerous efforts have been made to limit police discretion, as mentioned previously. The courts have placed controls on what police can do during investigations and interrogations. Police administrators have attempted to establish guidelines for police officers' operating behavior.[82] Some have established special units to oversee patrol activities; others have created boundaries of police efficiency and suggested that any behavior in excess of these limits would not be tolerated in the department.[83]

Despite some success, limiting police discretion has proven to be a difficult task. It has proven harder to control police officers' behavior when they refuse to take action than when they invoke their police powers.

With but a few exceptions, no clear answer to the management of police discretion exists.[84] Advocates of specialized units, policy statements, legal mandates, and other approaches can only assume that the officer in the field will comply with the intent and spirit of the administrator's desire. Little information is currently available concerning what the specific influence of any particular legal or administrative measure on police discretion will be, whether it will affect all officers equally, or why some officers will respond in one way and others in an opposite way. It is not known what police officers are really like, how they differ from or resemble one another, or how they react to pressures from above.

POLICE DISCRIMINATION?

One important issue in the study of police discretion is whether police discriminate on the basis of sex, race, ethnic origin, or class. Early studies indicated that police discretion worked against the poor, minorities, and women.[85] However, efforts to improve police sensitivity to minority rights may have helped reduce racial and sex discrimination. For example, Marvin Krohn and his associates examined almost 20,000 cases in a north-central American city in order to identify whether sex bias exists in the disposition of police contacts.[86] Though sex bias existed during the entire period of their examination, they also discovered that a consistent pattern of diminishing differences existed over time. And even during the years of greatest differences, the disposition of males and females were closer than the authors expected. They concluded that sex bias was a long-term problem but not one of great magnitude. In another study of police arrest decision making, Douglas Smith and Jodie Klein also failed to discover racial bias in the police use of discretion, though they did find that sex and socioeconomic variables were taken into account when police made decisions: Police tended to disregard nonviolent disputes involving female complainants in lower-class neighborhoods.[87]

Similarly, Richard Hollinger studied the use of police discretion in arresting drunk drivers in Georgia.[88] He found that police "bias" was a function of the socioeconomic status of the culprit and not their racial background. If blacks were overrepresented in the arrested group, it was because of their overrepresentation in the lower economic classes.

One possible area of police arrest discrimination overlooked by most research is the influence of the victim of crime on the arrest decision (most studies focus on the offender). In one such study, Douglas Smith and his associates uncovered little evidence of racial bias in police decision making.[89] However, police are more likely to take action if whites rather than blacks were the victims of crime. Thus, the sexual and racial background of the victims of crime may be a more important determinant of arrest decision making than the race and sex of the suspect.

Though racial bias in arrest decisions violates constitutional rights, courts have upheld the use of race as a personal identifying factor that helps narrow police searches for suspects. Police manuals also suggest that officers be aware of race when on the lookout for suspicious characters (for example, questioning those who do not "belong" on their beat). Similarly, courts have upheld the government's use of race as a condition of determining probable cause in searches for illegal aliens and in drug courier profiles.[90]

In sum, current research indicates that the effect of offenders' class, race, and sexual characteristics may be diminishing in magnitude, but it continues to influence police discretion.

HIGHER EDUCATION AND POLICE EFFECTIVENESS

In recent years, police departments have stressed the advantages of college education for their recruits. Though the great majority of U.S. police departments

Police Officers' Style

One important factor influencing police officers' use of discretion is their personal style, or approach to police work. Numerous attempts have been made in recent years to identify typologies of police behavior and describe "ideal" cop types. In a recent paper, Ellen Hochstedler has tried to synthesize these various attempts into four distinct types that describe the bulk of working police officers. According to Hochstedler, the following types of police merge from the literature:

SUPERCOP

Supercops take their role as law enforcers quite seriously. They do not refrain from using force when they have to and sometimes use it too quickly and excessively. Their view of the police task tends to be narrow, emphasizing fighting "real crimes" such as rape and robbery and ignoring service functions. They view themselves as part of the "thin blue line" that protects society from the forces of evil. In using discretion, the supercop probably ignores minor law violations and domestic squabbles, considering them not police business. They only are interested in arresting serious street criminals.

PROFESSIONAL

Professionals have a broad, inclusive definition of their task and a balanced perception of their professional identity. They are not crusaders on a mission but skilled workers performing a difficult and complex task. They are the officers best able to separate the individual from the job and to avoid feeling personally harmed when the police role is attacked. These police officers are able to see both sides of many issues and can therefore think coolly and rationally in many situations. Their use of discretion is professional, reasoned, and competent.

SERVICE ORIENTED

Service-oriented officers are not interested in crime fighting but are totally committed to helping people. They rely heavily on persuasion and talk. Their approach is that of a change agent and their stance is that of a social worker. They regard their clients with respect and hope to have a positive effect on anybody with whom they come into contact. Service-oriented officers are dedicated to their jobs but also experience some frustration because they want to effect lasting change but are unable to do so. These officers try to use the treatment resources of the community rather than their arrest powers, if at all possible.

AVOIDER

The avoider is characterized as a shirker. These officers do as little as possible, either by design or because they are inept or inefficient. They are not necessarily lazy but may be confused, frightened, or burned out. The avoider probably takes as little action as possible in any situation.

In a research study using officers in the Dallas Police Department, Hochstedler tried to empirically test the existence of these ideal types. Her results proved inconclusive. Though further research is necessary, the existence of ideal types of police officers who share similar attitudes and operating styles, and who use their discretion accordingly, may be more a matter of police folklore than a true picture of reality. Hochstedler's views challenge the traditional beliefs of many well-known police authorities.

DISCUSSION QUESTIONS

1. Do you think that supercops, who abound in TV programs and movies, really exist?
2. Can you create typologies for other professions—for example, college professors?

SOURCE. Ellen Hochstedler, "Testing Types, a Review and Test of Police Types," *Journal of Criminal Justice* 9 (1981):451–66. For more information on police types, see J. Broderick, *Police in a Time of Change* (Morristown, N.J.: General Leasing Press, 1977); M. Brown, *Working the Street* (New York: Russel Sage Foundation, 1981); W. Muir, *Police: Streetcorner Politicians* (Chicago: University of Chicago Press, 1977); M. O'Neill, "The Role of the Police—Normative Role Expectations in a Metropolitan Police Department (Ph.D. diss., State University of New York at Albany, 1974); J. Q. Wilson, *Varieties of Police Behavior* (Cambridge, Mass.: Harvard University Press, 1968).

still do not require a college degree of recruits, many give credit for education when considering candidates for promotion or special assignments.

There has been some debate over the value of a college education for police officers. Some people suggest that a college education can do little to help the "average" police officer perform daily activities.[91] The diversity of the police role, the need for split-second decision making, and the often boring and mundane tasks police officers are required to do are all considered reasons why formal education for police officers may be a waste of time.[92] Moreover, as Solomon Gross has argued, a college education may simply frustrate officers who must perform many routine jobs. Consequently, there may be a higher dropout rate among college-trained officers.[93]

However, a growing body of literature suggests that education benefits the officer's performance and job satisfaction. Studies conducted by R. P. Witte, Wayne Cascio, Merlyn Moore, James Finnegen, B. E. Sanderson, and others have found that higher education correlates favorably with such factors as training academy performance, citizens' attitudes toward police, low absentee rates, and promotion.[94]

Another important question involves what type of education police officers should receive. One approach favors hands-on training programs; another suggests an academically oriented general liberal arts or criminal justice approach. This important issue has been addressed in a report by the National Advisory Commission on Higher Education for Police Officers (commonly called the **Sherman Report**.[95] The Sherman Report examined the findings of a national study of existing college curriculums and educational delivery systems for police education in the United States. Generally critical of current police education techniques, the Sherman Report recommended that several basic changes be made: it called for a halt to federal tuition assistance for programs with narrow curriculums and unqualified faculty. The report was especially critical of police educational programs with limited, academic orientations. The Sherman Report instead advocated a limit to the number of criminal justice courses that could be allowed in any in-service or pre-service student program. It also called for discontinuing the practice of granting academic credit for in-service training programs such as those conducted by various state police academies. Finally, the report stressed that courses and course material should emphasize ethical considerations and moral values in law enforcement, not the "nuts and bolts" of police procedures.

Despite the controversy surrounding higher education for police, it is evident that today's officer realizes that the road to advancement in the police field necessitates receiving proper academic credentials. Higher education for police officers is here to stay.[96]

WOMEN AND MINORITY POLICE OFFICERS

For the past decade, U.S. police departments have made a concerted effort to attract women and minority police officers. The latter group includes blacks, Orientals, Hispanics, native Americans, and members of other racial minorities. The reasons for recruiting minority and female officers are varied. Viewed in its most positive light, such recruitment reflects police departments' desire to field a more balanced force that truly represents the community it serves. A heterogeneous police force can be instrumental in gaining the public's confidence by helping to dispel the view that police departments are generally bigoted or biased organizations. Furthermore, women and minority police officers possess special qualities that can improve police performance.

Another important reason for recruiting women and minority police officers is the need to comply with various federal guidelines on hiring.[97] A series of legal actions brought by minority representatives have resulted in local, state, and federal courts' ordering police departments to either create hiring quotas to increase minority representation or rewrite entrance exams and requirements to encourage the employment of women and minorities.[98] Several of the lawsuits have resulted in either court-ordered hiring judgments or voluntary compliance. Consequently, the numbers of women and minorities in police departments have increased dramatically.

Ellen Hochstedler and her associates studied recruitment of women and minorities in twenty large U.S. police departments.[99] They found impressive increases in representation between 1967 and 1981, the mean being a 330-percent increase in the number of minority and female officers hired during this period. However, women only made up about 6 percent of the officers in the sample and consequently progress in recruiting females was judged inadequate.

Despite such changes, there seems little question that the federal government is easing pressure on minority and female hiring. In 1985, the Justice Department requested police departments in Buffalo, Chicago, Cincinnati, Indianapolis, Los Angeles, and San Francisco (among other cities) to end quota hiring, charging that it violated the legal rights of white males. The department cited the 1984 case of *Firefighters Local Union No. 1784* v. *Stotts*, which stated that affirmative action rules could interfere with a legitimate union seniority system.[100] The Justice Department may receive further aid from the case of *Wygant* v. *Jackson*, to be decided during the 1985 term, which involves whether racial quotas violate the Fourteenth Amendment's equal protection clause.

Even if legally possible, many jurisdictions will probably not wish to end quota hiring, which is viewed as a means of protecting the interests of women and minority group members, and consequently of maintaining the support of the minority community for police. Even without federal government pressure, there should be an increasing number of female officers on the nation's police forces in the years to come.

Black Police Officers. Blacks have served on police forces since the mid-nineteenth century. A Republican mayor appointed the first black police officer in Chicago in 1872; and by 1894, there were twenty-three black officers serving in that city.[101] Nonetheless, even today, blacks are sorely underrepresented on the police forces of the nation's larger cities; and as mentioned previously, legal and social pressure has been mounted to increase their numbers. The reduction in local operating funds experienced in recent years has not helped alleviate this problem.

The life of the black officer can be difficult. As Nicholas Alex points out, black police officers suffer "double marginality."[102] On the one hand, the black officers must deal with the expectation that they will give members of their own race "a break." On the other hand, black officers often experience overt racism from police colleagues.

Alex found that black officers' treatment of other blacks ranges from denying that blacks should be treated differently from whites to treating black offenders more harshly than white offenders to prove lack of bias. Alex offers various reasons why some black police officers are tougher on black offenders: They desire acceptance from their white colleagues; they are particularly sensitive to any disrespect given them by black teenagers; they view themselves as the protectors of the black community.[103]

The problems of the black officer can also be exacerbated by the cool reception they are given by their white colleagues, who see them as potential competitors for promotions and special assignments. As James Jacobs and Jay Cohen point out, white police officers view affirmative action hiring and promotion programs as a threat to their job security.[104] They note that in Chicago, white officers intervened on the side of the city when a black police officers' organization filed suit to change criteria for promotion.[105]

As a greater number of minorities join U.S. police forces, it is likely that they will experience the same problems encountered by white officers. For example, Stephen Leinen interviewed black police officers in New York City and found that their attitudes toward policing were similar to those of white police officers.[106] They were dissatisfied that people in the black community still expressed mistrust and contempt for police even though an increasing number of black officers had been assigned to these areas. They believed that black cops would be better able to deal with problems in minority communities than whites. Nonetheless, their job perception seemed to mirror the cynicism and apathy that have plagued white police officers.

Female Police Officers. The first female police officers were appointed in New York as early as 1845; but they were designated as "matrons," and their duties were restricted to handling females in jail custody.[107] In 1893, Chicago hired policewomen but again restricted their activities to making court visitations and assisting male detectives with cases involving women and children. However, it was not until the passage of the final version of Title VII of the Civil Rights Act in 1972 that police departments around the nation began to hire females and assign them to regular patrol duties.

In general, evaluations of policewomen show them to be equal or superior to male officers in some areas of police work. In the most highly regarded study of policewomen, Catherine Milton found that female officers in Washington, D.C., responded to similar types of calls as their male colleagues and that the arrests they made were as likely to result in conviction.[108] Women were more likely to receive support from the community and less likely to be charged with police misconduct. On the negative side, policewomen made fewer felony and misdeameanor arrests and received lower supervisory ratings than male officers. The generally favorable results obtained by Milton have also been found in other studies assessing policewomen's performance.[109]

Despite their relative proficiency, female police officers have not received general support from their colleagues or the public. One study found that male officers perceive the public to be less cooperative toward them if females are on patrol and report that they receive more insults and threats when patrolling with female partners.[110] Consequently, surveys have shown a relatively low acceptance rate for females in police functions, especially those involving hazardous duties.[111] Some jurisdictions still assign women officers to secretarial and clerical posts; and in some cities, when budget cutbacks require layoffs, women officers are released in disproportionate numbers.[112]

In a study of women entering police training in Florida, Sally Gross found that though subjects had a high degree of self-confidence and idealism on entry, their self-perceptions diminished significantly after eight weeks of academy life.[113] Sex-role conflicts produced disillusionment with police work, accompanied by denial, self-doubt, repressed anger, and confusion.

POLICE VIOLENCE

Police officers are empowered to use force and violence in pursuit of their daily task. Some scholars have argued that this is the core of the police role:

The role of the police is best understood as a mechanism for the distribution of non-negotiably coercive force employed in accordance with the dictates of an intuitive group of situational exigencies.[114]

Police violence first became a major topic for discussion in the 1940s, when rioting provoked serious police backlash. Thurgood Marshall, then of the NAACP, referred to the Detroit police as a "gestapo" after a 1943 race riot left thirty-four people dead.[115] Twenty-five years later, excessive police force was again an issue when television cameras captured police violence against protestors at the Democratic National Convention in Chicago. However, general day-to-day police brutality against individual citizens seems to be diminishing. In 1967, the President's Commission on Criminal Justice concluded:

The Commission believes that physical abuse is not as serious a problem as it was in the past. The few statistics which do exist suggest small numbers of cases involving excessive use of force. Although the relatively small number of reported complaints cannot be considered an accurate measurement of the total problem, most persons, including civil rights leaders, believe that verbal abuse and harassment, not excessive use of force, is the major police-community relations problem today.[116]

Similarly, a study by Albert Reiss found that police abuse was verbal and coercive rather than physically violent. Reiss found little difference in the way police treated blacks and whites; when force was used, it was used more selectively, against those who showed disrespect or disregard for police authority once they had been arrested.[117] Thus, while not perfect, police officers do seem to have improved their relationships with citizens of all races.

A more recent area of concern has been the use of deadly force in apprehending fleeing or violent offenders. As commonly used, **deadly force** refers to the actions of a police officer who shoots and kills a suspect who is either fleeing from arrest, assaulting a victim, or attacking the police officer.

The justification for the use of deadly force can be traced to English common law, in which almost every criminal offense merited a felony status and subsequent death penalty. Thus, execution effected during the arrest of a felon was considered expedient, saving the state from the burden of trial. Research shows that between 250 and 350 citizens are killed by police each year.[118] The numbers of shooting incidents have been declining, reflecting efforts to control police use of deadly force (see later in this section).

Research studies indicate that the following factors have been related to police violence:[119]

- *Exposure to threat and stress.* Areas with an unusually high incidence of violent crime are likely to experience shootings by police.
- *Police workload.* Violence corresponds with the number of police officers on the street, the number of calls for service, the number and nature of police dispatches, and the number of arrests made in a given jurisdiction.
- *Firearm availability.* Cities that experience a large number of crimes committed with firearms are also likely to have high police violence rates. Houston, which ranks first in firearm availability, had 21.5 police shootings per 1,000 arrests for violent crimes, while San Francisco, which ranks tenth, had only 1.5 shootings per 1,000 such arrests.
- *Population type and density.* Jurisdictions swollen by large numbers and varied types of transients and nonresidents also experience a disproportionate

amount of police shootings. Research findings suggest that many individuals shot by police are nonresidents caught at or near the scenes of robberies or burglaries of commercial establishments.

- *Racial variations.* It is alleged that blacks and other racial minorities are killed at a significantly higher rate than whites. Catherine Milton and her associates found that 79 percent of those shot by police in the seven cities they studied were black (blacks made up 39 percent of the population of the cities). In a similar study, Betty Jenkins and Adrienne Faison found that 52 percent of those killed by police in 1970–1973 were black and 21 percent Hispanic. It is common to focus on the racial factor as the primary predictive factor in police violence.[120]

Despite the evidence indicating that police shootings are motivated by racial bias, research conducted by James Fyfe reveals some contradictory results. In a study of New York City shootings occurring over a five-year period (1971–1975), Fyfe found that police officers were most likely to shoot suspects when they attacked police officers, that many shootings stemmed from incidents in which police officers themselves were injured or killed, and that minorities were more likely to be involved in weapon assaults on police officers than whites (37 percent of events involving white citizens were gun incidents, while the rates for blacks and Hispanics were 58 and 56 percent).[121]

Fyfe's data revealed that minority police officers in New York were responsible for a disproportionate number of police shootings. Fyfe found that minority officers were often assigned to inner-city ghetto areas in which violence against police was common; it is therefore not surprising that minority officers' use of violence was relatively more frequent. However, in a more recent analysis of police shootings in the city of Memphis, Tennessee, Fyfe found that police were more likely to shoot black citizens than white and that "police there did differentiate racially with their trigger fingers, by shooting blacks in circumstances less threatening than those in which they shot whites."[122] Thus, the charge that police "have one trigger finger for whites and another for blacks" may have more validity in some areas than in others.

Not all research suggests that personal factors account for police shooting. Some points to the nature of the criminal interaction itself. Peter Scharf and Arnold Binder found that police shootings are influenced by the nature of the opponent the officer faced; whether they were on duty or off duty; the number of officers present; and the nature of the physical environment.[123] Rather than being purely spontaneous, Binder and Sharf found that shootings actually can be described as following a five-step model involving anticipation, confrontation, dialogue, shooting, and aftermath stages. Their research led them to suggest that police departments develop policies stressing containment of armed offenders while specially trained backup teams are sent to take charge of the situation. Similarly, training might emphasize the choices available in situations involving violence and conflict.

Controlling Deadly Force. In 1985, the Supreme Court moved to restrict police use of deadly force when in *Tennessee* v. *Garner* it banned the shooting of unarmed or nondangerous fleeing felons.[124] The Court based its decision on the premise that shooting an unarmed, nondangerous suspect was an illegal seizure of his body under the Fourth Amendment. According to the ruling, police could not justifiably use force unless it was "necessary to prevent the escape, and the officer has probable cause to believe that the suspect poses a significant threat of death or serious physical injury to the officers or others," for example, if the suspect threatens the officer or the officer has probable cause to believe that he has committed a crime involving serious physical harm. Before *Garner*, the policy of shooting unarmed fleeing felons had still been used in seventeen states.

Another method of controlling police shootings is through internal review and policy making by police departments themselves. For example, in New York City, the police department established a new firearms policy based on the American Law Institute's Model Penal Code. The new policy stated:

a. *In all cases, only the minimum amount of force will be used which is consistent with the accomplishment of a mission. Every other reasonable means will be utilized for arresting, preventing or terminating a felony or for the defense of oneself or another before a police officer resorts to the use of his firearm.*
b. *A firearm shall not be discharged under circumstances where lives of innocent persons may be endangered.*
c. *The firing of a warning shot is prohibited.*
d. *The discharging of a firearm to summon assistance is prohibited, except where the police officer's safety is endangered.*
e. *Discharging a firearm at or from a moving vehicle is prohibited unless the occupants of the other vehicle are using deadly physical force against the officer or another, by means other than the vehicle.*[125]

The New York police department also created the Firearm Discharge Review Board to evaluate shooting incidents. In an examination of the effects of this policy, James Fyfe found that a considerable reduction in the frequency of police shootings followed the policy change.[126]

Change in law and policy may not always work in changing police behavior. William Waegel studied police shootings in Philadelphia before (1970–1972) and after (1974–1978) the "fleeing felon" rule was abandoned. He found that after the state had restricted the police use of deadly force, about 20 percent of all shootings violated the new shooting code. In the five-year period after the rule change, police continued to violate shooting rules, and few officers were punished for their transgressions. Waegel found that shooting restrictions clash with the informal rules of the police culture. Unless police departments actively counteract informal pro-violence attitudes, changes in law and policy may be ineffective.[127]

Summary

Police officers are the gatekeepers of the criminal justice process. They use their power to arrest to initiate the justice process.

U.S. police agencies are modeled after their British counterparts. Early in British history, law enforcement was a personal matter. Later, constables were appointed to keep peace among groups of a hundred families. From this rudimentary beginning came the seed of today's police departments. In 1838, the first true U.S. police department was developed in Boston.

The first U.S. departments were created because of the need to control mob violence, which was common during the nineteenth century. The police were viewed as being dominated by political bosses who controlled their hiring practices and policies.

Reform movements begun during the 1920s culminated in the concept of professionalism in the 1950s and 1960s. Police professionalism was interpreted to mean tough, rule-oriented police work featuring advanced technology and hardware. However, the view that these measures would quickly reduce crime proved incorrect.

There are several major law enforcement agencies. On the federal level, the FBI is the premier law enforcement organization. Other agencies include the Drug Enforcement Administration, the U.S. marshals, and the Secret Service. County-level law enforcement is provided by sheriff's departments, and most states maintain state police agencies. However, the great bulk of law enforcement activities are carried out by local police agencies.

The police role is multilevel. Police officers fight crime, keep the peace, and provide community services. The conflicts and burdens involved in their work insulate them from the community and create great stress. Police officers suffer from high alcoholism, divorce, and suicide rates.

In carrying out their roles, police departments provide various services. The patrol function is designed to deter crime, keep the peace, and provide services. There is some question whether police patrol is actually effective. One important study conducted in Kansas City found that the extent of patrol had little effect on the crime rate or on citizens' satisfaction. Police departments have responded by creating innovative patrol mechanisms such as computer-dictated beats, hidden cameras, and team policing.

The second prominent police role is investigation. Detectives collect evidence in order to identify perpetrators. Although detectives use various techniques, including the successful sting operations, studies have shown that detective work is generally ineffective.

Other police functions include traffic control, departmental administration and maintenance, improvement of relations between police and community, and so on.

In recent years, many police operations have been controlled by court decisions. Most importantly, the courts have set limits on the extent of police interrogations and search and seizure of evidence.

Police departments face critical issues today. One involves understanding the police personality and its effect on performance. Another involves police personality and its effect on performance. Another involves police officers' use of discretion and how it can be controlled. Debate also continues over whether police officers should receive a higher education and what that education should include. Women and minority officers probably will become more prevalent on police departments, and their worth must be more fully appreciated by rank-and-file patrolmen. Police violence has received much attention. There is some debate whether police officers kill members of minorities more frequently than white citizens. Recent evidence indicates that may be the case in some cities.

Notes

1 "San Francisco, New York Police Troubled by Series of Scandals," *Criminal Justice Newsletter* 16 (1 May 1985):2–4.
2 Frank Tippett, "It Looks Just Like a War Zone," *Time*, 27 May 1985, pp. 16–22.
3 This section relies heavily on Daniel Devlin, *Police Procedure, Administration and Organization* (London: Butterworth, 1966); Robert Fogelson, *Big City Police* (Cambridge, Mass.: Harvard University Press, 1977); Roger Lane, *Policing the City, Boston 1822–1885* (Cambridge, Mass.: Harvard University Press, 1967); Roger Lane, "Urban Police and Crime in Nineteenth Century America," in *Crime and Justice*, vol. 2, ed. N. Morris and M. Torrey (Chicago: University of Chicago Press, 1980), pp. 1–45; J. J. Tobias, *Crime and Industrial Society in the Nineteenth Century* (New York: Schoken Books, 1967);

Samuel Walker, *A Critical History of Police Reform: The Emergence of Professionalism* (Lexington, Mass.: Lexington Books, 1977); Samuel Walker, *Popular Justice* (New York: Oxford University Press, 1980); President's Commission on Law Enforcement and the Administration of Justice, *Task Force Report: The Police* (Washington, D.C.: Government Printing Office, 1967), pp. 1–9.

4 Devlin, *Police Procedure, Administration and Organization*, p. 3.

5 Walker, *Popular Justice*, p. 18.

6 Lane, "Urban Police and Crime in Nineteenth Century America," p. 5.

7 Walker, *Popular Justice*, p. 61.

8 National Commission on Law Observance and Enforcement, *Report on the Police* (Washington, D.C.: Government Printing Office, 1931), pp. 5–7.

9 Preston William Slossom, *A History of American Life*, 12 vols., ed. 35. Arthur M. Schlesinger and Dixon Ryan Fox, vol. 12, *The Great Crusade and After, 1914–1929* (New York: Macmillan, 1931), p. 102.

10 See generally Walker, *A Critical History of Police Reform*.

11 This section was adapted from Law Enforcement Assistance Administration, *Two Hundred Years of American Criminal Justice* (Washington, D.C.: Government Printing Office, 1976).

12 Thomas Adams, *Law Enforcement* (Englewood Cliffs, N.J.: Prentice-Hall, 1968), p. 99.

13 Walker, *Popular Justice*, p. 238.

14 John Sullivan, *Introduction to Police Science* (New York: McGraw-Hill, 1968), p. 24.

15 The personnel distribution of local police agencies is listed in Federal Bureau of Investigation, *Crime in the United States, 1981* (Washington, D.C.: Government Printing Office, 1982).

16 See Clarence Schrag, *Crime and Justice: American Style* (Washington, D.C.: Government Printing Office, 1970), p. 47.

17 Egon Bittner, *The Functions of Police in Modern Society* (Cambridge, Mass.: Delgeschlager, Gunn and Hain, 1980), p. 149.

18 J. Q. Wilson, *Varieties of Police Behavior: The Management of Law and Order in Eight Communities* (Cambridge, Mass.: Harvard University Press, 1968).

19 Richard Sykes and Edward Brent, *Policing: A Social Behaviorist Perspective* (New Brunswick, N.J.: Rutgers University Press, 1983).

20 Peter Manning, *Police Work: Essays on the Social Organization of Policing* (Cambridge, Mass.: MIT Press, 1977), pp. 101–102.

21 Bittner, *The Functions of Police in Modern Society*, pp. 63–72.

22 James Q. Wilson and George Kelling, "Broken Windows: The Police and Neighborhood Safety," *Atlantic Monthly*, March 1982, pp. 29–38.

23 Ibid., p. 37.

24 Samuel Walker, "Broken Windows and Fractured History: The Use and Misuse of History in Recent Police Patrol Analysis," *Justice Quarterly* 1 (1984):75–90.

25 See Harlan Hahn, "A Profile of Urban Police," in *The Ambivalent Force*, ed. A. Niederhoffer and A. Blumberg (Hinsdale, Ill.: Dryden Press, 1967), p. 59.

26 George Kelling, Tony Pate, Duane Dieckman, and Charles Brown, *The Kansas City Preventive Patrol Experiment: A Summary Report* (Washington, D.C.: Police Foundation, 1974).

27 Ibid., pp. 3–4.

28 Albert J. Reiss, *The Police and the Public* (New Haven, Conn.: Yale University Press, 1971), p. 19.

29 Bittner, *The Functions of Police in Modern Society*, p. 127.

30 David Greenberg, Ronald Kessler, and Colin Loftin, "The Effect of Police Employment on Crime," *Criminology* 21 (1983):375–94.

31 Laurence Sherman and Richard Berk, "The Specific Deterrent Effects of Arrest for Domestic Assault," *American Sociological Review* 49 (1984):261–72.

32 Perry Shapiro and Harold Votey, "Deterrence and Subjective Probabilities of Arrest:

Modeling Individual Decisions to Drink and Drive in Sweden," *Law and Society Review* 18 (1984):111–49.

33 See generally L. Sherman et al., *Team Policing—Seven Case Studies* (Washington, D.C.: Police Foundation, 1973).

34 John Angell, "The Democratic Model Needs a Fair Trial: Angell's Response," *Criminology* 12 (1975):379–84.

35 "Many Cities Experimenting with Foot Patrol," Criminal Justice *Newsletter* 16 (15 May 1985):1–2.

36 See generally P. Greenwood and J. Petersilia, *The Criminal Investigation Process, Volume 1: Summary and Policy Implications* (Santa Monica, Calif.: Rand Corporation, 1975); P. Greenwood, J. Chaiken, J. Petersilia, and L. Prusoff, *The Criminal Investigation Process, Volume III: Observations and Analysis* (Santa Monica, Calif.: Rand Corporation, 1975).

37 C. Cotter and J. Burrows, *Property Crime Program, a Special Report: Overview of the STING Program and Project Summaries* (Washington, D.C.: Criminal Conspiracies Division, Office of Criminal Justice Programs, Law Enforcement Assistance Administration, U.S. Department of Justice, 1981).

38 Ibid., p. 8.

39 Ibid., p. 120.

40 Greenwood and Petersilia, *The Criminal Investigation Process, Volume I.*

41 Mark T. Willman and John R. Snortum, "Detective Work: The Criminal Investigation Process in a Medium-Size Police Department," *Criminal Justice Review* 9 (1984):33–39.

42 Thomas Reppetto, "The Uneasy Milieu of the Detective," in *The Ambivalent Force*, ed. A. Niederhoffer and A. Blumberg (Hinsdale, Ill.: Dryden Press, 1967), pp. 133–35.

43 See generally Robert Sheehan and Gary Cordner, *Introduction to Police Administration* (Reading, Mass.: Addison-Wesley, 1979).

44 Miranda v. Arizona, 384 U.S. 436 (1966).

45 Harris v. New York, 401 U.S. 222 (1971).

46 Michigan v. Tucker, 417 U.S. 433 (1974).

47 Michican v. Mosley, 423 U.S. 96 (1975); California v. Prysock, 453 U.S. 355 (1981).

48 Nix v. Williams, 104 S. Ct. 2501 (1984).

49 New York v. Quarles, 104 S. Ct 2626 (1984).

50 Oregon v. Elstad, 105 S. Ct. 1285 (1985).

51 Illinois v. Gates, 104 S. Ct. 2626 (1984).

52 David Fellman, *The Defendant's Rights Today* (Madison, Wis.: University of Wisconsin Press, 1976).

53 United States v. Chadwick, 433 U.S. 1 (1977).

54 Chimel v. California, 395 U.S. 752 (1969).

55 United States v. Hensley, 105 S. Ct. 675 (1985).

56 Terry v. Ohio, 392 U.S. 1 (1968).

57 Carroll v. United States, 267 U.S. 132 (1925).

58 United States v. Ross, 102 S. Ct. 2147 (1982).

59 Bumper v. North Carolina, 391 U.S. 543 (1960).

60 Katz v. United States, 389 U.S. 347 (1967).

61 United States v. Sharpe, No. 83-259 (1985).

62 Hayes v. Florida, No. 83-6766 (1985).

63 California v. Carney, No. 83-859 (1985).

64 New Jersey v. TLO, No. 83-712 (1985).

65 United States v. Johns, No. 83-1625 (1985).

66 Richard Lundman, *Police and Policing* (New York: Holt, Rinehart and Winston, 1980); see also Jerome Skolnick, *Justice without Trial* (New York: Wiley, 1966).

67 Cited in Arthur Niederhoffer, *Behind the Shield: The Police in Urban Society* (Garden City, N.Y.: Doubleday, 1967), p. 65.

68 See, for example, Richard Bennett and Theodore Greenstein, "The Police Personality: A Test of the Predispositional Model," *Journal of Police Science and Administration* 3 (1975):439–45.

69 Milton Rokeach, Martin Miller, and John Snyder, "The Value Gap between Police and Policed," *Journal of Social Issues* 27 (1971):155–71; for a similar view, see James Teevan and Bernard Dolnick, "The Values of the Police: A Reconsideration and Interpretation," *Journal of Police Science and Administration* 1 (1973):366–69.

70 John Van Maanen, "Observations on the Making of Policemen," in *Order under Law*, ed. R. Culbertson and M. Tezak (Prospect Heights, Ill.: Waveland Press, 1981), p. 59.

71 Ibid., p. 66.

72 George Kirkham, "A Professor's 'Street Lessons'," in *Order under Law*, ed. R. Culbertson and M. Tezak (Prospect Heights, Ill.: Waveland Press, 1981), p. 81.

73 Bittner, *The Functions of Police in Modern Society*, p. 63.

74 Niederhoffer, *Behind the Shield.*

75 William Westly, *Violence and the Police: A Sociological Study of Law, Custom and Morality* (Cambridge, Mass.: MIT Press, 1970); W. Westly, "Violence and the Police," *American Journal of Sociology* 49 (1953):34–41.

76 Niederhoffer, *Behind the Shield*, pp. 216–20.

77 See, for example, Richard Harris, *The Police Academy: An Inside View* (New York: Wiley, 1973); John Van Maanen, "Observations on the Making of Policemen," *Human Organization* 32 (1973): 407–18; Jonathan Rubenstein, *City Police* (New York: Ballantine, 1973); John Broderick, *Police in a Time of Change* (Morristown, N.J.: General Learning Press, 1977).

78 Joseph Goldstein, "Police Discretion Not to Invoke the Criminal Process," *Yale Law Journal* 69 (1960):543–94.

79 Richard C. Donnelly, "Police Authority and Practices," *Annals of the American Academy of Political and Social Science* 339 (January 1962), pp. 91–92.

80 See generally Kenneth C. Davis, *Discretionary Justice—A Preliminary Inquiry* (Baton Rouge: Louisiana State University Press, 1969).

81 See, for example, Nathan Goldman, *The Differential Selection of Juvenile Offenders for Court Appearance* (New York: National Council on Crime and Delinquency, 1963); Aaron Cicourel, *The Social Organization of Juvenile Justice* (New York: Wiley, 1968); Irving Piliavin and Scott Briar, "Police Encounters with Juveniles," *American Journal of Sociology* 70 (1964):206.

82 Jerome Skolnick and J. Richard Woodworth, "Bureaucracy, Information and Social Control: A Study of a Morals Detail" in *The Police, Six Sociological Essays*, ed. David Bordua (New York: Wiley, 1960).

83 John Gardiner, *Traffic and the Police: Variations in Law Enforcement Policy* (Cambridge, Mass.: Harvard University Press, 1969).

84 One notable exception is control of deadly force, which will be discussed later in this chapter.

85 See note 81.

86 Marvin Krohn, James Curry and Shirley Nelson-Kilger, "Is Chivalry Dead? An Analysis of Changes in Police Dispositions of Males and Females," *Criminology* 21 (1983):417–37.

87 Douglas Smith and Jody Klein, "Police Control of Interpersonal Disputes," *Social Problems* 31 (1984):468–81.

88 Richard C. Hollinger, "Race, Occupational Status and Pro-Active Police Arrest for Drinking and Driving," *Journal of Criminal Justice* 12 (1984):173–83.

89 Douglas A. Smith, Christy A. Visher, and Laura A. Davidson, "Equity and Discretionary Justice: The Influence of Race on Police Arrest Decisions," *Journal of Criminal Law and Criminology* 75 (1984):234–49.

90 Sherri Lynn Johnson, "Race and the Decision to Detain a Suspect," *Yale Law Journal* 93 (1983):214–58.

91 See, for example, James Erickson and Mathew Neary, "Criminal Justice Education: Is It Criminal?" *Police Chief* 42 (1975):38–40.

92 See Lawrence Sherman and Warren Bennis, "Higher Education for Police Officers: The Central Issues," *Police Chief* 44 (1977):32–33.

93 Solomon Gross, "Higher Education and Police: Is There a Need for a Closer Look," *Journal of Police Science and Administration* 1 (1973):336–44.

94 See, for example, B. E. Sanderson, "Police Officers: The Relationship of College Education to Job Performance," *Police Chief* 44 (1977):62; James Finnegan, "A Study of Relationships between College Education and Police Performance in Baltimore, Maryland," *Police Chief* 43 (1976):50; R. Trojanowicz and Thomas Nicholson, "A Comparison of Behavioral Styles of College Graduate Police Officers v. Non-College-Going Police Officers," *Police Chief* 43 (1967):57; R. P. Witte, "The Dumb Cop," *Police Chief* 36 (1969):38; Wayne Cascio, "Formal Education and Police Officer Performance," *Journal of Police Science and Administration* 5 (1977):89; Merlyn Moore, "The Field and Academia—a Message," *Police Chief* 42 (1975):66–69.

95 Lawrence Sherman et al., *The Quality of Police Education* (San Francisco: Jossey-Bass, 1978).

96 Robert Fischer, "Is Education Really an Alternative? The End of a Long Controversy," *Journal of Police Science and Administration* 9 (1981):313–16.

97 Most important is the Equal Employment Opportunity Act of 1972, amending Title VII of the Civil Rights Act of 1964.

98 See, for example, Arnold v. Ballard, 390 F. Supp. 723 (1975). Evidence showed that between 1965 and 1971, 10 blacks and 277 whites had been appointed to the Akron, Ohio, police department. Similar cases have been decided in many major U.S. cities.

99 Ellen Hochstedler, Robert M. Regoli, and Eric D. Poole, "Changing the Guard in American Cities: A Current Empirical Assessment of Integration in Twenty Municipal Police Departments," *Criminal Justice Review* 9 (1984):8–14.

100 Firefighters Local Union No. 1784 v. Stotts, 104 S. Ct. 2576 (1984).

101 Walker, *Popular Justice*, p. 61.

102 Nicholas Alex, *Black in Blue: A Study of the Negro Policeman* (New York: Appleton Century Crofts, 1969).

103 Ibid., p. 154.

104 James Jacobs and Jay Cohen, "The Impact of Racial Integration on the Police," *Journal of Police Science and Administration* 6 (1978):182.

105 See Afro-American Patrolmen's League v. Duck, 366 F. Supp. 1095 (1973); 503 F. 2d 294 (6th Cir., 1974); 538 F. 2d 328 (6th Cir., 1976).

106 Stephen Leinen, *Black Police, White Society* (New York: New York University Press, 1984).

107 See generally David J. Bell, "Policewomen: Myths and Reality," *Journal of Police Science and Administration* 10 (1982):112–20.

108 Catherine Milton, *Women in Policing* (Washington, D.C.: Police Foundation, 1972).

109 See generally A. Bouza, "Women in Policing," *FBI Law Enforcement Bulletin* 44 (1975):2–7; Joyce Sichel, Lucy Friedman, Janet Quint, and Micall Smith, *Women on Patrol. A Pilot Study of Police Performance in New York City* (Washington, D.C.: National Criminal Justice Reference Service, 1978); William Weldy, "Women in Policing: A Positive Step toward Increased Police Enthusiasm," *Police Chief* 43 (1976):47.

110 Patricia Marshall, "Policewomen on Patrol," *Manpower* 5 (1973):14–20.

111 R. Hindman, "A Survey Related to Use of Female Law Enforcement Officers," *Police Chief* 42 (1975):58–60.

112 Bell, "Policewomen: Myths and Realities," p. 114.

113 Sally Gross, "Women Becoming Cops: Developmental Issues and Solutions," *Police Chief* 51 (1984):32–35.

114 Bittner, *The Functions of Police in Modern Society*, p. 46.

115 Walker, *Popular Justice*, p. 197.

116 President's Commission on Law Enforcement and the Administration of Justice, *Task Force Report: The Police*, pp. 181–82.

117 Albert Reiss, *The Police and the Public*.

118 Kenneth Mattulla, *A Balance of Forces* (Washington, D.C.: U.S. Government Printing Office, 1982), p. 17.

119 This discussion is adapted from James Fyfe, "Toward a Typology of Police Shootings," (Paper presented at the annual meeting of the Academy of Criminal Justice Sciences, Oklahoma City, March 1980, to be included in James J. Fyfe, ed., *Contemporary Issues in Law Enforcement* (Beverly Hills, Calif.: Sage Publications, forthcoming).

120 Milton et al., *Use of Deadly Force*; Betty Jenkins and Adrienne Faison, *An Analysis of 248 Persons Killed by New York City Policemen* (New York: Metropolitan Applied Research Center, 1974).

121 James Fyfe, "Race and Extreme Police-Citizen Violence," in *Race, Crime and Criminal Justice*, ed. R. L. McNeely and Carl Pope (Beverly Hills, Calif.: Sage Publications, 1981).

122 James Fyfe, "Blind Justice? Police Shooting in Memphis" (Paper prepared for the annual meeting of the Academy of Criminal Justice Science, Philadelphia, March 1981), p. 18.

123 Peter Scharf and Arnold Binder, *The Badge and the Bullet: Police Use of Deadly Force* (New York: Praeger, 1983).

124 Tennessee v. Garner, 105 S. Ct. 1694 (1985).

125 New York City Police Department, *Temporary Operating Procedure 237*, p. 1.

126 James Fyfe, "Administrative Interventions on Police Shooting Discretion: An Empirical Examination," *Journal of Criminal Justice* 7 (1979):309–23.

127 William Waegel, "The Use of Lethal Force by Police: The Effect of Statutory Change," *Crime and Delinquency* 30 (1984):121–40.

16 The Adjudicatory Process

CHAPTER OUTLINE

Introduction

Court Structure
State Courts
Federal Courts

Actors in the Adjudicatory Process
Prosecutor
Defense Attorney
Judge

Pretrial Procedures
Bail
Plea Bargaining
Alternatives to Prosecution: Diversion

The Criminal Trial
Jury Selection
Trial Process
Trials and the Rule of Law

Sentencing
Purposes of Sentencing
Sentencing Dispositions
Sentence to an Extended Term in Prison
Sentencing Disparity and Control
Extralegal Factors in Sentencing
Sentencing in the 1980s: A Final Word

Summary

KEY TERMS

United States District Court
Federal Circuit Court of Appeals
United States Supreme Court
prosecution
affidavit
discretion
defense
attorney list/assigned counsel
public defender

judge
charge the jury
Missouri Plan
Bill of Indictment
information
complaint
nolo contendere
bail

preventive detention
Vera Foundation
release on recognizance
plea bargaining
diversion
venire
voir dire
peremptory challenge

Introduction

The adjudicatory process is designed to provide an open and impartial forum for deciding the justice of a conflict between two or more parties. The conflict may be between criminal and victim, law enforcement agents and violators of the law, parent and child, federal government and violators of governmental regulations, and so on. Regardless of the parties or issues involved, their presence in a courtroom should guarantee that their hearing will be conducted under regulated rules of procedure, that the outcome of the hearing will be clear, and that the hearing will take place in an atmosphere of fair play and objectivity. If either party, defendant or complainant, believes that these ground rules have been violated, that party may take the case to a higher court, where the procedures of the original trial will be examined. If, upon reexamination, it is found that a violation of the rights of either the defendant or the complainant has occurred, the appellate court may deem the findings of the original trial improper and either order a new hearing or hold that some other measure must be carried out—for example, the court may dismiss the charge outright.

The court is a complex social agency with many independent but interrelated subsystems—police, prosecutor, defense attorney, judge, and probation department—each having a role in the court's operation. It is also the scene of many important elements of criminal justice decision making—detention, jury selection, trial, and sentencing.

Ideally, the adjudicatory process operates under a cloak of absolute fairness and equality. The entire process—from the filing of the initial complaint to final sentencing of the defendant—is governed by precise rules of law designed to insure that fairness exists. No defendant being tried before a U.S. court should suffer, or benefit, because of his or her personal characteristics, beliefs, or affiliations.

However, as suggested in chapter 14, U.S. criminal justice can be a very selective process. Decision makers' discretion follows the defendant through every step of the process of justice. For every hundred adults arrested on felony charges, fewer than three are sent to prison.[1] Most of the others receive little or no punishment, although their offenses may at first seem indistinguishable from the offenses of those who are dealt with harshly.[2] Thus, although the adjudicatory process should be impartial and fair, very often it is marked by the same informal, low-visibility decision making that characterizes the law enforcement process.[3]

This chapter will review some of the institutions and processes involved in adjudication and trial. First, the chapter will briefly describe the court structure. Then, a discussion of the actors in the process—prosecution, defense, judges, and juries—will be undertaken. The preadjudicatory stage of the justice process will next be the focus of attention. Issues such as bail and plea bargaining are described. The criminal trial will then be discussed in some detail; and finally, sentencing formats will be explained.

Court Structure

The criminal adjudication process is played out within the confines of the court system. As mentioned in chapter 14, there are over 17,000 courts operating in the United States. They are organized on the municipal, county, state, and federal levels of jurisdiction.

STATE COURTS

The typical state court structure is illustrated in figure 16.1. As noted in chapter 14, most states employ a three- or four-tiered court structure. Lower (county) courts

FIGURE 16.1

State judicial systems

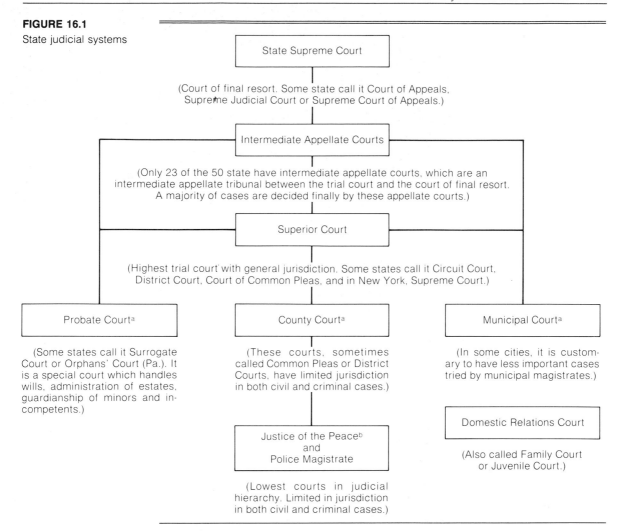

State Supreme Court

(Court of final resort. Some state call it Court of Appeals,
Supreme Judicial Court or Supreme Court of Appeals.)

Intermediate Appellate Courts

(Only 23 of the 50 state have intermediate appellate courts, which are an
intermediate appellate tribunal between the trial court and the court of final resort.
A majority of cases are decided finally by these appellate courts.)

Superior Court

(Highest trial court with general jurisdiction. Some states call it Circuit Court,
District Court, Court of Common Pleas, and in New York, Supreme Court.)

Probate Court[a]

(Some states call it Surrogate
Court or Orphans' Court (Pa.). It
is a special court which handles
wills, administration of estates,
guardianship of minors and in-
competents.)

County Court[a]

(These courts, sometimes
called Common Pleas or District
Courts, have limited jurisdiction
in both civil and criminal cases.)

Municipal Court[a]

(In some cities, it is customary to have less important cases
tried by municipal magistrates.)

Domestic Relations Court

(Also called Family Court
or Juvenile Court.)

Justice of the Peace[b]
and
Police Magistrate

(Lowest courts in judicial
hierarchy. Limited in jurisdiction
in both civil and criminal cases.)

[a]Courts of special jurisdiction, such as Probate, Family or Juvenile, and the so-called inferior courts, such
as Common Pleas or Municipal courts, may be separate courts or may be part of the trial court of general
jurisdiction.
[b]Justices of the Peace do not exist in all states. Their jurisdictions vary greatly from state to state when
they do exist.

SOURCE. American Bar Association, *Law and the Courts* (Chicago: American Bar Association, 1974),
p. 20.

handle misdemeanors and petty offenses. Superior trial courts have jurisdiction
over felony cases. Appellate courts review the criminal procedures of trial courts
to determine whether the offenders were treated fairly. Superior appellate courts
or state supreme courts, used in about half the states, review lower appellate court
decisions.

FEDERAL COURTS

The federal court system maintains a three-tiered model of court jurisdiction, as
shown in figure 16.2. The **United States District Courts** are the trial courts of
the system; they maintain jurisdiction over cases involving violations of federal
law, such as interstate transportation of stolen vehicle and RICO prosecution.

FIGURE 16.2

Federal judicial system

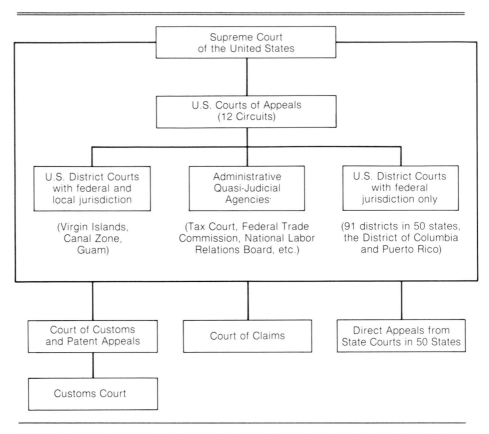

SOURCE. American Bar Association, *Law and the Courts* (Chicago: American Bar Association, 1974), p. 21.

Appeals from the district court are heard in one of the intermediate-level **Federal Circuit Courts of Appeal.** However, the highest federal appeals court is the **United States Supreme Court.**

The United States Supreme Court, as the nation's highest appellate body, is the court of last resort for all cases tried in the various federal and state courts. In certain rare instances, however, the Supreme Court can actually sit as a trial court—for example, in cases involving ambassadors or in suits between states.

The Supreme Court is composed of nine members, appointed for lifetime terms by the president with the approval of Congress. In general, the Court has discretion as to which cases it will consider and may choose to hear only those it deems important, appropriate, and worthy of its attention. When the Court decides to hear a case it usually grants a *Writ of Certiorari*, requesting a transcript of the proceedings of the case for review.

The Supreme Court must accept jurisdiction in all cases in which:

- A federal court holds an act of Congress to be unconstitutional.
- A United States Court of Appeals finds a state statute unconstitutional.
- A state's highest court holds a federal law to be invalid.
- An individual's challenge to a state statute on constitutional grounds is upheld by a state supreme court.

When the Supreme Court chooses to, it can word a decision so that it becomes a precedent that must be honored by all lower courts. For example, if the Court grants a particular litigant the right to counsel at a police lineup, then all people in similar situations must be given the same right. This type of ruling is usually referred to as a *landmark decision*. The use of precedent in the legal system gives the Supreme Court power to influence and mold the everyday operating procedures of police agencies, trial courts, and corrections institutions. In the past, this influence was not nearly as pronounced as it has been during the tenure of the two most recent chief justices, Earl Warren and Warren Burger, who have greatly amplified and extended the power of the Court to affect criminal justice policies.

Court Caseloads. The American court system is a vast enterprise. In 1983, the last year statistics were available, about 81 million cases were brought before the trial courts of the 50 states and the District of Columbia.[4] In addition to trial court cases, there were 189,937 appeals filed in state appellate courts. In addition, federal courts handled about 34,000 criminal cases and 4800 appeals in 1983.

These statistics can be misleading since about 60 to 70 percent of all cases are traffic violations handled by municipal or traffic court. Nonetheless, about 12 million cases involving criminal actions are handled by the courts each year.

The trend toward a rapidly expanding criminal court caseload may be ending due to the recent declines in the nation's crime rate. Nonetheless, if currently popular get-tough policies persist, the percentage of apprehended offenders brought to trial may increase, helping to maintain the court system's overwhelming criminal caseload.

Actors in the Adjudicatory Process

This section describes the major actors in the pretrial, trial, and sentencing process—the prosecutor, the defense attorney, and the judge.

PROSECUTOR

The major role of the **prosecution** is to represent the state in criminal matters that come before the court system. Among prosecutors' major duties are included:

- *Conducting investigations of law violations.* Prosecutors are empowered to conduct their own investigations into alleged violations of the law. In some jurisdictions, they maintain their own staff of detectives and investigators; in others they rely on local or state police. In jurisdictions with grand jury systems, the prosecutor can convene the grand jury to act as a fact-finding body to collect information and interview witnesses for the purpose of accumulating enough evidence to indict suspects in criminal conspiracies.
- *Cooperating with police.* The prosecutor's office usually maintains a close working relationship with police agencies. Police prepare the investigation report of a crime according to the format desired by the prosecutor's office. Prosecutors also advise police agents about the legal issues in a given case. For example, they supervise the drawing up of requests (**affidavits**) for search warrants and then make sure that the police understand the limitations presented by the warrant. Some prosecutor's offices help train police officers, making them aware of the legal issues involved in securing a warrant or a legal arrest, interrogating a suspect, and so on.

- *Determining charges.* It is the prosecutor who makes the final determination of the charges to be brought against the suspect. The charge on which persons are brought to trial may have little resemblance to the original reasons for which they were arrested. For example, a suspect picked up for disorderly conduct may later be identified at a police lineup as the perpetrator of a string of liquor store robberies. The disorderly conduct charge may then be dropped in favor of prosecution on the more serious robbery charges.
- *Representing the government in pretrial hearings and motions.* The prosecutor is charged with bringing the case to trial. Prosecutors make contact with witnesses and prepare them to testify; secure physical evidence; and discuss the victim's testimony. If the defendant attempts to have evidence suppressed at a pretrial hearing (for example, because of violations of the exclusionary rule), the prosecutor represents the state's position on the matter.
- *Plea bargaining.* The prosecutor is empowered to negotiate a guilty plea with the defendant, thereby ending the formal trial process.
- *Trying criminal cases.* The prosecutor acts as the state's attorney at criminal trials. Consequently, another name for the prosecutor is *people's attorney.*
- *Sentencing.* The prosecutor recommends dispositions at the completion of the trial. Usually, the type of sentence recommended is influenced by plea bargaining cooperation, public opinion, the seriousness of the crime, the offender's prior record, and other factors related to the case.
- *Representing the government at appeals.* If the defendant is found guilty as charged, he or she may appeal the conviction before a higher court. It is part of the prosecutor's overall duties to represent the government at these hearings.
- *Conducting special investigations.* Some jurisdictions empower special prosecutors to seek indictments for serious crimes considered of importance to public interest. This practice became well known during the Watergate investigation, when first Archibald Cox and then Leon Jaworski were appointed special prosecutors to investigate the break-ins and subsequent cover-up.

Types of Prosecutors. In the federal system, prosecutors are known as United States attorneys and are appointed by the president. They are responsible for representing the government in federal district courts. The chief prosecutor is usually an administrator, while assistants normally handle the actual preparation and trial work. Federal prosecutors are professional civil service employees with reasonable salaries and job security.

At the state level, the chief prosecutorial officer is the attorney general; at the county level, the district attorney. Both are elected officials. Again, the bulk of criminal prosecution and staff work is performed by scores of full-time and part-time attorneys, police investigators, and clerical personnel. Most attorneys who work for prosecutors at state and county levels are political appointees who earn low salaries; handle many cases; and in some jurisdictions, maintain private law practices. Many young lawyers serve in this capacity to gain trial experience, and leave when they obtain better-paying positions. In some state, county, and municipal jurisdictions, however, the office of the prosecutor can be described as meeting the highest standards of professional skill, personal integrity, and working conditions.

In urban settings, the structure of the district attorney's office is often specialized, with separate divisions for felonies, misdemeanors, and trial and appeal assignments. In rural offices, chief prosecutors handle many of the criminal cases themselves. Where assistant prosecutors are employed, they often work part-time, have limited professional opportunities, and depend on the political patronage of chief prosecutors for their positions.

Prosecutorial Discretion. Prosecutors maintain broad **discretion** in the exercise of their duties. In fact, full enforcement of the law is so rare that it is assumed that prosecutors will pick and choose the cases they decide to bring to court. Over forty years ago, Newman Baker discussed the problems of prosecutorial decision making when he said:

> *"To prosecute or not to prosecute?" is a question which comes to the mind of this official scores of times each day. A law has been contravened and the statute says he is bound to commence proceedings. His legal duty is clear. But, what will be the result? Will it be a waste of time? Will it be expensive to the state? Will it be unfair to the defendant (the prosecutor applying his own ideas of justice)? Will it serve any good purpose to society in general? Will it have good publicity value? Will it cause a political squabble? Will it prevent the prosecutor from carrying the offender's home precinct when he, the prosecutor, runs for Congress after his term as prosecutor? Was the law violated a foolish piece of legislation? If the offender is a friend, is it the square thing to do to reward friendship by initiating criminal proceedings? These and many similar considerations are bound to come to the mind of the man responsible for setting the wheels of criminal justice in motion.*[5]

Prosecutors exercise their discretion in a variety of circumstances. One major decision involves the choice of either acting on the information brought by police, or deciding not to file for an indictment. The prosecutor can also attempt to prosecute and then decide to take official action to drop the case; this is known as a *nolle prosequi*.

Figure 16.3 shows the pattern of decision making exercised by prosecutors in three large urban jurisdictions: New Orleans, Washington, D.C., and Manhattan Borough court in New York. As figure 16.3 indicates, the number of felony cases screened out before trial varies widely between jurisdictions. Nolle prosequi cases ranged from 8 percent to 32 percent. Prosecutorial discretion resulted in the dismissal of between 40 and 55 percent of the felony cases filed in the three jurisdictions.[6]

In making their decision, prosecutors have a significant effect on the criminal justice process. If they attempted to formally handle all suspects arrested by police, they would clog the courts with many petty crimes and prosecute others in which there was little chance for conviction. By effectively screening out cases in which conviction could not reasonably be expected, cases inappropriate for criminal action (such as minor thefts by first offenders), and cases involving offenders with special needs (such as the emotionally disturbed or mentally retarded), the prosecutor can concentrate on bringing to trial those who commit more serious criminal offenses.

Factors Influencing Decision Making. What factors influence prosecutorial discretion? Numerous attempts have been made to examine the charging decision. Best known is the classic work *Prosecution: The Decision to Charge a Subject*, by

FIGURE 16.3 Differences in how prosecutors handle felony cases in three jurisdictions

Differences in how prosecutors handle felony cases
in 3 jurisdictions

Outcome of felony cases presented to prosecutor

New Orleans, Louisiana

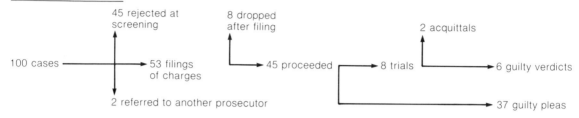

Washington, D.C.

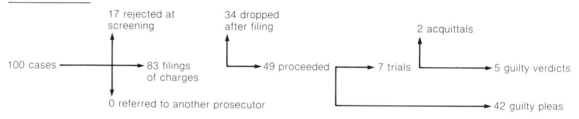

Manhattan Borough, New York

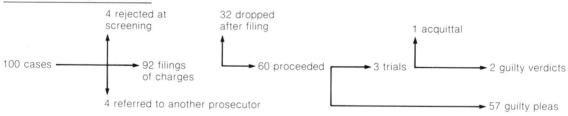

SOURCE. B. Boland, INSLAW, Inc., *The prosecution of felony arrests*, 1983.

Frank Miller.[7] In his incisive analysis, Miller pinpoints factors influencing prose-cutorial discretion, including (1) the attitude of the victim; (2) the cost of pros-ecution to the criminal justice system; (3) the possibility of undue harm to the suspect; (4) the availability of alternative procedures; (5) the availability of civil sanctions; and (6) the willingness of the suspect to cooperate with law enforcement authorities.

In another classic work, Wayne LaFave also identified factors related to the decision to invoke prosecutorial discretion.[8] According to LaFave, when acts have been *overcriminalized*—such as when laws provide stiff sentences for neighborhood poker games—they are not prosecuted. Further, limited resources force the pros-ecutor to select only the most serious cases. Finally, alternatives to prosecution are used whenever possible to spare the offenders the stigma of a criminal conviction.

In some instances, LaFave found that the prosecutor may decide to take no action; this occurs when the victim expresses the desire not to prosecute, when the cost would be excessive, when the harm of prosecution outweighs the benefits, or when the harm done by the offender can be corrected without a criminal trial. LaFave also points out that prosecutors have tools at their disposal to invoke obscure statutes to punish unrepentant offenders or refuse leniency to defendants who will not cooperate with them. Thus, to LaFave, prosecutorial discretion is a two-edged sword.

In addition, the following have been identified as influencing prosecutorial discretion:

- *Evidence problems* that result from a failure to find sufficient physical evidence that links the defendant to the offense
- *Witness problems* that arise, for example, when a witness fails to appear, gives unclear or inconsistent statements, is reluctant to testify, or is unsure of the identity of the offender
- *Office policy*, wherein the prosecutor decides not to prosecute certain types of offenses, particularly those that violate the letter but not the spirit of the law (for example, offenses involving insignificant amounts of property damage)
- *Due process problems* that involve violations of the Constitutional requirements for seizing evidence and for questioning the accused
- *Combination with other cases*, for example, when the accused is charged in several cases and the prosecutor prosecutes all of the charges in a single case
- *Pretrial diversion* that occurs when the prosecutor and the court agree to drop charges when the accused successfully meets the conditions for diversion, such as completion of a treatment program.[9]

Is prosecutorial discretion inherently harmful? Not according to most experts, who view it as a necessary component of efficiency in the criminal justice system. For example, Judge Charles Breitel has stated:

> *If every policeman, every prosecutor, every court, and every postsentence agency performed his or its responsibility in strict accordance with rules of law, precisely and narrowly laid down, the criminal law would be ordered but intolerable. Living would be a sterile compliance with soul-killing rules and taboos. By comparison, a primitive tribal society would seem free, indeed.*[10]

Although eliminating prosecutorial discretion may not always be desirable, efforts have been made to control its content and direction. For example, national commissions have established guidelines for the exercise of appropriate prosecutorial actions.[11] Other methods of controlling prosecutorial decision making include: (1) identification of the reasons for charging decisions; (2) publication of prosecution office policies; (3) reviews by nonprosecutorial groups; (4) charging conferences; and (5) evaluation of charging policies and decisions and development of screening, diversion, and plea negotiation procedures.[12]

DEFENSE ATTORNEY

The **defense** counsel performs many functions while representing the accused in the criminal process. They include, but are not limited to, the following:

- Investigating the incident.
- Interviewing the client, police officers, and other witnesses.

Judges and attorneys may meet informally to discuss sentencing alternatives such as community treatment or rehabilitation programs.

- Discussing the matter with the prosecutor.
- Representing the defendant at the various prejudicial procedures, such as arrest, interrogation, lineup, and arraignment.
- Entering into plea negotiations.
- Preparing the case for trial, including developing the tactics and strategy to be used.
- Filing and arguing legal motions with the court.
- Representing the defendant at trial.
- Providing assistance at sentencing.
- Determining the appropriate basis for appeal.

Despite the numerous prominent criminal defense lawyers in the United States, the majority of criminal defendants are indigents who cannot afford legal counsel. The Supreme Court has interpreted the Sixth Amendment of the Constitution to mean that people facing trial for offenses that can be punished by incarceration have the right to legal counsel.[13] If they cannot afford counsel, the state must provide an attorney free of charge. Consequently, three systems have been developed to provide legal counsel to the indigent:

1. Assigning private attorneys to represent indigent clients on a case-by-case basis (sometimes referred to as an attorney list system), with the state paying their fees.
2. Contracting with a law firm or group of private attorneys to regularly provide defense services to indigents.
3. Creating a publicly funded defenders' office.

These three systems can be used independently or in combination. In general, the **attorney list/assigned counsel** system is used in less populated areas, where case flow is minimal and a full-time public defender unneeded. **Public defenders** are usually found in larger urban areas with high case flow rates. Thus, although a proportionately larger area of the country is served by the assigned counsel system, a significant portion of criminal defendants receive public defenders. Public defenders can be part of a state-wide agency (25 percent), county government (38 percent), the judiciary (23 percent); or they can be set up as an independent nonprofit organization or other institution (14 percent).

A recent government survey found that of the 3,082 counties served by indigent defendant services, 1,833 (60 percent) had assigned counsel systems, 1,048 had public defenders (34 percent), and 201 (6 percent) had contract attorneys.[14] However, public defenders were found in the most populous counties, containing 68 percent of the U.S. population. Since crime rates are also higher in larger metropolitan areas, public defenders serve a majority of all criminal defendants.

The survey also found that indigent defense systems handle about 3 million cases annually and cost taxpayers around $600 million.

Conflicts of Defense. Because of the way the U.S. system of justice operates today, criminal defense attorneys face many role conflicts. They are viewed as prime movers in what is essentially an *adversarial process*: The prosecution and the defense engage in conflict over the facts of the case at hand, with the prosecutor arguing the case for the state and the defense counsel using all the means at his or her disposal to aid the client.

However, as members of the legal profession, defense counsels must be aware of their role as officers of the court. As an attorney, the defense counsel is obligated to uphold the integrity of the legal profession and to observe the requirements of the Code of Professional Responsibility of the American Bar Association in the defense of a client. The code makes the following statement regarding the duties of the lawyer in the adversary system of justice:

> *Our legal system provides for the adjudication of disputes governed by the rules of substantive, evidentiary, and procedural law. An adversary presentation counters the natural human tendency to judge too swiftly in terms of the familiar that which is not yet fully known; the advocate, by his zealous preparation of facts and law, enables the tribunal to come to the hearing with an open and neutral mind and to render impartial judgements. The duty of a lawyer to his client and his duty to the legal system are the same: To represent his client zealously within the boundaries of the law.*[15]

In this dual capacity of being both a defensive advocate and an officer of the court, the attorney is often confronted with conflicting obligations to client and profession. Monroe Freedman identifies three of the most difficult problems involving the professional responsibility of the criminal defense lawyer:

1. *Is it proper to cross-examine for the purpose of discrediting the reliability or credibility of an adverse witness whom you know to be telling the truth?*
2. *Is it proper to put a witness on the stand when you know he will commit perjury?*
3. *Is it proper to give your client legal advice when you have reason to believe that the knowledge you give him will tempt him to commit perjury?*[16]

These questions and others reveal serious difficulties with respect to a lawyer's ethical responsibilities.

There are other, equally important issues. Suppose, for example, that a client confides that she is planning to commit a crime. What are the defense attorney's ethical responsibilities in this case? Obviously, the lawyer must counsel the client to obey the law; if he assisted the client in engaging in illegal behavior, he would be subject to charges of unprofessional conduct and even criminal liability. In another area, what is the duty of the defense attorney who is well aware that her client committed the act of which he is accused, but is also aware that the police made a procedural error in the case and that the client could be let off on a technicality? The criminal lawyer must be aware of these troublesome situations in order to properly balance the duties of being an attorney with those of being an officer of the court.

Another problem defense lawyers face is a reputation for underhanded methods and unscrupulous conduct, which may or may not be deserved:

> Criminal lawyer is identified unjustifiably in the public eye with the client he represents. Indeed some criminal lawyers are in fact house counsel for criminal groups engaged in gambling, prostitution, and narcotics. The reprehensible conduct of the few sometimes leads the public to see honest, competent practitioners as "mouthpieces" also. Furthermore, in nearly every large city a private defense bar of low legal and dubious ethical quality can be found. Few in number, these lawyers typically carry large caseloads and in many cities dominate the practice in routine cases. They frequent courthouse corridors, bondsmen's offices, and police stations for clients, and rely not on legal knowledge but on their capacity to manipulate the system. Their low repute often accurately reflects the quality of the services they render. This public image of the criminal lawyer is a serious obstacle to the attraction of able young lawyers, and reputable and seasoned practitioners as well, to the criminal law. [17]

Career Conflicts. Beyond their ethical problems, criminal defense attorneys often find themselves at the bottom of the legal profession's financial hierarchy. Whereas partners in a high-powered commercial law firm can make between $250 and $600 thousand per year, a public defender averages between $20 and $30 thousand. [18] Consequently, talented criminal attorneys feel pressure to leave the field and enter more lucrative areas of the law. Because of this inducement, public defenders and other attorneys for the indigent have been accused of caring more about their reputation in court, and their relationships with other attorneys and judges, than their own clients. This relationship has been described as a *courtroom work group*, which functions to streamline the process of justice through the extensive use of plea bargaining rather than to provide a spirited defense. In most criminal cases, cooperation rather than conflict between prosecution and defense appears to be the norm. It is only in the widely publicized "heavy" criminal cases involving rape or murder that the adversarial process is called into play. [19]

What has developed is a system in which criminal defense can be viewed as a training ground for young attorneys looking for seasoning and practice, a means for newly established lawyers to receive government compensation for cases taken to get their practice going, or an arena in which established firms can place their new associates for seasoning before they are assigned to paying clients. The following Close-Up, entitled "Law as a Con Game," describes Abraham Blumberg's well-known view of the problems associated with the criminal defense system.

JUDGE

The third major participant in the criminal trial is the **judge**—the senior officer in a court of criminal law. Judges' duties are quite varied and are far more extensive

Law as a Con Game

In a widely read and provocative article, Abraham Blumberg compares the practice of criminal law to a con game.

According to Blumberg, criminal lawyers—whether private or court appointed—are not the fighters for clients' rights the media makes them out to be. Blumberg finds that most defense attorneys are more committed to the demands and conditions of their profession and the court organization than they are to their own clients. "All court personnel," he argues, "including the accused's own lawyer, tend to be co-opted to become 'agent-mediators' who help the accused redefine his situation and restructure his perceptions." To Blumberg, the lawyer is a "company man" rather than an adversary of the system.

Defense attorneys are above all officers of the court, and that is where their loyalties lie. This is particularly true of the attorneys—Blumberg calls them "lawyer-regulars"—who specialize in criminal cases and whose ties reach into the judge's chambers and the prosecutor's office. "The client, then, is a secondary figure in the court system. . . . He becomes a means to the other ends of the organization's incumbents. . . . The accused's lawyer has far greater professional, economic, intellectual and other ties to the various elements of the court system than he does to his own client," states Blumberg.

How do these ties influence the relationship of lawyer to client? First, to foster court efficiency and maintain a good working relationship with their colleagues, defense lawyers convince or pressure their clients into pleading guilty as charged. Moreover, the plea may be tailored more to the needs of their friends in the prosecutor's office than it is to their clients' best interest.

Second, lawyers often manipulate their clients' emotions so that they can charge higher fees and be guaranteed of receiving them. They seek to keep their clients in a proper state of tension "and to arouse in them the precise edge of anxiety which is calculated to encourage prompt fee payment." By telling their clients that they have "connections" in the courthouse and that they will only be able (and willing) to use them if they get paid, these lawyers use their insider's knowledge to take advantage of their clients. Some court personnel actually aid the lawyer in creating and keeping an image of power and strong connections, helping to solidify the attorney's loyalty to the court. In contrast, "his relationship with his client . . . is transient, ephemeral, and often superficial."

Blumberg charges that defense lawyers are "double agents" for the state. In this capacity, they convince their clients to plead guilty, thereby aiding court organization and efficiency. At the same time, clients are told that only attorneys can save them from a harsh sentence and that they are truly the clients' only friends in court. Clients are afraid to question any aspect of the deals lawyers work out for fear of upsetting the supposedly "lesser charge" or "reduced sentence" they have been tricked into accepting.

In a study of over 700 defendants processed through a metropolitan court, Blumberg found that most pleaded guilty at advice of counsel and that most seemed so unsure of what was taking place that they blindly followed their attorney's suggestion to "cop a plea." He concludes: The defense counsel becomes the ideal agent-mediator since as "officer of the court" and confidant of the accused and his kin, he lives astride both worlds and can serve the ends of the two as well as his own.

DISCUSSION QUESTIONS

1. Is it possible or desirable to make lawyers independent of the court organization?

2. Would the public defender be less or more susceptible to the pressures that influence private counsel?

SOURCE. Abraham Blumberg, "The Practice of Law as a Confidence Game: Organizational Co-optation of a Profession," *Law and Society Review* 1 (1967):15–39.

than the average citizen might suspect. During trials, the judge rules on the appropriateness of conduct, settles questions of evidence and procedure, and guides the questioning of witnesses. When a jury trial occurs, the judge must instruct jury members on which evidence is proper to examine and which should be ignored. The judge also formally **charges the jury** by instructing its members on what points of law and evidence they must consider before reaching a decision of guilty or innocent. When a jury trial is waived, the judge must decide whether to hold for the complainant or the defendant. Finally, in the event that a defendant is found guilty, the judge has the authority to decide on the sentence (in some cases, the sentence is legislatively determined). This duty includes choosing the type of sentence, its length, and—in the case of probation—the conditions under which it may be revoked. Obviously, this decision has a significant effect on an offender's future.[20]

Beyond these stated duties, the trial judge has extensive control and influence over the other service agencies of the court: probation agencies, court clerks, police agencies, and the district attorney's office. Probation and the clerk may be under the judge's explicit control. In some courts, the operations, philosophy, and procedures of these agencies are within the magistrate's administrative domain. In other courts—for example, where a state agency controls the probation department—the attitudes of the county or district court judge still have a great deal of influence on how a probation department is run and how its decisions are made.[21]

The magistrate also has considerable influence on the operations of the local police and prosecutor's offices. For example, if a judge usually chooses a minimal sentence—such as a fine—for a particular offense, then police may be reluctant to arrest offenders for that crime, knowing that the outcome of the criminal justice procedure for that offense will not justify the time spent. Similarly, if a judge is known to have a liberal attitude toward police discretion, then the local department may be more inclined to engage in practices that border on entrapment; or they may become involved in cases requiring the use of easily obtained wiretaps. However, a magistrate oriented toward strict use of due process guarantees would stifle such activities by dismissing all cases involving apparent police abuses of personal freedoms. The district attorney's office may also be sensitive to judicial attitudes. The district attorney might forgo indictments for offenses the presiding magistrate expressly considers trivial or quasi-criminal and for which he or she has been known to take only token action, such as the prosecution of pornographers.

Finally, the judge considers requests by police and prosecutors for leniency (or severity) in sentencing. The judge's reaction to these requests is important if police officers or the district attorney are to honor the bargains they have made with defendants to secure information, cooperation, or guilty pleas. For example, when police officers tell informers that they will try to convince the judge to be lenient with them in exchange for required information, they have to be sure that their requests will later be honored, or at least considered, by the presiding magistrate.

Judicial Selection. Several methods are used to select state court judges.[22] In some jurisdictions, the governor simply appoints judges. In others, judicial recommendations must be confirmed by either (1) the state senate, (2) the governor's council, (3) a special confirmation committee, (4) an executive council elected by the state assembly, or (5) an elected review board. Some states employ screening bodies who submit names to the governor for approval.

Another form of judicial selection is through popular election, either partisan or nonpartisan. This practice is used in a majority of states.

About eleven states have adopted what is known as the **Missouri Plan** to select judges. This three-part approach consists of: (1) a judicial nominating commission to nominate candidates for the bench, (2) an elected official (usually from the executive branch) to make appointments from the list submitted by the commission, and (3) subsequent nonpartisan and noncompetitive elections in which incumbent judges run on their records.

There has been great concern about the qualification of judges. In most states, people appointed to the bench have had little or no training in the role of judge. Others may have held administrative posts and may not have appeared before a court in years. In fact, if local justices of the peace are included, the majority of U.S. judges have not graduated from law school or even college.

Several agencies have been created to improve the quality of the judiciary. The National Conference of State Court Judges and the National College of Juvenile Justice both operate judicial training seminars and publish manuals and guides on state-of-the-art judicial techniques. Their ongoing efforts are designed to improve the quality of the nation's judges.

Now that the actors in the adjudicatory process have been introduced and the structure within which they work defined, our attention will turn to the three main stages of the process itself: pretrial procedures, the trial, and sentencing.

Pretrial Procedures

After arrest, or if an arrest warrant has been served, a criminal charge is drawn up by the appropriate prosecutor's office. The charge is a formal written document identifying the criminal activity, the facts of the case, and the circumstances of the arrest. If the crime is a felony, the charge is called a **Bill of Indictment**, if it is to be considered by a grand jury, or an **information**, if that particular jurisdiction uses the preliminary hearing system; misdemeanants are charged with a **complaint**.

After an indictment or information in a felony offense is filed, the accused is brought before the trial court for arraignment, at which time the judge informs the defendant of the charge, insures that the accused is properly represented by counsel, and determines whether the person should be released on bail or some alternative plan pending a hearing or trial.

The defendant who is arraigned on an indictment or information can ordinarily plead guilty, not guilty, or **nolo contendere**, which is equivalent to a guilty plea. When a guilty plea is entered, the defendant admits to all the elements of the crime and the court begins to review the person's background for sentencing purposes. A plea of not guilty sets the stage for a trial on the merits of the case or for negotiations between the prosecutor and defense attorney with the aim of reaching a guilty plea arrangement.

This section will review in more detail three important issues related to pretrial procedures: bail, plea bargaining, and noncriminal alternatives to prosecution.

BAIL

Bail represents money or some other security provided to the court to insure the appearance of the defendant at trial. The amount of bail is set by a magistrate, who reviews the facts of the case and the history of the defendant. Defendants who cannot afford bail are kept in secure detention, usually in a county jail, until their trial date.

The bail system goes back to Great Britain and the English common law. At one time, the legal relationship existing in the contract law of bailment even permitted the trying and sentencing of the bailor (the person who posted bail) if the bailee did not appear for trial.[23]

Under the U.S. system of justice, the right to bail comes from the Eighth Amendment of the Constitution. However, the Eighth Amendment does not guarantee bail; rather, it states that people can expect to be released on reasonable bail in all but capital cases. Thus, in most cases, accused persons have the right to be released on reasonable bail in order to prepare their defense and continue their life in the community.

The issue that determines the amount of bail is the probability that the defendant will return for trial. Some jurisdictions, such as Washington, D.C., have **preventive detention** statutes that allow a judge, after a hearing, to hold defendants in jail if they are considered to present a danger to the community.[24] In other jurisdictions—for example, Nebraska—state laws have been passed to deny bail for some noncapital crimes, such as rape, if substantial evidence exists ("the proof is evident or the presumption great") as to the defendant's guilt.[25] However, bail cannot be used to punish the accused, nor can it be denied or revoked at the whim of the court. Most states hold bail review hearings in a higher court in cases in which the defendant is detained because of what might be considered excessive bail requirements set by a judge.

Many experts believe that money bail is one of the more unacceptable elements of the criminal justice process. First, it discriminates against the poor, who cannot put up money to secure their freedom. Caleb Foote, one of the nation's leading experts on bail, has said:

> The basic problem—poor people and those being locked up before trial—remains. I still think pretrial detention is the most pervasive denial of equal protection and equal rights in American law.[26]

The bail system is also costly since it causes the state to pay for the detention of offenders who are unable to raise bail and who might otherwise remain in the community. The significance of bail is further amplified because both the amount of bail ordered and length of stay in pretrial detention for those who cannot raise bail are associated with a greater likelihood of conviction and a longer prison sentence after conviction.[27]

Bail Bondsmen. To help indigent people make bail, the institution of the professional bail bondsman was created. Normally, bail bondsmen put up 90 percent of a bond fee and the defendant the remaining 10 percent. When the defendant appears at trial, the bail is returned and the bondsman keeps the entire amount, the defendant's 10 percent serving as the bondsman's commission. If the defendant does not show up for trial, the bondsman must pay the entire bail. Usually, bondsmen expect defendants, their friends, or their relatives to put up further collateral (such as the deed to their house) to cover the risk. If collateral is unavailable or the bondsman believes the offender presents too great a risk, the bondsman will refuse bond, relegating the defendant to a jail stay until the trial date.

Bail bondsmen have often been accused of unscrupulous practices, such as bribing police and court personnel to secure referrals. Some judges have been accused of refusing to collect forfeited bail owed from professional bondsmen.[28] Abuses of the system have prompted bail reform movements and many jurisdictions have set up systems to replace bondsmen.

Bail Reform. The bail reform movement was started in 1961 to help alleviate the problems presented by the bail process. In New York, the **Vera Foundation**, set up by the philanthropist Louis Schweitzer and later supported by the Ford Foundation, pioneered the concept of **release on recognizance** (ROR).[29] This project found that if the court had sufficient background information about the defendant, it could make a reasonably good judgment about whether the accused would return to court. The project found that most defendants, selected on the basis of such information as the nature of the offense, family ties, employment record, and other factors, returned to court when placed in the community on their own recognizance. Their findings suggested that releasing a person on the basis of verified information more effectively guaranteed appearance in court than did money bail.

The Vera Project employed college students to evaluate potential candidates on five criteria:

1. *Residence.* Whether defendants lived in the area, as well as their record of domicile (for example, how often they moved).
2. *Community ties.* Whether defendants had family ties and contacts in the area.
3. *Employment record.* Present job and history of employment.
4. *Prior record.* Past convictions and record of showing up for trial.
5. *Character.* Referees' assessments of defendants' character.

The project proved to be a great success. A significant majority of clients returned for trial when released on their own recognizance. The success of ROR in New York prompted its adoption in many other large cities around the country.

Bail reform has been considered one of the great successes in criminal justice reform, but some research efforts indicate greate disparity in the way judges handle bail decisions. They also show that racial and socioeconomic disparity might be a factor in decision making.[30] If this is so, then the original purposes of creating bail reform would be negated by bias in the justice system.

Bail Today. Research studies indicate that today, thanks to bail reform, the great majority of criminal defendants are released before trial—upwards of 85 percent.[31] Similarly, it has been found that about 85 percent of those granted pretrial release do return for their hearings, and that the most serious offenders are the ones most likely to return.[32]

How successful are judges in predicting the dangerousness of defendants granted pretrial release? In one study of eight jurisdictions, Mary Toborg found that about 15 percent of defendants released by local courts were rearrested before trial.[33] A more recent study conducted by the Bureau of Justice Statistics found that about 10 percent of defendants released by federal district courts were rearrested before trial.[34] Those rearrested tended to (1) be on bail longer (nine months or more); (2) have a serious prior record; (3) be drug abusers; (4) have a poor work record; and (5) be disproportionately young, male, and nonwhite. The Bureau of Justice Statistics study also found that people detained before trial get significantly longer sentences than those granted pretrial release.

Because of the concern over defendant misconduct while on bail, about thirty states have made provisions to limit bail for certain offenses; these are summarized in table 16.1. Similarly, the U.S. Supreme Court, in the case of *Schall* v. *Martin*, has upheld the constitutionality of laws providing for the preventive detention of a juvenile offender if the judicial authority believes the offender will be a danger to community safety.[35]

In sum, bail reform movements have encouraged the use of pretrial release. Studies show that most defendants to return for trial and that most bailees do not commit more crime while in the community. Nonetheless, concern for public safety in the conservative eighties has prompted states to restrict the use of bail for serious offenders.

PLEA BARGAINING

The majority of defendants in criminal trials are convicted by their own pleas of guilty. A leading authority, Donald Newman, estimates that 90 percent of all those

TABLE 16.1

Preventive detention provisions

Type of provision	States that have enacted the provision
Exclusion of certain crimes from automatic bail eligibility	Colorado, District of Columbia, Florida, Georgia, Michigan, Nebraska, Wisconsin
Definition of the purpose of bail to ensure appearance and safety	Alaska, Arizona, California, Delaware, District of Columbia, Florida, Hawaii, Minnesota, South Carolina, South Dakota, Vermont, Virginia, Wisconsin
Inclusion of crime control factors in the release decision	Alabama, California, Florida, Georgia, Minnesota, South Dakota, Wisconsin
Inclusion of release conditions related to crime control	Alaska, Arkansas, Delaware, District of Columbia, Florida, Hawaii, Illinois, Minnesota, New Mexico, North Carolina, South Carolina, Vermont, Virginia, Washington, Wisconsin
Limitations on the right to bail for those previously convicted	Colorado, District of Columbia, Florida, Georgia, Hawaii, Michigan, New Mexico, Texas, Wisconsin
Revocation of pretrial release when there is evidence that the accused committed a new crime	Arkansas, Colorado, Illinois, Indiana, Massachusetts, Nevada, New York, Rhode Island, Virginia, Wisconsin
Limitations on the right to bail for crimes alleged to have been committed while on release	Colorado, District of Columbia, Florida, Maryland, Michigan, Nevada, Tennessee, Texas, Utah
Provisions for pretrial detention to ensure safety	Arizona, California, District of Columbia, Florida, Georgia, Hawaii, Michigan, Wisconsin

SOURCE. Updated as of December 1982 from *Typology of State Laws which Permit Consideration of Danger in the Pretrial Release Decision*, by Elizabeth Gaynes for the Pretrial Services Resource Center, Washington, D.C., 1982; in *Report to The Nation on Crime and Justice*.

charged with serious crimes plead guilty; if minor crimes are included, the percentage jumps to 98 percent.[36]

The **plea bargaining** process usually occurs between arraignment (or initial appearance, in the case of a misdemeanor) and the onset of trial. Normally, there are four ways a bargain can be made between the prosecutor and the defense attorney: (1) the initial charges may be reduced to those of a lesser offense, thus automatically reducing the sentence imposed; (2) in cases in which many counts are charged, the prosecutor may reduce the number of counts; (3) the prosecutor may promise to recommend a lenient sentence, such as probation; and (4) when the charge imposed has a negative label attached (for example, child molestor), the prosecutor may alter the charge to a lesser one (for example, assault) in exchange for a plea of guilty. In a jurisdiction in which it is common knowledge that sentencing disparity between judges exists, the prosecutor may even agree to arrange that the defendant appear before a lenient judge to insure the court's agreement to the bargain.

There are a number of different motivations for plea bargaining. Defendants, well aware of the evidence against them, plea bargain for obvious reasons. They wish to minimize their sentence and avoid negative labels and the harmful publicity of a conviction for a serious crime. Occasionally, people accept a bargain to protect accomplices or confederates by "taking the rap" themselves.[37] It is also possible that defendants who actually are innocent will accept a plea to a reduced charge because they fear the consequences of a trial on a much more serious charge.

The defense attorney may seek a bargain to limit his or her own involvement in the case. In some instances, counsel for the defense may wish to increase their operating profits by minimizing the effort they put forth for an obviously guilty client.[38] In other instances, they may simply wish to adapt to the bureaucratic structure favorable to plea bargaining that exists in most U.S. criminal courts.[39] In some cases, defense attorneys may wish to secure noncriminal dispositions for their clients, such as placement in a treatment program, and may advise them to plead guilty in exchange for this consideration.

The prosecution may also seek to plea bargain, for various reasons. For one thing, the prosecutor's case may be weaker than hoped for; and it may therefore be safer to accept a plea to a lesser charge than to risk a trial. Or perhaps the prosecutor believes police officers have made a serious error in securing evidence, and is therefore afraid to bring the case to trial. When a defendant pleads guilty, it voids all prior constitutional errors made in that case. And, of course, no matter how strong the state's case, there is always the chance that a jury will render an unfavorable decision. Prosecutors also bargain to gain the cooperation of informers and codefendants.

Some prosecutors may be reluctant to press charges against some offenders whose conviction could result in their receiving long sentences without chance of parole. For example, some states, such as New York, have passed drug laws that provide mandatory sentences for convicted offenders. However, when the legislature passed these statutes, its intent was to control serious, professional drug dealers. Therefore, the amateur "campus pusher" who falls into police hands may be originally charged with a lesser offense.

The nature and extent of plea bargaining was analyzed by a recent federal survey of felony plea negotiations in fourteen jurisdictions.[40] The survey found wide disparity in the use of pleas; some jurisdictions averaged four pleas per trial, while others conducted more than twenty; overall, pleas were used in 80 percent of felony cases. The survey found that, surprisingly, 60 percent of the pleas were to the top charge filed. This implies that most plea negotiations are directed at achieving a reduced sentence, or dropping lesser included charges that could add to the sentence (such as possession of a firearm), rather than at lowering the most serious charge filed against the defendant. Even in jurisdictions where prosecutors are reluctant to reduce charges or engage in bargaining, a majority of defendants still enter a guilty plea.

Plea Bargaining Issues. Those who favor plea bargaining argue that it actually benefits both the state and the defendant in the following ways: (1) the overall financial costs of criminal prosecution are reduced; (2) the administrative efficiency of the courts is greatly improved; (3) the prosecution is able to devote more time to cases of greater seriousness and importance; and (4) the defendant avoids possible detention and extended trial and may receive a reduced sentence.[41] Thus, those who favor plea bargaining believe it is appropriate to enter into plea discussions where the interests of effective administration of justice will be served.

It has been argued, however, that plea bargaining is basically objectionable because it encourages a defendant to waive the constitutional right to a trial. In addition, some experts suggest that sentences tend to be less severe in guilty plea situations than in actual trials and that plea bargains result in even greater sentencing disparity. Particularly in the eyes of the general public, this allows the defendant to beat the system and further tarnishes the criminal justice process. Plea bargaining also raises the danger than an innocent person will be convicted of a crime if convinced that the lighter treatment resulting from a guilty plea is preferable to the possible risk of a harsher sentence following a formal trial. Richard Kuh argues that plea bargaining allows dangerous offenders to get off lightly and therefore weakens the deterrent effect of the criminal law.[42] Albert Alschuler, a legal scholar, has forcibly argued that whereas plea bargains may have an internal, administrative logic, the general public views their outcome as illogical.[43]

Control of Plea Bargaining. It is unlikely that plea negotiations will be eliminated or severely curtailed in the near future. Those who support their total abolition are in the minority. As a result of abuses, however, efforts are being made to improve plea bargaining operations. Such reforms include (1) the development of uniform plea practices, (2) the presence of counsel during plea negotiations, and (3) the establishment of time limits on plea negotiations.[44]

In recent years, some efforts have been made to convert the practice of plea bargaining into a more visible, understandable, and fair dispositional process. On the one hand, safeguards and guidelines have been developed in many jurisdictions to prevent violations of due process and to insure that innocent defendants do not plead guilty under coercion. Such safeguards include the following: (1) the judge questions the defendant about the facts of the guilty plea before accepting the plea; (2) the defense counsel is present and able to advise the defendant of his or her rights; (3) open discussions about the plea occur between prosecutor and defense attorney; (4) full and frank information regarding the offender and offense is made available at this stage of the process. In addition, judicial supervision is an effective mechanism to insure that plea bargaining is undertaken fairly.

Another method of reform has involved the development of specific guidelines by the office of the chief prosecutor. Also, some jurisdictions have adopted the use of prepleading investigations, which are summaries of the case prepared before a plea is made rather than after the plea is given to the court. The use of the prepleading report helps provide information to all the participants in the negotiations. The pretrial settlement conference is another method used to improve the visibility and fairness of plea bargaining. In such a conference, the participants include the judge, victim, defendant, and police as well as the prosecutor and defense attorney. Generally, the defendant's guilt is assumed by the parties, and efforts are made to contribute to a settlement of the case. If a settlement is reached and approved by the judge, the defendant enters a plea in open court.

The most extreme method of reforming plea bargaining has been to abolish it completely. A ban on plea bargaining has been tried in numerous jurisdictions throughout the country. In 1975, the state of Alaska eliminated the practice. In Honolulu, Hawaii, efforts were made to abolish plea bargaining. Jurisdictions in other states, including Iowa, Arizona, the District of Columbia, and Delaware, have also sought to limit the use of plea bargaining.[45] What this meant was that these jurisdictions would give no consideration or concessions to the defendant in exchange for a guilty plea.

Efforts to control plea bargaining have met with mixed results. Evaluation of the Alaska experiment found that the number of pleas did not change significantly after plea bargaining was eliminated, nor did it increase the prison sentences given to the most serious offenders.[46] This and other similar efforts indicates that attempts to eliminate plea bargaining will most likely move prosecutorial discretion further up in the system. For example, eliminating felony plea bargaining may cause prosecutors to automatically charge offenders with a misdemeanor, so they can retain the option of offering them a "deal" in exchange for their cooperation before trial.

Legal Issues in Plea Bargaining. The United States Supreme Court has reviewed the propriety of plea bargaining in several court decisions, particularly in regard to the voluntariness of guilty pleas. In *Boykin* v. *Alabama*, the court held that an effort must be made in open court to question the defendant on the voluntariness of the admission of guilt before a trial judge may accept a guilty plea.[47] This is essential, since a guilty plea constitutes a waiver of the defendant's Fifth Amendment right to avoid self-incrimination and Sixth Amendment right to a jury trial. After the *Boykin* case, the Court ruled, in the case of *Brady* v. *United States*, that a guilty plea is not invalid merely because it is entered to avoid the possibility of the death penalty.[48] And in *Santobello* v. *New York*, which involved a guilty plea made after plea bargaining, the Court held that the promise of the prosecutor must be kept and that the breaking of a plea bargaining agreement by the prosecutor required a reversal for the defendant.[49] The Court ruled in the 1978 case of *Brodenkircher* v. *Hayes* that a defendant's due process rights are not violated when a prosecutor threatens to reindict the accused on more serious charges if he or she does not plead guilty to the original offense.[50]

The problem of controlling plea bargaining remains. Despite calls for its abolishment, it flourishes in U.S. trial practice. As Donald Newman states:

> *There are at present, no good answers to all of the unresolved bargaining issues. One thing, however, is abundantly clear; plea bargaining is with us and is probably here to stay in most jurisdictions throughout the country.*[51]

ALTERNATIVES TO PROSECUTION: DIVERSION

In the past fifteen years, great effort has been made to remove as many people as possible from the formal criminal justice process and to deal with them in an informal, treatment-oriented fashion.

Several reasons underlie this movement. On the one hand, advocates of the labeling perspective forcefully argue that the stigma of criminal conviction serves only to reinvolve the offender in crime. Thus, noncriminal alternatives can, in the long run, help reduce criminal activity.

From another viewpoint, it is alleged that pretrial alternatives to prosecution are usually cheaper than full trials, and more importantly, that they free the justice system to concentrate on more serious offenders. Alternatives to prosecution can reduce the need for plea bargaining by reducing caseload pressure to settle cases.

In most instances, pretrial programs are designed to treat offenders rather than punish them. Some pretrial programs are organized around a particular type of rehabilitation effort. For example, a judge may allow a case to continue indefinitely without a hearing if the offender voluntarily enrolls in a residential alcohol or drug treatment program.

More common today are formalized **diversion** programs operating out of the local police, prosecutor's, or probation department. Involvement with the diversion program usually begins after the arrest and arraignment of the individual but before trial. The selected individual is released on a continuance to the diversion program—that is, the trial is postponed—if the relevant court personnel (judge, probation officer, assistant district attorney, defense lawyer, arresting officer) and the program representative (usually called a screener) agree on the potential suitability of the accused for the program.

Services rendered by most adult pretrial diversion programs can be classified into three complementary areas:

1. Counseling is undertaken by an advocate, who conducts individual and group sessions with clients throughout the initial period.
2. Employment services are offered by a career developer, who evaluates and implements career goals in a team effort with the client and the advocate.
3. Human services are provided, including health care, educational programs, emergency housing, and a variety of testing to assess needs and capabilities.[52]

The diversion movement was originally supported by federal government money funneled to local jurisdictions. However, some programs begun with federal funds are now being underwritten by local money. Consequently, the uncertainty of local budgets often makes programs temporary. Nonetheless, several pretrial programs have achieved both longevity and apparent success.

Despite the prevalence of diversion, critics have claimed that the practice is no more successful than the formal justice system. In some cases it entangles the offender in the social service area more intensely than if he or she had gone to trial; this effect is known as *widening the net.*

The Criminal Trial

Although the jury trial is a relatively rare occurrence, it is still one of the cornerstones of the criminal justice process:

> *Although most criminal prosecutions do not involve the adversary determination of guilt or innocence that occurs at the formal trial of a criminal case, the trial process remains a matter of vital importance to the criminal justice system. Whether or not a defendant chooses to invoke his right to trial, he has an interest in the trial process because in many cases it represents to him a legal option guaranteed by the Constitution of the United States. The opportunity to go to trial provides a valuable safeguard against abuse of informal processing and a basis for encouraging faith in the system on the part of those who acknowledge that their situation does not present any contestable issues.*
>
> *Since informal disposition of a case often occurs only after the case proceeds along the formal route towards trial, procedures for formal processing at the earlier court stages may be used for a much greater number of cases than actually come to trial. Because all other means of processing cases must be evaluated as alternatives to formal trial, the attractiveness of trial is a major consideration in both prosecution and defense willingness to process a case administratively.*[53]

Because of its importance, jury trial stages, critical issues, and associated legal rights are discussed below.

JURY SELECTION

The first stage of the trial process involves jury selection. Jurors are selected randomly in both civil and criminal cases from tax assessment or voter registration

The most dramatic element of the adjudacatory process, the jury trial, actually occurs relatively infrequently.

lists within each court's jurisdiction. The initial list of persons chosen, which is called a **venire**, or jury array, provides the state with a group of potentially capable citizens able to serve on a jury. Many states, by rule of law, review the venire to eliminate unqualified persons and to exempt those who by reason of their professions are not allowed to be jurors; this latter group may include (but is not limited to) physicians, the clergy, and government officials. The actual jury selection process begins with those remaining on the list.

The court clerk, who handles the administrative affairs of the trial—including the processing of the complaint, the evidence, and other documents—randomly selects enough names (sometimes from a box) to fill the required number of places on the jury. In most cases, the jury in a criminal trial consists of twelve persons, with two alternate jurors standing by to serve should one of the regular jurors be unable to complete the trial. Once the prospective jurors have been chosen, the process of **voir dire** is begun; all persons selected are questioned by both the prosecutor and the defense to determine their appropriateness to sit on the jury. They are examined under oath by the government, the defense, and sometimes the judge about their backgrounds, occupations, residences, and possible knowledge or interest in the case. A juror who acknowledges any bias for or prejudice against the defendant—a juror who is a friend or relative of the defendant, for example, or who has already formed an opinion about the case—is removed for *cause* and replaced with another. Thus, any prospective juror who reveals an inability to be impartial and render a verdict solely on the basis of the evidence to be presented at the trial may be removed by attorneys for either the prosecution or defense. Because normally no limit is placed on the number of challenges for cause that can be offered, it often takes considerable time to select a jury for controversial and highly publicized criminal cases.

In addition to challenges for cause, both the prosecution and the defense are allowed **peremptory challenges**, which allow the attorneys to excuse jurors for no particular reason or for reasons that remain undisclosed. For example, a prosecutor might not want a bartender as a juror in a drunken driving case, believing that a person in that occupation might be sympathetic to the accused. Or a defense attorney might excuse a male prospective juror because the attorney prefers to have a predominantly female jury for the client. The number of peremptory challenges permitted is limited by state statute and often varies by case and jurisdiction.

Recently, the peremptory challenge has been criticized by legal experts who question the fairness and propriety with which it has been employed.[54] Generally, the courts have left the challenge immune from judicial review, applying the nonintervention doctrine dictated by the U.S. Supreme Court case of *Swain* v. *Alabama*.[55] In *Swain*, the Court upheld the use of peremptory challenges in isolated cases to exclude jurors because of racial or other group affiliations.

The Sixth Amendment to the United States Constitution provides for the right to a speedy and public trial by an impartial jury. The United States Supreme Court has sought to insure compliance with this constitutional mandate of impartiality through recent decisions eliminating racial discrimination in jury selection. For instance, in *Ham* v. *South Carolina*, in 1973, the court held that the defense counsel of a black civil rights leader was entitled to question each juror on the issue of racial prejudice.[56] And in *Taylor* v. *Louisiana*, in 1975, the Court overturned the conviction of a man by an all-male jury because a Louisiana statute allowed women but not men to exempt themselves from jury duty.[57] These and other similar decisions have had the effect of providing safeguards against jury bias. Nonetheless, there is still evidence that women, minorities, and the poor are underrepresented on U.S. juries. Similarly, evidence shows that juries have trouble understanding the intricacies of the legal process and misinterpret the instructions given them by the judge.

TRIAL PROCESS

The trial of a criminal case is a formal process conducted in a specific and orderly fashion in accordance with rules of criminal law, procedure, and evidence. Unlike trials in popular television programs, where witnesses are often asked leading and prejudicial questions and where judges go far beyond their supervisory role, the modern criminal trial is a complicated and often time-consuming technical affair. It is a structured adversary proceeding in which both the prosecution and the defense follow specific procedures and argue the merits of their cases before the judge and jury. Each side seeks to present its case in the most favorable light. Where possible, the prosecutor and the defense attorney object to evidence they consider damaging to their individual points of view. The prosecutor uses direct testimony, physical evidence, and a confession, if available, to convince the jury that the accused is guilty beyond a reasonable doubt. The defense attorney rebuts the government's case with his or her own evidence, makes certain that the rights of the criminal defendant under the federal and state constitutions are considered during all phases of the trial, and determines whether an appeal is appropriate if the client if found guilty. From the beginning of the process to its completion, the judge promotes an orderly and fair administration of the criminal trial.

Although each administration in the United States differs in its trial procedures, all conduct criminal trials in a generally similar fashion. The basic steps of the criminal trial proceed in the following established order.

1. *Opening statements.* As the trial begins, both prosecution and defense address the jury and present their cases. They alert the jury to what they will attempt to prove and what the major facts of the case are. They introduce the witnesses, prepare the jury for their testimony, and tell them what information to be sure to listen for. The defense begins to emphasize that any doubts about the guilt of the accused must be translated into an acquittal; the prosecution dwells on civic duty and responsibility.

2. *The prosecution's case.* Following the opening statement, the government begins its case by presenting evidence to the court through its witnesses. Those called as witnesses—such as police officers, victims, or expert witnesses—provide testimony via *direct examination*, during which the prosecutor questions the witness to reveal the facts believed pertinent to the government case. Testimony involves what the witness actually saw, heard, or touched, and does not include opinions. However, a witness's opinion can be given in certain situations, such as in describing the motion of a vehicle or indicating whether a defendant appeared to act intoxicated or insane. Witnesses may also qualify to give their opinions because of their professions as experts on a particular subject relevant to the case; for example, a psychiatrist may testify as to a defendant's mental capacity at the time of the crime.

   After the prosecutor finishes questioning a witness, the defense cross-examines the same witness by asking questions in an attempt to clarify the defendant's role in the crime. If desired, the prosecutor may seek a *redirect examination* after the defense attorney has completed cross-examination; this allows the prosecutor to ask additional questions about information brought out during cross-examination. Finally, the defense attorney may question or cross-examine the witness once again. All witnesses for the trial are sworn in and questioned in the same basic manner.

3. *The defense's case.* At the close of the prosecution's case, the defense usually asks the presiding judge to rule on a *motion for a directed verdict.* If this motion is sustained, the judge will direct the jury to acquit the defendant, thereby ending the trial. A directed verdict means that the prosecution did not present enough evidence to prove all the elements of the alleged crime. If the judge fails to sustain the motion, the defense will present its case. Witnesses are called to testify in the same manner used by the prosecution.

   After the defense concludes its case, the government may present *rebuttal evidence.* This normally involves bringing evidence forward that was not used when the prosecution initially presented its case. The defense may examine the rebuttal witnesses and introduce new witnesses in a process called *surrebuttal.* After all the evidence has been presented to the court, the defense attorney may again submit a motion for a directed verdict. If the motion is denied, both the prosecution and the defense prepare to make closing arguments; and the case on the evidence is ready for consideration by the jury.

4. *Closing arguments.* Closing arguments are used by the attorneys to review the facts and evidence of the case in a manner favorable to their positions. At this stage of the trial, both prosecution and defense are permitted to draw reasonable inferences and show how the facts prove or refute the defendant's guilt. Often, both attorneys have a free hand in arguing about facts, issues, and evidence, including the applicable law. They cannot

comment on matters not in evidence, however; nor, where applicable, can they comment on the defendant's failure to testify. Normally, the defense attorney makes a closing statement first, followed by the prosecutor. Either party can elect to forgo the right to make a final summation to the jury.

5. *Instructions to the jury.* In a criminal trial, the judge instructs, or charges, the jury on the principles of law that ought to guide and control the decision on the defendant's innocence or guilt. Included in the charge are information about the elements of the alleged offense, the type of evidence needed to prove each element, and the burden of proof required to obtain a guilty verdict. Although the judge commonly provides the instructions, he or she may ask the prosecutor and the defense attorney to submit instructions for consideration; the judge then uses discretion in determining whether to use any of their instructions. The instructions that cover the law applicable to the case are extremely important, since they may serve as the basis for a subsequent criminal appeal.

    One important aspect of instructing the jury is to explain the level of proof needed to find the person guilty of a crime. As mentioned, the U.S. system of justice requires guilt to be proved *beyond a reasonable doubt.* The judge must inform the jurors that if they have even the slightest suspicion that the defendant is not guilty, then they cannot find for the prosecution. Also, the judge must explain how, in criminal cases, the burden of proof is on the prosecution to prove the defendant guilty; the accused does not have to prove his or her innocence.

6. *Verdict, sentence, and appeal.* Once the charge has been given to the jury, the jurors retire to deliberate on a verdict. As previously mentioned, the verdict in a criminal case—regardless of whether the trial involves a six-person or a twelve-person jury—is usually required to be unanimous. A review of the case by the jury may take hours or even days. The jurors are always sequestered during their deliberations; and in some lengthy, highly publicized cases, they are kept overnight in a hotel until the verdict is reached. In less sensational cases, the jurors may be allowed to go home but are often cautioned not to discuss the case with anyone. If a verdict cannot be reached, the trial may result in a hung jury; in this case, the prosecutor has to bring the defendant to trial again if the prosecution desires a conviction. If found not guilty, the defendant is released from the criminal process. On the other hand, if the defendant is convicted, the judge normally orders a presentence investigation by the probation department preparatory to imposing a sentence. Prior to sentencing, the defense attorney often submits a motion for a new trial, alleging that legal errors occurred in the trial proceedings. The judge may deny the motion and impose a sentence immediately, a practice quite familiar in most misdemeanor offenses. In felony cases, however the judge sets a date for sentencing and the defendant is either placed on bail or held in custody until that time.

Sentencing usually occurs a short time after trial. In most jurisdictions, the typical criminal penalties include fines, community supervision, incarceration, and the death penalty.

After sentencing, defendants have the right to appeal the case, charging either that the law under which they were tried was unconstitutional (for example, discriminatory or vague) or that the procedures used by agents of the justice system violated their constitutional rights (for example, police did not give them a proper Miranda warning or that improperly obtained evidence was used at trial). If the appeal is granted, a new trial may be ordered. If the appeal is not sustained, the convicted offender will begin serving the sentence imposed, thus marking the end of the adjudicatory process.

TRIALS AND THE RULE OF LAW

Every trial has its constitutional issues, complex legal procedures, rules of court, and interpretations of statutes, all designed to insure that the accused will have a fair trial. This section discusses the most important constitutional rights of the accused at the trial stage of the criminal justice system and reviews the legal nature of the trial process.

Right to a Speedy and Public Trial. The Sixth Amendment guarantees a defendant the right to a speedy trial. This means that an accused is entitled to be tried within a reasonable period of time. If a person's right to a speedy trial is violated, then a complete dismissal of the charges against him or her is required, according to *Strunk v. United States*.[58] The right to a speedy trial was made applicable to state courts through the Due Process Clause of the Fourteenth Amendment in the case of *Klopfer v. North Carolina*.[59] It should be noted, however, that a defendant can waive the right to a speedy trial. A waiver of the right is implied when defendants cause the delay or when they do not assert their right even though the trial takes too long to get under way.

In determining whether a violation of a defendant's right to speedy trial has occurred, several factors are taken into consideration; length of the delay alone is not enough to constitute a violation. The Supreme Court, in the case of *Barker v. Wingo*, enumerated the factors that should be considered in determining whether the speedy trial requirement has been complied with: (1) the length of the delay, (2) the reason for the delay, (3) the timeliness of the defendants' assertion of their right to a speedy trial, and (4) the prejudice to the defendant.[60]

How speedy does a speedy trial have to be? There is no set standard, but the Federal Speedy Trial Act of 1974 mandates 30 days from arrest to indictment and 70 days from indictment to trial. However, the states vary widely in their definitions of a speedy trial. For example, in Louisiana the limit is 730 days (2 years) in a noncapital case and 1,095 days in capital cases; in New York, the time limit is 180 days.[61]

Right to a Jury Trial. Because a jury trial is considered a fundamental right, the Supreme Court, in the case of *Duncan v. Louisiana*, made the guarantee applicable to the states through the Fourteenth Amendment.[62] However, the question arises as to whether this right extends to all defendants—those charged with misdemeanors as well as felonies. The Supreme Court addressed this issue in the case of *Baldwin v. New York*, in which it decided that an accused facing the possibility of a prison sentence of more than six months is entitled to a jury trial.[63]

Although most people think of a jury as having twelve members, and historically most juries have had twelve members, the Sixth Amendment does not specify that a twelve-person jury is required. In fact, in the case of *Williams v. Florida*, the Supreme Court held that a six-person jury fulfilled a defendant's right to a trial by jury.[64] However, a unanimous verdict is required when a six-person jury is used.

When a twelve-person jury is used, the Supreme Court has maintained that the Sixth Amendment does not require a unanimous verdict, except in first-degree murder cases. In *Apodica* v. *Oregon*, the Court found constitutional an Oregon statute that required a finding of guilty by ten out of twelve jurors in cases dealing with assault with a deadly weapon, burglary, and larceny.[65] However, it should be noted that the majority of states and the federal courts still require a unanimous verdict.

Right to be Free From Double Jeopardy. The Fifth Amendment provides that no person shall "be subject for the same offense to be twice put in jeopardy of life or limb." This means that a defendant cannot be prosecuted by a jurisdiction more than once for a single offense. For example, if a defendant is tried and convicted of murder in the state of Texas, he cannot be tried again for the same murder in Texas. The right to be protected from double jeopardy was made applicable to the states through the Fourteenth Amendment in the case of *Benton* v. *Maryland*.[66] Thus, a person is protected against double jeopardy in both the federal and state courts, though a person tried in federal court can be tried in state court, and vice versa.

Right to Legal Counsel. Regardless of the legal rights citizens command at trial, without legal counsel to aid them they would be rendered defenseless before the law. Consequently, the Sixth Amendment provides the right to be represented by an attorney in criminal trials. However, the vast majority of criminal defendants are indigents who cannot afford private legal services. In a series of cases beginning in the 1930s, the U.S. Supreme Court established the defendant's right to be represented by an attorney and, in the event they cannot pay for representation, to have the state provide free legal services. First, in *Powell* v. *Alabama*, the court held that an attorney was essential in capital cases where the defendant's life was at stake.[67] Then, in the critically important case of *Gideon* v. *Wainwright*, the court granted the absolute right to counsel in all felony cases.[68] Finally, in *Argersinger* v. *Hamlin*, the defendant's right to counsel in misdemeanor cases was established.[69] Today, most defendants are represented by attorneys from the time they are in police custody until their final sentencing and appeal.

Right to Competent Legal Representation. In the 1984 case of *Strickland* v. *Washington*, the Supreme Court found that defendants also have the right to *reasonably effective assistance* of counsel. The court enumerated the qualities characterizing competent representation:

> *Representation of a criminal defendant entails certain basic duties. Counsel's function is to assist the defendant, and hence counsel owes the client a duty of loyalty, a duty to avoid conflicts of interest. From counsel's function as assistant to the defendant derive the overarching duty to advocate the defendant's cause and the more particular duties to consult with the defendant on important decisions and to keep the defendant informed of important developments in the course of the prosecution. Counsel also has a duty to bring to bear such skill and knowledge as will render the trial a reliable adversarial testing process.*[70]

If convicted, defendants can have their sentence overturned if they can prove that (1) counsel's performance was so deficient that they were not functioning as the counsel guaranteed by the Sixth Amendment, and (2) the deficient performance prejudiced the case and deprived them of a fair trial.

Sentencing

After a defendant has been found guilty of a criminal offense or has entered a plea of guilty, he or she is brought before the court for imposition of a criminal penalty— sentencing.

Historically, a full range of punishments has been meted out to criminal offenders: corporal punishments, such as whipping or multilation; fines; banishment; incarceration; death. The evolution of punishment as a means of correction will be discussed in chapter 17.

In U.S. society, incarceration in a federal, state, or local institution is generally the most serious penalty meted out to offenders. Although the death penalty remains on the statute books of most jurisdictions, it has been used rather sparingly (though at an increasing rate) in recent years. Since this topic was discussed in chapter 5, the discussion here will be confined to sentencing formats that involve community supervision and incarceration.

PURPOSES OF SENTENCING

There are many purposes behind the imposition of a criminal sentence.[71] It is safe to say no single philosophy of justice holds sway when sentencing decision is made. Each jurisdiction employs its own sentencing philosophies, and each individual decision maker views the purpose of sentencing differently. Thus, a twenty-three-year-old college student arrested for selling cocaine might be seen as essentially harmless by one judge and therefore given a light sentence. Another judge might see the young drug dealer as a dangerous destroyer of the moral fabric of society, deserving the harshest punishment possible. Thus, one of the great flaws of the U.S. system of justice has been the extraordinary amount of *disparity* in the way criminal punishment has been meted out.[72]

In general, four goals—deterrence, incapacitation, rehabilitation, and desert/ retribution—are associated with imposition of a sentence.[73]

1. *Deterrence.* By imposing a sentence on the convicted criminal, the court hopes to deter others from committing similar crimes. The validity of deterrence rests on the premise that punishing the offender will have a future payoff in a reduced crime rate.

2. *Incapacitation.* Incapacitation is used because, at least for the period during which offenders are under control, they will not repeat their criminal behavior. In some instances, incapacitation involves keeping offenders under supervision while they remain in the community. In others, it calls for their confinement in an institution. Incapacitation involves prediction of behavior patterns: Offenders are confined not for what they have done but for what it is feared they might do in the future.

3. *Rehabilitation.* Correctional treatment is another goal of sentencing. Its purpose is to lessen the probability that the offender will commit additional criminal acts by administering some type of rehabilitory therapy under supervision of correctional agents. Rehabilitation may help offenders deal emotionally with the stresses of modern life, enroll them in vocational training, provide them with an education, and so on. Again, the concept complies that current actions by the justice system can help change future behaviors.

4. *Desert/Retribution.* The final goal of sentencing is to exact punishment on offenders for what they have already done. Whereas the goals of deterrence, incapacitation, and rehabilitation are based on what might happen or what

the offender might do, desert focuses on the event that led to conviction. Desert/retribution is grounded in equity: criminals benefited from their acts; they must now pay society back to make things even.

Each of these goals is in operation when a person is sentenced. Sometimes, one policy or goal becomes popular in public opinion and for a while dominates sentencing considerations. In the 1960s and 1970s, rehabilitation became the prime goal of sentencing; and innovative treatment methods were stressed. Today, rising crime rates, the supposed failure of rehabilitation, and a generally conservative outlook make desert, deterrence, and incapacitation the primary sentencing goals.

SENTENCING DISPOSITIONS

Generally, four kinds of sentences or dispositions are available to the court:

1. A fine.
2. A suspended sentence.
3. Probation.
4. Incarceration.

A fine is usually exacted for a minor and may also be combined with other sentencing alternatives, such as probation or confinement. A suspended sentence represents an effort by the court to refrain from enforcing a sentence, instead allowing the offender to remain in the community, often without supervision. The most common sentence is community supervision, or probation, by which the offender is permitted to live in the community subject to compliance with legally imposed conditions. Finally, the sentence of total confinement, or incarceration, is imposed when it has been decided that the general public needs to be protected from further criminal activity by the defendant.

When an accused is convicted of two or more charges, they must be sentenced on each charge. If the sentences are concurrent, they begin the same day and sentence has been completed after the longest term has been served. For example: a defendant is sentenced to three years imprisonment on a charge of assault and ten years for burglary, the sentences to be served concurrently. After ten years in prison the sentences would be completed. Conversely, a consecutive sentence means that upon completion of one sentence the other term of incarceration begins. For example: a defendant is sentenced to three years imprisonment on a charge of assault and ten years for burglary, the sentences to be served consecutively. After three years are served on the assault charge, the offender begins serving the burglary sentence. Therefore, the total term on the two charges would be thirteen years. In most instances, sentences are given concurrently.

The sentence itself is generally imposed by the judge, and sentencing is one of the most crucial functions of judgeship. Sentencing authority may also be exercised by the jury, an administrative body, or a group of judges, or may be mandated by statute. As previously mentioned, the length of the sentence is determined by the limits of the statute defining the particular offense. It is also determined by the discretion of the judge, who bases his or her decision on information received about the defendant before imposing the sentence. In the case of a minor offense, the judge generally places the defendant on probation; he or she requires only limited information to make such a decision. In a felony case, the court usually delays the sentence until the completion of a *presentence investigation report* by the probation department; this report, which is a social and personal history as well as an evaluation of the defendant, is used by the judge in making a sentencing decision. Some judges heavily weigh the presentence investigation report; others may dismiss it completely or rely only on certain portions of it. However, such criteria as the nature of the offense and the previous record of the defendant are of prime importance to most judges in determining the type and length of sentence to be imposed. Thus, in most jurisdictions, the judge has the choice of treating offenders in the community or giving them prison terms.

SENTENCE TO AN EXTENDED TERM IN PRISON

When a convicted offender is sentenced to prison, the statutes of the jurisdiction in which the crime was committed determine the penalties that may be imposed by the court. Over the years a variety of sentencing structures have been used in the United States. They include determinate sentences, indeterminate sentences, mandatory sentences, and presumptive sentences.

Determinate Sentences. Determinate sentences were the first kind used in the United States, and are still employed today in some jurisdictions. A determinate sentence is a fixed term of years, set by the legislature, to be served by the offender sentenced to prison for a particular crime. For example, in one type of determinate sentencing structure, the legislature may set a term of ten years for all people convicted of robbery who are not eligible for community supervision. If the judge decides to impose a prison sentence, it must be ten years and it must be served in its entirety without parole. This approach is known as *flat*, or *fixed*, sentencing. Maine is a state that imposes flat sentences.

Another variation of the determinate sentence is to have the legislature create the maximum sentence a person can serve for a crime, but to allow the judge discretion within that limit. For example, the maximum sentence for robbery may be ten years, but judges may be given the opportunity to reduce the sentence at their discretion (for example, to seven years, to three years, or even to grant probation).

Though determinate sentences provide a single term of years to be served, the actual time spent in prison can be reduced by several methods. Inmates can accrue *good time*—time off for good behavior—at a rate ranging from ten to fifteen days per month. In some states, like California, half of a determinate sentence can be erased by accumulating good time. In addition, some correctional authorities grant sentence reductions to inmates who participate in treatment programs such as educational and vocational training.

Indeterminate Sentences. In the 1870s, prison reformers such as Enoch Wines and Zebulon Brockway called for creation of indeterminate sentences. They believed that prison sentences should be tailored to fit individual needs and that offenders should only be placed in confinement until they were rehabilitated. Indeterminate sentencing was influenced by positivist criminology and the belief that criminals were "sick" people who could be treated in prison. The wisdom of putting an offender away for a fixed period of time was disputed. Rather than the "punishment fitting the crime," reformers believed the "treatment should fit the offender." The indeterminate sentence became the most widely used type of sentence in the United States.[74]

This concept, still used in the majority of states, gives convicted offenders who are not eligible for community of supervision a light minimum sentence that must be served and a lengthy maximum sentence that is the outer boundary of the time that can be served. For example, the legislature might set a sentence of a minimum of one year and a maximum of twenty years for burglary.

Under this scheme, the actual length of time served by the inmate is controlled by the correction agency. The inmate can be paroled from confinement after serving the minimum sentence whenever the institution and parole personnel believe that he or she is ready to live in the community. The basic purpose underlying the indeterminate sentencing approach, particularly during the middle of the twentieth century, has been to individualize each sentence in the interests of rehabilitating the offender. This type of sentencing allows for flexibility not only in the type of sentence to be imposed but also in the length of time to be served. Indeterminate sentences are also subject to reduction for good time. Following are some variations on the indeterminate sentence:

- The legislature determines minimum and maximum sentence and the judge cannot change either. For example, each offender sent to prison for burglary receives a sentence of one to twenty years.
- Maximum sentence is set by legislature and cannot be changed; minimum is determined by judge. For example, offender A receives one to twenty years for burglary; offender B, sixteen to twenty, offender C, ten to twenty, and so on.
- Judge sets both maximum and minimum sentence within guidelines set up by legislature. For example, minimum and maximum sentence for burglary is one to twenty years. Offender A gets one to twenty; offender B, four to ten; offender C, three to six. The maximum the judge uses cannot exceed twenty years; the minimum cannot be less than one.
- Maximum set by judge within upper limit, minimum determined by legislature. For example, all sentenced burglars do at least one year in prison but no more than twenty. Offender A receives one to ten; offender B, one to twenty; offender C, one to five.

The indeterminate sentence has come under attack in recent years for various reasons. One group of critics charges that it produces great disparity in the way people are treated in the correctional system. For example, one offender may serve one year and another may serve twenty for the same crime. Further, the indeterminate sentence is believed to take control of sentencing out of the hands of the judiciary and place it within the framework of corrections. The protections of due process that a person maintains in the courtrooms are absent in the correctional setting.

Finally, conservatives charge that serious criminals are given the opportunity to serve little or no time in prison, thereby weakening the power of the criminal law to deter crime.

In response to these charges, new sentencing structures have been developed. Two of the more important ones are described below.

Mandatory Sentences. One effort to limit judicial discretion has been the development of the mandatory sentence. Some states, for example, prohibit people convicted of certain offenses, such as violent crimes, or multiple offenders (recidivists) from being placed on probation; still others bar certain offenders from being considered for parole. Mandatory sentencing legislation may impose minimum and maximum terms or fixed prison sentences. Crimes that often call for mandatory prison sentences include murder and multiple convictions for crimes such as rape, drug violations, and robbery. Mandatory sentencing generally limits the judge's discretionary power to impose any disposition but that authorized by the legislature; as a result, it limits the idea of the individualized sentence and restricts sentencing disparity. Mandatory sentencing provides equal treatment for all offenders who commit the same crime, regardless of age, sex, or other individual characteristics.

One illustration of a mandatory sentence is the Massachusetts Gun Control Law, which requires a sentence of imprisonment for not less than one year nor more than two and one-half years for illegally carrying a firearm.[75] The unique feature of this statute is that the punishment is a mandatory sentence of at least one year in prison, which cannot be suspended by the court. Neither can the offender be considered for probation, parole, or other forms of early release until completion of the one-year sentence.

Another type of mandatory sentence is designed for chronic, multiple, or career criminals. Habitual offender statutes can be found in the criminal codes of most states. They are employed at the discretion of the prosecutor when an offender is found to have been convicted for previous felony offenses. If found guilty when charged as a habitual felon, the defendant is given a long prison sentence, sometimes life in prison without hope of parole. Habitual offender statutes are aimed at the career criminal and represent the dominance of the conservative incapacitation philosophy in the nation's sentencing policies.

More than thirty-five states have already replaced discretionary sentencing with fixed-term mandatory sentences for such crimes as the sale of hard drugs, kidnapping, gun possession, and arson. The primary purpose behind such laws is to impose swift and certain punishment on the offender. It is difficult to say if depriving the judiciary of discretion and placing all sentencing power in the hands of the legislature will have a deterrent effect on the commission of these offenses. Only time and further research will provide the answer.

Presumptive Sentences. Presumptive sentencing plans create a statutorily determined sentence convicted offenders should "presume" they will receive if sent to prison. Offenders convicted under this scheme are given this specific sentence unless mitigating or aggravating circumstances are found in the commission of the offense or the offender's personal background. In other words, a judge is permitted to sentence below or above the maximum but is required to write an opinion justifying such action. For example, the legislature might set a penalty of six years for armed robbery with a mitigation factor of plus or minus two years. Thus, the "ordinary" robber should be given six years in prison. The first offender who has had a good prior record might have the sentence reduced to four years; the multiple offender who used excess brutality could receive up to eight years. However, the range of possible sentence length is reduced and thus sentencing disparity should be limited.

In addition, most presumptive sentencing statutes abolish early release via parole, though maintaining the use of good-time credit. Forms of this method have already been adopted in states such as California, Illinois, and Indiana. Although presumptive sentencing is a rather new device, critics maintain that it will help increase the size of prison populations to a dangerous level.[76] On the other hand, its supporters believe that it creates a fairness in the justice process, helps eliminate sentencing disparity, and increases the deterrent effect of punishment.[77]

SENTENCING DISPARITY AND CONTROL

Sentencing disparity has long been a problem in the justice system. Simply put, people who commit the same criminal acts receive widely different sentences. Though many legal and extralegal factors (see following section) enter into the sentencing decision, it seems a violation of due process and equal protection to maintain a sentencing system that results in wide variations in punishment. However, some argue that sentences should be tailored to the individual needs of offenders, and therefore it is logical to give each defendant a different sentence.

One approach to reducing sentencing disparity has been to legislate flat, mandatory, or presumptive sentences that are designed to reduce discretion in sentencing decision making. However, these measures can be bypassed by judges and prosecutors who wish to maintain their independence by shifting discretion further up the justice system. For example, if a mandatory one-year sentence exists for firearm possession, a prosecutor can arrange a plea bargain to a lesser charge in order to retain discretion.

Another approach to reducing disparity has been to create judicial sentencing councils. Sentencing councils are meetings of the judges who sit regularly in a particular court. During a sentencing council, the judges discuss appropriate dispositions of defendants awaiting sentencing. The sentencing judge retains the ultimate responsibility for selecting and imposing the sentence while the other judges act in an advisory capacity. Normally, the judges meet in groups of three to consider the sentencing alternatives in pending cases. The sentencing council has the following advantages: (1) it reveals to judges their differences in sentencing philosophies; (2) it provides an opportunity for judges to debate their differences; and (3) it provides a forum for periodic evaluation of a court's sentencing practice.

Ordinarily, the sentencing decision for a particular case is in the hands of a single judge. Sentencing councils provide a departure from this individual approach and are particularly useful in that they serve to lessen the amount of disparity in sentencing practices. One major difficulty regarding the sentencing council is that information gathered from other judges may impair the ability of the sentencing judge to give open-minded consideration to all arguments at the dispositional hearing.

The United States District Court for the Eastern District of Michigan originally developed the idea for the sentencing council, and such councils have since been implemented in other federal courts as well as state court systems.

Another approach is the sentencing guidelines model developed by Leslie Wilkins and currently used in the federal court system. Guidelines assign a score to each offender based on personal factors such as age, prior offense history, and current criminal behavior (for example, narcotics violations, robbery, or theft). The typical sentence given to, for example, young, first-offense narcotics violators or robbers can then be computed. Sentencing judges know whether their decision in the case at hand differs significantly from decisions made by their colleagues in similar cases. Guidelines can be used to control disparity, but judges still make their own decisions in each case.[78] The use of guidelines has been adapted in Michigan, Minnesota, and other states; the federal government's Criminal Code revision of 1984 mandates the creation of a federal sentencing guideline commission

TABLE 16.2 Minnesota sentencing guidelines grid

SEVERITY LEVELS OF CONVICTION OFFENSE		CRIMINAL HISTORY (# OF PRIOR OFFENSES) (presumptive sentence lengths in months)						
		0	1	2	3	4	5	6 or more
Unauthorized use of motor vehicle Possession of marijuana	I	12*	12*	12*	15	18	21 24 23-25	
Theft related crimes ($150-$2500) Sale of marijuana	II	12*	12*	14	17	20	23	27 25-29
Theft crimes ($150-$2500)	III	12*	13	16	19	22 21-23	27 25-29	32 30-34
Burglary - Felony intent Receiving stolen goods ($150-$2500)	IV	12*	15	18	21	25 24-26	32 30-34	41 37-45
Simple robbery	V	18	23	27	30 29-31	38 36-40	46 43-49	54 50-58
Assault, 2nd degree	VI	21	26	30	34 33-35	44 42-46	54 50-58	65 60-70
Aggravated robbery	VII	24 23-25	32 30-34	41 38-44	49 42-53	65 60-70	81 75-87	97 90-104
Assault, 1st degree Criminal sexual conduct, 1st degree	VIII	43 41-45	54 50-58	65 60-70	76 71-81	95 89-101	113 106-120	132 124-140
Murder, 3rd degree	IX	97 94-100	119 116-122	127 124-130	149 143-155	176 168-184	205 192-215	230 218-242
Murder, 2nd degree	X	116 111-121	140 133-147	162 153-171	203 192-214	243 231-255	284 270-298	324 309-339

Italicized numbers within the grid denote the range within which a judge may sentence without the sentence being deemed a departure.
1st Degree murder is excluded from the guidelines by law and continues to have a mandatory life sentence.
Cells below heavy line receive a presumptive prison sentence.
Cells above line receive a presumptive non-prison sentence.
The numbers in these cells refer to duration of confinement if probation is revoked.
*One year and one day.

SOURCE. Minnesota Sentencing Guidelines Commission, 1981.

to review and revise all federal punishments. The guidelines used in Minnesota are illustrated in Table 16.2.

The jury is still out on the effectiveness of guidelines. An evaluation of the Minnesota experiment found mixed results.[79] Minnesota's judges strictly adhered to guideline recommendations the first year they were in effect (1980), but began to deviate from them after two years. Some racial disparity was indicated the first year after the guidelines were adapted, but it diminished over time. Most importantly, there was a 73-percent increase in incarceration for serious offenders and

Sentencing Practices

What factors influence sentencing? What is the average sentence given for various crime categories? What effect does pleading guilty have on sentencing? To answer these and other questions about sentencing practices, and federal government's Bureau of Justice Statistics evaluated 15,000 cases in 18 jurisdictions. The following were the major findings of the analysis.

- Forty-five percent of the sentences for the felonies studied were to state prison; 26 percent were to county jail (with or without an additional probation sentence); and 28 percent were to probation only (see table A).
- Those convicted of homicide were most likely to be sentenced to prison (85 percent) and those convicted of drug trafficking were least likely (23 percent) (see table B).
- Average prison sentences for each crime varied greatly among the jurisdictions, but within each jurisdiction sentence lengths were ordered with great consistency (see table C).
- The use of jail in felony sentencing varied substantially among the participating jurisdictions, ranging from less than 1 percent of the sentences in Baltimore City to half of the sentences in Hennepin County (Minneapolis).
- The average prison term imposed in determinate sentencing jurisdictions was 40 percent to 50 percent shorter than in jurisdictions using indeterminate sentencing.
- Nearly three-fourths (74 percent) of the sentences to life imprisonment or death were for those convicted of homicide; 26% of all homicide sentences were to life in prison or death.
- For robbery and burglary, those convicted of an attempted offense were less likely to be sentenced to prison and received shorter average prison terms than those convicted of the completed offense.
- The number of charges on which a person was convicted affected sentencing outcomes. Forty percent of those convicted on a single charge received prison sentences, averaging 5.3 years; in contrast, 69 percent of those convicted on four or more charges received prison terms averaging 13.5 years.
- About 1 in 9 of those convicted of multiple charges and sentenced to prison received consecutive rather than concurrent sentences. The average prison term imposed on those with consecutive sentences was 18.9 years; for those with concurrent sentences it was 8.9 years.
- Nearly six times as many offenders were convicted on the highest original charge rather than on a lesser charge (85 percent vs. 15 percent).
- There were about five times as many convictions through guilty pleas as by trial. About five-sixths (83 percent) of all guilty pleas were to the highest original charge. Those pleading guilty were slightly less likely to be sentenced to prison (44 percent) than those found guilty at trial (51 percent). Those pleading guilty also received shorter average prison terms than those found guilty at trial for each of the crimes studied (table D).

This remarkable study tells us a great deal about sentencing practices around the United States. As expected, people who plead guilty receive shorter sentences per crime, indicating the influence of plea bargaining. Similarly, people who commit serious crimes were punished more severely, as were offenders who had prior convictions.

a 72-percent reduction for nonserious offenders. In sum, the guidelines had an initial effect, but judges tended to stray from the recommended sentences as time wore on.

With the establishment of a federal guideline commission, attempts at reducing sentencing disparity should receive a boost. Several states, including New York, are attempting to control judicial discretion through the use of guideline-setting bodies.

EXTRALEGAL FACTORS IN SENTENCING

Logically, various factors should influence the length of prison sentences, including:

- How severe the offense is
- Offender's prior criminal record

TABLE A. A typical 100 sentences in felony court

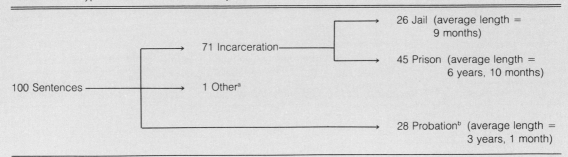

aOther includes such sentences as restitution to the victim or a fine.
bProbation refers to probation *only* and does not include sentences to a split term of incarceration and probation.

TABLE B. Distribution of sentences, by type of sentence and conviction offense

Conviction offense	Prison	Jail only	Jail and probation	Probation only	Other	Total
Violent						
Homicide	85	1	5	9	.5	100
Rape	69	2	10	18	1	100
Robbery	65	4	12	17	1	100
Aggravated assault	39	11	19	31	2	100
Property						
Burglary	46	8	17	28	1	100
Larceny	29	15	17	38	2	100
Other						
Drug trafficking	23	6	35	35	2	100
Total	45%	3%	18%	28%	1%	100%

Note: May not total 100% because of rounding.

cont'd

- Whether the offender used violence
- Whether the offender used weapons

Research studies do in fact show a strong correlation between these variables and the type and length of sentence received (see Close-Up entitled "Sentencing Practices"). Some experts have also suggested that sentencing outcome may depend on whether the defendant had a private attorney or public defender, though research does not always support this contention.[80]

Of greater importance is the charge that race, sex, and economic status influence sentencing outcomes. These factors appear to influence sentencing because the inmate population is predominantly male, black, and lower-class. Although this phenomenon may be a result of discrimination, it could also be simply a function of existing crime patterns—males, minorities, and members of the lower class commit the crimes that are most likely to result in a prison sentence (homicide,

Sentencing Practices—cont'd

TABLE C. Average prison sentence length in years for each conviction offense, by jurisdiction

Jurisdiction	Average prison sentence length in years for:						
	Homicide	Rape	Robbery	Aggravated assault	Burglary	Larceny	Drug trafficking
Average for all jurisdictions	14.9	12.6	8.7	6.7	4.6	3.3	4.2
Determinate sentencing jurisdictions							
Hennepin County	10.0	5.8	4.1	3.7	2.2	2.1	1.5
Los Angeles	6.5	11.5	3.8	5.2	2.5	2.1	2.6
Riverside County	5.2	9.7	4.6	3.8	3.0	2.6	3.1
Kane County	9.3	8.6	5.8	4.0	4.2	2.2	5.4
Denver	7.6	11.8	7.1	5.7	4.8	4.7	4.5
Median	7.6	9.7	4.6	4.0	3.0	2.2	3.1
Indeterminate sentencing jurisdictions							
Maricopa County	11.2	7.6	7.4	5.3	3.9	3.1	5.4
Milwaukee County	12.7	8.3	7.6	9.1	4.0	3.3	3.6
Lancaster County	7.5	11.0	4.6	6.8	2.7	2.0	2.4
Davidson County	15.4	12.1	13.2	7.9	5.8	5.0	5.8
Philadelphia	14.7	11.9	8.4	5.3	5.8	3.9	5.7
Jefferson Parish	11.6	3.5	16.8	11.3	4.7	2.9	7.6
New Orleans	15.4	18.4	9.8	9.3	4.7	2.6	5.0
Oklahoma County	13.7	21.3	13.5	10.0	6.2	4.1	4.9
Lucas County	22.5	18.2	20.6	11.4	10.2	4.2	9.2
Baltimore City	17.4	11.2	6.7	14.4	3.3	*	*
Baltimore County	25.3	20.3	10.4	10.5	6.3	2.0	3.5
Dade County	28.7	28.2	15.6	4.3	5.9	3.3	6.4
Jefferson County	13.9	15.7	13.7	7.1	7.4	4.1	4.9
Median	14.7	12.1	10.4	9.1	5.8	3.3	5.0/5.4

Note: Persons receiving life or death sentences (less than 2% of all cases but 26% of all homicide cases) were excluded in computing the average prison terms.
*Sentencing data were not collected for these crimes in Baltimore City.

rape, armed robbery, and so on). They may also be the defendants least likely to make bail, another factor often correlated with imprisonment.

Numerous research studies have been conducted to measure racial, sexual and economic discrimination in sentencing. And though the evidence shows that these factors do produce differential outcomes, the effect of legal factors (crime, prior record, and so on) seems much stronger.[81] For example, Joan Petersilia's recent study of racial disparities in criminal justice found that, all things considered, blacks did receive longer sentences than whites.[82] Nonetheless, Petersilia attributes these differences to white defendants' use of plea bargains and the favorable outcome of their (probation department) presentence reports, and not discrimination by judicial decision makers. Also, the extra time served by blacks is only a matter of months (for example, 2.4 more in California and 7.7 in Texas) and not years, which overt discrimination would lead us to expect. Whereas racial discrimination may have been an important factor in the past, some evidence shows that it is decreasing today.[83]

TABLE D. Sentences to prison, by method of conviction

Conviction offense	Percent of sentences to prison for those convicted by:		Average prison sentence length for those convicted by:	
	Trial	Guilty plea	Trial	Guilty plea
Violent				
Homicide	92	82	16.2	14.2
Rape	81	65	16.2	10.9
Robbery	66	65	12.7	7.3
Aggravated assault	47	36	9.8	5.6
Property				
Burglary	42	48	6.4	4.3
Larceny	24	30	4.2	3.1
Other				
Drug trafficking	27	21	5.7	3.8
Total	51%	44%	10.7 years	6.0 years

Note: Table excludes those cases (9%) where the study could not ascertain how the person was convicted.

What may be surprising is the relative similarity of sentence length used across the United States. Regardless of whether jurisdictions use determinate or indeterminate sentences, judges seem to take sentence reduction factors into account (parole, good time, earned credit) when making sentence decisions. So while at first glance indeterminate sentences seem longer, the actual time served per offense may be quite similar.

Finally, whereas crime seriousness and prior convictions predict both probability of incarceration and length of sentence, it is surprising to find that many multiple offenders do not get prison sentences—40 percent of those convicted of three charges and 31 percent of those convicted of four charges did not go to prison. Thus, although the American judicial system has been accused of being overly harsh, it is still quite likely that multiple-felony offenders will avoid a prison stay.

DISCUSSION QUESTIONS

1. Should all convicted felons receive some time in prison?
2. Should plea bargains be allowed to reduce sentence length?

SOURCE. Bureau of Justice Statistics, *Felony Sentencing in 18 Local Jurisdictions* (Washington, D.C.: U.S. Department of Justice, 1985).

This evidence should not be interpreted as meaning that the fight against sentencing disparity has been won. You may recall from chapter 6 that research indicates a pattern of racial discrimination in death penalty sentencing. Similarly, some studies have found that males are treated more harshly than females who commit the same crime, though this pattern may also be changing.[84] Discrimination may be shifted either up the criminal justice ladder—to prosecutorial discretion and bail decisions—or downward, to the choice of correctional facilities, the granting of parole, and so on. So, one primary goal of sentencing reform in the 1980s has been to reduce disparity, both legal and extralegal, by creating flat sentences, eliminating parole, creating guidelines, and so on.

SENTENCING IN THE 1980s: A FINAL WORD

In the 1980s, sentencing practices have been controlled by the need to deter crime and incapacitate dangerous offenders. The rehabilitation/treatment goal of sentencing has been subordinated to the need to protect public safety. Jurisdictions that previously had employed indeterminate sentences, which allow early release from prison after correctional authorities deem the inmate rehabilitated, have been replacing them with determinate and mandatory sentences, which insure that they will be separated from society for a predictable number of years. Consequently, the number of people behind bars has risen at the same time the crime rate has declined.

Sentencing practices reflect the dominance of conservative/classical theory. That dominance has caused consternation among liberal/radical thinkers, who view it as a threat to the justice system's humanistic principles. Conservatives counter with the view that modern sentences are more fair, eliminate disparity, and increase the inmate's sense of justice. Regardless of the merits of either argument, removing uncertainty in sentences seems to be a trend that is here to stay.

Summary

The adjudicatory process is designed to provide an important forum for deciding the justice of a conflict between two or more parties. Unfortunately, discretion and personal decision making interfere with the equality that should be built into the law.

The adjudicatory process is played out in the nation's court system. State courts usually involve a three- or four-tiered system—lower trial courts; superior trial courts; appellate courts, supreme court. The federal system is similar; it contains trial courts, appellate courts, and the Supreme Court. The U.S. Supreme Court is the final court of appeals for all cases on both state and federal levels.

There are three main actors in the adjudicatory process. The prosecutor brings charges against the offender and then represents the state in all criminal matters. The defense attorney represents the accused at all stages of the adjudicatory process. Some defense attorneys offer private counsel, but the majority are appointed and paid for by the state. The judge controls the trial, rules on issues of evidence, charges the jury, and in some cases can choose the type and length of sentence.

The pretrial stage of the justice process involves such issues as bail, plea bargaining, and alternatives to prosecution. Bail is a money bond the defendant puts up to secure freedom before trial. It is controversial, since those who cannot make bail must spend their time in detention. Critics charge that bail discriminates against the poor, who can neither afford bond nor borrow it from bondsmen. Consequently, reform programs such as release on recognizance have been started.

Plea bargaining involves the prosecutor's allowing people to plead guilty as charged in return for some consideration—for example, a reduced sentence or dropped charges. Plea bargaining has been criticized, since it represents the un- checked use of discretion by prosecutors. Often, serious criminals can receive light sentences by bargaining, while some people may be coerced into pleading guilty because they fear a harsh sentence if they go to trial. An effort has been made to control plea bargains; but they are still frequently used.

One way of influencing plea bargains is through noncriminal alternatives to prosecution. These include diversion and other types of treatment-oriented pro- grams.

The second stage of the adjudicatory process is the criminal trial. The trial has a number of distinct stages, including jury selection; opening statements; pre- sentation of evidence by prosecution and defense; closing arguments; instructions to the jury; and verdict, sentence, and appeal. The rule of law also affects criminal trials. The Supreme Court has required that trials be speedy, public, and fair, and has ruled that people have a right to be free from double jeopardy and to be represented by competent counsel.

After a conviction, sentencing occurs. Each state, as well as federal, government has its own type of sentences and punishments. In all, fines, suspended sentences, community supervision, and prison are the most common forms of punishment. Prison sentences are divided into determinate, indeterminate, mandatory, and presumptive types. Efforts to control sentencing disparity include the use of sentencing councils and sentencing guidelines, as well as determinate, mandatory, and presumptive sentences.

Notes

1 Arthur Rossett and Donald Cressey, *Justice by Consent* (New York: J. B. Lippincott, 1976), p. 4.

2 Ibid.

3 See generally Jerome Skolnick, *Justice without Trial* (New York: Wiley, 1966).

4 Bureau of Justice Statistics, *Case Filings in State Courts, State Court Caseload Statistics* (Washington, D.C.: U.S. Department of Justice, 1984).

5 Newman Baker, "The Prosecutor Initiation of Prosecution," *Journal of Criminal Law, Criminology and Police Science* 23 (1933):770–71.

6 Bureau of Justice Statistics, *Report to the Nation on Crime and Justice* (Washington, D.C.: U.S. Department of Justice, 1983), p. 55.

7 Frank W. Miller, *Prosecution: The Decision to Charge a Suspect with a Crime* (Boston: Little Brown; 1970).

8 Wayne LaFave, "The Prosecutor's Discretion in the United States," *American Journal of Comparative Law* 18 (1970):532–48.

9 Bureau of Justice Statistics, *Report to the Nation on Crime and Justice*, p. 56.

10 Charles Breitel, "Controls in Criminal Law Enforcement," *University of Chicago Law Review* 27 (1960):427–35.

11 See generally "A Symposium on Prosecutorial Discretion," *American Criminal Law Review* (1976):379–99.

12 George Cole, "The Decision to Prosecute," *Law and Society Review* 4 (1970):331–43.

13 Gideon v. Wainwright, 372 U.S. 335 (1963); Argersinger v. Hamlin, 407 U.S. 25 (1972).

14 Bureau of Justice Statistics, *Criminal Defense Systems* (Washington, D.C.: U.S. Department of Justice, 1984).

15 See American Bar Association, Special Committee on Evaluation of Ethical Standards, *Code of Professional Responsibility*, (Chicago, Ill, American Bar Association) p. 81.

16 Monroe H. Freedman, "Professional Responsibility of the Criminal Defense Lawyer: The Three Hardest Questions," *Michigan Law Review* 64 (1966):1468.

17 President's Commission on Law Enforcement and the Administration of Justice, *The Challenge of Crime in a Free Society* (Washington, D.C.: Government Printing Office, 1967), p. 152.

18 See generally Malcolm Feeley, *The Process is the Punishment* (New York: Russell Sage Foundation, 1979); James Eisenstein and Jacob Herbert, *Felony Justice* (Boston: Little, Brown; 1977).

19 Marcia Lipetz, *Routine Justice: Processing Cases in Women's Court* (New Brunswick, N.J.: Transaction Books, 1983); Michael Gottfredson and Donald Gottfredson, *Decision Making in Criminal Jusstice: Toward the Rational Exercise of Discretion* (Cambridge, Mass.: Ballinger, 1980).

20 William Lineberry, ed., *Justice in America: Law, Order and the Courts* (New York: H. W. Wilson Co., 1972).

21 John MacKenzie, *The Appearance of Justice* (New York: Charles Scribner's Sons, 1974).

22 Sari Escovitz with Fred Kurland and Nan Gold, *Judicial Selection and Tenure* (Chicago: American Judicature Society, 1974), pp. 3–16.

23 M. Ozanne, R. Wilson, and D. Gedney, Jr., "Toward a Theory of Bail Risk," *Criminology* 18 (1980):149.

24 Stephen Gettinger, "Bail Reform," in *Legal Process and Corrections*, ed. N. Johnston and L. Savitz (New York: Wiley, 1982), p. 84.

25 Parker v. Roth, 278 NW 2d 106 (1979). The Supreme Court refused to rule on the merits of the case, thus allowing it to stand. Murphy v. Hunt, 80-2165, 30 CrL 3075 (1982).

26 Cited in Gettinger, "Bail Reform," p. 83.

27 A. Rankin, "The Effects of Pre-Trial Detention," *New York University Law Review* 39 (1964):641–55; V. Swigert and R. Farrell, "Normal Homicides and the Law," *American Sociological Review* 42 (1977):16–32.

28 See generally Gettinger, "Bail Reform."

29 Vera Institute of Justice, *Programs in Criminal Justice* (New York: Vera Institute, 1972).

30 Malcolm Feeley, *Court Reform on Trial* (New York: Basic Books, 1983); John Goldkamp, "Judicial Reform of Bail Practices: The Philadelphia Experiment," *Court Management Journal* (1983):16–20.

31 Mary Toborg, *Pretrial Release: A National Evaluation of Practices and Outcomes*, National Institute of Justice, U.S. Department of Justice (Washington, D.C.: USGPO, 1981).

32 Donald Pryor and Walter Smith, "Significant Research Findings Concerning Pre-Trial Release," *Pretrial Issues*, Pretrial Services Resource Center, Washington, D.C., 1982.

33 Toborg, *Pretrial Release.*

34 Bureau of Justice Statistics, *Pretrial Release and Misconduct* (Washington, D.C.: U.S. Department of Justice, 1985).

35 Schall v. Martin, 104 S.Ct. 2403 (1984).

36 Donald Newman, "Making a Deal," in *Legal Process and Corrections*, ed. N. Johnston and L. Savitz (New York: Wiley, 1982), p. 93.

37 Ibid., pp. 96–97.

38 These sentiments are similar to those expressed by Abraham Blumberg in "The Practice of Law as a Confidence Game: Organizational Co-optation of a Profession," *Law and Society Review* 1 (1967):15–39.

39 Again, these thoughts are similar to Blumberg's views as expressed in "Law as a Confidence Game."

40 Bureau of Justice Statistics, *The Prevalence of Guilty Pleas* (Washington, D.C.: U.S. Department of Justice, 1984).

41 National Advisory Commission in Criminal Justice Standards and Goals, *Courts* (Washington, D.C.: Government Printing Office, 1976).

42 Richard Kuh, "Plea Copping," *Bar Bulletin* 24 (1966-1967):160.

43 Alan Alschuler, "The Defense Counsel's Role in Plea Bargaining," *Yale Law Journal* 84 (1975):1179.

44 See generally Milton Heuman, "A Note on Plea Bargaining and Case Pressure," *Law and Society Review* 9 (1975):515.

45 National Institute of Law Enforcement and Criminal Justice, *Plea Bargaining in the United States* (Washington, D.C.: Georgetown University, 1978), p. 8.

46 Michael Rubenstein, Stevens Clarke, and Teresa White, *Alaska Bans Plea Bargaining* (Washington, D.C.: U.S. Department of Justice, 1980).

47 Boykin v. Alabama, 395 U.S. 238, 89 S.Ct. 1709, 23 L.Ed. 2d 274 (1969).

48 Brady v. United States, 397 U.S. 742, 90 S.Ct. 1463, 25 L.Ed. 2d 747 (1970).

49 Santobello v. New York, 404 U.S. 257, 92 S.Ct. 495, 30 L.Ed. 2d 427 (1971).

50 Brodenkircher v. Hayes, 434 U.S. 357 (1978).

51 Newman, "Making a Deal," p. 102.

52 National Pretrial Intervention Service Center, American Bar Association, *Portfolio of Descriptive Profiles on Selected Pretrial Criminal Justice Intervention Programs* (1974); A.B.T. Associates, *Pretrial Intervention Program of the Manpower Administration* (Washington, D.C.: Department of Labor, 1971-1972).

53 National Advisory Commission on Criminal Justice Standards and Goals, *Courts*, p. 66.

54 See, for example, "Limiting the Peremptory Challenge: Representation of Groups on Petit Juries," *Yale Law Journal* 86 (1977):1715.

55 Swain v. Alabama, 380 U.S. 202 (1964).

56 Hamm v. South Carolina, 409 U.S. 524, 93 S.Ct. 848, 35 L.Ed. 2d 46 (1973).

57 Taylor v. Louisiana, 419 U.S. 522, 42 L.Ed. 2d 690, 95 S.Ct. 692 (1975).

58 Strunk v. United States, 412 U.S. 434 (1973).

59 Klopfer v. North Carolina, 38 U.S. 213 (1967).

60 Barker v. Wingo, 404 U.S. 307 (1971).

61 Bureau of Justice Statistics, *Report to the Nation on Crime and Delinquency*, p. 66.

62 Duncan v. Louisiana, 391 U.S. 145 (1968).

63 Baldwin v. New York, 399 U.S. 66 (1970).

64 Williams v. Florida, 399 U.S. 78 (1970).

65 Apodica v. Oregon, 406 U.S. 404 (1972).

66 Benton v. Maryland, 395 U.S. 784 (1969).

67 Powell v. Alabama, 287 U.S. 45 (1932).

68 Gideon v. Wainwright, 372 U.S. 335 (1963).

69 Argersinger v. Hamlin, 407 U.S. 25 (1972).

70 Strickland v. Washington, 104 S.Ct. 2052 (1984).

71 See Marvin E. Frankel, *Criminal Sentences—Law without Order* (New York: Hill & Wang, 1973).

72 See generally, Norval Morris, *Equal Justice under the Law* (Washington, D.C.: Government Printing Office, 1977).

73 See V. O'Leary, M. Gottfredson, and A. Gelman, "Contemporary Sentencing Proposals," *Criminal Law Bulletin* 11 (1975):558–60.

74 Marvin Zalman, "The Rise and Fall of the Indeterminate Sentence," *Wayne Law Review* 24 (1978):857.

75 See Massachusetts General Laws, Chap. 369:10, Chap. 649, Acts of 1974.

76 T. R. Clear, R. D. Hewitt, and R. M. Regoli, "Discretion and the Determinate Sentence: Its Distribution, Control and Effect on Time Served," *Crime and Delinquency* 20 (1974):428–45.

77 See David Fogel, *Justice as Fairness* (Cincinnati: W. H. Anderson, 1981).

78 See Leslie Wilkins, *The Principle of Guidelines for Sentencing* (Washington, D.C.: Government Printing Office, 1981).

79 Minnesota Sentencing Guidelines Commission, *The Impact of the Minnesota Sentencing Guidelines: Three-Year Evaluation*, St. Paul, Minn., 1984, p. 162.

80 David Willison, "The Effects of Counsel on the Severity of Criminal Sentences: A Statistical Assessment," *Justice System Journal* 9 (1984):87–101.

81 Alan Lizotte, "Extra-Legal Factors in Chicago's Criminal Courts: Testing the Conflict Model of Criminal Justice," *Social Problems* 25 (1978):564–80; P. Burke and A. Turk, "Factors Affecting Post-Arrest Dispositions: A Model for Analysis," *Social Problems* 22 (1975):313–32; and Terrence Thornberry, "Race, Socioeconomic Status and Sentencing in the Juvenile Justice System," *Journal of Criminal Law and Criminology* 64 (1973): 90–98.

82 Joan Petersilia, *Racial Disparities in The Criminal Justice System* (Santa Monica, Cal.: Rand Corporation, 1983).

83 Charles R. Pruitt and James Q. Wilson, "A Longitudinal Study of the Effect of Race on Sentencing," *Law and Society Review* 17 (1983):613–35; Candace Kruttschnitt, "Sex and Criminal Court Dispositions," *Journal of Research in Crime and Delinquency* 21 (1984):213–32; Cynthia Kempinen, "Changes in the Sentencing Patterns of Male and Female Defendants," *Prison Journal* 63 (1983):3–11.

Corrections

CHAPTER OUTLINE

Introduction

History of Punishment and Corrections

The Middle Ages

Punishment in the Seventeenth and Eighteenth
  Centuries

Corrections in the Late Eighteenth and Nineteenth
  Centuries

Post-Civil War Developments

The Progressive Era and Beyond

The Modern Era

Corrections Today

Community-Based Corrections

Jails

Closed Institutions: The Prison

Parole

The Criminal Justice System: A Final Consideration

Summary

KEY TERMS

prison

jail

community-based correctional
  institution

halfway house

punishment

capital and corporal punishment

Poor Laws

Society for Alleviating the Miseries
  of Public Prisons

Walnut Street Prison

Auburn system

Z.R. Brockway

penologists

shock probation

probation subsidy

restitution

revoke

technical violation

maximum security prison

hustle

inmate subculture

social code

argot

prisonization

work furlough

free venture

conjugal visit

coeducational prison

hands-off doctrine

parole

Introduction

When a person is convicted for a criminal offense, society exercises the right to punish or *correct* his or her behavior. Equating crime and punishment is certainly not a new practice. Criminal offenders have been subjected to punishment by governmental authority throughout recorded history. Over the centuries, there has been significant debate as to why people should be punished and what type of punishment is most appropriate to correct, treat, or deter criminal offenders. The style and purpose of criminal correction has gone through many evolutionary stages and has featured a variety of penal sanctions.

In U.S. society, correctional jurisdiction is divided among the federal, state, and local levels of government.

If they are not eligible for leniency and some sort of community supervision program because of the seriousness of their crimes, felons are usually incarcerated in state or Federal **prisons**. Misdemeanants are housed in county **jails** or reformatories. In addition, there exist a wide variety of **community-based correctional institutions** and **halfway houses**.

The entire correctional system has been a source of great controversy. Prisons have been viewed as warehouses that, far from helping rehabilitate inmates, are places of violence and degradation. Jails have been the scene of suicides and rapes. Some critics call for the tearing down of the prison, while others argue that new ones should be built and sentences lengthened.[1] Well-publicized riots and conflicts have made the prison the subject of much public attention.

This chapter reviews some of the basic elements of correctional treatment in U.S. society. First, a brief history of corrections will be undertaken. Then, the concept of community-based corrections will be explored. Finally, the closed institution will be the focus of attention. Such issues as penal institutions, the prisoner's social world, correctional treatment, and prisoners' rights will be discussed.

History of Punishment and Corrections

Throughout history punishment, in its severest physical forms, has been present in all major institutions.[2]

The **punishment** of criminals has undergone many noteworthy changes, reflecting custom, economic conditions, and religious and political ideals.[3]

In ancient times, the most common state-administered punishment was banishment or exile. Only slaves were commonly subject to harsh physical punishment for their misdeeds. In Rome, for example, the only crime for which capital punishment could be administered was *furtum manifestum*—a thief caught in the act was executed on the spot. More common were economic sanctions and fines, levied for such crimes as assault on a slave, arson, or housebreaking.

In both ancient Greece and ancient Rome, interpersonal violence, even when it resulted in death, was viewed as a private matter. Neither Greek nor Roman (until quite late in its history) state laws provided for the punishment of a violent crime. Execution of an offender was looked upon as the prerogative of the deceased's family.

THE MIDDLE AGES

As noted in chapter 2, little law or governmental control existed during the early Middle Ages (fifth century to eleventh century A.D.). Offenses were settled by

Perspectives on Corrections

The major criminological perspectives maintain differing views on the functions and purpose of corrections. Below, each is briefly described.

Criminological perspective	Correctional viewpoint
Classical Perspective	Correctional institutions are designed to incapacitate known criminals and make them so fearful of punishment that they will not risk repeating their criminal behavior. The threat of punishment should also deter potential criminals. Punishment should be fair and should fit the crime. Crime causes the need for correction.
Positivist Perspective (Individual)	Corrections should be used to treat the offender. Correctional institutions should be turned into "therapeutic communities." Psychologists and psychiatrists should help formulate prison policy and plan treatment routines. Inmates should be released when they are rehabilitated. Treatment should fit the inmate. Social pathology causes the need for correction.
Positivist Perspective (Sociological)	Corrections should help the inmate readjust to society. Vocational and educational training should be stressed. If inmates can learn to adjust to prison, then they will be better able to adjust to society when released. Maintaining social order causes the need for correction.
Interactionist Perspective	Prisons stigmative inmates. Every effort should be made to keep offenders in the community. Use of community-based corrections should be emphasized. Correction causes crime.
Social Conflict Perspective (Conflict)	The "have-nots" go to prison while the "haves" go free. Prisons should not be used to punish the lower class while the wealthy are treated leniently. Criminals of all classes should be treated equally. Social power struggles produce the need for correctional institutions.
Social Conflict Perspective (Marxist)	Prisons are an element of class struggle used to punish people who rebel against class-created laws. Corrections should be used to treat the "true capitalist criminals." In a Marxist society, corrections would not be needed. Capitalism creates the need for correction.

DISCUSSION QUESTIONS

1. Which perspective on corrections do you agree with?

2. Can a society exist without corrections institutions?

blood feuds carried out by the families of the injured parties. When possible, the Roman custom of settling disputes by fine or an exchange of property was adopted as a means of resolving interpersonal conflicts with a minimum of bloodshed.

After the eleventh century, during the feudal period, forfeiture of land and property was common punishment for persons who violated law and custom or who failed in their feudal obligations to their lord. The word felony actually comes from the twelfth century, when the term *felonia* referred to a breach of faith with one's feudal lord.

During this period in history, the main emphasis on criminal law and punishment lay in maintaining public order.[4] If in the heat of passion or in a state of intoxication one person severely injured or killed his neighbor, free men in the area would gather to pronounce a judgment and make the culprit do penance or pay a fine called *wergild* (see chapter 2). The purpose of the fine was to assuage the vengeance of the injured party and insure that the conflict would not develop into a blood feud and anarchy. The inability of the lower-class offender to pay a fine led to the development of corporal punishment such as whipping or branding as a substitute penalty.

By the fifteenth century, changing social conditions influenced the relationship between crime and punishment. First the population of England and Europe began to increase, after a century of being decimated by constant warfare and plague. At the same time, the developing commercial system caused large tracts of agricultural fields to be converted to grazing lands. Soon, unemployed peasants and landless noblemen began flocking to newly developing urban centers, such as London and Paris, or taking to the roads as highwaymen, beggars, or vagabonds.

The later Middle Ages also saw the rise of strong monarchs such as Henry VIII and Elizabeth I of England, who were determined to keep a powerful grip on their realm. The administration of the "King's Peace" under the shire reeve and constable became stronger.

These developments led to the increased use of **capital** and **corporal punishment** to control the criminal poor. While the wealthy could buy their way out of punishment and into exile, the poor were executed and mutilated at ever-increasing rates. It is estimated that 72,000 thieves were hung during the reign of Henry VIII alone.[5] Execution, banishment, mutilation, branding, and flogging were used on a wide range of offenders, from murderers and robbers to vagrants and gypsies. Punishments became unmatched in their cruelty, featuring a gruesome variety of physical tortures. Also during this period, punishment became a public spectacle, presumably so the sadistic sanctions would act as a deterrent. But the variety and imagination of the tortures inflicted on even minor criminals before their death suggests that sadism and spectacle were more important than any presumed deterrent effect.

PUNISHMENT IN THE SEVENTEENTH AND EIGHTEENTH CENTURIES

By the end of the sixteenth century, the rise of the city and overseas colonization provided tremendous markets for manufactured goods. In England and France, population growth was checked by constant warfare and internal disturbances. Labor was scarce in many manufacturing areas of England, Germany, and Holland. The Thirty Years' War in Germany and the constant warfare among England, France, and Spain helped drain the population.

The punishment of criminals changed to meet the demands created by these social conditions. Instead of the wholesale use of capital and corporal punishment, many offenders were made to do forced labor for their crimes. **Poor Laws** developed in the early seventeenth century required that the poor, vagrants, and vagabonds be put to work in public or private enterprise. Houses of correction were developed to make it convenient for petty law violators to be assigned to work details. Many convicted offenders were pressed into sea duty as galley slaves, a fate considered so loathsome that many convicts practiced self-mutilation rather than submit to it.

The constant shortage of labor in the colonies also prompted the authorities to transport convicts overseas. In England, *The Vagrancy Act of 1597* legalized deportation for the first time. Similarly. *An Order in Council of 1617* granted a reprieve and stay of execution to people convicted of robbery and other felonies who were strong enough to be employed overseas. Similar measures were employed in France and Italy to recruit galley slaves and workers.

Transportation to the colonies became popular; it supplied labor, cost little, and was actually profitable for the government, since manufacturers and plantation owners paid for convicts' services. The Old Bailey Court in London supplied at least 10,000 convicts between 1717 and 1775.[6] Convicts would serve a period as workers and then become free again.

Transportation to the colonies waned as a method of punishment with the increase in colonial population, the further development of the land, and the increasing importation of African slaves in the eighteenth century. The American Revolution ended transportation of felons to North America; the remaining areas used were Australia, New Zealand, and African colonies.

CORRECTIONS IN THE LATE EIGHTEENTH AND NINETEENTH CENTURIES

Between the American Revolution in 1776 and the first decades of the nineteenth century, the population of Europe and America increased rapidly. The gulf between poor workers and wealthy landowners and merchants widened. The crime rate rose significantly, prompting a return to physical punishment and the increased use of the death penalty. During the last part of the eighteenth century, 350 types of crime in England were punishable by death.[7] Although many people sentenced to death for trivial offenses were spared the gallows, there is little question that the use of capital punishment rose significantly between 1750 and 1800.[8] Prompted by these excesses, legal philosophers such as Jeremy Bentham and Cesare Beccaria (see chapter 5) argued that physical punishment should be replaced by periods of confinement and incapacitation in prison.

It was in the United States that correctional reform was first instituted. The U.S. correctional system originated in Pennsylvania under the leadership of William Penn.[9] At the end of the seventeenth century, Penn revised Pennsylvania's criminal code to forbid torture and the capricious use of mutilation and physical punishment. These devices were replaced by the penalties of imprisonment at hard labor, moderate flogging, fines, and forfeiture of property. All lands and goods belonging to felons were to be used to make restitution to the victims of crimes, with restitution being limited to twice the value of the damages. Felons who owned no property were required by law to labor in the prison workhouse until the victim was compensated.

Penn ordered that a new type of institution be built to replace the widely used public forms of punishment—stocks, pillories, the gallows, and the branding iron. Each county was instructed to build a house of corrections similar to today's jails. These measures remained in effect until Penn's death in 1718, when the criminal penal code reverted to its earlier format of open public punishment and harsh brutality.

In 1776, postrevolutionary Pennsylvania again adopted William Penn's code, and in 1787 a group of Quakers led by Dr. Benjamin Rush formed the Philadelphia **Society for Alleviating the Miseries of Public Prisons**. The aim of the society was to bring some degree of humane and orderly treatment to the growing penal system. The Quakers' influence on the legislature resulted in limiting the use of the death penalty to cases involving treason, murder, rape, and arson. Their next step was to reform the existing institutional system so that the prison could serve as a suitable alternative to physical punishment.

The only models of custodial institutions at that time were the local county jails that Penn had established. These facilities were designed to detain offenders, to securely incarcerate convicts awaiting other punishment, or to hold offenders who were working off their crimes. The Pennsylvania jails placed men, women, and children of all ages indiscriminately in one room. Liquor was often freely sold. Under pressure from the Quakers to improve these conditions, the Pennsylvania State Legislature in 1790 called for the renovation of the prison system. The ultimate result was the creation of Philadelphia's **Walnut Street Prison**. At this institution, most prisoners were placed in solitary cells, where they remained in isolation and did not have the right to work.[10] Quarters that contained the solitary or separate cells were called the *penitentiary house*, as was already the custom in England.

The new Pennsylvania prison system took credit for a rapid decrease in the crime rate—from 131 convictions in 1789 to 45 in 1793.[11] The prison became known as a school for reform and a place for public labor. The Walnut Street Prison's equitable conditions were credited with reducing escapes to none in the first four years of its existence (except for fourteen on opening day).

However, the Walnut Street jail was not a total success. Overcrowding undermined the goal of solitary confinement of serious offenders, and soon more than one inmate was placed in each cell. Despite these difficulties, similar institutions were erected in New York (Newgate in 1791), New Jersey (Trenton in 1798), Virginia (1800), and Kentucky (1800).

The Auburn System. In the early 1800s, both the Pennsylvania and the New York prison systems were experiencing difficulties maintaining the ever-increasing numbers of convicted criminals. Initially, administrators dealt with the problem by increasing the use of pardons, relaxing prison discipline, and limiting supervision.

In 1816, the state of New York built a new prison at Auburn, hoping to alleviate some of the overcrowding at Newgate. The Auburn Prison design became known as the *tier system*, because cells were built vertically on five floors of the structure. It was sometimes also referred to as the *congregate system*, since most prisoners ate and worked in groups. Later, in 1819, construction was started on a wing of solitary cells to house unruly prisoners. Three classes of prisoners were then created: one group remained continually in solitary confinement as a result of breaches of prison discipline; the second group was allowed labor as an occasional form of recreation; and the third and largest class worked and ate together during the days and only went into seclusion at night.

The philosophy of the **Auburn system** was crime prevention through fear of punishment and silent confinement. The worst felons were to be cut off from all contact with other prisoners; and although they were treated and fed relatively well, they had no hope of pardon to relieve their isolation. For a time, some of the worst convicts were forced to remain totally alone and silent during the entire day; this practice caused many prisoners to have mental breakdowns, resulting in many suicides and self-mutilations. This practice was abolished in 1823.[12]

The combination of silence and solitude as a method of punishment was not abandoned easily. Prison officials sought to overcome the side effects of total isolation while maintaining the penitentiary system. The solution Auburn adopted was to keep convicts in separate cells at night but allow them to work together during the days under enforced silence. Hard work and silence became the foundation of the Auburn system wherever it was adopted. Silence was the key to prison discipline; it prohibited the formulation of escape plans, it averated plots and riots, and it allowed prisoners to contemplate their infractions.

The concept of using harsh discipline and control to "retrain" the heart and soul of offenders has been the subject of an important book on penal philosophy—*Discipline and Punish,* by the French sociologist Michel Foucault.[13]

Foucault's thesis is that as societies evolve and become more complex, they create increasingly more elaborate mechanisms to discipline their recalcitrant members and make them "docile" enough to obey social rules.[14] In the seventeenth and eighteenth centuries, discipline was directed toward the human body itself, through torture. In the development of the nineteenth-century prison, the object was to discipline the offender psychologically; "the expiation that once rained down upon the body must be replaced by a punishment that acts in the depths of the heart."[15] We can still see remnants of that philosophy in today's prisons.

According to one historian, David Rothman, regimentation became the standard mode of prison life. Convicts did not simply walk from place to place; rather, they went in close order and single file, each looking over the shoulder of the preceding person, faces inclined to the right, feet moving in unison. The lockstep prison shuffle was developed at Auburn and is still employed in some institutions today.[16]

When discipline was breached in the Auburn system, punishment was applied in the form of a rawhide whip on the inmate's back. Immediate and effective, Auburn discipline was so successful that when a hundred inmates were chosen to build the famous Sing-Sing prison in 1825, not one dared escape, although they were housed in an open field with only minimal supervision.[17]

The New Pennsylvania System. In 1818, the state of Pennsylvania took the radical step of establishing a prison that placed each inmate in a single cell and did not provide them with any work to do. Classifications were abolished, because each cell was intended as a miniature prison that would prevent the inmates from contaminating one another.

The new Pennsylvania state prison, called the Western Penitentiary, had an unusual architectural design. It was built in a semicircle, with the cells positioned along its circumference. Built back-to-back, some cells faced the boundary wall while others faced the internal area of the circle. Its inmates were kept in solitary confinement almost constantly, being allowed about an hour a day for exercise. In 1820, a second, similar penitentiary using the isolate system was built in Philadelphia and called the Eastern Penitentiary.

The supporters of the Pennsylvania system believed that the penitentiary was truly a place to do penance. By advocating totally removing the sinner from society and allowing the prisoner a period of isolation in which to reflect alone upon the evils of crime, the supporters of the Pennsylvania system reflected the influence of religion and religious philosophy on corrections. In fact, its advocates believed that solitary confinement (with in-cell labor as a recreation) would eventually make working so attractive that upon release the inmate would be well suited to resume a productive existence in society. The Pennsylvania system obviated the need for large numbers of guards or disciplinary measures. Isolated from each other, inmates could not plan escapes or collectively break rules. When discipline was a problem, however, the whip and the iron gag were used.

Many fiery debates occurred between advocates of the Pennsylvania system and the Auburn system. Those supporting the latter position boasted of its supposed advantages; their system was the cheapest and most productive way to reform prisoners. They criticized the Pennsylvania system as cruel and inhumane, suggesting that solitary confinement was both physically and mentally damaging. The Pennsylvania system's devotees, on the other hand, argued that their system was quiet, efficient, humane, well ordered, and provided the ultimate correctional facility.[18] They chided the Auburn system for tempting inmates to talk by putting them together for meals and work and then punishing them when they did talk. Finally, the Auburn system was accused of becoming a breeding place for criminal associations by allowing inmates to get to know one another.

The Auburn system eventually prevailed and spread throughout the United States; many of its features are still used today. Its innovations included congregate working conditions, the use of solitary confinement to punish unruly inmates, military regimentation, and discipline. In Auburn-like institutions, prisoners were marched from place to place; their time was regulated by bells telling them to wake up, sleep, and work. The system was so like the military that many of its early administrators were recruited from the armed services.

Although the prison was viewed as an improvement over capital and corporal punishment, it quickly became the scene of depressed conditions; inmates were treated harshly, and routinely whipped and tortured. As one historian, Samuel Walker, notes:

> *Prison brutality flourished. It was ironic that the prison had been devised as a more human alternative to corporal and capital punishment. Instead, it simply moved corporal punishments indoors where, hidden from public view, it became even more savage.*[19]

POST-CIVIL WAR DEVELOPMENTS

The prison of the late nineteenth century was remarkably similar to that of today. The congregate system was adapted in all states except Pennsylvania. Prisons experienced overcrowding, and the single-cell principle often was ignored. The prison, like the police department, became the scene of political intrigue and efforts by political administrators to control the hiring of personnel and dispensing of patronage.

Prison industry developed and became the predominant theme around which institutions were organized. Some prisons used the *contract system,* in which officials sold the labor of inmates to private businesses. Sometimes, the contractor supervised the inmates inside the prison itself. Under the *convict-lease system,* the state leased its prisoners to a business for a fixed annual fee and gave up supervision and control. Finally, the *state account system* had prisoners produce goods in prison for state use.[20]

The development of prison industry quickly led to abuse of inmates, who were forced to work for almost no wages, and to profiteering by dishonest administrators and businessmen. During the Civil War era, prisons were major manufacturers of clothes, shoes, boots, furniture, and the like. During the 1880s, opposition by trade unions sparked restrictions on interstate commerce in prison goods and ended their profitability.

There were also reforms in prison operations. **Z. R. Brockway**, warden at the Elmira Reformatory in New York, advocated individualized treatment, the indeterminate sentence, and parole. The reformatory program initiated by Brockway included elementary education for illiterates, designated library hours, lectures by faculty members of the local Elmira College, and a group of vocational training shops. The cost to the state of the institution's operations was to be held to a minimum. Although Brockway proclaimed Elmira to be an ideal reformatory, his actual achievements were limited. The greatest significance of his contribution was the injection of a degree of humanitarianism into the industrial prisons of that day. However, although many institutions were constructed across the country and labeled reformatories as a result of the Elmira model, most of them continued to be industrially oriented.[21]

THE PROGRESSIVE ERA AND BEYOND

The early twentieth century was a time of contrasts in the prison system of the United States.[22] At one extreme were those who advocated reform, such as the Mutual Welfare League, led by Thomas Mott Osborne. Prison reform groups proposed better treatment for inmates, an end to harsh corporal punishment, and the creation of meaningful prison industries and educational programs. Reformers argued that prisoners should not be isolated from society, but that the best elements of society—education, religion, meaningful work, self-governance—should be brought to the prison. Osborne went so far as to spend one week in New York's notorious Sing-Sing Prison to learn about its conditions firsthand.

Opposed to the reformers were conservative prison administrators and state officials, who believed that stern disciplinary measures were needed to control dangerous prison inmates. They continued the time-honored system of regimentation and discipline. Although the whip and the lash were eventually abolished, solitary confinement in dark, bare cells became a common penal practice.

In time, some of the more rigid prison rules gave way to liberal reform. By the mid-1930s, few prisons required inmates to wear the red-and-white-striped convict suit and substituted nondescript gray uniforms. The code of silence ended, as did the lockstep shuffle. Prisoners were allowed "the freedom of the yard" to mingle and exercise an hour or two each day.[23] Movies and radio appeared in the 1930s. Visiting policies and mail privileges were liberalized.

A more important trend was the development of specialized prisons designed to treat particular types of offenders. For example, in New York the prisons at Clinton and Auburn were viewed as industrial facilities for hard-core inmates, Great Meadow as an agricultural center to house nondangerous offenders, and Dannemora as a facility for the criminally insane. In California, San Quentin housed inmates considered salvageable by correctional authorities, while Folsom was reserved for the hard-core offender.[24]

Prison industry also evolved. Opposition by organized labor helped put an end to the convict lease system and forced inmate labor. Although some vestiges of private prison industry existed into the 1920s, most convict labor was devoted to state-use items, such as license plates and laundry.

Despite these changes and reforms, the prison in the mid-twentieth century remained a destructive total institution. Although some aspects of inmate life improved, severe discipline, harsh rules, and solitary confinement were the way of life in prison.

THE MODERN ERA

In the modern era we have witnessed a period of change and turmoil in the nation's correctional system. Three trends stand out. First, a great deal of litigation has been brought by inmates seeking greater rights and privileges. Since 1960, state and federal courts have ruled in numerous cases concerning an inmate's right to freedom of religion and speech and rights to medical care, due process, and proper living conditions. In many areas inmates have won rights unheard of in earlier nineteenth- and twentieth-century prisons.

Second, violence within the correctional system became a national scandal. Well-publicized riots at New York's Attica Prison and the New Mexico State Penitentiary have drawn attention to the potential for death and destruction that lurks in every prison. One reaction has been to improve conditions and provide innovative programs that give inmates a voice in running the institution. Another has been to tighten discipline and call for the building of new maximum-security prisons to control dangerous offenders.

Third, the alleged failure of correctional rehabilitation has prompted many **penologists** (criminologists who deal with prison management and the treatment of offenders) to reconsider the purpose of incapacitating criminals. Today it is more common to view the correctional system as a mechanism for control and punishment than as a device for rehabilitation and reform.

The alleged failure of correctional treatment has prompted the development of alternatives to incarceration: diversion, restitution, and community-based corrections. As the mid-1980s approach, the nation's correctional policy seems to be to keep as many nonthreatening offenders out of the correctional system as possible by means of community-based programs, and conversely to incarcerate dangerous, violent offenders for long periods of time.[25] Unfortunately, despite the development of alternatives to incarceration, the number of people under lock and key has skyrocketed.

The following section reviews the most prominent types of correctional facilities in use today.

Corrections Today

Correctional treatment can be divided into four main components—community-based corrections, jails, prisons, and parole. Community-based corrections programs include probation—community supervision under the control of the sentencing court—and an array of institutional facilities located in the community, usually called halfway houses or community correctional centers. The jail, the second component of the correctional system, houses misdemeanants (and some felons) serving their sentences as well as felons and misdemeanants awaiting trial who have not been released on bail. State and federal prisons are used to incarcerate felons for extended periods of time. Finally, parole and aftercare agencies supervise prisoners who have been given early release from their sentences. Each of these institutions will now be briefly discussed.

COMMUNITY-BASED CORRECTIONS

Treatment in the community is viewed as a viable alternative to traditional correctional practices.[26] First, it is significantly less expensive to supervise inmates in the community than to house them in secure institutional facilities. Second, community-based corrections are necessary if the prison system is not to be overwhelmed by an influx of offenders. Third, community-based treatment is viewed as a charitable gesture given to less serious offenders so they can avoid the stigma and pains of imprisonment and be rehabilitated in the community. The major forms of community treatment are discussed below.

Probation. Probation usually involves the suspension of the offender's sentence, in return for the promise of good behavior in the community, under the supervision of the probation department. It usually replaces a term in an institution, although minors can simply be placed on probation without the threat of detention. In about one-fourth of the states, the offender is first sentenced to a prison term, and then the sentence is suspended and the defendant placed on probation. In another one-fourth of the states, the imposition of a prison sentence is delayed while the offender is put on probation. In the rest, courts may use either mechanism.[27]

As practiced in all fifty states and by the federal government, probation implies a contract between the court and the offender in which the former promises to hold a prison term in abeyance while the latter promises to adhere to a set of rules or conditions required by the court. If the rules are violated, and especially if the probationer commits another criminal offense, probation may be *revoked*; this means that the contract is terminated and the original sentence enforced. If an offender on probation commits a second offense that is more severe than the first, he or she may also be indicted, tried, and sentenced on that second offense. Probation may be revoked simply because the rules and conditions of probation have not been met, even if the offender has not committed a further crime.

Each probationary sentence is for a fixed period of time, depending on the seriousness of the offense and the statutory law of the jurisdiction. Probation is considered served when the offender fulfills the conditions set by the court for that period of time; he or she can live without interference from the state.

Probation Sentences. Probationary sentences may be granted by state and federal district courts and state superior (felony) courts. Probation has become an accepted and widely used sentence for adult felons and misdemeanants and juvenile delinquents.

In some states, juries may grant probation as part of their sentencing power; or they may make recommendations to judges, which judges will usually follow if the case meets certain legally regulated criteria (for example, if it falls within a certain class of offenses as determined by statute).[28] Juries can recommend probation, but the judge has the final say in the matter and can grant probation at his or her discretion. In nonjury trials, probation is granted solely by judicial mandate.

In most jurisdictions, all juvenile offenders are eligible for probation, as are most adults. Some state statutes prohibit probation for certain types of adult offenders, usually those who have engaged in repeated and serious violent crimes such as murder or rape. Mandatory sentences have also made some offenders ineligible for probation.

The term of the probationary sentence may extend to the limit of the suspended prison term; or the court may set a time limit that reflects the sentencing period. For misdemeanors, probation usually extends for the entire period of the jail sentence. For felonies, probationary periods are likely to be shorter and more limited than the prison sentences would have been. The federal criminal code recommends that probation for felons last five years; juveniles are typically placed on probation for periods from six to twenty-four months. Some state court judges may also impose monetary fines when granting probation; this practice is commonly applied to white-collar crimes, by which an offender may have profited from an illegal business practice.

Some judges may wish to grant an offender probation only after the offender has sampled prison life, perhaps to emphasize that the rules of probation must be kept. Probation cannot be granted after the offender has actually been incarcerated (since this practice is known as parole), but a judge does have available several devices to allow institutionalizing a convicted offender for limited period of time before probation. For example, when the offender is charged with a variety of offenses, the judge may impose a short jail term on one criminal count and probation on the others. In some state codes and in the federal criminal code, a jail term can actually be a condition of probation. The federal probation statute states that the court "may impose a sentence in excess of six months and provide that the defendant be confined in a jail-type institution for a period not exceeding six months and that the execution of the remainder of the sentence be suspended and the defendant placed on probation for such period and upon such terms and conditions as the court deems best."[29]

However, the granting of probation to follow a jail sentence is frowned upon by some experts, who believe that even a brief period of incarceration can mitigate the purpose of probation, which is to provide the offender with nonstigmatized, community-based treatment.

At last tally, there were 1,502,247 adult probationers, an increase of 145,000 from the preceding year.[30] Between 1979 and 1983 the probation population increased by 38 percent, which paralleled the increase in the prison population (39 percent) during that same period. During a given year (1983), about 891,133 people were placed on probation and 746,170 finished their probationary sentence. In 1983, about 877 people per 100,000 population were on probation; probationers made up 63 percent of all people under correctional supervision.

Probation Organizations. About 1,920 agencies nationwide list adult probation as their major function. Most of them (56 percent) are state-level agencies; the remainder are organized at the county or municipal level of government. About thirty states combine probation and parole agencies into a single state agency.[31]

There are arguments both for placing probation services under the supervision of individual courts and for creating statewide agencies. Local supervision makes probation more responsive to court discretion and helps judges get better information on the effectiveness of their decisions. Since the bulk of the probation department's work is in the local courts, it seems appropriate that the agencies should be organized at the county level of government.

Those who advocate large state probation agencies argue that probation is a correctional service and therefore should be part of the executive level of government.[32] Larger agencies can facilitate coordination of programs and staff, establishment of training programs, and distribution of budget. However, as of this writing, no one position prevails; probation remains organized at both the state and the local level.

Probation Services. After a person is convicted of a crime, the probation department investigates the case to determine the factors related to the criminality of the offender. Based on this presentence investigation, the department recommends to the sentencing judge whether the offender should be given eligibility for community release. In the event the offender is placed on probation, the investigation findings will be used as the basis for treatment and supervision.

If the offender is placed on probation, the department makes a diagnosis of his or her personality and treatment needs. Based on this evaluation, some offenders will be given little supervision, perhaps a monthly phone call or visit, while others will be maintained under close supervision and will receive intensive care and treatment.

The probation officer also participates in treatment supervision. Based on concepts of psychology, social work, or counseling, and on the diagnosis of the offender, the probation officer plans a treatment schedule that, it is hoped, will allow the probationer to fulfill the probation contract and make a reasonable adjustment to the community.

The treatment function is a product of both the investigative aspect and the diagnostic aspect of probation. It is based on the probation officer's perceptions of the probationer, including family problems, peer relationships, and employment background. Treatment may also involve the use of community resources. For example, a probation officer who discovers that a client has a drinking problem may help to find a detoxification center willing to accept the case, while a chronically underemployed offender may be given job counseling or training. Or, in the case of juvenile delinquency, a probation officer may work with teachers and other school officials to help a young offender stay in school. Of course, most cases do not (or cannot) receive such individualized treatment; some treatment mechanisms merely involve a weekly or biweekly phone call to determine whether a job is being maintained or school attended.[33]

Innovative Probation Services. Probation departments have attempted numerous innovative programs to service clients:

- *Shock probation.* **Shock probation** has been used in a few states, such as Kentucky and Ohio.[34] Under this plan, offenders begin serving their prison sentence but, after a brief stay, may petition to serve the rest of their sentence in the community. The belief is that the shock of a prison stay will jolt the offender into conventional behavior. Several studies that have attempted to test the effectiveness of this approach have failed to indicate that it reduces recidivism. Critics argue that even a short prison stay can damage offenders and mitigate the purpose of probation.
- *Probation subsidies.* Some states, including California, Michigan, and Washington, have created **probation subsidy** programs. Rather than pay the high cost of incarcerating offenders, the state gives a special subsidy to local probation departments to provide special intensive services for clients who might otherwise be placed in a residential prison setting. There is little evidence that subsidy programs reduce crime, but they do reduce institutional populations, and their low cost eases the taxpayers' burdens. The success of probation subsidy programs is similar to regular probation, even though they deal with higher-risk clients.[35]
- *Pretrial programs.* Probation departments have become active in maintaining pretrial programs, designed to minimize the interaction between offenders and the justice system. These programs include Release on Recognizance

(ROR) efforts and diversion programs that provide noncriminal alternatives for first or petty offenders (see chapter 14).

- *Volunteers.* Since probation services are so widely used, the burden on individual probation officers is tremendous. It is not unusual for probation officers to maintain over a hundred clients. To meet this challenge, it has become commonplace for probation departments to employ paraprofessionals and volunteers in what might be considered regular line positions. Volunteers often make up a significant portion of probation department staffs.

  This practice is not without controversy. Volunteers and paraprofessionals can certainly make an important contribution, but their employment has not always been met with enthusiasm by regular probation staff members. They are sometimes viewed as a threat to job security and as an excuse for legislatures to deny budgetary increases for probation services.

  The principal method of using volunteers is to establish teams consisting of a probation officer, an assistant, and three to five volunteers who share a common responsibility for managing otherwise unreasonable caseloads, some of which run as high as two hundred cases.

- *Restitution and probation.* Probation officers have also been assigned to operate court-based **restitution** programs. The restitution concept requires defendants to either pay back the victims of their crimes (monetary restitution) or serve the community to compensate for their criminal acts (community service restitution). The restitution concept received its impetus from federal funding, but the termination of support has caused ongoing programs to be incorporated into existing court structures such as probation departments.[36]

  Ordinarily, as mentioned, restitution programs require offenders to pay back victims of crime or serve the community as a condition of probation. The process thus offers the convicted offender a chance to avoid a prison sentence or a more lengthy probationary period. Restitution may also be used as a diversionary device to offer some offenders the chance to avoid a criminal record altogether. In this instance, the judge continues the case "without a finding" while the defendant completes the restitution order; after the probation department determines that restitution has been made, the case is dismissed.

  Some restitution programs, such as the Win-Onus program in Winona, Minnesota, and the EARN-IT program in Quincy, Massachusetts, have proven highly successful.[37] A national evaluation of juvenile restitution programs found that 87 percent of 12,000 probationers successfully completed their restitution orders and that 86 percent of the clients had no further contact with authorities because of new offenses.[38]

Probation Rules and Revocation. Each offender granted probation is given a set of rules to guide his or her behavior. Most jurisdictions have a standard set of rules, which include behaviors such as: (1) maintaining steady employment; (2) making restitution for loss or damage; (3) cooperating with the probation officer; (4) obeying all laws; and (5) meeting family responsibilities. Sometimes an individual probationer is given specific rules that relate to his or her particular circumstances, such as the requirement to enroll in a drug treatment program.

If rules are violated, a person's probation may be **revoked** by the court, and the person either begins serving the sentence or, if he or she has not yet been sentenced, receives a prison sentence from the court. Revocation for violation of probation rules is called a **technical violation**; probation also can be revoked if the offender commits another offense.

In a series of cases, most importantly *Gagnon v. Scarpelli*,[39] the Supreme Court has ruled that before probation can be revoked, the offender (1) must be given a hearing before the sentencing court and (2) must be provided with counsel if there is a substantial reason for him or her to require the assistance of an attorney.

Success of Probation. There is some question as to how successful probation actually is. That is, how often do probationers commit new crimes while they are under supervision? A recent federal survey found that 27 percent of people entering prison for the first time were on probation for a prior offense, and that 21 percent of all entering inmates were on probation.[40]

In a similar vein, Joan Petersilia and her colleagues at the Rand Corporation followed the careers of 1,672 California men granted probation for felony offenses.[41] They found that 1,087 (65 percent) were rearrested, 853 (51 percent) were convicted, and 568 (34 percent) were incarcerated! The researchers uncovered the disturbing fact that 75 percent of the new charges were for serious crimes including larceny, burglary, and robbery; and that 18 percent were convicted on serious violent crime charges. They also found that about 25 percent of felons granted probation had personal and legal characteristics indistinguishable from people put in prison for the same original charge.

So, although probation remains the predominant criminal sentence, its success may be undermined by the pressure to keep the prison population down by granting probation to serious felony offenders. It costs far less to maintain an offender in the community than in prison, and with continued prison overcrowding, there is constant economic pressure to grant probation to serious felony offenders.

The answer to this dilemma may be to place high-risk offenders in probation programs that have small caseloads and intensive supervision. Such programs cost upwards of $5 thousand per client annually, but their cost is still far less than the $15 to $20 thousand needed to keep someone behind bars. Intensive probation is now being used around the country, and may yet prove to be more effective than traditional probation models.[42]

Community-Based Institutions. Community-based institutions have come into prominence in the past twenty years; today, hundreds of community-based programs are operating around the country.

Community-based institutions can be classified into three types: halfway houses that serve as a bridge between prison and the community and hold inmates just before their release; community facilities that serve as an original treatment alternative for offenders who are judged to be in need of a structured environment but whose behavior does not warrant a prison sentence; finally, some facilities that house both types of clients.

The theoretical basis of community-based institutions is founded on four major concepts.[43]

1. It is considered more humane to treat offenders in the community than in large, fortress-like prisons. The community-based institution can help integrate the offender back into society.

2. Community-based institutions are viewed as a way to divert offenders from the traditional prison system. When community institutions are used as

the primary correctional measure, the offender is spared the stigma of the prison experience.

3. Community corrections have also been viewed as a more effective rehabilitation device than the prison. When the offender's ties with family, friends, job, and neighborhood are maintained, the dehumanizing effect of prison is avoided.

4. Community institutions are cost-effective, since the needs for high security and large staff of the traditional prison are avoided.

Most community institutions are used to service inmates before their release into society. Several different community corrections strategies have been employed recently. The traditional halfway house serves as a transitional setting between institution and community for selected inmates. An inmate is transferred to a halfway house just before being granted parole. He or she works during the day and usually receives counseling at night. The group living experience in the community helps prepare inmates for success when they are eventually released.

A more recent model is for offenders to serve their entire term within the halfway house setting. For example, Portland House, a private residential center in Minneapolis, Minnesota, operates as an alternative to county jail or state prison commitment for young adult felony offenders. Residents regularly receive group therapy and counseling on financial, employment, educational, family, and personal matters. With funds withheld from their earnings at work-release employment, residents pay room and board, family support, self-support, and income taxes.[44]

Despite attempts at innovation, nagging doubts persist about the overall effectiveness of community-based corrections. Conflict theorist Andrew Scull suggests that community-based corrections are simply a way of managing offenders at a lower cost than prison.[45] And John Hylton argues that they help "widen the net": "Persons who were not subjected to control previously," he charges, "may now be controlled under the guise of community treatment."[46]

Thus, although many community-based correctional programs are still in operation, and new ones are being created, the jury is still out on their overall efficiency and effectiveness.[47]

JAILS

The jail, sometimes referred to as a house of correction, is a secure institution used to (1) detain offenders before trial if they cannot afford or are not eligible for bail, and (2) serve as an institution to house misdeameanant offenders sentenced to terms of one year or less as well as some nonserious felons.

The jail is of European design, it originated in the sixteenth century and was used to house those awaiting trial and punishment. Jails were not used to house sentenced criminals, since at that time punishment was either by fine, exile, corporal punishment, or death.

Throughout their history, jails have been considered hell holes of pestilence and cruelty. In early English history, they were used to house offenders awaiting trial as well as vagabonds, debtors, the mentally ill, and assorted others. The cost of running the jail was paid by the prisoners themselves.

In 1748 the admission to Southwark prison was eleven shillings and four pence. Having got in, the prisoner had to pay for having himself put in irons, for his bed, of whatever sort, for his room if he was able to afford a separate room. He had to pay for his food, and when he had paid his debts and was ready to go out, he had to pay for having his irons struck off, and a discharge fee. . . . The gaolers [jailers] were usually 'low-bred, mercenary and oppressive, barbarous fellows, who think of nothing but enriching themselves by the most cruel extortion, and have less regard for the life of a poor prisoner than for the life of a brute.'[48]

The early colonists adopted the European custom of detaining prisoners in jail. As noted previously, William Penn instituted the first jails to house convicted offenders while they worked off their sentence. The Walnut Street jail, built in 1790, is considered the first modern jail.

Jail Populations. There were 223,551 people held in the nation's 3,338 jails at the time of the last jail census (June, 1983).[49] Whereas the number of jails has declined from a high of 4,037 in 1970 to 3,338 in 1983, the number of inmates increased about 40 percent (from 160,683); thus, there is a trend toward fewer but larger jails (see table 17.1). During a single year (1983), 8,084,344 people were admitted to jails, including 708,315 women and 102,000 juveniles. Though the jail population was only 7 percent female, the number of women admitted to jails increased 65 percent in a five-year period (1978–1983).

A federal survey of jail inmates found that they were disproportionately young, single, minority males whose annual income was around $3,700; 60 percent had

TABLE 17.1
Ten largest jails in the United States, 30 June 1983

Rank	Jail	Rated capacity	Under court order to reduce crowding	Court-ordered capacity
1	Men's Central Jail Los Angeles, California	5,136	no	
2	Cook County Jail Chicago, Illinois	4,600	yes	4,500
3	Harris County Jail (Houston) Humble, Texas	2,450	no	
4	New York City Correctional Institution New York, New York	2,096	no	
5	Anna M. Kross Center New York, New York	2,045	yes	2,045
6	Baltimore City Jail Baltimore, Maryland	1,815	yes	1,057
7	Hall of Justice Jail Los Angeles, California	1,750	no	
8	Orange County Jail Santa Ana, California	1,461	no	
9	New York City House of Detention for Men New York, New York	1,445	yes	1,445
10	New York City Adolescent Reception and Detention Center New York, New York	1,431	yes	1,431

SOURCE. *The 1983 Jail Census*, p. 6.

not finished high school.[50] One in four had been financially dependent on welfare, Social Security, unemployment insurance, family, and friends rather than their own wages. This was particularly true of black female inmates, whose poverty level was extremely high. The survey also found a great many inmates were involved in daily drug use (40 percent). About 20 percent were under the influence of drugs at the time of their offense and 25 percent reported being drunk.

In sum, the jail population reflects the social and economic factors typically associated with crime: poverty, lack of education, unemployment and substance abuse.

Jail Conditions. Jail conditions have become a national scandal. Throughout the United States, jails are marked by violence, overcrowding, deteriorated physical conditions, and lack of treatment or rehabilitation efforts. Suicides are common, as are fires and other natural calamities.[51] Another problem is the housing together of convicted offenders and detainees. And, despite government efforts to end the practice, many juvenile offenders occupy cells within adult jail facilities.

The deplorable conditions of jails today are highlighted by the results of a General Accounting Office survey, which reviewed conditions in twenty-two jails that had received federal assistance. Findings include the following:

- Seven of the twenty-two jails did not have operable emergency exits, and at least nine did not have fire extinguishers.
- Sanitary conditions were inadequate. Elementary commodities such as soap, toothbrushes, and clean bedding were in short supply or totally absent from the jails.
- Six of the jails had cells that did not contain toilets or had toilets that were inoperable when the survey team visited.
- Eating facilities in fifteen of the twenty-two jails were in the cell block in full view of the sanitary facilities.
- Only three jails provided space in which inmates could have private conversations with visitors.
- Eight of the twenty-two jails did not have a private area in which to search the prisoners. In fact, in one jail, searches were done in an open corridor between the two main cell blocks.[52]

Some effort has been made to ameliorate jail conditions. The American Correctional Association has set up the Commission on Accreditation for Corrections, which has defined standards for health care, treatment, and visitations. A multistate pilot project has helped local facilities to improve conditions so they may be accredited by the commission.[53]

In a similar vein, the states of Washington and New York have passed minimum standard acts to force local counties to improve their jail conditions. State funding is made available to areas that cannot comply with conditions because of budgetary problems.[54] When state efforts have not been sufficient, national agencies have sometimes helped. The National Institute of Corrections has established a national jail center in Boulder, Colorado, to develop training materials and hold workshops for jail personnel.

Despite such improvements, the future of jails probably does not lie in improving them or building newer, more modern facilities. Rather, community institutions will be developed to ease jail overcrowding and remove many people from their harsh conditions.

Alternatives to Jail. The cost of jailing an inmate is exorbitant—between $20 thousand and $40 thousand per year—and the benefits for many offenders are negligible.[55] Therefore, programs have been developed around the country to place detainees and convicted offenders in alternative programs. One method was diversion into noncriminal community treatments (see chapter 14). A growing trend, discussed earlier in this chapter, is the use of restitution as an alternative to confinement. The accompanying Close-Up describes some innovative alternatives to jail that have been in operation around the country.

CLOSED INSTITUTIONS: THE PRISON

The various state and federal governments maintain closed correctional facilities to house convicted felons. Usually called prisons or penitentiaries, these institutions have become familiar to most people as harsh, frightening places filled with dangerous men and women. San Quentin (California), Attica (New York), Statesville/Joliet (Illinois), Leavenworth (Kansas), and Pontiac (Michigan) are but a few of the large state and federal prisons made well known by films, books, or the media.

This section will discuss types of correctional institutions, life and treatment in prison, and the prisoners' rights movement.

Types of Institutions. Of the more than five hundred adult prisons operating in this country, the overwhelming majority are state institutions.[56] These prison systems are usually subdivided—according to the level of security they maintain and their inmate populations—into maximum, medium, and minimum security institutions. The 153 **maximum security prisons** are surrounded by high walls and have elaborate security measures and armed guards. They house inmates classified as potentially dangerous. The 224 medium security prisons have similar protective measures but usually contain less violent inmates. Consequently, they are more likely to offer a variety of treatment and educational programs to their residents.

The United States Federal Penitentiary in Leavenworth, Kansas, is a maximum security prison.

Alternatives to Jail

Many alternative jail programs are in operation around the country. Below, a few of the more innovative ones to be attempted are described.

PRETRIAL PROGRAMS

In Indianapolis, Indiana, the Pretrial Services Agency of the Marion County Municipal Court employs law students on a part-time basis to provide round-the-clock coverage of the jail at lower cost than would be possible with full-time salaried employees. Experienced interviewers in their senior year of law school are appointed bail commissioners. They have the authority to release misdemeanants on recognizance (ROR) without referral to court, greatly reducing the time required for decision making about such releases. Bail commissioners may recommend ROR, supervised release, or reduced bail (that is, less than that provided for in the bail schedule). In addition, they investigate eligibility for indigent defense services, handle diversion of public inebriates, and perform initial screening for drug-dependency services. From its inception, the agency has been dynamic and innovative, adding new features and options and expanding its capacity to meet the needs of the community.

In Washington, D.C., the D.C. Bail Agency monitors and supervises not only recognizance and conditional release cases but also persons released on percentage bail. Private social service agencies and self-help groups are used extensively in third-party release cases. Recently, the agency has experimented with a mobile field unit, which can be contacted by radio. The functions of this unit are diverse—from helping to verify facts in the case of a person just arrested to making contact with absentees from court to making supervisory or service contacts with persons on conditional release.

POST-TRIAL PROGRAMS

In Dade County, Florida, the state probation and parole division operates halfway houses in several more populous communities. One of these, the Multiphasic Diagnostic and Treatment Center in Miami, serves young adult offenders (eighteen to twenty-five years old) who would otherwise be sentenced to jail or state prison. Typically, residents of the center have been charged with violations while on probation and transferred to the institutional program.

The 182 minimum security prisons operate without armed guards or walls; usually, they are constructed in compounds surrounded by a cyclone fence.

Minimum security prisons usually house the most trustworthy and least violent offenders; white-collar criminals may be their most common occupants. Work furloughs and educational releases are encouraged, and vocational training is of the highest level. Dress codes are lax.

Minimum security facilities may employ dormitory living or have small private rooms for inmates. Prisoners are allowed much discretion in keeping with them personal possessions that might be deemed dnagerous in a maximum security prison. The major security measure in minimum security institutions is the threat that an escape will lead to transfer to a more secure facility.

Prisoners in the United States. According to a federal government survey, there were 463,866 prisoners in state and federal institutions as 1985 began—an increase of 6.1 percent over the previous year. The prison population has increased 50 percent since 1980, when 300,024 adults were incarcerated.[57] This is a continuation of a trend of sharp increases in the prior population, despite the reduction in the crime rate and attempts to use alternatives to incarceration. As table 17.2 shows, the percentage of people sentenced to prison per 100 reported crimes, arrests, cleared crimes, and crimes reported by NCS surveys has increased substantially in the past few years. This is further evidence of the influence of conservative, get-tough trends in the criminal justice system.

The program is treatment-oriented. Residents are expected to cooperate in identifying the problems associated with their law-breaking activity and to agree to undertake efforts to deal with them. All are expected to attend school, work full time, or engage in some combination of work and study. Nightly group counseling sessions as well as individual counseling sessions are directed toward resolving personal difficulties and achieving personal goals. Community agencies and educational institutions are used extensively. Employed residents pay $4 per day to help defray program costs. Residents also perform tasks associated with maintenance at the center. Rewards and sanctions—for example, granting or withholding of furloughs, early release to probation, greater privacy in sleeping quarters, and extra housekeeping chores—are used to reinforce counseling efforts and behavior limits. The ultimate sanction, which is used only rarely, is referral back to court as a program failure.

A similar program in Baton Rouge, Louisiana, is available for youthful offenders as a condition of probation. The alternative is a jail or state prison term. Residents generally stay three or four months, with the release decision made by the judge on the basis of progress reports submitted periodically by the probation department. Residents participate in policy planning, disciplinary decisions, grievance settlement, and orientation of new residents through service on elected committees. Extensive use is made of volunteers and student interns.

With some exceptions, new residents are confined to the center for the first three or four weeks. They work thirty hours a week in center maintenance, earning $30 a week and contributing $21 of this amount toward the costs of room and board. After evaluation and guidance, they can choose full-time employment in the community, full-time school, or a mixed schedule. All residents are required to pay room and board and perform some chores during their leisure hours. The program is oriented toward behavior modification, with residents earning points for good performance and losing them for infractions.

DISCUSSION QUESTIONS

1. What other alternatives might be used instead of jail?
2. Should offenders accused of violent crimes be given pretrial release opportunities?

SOURCE. Adapted from John Galvin and Walter Busher, "Instead of Jail: Pre- and Post-Trial Alternatives to Jail Incarceration," vol. 1., *Issues and Programs in Brief* (Washington, D.C.: Government Printing Office, 1977), pp. 13, 30.

TABLE 17.2
Change in the ratio of prison admissions to crime, 1980-83

Year	Admissions per 100 UCR crimes	Admissions per 100 NCS crimes[a]	Admissions per 100 cleared crimes[b]	Admissions per 100 arrests[b]
1980	2.6	1.3	12.6	13.3
1981	2.9	1.4	14.1	14.1
1982	3.5	1.7	16.3	15.6
1983	4.0	2.0	17.7	17.7
Change, 1980–83	53.8%	53.8%	40.5%	33.1%

[a]Completed rapes, robberies, aggravated assaults, and burglaries (as reported in the National Crime Survey) are counted in the denominator.
[b]Cleared crimes and arrests refer to murder, non-negligent manslaughter, forcible rape, robbery, aggravated assault, and burglary (as reported in the *Uniform Crime Reports*).
SOURCE. Bureau of Justice Statistics, *Prisoners in 1984* (Washington, D.C.: U.S. Department of Justice, 1985), p. 8.

Because of this influx of offenders, the nation's prisons were operating at 110 percent of capacity, even though over eight thousand prisoners were being held in local jails because of overcrowding. In 1984, eight jurisdictions were operating under court order to reduce overcrowding. The cost of this vast system to taxpayers: $7.2 billion.

Profile of Prison Inmates. What are the personal characteristics of U.S. prison inmates? As would be expected, they reflect the same qualities that were found in the analysis of serious criminal behavior (chapter 4).[58]

Inmates of state prisons are predominantly poor young adult males with less than a high school education. Prison is not a new experience for them; they have been incarcerated before, many first as juveniles. The offense that brought them to prison was a violent crime or a burglary. On the average, they have already served one and one-half years on a maximum sentence of eight and one-half years. Along with a criminal history, they have a history of drug abuse and are also likely to have a history of alcohol abuse. They are typically housed in a maximum or medium security prison where they are likely to be sharing their living space with at least one other person.

There are other important characteristics of the incarcerated inmate population. Blacks are overrepresented, making up 48 percent of the inmate population. Hispanics represent only a small percentage of prisoners, but their numbers have doubled in the past five years to about 9 percent.

The largest group of inmates is aged eighteen to twenty-nine (63 percent); only 4 percent are over fifty years old. About 60 percent have not finished high school, and nearly 30 percent were unemployed during the year before the arrest that led to their incarceration. Their median income was $6,660, far below the national average.

About 52 percent of the inmates had been arrested for violent crimes. It is not surprising that more than half had received a maximum sentence of ten years or more. Also, about 64 percent of the inmates were repeat offenders.

A majority of the state inmates had been regular drug users at some time in their lives. Forty percent had been heroin addicts; most of the others had been habitual users of marijuana. Among prisoners who said they had used drugs only occasionally (23 percent), most had been marijuana users; but 8 percent of all inmates said they had used heroin occasionally. About half the inmates had drunk daily, or almost daily, in the year before their arrest. Most had drunk heavily, consuming the equivalent of eight cans of beer, seven glasses of wine, or ten ounces of hard liquor. Another 26 percent had drunk weekly. Some 18 percent said they had not drunk at all. About half of all inmates admitted to having been drinking, most of them heavily, just before the offense that brought them to prison. In the following Close-Up, the time these inmates serve in prison for their offenses is discussed.

Prison Life: Males. Inmates in large, inaccessible prisons find themselves physically cut off from families, friends, and former associates. Visitors may find it difficult to travel great distances to visit them; mail is censored and sometimes destroyed. The prison is a "total institution" regulating dress, work, sleep, and eating habits.[59]

Inmates soon find themselves in a totally new world with its own logic, behavior, rules, and language. They must learn to live with the stress of prison life. According to Gresham Sykes, the major losses are goods and services, liberty, heterosexual relationships, autonomy, and security.[60] Prisoners find they have no privacy; even when locked in their own cells, they are surrounded and observed by others.

Inmates must adjust to the incentives prison administrators have created to promote security and control behavior:[61] One type of incentive involves the level of comfort provided the inmate. Those obeying rules are given choice work assignments, privileges, and educational opportunities. Those who flout prison rules may be segregated, locked in their cells, or put in solitary confinement (*the hole*).

Administrators can also control the amount of time spent in prison. Furloughs can be dispensed to allow prisoners the opportunity to work or visit outside the prison walls. Good-time credit can be extended to lower the minimum sentence. Parole decisions can be influenced by reports on inmates' behavior.

The inmate must learn to deal with sexual exploitation and violence in the prison. One position says that this phenomenon is a function of racial conflict; another holds that victims are targets because they are physically weaker and less likely to form cohesive defensive groups.[62] In one study, Daniel Lockwood found that inmate aggressors come from a street culture that stresses violence and continue to behave violently while in prison.[63]

To cope with sexual aggression, inmates can fight back to indicate that they are not people to be taken advantage of, or they can join cliques and seek out mutual protection from other inmates. Some seek transfers to a different cell block or prison, ask for protective custody, or simply remain in their cells all the time.

Part of inmates' early adjustment involves their becoming familiar with and perhaps participating in the hidden, black-market economy of the prison—the **hustle**. Hustling provides inmates with a source of steady income and the satisfaction of believing they are beating the system.[64]

Hustling involves sales of such illegal commodities as drugs (uppers, downers, pot), alcohol, weapons, and illegally obtained food and supplies. When prison officials crack down on hustled goods, it merely serves to drive the price up—giving hustlers a greater incentive to promote their black-market activities.[65]

Inmates must also learn to deal with the racial conflict that is a daily fact of life. Prisoners tend to segregate themselves and, if peace is to reign in the institution, stay out of each other's way. Often, racial groupings are quite exact; for example, Hispanics may separate themselves according to their national origin (Mexicans, Puerto Ricans, Colombians, and so on). Prisons represent one area in which minorities often hold power; as one sociologist, James B. Jacobs, observed, "Prison may be the one institution in American society that blacks control."[66]

Prisoners must learn to deal with their frustrations over getting a "rotten deal." They may find that some other inmates received far lower sentences for similar crimes. They may be turned down for parole and then observe that others with similar records are granted early release. There is some evidence that perceived discrimination in the distribution of rewards and treatment may contribute to dissatisfaction, maladjustment, and prison violence.[67]

Finally, as the inmate's sentence winds down and his parole date nears, he must learn to cope with the anxiety of being released into the outside world. During this period, inmates may question their ability to make it in an environment in which they have failed before. Have their families stood by them? Are they unwanted outcasts?

Thus, adapting to prison requires coping with a whole series of new conditions and personal crises. Failure to cope can lead to mental breakdown and suicide.

Inmate Society. A significant element of the inmate's adjustment to prison is the encounter with what is commonly known as the **inmate subculture**.[68] One major aspect of the inmate subculture is a unique **social code**, unwritten guidelines that express the values, attitudes, and types of behavior that the older inmates demand

Time Served in Prison

How much time do convicted offenders actually serve in prison? This question is the subject of two studies conducted for the Bureau of Justice Statistics by Herbert Koppel and Lawrence Greenfield.

Using data from twelve states, Koppel found that the average prison stay for all felonies is 1.5–2.5 years, and for violent ones 2.5–4 years. As table A indicates, people convicted for the most serious crimes such as homicide, rape, and robbery do in fact spend the longest time in prison. Yet, there were great differences between the states in the amount of time served. For example, murderers in Oklahoma average just over 3 years in prison; in Ohio they average more than 6. Similarly, an arsonist in Iowa is behind bars four times longer than one in Delaware, but murderers in these states receive comparable incarceration periods.

Koppel cautions that these data must be interpreted in light of different justice system practices within the various jurisdictions. For example, some states give credit for jail time while others do not, each state has different good-time procedures, and so on.

Greenfield's study reviewed incarceration trends in twenty-nine states and the District of Columbia. He found that the median confinement period for felonies in 1982 was 16 months, an historic low. For example, in 1926 the median was 19 months. Since then the average amount of time served for burglary and robbery has declined 6 months, while time for larceny incarcerations

TABLE A. Average (mean) time served for specific offenses, in months

State and release period	Criminal homicide[a]	Rape	Rob- bery	Aggra- vated assault	Burg- lary	Lar- ceny	Auto theft	Arson	Drug offenses[b]
Delaware, 1980–82[c]	74.3	25.5	39.3	18.6	15.7	6.5	12.8	9.4	15.0
Illinois, 1978–82	52.1	46.0	29.1	18.7	20.7	14.1	*	*	*
Iowa, 1979–83[c]	72.4	47.1	51.7	33.1	30.5	22.7	15.5	29.9	24.0
Maryland, 1982[c]	63.1	63.7	61.5	30.0	29.2	14.2	20.9	35.6	15.9
North Carolina, 1977–81[c,d]	51.3	*	40.8	19.7	22.2	*	19.4	*	15.7
Ohio, 1980–81	78.6	50.0	34.9	26.6	27.0	15.4	24.9	22.5	17.3
Oklahoma, 1982	39.3	35.6	29.7	17.4	13.8	11.8	15.1	16.4	11.4
Oregon, 1979–82	41.2	36.0	25.2	23.1	15.3	11.3	11.9	25.5	10.4

continued

of younger inmates. Passed on from one generation of inmates to another, the inmate social code represents the values of interpersonal relations within the prison.

National attention was first drawn to the inmate social code and subculture by Donald Clemmer. In his *The Prison Community*, Clemmer set out to present a detailed sociological study of life in a maximum security prison.[69] Referring to thousands of conversations and interviews, as well as to inmate essays and biographies, Clemmer was able to identify a unique language **(argot)** that prisoners use. In addition, Clemmer found that prisoners tend to group themselves into cliques on the basis of such personal criteria as sexual preference, political beliefs, and offense history. He found that there were complex sexual relationships in prison and concluded that many heterosexual men will turn to homosexual relationships when faced with long sentences and the loneliness of prison life.

Clemmer's most important contribution may have been his identification of the **prisonization** process. This he defined as the inmate's assimilation into the existing prison culture through acceptance of its language, sexual code, and norms

TABLE A. Average (mean) time served for specific offenses, in months—cont'd

State and release period	Criminal homicide[a]	Rape	Rob-bery	Aggra-vated assault	Burg-lary	Lar-ceny	Auto theft	Arson	Drug offenses[b]
Pennsylvania, 1981–82[c]	57.4	47.7	33.5	25.4	22.6	16.8	14.8	28.2	18.9
Washington, 7/81–6/82	63.2	36.3	38.8	37.0	*	*	*	*	17.8
Wisconsin, 1/80–5/83	41.8	33.5	42.3	30.7	26.5	22.6	20.6	24.7	22.3
Wyoming, 7/80–6/83[c]	59.5	51.5	29.5	29.4	22.5	15.8	18.2	25.8	15.2

[a]Includes murder and non-negligent manslaughter.
[b]Includes sale and possession.
[c]Includes credited jail time.
[d]Derived from data in Clarke, Stevens H. et al., *North Carolina's Determinate Sentencing Legislation: An Evaluation of the First Year's Experience*, Institute of Government, University of North Carolina at Chapel Hill, October 1983.
*Data not available.

SOURCE. *Time Served in Prison*, p. 3.

declined 7 months. Although nearly half of all murderers received life sentences, those convicted of murder but not given life sentences served about 5 years and 9 months for their crimes; rapists served 3 years or less. In sum, whereas the proportion of the population behind bars is at an all-time high—9.8 people per 100,000 population—the time they serve is at an all-time low.

These data raise questions about the concept of punishment in the American justice system. Most criminologists believe that conservative, get-tough policies dominate the system, but these surveys only partially support that assumption. Though more people are in prison than ever before, the time they serve has actually declined. The get-tough approach seems to be translated into more frequent but shorter prison sentences for felony offenders. Whether three years for rape or six for murder is too little, or too much, may be a matter of individual preference. Nonetheless, those who believe that punishment has gotten out of hand may have second thoughts after considering these data.

DISCUSSION QUESTIONS

1. Do criminals spend less time in prison than you believed?

2. Should a uniform criminal code be applied to all people in all states?

SOURCE. Herbert Koppel, *Time Served in Prison* (Washington, D.C.: Bureau of Justice Statistics, 1984); Lawrence Greenfield, *Prison Admissions and Releases, 1982* (Washington, D.C.: Bureau of Justice Statistics, 1985).

of behavior. Those who become the most "prisonized" will be the least likely to reform on the "outside."

Using Clemmer's work as a jumping-off point, some prominent sociologists have set out to explore more fully the various roles in the prison community. For example, in one important analysis entitled *The Society of Captives*, Gresham Sykes further defined prison argot and argued that prison roles exist because of the deprivations presented by the prison.[70] Later, writing with Sheldon Messinger, Sykes identified the following as the most important principles of the prison community:

- *Don't interfere with inmates' interests.* Within this area of the code are maxims concerning the serving of the least amount of time in the greatest possible comfort. For example, inmates are warned . . . never [to betray another] inmate to authorities; . . . [in other words,] grievances must be handled personally. Other aspects of the noninterference doctrine include "Don't

Prisons reshape the lives and personalities of their inmates. The State Penitentiary in Joliet, Illinois, is such a total institution.

be nosy," "Don't have a loose lip," "Keep off [the other inmates' backs"], and "Don't put [another inmate] on the spot."

- *Don't lose your head.* Inmates are also cautioned to refrain from arguing, [quarreling, or engaging in] other emotional displays with fellow inmates. The novice may hear such warnings as "Play it cool" and "Do your own time."
- *Don't exploit inmates.* Prisoners are warned not to take advantage of one another—"Don't steal from cons," "Don't welsh on a debt," "Be right."
- *Inmates are cautioned to be tough and not lose their dignity.* While rule 2 forbids conflict, once it starts an inmate must be prepared to deal with it effectively and [thoroughly]. Maxims include "Don't cop out," "Don't weaken," "Be tough; be a man."
- *Don't be a sucker.* Inmates are cautioned not to make fools . . . of themselves and support the guards or prison administration over the interest of the inmates—"Be sharp."[71]

Not all prison experts believe that the prison culture is a function of the harsh conditions existing in a total institution. In 1962, John Irwin and Donald Cressey published a paper in which they conceded that a prison culture exists but claimed that its principles are actually imported from the outside world.[72] In their *importation model,* Irwin and Cressey conclude that the inmate culture is affected as much by values of newcomers:

> *Many inmates come to any given prison with a record of many terms in correctional institutions. These men, some of whom have institutional records dating back to early childhood, bring with them a ready made set of patterns which they apply to the new situation, just as is the case with participants in the criminal subculture.*[73]

Irwin and Cressey found that the inmate world was actually divided into three groups, each corresponding to a role in the outside world. The *thief subculture* is made up of professional criminals who stick to themselves and always try to "do their own time." Members of the *convict subculture* try to obtain power in the prison and control others for their own needs. The *conventional subculture* is made up of inmates who try to retain legitimate elements of the outside world in their daily life (that is, they identify with neither of the deviant prison subcultures).

Although the debate between the prisonization and importation models has not been concluded, there may actually be a middle ground between them. For example, Charles Thomas suggests that an inmate's preincarceration personal characteristics, such as social class, attitudes, and values, will significantly influence the way he or she assimilates the prison culture.[74] Consequently, the development of an inmate culture may contain elements of both prisonization and importation.

The traditional prison subculture may be vanishing. The growing number and power of black and Hispanic inmates has created an advanced degree of racial segregation in some prisons. There appears to be separation along cultural and racial lines in the prison community today, so that the traditional, unified inmate subculture now appears to be divided into distinct racial groupings. If solidarity exists, it takes the form of loyalty to one's clique or perhaps to one's old street gang. Future research on inmate subcultures will have to be cognizant of prison race relations and their influence on convict life.[75]

Prison Life: Females. Women make up about 4 percent of the adult prison population. Usually, they are housed in minimum security institutions more likely to resemble college dormitories than high security male prisons.

Women in prison tend to be of three basic types, described by Esther Heffernan as: "the square," who is basically a noncriminal but who, in a fit of rage, may have shot or stabbed a husband or boyfriend; "the life," who is a repeat offender—shoplifter, prostitute, drug user, or pusher; and "the cool," who is part of the sophisticated criminal underworld. The square usually espouses conventional values and wants to follow the rules; the life rejects prison authority and is a rebel; the cool is aloof, manipulates the environment, and does not participate in prison life.[76]

Daily life in the women's prison community is also somewhat different from that in male institutions. For one thing, women usually do not present the immediate physical danger to staff and fellow inmates that many male prisoners do. For another, the rigid, antiauthority inmate social code found in many male institutions does not exist in female prisons. Confinement for women, however, may produce severe anxiety and anger, because they are separated from families and loved ones and unable to function in normal female roles. Unlike men, who direct their anger outward, female prisoners may revert to more self-destructive acts to cope with their problems. Female inmates are perhaps more likely than males to mutilate their own bodies and attempt suicide.

One common form of adaptation to prison employed by women is the surrogate family. This group contains masculine and feminine figures acting as fathers and mothers; some even act as children and take on the role of either brother or sister. Formalized marriages and divorces may be conducted. Sometimes, multiple roles are held by one inmate, so that a "sister" in one family may "marry" and become the "wife" in another.[77]

Correctional Treatment. Correctional treatment has been an integral part of prison life since Z. R. Brockway introduced it as part of the daily regime at the Elmira reformatory.

There are many approaches to treatment. Some, based on the medical model, rely heavily on counseling and clinical therapy. Others, reflecting interactionist theory, attempt to reintegrate the offender into the community; they rely on work release, vocational training, and other such programs. Although it is beyond the scope of this book to describe the vast number of correctional treatment programs, a few important types will be discussed.

Therapy and Counseling. The most traditional type of treatment in prison involves psychological counseling and therapy. Counseling programs exist in almost every major institution. Some stress individual treatment with psychotherapy or other techniques. However, because of lack of resources, it is more common for group methods to be used. Some groups are led by trained social workers, counselors, or therapists; others rely on lay personnel as leaders.

Group counseling in prison usually tries to stimulate inmates' self-awareness and their ability to deal with everyday problems.[78] Since the group is a microcosm of the real world, containing winners, losers, toughs, straights, and others, successful adaptation to the group process is believed to be analogous to improving relationships with other social groups. Thus, by identifying roles and behaviors that occur within the group and uncovering the motivations underlying them, inmates learn to understand why they act as they do and how others react to their behavior.

A wide variety of innovative psychological treatment approaches have been used in the prison system: *behavior therapy* uses tokens to reward conformity and help develop positive behavior traits; *reality therapy* is meant to help satisfy individuals' needs to feel worthwhile to themselves and others; *transactional analysis* encourages inmates to identify the different aspects of their personalities and to be their own therapists; *milieu therapy* uses the social structure and processes of the institution to influence the behavior patterns of offenders.[79]

Educational Programs. The first prison treatment programs were educational in nature. A prison school was opened at the Walnut Street Prison in 1784. Elementary courses were offered in New York' prison system in 1801, and in Pennsylvania's in 1844. An actual school system was established in Detroit's House of Corrections in 1870, and Elmira Reformatory opened a vocational trade school in 1876.

Today, most institutions provide some type of educational program. At some prisons, inmates are given the opportunity to obtain a high school diploma through equivalency exams or general educational development (GED) certificates. Other institutions provide an actual classroom education, usually staffed by full-time certified teachers or by part-time teachers who work at an institution after a full day's teaching in a nearby school.[80] Many institutions also offer college-level courses. A survey of prison education programs found that 96 percent of surveyed institutions had both basic education (basic literacy) programs and secondary education (high-school level) programs, 83 percent had postsecondary education (college level) programs, 89 percent had vocational (skilled job training) programs, and 44 percent had programs offering social education (life skills, consumer education, problem-solving skills).[81]

Vocational Rehabilitation. Most prisons operate numerous vocational training programs designed to help inmates develop skills to help them secure employment on their release. In the past, the traditional prison industries of laundry and license plate manufacture failed to provide skills that helped inmates secure employment upon release. Today, programs stress such marketable skills as dental laboratory work, computer programming, auto repair, and radio and television work.

Unfortunately, it is often difficult to obtain the necessary equipment to run meaningful programs. Therefore, many prisons have adopted **work furlough** programs to allow inmates to work in the community during the day and return to the institution at night.

In addition to work furlough programs, several state correctional departments have instituted prerelease and postrelease employment services. Employment program staff members assess inmates' backgrounds to determine their abilities, interests, goals, and capabilities. They also consult with clients to help them create job plans (which are essential to their receiving early release, or parole) and to help them successfully reintegrate themselves into the community. Some programs use community correctional placements in sheltered environments to help inmates bridge the gap between institutions and the outside world; services include job placement, skill development, family counseling, and legal and medical attention.

Free Venture. A new version of vocational rehabilitation is the **free venture** programs developed in the 1980s in Minnesota, Kansas, and other areas.[82] The programs involve businesses to be set up by private entrepreneurs within the institution. Inmates are hired at free-market wages and produce goods that are competitively marketed. Inmates can be fired by being sent back to the general population.

On paper, free venture is quite attractive. It teaches inmates skills in usually desirable commercial areas such as data processing. It increases employment opportunities on the outside in areas where the ex-offender can earn enough to forgo a life of crime. Various evaluations of the programs have given them high marks. However, free venture programs have so far used relatively few inmates. It is also questionable whether they could be applied to the general prison population, which contains many people with educational deficiencies and a history of substance abuse.

Another new approach is to have major corporations manage prisions for profit. The idea is that private corporations can run correctional institutions more economically than state correctional authorities. Several institutions are now being run privately in Minnesota and Tennesee as well as other states. This young program has not yet been evaluated in depth.

Coed Programs. The **conjugal visit** is another mode of treatment that has received renewed emphasis from correctional administrators. During conjugal visits, prisoners are regularly able to have completely private meetings with their wives. The explicit purpose of the program is to grant inmates access to normal sexual outlets and thereby counteract the pains of imprisonment. Though it is a relatively new and infrequently used phenomenon, the conjugal visit has provoked much debate. Detractors view it as degrading. They also say it creates sexual tension among single prisoners who cannot share in the program, and may produce children who cannot be adequately supported by their fathers. Supporters view it as a major development in maintaining normal relationships among incarcerated felons, and a mechanism for keeping prison families together.[83]

Another recent trend, one with strong historical roots, is the **"coedu-cational" prison**. Since 1973, prisons housing both men and women have pro-liferated throughout the United States. Examples of coed institutions include the Renz Correctional Center in Cedar City, Missouri, established in 1975, and the Maine Correctional Center in South Windham, Maine, established in 1976.[84]

In all, it is estimated that in the federal prison system, 58.1 percent of females and 7.5 percent of males are in coed prisons; the figures for state systems are much smaller—9.7 percent of females and 0.53 percent of males.[85]

Generally speaking, the typical coed prison is a small, low security institution, predominantly of one sex (either mostly male or mostly female), populated by nonviolent, carefully screened offenders. In most instances, males and females live in physically separate housing—either in different buildings or in separate cottages. Again, the purpose of this method is to provide a more normal environment for prison inmates.

Does Rehabilitation Work? Despite the variety and number of treatment programs in operation, there is some question about their effectiveness. In their highly regarded research, Robert Martinson and his associates found that a majority of treatment programs were failures.[86] Martinson found in a national study that, with few exceptions, rehabilitative efforts seemed to have no appreciable effect on recidivism.

Martinson's work was followed by efforts that found, embarrassingly, that some high-risk offenders were more likely to commit crimes after they had been placed in treatment programs than before the onset of rehabilitation efforts.[87] Even Cal-ifornia's highly touted community treatment program, which matched youthful offenders and counselors on the basis of their psychological profiles, was found by Paul Lerman to exert negligible influence on its clients.[88]

These devastating reviews of correctional rehabilitation helped develop a more conservative view of corrections, which holds that prisons are places of incapa-citation and punishment and should not be used for treatment. Current social policy stresses eliminating the nonserious offender from the correctional system, but at the same time increasing the sentences of serious, violent offenders. Thus, the late 1970s and early 1980s have seen the development of lengthy mandatory and determinate sentences of serious offenders; and the simultaneous development of restitution, diversion, and pretrial release programs to limit the nonserious offender's interface with the system.

Though liberals such as Ted Palmer, Francis Cullen, and Karen Gilbert have challenged the "nothing works" philosophy, their voices have been drowned out by a sea of professional and public opinion calling for longer sentences and high security rather than care and treatment.[89] The trend toward imprisonment will most likely continue until the reality of its costs is fully appreciated by the public.

Prison Violence. One of the more significant problems facing prison adminis-trators is the constant fear of interpersonal and collective violence. Hans Toch, an expert on violence, has said:

> *Jails and prisons . . . have a climate of violence which has no free-world counter-part. Inmates are terrorized by other inmates and spend years in fear of harm. Some inmates request segregation, others lock themselves in and some are hermits by choice. Many inmates injure themselves.[90]*

What are the causes of prison violence? Though there is no single explanation for either collective or individual violence, theories abound. One position holds that inmates are often violence-prone individuals who have always used force to get their own way. In the crowded, dehumanizing world of the prison, it is not surprising that they resort to force to exert their dominance over others.[91]

A second view is that prisons convert people to violence by their inhumane conditions, including overcrowding, depersonalization, and threats of homosexual rape. One social scientist, Charles Silberman, suggests that even in the most humane prisons, life is a constant put-down and prison conditions threaten the inmates' sense of self-worth; that violence is a consequence of these conditions is not surprising.[92]

Still another view is that prison violence stems from mismanagement, lack of strong security, and inadequate control by prison oficials.[93] This view has contributed to the escalated use of solitary confinement in recent years as a means of control. Also contributing to prison violence is the changing prison population. Younger, more violent inmates, who often have been members of teenage gangs, now dominate prison life. The old code of "do your own time" and "be a right guy" may be giving way to a prison culture dominated by gangs and their leaders, whose very nature breeds violence.

Sometimes prison violence generates large-scale rioting. The American Correctional Association gives these reasons for prison flare-ups: (1) unnatural institutional environment; (2) antisocial characteristics of inmates; (3) inept management; (4) inadequate personnel practices; (5) inadequate facilities; (6) insufficient constructive, meaningful activity; (7) insufficient legitimate rewards; (8) basic social values and unrest in the larger community; (9) inadequate finances; (10) inequities and complexities in the criminal justice system.[94]

In an analysis of the similarities between the two worst prison riots of recent times, Attica in 1971 and New Mexico State in 1980, the following phenomena were observed:

- Prisoners felt they were not being treated like human beings.
- Line officers were unprepared; they were not informed of plans and regulations at the prison.
- Administrators lacked consistency. Their policies lacked stability.
- Legislators were insensitive to the needs of the penal system.
- The public and media were unconcerned about the corrections system.[95]

Overcrowding and Violence. Another recent trend in prisons that may be associated with violence is the overcrowding caused by rapid increases in the prison population. Data from Texas indicate that a large increase in the inmate population, unmatched by creation of new space, was associated with increases in suicide, violent death, and disciplinary action rates. The largest prisons in Texas (with populations of over 1,600) demonstrated violence rates higher than the smaller prisons (800 or less).[96] Similar data from Oklahoma on crowding and violent deaths corroborate the Texas findings. One explanation: high population in an institution exerts a negative influence that is associated with violence.

Other recent research efforts have reached similar conclusions. Paul Paulus and his associates found that feelings of crowding and blood pressure rates increased in cells occupied by more than one person.[97] E. I. Megargee found that crowding was associated with increased disciplinary infractions.[98] P. L. Nacci and his associates found that the federal correctional institutions that were most overcrowded also had the highest disciplinary infraction rates.[99]

Others disagree that prison overcrowding by itself can cause violence. For example, Sheldon Ekland-Olson and his associates found that the age of the prison population and not overcrowding was the factor producing violence; younger prisoners are the most likely to be violence-prone.[100] Despite this evidence, most studies do conclude that a violence/overcrowding link exists.[101]

It seems evident, then, that as the prison population continues its upward climb, unmatched by expanded correctional capacity, prison violence may increase. Though judges in some states have ordered the mandatory release of prisoners because of overcrowded conditions, the problem of overcrowding may become even more acute in future years. Consequently, prison administrators have attempted to reduce tension levels by (1) creating inmate councils to help govern the institution (self-governance), and (2) creating grievance mechanisms so that inmates' complaints will be taken into account. Such measures have worked rather effectively in some institutions.

Corrections and the Rule of Law. For many years, the nation's courts did not interfere in the operation of the prison, maintaining what is called the **hands-off doctrine**. The court's reluctance to interfere in prison matters was based on (1) the belief that it lacked technical competence in prison administration, (2) society's general apathy toward the prison, and (3) the belief that prisoners' complaints involved privileges rather than rights.[102] Consequently, prisoners had no legal rights and were "slaves of the state."

The hands-off doctrine was lifted in the 1960s. General concern with civil and human rights, an increasing militancy in the prison population, and the reformist nature of the Warren Court created a climate conducive to reform.

The first area of change came in the First Amendment right of freedom of religion. The Black Muslims, a politically active religious organization led by Elijah Muhammed of Chicago, had many adherents in the prison system. Using their legal and financial clout, the Muslims litigated claims that their followers were being denied the right to worship according to their faith. A series of Supreme Court cases upheld the Muslim's freedom of religion and opened the door to further issues of inmates' rights.[103]

Today, most litigation is brought under the federal Civil Rights Act, 28 USC 1983, which states:

> *Every person who, under color of any statute, ordinance, regulation, custom, or usage of any State or Territory subjects, or causes to be subjected, any citizen of the United States or other person within the jurisdiction thereof to the deprivation of any rights, privileges, or immunities secured by the Constitution and laws shall be liable to the party injured in an action at law, suit in equity or other proper proceeding for redress.*

Although the Supreme Court has recently limited the methods by which inmates can seek release or redress, it has consistently upheld the rights of inmates to seek legal remedies. For example, in *Johnson* v. *Avery* the Supreme Court upheld the right of legally trained inmates (*jail house lawyers*) to help fellow inmates prepare legal documents.[104] In *Gilmore* v. *Lynch*, the Court maintained that prisons must have an adequate law library and make it available to inmates.[105] Consequently, there has been a revolution in the area of prisoners' rights and their ability to seek help with their institutional problems.

Next, some of the more important areas of prisoners' rights will be briefly discussed.

Freedom of Press and Speech. The courts have ruled that inmates retain freedom of speech and press unless correctional authorities can show that it interferes with or threatens institutional freedom. For example, in *Procunier* v. *Martinez*, a court ruled that an inmate's mail could be censored only if there existed substantial belief that its contents would threaten security. Similarly, in *Nolan* v. *Fitzpatrick*, a federal court upheld the right of prisoners to write to newspapers unless their letters discussed escape plans or contained contraband.[106] However, in *Saxbe* v. *Washington Post*, the right of an inmate to grant press interviews was limited, since the Supreme Court argued that such interviews would enhance the reputations of particular inmates and jeopardize the authorities' desire to treat everyone equally.[107]

Medical Rights. After many years of indifference, inmates have only recently been given the right to secure proper medical attention. To gain their medical rights today, prisoners have generally resorted to class actions (suits brought on the behalf of all individuals governed by similar circumstances, in this case poor medical attention). In one such case, *Newman* v. *Alabama*, the entire Alabama prison system's medical facilities were declared inadequate. The court cited the following factors as contributing to inadequate care: insufficient physicians and nurses; reliance on untrained inmates for paramedical work; intentional failure to treat the sick and injured; and failure to conform to proper medical standards.[108]

In 1976, after reviewing the legal principles established over the preceding twenty years in cases such as *Newman* v. *Alabama*, the Supreme Court, in *Estelle* v. *Gamble*, clearly stated the inmate's right to have medical care.[109]

Gamble had hurt his back in a Texas prison and filed suit to contest the type of treatment he had recieved, and also to question the lack of interest prison guards had shown in his case. Although the Supreme Court referred Gamble's case to a lower court to determine whether he had actually been treated negligently, it laid down the following standard for judging future complaints:

> *Deliberate indifference to serious medical needs of prisoners constitutes the "unnecessary and wanton infliction of pain,"* . . . *proscribed by the Eighth Amendment. This is true whether the indifference is manifested by prison doctors in their response to the prisoner's needs or by prison guards in intentionally denying or delaying access to medical care or intentionally interfering with the treatment once prescribed.*[110]

Lower courts will now decide, case by case, whether "deliberate indifference" actually occured.

Cruel and Unusual Punishment. Prisoners have long suffered severe physical punishments in prison, ranging from whipping to extended periods of solitary confinement. The courts have held that such treatment is unconstitutional when it:

- Degrades the dignity of human beings.[111]
- Is more severe than the offense for which it has been given.[112]
- Shocks the general conscience and is fundamentally unfair.[113]

The courts have also ruled on the necessity for maintaining the general prison system in a humane manner. For example, in 1970, the entire prison system in Arkansas was declared unconstitutional, because its practices of overt physical punishment were ruled to be in violation of the Eighth Amendment.[114]

Two recent cases have been interpreted as signalling a slowdown in the Court's restrictions on oppressive prison conditions. In *Bell* v. *Wolfish*[115] and *Rhodes* v. *Chapman*,[116] the Supreme Court upheld the practice of double-bunking two or more inmates in a small cell (fifty square feet). "Conditions of confinement," they argued, "must not involve the wanton and unnecessary infliction of pain nor may they be grossly disproportionate to the severity of the crime warranting imprisonment"; but "conditions that cannot be said to be cruel and unusual under contemporary standards are not unconstitutional. To the extent that such conditions are restrictive and even harsh, they are part of the penalty that criminal offenders pay for their offenses against society."[117]

Procedural Due Process. Another critical element of prisoners' rights is in the area of procedural due process. This issue arises when the inmate is subject to disciplinary actions involving the loss of privileges, good time, or parole. In the landmark case of *Wolff* v. *McDonnell*, the Supreme Court established these guidelines for disciplinary hearings.[118]

1. Advance written notice of the charges must be given to the inmate no less than twenty-four hours before the prisoner's appearance at the disciplinary committee hearing.
2. There must be a written statement by the fact-finders as to the evidence relied upon and the reasons for the disciplinary action.
3. The inmate should be allowed to call witnesses and present documentary evidence as defense if these activities will not jeopardize institutional control.
4. The inmate has no constitutional right to confrontation and cross-examination in prison discipline proceedings.
5. The inmate has no right to retained or appointed counsel, although substitute counsel, such as a staff member or another inmate, may be provided in certain cases.
6. The inmate has the right to have an impartial group conduct disciplinary hearings.
7. In regard to regulations governing inmate mail, the Court held that the state may require that mail from an attorney to a prisoner be identified as such and that the attorney's name and address appear on the communication. In addition, as a protection against contraband, prison authorities may open mail in the inmate's presence.

Despite the liberalization of due process rights brought about by *Wolff*, the Court has limited them by denying inmates the right to counsel at parole hearings and at hearings to consider transfer to another institution. The legal rules of thumb appear to be (1) prisoners have a right to personal freedom as long as it cannot be construed as interfering with prison security; and (2) prisoners have procedural rights when something is to be taken from them thay they already have, but relatively few legal rights when they are denied special privileges that other inmates may have obtained.

PAROLE

The final component of corrections is **parole**. Parole is the planned release and supervision of incarcerated offenders before the actual expiration of their prison sentences. It is usually considered to be a way of completing a prison sentence in the community and is not the same as a pardon; the paroled offender can be legally recalled to serve the remainder of his or her sentence in an institution if the parole authorities deem the offender's adjustment inadequate or if while on parole the offender commits a further crime.

The decision to parole is determined by statutory requirement and usually involves the completion of a minimum sentence. Parole is granted by a state *parole board*, a body of men and women whose task it is to review cases and determine whether an offender has been rehabilitated sufficiently to deal with the outside world. The board also dictates what specific parole rules a parolee must obey. Some states with determinate sentencing statutes, such as Indiana and California, do not use parole boards but release inmates at the conclusion of their maximum term less accumulated good time. This is referred to as mandatory parole release.

Once community release has begun, the offender is supervised by a trained staff of parole officers who help the offender adjust to the community, help in the search for employment, and monitor behavior and activities to insure that the offender conforms to the conditions of parole.

Parolees are subject to a strict standardized and/or a personalized set of rules that guide their behavior and set limits on their activities. If at any time these rules are violated, the offender can be returned to the institution to serve the remainder of the sentence; this is known as a technical parole violation. Inmates released in determinate sentencing states can have part or all of their good time revoked if they violate the conditions of their release.

Parole can also be revoked if the offender commits a second offense; the offender may also be tried and sentenced for this subsequent crime. The Supreme Court has granted parolees due process rights similar to those of probationers at revocation hearings.

Parole is viewed as an act of grace on the part of the criminal justice system. It represents an actual manifestation of the policy of returning the offender to the community. There are two conflicting sides to parole, however; on one hand, the paroled offender is given a break and allowed to serve part of the sentence in the community; on the other hand, the sentiment exists that parole is a privilege and not a right and that the parolee is in reality a dangerous criminal who must be carefully watched and supervised. The conflict between the treatment and enforcement aspects of parole has not been reconciled by the criminal justice system, and the parole process still contains elements of both orientations.

Extent of Parole. As 1984 began, there were 251,708 adults on parole in the United States, an increase of 27,000 (12 percent) over the previous year.[119] However, due to increased use of mandatory and determinate sentences, the number of parolees grew only 15 percent between 1979 and the beginning of 1984. A total of 176,214 were paroled in 1983 and 149,110 were discharged from supervision. Of those released from parole, a federal government survey found that 60 percent had completed their term, 31 percent were incarcerated on new or current charges, and 9 percent either absconded, died, were transferred to another jurisdiction, and so on.

Parole Decision Making. Most inmates become eligible for parole at the completion of their minimum sentence. The actual parole decision is made at a *parole grant hearing.* There, the full board or a selected subcommittee reviews information, may meet with the offender, and then decides whether the parole applicant has a reasonable probability of succeeding outside of prison. Candidates for parole may be chosen by statutory eligibility on the basis of time served in relation to their sentences. In most jurisdictions, the minimum sentence imposed by the judge regulates eligibility for parole; when no minimum sentence is set, parole eligibility is based on the policy of the board or the corrections department. Finally, in most jurisdictions, the good time an offender accumulates can serve to reduce the minimum sentence and therefore hasten eligibility for parole.

Each parole board works in a unique way and has its own administrative setup for reviewing cases. In some, the full board meets with the applicant; in others, only a few members are required. In some jurisdictions, a single board member can conduct a personal investigation and submit the findings to the full board for a decision.

What factors influence parole board decision making?[120] Of primary concern is whether board members believe that the offender can make an adjustment in the community or that continued confinement would be more beneficial. Boards are also interested in whether offenders have paid their debt to society. Does the time served seem adequate to compensate for the seriousness of the crime? Have other inmates been treated similarly?

The parole board is also concerned with inmates' preparation to make it "outside." Do they have families who can help them? Jobs waiting? Have they taken vocational and educational training courses while in prison?

The parole board also considers the conditions existing within the penal institution. Is overcrowding a problem? Are the inmates tense because some recent parole requests have been turned down? What are the feelings of the correctional administrators about parole decisions?

To help parole decision makers, parole prediction tables have been developed.[121] These tables correlate personal information on inmates who were released in the past with their rates of rearrest.

The best known predictive device is the Salient Factor Score Index developed by members of the federal parole system. The salient factor score includes age, type of offense, prior parole revocations, history of heroin use, and employment background.

A six-year follow-up of the effectiveness of the salient score index revealed mixed results. During the first year of the evaluation, there were considerable differences in the arrest rates of the four risk groups identified by the index (those judged very good risks were arrested less; poor risks tended to be arrested more). However, this trend diminished over time; and by the sixth year of the follow-up study, the arrest rates for all categories were quite similar.[122]

How Effective is Parole? Conservative thinkers criticize parole because it allows possibly dangerous offenders into the community before the completion of their sentence. Since parole decision making relies on human judgement, it is quite possible for dangerous offenders, who should actually have remained inside a secure facility, to be released into society while others who would probably make a good adjustment to the community are denied release.

The evaluation of parole effectiveness is still undecided since various studies have produced conflicting results. For example, a study of a sample of over 104,000 parolees released between 1965 and 1970 indicated that success (lack of recidivism) was quite high. Rates of nonrecidivism ranged from 90.1 percent for homicide offenders to 64.9 percent for motor vehicle theft violators.[123] In every offense category, offenders with prior records had somewhat lower success rates than first offenders, though the differences were not enough to discourage the continued use of parole for recidivists.

Similarly, a three-year Bureau of Justice Statistics study of the parole experiences of the 64,000 people paroled during 1974 and 1975 found that only 25 percent had their parole revoked or were returned to prison before their parole ended.[124]

However, not all studies of parole effectiveness reach the same optimistic conclusions. A recent six-year follow-up of 1,806 federal releases (parolees and people whose sentences had expired) found that 1,129 cases (62.5 percent) were arrested at least once after release or had their parole revoked on a technical violation. In 738 cases (40.9 percent), more than one criminal arrest was recorded. All told, more than 2,788 separate criminal arrests were recorded.[125] In the following Close-Up, entitled "Returning to Prison," further information on recidivism is presented.

Because of these alleged failures of parole, some critics have called for its abolition.

Should Parole Be Abolished? There have been many attacks on early release via parole, and there have been calls to eliminate the practice. The criticism leveled against parole is threefold:

1. The procedures that control the decision to grant parole are vague and have not been controlled by due process considerations. Consequently, some inmates may be subject to the unfair denial of parole, while some who are undeserving may benefit.

2. It is beyond the capacity of parole authorities to either predict who will make a successful adjustment on parole or to accurately monitor parolees' behavior in the community.

3. It is unjust to decide whether to release an individual from prison based on what we expect that person to do in the future. After all, we have no way of determining that accurately.[126]

Beyond these considerations, the parole process has been criticized as heightening the inmate's sense of injustice and powerlessness in the face of an omnipotent prison administration that has absolute control over the release date. As one prison expert, David Fogel, suggests:

Parole board decisions are also unreviewable and are not hammered out in an adversary clash; rather they are five to fifteen minute sessions with members frequently using a combination of whim, caprice, and arbitrariness.[127]

The indeterminate sentence, the heart of the parole process, is being replaced in many jurisdictions by mandatory, flat, and presumptive sentences (see chapter 16), which severely limit parole eligibility. Some states—Illinois, Maine, Indiana, and New Mexico—have abolished parole completely. Others, like California, have

Returning to Prison

What is the likelihood an offender will return to prison once released? Two recent studies sponsored by the Bureau of Justice Statistics help answer this important question.

The first examined aggregate data from fourteen reporting states to determine the probability of recidivism. Although these data include parolees, they also account for returnees who served their full sentence.

As table A shows, about 30 percent of all people released from prison return within three years; this sum does not include people released from one prison system who are incarcerated in another jurisdiction. The study found that most returnees are reincarcerated during the first year and that the probability of recidivism declines in each succeeding year. Most of the returnees were parolees or those released with special conditions who either violated parole rules or committed a new offense. The percentage of inmates released outright who returned to prison was relatively low in most states.

The study also found that property offenders are more likely to return than violent offenders (37 percent versus 31.5 percent). Also, the more prior prison experiences a person had, the more likely they were to recidivate for their current offense. As far as personal variables influenced recidivism; it was shown that males, minority, and younger inmates were more likely to recidivate than female, white, and older inmates.

A second federal study reviewing recidivism made use of data collected from a nationwide survey of inmates. Some of the chief findings of the study are listed below.

- An estimated 61 percent of those admitted to prison in 1979 were recidivists (i.e., they had previously served a sentence of incarceration as a juvenile, adult,

or both). Of those entering prison without a history of incarceration (an estimated 39 percent of all admissions), nearly 60 percent had prior convictions that resulted in probation and an estimated 27 percent were on probation at the time of their prison admission.
- An estimated 46 percent of the recidivists entering prison in 1979 would still have been in prison in 1979 would still have been in prison at the time of their admission if they had fully served the maximum term* of their last sentence to confinement. This group, referred to as "avertable recidivists," constituted approximately 28 percent of all those who entered prison in 1979.
- Recidivists were estimated to account for approximately two-thirds or more of the burglaries, auto thefts, and forgery/fraud/embezzlement offenses attributable to all the admissions. When their past criminal histories were examined, however, recidivists were found to be as likely as first-time admissions to have a current or prior violent offense.
- Of the estimated 200,000 offenses reported by the 1979 prison admissions, the "avertable recidivists" ac-

*The maximum term of confinement is defined in the Inmate Survey as the maximum sentence to incarceration imposed upon an offender by a sentencing court. Often courts impose a minimum and maximum sentence so that the sentence reflects a range of duration (e.g., one to three years). For purposes of this study, the maximum of the range imposed is considered to be the maximum sentence. Note that the maximum imposed sentence is not necessarily the same as the maximum sentence allowed by the statutes of a state.

retained parole but use it as a postrelease supervisory authority for inmates who have completed their prison sentences. Monitored by the community release board, inmates can have their good time revoked for behavioral indiscretions and can therefore be returned to prison.

It is likely that the abolition of parole would shift the burden of discretion from the prison authorities to the district attorney (who charges the defendants and conducts plea bargains), the judge (who sentences), and the prison authorities, who control good time violations. Of course, the inmates' sense of frustration might still remain; and sentencing disparity could still occur. Moreover, critics allege that abolishing parole would hurt prison discipline (except in states that maintained extremely liberal good time allowances of up to 50 percent of the prison sentence—almost an equivalent to parole). Despite these factors, the antiparole movement probably will continue in the years ahead, especially now that the federal government's new criminal code replaces parole with determinate sentences.

TABLE A. Percents of releasees returned to prison

State and year of release reported	Number of releases	The cumulative percent of prison releasees who returned to prison within:		
		1 year	2 years	3 years
Colorado, 1980	1,288	8.2%	18.5%	24.1%
Georgia, 1980	6,583	14.5	26.8	34.9
Iowa, 1980	605	16.3	21.8	23.3
Massachusetts, 1976	923	18.0	28.0	32.0
Minnesota, 1980	1,133	26.0	37.0	40.0[a]
Mississippi, 1978	1,417[b]	13.3	23.6	27.8
Nebraska, 1979[c]	646	14.1	22.5	27.9
New York, 1980	7,661	11.1	25.9	33.7
North Carolina, 1979	9,630[c]	14.9	26.3	31.6
Oklahoma, 1976–1977	1,906[d]	9.8	21.0	27.8
Oregon, 1979	1,782[e]	17.2	27.6	32.2
Rhode Island, 1978	401[f]	20.2	28.9	36.2
Washington, 1979	1,909	12.4	22.3	28.3
Wisconsin, 1980	1,616	16.8	25.7	31.3
Median of reporting States		14.9	26.1	31.5
Mean of reporting States		15.2	25.4	30.8

NOTE: Unless otherwise noted, number of releasees excludes persons being held for another agency, interinstitutional or interstate transfers, AWOLs, escapes, and deaths.
[a]Data are for July 1, 1983, resulting in a 2½-year follow-up period for the portion of the cohort released in the second half of 1980.
[b]Estimate based on half-year total.
[c]Fiscal 1978–79.
[d]Figure is half of a 2-year total of 3,812, from which a 15% sample was drawn.
[e]Excludes 100 inmates with offense data missing.
[f]Includes prison and jail inmates, for state has an integrated jail-prison system.

SOURCE. John Wallerstedt, *Returning to Prison* (Washington, D.C.: Bureau of Justice Statistics, 1984).

cont'd

The Criminal Justice System: A Final Consideration

Chapters 14 through 17 have reviewed the various components and processes of the criminal justice system. Taken as a whole, they illustrate the tension existing in today's justice system caused by competing philosophies and points of view. The conflicts that result from the need for due process; and the desires to rehabilitate and care for offenders, to protect the victims of crime and punish criminals, to incapacitate dangerous offenders, to provide fair treatment, etc. are apparent in our analysis of the system.

What, then, are some of the major findings or conclusions about the justice system?

1. The justice system is a vast enterprise involving millions of offenders, personnel, and policy makers. Its cost is in the billions of dollars.
2. The justice system is not effective in apprehending criminals or deterring crime. There is little evidence that police prevent crime or catch significant numbers of criminals after they violate the law.

Returning to Prison—cont'd

counted for approximately 20 percent of the violent crimes, 28 percent of the burglaries and auto thefts, 30 percent of the forgery/fraud/embezzlement offenses, and 31 percent of the stolen property offenses.

- Based on recidivist self-reports of how long it took them to reenter prison by 1979, it is estimated that nearly half (48.7 percent) of all those who exit prison will return within twenty years of release. Most of the recidivism, however, was found to occur within the first three years after release: an estimated 60 percent of those who will return to prison within twenty years do so by the end of the third year.
- Among the recidivists entering prison in 1979, those committing new offenses of robbery, burglary, and auto theft were found to return more rapidly than those committing other crimes.
- An estimated half of the recidivists had four or more prior sentences to probation, jail, or prison. About one in nine of the recidivists had more than ten prior convictions.
- An estimated 42 percent of those entering prison in 1979 were on probation or parole for prior offenses at the time of their admission.

How can these data be interpreted? Taken together, they indicate that a significant portion of people released from prison will one day return, and that a significant portion of people entering prison have had experience with the criminal justice system. A conservative view would be that the justice system fails to rehabilitate many offenders and that longer sentences are needed to protect the public. A liberal view is that a majority of people released from prison do not in fact return, and rather than focusing on the failures, we should look favorably on the successes. Nonetheless, the trend has been to abolish parole and view the prison as a place of confinement. This conclusion is certainly supported by the fact that nearly half the recidivists who entered prison would still have been there had they served the maximum term of their last confinement sentence. In other words, by toughening up penalties and forcing offenders to serve their full sentence, a significant portion of all offenses that result in prison sentences could be avoided.

DISCUSSION QUESTIONS

1. Should parole be abolished?
2. Should recidivists have an extra mandatory prison term tacked onto their sentences?

SOURCE. John Wallerstedt, *Returning to Prison* (Washington, D.C.: Bureau of Justice Statistics, 1984); Lawrence Greenfield, *Examining Recidivism* (Washington, D.C.: Bureau of Justice Statistics, 1985). Quote from p. 1.

---

3. The court system processes millions of cases annually. The overwhelming number of offenders causes most cases to be plea bargained. The criminal trial is a relatively rare event.

4. Efforts to rehabilitate criminals through treatment programs or mild forms of punishment such as probation have not been successful. Recent evidence indicates that people out on bail or on probation commit significant amounts of crime.

5. Prisons also seem to have little effect on crime prevention. Many people returning to prison have prior records and many inmates placed on parole recidivate.

6. Despite its questionable success, more people are being sent to prison than ever before. Prisoners tend to be poor, uneducated, and minorities. Studies of sentencing indicate that discrimination may play a role in the decision to incarcerate.

7. Prison stays are getting shorter! Though most scholars believe the opposite, surveys indicate that the average stay in prison has declined.

8. The get-tough approach, based on classical criminology, dominates the justice system today. It has resulted in the creation of mandatory sentences and preventive detention statutes, abolition of parole in some jurisdictions, control of plea bargains, and so on. At the same time, the crime rate has been reduced.

9. The Supreme Court has limited the constitutional protections of defendants in such areas as search and seizure, custodial interrogation, and rights of prisoners. However, they have increased rights in other areas such as right to counsel and protection from discriminatory treatment.

10. Overall, the conflicting goals of the criminal justice system have prevented it from operating in an efficient and effective manner. There seems little hope that these conflicts will be reconciled in the near future.

The information flow in the criminal justice system has been vastly improved. We know more about the numbers of people who are processed through the system, what happens to them, and why. If there is hope for the system, it will be to use this information in a more rational way. Police will have to become more efficient crime preventers, courts will have to dispense justice more evenhandedly, prisons will have to develop more effective treatment methods. But even then, it is unlikely that the justice system by itself can affect crime. If crime is to be reduced, society must be prepared to deal with its root causes: poverty, racism, economic inequality, educational dysfunction, family conflict, and social disorganization.

Summary

Corrections involve the punishment, treatment, and incapacitation of convicted criminal offenders. Methods of punishing offenders have undergone many changes through history. At first, fines were levied to compensate the victims and their families for losses. Then, cruel corporal and capital punishments were developed. The mercantile system and the development of overseas colonies created the need for labor; so slavery and forced labor began to replace physical punishments. However, in the late eighteenth century, the death penalty began to be used once again.

Reformers pushed for alternatives to harsh, brutal, physical punishment. The prison developed as an alternative that promised to reform and rehabilitate offenders. However, early institutions were brutal places featuring silence, corporal punishment, work details, and warehousing of prisoners. Around the turn of the century, reformers began to introduce such measures as educational training and counseling for inmates.

Today, corrections can be divided into four components—community-based corrections, jails, prisons, and parole programs.

Many convicted offenders are treated in the community. Some are put on probation under supervision of local probation departments. If they obey the rules of probation, they are allowed to serve their sentences in the community. A new development is community-based correction facilities. These institutions allow the offender to remain in the community but live in a regulated environment. Some community institutions are used to house probationers who need a regulated living situation and intensive treatment. Others house prison inmates just before their release into the community. A third institution type allows inmates to serve their entire sentence in a community correctional facility. Despite their promise, community corrections methods generally have not experienced lower recidivism rates than traditional methods.

The jail is the second element of corrections. It houses misdemeanant offenders serving their sentences, and both felons and misdemeanants awaiting trial. The jail is a sore spot in the criminal justice system, because jails are usually old and dilapidated and lack rehabilitory programs.

Prisons are used to house convicted felony offenders. Recently, shifts in criminal justice philosophy and the passage of laws requiring mandatory and presumptive sentences hav ecaused a large upswing in the U.S. prison population and consequent overcrowding.

Prisons are total institutions. Inmates must adjust to a new regime that controls every aspect of their lives. Prison is a violent, stressful place with its own unique subculture and language.

Various rehabilitation devices are used in the prison system, including counseling, educational programs, vocational training, coed prisons, and conjugal visits. However, critics charge that these methods do not seem to work. Consequently, the most recent philosophy to dominate the justice system holds that prisons are places of punishment and incapacitation and not treatment.

In the past twenty years, prisoners have been awarded some legal rights by the nation's courts. Today, their rights include medical treatment, freedom of religion, procedural due process, and correspondence with the media.

The fourth component of corrections is aftercare. About 70 percent of inmates are released on parole. Parole officers supervise inmates in the community while they complete their sentences. Recently, parole has been under attack; four states have actually abolished the practice. Flat and mandatory sentences without parole are viewed as promoting fairness and ending sentencing disparity.

Notes

1 For a general discussion of this issue, see Donald Newman, "In Defense of Prisons," *Psychiatric Annals* 4 (1974):6–17.
2 Graeme Newman, *The Punishment Response* (Philadelphia: J. B. Lippincott, 1978), p. 13.
3 Among the most helpful sources for this section are Benedict Alper, *Prisons Inside-Out* (Cambridge, Mass.: Ballinger, 1974); Gustave de Beaumont and Alexis de Tocqueville, *On the Penitentiary System in the United States and Its Application in France* (Carbondale: Southern Illinois University Press, 1964); Orlando Lewis, *The Development of American Prisons and Prison Customs 1776-1845* (Montclair, N.J.: Patterson-Smith, 1967); Leonard Orland, ed., *Justice, Punishment and Treatment* (New York: Free Press, 1973); J. Goebel, *Felony and Misdemeanor* (Philadelphia: University of Pennsylvania Press, 1976); Georg Rusche and Otto Kircheimer, *Punishment and Social Structure* (New York: Russell and Russell, 1939); Samuel Walker, *Popular Justice* (New York: Oxford University Press, 1980); Newman, *The Punishment Response*.
4 Rusche and Kircheimer, *Punishment and Social Structure*, p. 9.
5 Ibid., p. 19.
6 G. Ives, *A History of Penal Methods* (Montclair, N.J.: Patterson-Smith, 1970).
7 Leon Radzinowicz, *A History of English Criminal Law*, vol. 1 (London: Stevens, 1943), p. 5.
8 Newman, *The Punishment Response*, p. 139.
9 Walker, *Popular Justice*, p. 34.
10 Lewis, *Development of American Prisons and Prison Customs*, p. 17.
11 Ibid., p. 29.
12 Beaumont and de Tocqueville, *On the Penitentiary System in the United States*, p. 42.
13 Michel Foucault, *Discipline and Punish* (New York: Vintage Books, Random House, 1978).
14 Ibid., p. 139.
15 Ibid., p. 16.
16 David Rothman, *The Discovery of the Asylum* (Boston: Little, Brown; 1970).
17 Orland, *Justice, Punishment and Treatment*, p. 143.
18 Ibid., p. 144.

19 Walker, *Popular Justice*, p. 70.

20 Ibid., p. 71.

21 See Z. R. Brockway, "The Ideal of a True Prison System for a State," in *Transactions of the National Congress on Penitentiary and Reformatory Discipline*, reprint ed. (Washington, D.C.: American Correctional Association, 1970), pp. 38–65.

22 This section relies heavily on Rothman, *Conscience and Convenience*.

23 Ibid., p. 23.

24 Ibid., p. 133.

25 See generally, Jameson Doig, *Criminal Corrections: Ideals and Realities* (Lexington, Mass.: Lexington Books, 1983).

26 See generally Chris Eskridge, Richard Seiter, and Eric Carlson, "Community Based Corrections: from the Community to the Community," in *Critical Issues in Corrections*, ed. V. Webb and R. Roberg (St. Paul, Minn.: West Publishing Company, 1981), pp. 171–203.

27 H. Allen, E. Carlson, and E. Parks, *Critical Issues in Adult Probation* (Washington, D.C.: Government Printing Office, 1979), p. 11.

28 G. Killinger, H. Kerper, and P. Cromwell, *Probation and Parole in the Criminal Justice System* (St. Paul, Minn.: West Publishing Company, 1976), p. 35.

29 18 U.S.C.A. 3651 ff.

30 Bureau of Justice Statistics, *Probation and Parole* (Washington, D.C.: U.S. Department of Justice, 1984).

31 Allen, Carlson, and Parks, *Critical Issues in Adult Probation*, p. 47.

32 Ibid.

33 See generally, Patrick McAnany, Doug Thomson, and David Fogel, *Probation and Justice: Reconsideration of Mission* (Cambridge, Mass.: Oelgeschlager, Gunn and Hain; 1984).

34 Paul Friday, David Petersen, and Harry Allen, "Shock Probation: A New Approach to Crime Control," *Georgia Journal of Corrections* 1 (1973):1–13.

35 Larry Travis, "Intensive Supervision in Probation and Parole," *Corrections Today* 46 (1984):34–40.

36 For a further analysis of restitution, see Larry Siegel, "Court-Ordered Victim Restitution: An Overview of Theory and Action," *New England Journal of Prison Law* 5 (1979):135–50.

37 Descriptive materials can be obtained from the EARN-IT Program, District Court of East Norfolk, 50 Chestnut Street, Quincy, MA 02169.

38 "Expanded Use of Financial Restitution Urged," *Justice Assistance News* 2 (August 1981):6.

39 Gagnon v. Scarpelli, 411 U.S. 778, 93 S.Ct. 1756, 36 L.Ed. 2d 655 (1973).

40 Lawrence Greenfield, *Examining Recidivism* (Washington, D.C.: Bureau of Justice Statistics, 1985).

41 Joan Petersilia, Susan Turner, James Kahan, and Joyce Peterson, *Granting Felons Probation: Public Risks and Alternatives* (Santa Monica, Calif.: Rand Corporation, 1985).

42 See Travis, "Intensive Supervision in Probation and Parole."

43 Eskridge, Seiter, and Carlson, "Community Based Corrections: From the Community to the Community," pp. 183–85.

44 This program is evaluated in E. Kim Nelson, Howard Ohmart, and Nora Harlow, *Promising Strategies in Probation and Parole* (Washington, D.C.: Government Printing Office, 1978), pp. 25–26.

45 Andrew Scull, *Decarceration: Community Treatment and the Deviant: A Radical View* (Englewood Cliffs, N.J.: Prentice-Hall, 1977).

46 John Hylton, "Rhetoric and Reality: A Critical Appraisal of Community Correctional Programs," *Crime and Delinquency* 28 (1982):341–73.

47 For example, see Howard Kaplan and Joseph Meyerowitz, "Evaluation of a Halfway House: Integrated Community Approach in the Rehabilitation of Narcotic Addicts,"

International Journal of Addictions 4 (Winter 1969):65–66; James Beck, "An Evaluation of Federal Community Treatment Centers," *Federal Probation* 43 (1979):36–40.

48 Margaret Wilson, *The Crime of Punishment*, Life and Letter Series no. 64 (London: Jonathon Cape Ltd., 1934), p. 186.

49 Bureau of Justice Statistics, *The 1983 Jail Census* (Washington, D.C.: U.S. Department of Justice, 1984).

50 Bureau of Justice Statistics, *Profile of Jail Inmates* (Washington, D.C.: U.S. Department of Justice, 1980).

51 See generally Daniel Kennedy, "A Theory of Suicide While in Police Custody," *Journal of Police Science and Administration* 12 (1984):191–200.

52 Sherman Day, "Community Action Needed to Upgrade Local Jails," *LEAA Newsletter* 6 (1977):2.

53 Note, *Jail Administration Digest* 3 (1980):4.

54 See Note, *Jail Administration Digest* 2 (1979):6.

55 Diane Steelman, *New York City Jail Crisis: Causes, Costs, and Solutions* (New York: Correctional Association of New York, 1984).

56 Bureau of Justice Statistics, *Prisons and Prisoners* (Washington, D.C.: Government Printing Office, 1982).

57 Bureau of Justice Statistics, *Prisoners in 1984* (Washington, D.C.: U.S. Department of Justice, 1985).

58 Bureau of Justice Statistics, *Prisons and Prisoners.*

59 See E. Goffman, "Characteristics of Total Institutions," in *Justice, Punishment and Treatment*, ed. Leonard Orland (New York: Free Press, 1973), pp. 153–58.

60 Gresham Sykes, *The Society of Captives* (Princeton, N.J.: Princeton University Press, 1958), pp. 79–82.

61 Nicolette Parisi, "The Prisoner's Pressures and Responses," in *Coping with Imprisonment*, ed. N. Parisi (Beverly Hills, Calif.: Sage Publications, 1982), pp. 9–16.

62 Daniel Lockwood, "The Contribution of Sexual Harrassment to Stress and Coping in Confinement," in *Coping with Imprisonment*, ed. N. Parisi (Beverly Hills, Calif.: Sage Publications, 1982), p. 47.

63 Ibid.

64 Sandra Gleason, "Hustling: The 'Inside' Economy of a Prison," *Federal Probation* 42 (1978), pp. 32–39.

65 Ibid., p. 39.

66 "The Killing Ground," *Newsweek*, 18 February 1980, p. 75.

67 Parisi, "The Prisoner's Pressures and Responses."

68 John Irwin, "Adaptation to Being Corrected: Corrections from the Convict's Perspective," in *Handbook of Criminology*, ed. Daniel Glazer, (Chicago: Rand McNally & Co. 1974), pp. 971–93.

69 Donald Clemmer, *The Prison Community* (New York: Holt, Rinehart & Winston, 1958).

70 Sykes, *The Society of Captives.*

71 Gresham Sykes and Sheldon Messinger, "The Inmate Social Code," in *The Sociology of Punishment and Corrections*, ed. Norman Johnston et al. (New York: John Wiley & Sons, 1970), pp. 401–408.

72 John Irwin and Donald Cressey, "Thieves, Convicts, and the Inmate Culture," *Social Problems* 10 (1962):142–155.

73 Ibid., p. 145.

74 Charles Thomas, "Prisonization or Resocialization? A Study of External Factors Associated with the Impact of Imprisonment," *Journal of Research in Crime and Delinquency* 10 (1973):18–20.

75 James Jacobs, "Race Relations and the Prison Subculture," in *Crime and Justice*, vol. 1, ed. N. Morris and M. Tonry (Chicago: University of Chicago Press, 1979), pp. 1-28.

76 Esther Heffernan, *Making It in Prison: The Square, the Cool and the Life* (New York: Wiley, 1972).

77 Rose Giallombardo, *Society of Women: A Study of a Women's Prison* (New York: Wiley, 1966), pp. 165–89.

78 See generally G. Kassebaum, D. Ward, and D. Wilner, "Group Counseling," in *Legal Process and Corrections*, ed. N. Johnston and L. Savitz (New York: Wiley, 1982), pp. 255–70.

79 See William Glasser, *Reality Therapy* (New York: Harper & Row, 1965). For further use of this technique, see Richard Rachin, "Reality Therapy: Helping People Help Themselves," *Crime and Delinquency* 16 (1974), pp. 143–45; Eric Berne, *Transactional Analysis in Psychotherapy* (New York: Grove Press, 1961); Richard Nicholson, "Transactional Analysis: A New Method for Helping Offenders," *Federal Probation* 34 (1970), pp. 29–31; Gaylord Thorne, "Behavior Modification Techniques: New Tools for Probation Officers," *Federal Probation* 31 (1967), pp. 21–23; Ralph Schwitzgabel, *Street Corner Research* (Cambridge, Mass.: Harvard University Press, 1964); J. T. Saunders and N. D. Reppucci, "Reward and Punishment: Some Guidelines for Their Effective Application in Correctional Programs for Youthful Offenders," *Crime and Delinquency* 18 (1972), p. 284.

80 Sylvia McCollum, "New Designs for Correctional Education and Training Programs," *Federal Probation* 37 (June 1973), p. 6.

81 R. Bell et al., *Correctional Education Programs for Inmates* (Washington, D.C.: Government Printing Office, 1979), pp. 18–19.

82 See generally Michael Fedo, "Free Enterprise Goes to Prison," *Corrections Magazine* 7 (1981): 11–18.

83 Ann Goetting, "Conjugal Association in Prison: Issues and Perspectives," *Crime and Delinquency* 28 (1982):52–62.

84 J. G. Ross, E. Hefferman, J. R. Sevick, and F. T. Johnson, *Assessment of Coeducational Corrections* (Washington, D.C.: Government Printing Office, 1978).

85 Ibid.

86 D. Lipton, R. Martinson, and J. Wilks, *The Effectiveness of Correctional Treatment: A Survey of Treatment Evaluation Studies* (New York: Praeger, 1975).

87 Charles Murray and Louis Cox, *Beyond Probation: Juvenile Corrections and the Chronic Delinquent* (Beverly Hills, Calif.: Sage Publications, 1979).

88 Paul Lerman, *Community Treatment and Social Control* (Chicago: University of Chicago Press, 1975).

89 Francis Cullen and Karen Gilbert, *Reaffirming Rehabilitation* (Cincinnati: Anderson Publications, 1982).

90 Hans Toch, *Police, Prisons and the Problems of Violence* (Washington, D.C.: Government Printing Office, 1977), p. 53.

91 For a series of papers on the position, see A. Cohen, G. Cole, and R. Baily, eds., *Prison Violence* (Lexington, Mass.: Lexington Books, 1976).

92 Charles Silberman, *Criminal Violence, Criminal Justice* (New York: Vintage Books, 1978).

93 See Hans Toch, "Social Climate and Prison Violence," *Federal Probation* 42 (1978), pp. 21–23.

94 American Correctional Association, *Riots and Disturbances in Correctional Institutions* (Washington, D.C.: American Correctional Association, 1970), p. 1.

95 Sue Mahar, "An 'Orgy of Brutality' at Attica and the 'Killing Crowd' at Santa Fe: A Comparison of Prison Riots," in *Coping with Imprisonment*, ed. N. Parisi (Beverly Hills, Calif.: Sage Publications, 1982), p. 75.

96 Cited in G. McCain, V. Cox, and P. Paulus, *The Effect of Prison Crowding on Inmate Behavior* (Washington, D.C.: Government Printing Office, 1981), p. vi.

97 P. Paulus, V. Cox, G. McCain, and J. Chandler, "Some Effects of Crowding in a Prison Environment," *Journal of Applied Social Psychology* 5 (1975):86–91.

98 E. Megargee, "The Association of Population Density, Reduced Space, and Uncomfortable Temperatures with Misconduct in a Prison Community," *American Journal of Community Psychology* 5 (1977):289–98.

99 P. Nacci, H. Teitelbaum, and J. Prather, "Population Density and Inmate Misconduct Rates in the Federal Prison System," *Federal Probation* 41 (1977), pp. 26–31.

100 Sheldon Ekland-Olsen, Dennis Barrick, and Lawrence Cohen, "Prison Overcrowding and Disciplinary Problems: An Analysis of the Texas Prison System," *Journal of Applied Behavioral Science* 19 (1983):163–76.

101 D. D'Atri, "Psychophysiological Response to Crowding," *Environment and Behavior* 7 (1975):237–52; D. D'Atri and A. Ostfeld, "Crowding: Its Effects on the Elevation of Blood Pressure in a Prison Setting," *Preventative Medicine* 4 (1975):550–66; J. Freedman, *Crowding and Behavior* (San Francisco: Freeman, 1975).

102 National Advisory Commission on Criminal Justice Standards and Goals, *Volume on Corrections* (Washington, D.C.: Government Printing Office, 1973), p. 18.

103 See, for example, Cooper v. Pate, 378 U.S. 546 (1964).

104 Johnson v. Avery, 393 U.S. 483 (1969).

105 Gilmore v. Lynch, 319 F.Supp. 105 (N.D.Cal. 1970).

106 Nolan v. Fitzpatrick, 451 F.2d 545 (1st Cir., 1971).

107 Saxbe v. Washington Post, 41 L.Ed. 2d 514 (1974).

108 Newman v. Alabama, 349 F.Supp. 278 (M.D.Ala. 1974).

109 Estelle v. Gamble, 429 U.S. 97 (1976).

110 97 S.Ct. 291 (1976).

111 See, for example, Trop v. Dulles, 356 U.S. 86, 78 S.Ct. 590, 2d 630 (1958); see also Furman v. Georgia, 408 U.S. 238, 92 S.Ct. 2726, 33 L.Ed. 2d 346 (1972).

112 See, for example, Weems v. United States, 217 U.S. 349, 30 S.Ct. 544, 54 L.Ed. 793 (1910).

113 See, for example, Lee v. Tahash, 352 F.2d 970 (8th Cir. 1965).

114 309 F.Supp. 362 (E.D.Ark. 1970); aff'd 442 F.2d 304 (8th Cir. 1971).

115 Bell v. Wolfish, 99 S.Ct. 1873-1874 (1979).

116 Rhodes v. Chapman, 452 U.S. 337 (1981).

117 Ibid. 337.

118 Wolff v. McDonnell, 418 U.S. 539 (1974).

119 Bureau of Justice Statistics, *Probation and Parole, 1983.*

120 See generally Vincent O'Leary and Joan Nuffield, *The Organization of Parole Systems in the United States* (Hackensack, N.J.: National Council on Crime and Delinquency, 1972).

121 See Peter Hoffman and Lucille DeGostin, "Parole Decision-Making: Structuring Discretion," *Federal Probation* 38 (1974):19–21.

122 Peter Hoffman and Barbara Stone-Meierhoefer, "Post-Release Arrest Experiences of Federal Prisoners: A Six Year Follow-Up," *Journal of Criminal Justice* 7 (1979):193–216.

123 Don M. Gottfredson, M. G. Neithercutt, Joan Nuffield, and Vincent O'Leary, *Four Thousand Lifetimes: A Study of Time Served and Parole Outcome* (Fort Lee, N.J.: National Council on Crime and Delinquency, 1973).

124 National Council on Crime and Delinquency, *Parole in the United States, 1979* (Washington, D.C.: Government Printing Office, 1981).

125 Hoffman and Stone-Meierhoefer, "Post-Release Arrest Experiences," p. 202.

126 Listed in Andrew Von Hirsch and Kathleen Hanrahan, *Abolish Parole?* (Washington, D.C.: Government Printing Office, 1978).

127 David Fogel, . . . *We are the Living Proof . . . : The Justice Model for Corrections* (Cincinnati: Anderson, 1979), p. 197.

Subject Index

Name Index

Table of Cases